FIFTH EDITION

# Learning Disabilities

## The Interaction of Students and Their Environments

Corinne Roth Smith
*Syracuse University*

Boston New York San Francisco
Mexico City Montreal Toronto London Madrid Munich Paris
Hong Kong Singapore Tokyo Cape Town Sydney

Executive Editor: Virginia Lanigan
Editorial Assistant: Robert Champagne
Executive Marketing Manager: Amy Cronin Jordan
Editorial Production Service: Tom Conville Publishing Services, LLC
Manufacturing Buyer: Andrew Turso
Cover Administrator: Kristina Mose-Libon
Electronic Composition: Omegatype Typography, Inc.

For related titles and support materials, visit our online catalog at www.ablongman.com.



Between the time Website information is gathered and then published, some sites may have closed. Also, the transcription of URLs can result in typographical errors. The publisher would appreciate being notified of any problems with URLs so that they may be corrected in subsequent editions.

**Library of Congress Cataloging-in-Publication Data**

Smith, Corinne Roth.
Learning disabilities: the interaction of students and their environments / Corinne Roth Smith.—5th ed.
p. cm.
Includes bibliographical references (p. ) and indexes.
ISBN 0-205-31952-1
1. Learning disabilities. 2. Learning disabled children—Education. I. Title.
LC4704.S618 2004
371.92'6—dc21

2003043850

Printed in the United States of America

10 9 8 7 6 5 4 3 2 1 RRD–IN 08 07 06 05 04 03

**Photo Credits:** Page 1: Rob Lewine/Corbis; page 4: Jim Craigmyle/Corbis; page 29: Ariel Skelley/Corbis; page 54: Larua Dwight/Corbis; page 96: Richard Hutchings/PhotoEdit; page 126: Tom Steward/Corbis; page 155: Paul Barton/Corbis; page 210: Ariel Skelley/Corbis; page 261: Royalty-Free/Corbis; page 307: Michael Newman/PhotoEdit; page 350: Royalty-Free/Corbis; page 396: Bock/Corbis; page 441: Ariel Skelley/Corbis; page 477: Courtesy of Rachael E. Smith; page 516: Dana White/PhotoEdit.

*With love to*
*Lynn, Juli, and Justin,*
*Rachael and Brian,*
*and my precious granddaughter*
*Ariel Elizabeth*

# CONTENTS

## Part Two | CAUSES OF LEARNING DISABILITIES

CHAPTER FIVE



Part Three | THE STUDENT

CHAPTER SIX

## Part Four | THE CURRICULUM

### CHAPTER NINE

### Assessment 307

# FEATURES

## Research Boxes



## Case Studies

## Simulations

# PREFACE

**HAVING JUST COMPLETED** a ten year term as Dean and Associate Dean of Syracuse University's School of Education, I undertook the revisions for this fifth edition with newfound zeal and pride. As a Dean, I learned that my message was more effective when I kept my language short, simple, and to the point. As I took pen to paper for this book, I asked myself why I wouldn't also want to write a book in the same manner in which I wrote my Dean's messages. Wouldn't students grasp the big picture faster? Wouldn't the most important points in my textbook be clearer if I eliminated unnecessary tangents and detail? And wouldn't the text be equally scholarly? I learned from my deanship experience that the answer to all these questions had to be *yes.* Hence I attacked this edition with purpose, maintaining the strict scholarship that faithful users of this book have grown to count on, but revising the language to be friendlier to undergraduates. References have been moved to a new section, Helpful Resources, at the end of each chapter, offering students both classic and up-to-date resources for further study. The text still brings together the most valid and current research and concepts from psychology, medicine, child development, and special education to help us understand and intervene with children with learning disabilities—but in a more down-to-earth, straight-forward manner than prior editions. The text clarifies the big ideas in learning disabilities—those most important to hold on to—while the Research Boxes discuss in greater depth pertinent methodological and theoretical research controversies.

I have always been proud of the unique focus of this text, which brings together the most useful information on how children's strengths and weaknesses in learning can be helped or aggravated by the learning expectations and behavioral styles they encounter in their homes and schools. The many individual, home, and school factors that must be assessed and perhaps modified in order to promote a child's learning and behavioral development were put forth as a model in the very first edition of this book in 1983. This interactionist model has withstood the test of time, and an ecological approach to learning disabilities is now the gold standard. Even if children are born with inefficiently wired brains, parents and teachers can do much to overcome what might have been devastating learning problems. Therefore, equal scrutiny of student, curriculum, and family and school environment variables that impact a child's development is critical.

I am proud of the model I put forth two decades ago. But, just as their environments influence children with learning disabilities, I have come to realize that I might not have generated this interactionist model had I not been first schooled by, and then a faculty member for over thirty years at, such a cutting-edge bastion of special education innovation as Syracuse University. It is here that William Cruickshank honed his structured approaches to help children focus their attention. It is here that Louis DiCarlo produced magic when children who were electively mute would begin speaking in sentences within minutes of meeting this great man. It is at Syracuse University that Burton Blatt asked why we were segregating children with special needs in special classes, with little benefit—and so Syracuse University became a pioneer in inclusive practices. The walls of institutions for the mentally retarded came crashing down after Blatt exposed their inhumane conditions, and community living became the standard. At Syracuse University, Benita Blachman is doing her groundbreaking research on how nonreaders benefit from exposure to systematic, intense phonological awareness and linguistic reading interventions—and brain imaging studies show that these children's brains are in fact becoming more capable of supporting learning. Our neuropsychologists are discovering for whom multimodal instruction via voice activated computers works, and for whom not. Our behaviorists are honing curriculum-based assessment approaches. Our math professors have revolutionalized teaching approaches by showing how math can be learned through design projects. Our reading professors are perfecting comprehension strategies that increase children's independence in learning. The Psychoeducational Teaching Laboratory that I direct created a model for what is now known as "dynamic assessment"—assessing not just *what* a child knows and doesn't know, but *how* he or she learns best by measuring learning rate with different teaching approaches. All these teachings informed my approach to this book.

The "to-the-point" communication in this text would not have been possible without the editorial assistance of Kathryn Lee, who translated my scholarly talk into pure, simple English. Kathryn teaches writing courses at Syracuse University's Newhouse School of Public Communications. She knows first hand what it takes to communicate clear messages to undergraduates, to inspire their questions, and to make information memorable. I thank her for helping me make the latest scholarship in learning disabilities accessible to all readers.

It is interesting to consider that a book on learning disabilities is necessary only because of the times in which we live. It is society's priorities that determine who is considered disabled. In every age there have been people who had difficulty meeting the demands society placed on them, whether it be the value on physical prowess in Greek and Roman times, musical talent in the Elizabethan era, or social repartée in Edwardian days. Today, it is the academic expectations that our society has for its citizens that render some "learning disabled."

An unfortunate consequence of society's focus on a disability is that we often look so much at students' weaknesses that we tend to overlook nurturing strengths and talents. We also focus so much on student weaknesses that we forget to scrutinize the many ways in which home and school environments influence the extent of the disability and its impact on life adjustment. Since it is our expectations and interventions that help shape whether a student's learning will be optimized or whether difficulties will become lifelong handicaps, we must not only assess the student's characteristics and needs but we must also look inward at ourselves. We must seriously consider how our families and schools may contribute to the individuals' difficulties, and how they can help. This book looks at the student, curriculum, and environmental contributors to learning disabilities, and sets these against the backdrop of what would be expected in normal development.

This book also gives voice to the fears, frustrations, and triumphs of parents, teachers, and individuals with learning disabilities. Throughout the text they tell their own stories in a way that teaches best. Illustrations of student work offer helpful examples, and simulations help the reader gain some notion of what it might be like to have a learning disability, if only for a moment. The text also examines the role of multicultural diversity in learning disabilities and offers suggestions on how to build schools that value the richness that diverse family traditions, cultures, and languages bring to the educational process. Throughout the text, margin notes highlight the "big ideas."

This book reviews the most recent work in learning disabilities from an eclectic vantage point, as much can be learned from different perspectives. Part One introduces students to the history of the field of learning disabilities, as well as current LD definitions, identification practices, and prevalence. Part Two reviews the many student, curriculum, and environmental factors that may contribute to learning disabilities, from inherited neuropsychological patterns to the effects of poverty and poor teaching. Part Three contrasts the normal development of academic skills, learning strategies, information-processing abilities, and social–emotional adjustment with that of the learning disabled—from preschool through transition planning for adulthood. Part Four focuses on the academic accomplishments we expect of students by examining multidimensional assessment approaches and programming strategies that best match different students' abilities and learning styles. Part Five sheds light on the students' learning and behavior from the context of their parents as models, advocates, and teachers, and their schools' human, physical, and organizational characteristics. Only by understanding how the student's characteristics interact with the nature of the curriculum he or she is expected to master and the expectations and personalities within his or her social settings can we comprehend the student's learning and adjustment needs and how best to intervene.

An Instructor's Manual with test items is available with the fifth edition. Please ask your Allyn & Bacon representative for details. We have created a Companion Website to accompany this new edition, which can be found at www.ablongman.com/SmithLD5e

Writing a major textbook involves the assistance of many people. I am especially indebted to Virginia Lanigan, Executive Editor, for guiding this revision. I thank the following reviewers for their suggestions: Jean C. Faieta, Edinboro University of Pennsylvania; Kimberly Fields, Albany State University; Lori J. Ladiges, Cardinal Stritch University; Susan M. Munson, Duquesne University; Ann M. Richards, West Virginia University; and Ralph Zalma, Hofstra University.

My students deserve special acknowledgment. In more ways than they will ever know, they have influenced this text's philosophical approach.

Finally, I thank the many children, parents, and teachers who, over the years, trusted those of us at Syracuse University's Psychoeducational Teaching Laboratory to join them in problem solving. Their reflections taught me and led me as I explored an interactionist approach to learning disabilities. Both my students and I have been enriched by being invited to share a small piece of their lives. I thank them for their wisdom, applaud their courage, and delight in watching these children, with the support of their parents and teachers, enter adulthood as more fulfilled and hopeful individuals.

CHAPTER ONE

# History of the Field

**TODAY OVER 2.8 MILLION** school children—1 child in every 20—are identified as *learning disabled* (LD). Children with LD are presumed to have a neurological handicap that affects their brain's ability to understand, remember, or communicate information. Their teachers and parents describe one characteristic that each and every student with LD shares in common—the *unexpected failure to learn.* Besides this unexpected underachievement, these children run the gamut. Some are brighter than others. Some are socially savvy and born leaders; others just can't seem to get in sync with their classmates. Some are avid risk takers, thinking themselves capable of accomplishing whatever they put their minds to; others are more fragile and any upset can set them off for days. Some are superb athletes; others seem to trip over anything in their path. Some are strong readers but terrible in math; others are math whizzes but can't catch on to even the basics of reading and spelling. Others read well but have no idea what they've read; memorizing social studies and science facts is their definition of torture. When these students listen to lectures, information often goes in one ear and out the other. Some can tell you the most intricate and fascinating stories, but if you ask them to write them down, the results are surprisingly immature.

*Despite adequate intelligence, schooling, and their parents' best attempts at nurturing, children with LD achieve far less academically than expected.*

Despite adequate intelligence, schooling, and their parents' best attempts at nurturing, children with learning disabilities achieve far less academically than one would have expected.

To illustrate just how different two students with learning disabilities can be, consider Ben and Rodney. Ben is a junior at Harvard. He has no trouble with the demanding courses in architectural design, physics, and engineering he's taking. He is vice president of his fraternity and a superb soccer player. But his sociology course, in fact all his heavy reading courses, are almost too much for him. It takes him three times as long to wade through a chapter in the SOC 101 text as it does for his roommate. Worse, when he finally gets through the reading, he realizes he hasn't absorbed much. He wonders how he'll ever manage to pass the course given the volumes of assigned reading.

Contrast Ben's case with Rodney's. Rodney is in tenth grade. He reads and understands his textbooks just fine. But even the simplest addition problems leave him in the dark. His handwriting is nearly illegible, he falls over his own feet, he stands out with his strange combinations of clothes, he can never think of anything to say in a social group, and he is friendless and lonely. He's in danger of flunking out of school, and he can't seem to hold on to a part-time job at a fast food restaurant because he's awkward with customers and is easily distracted from his duties.

*Students with LD have exceptionally uneven ability to learn, with some skills coming to them far easier than others.*

Both students come from loving homes. Both have attended highly regarded schools since kindergarten. Both have been willing to work hard to learn. Although their symptoms are different in type and severity, both of these students have learning disabilities. Like all students with learning disabilities, Ben and Rodney have exceptionally uneven ability to learn, with some skills coming to them far easier than others. The result is far lower achievement in some academic areas when compared with the expectations their parents and teachers had of them given their much higher aptitude.

*Although all children with LD have in common the extremely uneven development of learning abilities, the cause of their brains' inefficiency in processing information, the way it affects their learning and behavior, and the effect of families and schools can be very different from one individual to another.*

Both Ben and Rodney meet the classic definition of learning disability: they have demonstrated *unexpected underachievement in one or more areas of learning.* Through the centuries there have been individuals who haven't achieved up to society's expectations. Learning disabilities, the failure to achieve academically when one is otherwise quite able, is the modern-day version of this phenomenon. In simpler times, academic achievement was much less a priority for families. Children were expected to begin earning their keep as soon as possible by working on the farm or in the factories—or fighting wars or raising families. That some couldn't master reading, writing, and arithmetic wasn't very important. Today, however, academic achievement is critical if a person wants to secure a better job and enjoy a higher standard of living. Against this backdrop, the learning disabled are particularly handicapped by their comparatively limited capacity to process some kinds of information. Their brains appear to be quite capable at some tasks, but not others—especially when it comes to schoolwork. Although all children with learning disabilities have in common this extremely uneven development of learning abilities, the cause of their brains' inefficiency in processing information, the way it affects their learning and behavior, and the effect of families and schools can be very different from one individual to another, as we described in the cases of Ben and Rodney.

The official federal definition of a learning disability was first put forward in the Education for All Handicapped Children Act (1975) and later incorporated into the Individuals with Disabilities Education Act (IDEA, 1990), which was amended again in 1997:

> "Specific learning disability" means a disorder in one or more of the basic psychological processes involved in understanding or in using language, spoken or written, that may manifest itself in an imperfect ability to listen, think, speak, read, write, spell, or to do mathematical calculations, including conditions such as perceptual disabilities, brain injury, minimal brain dysfunction, dyslexia, and developmental aphasia. The term does not include learning problems that are primarily the result of visual, hearing, or motor disabilities, of mental retardation, of emotional disturbance, or of environmental, cultural, or economic disadvantage. (Federal Register, March 12, 1999, p. 12422)

In order for a learning disability to be identified, a child must have a severe discrepancy between intellectual aptitude and actual achievement in reading, math, written expression, or language skills. Put simply, there is a discrepancy between what the child ought to be able to learn, and what he or she actually can learn. These students achieve far less than expected for their age, intellectual ability, and their home and school backgrounds. Teachers and parents alike bemoan the fact that "Susie's bright enough and tries so very hard, but she just can't seem to keep up with the rest of the class."

Biology contributes significantly to learning disabilities, as we will discuss in Chapter 3. The way that children's brains develop influences the efficiency with which their brains process information, which in turn influences learning. Personality also contributes to learning, as does education, life experiences, and family background. Figure 1.1 presents a detailed picture of the various contributors to learning disabilities, any of which can influence the development and/or application of a person's information-processing capabilities. Any of these factors can influence whether a child will take in information, organize it, store it, and recall it—in other words, learn efficiently. Different combinations of these influences can constrain learning, so that mild, moderate, or severe learning disabilities result. On the other hand, when the school and family factors that have an effect on learning are most favorable, a potential learning disability can be reduced in severity or even averted. Depending on how sensitively parents and teachers respond to the children's learning strengths and weaknesses, children can be happy with who they are and motivated to keep plugging away, or their behavior can become complicated by significant emotional reactions. The cases of Brian, Aisha, Frank, and Joel on page 5 illustrate how important it is to get to the root of any learning and behavior problems as soon as possible, rather than assuming that children's failures are due to intellectual slowness, laziness, or lack of cooperation.

***When school and family factors that have an effect on learning are most favorable, a potential learning disability might be reduced in severity or even averted.***

Most of the time children like Brian, Aisha, Frank, and Joel function in a way that is consistent with what would be expected from their intellectual ability and their educational and family backgrounds. Ask them to learn certain types of school tasks, however, and their brains seem to stall. As a result, their performance in school is inconsistent: they are on target or even advanced in some areas, but fall far behind and perform much like a younger child in other areas. On the playground and at home, the same brain inefficiencies that affect academic learning can lead to social problems. It is natural for these children to be frustrated by their

***On the playground and at home, the same brain inefficiences that affect academic learning can lead to social problems.***

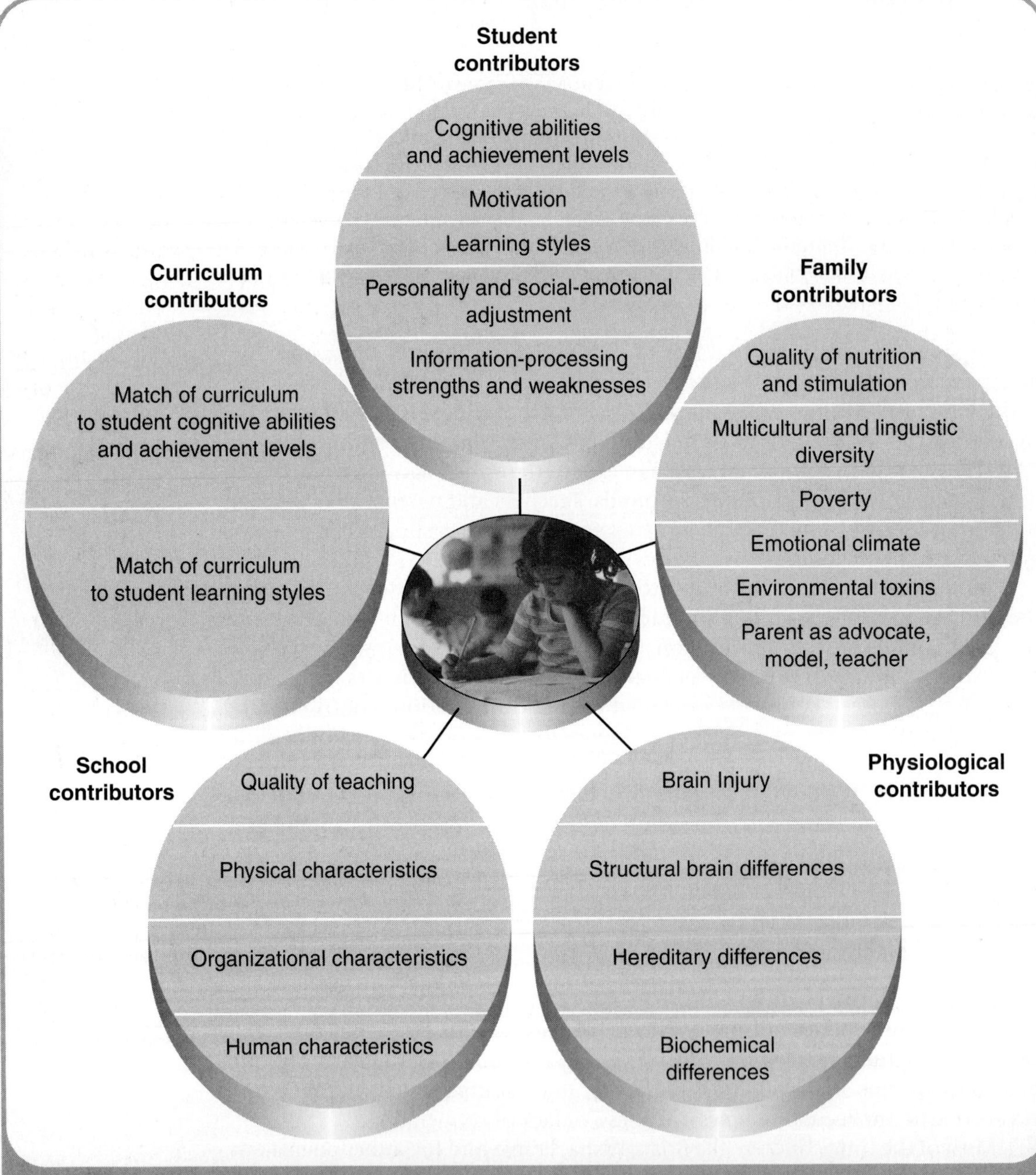


**Figure 1.1** Student, curriculum, and environmental factors that can facilitate or constrain learning.

## Brian, Aisha, Frank, and Joel

*Children whose disabilities were misunderstood.*

Brian's first-grade teacher describes him as "a human pinball machine." He never walks; he bolts. He leaves his desk every few minutes to sharpen his pencil, get more paper, look in on the class gerbils. He can't seem to resist commenting on everything he sees. Brian's classmates find his restlessness and interruptions annoying, but neither punishments nor rewards have produced any lasting change in his behavior. On his mid-term report, Brian's teacher writes: "Brian is bright and enthusiastic, but he needs to settle down. He is falling behind because he just won't pay attention."

Eleven-year-old Aisha is quiet and shy. She works hard, but her progress in school has always been slow. Now in fifth grade, she is more than a year behind her peers in both math and reading. Her teachers do not believe Aisha is smart enough to keep up with the class, and they have reduced their expectations of her. Aisha's parents say she grasps ideas well enough at home, and they are puzzled by her slow academic progress. They are also worried about the fact that Aisha is becoming increasingly withdrawn: she has no friends, and she spends most of her free time alone watching television.

Frank has been put on notice that he is failing eighth grade, and he will have to repeat it if he does not start handing in his assignments and stop cutting classes. He has been in trouble for other things this year: fighting, vandalism, and (most recently) showing up at a school dance drunk. Frank says he doesn't care if he fails—he plans to quit school at 16, so he's just "doing time" until then. All but one of Frank's teachers find him hostile and uncooperative. The teacher who runs the computer lab says Frank is attentive and capable; he even helps others who don't know what to do.

A popular tenth-grader, Joel has enjoyed sports since he was in elementary school. He has earned places on the high school wrestling, track, and baseball teams. He is also active in student government and sells advertising for the school yearbook. His grades, however, are mostly C's and D's. Joel's teachers complain that his homework is careless, sloppy, and incomplete; his handwriting is unreadable. "Maybe if he weren't so involved in extracurricular activities, he'd be able to focus on his work," Joel's history teacher comments. "He'll never get into college if he doesn't start making an effort!"

It can be easy to make assumptions about students like these. Brian is immature and lacks self-control. Aisha is a child who is slow intellectually. Frank has a "bad attitude" and emotional problems. Joel needs to overcome his lack of academic motivation.

If you take a closer look, however, a very different picture emerges:

Brian's wandering mind and restless drive to keep moving frustrate him and his family even more than they do his teacher, but this behavior is beyond his control. He lacks the ability to plan ahead and "screen out" distractions, so he can't concentrate no matter how hard he tries. Brian also cannot regulate his impulses to investigate and comment on anything he notices that is new. At the end of each day he is exhausted from responding to all the sights and sounds that swirl around him, yet he can't "turn himself off" until he falls asleep (which is a struggle in itself).

A psychologist found that Aisha's intelligence is in the gifted range. She must struggle to keep up with less able peers because she has difficulty making sense out of written symbols. The psychologist told Aisha's parents that Aisha has become depressed as a result of her school problems. "She sees herself as a total failure," he said.

*(continued)*

**Brian, Aisha, Frank, and Joel** (Continued)

Frank started avoiding classes and homework to hide the trouble he has understanding either verbal directions or very much of what he reads. Brighter than average, he is successful in learning situations that do not call for extensive use of language. Junior high, however, does not provide him with many opportunities of that kind. Frank feels like a misfit and longs to escape the endless failure and criticism that he faces in school.

Joel's success as an athlete masks his poor fine motor coordination. Difficulty controlling his hands makes it extremely hard for Joel to manipulate a pen or pencil (he is also "all thumbs" when it comes to chores like washing dishes or setting the table). Joel is a conscientious student and understands class material, but he finds it virtually impossible to express what he knows when he is required to write it down.

All of these students have *learning disabilities*, neurological handicaps that affect the brain's ability to understand, remember, or communicate information.

*Source:* Reprinted with the permission of The Free Press, a Division of Simon & Schuster Adult Publishing Group, from *Learning Disabilities A to Z: A Parent's Complete Guide to Learning Disabilities from Preschool to Adulthood* by Corinne R. Smith and Lisa W. Strick. Copyright © 1997 by Corrine R. Smith and Lisa W. Strick.

*It is natural for children with LD to be frustrated by their learning and social challenges, and to react emotionally.*

*Parents and teachers often become exasperated with children with LD because of their behavior, instead of searching for the real cause—a problem with attention, difficulty perceiving visual symbols, or a delay in language or motor development—that started the chain of learning and emotional problems in the first place.*

learning and social challenges, and to react emotionally. Unfortunately, parents and teachers often become exasperated with these children because of their behavior, instead of searching for the real cause—a problem with attention, difficulty perceiving visual symbols, or a delay in language or motor development—that started the whole chain of learning and emotional problems in the first place.

This chapter explores the history of the learning disabilities field and its research emphases from the 1800s to today. Two points in the history of LD are particularly important: the 1950s and 1960s when the LD concept gained popularity, and the landmark legislation of 1975 that mandated special education services for all students with handicapping conditions, including those with learning disabilities. These events were preceded by a rich legacy of research around how individuals process information and how learning can be accelerated through appropriate programming.

## Educational Philosophy and Practices

The birth of the distinct field of learning disabilities can be traced to the 1950s and 1960s, when parent and professional frustration grew regarding some children who, though appearing to be bright and eager to learn, had unexpected lags in their academic achievements. These were children who needed special education intervention of a nature not typically offered at the time. They required a multifaceted, individualized focus that was different in three important ways from practices prevalent in the 1950s and 1960s. This new approach was marked by

1. *A focus on individual learning strengths and weaknesses rather than instruction based on the category of disability.* In the 1950s and 1960s it was customary to group

children for instruction according to their diagnosed disability. Children with mental retardation, for example, were grouped together in one class, apart from those with emotional problems, because it was thought that their teaching needs were so different. More often than not, however, teachers and parents discovered that children's needs varied so widely within each disability category that the same teaching strategy was useful in all classes, regardless of diagnosis. Unfortunately, children often wouldn't get the most appropriate instruction because of a watered-down curriculum where "we don't do that for this type of child" (for example, teach reading to children who are mentally retarded). Those advocating for the learning disabled recognized that along with their children's weaknesses came areas of great strength and potential that were not being nurtured. The expectations of educators for all of the existing handicapping classifications were simply too low. Parents urged teachers to be more thoughtful about tailoring instruction to their children's individual needs—both their areas of strength and weakness. This individualized approach paved the way for serving the learning disabled, a group of students who did not clearly fit any of the existing special education classifications. Parents and educators urged that instruction for these children focus on their individual strengths, weaknesses, and learning styles: children needed to be taught at multiple levels without lowering overall expectations for academic and life success simply because the child was identified with a disability.

***Parents urged teachers to be more thoughtful about tailoring instruction to their children's individual needs—both their areas of strength and weakness.***

2. *A focus on intensive teaching.* Parents of children with learning disabilities challenged the prevailing "let's take it slow and easy, and in the meantime keep children happy" approach to instruction. It was widely believed in the 1950s and 1960s that children would begin to learn effortlessly "when they were ready." So why struggle now when children would automatically "catch on" when they became more mature? But despite being placed in segregated classes with smaller groups and specially trained teachers, many children in fact failed to make notable progress from year to year. Essentially, the special class was a low-achiever environment in which the emphasis was on disabilities rather than abilities, and expectations were lower as a result. Parents pressed for teachers to capitalize on students' strengths in their instructional approaches and to raise the bar of expectation. Teachers were asked to refocus on what children *can* do, and *how* they learn best, rather than the prior emphasis on primarily what children can't do. The challenge for teachers was to stop focusing on weaknesses and the elimination of disabilities, and instead teach to the children's strengths in order to develop their talents and skills. Teaching goals and approaches had to be matched to what children were ready to learn and how they learned best. Researchers were urged to develop a solid scientific foundation for intensive teaching practices tailored toward individual learning needs.

***Parents pressed to intensify teaching and raise expectations.***

3. *A focus on instruction to overcome behavioral and intellectual limitations.* The late 1960s saw the creation of Head Start, a federally funded program for preschoolers from economically disadvantaged homes. The gains made by these children caught the attention of parents and professionals who began to see that some children who were identified as mentally retarded or emotionally disturbed could make great strides when given intensive language

and reading remediation. One landmark study by Samuel Kirk showed that the IQs of institutionalized preschoolers with mental retardation enrolled in such an intensive program increased over time, whereas a group not enrolled showed losses in IQ scores. In fact, 6 of the original 15 children in the intensive program eventually left the institution. One graduated from college. None of the nonenrolled children ever left the institution. The investigator reasoned that many of these children had been misunderstood as retarded; rather they had specific learning disabilities in some areas but were normal in many other respects.

***The term* learning disabled *implied that the problem could be corrected and that the schools were responsible for doing so.***

The term *learning disabled* naturally appealed to parents since it meant their children could escape the segregation and stigma of the labels "mentally retarded" or "emotionally disturbed." Further, using the term *learning disabled* implied that the problem could be corrected and that the schools were responsible for doing so.

## Advocacy

As the term *learning disabilities* gained in stature, so too did the call for mandated services for the millions of children who qualified for this distinction. Moreover, the United States' attempt to upgrade its educational system in response to the Soviet launching of Sputnik I in 1957 made this unique population of children, who were smart enough but could not keep up, even more apparent and disturbing.

### Professional and Parent Organizations

Parents in the 1950s and 1960s understood better than anyone that some of their children were very bright in some ways but struggled a great deal in other ways. These children, the parents maintained, did not deserve to be called "stupid" or "lazy" or "mixed up." Their learning problems were subtle. They could learn, but only if instruction was matched to their unique strength and weakness patterns. Finally, parents put pressure on the schools and ultimately Congress to change the way their children were educated.

Parent advocacy groups started at the local level. In 1963, these smaller groups banded together at a national conference in Chicago, at which time the term *learning disabilities* was used in an address by Samuel Kirk. This led in 1964 to the formation of a strong national parent advocacy group, now called the Learning Disabilities Association of America.

In 1968, educators followed suit by forming what is now the Division for Learning Disabilities within the Council for Exceptional Children. Both parent and professional advocacy groups played a powerful role in bringing about the litigation and legislation that eventually led to the recognition of learning disabilities as a handicapping condition.

***Parent and professional advocacy groups played a powerful role in bringing about the litigation and legislation that eventually led to the recognition of learning disabilities as a handicapping condition.***

### The Federal Role in Special Education

In 1975, Congress enacted the Education for All Handicapped Children Act (Public Law 94-142) in response to court decisions mandating that children with disabilities be able to access a free public education (*Pennsylvania ARC* v. *Pennsylvania,* 1971; *Mills* v. *Board of Education,* 1972). Until this time, schools could and did refuse to admit a child with a disability. In 1971, one in seven children with disabilities were simply told to stay home.

PL 94-142 mandated special services for all children with disabilities, including for the first time children with specific learning disabilities. Before PL 94-142, the only recognized disability categories were those of mental retardation, hard of hearing, deaf, speech impaired, visually handicapped, seriously emotionally disturbed, crippled, and other health impaired.

***PL 94-142, passed in 1975, mandated special services for all children with disabilities, including, for the first time, children with specific learning disabilities.***

In the nine years preceding PL 94-142 Congress had bowed to pressure from several national advisory committees by authorizing money for teacher training, research, and demonstration projects in learning disabilities. Yet, no money had been appropriated for educational services to these children. The argument for the court mandate of equal educational opportunities for *all* children with disabilities was based on two points: (1) that unequal education practices violated the equal protection clause of the Fourteenth Amendment of the U.S. Constitution, and (2) that the Civil Rights Act of 1964 guaranteed equal opportunity for education to all citizens. Public Law 94-142 finally recognized the learning disabled and partially reimbursed schools for providing special education services to this population. All states accepting federal funds for education were required to implement the law by the 1978–1979 school year.

Public Law 94-142, reenacted in 1990 as the Individuals with Disabilities Education Act (IDEA, PL 101-476) and amended again in 1997 (PL 105-17), specifically mandated that states accepting federal funds for education (all 50 do) provide a free, appropriate education to all children with disabilities aged 6 to 17. IDEA mandates that these students be educated in the "least restrictive environment," that is, in as normal a setting as possible. It also requires that a variety of assessment procedures and observation of children in their classrooms be used when identifying children as disabled. The testing materials cannot be racially or culturally biased and must be administered in the student's native language if the child is not fluent in English. A student's curriculum must be detailed yearly in an *individualized education program* (IEP) to be prepared by the appropriate school personnel in consultation with the parents. Beginning at age 14 and each year thereafter, the IEP must designate the coursework that will meet the child's transition needs after high school. By age 16, a *transition service plan* must be written to prepare the student for vocational training, employment, postsecondary education, and independent living. Finally, IDEA's regulations give parents very specific rights to involvement in their child's educational planning process.

***Federal law mandates that students with disabilities be educated in the "least restrictive environment"—in as normal a setting as possible.***

***Parents have very specific rights to involvement in their child's educational planning process.***

If a student doesn't meet IDEA's eligibility criteria, he or she can still access special education services through the protections of Section 504 of the Rehabilitation Act of 1973. Section 504 requires public schools receiving federal funds to serve the needs of the disabled as adequately as the needs of the nondisabled. Its definition of *handicapped person* is broad: any person who has a physical or mental impairment that substantially limits a major life activity—in the case of the learning disabled, that major life activity is learning.

With the implementation of these laws, the learning disabled quickly grew to be the largest group of students with disabilities on record. Currently over 11 percent of school students, about 5.8 million, are being identified as disabled.

Among these, about half, over 2.8 million, are identified as learning disabled—5 in every 100 children. State percentages of children identified as disabled vary considerably, with New Jersey, Rhode Island, and West Virginia identifying over 50 percent more children as disabled than California, Arizona, and Colorado. The reasons for these disparities have a great deal to do with school budgets and identification philosophies.

All states permit adolescents with disabilities to stay in school until age 21, although IDEA requires this extension only if state law and practice provide education to nondisabled individuals in this age group. In 1986, Congress extended the mandate for free appropriate education to 3- to 5-year-olds with developmental delays through Public Law 99-457, an amendment to the Education for All Handicapped Children Act of 1975. Implementation had to be by the 1990–1991 schoolyear. Parents have the right to choose whether to enroll their children in any of these preschool programs. If a family chooses to enroll their child, an *individualized family service plan* is developed that describes the child's needs and the supports necessary to enhance the family's capacity to meet these needs. Funds also were appropriated to help states develop services for infants and toddlers with disabilities from birth through 2 years. Currently over 850,000 infants and preschoolers are benefiting from such services.

## Research and Program Development

*The LD field emerged from a long line of theory and research that began in the 1800s and investigated how people use their vision and language skills to learn.*

The LD field emerged from a long line of theory and research that began in the 1800s and investigated how people use their vision and language skills to learn. These researchers also were busy developing remedial programs that they hoped would spur student achievement. LD pioneers challenged popular assumptions and practices, and their insights laid the foundation for today's theories, research, and intervention strategies in learning disabilities.

Although each of these scientists approached the problem of learning disabilities from his or her own distinct perspective, most were influenced by and acknowledged the importance of the others' contributions. They understood that an eclectic approach was best because many different abilities and interventions can contribute to children's learning and behavior. Moreover, despite the early scientists' focus on what was wrong within the student, the effectiveness of their interventions at home and in the school highlighted the critical role of the family, the school, and the curriculum in capitalizing on strengths to overcome learning problems.

### Research on Learning through Vision

*Early research on learning disorders started with the study of brain-injured adults.*

Early research on learning disorders started with the study of brain-injured adults. The excerpt from Oliver Sacks's work on page 11 is an example of the intriguing behavior of a person whose brain is injured and therefore processes visual information in a highly unorthodox way. Fascinating case studies like this led scientists to conclude that the visual and motor difficulties of brain-injured people adversely affected their behavior and achievement. It wasn't long before the link to children with similar difficulties was made. Although we now know that brain injury and

## Dr. P.: The Man Who Mistook His Wife for a Hat

*An accomplished music teacher who, after a right hemisphere brain injury, processed visual information in a highly unorthodox way.*

Dr. P. was a musician of distinction, well-known for many years as a singer, and then, at the local School of Music, as a teacher. It was here, in relation to his students, that certain strange problems were first observed. Sometimes a student would present himself, and Dr. P. would not recognize him; or, specifically, would not recognize his face. The moment the student spoke, he would be recognized by his voice. Such incidents multiplied, causing embarrassment, perplexity, fear and, sometimes, comedy. For not only did Dr. P. increasingly fail to see faces, but he saw faces when there were no faces to see: genially, Magoo-like, when in the street, he might pat the heads of water-hydrants and parking-meters, taking these to be the heads of children; he would amiably address carved knobs on furniture, and be astounded when they did not reply. At first these old mistakes were laughed off as jokes, not least by Dr. P. himself. Had he not always had a quirky sense of humor, and been given to Zen-like paradoxes and jests? His musical powers were as dazzling as ever; he did not feel ill—he had never felt better; and the mistakes were so ludicrous—and so ingenious—that they could hardly be serious or betoken anything serious. The notion of there being "something the matter" did not emerge until some three years later. . . .

He was a man of great cultivation and charm, who talked well and fluently, with imagination and humor. I couldn't think why he had been referred to our clinic.

And yet there *was* something a bit odd. He faced me as he spoke, was oriented towards me, and yet there was something the matter—it was difficult to formulate. He faced me with his *ears,* I came to think, but not with his eyes. These, instead of looking, gazing, at me, "taking me in," in the normal way, made sudden strange fixations—on my nose, on my right ear, down to my chin, up to my right eye—as if noting (even studying) these individual features, but not seeing my whole face, its changing expressions, "me," as a whole. . . .

It was while examining his reflexes—a trifle abnormal on the left side—that the first bizarre experience occurred. I had taken off his left shoe and scratched the sole of his foot with a key—a frivolous-seeming but essential test of a reflex—and then, excusing myself to screw my ophthalmoscope together, left him to put on the shoe himself. To my surprise, a minute later, he had not done this. . . .

He continued to look downwards, though not at the shoe, with an intense but misplaced concentration. Finally his gaze settled on his foot: "That is my shoe, yes?" . . .

"No, it is not. That is your foot. *There* is your shoe."

"Ah! I thought that was my foot."

Was he joking? Was he mad? Was he blind? If this was one of his "strange mistakes," it was the strangest mistake I had ever come across. . . .

I resumed my examination. His visual acuity was good: he had no difficulty seeing a pin on the floor, though sometimes he missed it if it was placed to his left. He saw all right, but what did he see? I opened out a copy of the *National Geographic Magazine,* and asked him to describe some pictures in it.

His responses here were very curious. His eyes would dart from one thing to another, picking up tiny features, individual features, as they had done with my face. A striking brightness, a colour, a shape would arrest his attention and elicit comment—but in no case did he get the scene-as-a-whole. He failed to see the whole, seeing only details, which he spotted like blips on a radar screen. . . .

He had no sense whatever of a landscape or scene. I showed him the cover, an unbroken expanse of Sahara dunes.

"What do you see here?" I asked.

*(continued)*

**Dr. P.** (Continued)

"I see a river," he said. "And a little guest-house with its terrace on the water. People are dining out on the terrace. I see coloured parasols here and there." He was looking, if it was "looking," right off the cover, into mid-air and confabulating nonexistent features, as if the absence of features in the actual picture had driven him to imagine the river and the terrace and the coloured parasols.

I must have looked aghast, but he seemed to think he had done rather well. There was a hint of a smile on his face. He also appeared to have decided that the examination was over, and started to look round for his hat. He reached out his hand, and took hold of his wife's head, tried to lift it off, to put it on. He had apparently mistaken his wife for a hat! His wife looked as if she was used to such things. . . .

[At a later house visit] I turned on the television, keeping the sound off, and found an early Bette Davis film. A love scene was in progress. . . .

What was . . . striking was that he failed to identify the expressions on her face or her partner's, though in the course of a single torrid scene these passed from sultry yearning through passion, surprise, disgust and fury to a melting reconciliation. Dr. P. could make nothing of any of this. He was very unclear as to what was going on, or who was who or even what sex they were. His comments on the scene were positively Martian. . . .

On the walls of the apartment there were photographs of his family, his colleagues, his pupils, himself. I gathered a pile of these together and, with some misgivings, presented them to him. . . .

What had been funny, or farcical, in relation to the movie, was tragic in relation to real life. By and large, he recognised nobody: neither his family, nor his colleagues, nor his pupils, nor himself. He recognised a portrait of Einstein, because he picked up the characteristic hair and moustache. . . .

. . . he approached these faces—even of those near and dear—as if they were abstract puzzles or tests. . . .

He saw nothing as familiar. Visually, he was lost in a world of lifeless abstractions.

*Source:* Reprinted with the permission of Simon & Schuster Adult Publishing Group, from *The Man Who Mistook His Wife for a Hat and Other Clinical Tales* by Oliver Sacks. Copyright © 1970, 1981, 1983, 1984, 1985 by Oliver Sacks.

learning difficulties are not always linked in a cause-and-effect manner, the work of these pioneers established some very important building blocks for current LD practices.

In the late 1930s and early 1940s, Kurt Goldstein attributed the unusual behavior patterns of some brain-injured veterans of World War I (who had been shot in the head) to defective processing of and reaction to visual information. They had much the same difficulty you will have when you try to decipher the object in Figure 1.2. Their frustration with processing visual information extended into daily life as they tried to match their socks in the laundry or hold their attention on a speaker. Goldstein listed the following symptoms:

1. *Forced responsiveness to stimuli.* Subjects couldn't help being distracted by objects and people around them, the slightest noise or movement, or even a fleeting thought.
2. *Figure-ground confusion.* Subjects had trouble sorting out what was important (someone speaking to them) and what was not (the din of the dining

**Figure 1.2** Figure–ground problem. In this picture of a cow, the white space, which is customarily background, has become the "figure," the most important part to pay attention to. The dark space has become the irrelevant background. *Hint:* The cow's head is to the left and its upper torso extends to the right.

*Source:* Van Witsen, B. (1967). *Perceptual training activities.* New York: Teacher's College Press.

room noise). This presumably happened because everything, important or not, grabbed their attention.

3. *Perseveration.* Because they kept being distracted by the same stimuli, subjects repeated behaviors they had just engaged in over and over again, such as repeating themselves or continuing to tap a fork against a plate.
4. *Hyperactivity.* They showed extreme purposeless activity. This too was caused by their reactions to whatever caught their attention, however briefly.
5. *Catastrophic reaction.* Subjects broke down emotionally when they couldn't control their bizarre perceptions and chaotic behavior. Setting goals and systematic follow-through to achieve a goal were impossible.
6. *Meticulousness.* They became overly rigid in arranging their personal possessions and time schedules. This was a defense against the excessive stimulation and confusing misperceptions they were experiencing.

Many of these characteristics, though in a more subtle form, are found in children with learning disabilities who also have similar weaknesses with processing visual information.

Around the same time as Goldstein was making his observations, several psychologists and educators at the Wayne County Training School for Retarded Children near Detroit were developing interventions to try to speed up the development of their children who showed weaknesses in ability to process visual information. Heinz Werner, working with children who had trouble learning through their visual skills, concluded that it would be best to teach them following the normal developmental sequence from earlier- to later-developing skills. For example, teachers were advised to avoid introducing the written numeral "2" until the child first demonstrated an understanding of the concept "2" through manipulating real objects (such as sorting and counting piles of 2 blocks), followed by counting pictures of objects and less meaningful symbols (circles, dashes). Werner noted that some children were very organized in their learning styles while others were less so, and that some children adopted a global (attending to the whole) approach, whereas others were analytical (attending to the parts). These individual differences, Werner and other researchers cautioned, meant that it was very important to adapt one's remedial efforts to the particular child's learning patterns, instead of counting on a single method to be effective for everyone. Adapting teaching strategies to children's learning styles, and ordering the teaching process to parallel typical patterns of development, are key strategies used today in learning disabilities. In addition, Werner's observations that some children's learning and behavior are unlike anything known in normal development, while other children progress just like normal younger children, continue to be important in LD assessment today. Instructional approaches differ based on this distinction: very special teaching approaches versus approaches useful to younger, average achievers.

*Adapting teaching strategies to children's learning styles, and ordering the teaching process to parallel typical patterns of development, are key strategies still used today in LD.*

Werner and his colleagues, extrapolating from Goldstein's work with brain-injured soldiers, tended to infer that children with similar characteristics must also have damaged brains. Though that assumption has been convincingly refuted (there are many causes besides brain injury for inattention, hyperactivity, and visual-processing problems), the researchers' conclusion that even children who have the same diagnosis (e.g., brain injury, mental retardation) can differ greatly from one another, and therefore need unique teaching approaches, remains very important.

*Observations that some children's learning and behavior are unlike anything known in normal development, while other children progress just like normal younger children, continue to be important in LD today. Instructional approaches differ based on this distinction: very special teaching approaches versus approaches useful to younger, average achievers.*

Werner's partner, Alfred Strauss, was able to demonstrate that adapting the learning environment to deal with the distractibility of particular children can be very beneficial. He removed extraneous stimuli from the room in order to reduce distractions, and he incorporated movement and other attention-getters into the learning tasks. It was Strauss's idea, for example, to cover the pictures in books so that children would focus on the words. Similarly, he found that children read better when looking at only a few words at a time, rather than a whole sentence. Small group instruction, having teachers wear plain clothing and no jewelry, minimal room decorations, use of study carrels, and facing desks toward walls with children seated apart from one another are all Strauss's innovations. When visual-perceptual weaknesses were found, Strauss didn't recommend delaying academic instruction until this foundation was shored up. Instead, he applied special methods to work around the attention and figure-ground problems: heavy black crayon outlined a figure to be colored, confusable letters (such as *b* with *d*) were color-coded, only one math problem was presented on each page, and a rapid instructional pace was used to get through several steps before the child became distracted.

***LD pioneers demonstrated that adapting the learning environment to deal with the distractibility of particular children can be very beneficial.***

Research Box 1.1 describes some of the unique learning patterns observed by Werner and Strauss, all of which are commonly seen in children identified today as learning disabled. Strauss's methods led to remarkable academic, intellectual, and behavioral gains once attention was focused, as in the case of J. on page 16. Fifty years ago J. would have been called emotionally disturbed or brain injured. Today he would be identified as experiencing learning and behavioral difficulties as a result of an attention-deficit hyperactivity disorder.

William Cruickshank, a student of Werner and Strauss, noted that children with cerebral palsy (therefore known to have had a brain injury) who had near-

**RESEARCH BOX 1.1**

## Werner and Strauss's Observations of the Learning Styles of "Brain-Injured" Children

Werner and Strauss studied children with mental retardation, focusing particularly on children who they thought had become retarded as a result of a brain injury. They found that these children behaved very similarly to Goldstein's brain-injured soldiers: forced responsiveness to stimuli (impulsive and distractible), repetitiveness (they inappropriately fixated on a task or thought), visual-motor disorganization (hyperactivity), figure-ground confusion, attention to irrelevant elements when categorizing (e.g., instead of grouping pictures of "children" apart from "grown-ups," they might group by the color of their clothing), and inability to integrate parts into a whole (e.g., assemble puzzles or understand comic strips). When they looked through a telescope at common objects such as a hat or bird, these children often reported seeing the irrelevant background, not the object (Werner & Strauss, 1941). On a visual-motor task requiring copying a marble design on a marble board and then drawing the pattern, these children had no sense of the overall shape or pattern. Their approach was totally erratic (Werner & Bowers, 1941). When asked to sing simple melodies played on a piano, these children were at a loss. On all tasks, the errors of these children were "of a kind not known in normal development" (p. 98). In contrast, the children who were not presumed to be brain injured performed just like a typical, but younger, child.

Werner concluded that brain injury affects a child's perceptual and problem-solving styles, and therefore affects information being processed through all of the child's senses. The difference found between the problem-solving strategies of children with and without presumed brain injury (disorganized vs. organized, global vs. analytical) continues to be a major area of research in learning disabilities. Strauss's (Strauss & Kephart, 1955; Strauss & Lehtinen, 1947) emphasis on matching academic materials and classroom environments to these children's different learning styles remains a key element in learning disabilities practice today.

J

*An 8-year-old with attention-deficit hyperactivity disorder.*

J . . . Father a prominent attorney, mother educated according to the standards of the upper social class. Parents 31 and 17 years old respectively at the time of marriage. An only child. Pregnancy and delivery were both normal but the child was blue [oxygen deprived] at birth. . . . He walked and talked somewhat later than usual and had no serious childhood diseases. He was an extremely disobedient and "obstinate" child with destructive tendencies, very easily excited. He seemed to be fearless. Not accepted by other children because of his constant teasing and tormenting. . . . When 6 years old, he was entered in a private school but could not be admitted to a class with other children. Two teachers were employed for him alone since one teacher refused to stand it without relief for the entire day.

At 8 years and 6 months of age he was admitted to our clinic. He had a second grade school achievement; psychometric testing was impossible because of extreme restlessness and distractibility. He was always "on the move," exploring everything in the house, particularly technical equipment, electric switches, door bells, elevators, etc. Asked questions incessantly, like a machine gun. Very affectionate with all the persons in the house. When taken to bed, he did not sleep until midnight but asked another question every five minutes. On the days following his admission he was still very restless and disinhibited [did whatever he wished; continually active and impulsive] but meticulous and pedantic in the arrangement of his belongings and everything handled by him at the table or in the classroom. Play in the garden consisted in trying to destroy flowers or bushes but without ill-humor or anger. Always smiling and good-humored. At dinner time he ate enormous quantities of food and drank a glass of water or milk in one gulp. In church he was very distractible, wishing to give money to all the collection boxes. After two weeks in the clinic, he was more adjusted but still very distractible. He was discharged after one and one half years with an intelligence quotient within the normal range and admitted to a private school. Then attended class with children of his age and in an examination proved to be ninth in placement among 40 children.

*Source:* Strauss, A. A., & Lehtinen, L. E. (1947). *Psychopathology and education of the brain-injured child* (p. 2). New York: Grune & Stratton. Reprinted by permission.

average to above-average intelligence had visual-perceptual weaknesses similar to some of his mentors' retarded children. Because of these children's higher intelligence, Cruickshank reasoned that their perceptual disabilities must be the result of brain injury rather than mental retardation, and that any child could have them—even the emotionally disturbed. He used Werner's and Strauss's methods to teach children with visual-perceptual weaknesses, regardless of their intellectual levels. At Syracuse University's campus school Cruickshank even went so far as to paint all the desks and chairs gray and to paint over the lower halves of windows to limit distractions. Cruickshank supported the practice of grouping children by their instructional needs rather than their diagnoses, a forerunner of today's inclusive class placement practices.

Newell Kephart built on Werner's and Strauss's assumptions that perceptual and motor development was the basis for learning, and that incorporating movement into learning would help to catch and focus a student's attention. In order to make school information most meaningful and memorable, Kephart believed that all information that was seen or heard had to be linked with a spoken or movement response. For example, waving one's left and right hands would help clarify that the letter *b* faced one way and the letter *d* faced the opposite way. Kephart developed a perceptual-motor remediation program that worked on balance, coordination, eye movements, eye-hand coordination, and visual perception. Though his work did not lead to significant academic gains for his students, it did stimulate research into the relative role of motor and visual perceptual skills in academic development compared to factors subsequently found to be much more influential, such as language skills.

***LD pioneers found that incorporating movement into learning would help to catch and focus a student's attention.***

Finally, Marianne Frostig developed an assessment measure and a gross-motor and workbook program to help develop children's visual and motor skills so that they would be more efficient and supportive of learning. Initial excitement over her work gave way to disappointment when children with LD failed to produce significant reading gains. The poor showing was attributable to practitioners' reliance on Frostig's workbooks alone and their ignoring Frostig's caveat that intensive reading instruction must accompany the visual-perceptual activities. Frostig emphasized that appropriate programming for students with learning disabilities must take into account factors such as past education, social environment, interests, attitudes, temperament, abilities, and disabilities—concepts that are followed to this day when we assess the curriculum and environmental factors that contribute to a student's learning profile. Frostig's additional concern about developing moral and social behaviors was unusual at the time, but it is an important focus today in LD research and practice. The story Randal tells about himself on page 18 highlights how emotionally exhausting it is for people with learning disabilities to keep up academically, vocationally, and socially, a fact that Frostig began addressing nearly a half-century ago.

## Research on Learning through Language

Researchers in LD stress that the development of language competency is a key prerequisite for academic progress. After all, a child who cannot understand what he hears is likely to have difficulty understanding what he reads, because written words are simply oral language translated into a visual symbol system. Likewise, the child incapable of oral expression is likely to be at a severe disadvantage in writing, because writing requires the child to translate his or her spoken words into written form. Bobby's story (page 19) illustrates one type of language-impaired child with whom the pioneers in learning disabilities worked.

Like the work in the visual-perceptual field, this strand of research began in the 1800s. Franz Gall, a Viennese physician who practiced phrenology, the analysis of skull size and shape, hypothesized in the early 1800s that a person's loss of speech and ability to remember words is the result of injury to the brain's frontal lobes. In the 1860s, the French physician Pierre-Paul Broca further hypothesized that language ability was located in the left hemisphere of the brain. He based his

## Randal

*A 48-year-old college professor who battles daily to keep up with life's demands.*

Life for this 48-year-old college professor with an earned doctorate began on a very shaky foundation. At birth, there was identified brain damage on the right side of the brain. The first week of life was spent in an incubator, with only a fair chance to live. Early childhood was complete with eye surgery at three, a heart problem at nine, frailness, overweight, and awkwardness. Not exactly the most popular child in school. Teachers felt that as long as the behavior was OK, "just let him sit in the class."

High school was four years of struggle—mostly alone. Ignored by teachers and peers—"he's different," we don't "want him in our crowd." When graduation came finally, class rank was lower half. High enough to get into a state college. The independence of being away from home resulted in failing out in the sophomore year. Laying out five years, only made the desire for a degree stronger—"I'll show everybody."

During this return to college, my interest was peaked with the new field of learning disabilities. After many hours in the library "stacks," I came to the realization that I was not mildly retarded. That was the high water point of my life. I could learn, but I needed to find out how. As a special education major, I only needed to change my major emphasis to the new field. I will learn how I can learn while I learn how to teach others. Not a bad plan. To enhance the process, marriage came into the picture. She is a gifted learner who also majored in special education. Together, we finished the first degree, and marched together to receive our master's degrees. At last my life both professionally and personally was on the right track. . . .

In the workforce, my inability to handle large amounts of reading, and the comprehension of it, led to my loss of three special education jobs. Getting lost, no sense of direction, the inability to remember names, loss of details in planning meetings, and what appeared to be disinterest, caused me to job hunt on many occasions. It is frustrating, maddening, and yes, very depressing. Here is an individual who knows how it feels to be misunderstood, but I can't help myself, only everyone else.

When I get lost driving between schools, panic attacks take over for a time, and I am not able to function for ten to fifteen minutes. This is always seen as a poor attempt at getting out of work or making an excuse for not completing a task. The age of computers has been a godsend for all of us. Spell check is the most wonderful invention since sliced bread.

My goal for the rest of my professional life is to make a difference for others like me. I promise relentless work to assure that every needy child will receive the services deserved. Repeating my life will not be fun for anyone: avoid it; fight against it; realize that it will be a lifelong fight to have others understand that there are many of us out there in the work force who try harder than most people to function as normally as we can. It makes you crazy, angry, frustrated, and very tired.

*Source:* Reprinted by permission of Randal L. Becker.

theory on the autopsies of two men who had lost their power of speech *(expressive aphasia)*. Both showed atrophied areas of the left hemisphere of the brain in an anatomical region now known as *Broca's area*.

Interestingly, Broca observed that some children whose language-processing area in the left hemisphere had been destroyed nevertheless did develop normal

### Bobby

*A 2-year-old with an expressive language disorder mistakenly diagnosed as deafness.*

Bobby was seen at the center for auditory disorders in children when he was two years and ten months of age. His parents were professional people with deep concern about him but without handicapping anxiety. Bobby was the fourth pregnancy; the siblings were without defects. The parents stated frankly that although Bobby had no speech, they were confident that he had a great deal of hearing and doubted that his lack of speech could be attributed to peripheral deafness. The pregnancy was uneventful and of nine months' duration. Labor was precipitous, being of only two hours' duration. There was no evidence of injury at the time of birth. Birth weight was six pounds and there was no difficulty in swallowing or feeding immediately after birth. The illness history was negative. Bobby sat alone at eight months and walked at fourteen months. He was retarded in feeding and in acquiring toilet habits as compared to his siblings. He had a preference for the right hand and the parents had not observed unusual awkwardness or incoordination motorically. They reported that he had always been responsive to people, was playful and in general was a happy contented boy. The history of auditory behavior revealed responses to many environmental sounds including speech. He did not babble and only rarely produced meaningful sounds in play, such as "choo–choo" while engaging with a toy train. Moreover, he used a very few gestures and these had occurred only recently. . . . Interestingly, in view of the previous diagnosis of peripheral deafness, he comprehended speech rather readily. He made no attempts to intimate speech but used "mom" to refer to many objects and wants. . . . He was expressive in laughing, crying and smiling and these expressions manifested good emotional tone.

Bobby was a friendly boy who presented no unusual behavior symptoms with the exception of his lack of verbal ability. He was normally shy, inhibited, playful and manifested good relationship to his environment. He responded to simple verbal commands and engaged himself integratively and imaginatively with toys, crayons and other objects. His behavior was unlike that of children with peripheral or psychic deafness and was not typical of receptive aphasics [difficulty processing language input] or the mentally deficient. The clinical impression was distinctly one of predominantly expressive aphasia [difficulty expressing in speech what has been understood].

*Source:* Myklebust, H. R. (1954). *Auditory disorders in children* (pp. 331–333). New York: Grune & Stratton.

speech. He reasoned that their speech function must have transferred to the same region in the right hemisphere. Today we know that Broca was correct, and that good teaching and parenting can stimulate brain regions to take on new functions. Broca's work was an important beginning for subsequent theorists who studied the specialization of the cerebral hemispheres for specific functions; the readiness of certain brain areas to take over for malfunctioning areas; and how auditory information is received, understood, memorized, and repeated.

***LD pioneering work was an important beginning for the study of the specialization of the cerebral hemispheres for specific functions and the readiness of certain brain areas to take over for malfunctioning areas.***

In the 1870s, the German doctor Carl Wernicke began focusing on stroke patients' inability to understand speech *(receptive* or *sensory aphasia)*. When speaking, these patients struggled to think of even simple words such as *hat* or *pencil.* Their

*Word-finding problems are a common characteristic of learning disabilities that we continue to study today.*

inability to understand and use words was accompanied by a loss of ability to read and write. Interestingly, as these patients recovered their ability to understand words, their speech and reading also improved. However, the ability to call a word to mind quickly, or to express oneself in writing, remained poor. Wernicke was correct in suggesting that these losses were the result of damage to certain portions of the temporal lobe (now known as *Wernicke's area*) that had neural connections to Broca's area. He hypothesized that when these connections were damaged (*conduction aphasia*), stroke victims might be able to understand what others said, yet they could respond only with unrelated jargon. The difficulty Wernicke identified in his patients' inability to find the right word is a common characteristic of learning disabilities *(word-finding problem)*. Moreover, special educators now commonly analyze a child's learning along the receptive, expressive, and connectionist dimensions suggested by Wernicke.

Hughlings Jackson, a contemporary of Broca's, agreed that language is commonly located in the left hemisphere, but he was among the first to suggest that for some people, left-handers, for example, language could be located in the right hemisphere. Jackson felt that the right hemisphere controls certain types of speech messages because some of his patients who had suffered left hemisphere damage could still use emotional expressions ("Oh my God!") or respond with language that had become automatic habits ("yes," "very well"). Jackson also argued that, because behavioral disturbances often accompanied speech disorders, speech must be controlled by complex networks within the whole brain. In other words, damage to any single portion of the brain can reduce a person's abilities in multiple, seemingly unrelated areas. This reasoning led Jackson to propose that language is thought and is therefore critically linked to intelligence.

*LD pioneers observed that damage to any single portion of the brain can reduce a person's abilities in multiple, seemingly unrelated areas.*

Jackson's ideas about the right hemisphere's role in language have since been confirmed. This knowledge helps us understand the wide variety of differences in abilities among individuals. In addition, we now know that the loss of ability in one area because of brain injury may have an effect on other skills that also depend in part on that ability. For example, language weaknesses and the inability to sort out the order of sounds one hears in words can be linked to reading, writing, and comprehension difficulties. This link is particularly important in a culture like ours in which achievement and problem solving depend a great deal on verbal skills.

*Language weaknesses and the inability to sort out the order of sounds heard in words are linked to reading, writing, and comprehension difficulties.*

Sir Henry Head, editor of the British journal *Brain* from 1905 to 1922, monopolized its pages by criticizing Broca's and Wernicke's notion that each brain region served a different function. Like Jackson, Head saw the brain as a complex neural network crossing different brain regions. Therefore, injury to one area would affect many functions. Because of the complexity of understanding how the brain functions, Head thought it wisest to plan interventions based on what professionals observed in their patients' behavior. Trying to pinpoint the specific area of the brain that had been injured, as had Broca and Wernicke, was a waste of time and unlikely to help in educational planning. Likewise, Head spurned labels such as "aphasia" because they did not describe the specific skill that required remediation. Studying World War I victims of gunshot wounds to the head, Head followed Jackson's lead in noting that abstract conceptual ability is the most serious process affected by language losses. In other words, language disabilities dull a person's reasoning skills. Head observed that once these patients appeared less competent, others isolated them from the very communication and information that could have sharpened their intelligence—a practice unfortunately all too common in learning disabilities today when parents or teachers speak "at" these children or ignore them, rather than helping to draw them into the conversation to develop their thought processes.

*Pioneering work led to a key premise in current LD theory: that children with LD can display greater intellectual ability through one sensory channel rather than another, and they can handle some learning tasks easily but find others very difficult.*

Head's work is reflected in key premises in current LD theories: children may display greater intellectual ability through one sensory channel rather than another (such as visual perception vs. language), and they can handle some learning tasks easily but find others very difficult (such as singing vs. speaking); describing learning behaviors is more important than diagnosing sites of brain injury; and if language and intelligence are synonymous in this culture, then early language intervention is critical when weaknesses are noted.

In reaction to so much theorizing based on injured adult brains, in the 1950s Jon Eisenson suggested that, although children could experience poor language development because of brain injury before, during, or after birth, these delays also could have resulted simply from a lag in their brain's maturation. Unlike the adults his predecessors studied, the children whom Eisenson studied hadn't lost speech. Rather, they were slow to develop speech skills in the first place, such as vocabulary, grammar, and comprehension *(developmental aphasia)*. Moreover, these children frequently didn't recognize that someone was speaking to them; responded inconsistently to sound; had intellectual, attention, visual-perceptual, motor, and memory problems; had emotional ups-and-downs; and had some days that were better than others. Eisenson believed that these children could not speak correctly because they had a hard time figuring out the meaning of the speech they heard. This notion stimulated a great deal of important research into how auditory information is processed, and why breakdowns in auditory processing occur.

In contrast to Eisenson, who focused on impaired language processing in children, Charles Osgood proposed a normal language development model as a way of understanding learning disabilities. He proposed that there were two stages to all behaviors: *decoding* (interpreting what signals from the environment mean) and *encoding* (expressing oneself). Each stage has three levels of organization: (1) *projection,* in which incoming or outgoing signals are wired to appropriate brain areas, (2) *integration,* in which incoming or outgoing neural signals get organized, and (3) *representation,* in which meaning and thinking take place. The stronger the projection level, the better the integration and representation of information. Osgood's normal language development model helped shape the development of tests and remedial programs for children with learning problems.

By proposing that reading depends on inner language, comprehension, and speaking skills, and that composition skills depend on both language and reading skills, Helmer Myklebust firmly established the link between language disorders and learning disabilities. The work of this group of language development researchers reinforced the need for individually tailored, intensive, and early remediation efforts to raise not only children's language abilities but, as a result, also their intellectual, academic, and social skills.

## Program Development

By the 1960s the theoretical work in visual-perceptual and language development and a corresponding growth of new educational materials and methods made individualized instruction more sophisticated and manageable. The use of all senses to learn was emphasized. Specialized programming efforts expanded beyond reading instruction to include writing, arithmetic, comprehension, and content area learning (history and biology, for example). The pioneers in program development set the stage for creative remedial strategies for children who experienced mild to severe problems in one or more areas of development and learning.

The story of Percy F. is interesting not only because it dates back to 1896 but also because it's one of the earliest case studies of reading disorders. It shows the fascination and frustration of teaching a child who appears normal in every way but who has such great difficulty mastering reading. It's no wonder that researchers and other professionals have devoted whole careers to studying children like Percy.

James Hinshelwood, a Scottish ophthalmologist in the late 1800s, studied the effects of brain damage on adult reading skills. His case studies, summarized in

### Percy F.

*A bright 14-year-old who couldn't learn to read.*

Percy F.—a well-grown lad, aged 14—is the eldest son of intelligent parents, the second child of a family of seven. He has always been a bright and intelligent boy, quick at games, and in no way inferior to others of his age.

His great difficulty has been—and is now—his inability to learn to read. This inability is so remarkable, and so pronounced, that I have no doubt it is due to some congenital defect.

He has been at school or under tutors since he was 7 years old, and the greatest efforts have been made to teach him to read, but, in spite of this laborious and persistent training, he can only with difficulty spell out words of one syllable.

The following is the result of an examination I made a short time since. He knows all his letters and can write them and read them. In writing from dictation he comes to grief over any but the simplest words. For instance, I dictated the following sentence: "Now, you watch me while I spin it." He wrote: "Now you word me wale I spin it"; and, again, "Carefully winding the string round the peg" was written: "calfuly winder the sturng rond the pag."

In writing his own name he made a mistake, putting "Precy" for "Percy," and he did not notice the mistake until his attention was called to it more than once. I asked him to write the following words:

| | | |
|---|---|---|
| Song | he wrote | scone |
| Subject | " | Scojock |
| Without | " | wichout |
| English | " | Englis |
| Shilling | " | sening |
| Seashore | " | seasoiv |

He was quite unable to spell the name of his father's house though he must have seen it and spelt it scores of times. In asking him to read the

Research Box 1.2 on page 24, led him to hypothesize that the brain had separate centers to store visual memories of everyday objects, letters, numerals, and words. He based his theory on the fact that recognition of objects, letters, numerals, and words returned separately, rather than all at once, as adults recovered from a brain injury. Believing that we read by recalling the visual picture of words, Hinshelwood applied the term *congenital word blindness* to children of normal vision and intelligence who had reading problems similar to those of the adults he had studied. Hinshelwood's solution was to first teach letter sounds and then spell words aloud in order to use the child's good memory for letter sounds to work around his or her difficulty "picturing" words. The link to later phonics methods of teaching reading is obvious.

Also believing that reading at least in part involved storing the image of words, Samuel Orton, a neuropathologist working in the 1930s, proposed that when one cerebral hemisphere fails to establish dominance over the other, it can't suppress the mirror images of words coming in from the nondominant side. Such word reversals—reading and writing "backwards," in other words—were thought to be less serious concerns than if children couldn't decipher words by sounding out their component sounds.

**Percy F.** (Continued)

sentences he had just written a short time previously, he could not do so, but made mistakes over every word except the very simplest. Words such as "and" and "the" he always recognizes.

I then asked him to read me a sentence out of an easy child's book without spelling the words. The result was curious. He did not read a single word correctly, with the exception of "and," "the," "of," "that," etc.; the other words seemed to be quite unknown to him, and he could not even make an attempt to pronounce them.

I next tried his ability to read figures, and found he could do so easily. He read off quickly the following: 785, 852017, 20, 969, and worked out correctly: $(a + x)(a - x) = a^2 - x^2$. He could not do the simple calculation $4 \times \frac{1}{2}$, but he multiplied 749 by 867 quickly and correctly. He says he is fond of arithmetic, and finds no difficulty with it, but that printed or written words "have no meaning to him," and my examination of him quite convinces me that he is correct in that opinion. Words written or printed seem to convey no impression to his mind, and it is only after laboriously spelling them that he is able, by the sounds of the letters, to discover their import. His memory for written or printed words is so defective that he can only recognize such simple ones as "and," "the," "of," etc. Other words he never seems to remember no matter how frequently he may have met them. . . .

I may add that the boy is bright and of average intelligence in conversation . . . his eyesight is good. The schoolmaster who has taught him for some years says that he would be the smartest lad in the school if the instruction were entirely oral. It will be interesting to see what effect further training will have on his condition.

*Source:* Morgan, W. P. (1896). A case of congenital word blindness. *British Medical Journal, 2*, p. 1878. 

RESEARCH BOX 1.2

## Hinshelwood's Case Studies of "Word and Letter Blindness"

Hinshelwood's clients suffered from brain insults caused by strokes and chronic alcoholism, and they had acquired strange forms of "word blindness" or "dyslexia" (inability to read). One individual had lost the ability to read print or write more than the first few words of a line, after which the words lost meaning for him. He was a tailor and could not remember how to fit pieces together, where he had just placed objects, and where his home was located (Hinshelwood, 1896). Another client could not read words but could read letters and numbers, write from dictation, and copy words. If allowed to spell each word aloud, letter by letter, he could read the words laboriously (Hinshelwood, 1898).

Hinshelwood found that word blindness was often accompanied by letter blindness. One patient could not recognize letters but, if allowed to trace them with his finger, could eventually name them (Hinshelwood, 1898). Another client, Tom, exhibited letter blindness without word blindness. He could not read, write, or point to individual letters (with the exception of *T*, which he called "Tom"). However, Tom could read familiar and unfamiliar words rapidly and also wrote well (Hinshelwood, 1899). It was not long before Hinshelwood and others generalized their theoretical notions about the injured brain processes in these adults to children who also experienced significant difficulties acquiring reading and writing skills.

*Many pioneers in program development supported the phonetic approach to reading remediation, a method that has since been affirmed by reading and LD experts.*

Orton believed that the "look-say" approach in American schools at the time was making reading difficult since the nondominant hemisphere would interfere by reversing letter and word images. To counteract these images, he felt that the words' individual sounds should get the greatest emphasis in instruction. Orton was a strong proponent of the phonetic approach, a method that has since been affirmed by reading and LD experts. His reading remediation methods focused on building associations between auditory and visual information and feedback from body movements. For example, Orton suggested that children trace a letter or word while simultaneously giving the letter sounds. Consistent left-to-right tracing would help build "word pictures" and undo any confusion caused by the nondominant hemisphere's reversed images. Spelling, too, was to be trained through the analysis of the sequence of sounds in words. In extreme cases in which children still had not established a hand preference (and therefore what was believed to be a "dominant" brain hemisphere), Orton suggested training one side of the body's movements in order to strengthen cerebral dominance; this in turn was expected to overcome the interference from reversed images coming from the nondominant hemisphere.

Orton was influential in the learning disabilities field in many ways besides promoting a phonics approach to reading. He championed gearing teaching materials to the student's abilities and interests; individualizing instruction by analyzing the content and process of learning; and dealing head-on with the apathy, antagonism, and lack of self-esteem that often accompany learning failures. Most important by far, though, was his emphasis on phonetic analysis, which helped educators shift away from the then predominant visual-perceptual perspective on learning problems.

Many reading remediation experts developed Orton's methods further. Grace Fernald, author of the landmark book *Remedial Techniques in Basic School Subjects* (1943), had the most widespread influence. Because she believed that visual teaching methods didn't work for children who had difficulty remembering what they had seen, she suggested a multisensory approach that combined *kinesthetic* (touch and movement) methods such as tracing letters, with phonetic associations, such as blending the individual word sounds while looking at the whole word.

In the 1960s, Doris Johnson and Helmer Myklebust further developed Fernald's creative remedial approaches. Johnson and Myklebust categorized several forms of *dyslexia,* or reading failure: *auditory dyslexia,* the inability to process sounds; *visual dyslexia,* difficulty processing visual symbols; *comprehension disorders,* and *written production* problems. They believed that reading and spelling are so difficult because these tasks involve the *interneurosensory integration* of visual with vocal (as in reading) and auditory with motor (as in spelling) information. *Intraneurosensory integration,* staying within sensory systems (e.g., visual-motor as in copying designs; auditory-vocal as in repeating oral directions), was thought to be much easier. Based on these theories, Johnson and Myklebust developed several effective teaching strategies tailored to individual children's needs, many of which are still used today. They also stressed ongoing assessment while teaching, known as *clinical teaching,* with special attention to the sensory modality used to take in or express information. Their theories and practices greatly influenced the development of assessment strategies, teaching materials, and methods in the LD field.

***LD pioneers urged special attention to the sensory modality used to take in or express information, often recommending multisensory teaching approaches to facilitate learning.***

## The 1960s through 1990s

From the 1960s to the 1990s, the various theories and practices in learning disabilities rose and fell in popularity. Significant controversy resulted from the misapplication of some of the pioneers' beliefs. For example, some teachers aimed solely at remediating visual-motor or language causes of learning problems to the near exclusion of solid academic teaching.

Behavior modification moved from the laboratory to the classroom in the late 1960s as teachers learned to structure learning environments to reinforce appropriate behavior and learning. Rigidly sequenced reading and math programs were common, with teachers being told exactly what to teach next and precisely how to teach it—down to the specific words and motions to use. The students of Werner, Strauss, and Cruickshank modeled their mentors' structured approaches and developed many of these strategies. Behavior modification focused on teaching the actual academic skills, rather than building skills presumed to underlie the learning difficulties (such as form perception, auditory memory, coordination, or balance). Researchers found that an emphasis on underlying skills alone led to negligible academic gains if the building of these skills wasn't accompanied by solid teaching of academic skills.

***Researchers found that an emphasis on developing information-processing skills alone leads to negligible academic gains if the building of these skills isn't accompanied by solid teaching of academic skills.***

By the mid 1970s, language processing weaknesses and attention deficits gradually replaced the visual-motor emphasis in the understanding of learning

*By the mid-1970s it was recognized that language and attention delays have far more serious consequences for learning than visual or motor delays.*

*We still follow the lessons of the pioneers in the field, who advised teaching "through all the senses," limiting distractions to help children focus, not teaching too much too fast, and confronting reading delays by teaching phonics.*

*Because the causes and characteristics of LD vary from person to person, each child's teaching needs will differ from those of another.*

disabilities. The far more serious learning consequences of language and attention delays, when compared to visual or motor delays, gained greater notice. In this decade, sophisticated neuropsychological studies began to connect specific information-processing patterns to different kinds of academic delays. The pioneers' instructional approaches became second nature in the classroom, and they persist to this day. When we teach a child "through all his senses," that's Fernald. When we use a study carrel to help a child focus, that's Strauss. When we caution not to teach too much too fast, that's Werner. When we teach phonics, that's Orton. Despite this progress, however, it was disconcerting that learning disabilities didn't disappear as a child grew older. In fact, new hurdles seemed to appear as the demands of the academic, social, and work worlds became more complex. Therefore, research attention increasingly shifted to students at secondary and postsecondary levels, and to the social and emotional consequences of learning disabilities.

By the 1980s eclecticism had become the accepted approach to learning disabilities. Advances in neuropsychological research and the intricate interplay between biological and environmental influences on human development led experts to forego searching for a single theory of learning disabilities and to adopt a wide-ranging approach. Educators finally accepted the fact that learning disabilities are not a unitary deficit disorder. The causes and characteristics of LD vary from person to person, and therefore one person's teaching needs are markedly different from those of another.

In the 1990s several concerns rose in priority. As the learning disabilities concept gained in popularity and because so many different kinds of learning problems fell within the definition, embarrassingly large numbers of children were being misidentified as learning disabled. Normal variability in children's rates of development often was being identified as abnormal. The growing numbers of children with LD led some critics to question whether there even was such a thing as a learning disability. This situation pointed to the need for a refined definition of different subtypes of LD and more precise identification criteria.

Yet other concerns must be addressed as we move forward in this very young field. Among these are the need to continue developing valid curriculum-based assessment approaches (in contrast to standardized tests that don't inform us about precisely what or how to teach); helping adolescents transition from the school to adult worlds; finding the best preventative strategies; helping students access the curriculum and better negotiate their social worlds; and countering the inflexibility of the regular classroom curriculum by making the learning experience more meaningful, guided by each student's interests, creativity, and cultural and linguistic background. As we face these challenges, we continue to rely on the insights of the pioneers in the field who challenged us to conceptualize a child's learning disabilities as an outcome of the interaction among unique student, curriculum, and environmental factors.

## Summary

In the mid-1960s several forces came together to catalyze the birth of learning disabilities as a new field of special education. Parents whose children showed unexpected inability to learn and uneven patterns of development found that existing special education classification and placement practices did not meet their children's needs. Parents joined with professionals to advocate for intensified instruction and modification of teaching methods and settings to accommodate each child's unique strengths, weaknesses, and learning styles. Research relating visual-perceptual and language difficulties to learning disorders enhanced educators' understanding of these children's learning needs, and individualized instruction was augmented with the development of new programming materials and methods and the classroom application of behavior modification techniques. That a specific information-processing disorder could be responsible for learning difficulties had special appeal to parents because it avoided their children's identification as mentally retarded or emotionally disturbed, and encouraged intensive teaching efforts. Parent-professional advocacy groups and the backing of judicial decisions that gave the right to a free, appropriate education to all children with disabilities led the federal government in 1975 to mandate special education services to children with learning disabilities.

## Helpful Resources

### Educational Philosophy and Practices


Dunn, L. M. (1968). Special education for the mildly retarded—Is much of it justifiable? *Exceptional Children, 35*, 5–22.

Johnson, G. O. (1962). Special education for the mentally handicapped—A paradox. *Exceptional Children, 29*, 62–69.

Kirk, S. A. (1958). *Early education of the mentally retarded: An experimental study.* Urbana, IL: University of Illinois Press.

Kirk, S. A. (1976). Samuel A. Kirk. In J. M. Kauffman & D. P. Hallahan (Eds.), *Teaching children with learning disabilities: Personal perspectives.* Columbus, OH: Charles E. Merrill.

Morse, W. C., Cutler, R. L., & Fink, A. H. (1964). *Public school classes for the emotionally handicapped: A research analysis.* Washington, DC: Council for Exceptional Children, National Education Association.

Federal government educational publications and statistics: http://www.ed.gov/pubs


### Advocacy


Cruickshank, W. M. (1972). Some issues facing the field of learning disability. *Journal of Learning Disabilities, 5*, 380–388.

Gillespie, P. H., Miller, T. L., & Fielder, V. D. (1975). Legislative definitions of learning disabilities: Roadblocks to effective service. *Journal of Learning Disabilities, 8*, 660–666.

Individuals with Disabilities Education Act (IDEA). (1999, March 12). Final regulations and comments from the U.S. Dept. of Education. *Federal Register, 64*(48), 12406–12672.

Weintraub, F. J., & Abeson, A. (1974). New education policies for the handicapped: The quiet revolution. *Phi Delta Kappan, 55*, 526–529, 569.

IDEA implementation: http://www.ideapractices.org

International Dyslexia Association: http://www.interdys.org

Learning Disability Association of America: http://www.LDAamerica.org

Legislative updates: http://www.nasponline.org

National Center for Learning Disabilities: http://www.ncld.org

Special education law: http://www.wrightslaw.com

Twenty-Fourth Annual Report to Congress on the Implementation of the Individuals with Disabilities Education Act (2002): http://www.ideadata.org


### Research and Program Development


Anderson, P. L., & Meier-Hedde, R. (2001). Early case reports of dyslexia in the United States and Europe. *Journal of Learning Disabilities, 34*, 9–21.

Bijou, S. W. (1970). What psychology has to offer education—now. *Journal of Applied Behavior Analysis, 3*, 65–71.

Cruickshank, W. M., Bentzen, F. A., Ratzeburg, F. H., & Tannhauser, M. T. (1961). *A teaching method for brain-injured and hyperactive children.* Syracuse: Syracuse University Press.

Eggert, G. H. (1977). *Wernicke's works on aphasia: A sourcebook and review.* The Hague: Mouton Publishers.

Eisenson, J. (1968). Developmental aphasia: A speculative view with therapeutic implications. *Journal of Speech and Hearing Disorders, 33,* 3–13.

Fernald, G. M. (1943). *Remedial techniques in basic school subjects.* New York: McGraw-Hill.

Frostig, M. (1976). Marianne Frostig. In J. M. Kauffman & D. P. Hallahan (Eds.), *Teaching children with learning disabilities: Personal perspectives.* Columbus, OH: Charles E. Merrill.

Frostig, M., & Maslow, P. (1973). *Learning problems in the classroom.* New York: Grune & Stratton.

Goldstein, K. (1942). *Aftereffects of brain injuries in war.* New York: Grune & Stratton.

Head, H. (1926). *Aphasia and kindred disorders of speech.* London: Cambridge University Press.

Hinshelwood, J. (1917). *Congenital word blindness.* London: H. K. Lewis.

Jackson, H. (1931). *Selected writings of John Hughlings Jackson* (2 vols.). London: Hodder & Stoughton.

Johnson, D., & Myklebust, H. (1967). *Learning disabilities: Educational principles and practices.* New York: Grune & Stratton.

Kephart, N. C. (1960). *The slow learner in the classroom.* Columbus, OH: Charles E. Merrill.

Myklebust, H. R. (1954). *Auditory disorders in children.* New York: Grune & Stratton.

Myklebust, H. R. (1973). *Development and disorders of written language: Vol. 2. Studies of normal and exceptional children.* New York: Grune & Stratton.

Orton, S. T. (1937). *Reading, writing and speech problems in children.* New York: W. W. Norton.

Osgood, C. E. (1957). A behavioristic analysis of perception and language as cognitive phenomena. In J. S. Bruner (Ed.), *Contemporary approaches to cognition.* Cambridge: Harvard University Press.

Smith, C. R. (1985). Learning disabilities past and present. *Journal of Learning Disabilities, 18,* 513–517.

Smith, C. R. (1986). The future of the LD field: Intervention approaches. *Journal of Learning Disabilities, 19,* 461–472.

Strauss, A. A., & Kephart, N. C. (1955). *Psychopathology and education of the brain-injured child: Vol. 2. Progress in theory and clinic.* New York: Grune & Stratton.

Strauss, A. A., & Lehtinen, L. E. (1947). *Psychopathology and education of the brain-injured child.* New York: Grune & Stratton.

Strauss, A. A., & Werner, H. (1942). Disorders of conceptual thinking in the brain-injured child. *Journal of Nervous and Mental Disease, 96,* 153–172.

Wepman, J. M., Jones, L. V., Bock, R. D., & Van Pelt, D. (1960). Studies in aphasia: Background and theoretical formulations. *Journal of Speech and Hearing Disorders, 25,* 323–332.

Werner, H. (1937). Process and achievement: A basic problem of education and developmental psychology. *Harvard Educational Review, 7,* 353–368.

Werner, H., & Strauss, A. A. (1940). Causal factors in low performance. *American Journal of Mental Deficiency, 45,* 213–218.

CHAPTER TWO

# Definition, Identification, and Prevalence

**NOW THAT WE** have described the historical roots of learning disabilities, we explore the evolution of our LD definition and identification practices. The bottom line is that we are still searching for the best way to identify learning disabilities. Today's identification procedures boil down to a clinical judgment made after considering multiple dimensions, including a child's intelligence, achievement levels, quality of schooling, opportunities to learn at home, motivation, learning rate, and age. Although 1 in 20 schoolchildren qualifies for LD services, research tells us that many more children may in fact need special help but they do not get identified because of high school dropout, their ability to compensate for and mask weaknesses, opting for vocational education, or differences in identification practices from city to city and state to state. Today approximately 50 percent of school-children with disabilities are identified with learning disabilities. Although males are far more prevalent than females in our LD numbers, researchers feel that the male-to-female ratio is actually equal—but for a variety of reasons boys are more likely to come to our attention.

***1 in every 20 schoolchildren, approximately 50 percent of children with disabilities, are identified as learning disabled.***

## Definition

Before the term *learning disabilities* gained acceptance, nearly 40 terms were used interchangeably to describe children of near average or higher intelligence who, despite trying hard academically, couldn't succeed. Some of these children eventually did achieve, but at an extraordinary cost in terms of the effort needed to keep up. All of these children had unexpected underachievement, but they didn't fit into any of the existing disability classifications. They had characteristics similar to, but less striking than, children with a diagnosed brain injury. Instead of a dysfunctional limb because of a stroke, a child might be uncoordinated or have poor handwriting; a child could speak, but remembering a friend's name or calling to mind simple words like *house* was problematic. Terms used for these children included *organic brain damage, cerebral dysfunction, hyperkinetic behavior syndrome, primary reading retardation, clumsy child syndrome, slow learner, Strauss syndrome,* and even *cripple-brained.* None of these captured the overall problem, and some were very insulting.

*Early terms for learning disabilities such as* **brain injury** *and* **minimal brain dysfunction** *didn't survive long because they implied the situation was hopeless and they didn't inform instruction.*

Those terms that focused on the brain—such as *brain injury* and *minimal brain dysfunction* (MBD)—did not survive long in the lexicon. They were rejected because they implied the situation was hopeless (injured brain cells can't be repaired), they were too global to be meaningful (people with brain injury differ greatly), they were not helpful in determining an appropriate remedial approach, they often could not be verified as true, and they ignored a child's actual abilities by focusing on the hypothetical cause of the problem.

In the 1960s, Samuel Clements convened a national task force to come to grips with the terminology issue. The ten most agreed-on characteristics of these children that emerged were, in descending order of frequency, hyperactivity, perceptual-motor impairments, emotional lability, general coordination deficits, disorders of attention, impulsivity, disorders of memory and thinking, specific learning disabilities (reading, math, writing, spelling), disorders of speech and hearing, and equivocal neurological signs and electroencephalograph (EEG) irregularities. The task force recognized that seldom were two of these children identical in characteristics or teaching needs.

*Eventually the term* **specific learning disabilities** *gained popularity because of its educational, rather than medical, focus.*

Eventually, the term *specific learning disabilities* gained popularity, especially after Samuel Kirk used it in his keynote address in 1963 to a national conference on children with perceptual handicaps. The term had the advantage of an educational, rather than medical, focus.

The definition of learning disabilities that has the broadest current support was endorsed in 1988 by the National Joint Committee for Learning Disabilities, a group of nine national organizations dealing with the learning disabled:

> Learning disabilities is a general term that refers to a heterogeneous group of disorders manifested by significant difficulties in the acquisition and use of listening, speaking, reading, writing, reasoning, or mathematical abilities. These disorders are intrinsic to the individual, are presumed to be due to central nervous system dysfunction, and may occur across the life span. Problems in self-regulatory behaviors, social perception, and social interaction may exist with learning disabilities but do not by themselves constitute a learning disability. Although a learning disability may occur concomitantly with other disabilities (for example, sensory impairment, men-

> tal retardation, or serious emotional disturbance) or with extrinsic influences (such as cultural differences or insufficient/inappropriate instruction), it would not be a result of those conditions or influences. (National Joint Committee on Learning Disabilities, 1997, p. 29).

In contrast to the definition of LD in the Individuals with Disabilities Education Act (IDEA) of 1990 this definition shows that learning disabilities apply across the entire life span and clearly states that underachievement is due to a neurological dysfunction within the individual.

When the Education for All Handicapped Children Act (1975) recognized learning disabilities as a fundable handicapping condition, it set forth these identification criteria, which were subsequently incorporated into IDEA:

***A team may determine that a child has a specific learning disability if the child has a severe discrepancy between achievement and intellectual ability despite good educational opportunities.***

(a) A team may determine that a child has a specific learning disability if:

(1) The child does not achieve commensurate with his or her age and ability levels in one or more of the areas listed in paragraph (a) (2) of this section, if provided with learning experiences appropriate for the child's age and ability levels; and

(2) The team finds that a child has a severe discrepancy between achievement and intellectual ability in one or more of the following areas:

(i) Oral expression.
(ii) Listening comprehension.
(iii) Written expression.
(iv) Basic reading skill.
(v) Reading comprehension.
(vi) Mathematics calculation.
(vii) Mathematics reasoning.

(b) The team may not identify a child as having a specific learning disability if the severe discrepancy between ability and achievement is primarily the result of—

(1) A visual, hearing, or motor impairment;
(2) Mental retardation;
(3) Emotional disturbance; or
(4) Environmental, cultural or economic disadvantage.

(Federal Register, March 12, 1999, p. 12457)

The law stipulates that before a student can be identified as learning disabled, it must be documented that his or her learning outcome is poor in spite of good educational opportunities. In addition, the student must have disabilities that require special educational strategies different from those customary for typical learners at the same age and ability level.

Several key implications of our current LD definition and legal requirements deserve mention.

## Severe Discrepancy between Achievement and Intellectual Ability

*Each state determines the extent of discrepancy between intelligence and achievement that it considers "severe."*

Although all children with learning disabilities are achieving in some areas below what would be expected for their intellectual ability, each state determines the extent of discrepancy between intelligence and achievement that it considers "severe." Unevenness in skills is the norm in LD. A student, for example, may be an extraordinary artist, a talented mathematician, but a poor reader who has trouble comprehending and expressing himself or herself in writing or speech. Whether the reading and writing is poor enough to qualify as a learning disability is up to each state to determine.

## Educational Orientation

*Proving that a central nervous system dysfunction is at the root of the learning problem isn't necessary because IDEA states that underachievement is what determines LD identification.*

Proving that a central nervous system dysfunction is at the root of the learning problem isn't necessary because IDEA states that underachievement is what determines LD identification. IDEA's educational orientation doesn't mean, however, that the brain is irrelevant to learning disabilities. Although research is giving us more and more clues about how brain functions are linked to underachievement, we still don't know enough. The educational orientation of our current definition acknowledges that, because we are still learning about the neuropsychological processes underlying the different types of learning disabilities and deciding which approaches might work best for each individual, it is more pragmatic to identify LD based on academic criteria than on the basis of more theoretical information-processing weaknesses.

## Exclusion Clauses

Unfortunately, IDEA easily can be misinterpreted to mean that "if you're mentally retarded, emotionally disturbed, or physically handicapped, you can't also be learning disabled." That's simply not the case. A blind teenager who reads Braille may have great difficulty understanding what he or she has read because of language weaknesses. Youngsters who are emotionally disturbed may at first glance appear to lag behind their classmates because their minds seem to be everywhere but on schoolwork. Yet, such youngsters may also suffer from perceptual deficits that retard their ability to read: even when their attention is engaged and they try hard, they make no progress in reading.

The problem of telling whether mental retardation, emotional disturbance, or a physical disability is the cause of a child's underachievement, or whether a learning disability just happens to coexist with one of these disabilities, can be exacerbated when the experts chime in. Speaking of his client Jeffrey, a psychologist might argue that the child is emotionally disturbed because he has a difficult family life, and that he is learning disabled because of oxygen deprivation at birth. Jeffrey's pediatrician may argue that his developmental milestones were normal despite the oxygen deprivation, so it's really the emotional disturbance that's causing the underachievement. The special educator might protest that the academic and social frustrations that Jeffrey is experiencing has caused him to act out and be disobedient, which in turn caused the poor family relationships and ultimately the emotional disturbance. Similarly, Kayla, a teenager who is mildly retarded and whose reading comprehension lags behind her decoding and math skills, might simply have a cap on how far comprehension can progress because of her lower intelligence; alternatively, perhaps her intelligence is underestimated because her language weaknesses impede performance on IQ tests—she may be learning disabled and not retarded. It's the story of the blind men and the elephant, but with potentially serious consequences if, because of diagnostic uncertainty, children don't get the help they need.

IDEA also excludes environmental, cultural, and economic disadvantage as primary reasons for LD identification. It's clear that poor teaching, lack of familiarity with English, lack of parental encouragement to learn, cultural diversity, and lack of resources for even the basics like food and secure shelter can lead to underachievement. This underachievement might also be due to a learning disability, however, if it can be shown that the child fails to benefit from good schooling and requires very different teaching approaches from what is typical. Unfortunately, lower income children who do in fact have learning disabilities risk not being identified for special services if IDEA's exclusion clause is interpreted too literally. In other words, teachers and other professionals may be too quick to blame a child's background for underachievement rather than determine whether a learning disability actually exists.

***Professionals may be too quick to blame a child's cultural and economic background, low intelligence, physical or emotional difficulties for underachievement, rather than determining whether a learning disability actually exists.***

## Misidentification

The necessarily vague definition of learning disabilities has resulted in misidentification. Many students who are identified as learning disabled are really poorly motivated, have been poorly taught, have little support at home for learning, are immature, are slow learners in all areas of development, have English as a second language, or are in fact average learners out of place in above-average schools.

***Many students who are poorly motivated, have been poorly taught, have little home support for learning, are immature, are slow learners in all areas of development, have English as a second language, or are average learners out of place in above-average schools have been misidentified as LD.***

One study in Colorado revealed that 57 percent of the learning disabled really didn't belong in that category. Other studies have shown that one-third to one-half of children identified as learning disabled do not have a significant discrepancy between achievement and intellectual ability.

Although the intentions of those conducting the assessment and LD identification in these school districts may have been good, what they have really done is to diffuse the focus of LD programs that now must address the needs of students who really don't need this type of special help. Consequently, students with the most severe learning disabilities are sometimes cheated out of the intensive intervention imagined by the legislation. At the same time, the mislabeling unwittingly lets general educators avoid the responsibility of teaching those students functioning at the bottom of their classes. Moreover, since researchers often select LD subjects based on students whom school personnel already have identified as learning disabled, the mislabeling has contributed to confusing research findings regarding LD characteristics and the best intervention approaches. Research Box 2.1 on page 34 explores this research problem and offers recommendations for change.

RESEARCH BOX 2.1

## Dealing with the Contradictions in Learning Disabilities Research

Thousands of studies on LD have been published in the professional literature in the past 30 years. Unfortunately, this great activity has produced contradictory research findings, and the problem can't be explained away by simply saying "Well, the LD population is just so heterogeneous, what else would we expect?" There is a more basic problem that begins with researchers who, though very well meaning, are reporting on subject pools for whom they have very sparse descriptive data. Who are these children? What are their families like? How have they been taught? What are their learning patterns in different areas?

With the exception of some broad generalizations (e.g., many students with learning disabilities are slow information processors, have motor and language weaknesses, are poorly organized and not strategic in their learning, don't feel themselves capable of succeeding), very few additional generalizations hold true for the majority of students with learning disabilities. Because we are dealing with such a diverse group of individuals, in order for research to be most meaningful to the understanding of LD and the design of appropriate interventions, LD researchers must begin to conscientiously study subgroups of children who are alike on a subset of marker variables that affect learning. Segregating the data into subgroups acknowledges that individuals with LD are a "mixed" variety, and this categorization is our best hope for addressing the question of why particular children are struggling to learn and what we can do to help them.

Most researchers have studied heterogeneous groups of subjects, rather than subjects who fit one precise profile of learning disabilities. To complicate the matter, most of our subjects are identified by nonresearchers' standards and for nonresearch purposes by clinics or school districts (Keogh & Babbitt, 1986; Macmillan, Gresham, & Bocian, 1998). Because LD is a clinical judgment, who is called learning disabled differs markedly from one clinician and institution to another. Some clinics, for example, identify only children with neurological impairments as LD, whereas others identify only children with language impairments. Some school districts with tight budgets identify only children with severe delays, whereas wealthier districts and those with more intervention alternatives may decide to include children who are moderately underachieving.

If researchers begin to carefully choose subgroups of students who share specific variables, then we will be in a better position to sort out our research findings. That is, we may begin to understand why an information-processing weakness causes particular difficulties for one type of child but not for another, or why a specific teaching technique works for one type of child but not for another. With better descriptions of our subject populations, we will know which subjects to choose for replication studies.

To deal with this problem, Keogh and her colleagues (1982) suggested a group of important marker variables to specify when describing subject groups. Each of these variables can influence study outcomes:

| **Descriptive Markers** | **Topical Markers** |
|---|---|
| Number of subjects by sex | Activity level |
| Chronological age | Attention |
| Grade level | Auditory perception |

## RESEARCH BOX 2.1 (Continued)

**Descriptive Markers** *(continued)*
Race/ethnicity
Source of subjects
Socioeconomic status
Language background
Educational history
Educational placement
Physical and health status

**Substantive Markers**
Intellectual ability
Reading achievement
Arithmetic achievement
Behavioral and emotional adjustment

**Topical Markers** *(continued)*
Fine motor coordination
Gross motor coordination
Memory
Oral language
Visual perception

**Background Markers**
Month/year of study
Geographical location
Locale
Exclusionary criteria
Control/comparison group

Others urge that researchers specify:

- Children's time in special education; type of special and general education placement; family culture; community culture; school district size; socioeconomic level; philosophy toward inclusion; curriculum; student achievement levels; instructional materials and methods; resources; classroom variables such as teacher cultural background, experience, and educational philosophy; and classroom environment factors including grouping patterns, student-centeredness, challenge, level of language discourse, and incorporation of children's cultural backgrounds (Bos & Fletcher, 1997).
- Whether there was random assignment of participants to groups; control for the *Hawthorne effect* (subjects improve simply because they know they're being observed); use of the same teacher, setting, time period, and materials in both treatment and control groups; and whether learned skills were maintained over time or to new materials and settings (Simmerman & Swanson, 2001).
- The precise nature of the tasks subjects engaged in and the measurement techniques used (Keogh & Babbitt, 1986).
- How the intervention was monitored to make sure it was carried out as planned (Gresham et al., 2000).
- The LD identification criteria used as well as narrative information such as student motivation and history of teaching approaches (Rosenberg et al., 1993).
- The qualifications of the examiners (Morris et al., 1994).

An *age-matched control group* that matches the LD group on all variables but the one being studied is very important because it matches subjects for "years of experience." An *achievement-matched control group* also is important; this is a younger control group that equals the LD group's achievement level (Fisher & Athey, 1986). For example, when the ability to sequence sounds in words is found to be poorer in an LD group than for same-age peers, it may be that sound sequencing is not the cause of the observed reading delay. The results may simply be due to the reduced reading experience of the LD group, which

*(continued)*

## RESEARCH BOX 2.1 (Continued)

offers fewer opportunities to sharpen their sound-sequencing skills. But if the students with learning disabilities do differ in sequencing of sounds from even younger subjects who read and spell at comparable levels, then it is likely that a sound-sequencing deficit is contributing to their reading delays. The immature student who is merely behind for his or her age would be expected to progress at a steadier pace than the student whose learning characteristics are atypical at even younger developmental levels.

Torgesen (1987) describes the value of two additional control groups: (1) a longitudinal comparison of the developmental course of different types of children who have used different intervention approaches and (2) children who have experienced similar failure but who do not have the cognitive disability being investigated. In his reading investigations, Stanovich (1988) refers to the latter group as "garden variety" poor readers; they are of the same age and reading level as the learning disabled, but they have not been identified as disabled.

In a review of 900 studies published between 1963 and 1997, Simmerman and Swanson (2001) found that over three-quarters lacked a control condition, didn't report statistics (means, significance of effect levels), and reported on an intervention that lasted for fewer than three sessions. Clearly, we need to clean up our act if we are to trust the research we read and learn from it. By incorporating in our studies the types of descriptors and controls discussed here, the critical variables contributing to LD will begin to stand out. Simply comparing same-age students with and without LD tells us only what differences exist between the two without shedding light on the responsible factors.

Admonishing researchers who contribute to the confused state of research in learning disabilities, Senf (1987) reflects:

> LD is that flexible sponge that lives in the region between alleged normalcy and alleged handicap, expanding and contracting with a myriad of external events (philosophy of education, parental aspirations for their children, professional status, values) only a fraction of which concern the state of the individual so labeled. . . . In a "publish or perish" atmosphere . . . researchers might easily accept for research whatever is rung from the sponge. . . . A research sample squeezed from a public school (university clinic, hospital, or private practice) LD sponge would be a heterogeneous mess, containing subjects conforming to few knowledgeable persons' concept of LD (p. 92). . . . Squeeze the sample from the LD sponge: If a reasonably pure color appears, conduct the experiment. If the water is cloudy, so likely will be your results (p. 96).

Keogh (1987) poignantly adds:

> The heterogeneity within LD mirrors that of the sponge in its natural surround. . . . Many sponges harbor commensal worms, brittle stars, barnacles, shrimp, crabs, copepods, and amphipods. . . . Over 13,000 animals representing 19 species were found in a single Caribbean sponge (p. 56). . . . Some might argue that shrimp, barnacles, crabs, and brittle stars more accurately describe the researchers than the subjects of research (p. 97).

Currently, many researchers draw inappropriate conclusions due to these methodological problems. Clearly, better delineation of research samples, tasks, measurement tools, contexts, and control groups can help us understand the characteristics and needs of different subgroups of students with learning disabilities, even if they are drawn from the public school sponge.

### Further Concerns

Because of the vagueness of the federal LD definition and regulations, there is a need to establish more specific definitions, identification criteria, and service guidelines. These are some of the concerns that need to be addressed:

1. Describing a whole population as learning disabled mistakenly implies that they all have the same causes of learning disorders, the same characteristics, and the same educational needs.
2. The LD definition ignores associated problems such as poor social skills, planning ability, organization, and problem-solving strategies.
3. The LD definition does not include the adult who requires vocational, psychological, and independent living interventions because of persistent learning disabilities.
4. The LD definition implies that the problem is entirely within the student and that it must be cured, leaving the schools off the hook for addressing curriculum and learning environment factors that contribute to underachievement.
5. An LD label should be applied only when there is an extreme unevenness in abilities that requires intense, out-of-the-ordinary intervention. Uneven development is, by itself, quite normal, as any bright child who earns A's in everything except art will attest. Alexander's story on page 38 is one such example.
6. The LD definition may lead people to believe that the solution is simple, when, in fact, the learning disabled have very complex service needs.

***A child's underachievement can be assumed to be due to LD only if the child has failed to benefit from good schooling and requires very specialized teaching approaches.***

## Identification Practices

In this section we discuss in a general way the issues surrounding LD identification of the preschooler, the young child, and the older student. In Parts 3, 4, and 5 of the text you will find more detailed descriptions of diagnostic assessment procedures and programming options.

### The Preschooler

Identifying a preschooler as learning disabled is just a calculated guess because we don't really know whether, once the child reaches school age, a discrepancy between intellectual ability and achievement will develop. There is the danger that too quick an identification could lead to lowered expectations and stigmatizing. In order to avoid lowering expectations yet begin intervening as quickly as possible, the 1986 amendment to the Education for All Handicapped Children Act of 1975, (Public Law 99-457) is deliberately vague on the identification matter. The amendment refers to a "*developmental delay*" rather than "learning disability" or any other specific disability. This avoids inaccurate forecasts and provides schooling for all children exhibiting delays, no matter what the cause of the disability.

## Alexander

*A gifted fourth grader with writing difficulties.*

Alexander's mother and school psychologist referred him to Syracuse University's Psychoeducational Teaching Laboratory for evaluation. Because the 10-year-old fourth grader had persistent written language difficulties, they wondered whether it would be appropriate to identify him as "learning disabled."

Alexander's background revealed a great deal of turmoil. He had moved 17 times and attended 4 different schools. His parents divorced when he was 3 years old. His mother had recently remarried, and Alexander was having trouble accepting a new authority figure in the house. To complicate family matters, it was apparent that Alexander's biological father disliked and avoided Alexander, while he showered affection on his younger sister. Alexander claimed to have no close friends among his peers. He appeared to be a rather lonely and isolated little boy.

The assessment showed that Alexander was an incredibly gifted child. His vocabulary and reasoning ability were equal to those of most adults. He scored at high school levels in all areas of achievement, with the exception of written expression, where his achievement was average for his age and grade. Alexander's spelling, sentence structure, and punctuation were perfect, but he took an unduly long time getting words down on paper. He also developed his ideas in such a detail-oriented way that it was hard to discern the main thought he was trying to convey. In conversations, Alexander included many unnecessary details and had trouble getting to the point. This, in addition to his clumsiness and emotional difficulties, contributed to his lack of friends.

The evaluation revealed a captivating youngster struggling with many personal issues. Alexander's writing difficulties were found to be primarily due to very poor motor planning. He could not write a word without actually thinking about telling his hand how to move. It was also difficult for him to touch his thumb to each successive finger, figure out how to skip, or walk through a doorway without bumping the frame. When he was asked to stand upright with his eyes closed, he fell over. In his home, Alexander wasn't allowed to carry any breakables because they were sure to come crashing

***Preschoolers' rapid developmental spurts, followed by plateaus, make it impossible for tests to reliably predict whether developmental delays will actually become a learning disability. The level of confidence in predicting LD rises as the severity of the delays increases.***

There is no one test or group of tests that can predict whether preschoolers' developmental delays will actually become a learning disability once they enter school. The preschooler's rapid developmental spurts, followed by plateaus, make testing of preschoolers at any one point in time highly unreliable. The level of confidence for predicting a learning disability rises as (1) the severity of the delays in language, attention, visual-perception, or motor abilities increases; (2) the child nears kindergarten age and the assessment criteria become similar to what and how children are expected to learn in school (e.g., measuring letter knowledge, attention span, and number concepts); and (3) environmental circumstances, such as economic disadvantages or parental encouragement, that can cause or overcome developmental delays are taken into consideration. Because the earlier an intervention takes place the better off the child will be, the best solution is, as the law requires, to simply recognize a developmental delay and get on with good teaching—whatever the cause for the delay.

**Alexander** (Continued)

down. Putting a key into a keyhole, or a coin into a vending machine, were vexing for him. Given a little extra time to plan and think, however, Alexander could perform most of these tasks successfully.

Alexander's overanalytical personal style complicated his writing difficulties. Alexander was so concerned about getting in every minor point and detail that he lost track of how these contributed to his main theme. When he was given a "bubble" outline to separate and order each part of his story, instructed to begin each paragraph with a topic sentence, and allowed to dictate his assignments rather than write them out, however, Alexander quickly began to produce work that was very superior for his age and grade.

Alexander's school psychologist and mother thought he should be identified as "learning disabled." Without this classification, they feared they would be unable to convince Alexander's classroom teachers to give him extra time to do written work, reduce "busywork," or allow him to tape-record his assignments. Alexander couldn't understand all this. He argued that he would feel dumber if given any writing help from a special education teacher, and he didn't understand why labeling him was necessary. The solution was so simple. "Why not just let me tape?" he asked.

Alexander was right. The label "learning disabled" should be reserved for those who require a quality or intensity of instruction that is difficult to provide in an ordinary classroom without special education intervention. Although Alexander had some significant weaknesses, simple adaptations of his educational program were all that would be needed to promote success. The evaluation team recommended these minor accommodations, and pointed out that the stigma of an LD label might be more detrimental to Alexander than learning to live with his writing frustrations. The team suggested weekly counseling for emotional issues, and recommended that Alexander's school initiate a gifted program—and that Alexander be its first enrollee. The team explained Alexander's weaknesses to him and described how he could work around them. The team pointed out that his pattern of strengths and weaknesses was not unlike that of many bright people at the university! Fortunately, Alexander's school proved cooperative, and his teachers implemented the evaluation team's recommendations.

## The Young Elementary Student

Although assessment criteria are available, identification of the young elementary school student is still not easy to do, because it takes some time in school to determine whether the child can handle the curriculum as well as expected for his or her age, intelligence, and past learning opportunities. By age 9, though, the origins of a developmental delay and the gap between achievement and intellectual ability become clearer. That's why the 1997 IDEA amendments (Public Law 105-17) have added that a specific disability does not have to be designated until age 9. Until that time using the term "developmental delay" is sufficient to get special interventions under way. Basically, the law recognizes that it is better to get on with intervention than to waste professional time testing for the sake of labeling. We should be offering these children special education services, rather than waiting for years until severe discrepancies and failure develop.

*Until age 9, IDEA encourages identification of* **developmental delays** *in order to get special interventions under way, rather than waiting for years until severe discrepencies and failure develop.*

We have very good ways to determine which children should be offered the benefit of special help before age 9, so that gaps do not widen and the curriculum can be modified appropriately. For the kindergarten student, poor performance on the academic readiness skills listed in Figure 2.1 may signal a need for intervention. When a child performs poorly relative to his or her age, intelligence, and background on the visual, language, motor, or attention aspects of the listed tasks, this frequently forecasts later learning disabilities.

Tests can be administered to assess the readiness skills listed in Figure 2.1. Frequently, an even better predictor of learning problems are teacher ratings of how a child actually is faring in the classroom in terms of readiness skills, learning strategies, and behavior. This is because the teacher has observed the child's actual performance in the classroom's curriculum, rate of learning, mood, ability to focus attention, social relationships, independence, and motivation. Parent observa-

- Reciting the order of the alphabet; singing the alphabet song
- Pointing to alphabet letters as they are named
- Naming letters of the alphabet speedily and accurately
- Identifying rhyming words; adding a rhyming word where appropriate in a story
- Identifying which dictated words begin with a given sound, the same sound, or different sounds
- Clapping to the number of syllables heard in a word
- Segmenting dictated words into individual syllables and sounds; blending syllables and sounds into words
- Discriminating the position of sounds in words
- Naming common colors, shapes, objects, body parts, and signs (such as *McDonald's* and *Coca-Cola*)
- Comprehending age-appropriate vocabulary
- Recognizing and writing one's name
- Copying designs (circle, cross, square, X, triangle)
- Copying letters and simple words
- Telling one's full name, address, telephone number, and birthday
- Reciting familiar nursery rhymes
- Completing sequences *(breakfast, lunch, ____; yesterday, today, ____)*
- Completing analogies *(in daytime it is light, at night it is ______; birds fly, fish ____)*
- Responding to various question forms *(how many, where, who, what, why, what if, which)*
- Telling simple stories
- Succeeding at simple concentration-type games requiring matching pictures from memory
- Attending to a task for a reasonable period of time until done (such as a simple puzzle, listening to a story, a clay project)
- Developing friendships and playing cooperatively
- Succeeding on readiness tests that, in addition to the above skills, sample: vocabulary use, number concepts (*more–less,* matching sets, counting to ten, *beginning-middle-end, first-second-third*), numeral recognition to ten, sentence memory and comprehension, opposites, visual discrimination, following two- and three-step directions, categorization, substituting initial and final sounds in words, and general knowledge

**Figure 2.1** Academic readiness indicators.

tions also are valuable academic predictors, as are indicators such as the family's academic goals for the child and learning activities encouraged at home.

## The Older Elementary and Secondary Student

Numerous formulas have been used to calculate severe discrepancies between expected and actual achievement. Although all the formulas have inherent inaccuracies, they have several advantages:

1. They add objective balance to the subjective judgments in LD identification.
2. They enable researchers to choose sample populations with the same percentage of discrepancy, thereby making it possible to compare and interpret results more accurately.
3. They place no limits on intelligence levels, so that the degree of underachievement of even the mentally retarded can be evaluated.

**Severe Discrepancy.** As a rule, to be judged severe, a discrepancy between achievement and ability must be unusually large when compared to normal variability in individuals of similar age, intelligence, and backgrounds. States are left to decide how large of a discrepancy is considered severe. Cutoffs are generally determined by setting a percentage by which a child's achievement must lag behind age or grade expectations given his or her intellectual potential. For example, an average-intelligence fourth grader would be 50 percent behind his or her grade level expectations if the child achieved like a second grader.

***To be judged severe, a discrepancy between achievement and ability must be unusually large when compared to normal variability in individuals of similar age, intelligence, and backgrounds.***

Setting a rigid discrepancy cutoff is problematic because the meaning of a set percentage of discrepancy is more serious at lower grade levels than at higher ones. This is because children make the most rapid gains in basic skills in the primary grades, after which year-to-year progress slows. Therefore, children who are a few grade levels behind at younger ages may have far more serious problems than those who are many grade levels behind at older ages. For example, an average third grader who still hasn't mastered letter sounds that should be old hat to a first grader is more seriously behind than an eighth grader who reads at the fourth-grade level. Both are 50 percent behind expectations, but while the eighth grader can muddle through with reading, the third grader still hasn't even left the gate. Clearly, if the percentage discrepancy is set too high, then students with milder discrepancies will not be identified for help. Moreover, younger children will have to fail for years until their discrepancies grow large enough to qualify for special services—which only exacerbates their learning problems.

Relying on grade-level deviations—being a set number of years behind—to identify learning disabilities also is not a good idea for several reasons. First, a student's aptitude for achievement, as required by IDEA, is ignored. For example, a very bright sixth grader who is reading one year below grade level might not be identified as learning disabled, even though he or she is. At the same time, a slower student who is achieving two years below grade level might be considered learning disabled, even though the student is working to his or her capacity and is not disabled at all.

Second, grade-equivalent scores are of questionable validity. Errors in measurement and interpretation can be high because achievement tests sample only a handful of items at each difficulty level. Moreover, achievement tests do not reflect the actual curriculum the child has been expected to master. An average grade-level score merely means that the student got the same total number of items correct as his or her classmates; lows, highs, and peculiar patterns in specific areas do not become apparent. For example, Shekera may score average by reading every word she is expected to on a word list; the test, though, didn't pick up the fact that it took Shekera ten seconds to sound out each word, when she should have recognized the words instantly. This slow-reading rate will affect her comprehension and the time she needs to complete tests and assignments. In addition, tests aren't perfect and questions frequently are too easy for everyone. Therefore, a student who is learning disabled may score as high as his or her classmates, but this performance is not actually at grade level.

Third, because different academic subjects are acquired at different rates and because society doesn't value all of them equally, the same number of grade levels behind in different subjects may have different implications. For example, at age 15, a four-year lag in spelling is annoying mostly to the student, but not as ominous as the same lag in reading. Such considerations come into play when deciding whether or not to identify a child for special education services.

**Calculating Discrepancies.** Reading clinicians were the first to use formulas to determine the level at which students were expected to read. These formulas were later applied to the many achievement areas in which learning disabilities can be experienced.

Most formulas use an intelligence test score to estimate a student's expected level of achievement. A score of 100 is average for one's age. Achievement test scores are then compared with the IQ score to determine whether there is a gap that represents severe underachievement.

Harris's (1962) formula is the most frequently used and simplest method of quantifying a severe discrepancy:

$$\text{RE} = \text{MA} - 5$$

Where: RE = reading expectancy grade level

MA = mental age (mental age = chronological age × IQ/100)

5 = 5 years old at school entry

Using this formula, Harris charted expected reading grade levels for children of different IQs and ages. For example, Nancy, who is 8 years old and has an IQ of 100, would be expected to be reading at the third-grade level.

$$\begin{aligned} \text{RE} &= (8 \times 100/100) - 5 \\ &= 3 \end{aligned}$$

If her achievement is below the third-grade level, she is performing below her intellectual aptitude. It is up to the school to determine how much of a discrepancy qualifies as a learning disability.

**Statistical Weaknesses of Discrepancy Formulas.** Not surprisingly, formulas are not foolproof in identifying learning disabilities. One formula may identify a child as LD, whereas another one might not. This is because some formulas factor in math achievement levels, the number of years of schooling, current grade level, or they weight intelligence increasingly more than age as one gets older. Even among students who achieve at average levels, anywhere from 4 to 25 percent could be identified as learning disabled depending on the formula used. In fact, probability dictates that if 20 tests are administered, 1 test will show a discrepancy just by chance. To deal with the weaknesses of these formulas, experts recommend converting student test scores to standard scores or using regression equations.

The standard score method is illustrated in Figure 2.2 on page 44. This method compares standard scores on IQ and achievement tests and asks the question, "Is the child's percentile rank on one test roughly the same as the other?" Most often a standard score of 100 is set as the mean (50th percentile) and every 15 points above or below represents both a set percentile and a significant deviation (a standard score of 115 is at the 84th percentile; 130 is at the 98th percentile; 85 is at the 16th percentile; and 70 is at the 2nd percentile). A school district must decide how great the discrepancy between the IQ and achievement standard scores must be in order to indicate a learning disability.

A major problem with standard scores, as with all discrepancy formulas, is that they assume that as IQ goes up, achievement should go up equally. But this isn't true. At best, we can predict reading level from intelligence only about 50 percent of the time; many other things besides intelligence go into being a good reader. Achievement predictions become more and more inaccurate the higher or lower the IQ because these children's reading scores will tend to move closer toward the mean (this is called *regression toward the mean*). In other words, whenever two skills are tested and one score is above or below average, the other score is likely to be closer to average. Because standard score discrepancies don't take this "regression" into account, very bright children with average reading levels can be misidentified as learning disabled while less intelligent children who don't happen to test as poorly academically as you might expect may be underidentified.

The regression equation was developed to deal with the imperfect relationship between IQ and achievement by factoring in the actual correlation between the IQ and achievement measure and the likely degree of measurement error on each test. For example, using the regression equation, students with average intelligence who test low on the achievement measure might not be identified as learning disabled if, among all the students in that school, reading achievement is so variable that IQs are not very predictive of reading scores. In other words, the student's low achievement score is not at all unexpected given the student body. Regression equations are complicated to develop because they require giving the same IQ and achievement test to a sample of children who match the pupil in question in age, sex, socioeconomic status, and years of schooling. As a result, experts have agreed that, though imperfect, the standard score may be the method of choice for calculating discrepancies, as long as reliable standardized tests are used, the tests' norm samples are comparable to the child's school population, and the phenomenon of regression is taken into consideration.

***Despite its problems, the standard score is the method of choice for calculating discrepancies between learning aptitude and academic achievement.***

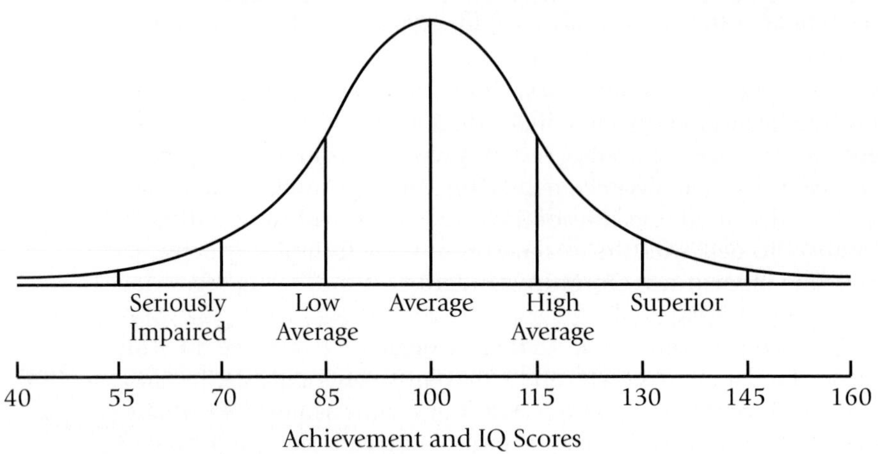


Each section of the chart represents one *standard deviation.* Most school districts state that a student's ability (as judged by an IQ test) and achievement (as judged by an achievement test) must be 1½ to 2 standard deviations apart (1½ to 2 sections apart on the chart) in order to determine that a learning disability exists. For example:

*Jim* has an IQ of 100 and a reading score of 70. These scores are 2 standard deviations apart—enough to identify a learning disability in most states.

*Jennifer* has an IQ of 100 and a math score of 85. Although she is behind, 1 standard deviation is considered within the normal range. She will need extra help in the classroom but will probably not be identified as learning disabled.

*Darryl* has an IQ of 130. His writing score is 105. Even though his achievement is average, it does not reflect his very superior intelligence. Darryl's discrepancy of 1½ standard deviations will identify a learning disability in some states.

*Alana's* IQ of 70 is considered retarded. Her reading comprehension score is 40, which suggests that she also has a specific learning disability. While not all states will recognize a mentally retarded student as learning disabled also, it should be recognized that Alana will need unusually intense instruction in reading comprehension in addition to other special education services.

**Figure 2.2** Using standard scores to calculate severe discrepancies.

*Source:* Reprinted with the permission of The Free Press, a Division of Simon & Schuster Adult Publishing Group, from *Learning Disabilities A to Z: A Parent's Complete Guide to Learning Disabilities from Preschool to Adulthood* by Corinne R. Smith and Lisa W. Strick. 

**Clinical Judgments.** Formulas can never be the only criteria for LD identification because they can't evaluate the many student, curriculum, and environmental factors that might have influenced the learning delays. Even if a severe discrepancy is found, it must be considered in light of factors such as a student's motivation to learn; the teacher's expectations, materials, and classroom setting; support at home for study; days of school missed due to illness; and so on.

Weighing all of these against other factors, such as the child's information-processing delays and learning rate, relies on the good clinical judgment that comes with experience.

Let us consider two students who have the same degree of discrepancy between intellectual ability and achievement according to the formulas. Autumn appears to be underachieving because she is impulsive and is delayed in acquiring language skills, both warning signs of a learning disability. Even though she is putting forth her best effort, the typical curriculum simply doesn't work for her. Trey, on the other hand, is underachieving because his family has moved so often that he's never had a consistent program of instruction and has all but given up on learning; he is underachieving, but he is not learning disabled. If he is taught like any average pupil and motivated, he will learn just fine.

*Discrepancy between learning aptitude and school achievement is a necessary, but not sufficient, condition for LD identification. Clinical judgment suggests whether there is any educational significance to the discrepancy.*

Discrepancy, therefore, merely points out that underachievement exists. Discrepancy is a necessary condition for LD identification, but not a sufficient one. It is clinical judgment that helps to fill in the picture and suggests whether there is any educational significance to the discrepancy. Too often professionals forego clinical judgment and identify every child who has a large discrepancy as LD. Others, in their zeal to get help for children, identify those who show only minor discrepancies. Left to their own judgment, different team members make different decisions about a child's LD eligibility because they have different conceptions of learning disabilities, different comfort levels with mislabeling, and different levels of understanding of the statistics needed for valid test interpretation. Too often teams interpret low scores as "meaningful" and indicative of LD, when in fact the low scores are due to nothing more than the student's erratic test-taking strategies or to invalid tests. One of the most important considerations that team members tend to miss is whether a student really does need a quality and intensity of instruction that differs markedly from the regular curriculum. To answer this last question effectively, teams need to carefully consider the possible curriculum and environmental influences on learning along with several issues that pertain to the student's intellectual abilities, achievement levels, past educational experiences, and age. They also must be open to alternative identification approaches.

***Intellectual Abilities.*** In general, IQ tests are the best predictors of school success, because both depend on one's fund of knowledge, cognitive processes (such as abstract reasoning and speed of information processing), motivation, and personality. But IQ tests are not perfect. There are several reasons why they should be used with care in identifying students who are learning disabled. When necessary, alternative measures should be substituted.

*IQ tests are not always the best measure of aptitude because they tend to underestimate the intellectual ability of low-income students, those with limited English proficiency, and those from some ethnic and cultural minority groups.*

1. IQ tests tend to underestimate the intellectual aptitude of lower income students, those with limited English proficiency, and those from some ethnic and cultural minority groups. In their home backgrounds, these students have learned concepts, languages, and information different from that assessed on IQ test questions. They also may not have benefited from experience with the kinds of problem-solving approaches and activities (puzzles, block designs, comic strips, mazes, or naming categories to which items belong—such as fruit or animals) required to do well on IQ tests. So, when children from these groups test low on traditional IQ tests, they aren't as likely to be identified as

learning disabled because the discrepancy between intellectual ability and achievement won't be as apparent. Chapter 9 explores the issue of intelligence test bias and the possible alternatives for testing lower income students and those from ethnic and cultural minority groups.

2. Intelligence tests that heavily tap a student's weaker skills—English language for children who are immigrants, or reading—may miss groups of students who won't show the appropriate degree of discrepancy because their intellectual aptitude is underestimated. Underestimation of a child's knowledge and reasoning abilities also arises when IQ test items draw too much on a student's weaknesses in short-term memory, rapid problem solving, fine-motor coordination, attention, or organization. Because different IQ tests have different types of items, it often is possible to select one that bypasses the weaker abilities and taps more of a student's strengths.
3. Although IQ becomes more stable by age 5 or 6, there still can be as much as a 15-point variation from one test to another because of test differences, the student's effort, the adverse effect of poor achievement on stimulation of intellectual growth, and administration and scoring differences across examiners. Therefore, when calculating discrepancies, it is always better to consider IQ as a range of probable functioning rather than as a fixed number.
4. As students with learning disabilities grow older, their learning problems diminish their vocabulary growth, knowledge acquisition, reasoning, and motivation, which in turn decreases their IQ scores. Therefore, gaps between IQ and achievement often are less apparent with time, as IQ becomes a poorer index of intellectual aptitude.
5. IQ tests are not equally good at predicting aptitude for achievement in all school subjects. For example, IQ contributes more strongly to reading comprehension than to handwriting performance. If the latter is an issue, then perhaps years of instruction in writing might be a more relevant index for evaluating expectations for handwriting quality, or examining the student's handwriting quality against writing samples for average achievers from each grade in that school.
6. Because IQ predicts no more than half of achievement, factors that influence aptitude for achievement such as interest in learning, willingness to try hard, or teacher and parent encouragement of learning should be given some weight in estimating expected levels of achievement.

***Achievement tests used for LD identification should match the child's classroom content as closely as possible to be fair.***

*Achievement Levels.* In choosing the best achievement tests to use for LD identification, keep in mind that these tests must match the child's classroom content as closely as possible to be fair. After all, we are trying to determine how much of what the student should have learned was actually learned. These tests must also evaluate achievement in the same way that the student is expected to demonstrate knowledge in the classroom. For example, because in class a child must write out correctly spelled words, it is of little help to administer an achievement test on which the child chooses correct spellings via a multiple-choice format. Fill-in-the-blank "writing" tests are very different from the composition requirements in a classroom. And reading word lists on a test certainly is not the same as reading a few paragraphs of a text and answering comprehension questions.

Special care also must be taken with children for whom our culture or language is new. Newly immigrated youngsters can't be expected to achieve the same levels as their native-born classmates. They should be tested in their native language and curriculum.

Finally, like IQ scores, achievement test scores should be interpreted in ranges rather than in absolute values. In part this is necessary because of validity problems with achievement tests. It also is necessary because the heightened reinforcement and attention in an individual testing situation raises the child's motivation and performance beyond what that child can do on his or her own in the classroom. Often achievement is overestimated by one year or more because of this attention, because test items are too easy for older students, or because of calculating scores based on the total points earned (which can mask gaps in lower level knowledge). Overestimates of achievement lead to denial of LD services to students who could benefit from them. Underestimates can lead to false identification.

*Educational Experience.* A student who continues to have severe, persistent learning difficulties in spite of good ability, effort, and quality educational opportunities at home and at school is probably learning disabled. If the opportunities to learn have been erratic and substandard, however, we may misidentify children as learning disabled because we overestimate what they should have achieved. Instructional failures too often are confused with learning problems.

***A student who continues to have severe, persistent learning difficulties in spite of good ability, effort, and educational opportunities is probably learning disabled.***

*Age.* Some children are mistakenly identified as learning disabled because they are young for their grade and too much is being expected of them. Age is important to consider in areas such as reading comprehension, which continues to develop over time. However, age declines in relevance in areas that mature fairly early, such as grammar and handwriting.

**Alternatives to Discrepancy Formulas.** Several alternatives used with or without discrepancy formulas can help broaden the approach to LD identification. Some experts have suggested that a much lower learning level and slower learning rate when compared to one's peers, even after adapting general education teaching approaches and offering intensive remediation, should be the key factor for LD identification. This is one of the major recommendations being considered for IDEA's next reauthorization. Low achievers who respond to conventional instruction adaptations in the classroom merely needed a more personalized learning environment and would not be identified as LD. These experts advocate that the IQ-achievement discrepancy criterion for LD identification be eliminated from the law, since there is very little difference between the achievement test profiles and intervention needs of children who show significant IQ-achievement discrepancies and those who score low in both intellectual and achievement areas; in other words, all children found to be underachieving should get special help, not just those showing severe discrepancies. It is believed that the truly "learning disabled" among these children will eventually emerge when they fail to make sufficient progress after intensive intervention.

***Many suggest that insufficient progress after intensive intervention should be the key to LD identification.***

Because learning disabilities are characterized by uneven maturation in information-processing abilities that underlie academic achievement, others have suggested that these be measured for LD identification purposes. When one modality for learning (such as language or visual perception) is weaker than the others, a learning disability might be present. The weakness in this premise, however, is that even average learners do not develop information-processing subskills at a uniform rate. Strengths and weaknesses are common and, using this method, typical learners may be misidentified as disabled. Besides, the subtest reliability and relation to academic learning on these types of tests are usually too inadequate to support such profile analyses.

Other professionals calculate discrepancies by assuming that a high achievement score in one academic area, contrasted with a low score in another, suggests a specific learning disability. The trouble with this approach is that a high score may simply show a special talent—number fact knowledge, for example—that has no relevance to what should be expected of the student in other areas of achievement. Instead, others suggest that skills highly related to the area of academic weakness, such as listening comprehension in the case of reading delays (listening comprehension is more highly predictive of reading than is IQ), be used as the measure of expected achievement.

Other experts encourage us to throw out all the tests in favor of monitoring performance on a regular schedule in the classroom. This faction advises providing special help when and where it's needed to all students making inadequate progress (e.g., all those achieving below the 20th percentile), and not being concerned with a specific disability diagnosis. This in effect is what the state of Massachusetts has done. Massachusetts students are identified for special services based on the percent of time they require for individualized instruction; whether they meet LD criteria is of little concern (except for reporting purposes to the U.S. Office of Education)—dealing with underachievement, no matter the cause, is the paramount objective. Such a system frees up a great deal of professional time now used for testing and identification and makes room for a great deal more time to be spent teaching and augmenting children's skills. Moreover, under this system young children who are struggling get intervention immediately because they don't have to wait for years until a significant discrepancy shows up before special help is provided. It is upsetting that, under the current discrepancy model, too many children with disabilities have to "wait to fail" before getting identified for early interventions that could have jump started their learning progress and perhaps even prevented a major disability from developing.

***It is upsetting that, under the current discrepancy model, too many children with disabilities have to "wait to fail" before getting identified for early interventions that could have jump started their learning progress and perhaps even prevented a major disability from developing.***

## Prevalence of Learning Disabilities

Empirical studies that administer individual tests to thousands of children and then apply the same discrepancy formula report a 4 to 7 percent incidence of learning disabilities in one or two areas of a child's achievement. Recent research suggests that, contrary to popular assumptions, the male-to-female ratio of learning disabilities may be equal. Nevertheless, depending on the geographical area or study, boys are 1.5 to 6 times more likely to be identified than girls. Figure 2.3 summarizes the various medical, maturational, sociological, and brain organization explanations for the greater numbers of males than females being identified as learning disabled.

***Boys are far more likely to be identified as LD despite research suggesting an equal incidence of LD among girls and boys.***

*(text continues on page 51)*

| Hypothesis | Investigator |
|---|---|
| *Medical Factors* | |
| • The male may be more biologically vulnerable to brain damage prenatally and postnatally than the female. Although more males than females are conceived, more males die in utero or in infancy, females outlive males, and males face a higher risk of disease that may lead to learning disorders (for example, meningitis). | • Bentzen (1963), Critchley (]1970), McMillen (1979), Novitski (1977) |
| • Boys tend to have greater birth weights and larger heads and are more often firstborns. These conditions are associated with increased risk of brain injury and learning disorders. | • Silver (1971), Strauss & Lehtinen (1947) |
| • More males than females experience difficulties during the birth process, resulting in more males than females with birth defects. Even in normal deliveries, births of males take an average of an hour longer than the births of females. | • Jacklin & Maccoby (1982) |
| • Boys experience one-and-one-half to three times greater numbers of head injuries than girls. | • Goethe & Levin (1984), Segalowitz & Lawson (1995) |
| • The left hemisphere, which is critical to language and reading achievement, develops more slowly prenatally than the right hemisphere. Therefore, it is vulnerable over a longer period of time to events that may alter development. The male's left hemisphere is particularly vulnerable because abnormalities in the development of the immune system are associated with excess testosterone, a male hormone. During fetal life, immune system malfunction can retard or disrupt migration of cells to the cortex. In addition, testosterone acts as a growth stimulus for the right hemisphere by decreasing the amount of normal cell death (which is intended to facilitate growth of more appropriate tissue). Not only can an overfunctioning right hemisphere block and distort left hemisphere processing, but if high levels of testosterone actually cause a shift in left-hemisphere handedness and language functions to the right hemisphere, developmental disorders may ensue. | • Galaburda (1986), Geshwind & Behan (1982) |
| • The inheritance of learning disabilities appears to be influenced by the offspring's sex, with a male to female inheritance ratio of 1.5:1.0. | • Pennington (1995) |
| • Impulsivity and certain types of information-processing disorders have been found to be male-linked genetically. | • Kinsbourne & Caplan (1979) |

*(continued)*

**Figure 2.3** Hypotheses regarding greater male than female incidence of learning disabilities identification.

| Hypothesis | Investigator |
|---|---|
| *Maturational Factors* | |
| • Males lag behind females from the start. At birth males are one month less mature than females; they complete maturation at age 18, 2 years later than girls. Growth rate is 80% that of the female through adolescence. Slow physical maturation often is correlated with slow behavioral maturation. | • Bayley (1943), Bayley & Jones (1955), Farnham-Diggory (1978) |
| • The male brain's protective sheath has been found to grow slower than the female's. Therefore, the male has more prenatal and postnatal opportunities for damage to later developing cortical functions. | • Goldman, Crawford, Stokes, Galkin, & Rosvold (1974) |
| • The neural maturation of boys' cortical regions is known to differ from that of females; these differences may increase the probability of learning failure. Males have been found to lag behind females in development of brain regions responsible for attention and such reading-related left hemisphere skills as verbal expression, articulation, and perception of the order of sounds in words; stuttering is more common in males than in females; the male delays may be related in part to girls experiencing a greater spurt in brain growth at 10 to 12 years of age. | • Bakker (1970, 1972), Denckla & Heilman (1979), Denckla & Rudel, in Denckla (1979), Epstein (1980), Goldman et al. (1974), Hier (1979), Hines (1990), Kinsbourne & Warrington (1963), Townes, Trupin, Martin, & Goldstein (1980) |
| • Males' greater variability in development may make them more susceptible to learning and behavior disorders. | • Kinsbourne & Caplan (1979) |
| • In both boys and girls, reading disabilities often are associated with attention-deficit hyperactivity disorder, inattentive type. But in boys reading disabilities also are associated with attention-deficit hyperactivity disorder, hyperactive-impulsive type, which are more disruptive than the inattentive behaviors exhibited by girls. This precipitates more frequent clinical referrals of boys. | • Willcutt & Pennington (2000) |
| *Sociological Factors* | |
| • Because males mature at a slower rate, research indicates that they often are unready for school entrance or the work of their grade. | • Ames (1968) |
| • It has been suggested that our society expects more achievement from boys than from girls and therefore is more apt to be aware of their learning difficulties or put pressures on them that they are too immature to meet; their more aggressive general behavior and reaction to failure seems to increase chances for LD referral. | • Bentzen (1963), Caplan (1977), Caplan & Kinsbourne (1974), Lambert & Sandoval (1980), Vernon (1957), in Critchley (1970) |

**Figure 2.3** *Continued*

| Hypothesis | Investigator |
|---|---|
| • Males and females show equal frequencies of low reading achievement relative to their intelligence, but because males are perceived by teachers as more active, inattentive, disruptive, aggressive and delayed in language, motor, and academic skills, this bias initiates a referral rate of males for assessment and identification that is more than twice the rate of referred girls. Girls get noticed if they have lower intellectual abilities and their academic difficulties are more pronounced. | • Flynn & Rahbar (1994), Shaywitz, Shaywitz, Fletcher, & Escobar (1990) |
| • Failing boys have been more apt to develop secondary behavioral difficulties; their socially sanctioned alternatives for success, being leaders and athletes, are harder to accomplish than girls' alternatives of being nice and quiet. | |
| • Males show more inappropriate physical activity than do females. This activity is particularly disturbing to female teachers, who are more apt than male teachers to refer such students for special education evaluation—and more teachers are females. | • McIntyre (1988) |
| • Boys have a greater tendency than girls to express feelings via action. This brings them more often to their teachers' attention. | |
| ***Brain Organization Factors*** | |
| • The male's cerebral hemispheres are known to be more strongly specialized than the female's (presumably due to increased levels of prenatal testosterone); therefore, in the event of left hemisphere damage, their right hemispheres are less flexible in assuming language functions important to academic achievement. In the event of right hemisphere damage, data indicate that boys' left hemispheres may become overloaded with inappropriate right hemisphere strategies (global, holistic), thereby compromising the left hemisphere analytic, sequential reasoning skills that are so important to reading. | • Davidoff, Cone, & Scully (1978), Hier (1979), Hier, LeMay, Rosenberger, & Perlo (1978), Witelson (1976, 1977) |

**Figure 2.3** *Continued*

*Currently over 2.8 million school-age children are identified as learning disabled.*

The latest count of school-age children actually receiving special education services indicates that over 2.8 million, about 50 percent of the 5.8 million "special education" students, are identified as learning disabled. More students probably could qualify as LD, but they are not identified because of an 11 percent teenage dropout rate, the development of compensations that mask the learning problem, and enrollment in high school vocational courses that have less rigorous academic requirements.

Large discrepancies exist from state to state in percentages of students identified as learning disabled, with some states identifying two times the percentage of students as others. Those states that identify fewer students as LD also tend to identify fewer children overall as disabled.

Although we know how many students are identified as learning disabled, we still don't know the nature and extent of these students' strengths and weaknesses, how many are falsely identified, and how many have been missed altogether.

## Summary

Our current LD definition defines learning disabilities as an information-processing disorder that causes achievement to be far below a student's intellectual aptitude. According to the federal definition in IDEA (1990), the retarded, emotionally disturbed, physically handicapped, and economically disadvantaged also can be considered learning disabled if these conditions are not directly responsible for their severe discrepancy from expected achievement.

Unfortunately, the conceptual vagueness of the LD definition has led to misidentification of many students as learning disabled. When these students then become part of our research samples, and researchers do not set firm criteria to decide which students really belong, we end up with confusing findings regarding the nature of learning disabilities and which interventions work best for whom.

The judgment of whether a learning disability exists is a difficult one to make. It involves consideration of the student's intelligence, achievement, past educational experiences, age, rate of learning with various instructional approaches, quality of present and past teaching, motivation, and many other personal, curriculum, and environmental factors. Currently, about 50 percent of all students with disabilities, over 5 percent of all students, are identified as learning disabled. However, studies suggest that even more pupils may be identifiable. The fact that boys are identified with learning disabilities in far greater numbers than girls has been linked to possible medical, maturational, sociological, and brain organization factors.

## Helpful Resources

### Definition

Ames, L. B. (1977). Learning disabilities: Time to check our roadmaps? *Journal of Learning Disabilities, 10,* 328–330.

Bateman, B. (1974). Educational implications of minimal brain dysfunction. *Reading Teacher, 27,* 662–668.

Clements, S. D. (1966). *Minimal brain dysfunction in children: Terminology and identification. Phase one of a three-phase project* (NINDS Monograph No. 3, U.S. Public Health Service Publication No. 1415). Washington, DC: U.S. Government Printing Office.

Gottlieb, J., Alter, M., Gottlieb, B. W., & Wishner, J. (1994). Special education in urban America: It's not justifiable for many. *The Journal of Special Education, 27,* 453–465.

Kavale, K. A., & Reese, J. H. (1992). The character of learning disabilities: An Iowa profile. *Learning Disability Quarterly, 15,* 74–94.

Kirk, S. A., & Elkins, J. (1975). Characteristics of children enrolled in the child service demonstration centers. *Journal of Learning Disabilities, 8,* 630–637.

Lyon, G. R. (1995). The definitional issue. *Annals of Dyslexia, 45,* 3–27.

McIntosh, D. K., & Dunn, L. M. (1973). Children with major specific learning disabilities. In L. M. Dunn (Ed.), *Exceptional children in the schools: Special education in transition* (2nd ed.). New York: Holt, Rinehart & Winston.

Mercer, C. D., Jordan, L., Allsop, D. H., & Mercer, A. R. (1996). Learning disabilities definitions and criteria used by state education departments. *Learning Disability Quarterly, 19,* 217–232.

Norman, C. A., Jr., & Zigmond, N. (1980). Characteristics of children labeled and served as learning disabled in school systems affiliated with child service demonstration centers. *Journal of Learning Disabilities, 13,* 542–547.

Shepard, L. A., & Smith, M. L. (1983). An evaluation of the identification of learning disabled students in Colorado. *Learning Disability Quarterly, 6,* 115–127.

Stevens, G. D., & Birch, J. W. (1957). A proposal for clarification of the terminology used to describe brain-injured children. *Exceptional Children, 23,* 346–349.

## Identification Practices

Badian, N. A. (1998). A validation of the role of preschool phonological and orthographic skills in the prediction of reading. *Journal of Learning Disabilities, 31,* 472–481.

Blachman, B. A. (1991). Early intervention for children's reading problems: Clinical applications of the research in phonological awareness. *Topics in Language Disorders, 12,* 51–65.

Bradley, L., & Bryant, P. (1985). *Rhyme and reason in reading and spelling.* Ann Arbor, MI: University of Michigan Press.

Cone, T. E., & Wilson, L. R. (1981). Quantifying a severe discrepancy: A critical analysis. *Learning Disability Quarterly, 4,* 359–371.

Fletcher, J. M., Francis, D. J., Shaywitz, S. E., Lyon, G. R., Foorman, B. R., Stuebing, K. K., & Shaywitz, B. A. (1998). Intelligent testing and the discrepancy model for children with learning disabilities. *Learning Disabilities Research & Practice, 13,* 186–203.

Furlong, M. J., & Yanagida, E. H. (1985). Psychometric factors affecting multidisciplinary team identification of learning disabled children. *Learning Disability Quarterly, 8,* 37–44.

Gregg, N., & Scott, S. S. (2000). Definition and documentation: Theory, measurement, and the courts. *Journal of Learning Disabilities, 33,* 5–13.

Gresham, F. M., MacMillan, D. L., & Bocian, K. M. (1997). Teachers as "tests": Differential validity of teacher judgments in identifying students at-risk for learning disabilities. *School Psychology Review, 26,* 47–60.

Horn, W. F., & Packard, T. (1985). Early identification of learning disabilities: A meta-analysis. *Journal of Educational Psychology, 77,* 597–607.

Jorm, A. F., Share, D. L., Maclean, R., & Matthews, R. (1986). Cognitive factors at school entry predictive of specific reading retardation and general reading backwardness: A research note. *Journal of Child Psychology and Psychiatry, 27,* 45–54.

Kavale, K. A. (1987). Theoretical issues surrounding severe discrepancy. *Learning Disabilities Research, 3,* 12–20.

Larsen, S. C., Rogers, D., & Sowell, V. (1976). The use of selected perceptual tests in differentiating between normal and learning disabled children. *Journal of Learning Disabilities, 9,* 85–90.

Lyon, G. R., Fletcher, J. M., Shaywitz, S. E., Shaywitz, B. A., Torgesen, J. K., Wood, F. B., Schulte, A., & Olson, R. (2001). Rethinking learning disabilities. In C. E. Finn, Jr., A. J. Rotherham, & C. R. Hokanson, Jr. (Eds.), *Rethinking special education for a new century* (pp. 259–287). Washington, DC: Thomas B. Fordham Foundation, Progressive Policy Institute.

McCall, R. B., Hogarty, P. S., & Hurlburt, N. (1972). Transitions in infant sensorimotor development and the prediction of childhood IQ. *American Psychologist, 27,* 728–748.

Meyer, M. S. (2000). The ability-achievement discrepancy: Does it contribute to an understanding of learning disabilities? *Educational Psychology Review, 12,* 315–337.

Sattler, J. M. (2001). *Assessment of children: Cognitive applications* (4th ed.). San Diego: J. M. Sattler.

Satz, P., Taylor, H. G., Friel, J., & Fletcher, J. (1978). Some predictive and developmental precursors of reading disability: A six-year follow-up. In D. Pearl & A. Benton (Eds.), *Dyslexia: A critical appraisal of current theory.* Oxford: Oxford University Press.

Scruggs, T. E., & Mastropieri, M. A. (2002). On babies and bathwater: Addressing the problems of identification of learning disabilities. *Learning Disability Quarterly, 25,* 155–168.

Stanovich, K. E. (1993). A model for studies of reading disability. *Developmental Review, 13,* 225–245.

Ysseldyke, J., Algozzine, B., & Epps, S. (1983). A logical and empirical analysis of current practice in classifying students as handicapped. *Exceptional Children, 50,* 160–166.

## Prevalence of Learning Disabilities

Shaywitz, S. E., Shaywitz, B. A., Fletcher, J. M., & Escobar, M. D. (1990). Prevalence of reading disability in boys and girls: Results of the Connecticut Longitudinal Study. *Journal of the American Medical Association, 264,* 998–1002.

Condition of Education: http://www.nces.ed.gov/programs/coe

Digest of Educational Statistics: http://www.nces.ed.gov/pubs2002/digest2001

CHAPTER THREE

# Physiological Differences

*LD is caused by neurological differences in the way children's brains are constructed and function. This results in information-processing inefficiencies that affect learning.*

**EXPERTS AGREE** that learning disabilities are caused by neurological differences in the way that human brains are constructed and function. This results in information-processing inefficiencies that affect learning. At the same time, experts are quite mindful of outside influences such as the curriculum, the school and home environments, tasks that demand more than the child can muster, inadequate nutrition, and stressful family life that can also strongly influence the development and use of a child's information-processing capabilities. Part Two examines physiological, curricular, and environmental influences on learning, all of which are critical to attend to if we are to appropriately assess and teach the large variety of students with learning disabilities.

*Different combinations of information-processing strengths and weaknesses of LD children result in unique learning and behavior patterns, so that one child's patterns will be very different from those of another.*

This chapter addresses the physiological differences and brain functioning patterns that relate to the information-processing weaknesses of individuals with learning disabilities. Different combinations of information-processing strengths and weaknesses in the learning disabled result in unique learning and behavior patterns, so that one child's patterns may be very different from those of another. Learning about these patterns helps us understand why children have learning disabilities and how we should go about teaching them. We begin by comparing the neuropsychological learning patterns of the learning disabled with the patterns of average achievers. We then explore the four physiological factors that are thought to underlie these inefficient learning patterns: brain injury, structural brain differences, heredity, and biochemical irregularities. In Chapter 5 we continue the discussion of the unique learning patterns of children with LD by examining the various types of information-processing weaknesses in greater depth.

## Neuropsychological Patterns of Learning

As a result of sophisticated research comparing the differences in patterns of brain functioning of typical and poor learners, we have learned much about the relationship between the brain, learning, and behavior. Research Box 3.1 on page 56 describes some of the fascinating scientific methods being used to discover these differences in brain functioning.

### Patterns of Typical Learners

The normal brain has a left and a right hemisphere. Each hemisphere includes a frontal, parietal, occipital, and temporal lobe. Figure 3.1 on page 61 shows how each part of the brain is responsible for different functions, and Figure 3.2 on page 64 depicts the arrangement of brain cells responsible for body movements and sensations. The *primary regions* are the brain sites that carry out the most basic functions such as sight, hearing, or movement. Complex neural systems connect these primary regions, and these carry out the higher-level functions such as learning to read, reason, and solve math problems.

*Adequate hemispheric specialization and attention processes are essential for children to learn normally.*

Adequate hemispheric specialization and attention processes are essential for children to learn normally. As a child grows, one cerebral hemisphere becomes more specialized than the other for certain functions. For example, both hemispheres are involved when we listen to music or speak, but the right hemisphere generally becomes more activated when we listen to music, and the left hemisphere predominates when we speak. The brain's specialization process continues through adolescence in a predictable fashion. Although this is desirable and natural, it's also true that the more specialized an area of the brain becomes, the less likely that it will be able to take over for another brain area that becomes damaged.

The difference in specialization between the two hemispheres is called *brain asymmetry*. During information processing, the left hemisphere appears to be more active approximately 65 percent of the time, and the right hemisphere is more active about 12 percent of the time. Brain asymmetry is important in learning disabilities because a person's efficiency and style of learning is influenced by the degree to which one hemisphere has become dominant over the other for given functions (e.g., visual-perceptual vs. language processing). A person's preference for a particular learning style also can influence which hemisphere he or she will use most during a certain activity.

*A person's efficiency and style of learning are influenced by the degree to which one hemisphere becomes dominant over the other for given functions.*

Music appreciation is a good example of how a person's preferred learning style can influence the hemisphere that will be most active. Music appreciation is usually a right hemisphere skill, but the hemisphere that is actually activated depends on *how* the person chooses to listen. If he simply enjoys the music, a person uses primarily the right hemisphere, listening to the overall patterns of the music. But if the person is a trained musician, he will activate the left hemisphere to a greater degree because his style is to analyze the precise notes and phrases of the

RESEARCH BOX 3.1

## Neuropsychological Research Methods

Researchers in the 1950s and 1960s studied brain–behavior relationships by noting behavior changes that occurred after brain injury or at the time of stimulation of specific brain sites during surgery (Penfield & Roberts, 1959). Advances in instrumentation and computer technology in the 1970s and 1980s brought rapid gains in knowledge concerning patterns of typical and atypical brain functioning. The left and the right brain hemisphere's preference for certain types of tasks, called *brain asymmetry,* was found to be very important to normal maturation and learning. The poor learner often showed atypical asymmetries. In the last decade, there has been an enormous expansion of methods for noninvasively imaging the working brain as it is actively processing different types of information. Several methods for studying brain–behavior relationships have been used with the learning disabled and are described below.

### Split-Brain Studies

Neuropsychologists isolated the function of one brain hemisphere from another by studying individuals whose severe seizures were terminated when the *corpus callosum,* a band of nerve fibers that connects the two cerebral hemispheres, was severed. Once this band is severed, it is possible to present information to either hemisphere alone, thereby isolating the function of each cerebral hemisphere and observing which activities are deterred because they necessitate interhemispheric communication.

Sperry's (1968) studies used the apparatus pictured on the next page. Visual information is presented only to the left or right halves (visual field) of each eye. A picture presented to the left visual field is represented in the right cerebral hemisphere. As a result of their severed corpus callosum, Sperry's patients could not report in speech or writing what they saw because the left hemisphere controls these language functions (and subjects were seeing with their right hemisphere, which couldn't communicate to the left hemisphere). Some subjects even reported seeing nothing or just a flash of light. However, these same subjects' left hands were able to find the objects through touch because both the left side of the body and vision in the left visual fields are controlled by the right cerebral hemisphere. Only input to the right visual field (which projects to the left hemisphere) could be described in speech or writing. Likewise, only objects placed in the right hand could be named because the left hemisphere controls all these functions. Even though they could perform the high-level task of naming when the object remained in their right hands, subjects could not match the object or name a picture of the object if the latter were projected to their right cerebral hemisphere (through the left visual field).

### Visual-Half Field, Dichotic Listening, and Dichhaptic Stimulation Techniques

Separate or simultaneous presentation of two different stimuli to both visual fields, or ears, or hands is one means of examining the relative efficiency of each brain hemisphere in processing certain types of information. Each visual field is represented in the opposite hemisphere. In contrast, the left and right ears project only approximately 60 percent of auditory information to the opposite hemisphere. By determining which hemisphere is more accurate on a task, investigators presume its greater specialization for that particular function.

RESEARCH BOX 3.1 (Continued)

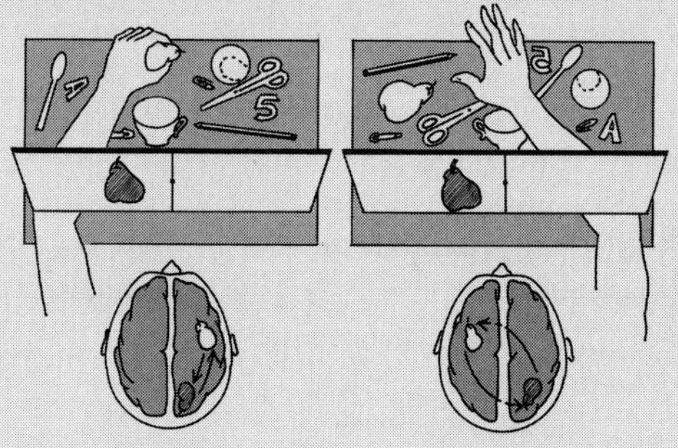

***Sperry's (1968, p. 730) Split-Brain Apparatus.*** When looking at the pear through the left visual field, the subject with a severed corpus collosum can find the corresponding object behind a screen only when using the left hand, which projects to the same hemisphere (right) that is seeing the pear.

*Source:* Sperry, R. W. (1968). Hemisphere deconnection and unity in conscious awareness. *American Psychologist, 23,* pp. 723–733. Copyright 1968 by the American Psychological Association. Reprinted by permission of the publisher and author.

These techniques have been adapted to a tactile *dichhaptic stimulation task* (Witelson, 1974). The subject is asked to use touch to perceive or name letters and meaningless shapes. Objects in the left hand are perceived primarily by the right cerebral hemisphere and vice versa. In naming letters, the right hemisphere is useful because it analyzes spatial information about the letter, while the left hemisphere provides the name. With nonlinguistic stimuli, however, the left hand's perceptions prove to be superior because their interpretation relies on the right hemisphere's spatial skills. These types of measures have shed light on the degree of specialization of each hemisphere for different functions, as well as the implications for the inefficiencies of the poor learner.

### Drugs

In the early years of hemispheric specialization research, drugs were used to anesthetize a hemisphere temporarily so that the researcher could observe which functions became impaired. Osgood and Miron (1963) used this technique to demonstrate that a numbing of the left hemisphere could induce language impairment in an adult. Their subject had been able to name common objects displayed to him: cigarette, spring, paper clip, colors, fingers. Injection of Nembutal (pentobarbital) into the right carotid artery (which feeds the right cerebral hemisphere) had no effect on this naming ability. An injection into the left carotid artery, however, produced jargonlike misnaming of the same articles. In addition, movement difficulties on the right side of the body became apparent (the left hemisphere controls movements of the right arm and leg). The Nembutal effect lasted four minutes, after which the subject again could identify the objects correctly. Obviously, his speech functions were located in his left hemisphere. This method has been named *Wada's technique,* after its discoverer. It is often used before brain surgery to detect whether the patient's language centers are in danger of being disturbed.

### Event-Related Potentials

*Event-related potentials* (ERP), the computer summing of *electroencephalogram* (EEG) recordings of electrical potentials, also reveal differences between good and poor learners.

*(continued)*

## RESEARCH BOX 3.1 (Continued)

Recordings may be taken from as many as 20 brain sites while the subject has eyes open/closed, reads letters/words, looks at meaningful/nonmeaningful shapes and objects, looks at light flashes, or listens to sounds or words. Usually 50 to 100 stimuli are presented at one-second intervals. For each presentation, the computer sums the amplitude (microvolts) of peaks and measures the milliseconds from the onset of stimulation to peaks, and the return to normal. This procedure allows the brain's responses to the stimuli to stand out against its background electrical activity. In the noncomputerized EEG, this background activity, as well as unreliable judgments, may obscure abnormal wave patterns.

### Brain Electrical Activity Mapping

The *average evoked potential* technique is used to create a moving visual display of brain wave activity. The computer divides the head into 4,096 picture elements (pixels), each of which takes on a color of the rainbow representing the electrode's reading. Electrodes measure the response to a stimulus (e.g., listening to spoken words) every 4 msec for a total of 512 msec. The 128 frames are viewed as a continuous movie of the spread of electrical activity in the brain. Using this technique, Duffy and McAnulty (1985) were among the first to demonstrate electroneurological differences among boys whose reading disabilities stemmed from three different types of language difficulties. *Magnetoencephalography* (MEG), also known as *magnetic source imaging* (MSI), uses over 100 magnetic field detectors placed around the head to record the tiny magnetic fields around the electrical currents that flow through neurons near the brain's surface. Simos et al. (2000) used MEG to show that normal readers activate their left temporoparietal areas when processing written words, but children with reading disabilities instead primarily activated the same region in the right hemisphere. Because the children with reading disabilities were similar to normal readers in the activation of visual association regions involved in looking at words, and auditory processing regions involved in listening to words, Simos and coworkers concluded that reading difficulties are associated with aberrant patterns of functional connections between brain areas involved in reading, that is, weaknesses in the connections that translate the printed word to sound. *Transcranial magnetic stimulation* (TMS) applies pulses to different areas of the scalp and records motor evoked potentials. Pascual-Leone's research group (1999) used this strategy to demonstrate the increase in area of brain activation after practice with a motor task.

### Computer-Assisted Tomographic Scanning (CAT Scan)

The *CAT scan* (also called *x-ray computed tomography—CT*) is a picture taken of an x-ray that scans the skull to detect the absorption differences between spinal fluid, bone, white and gray matter, and blood. Although brain lesion detection is enhanced by an intravenous injection of an x-ray-dense dye, the subtle brain differences of the learning disabled are hard to detect (Denckla, LeMay, & Chapman, 1985).

### Regional Cerebral Blood Flow, Positron Emission Tomography

In order for brain tissue to be activated, glucose and oxygen are required. These nutrients are supplied by means of the blood vessels. Consequently, measurement of blood flow in the cerebral hemispheres can indicate which hemisphere has been activated by a particular cognitive process.

## RESEARCH BOX 3.1 (Continued)

An extension of the CAT scan method, *regional cerebral blood flow* (rCBF, also called *positron emission tomography*, or *PET*) involves inhaling trace amounts of xenon or injecting radioactive isotopes into an arm vein. PET measures the decay of these radioactive isotopes. When a subject is asked to look at, listen to, or reason about something, blood flow concentrations change because the more active areas take up more oxygen and metabolize more glucose (80 percent of the brain's energy comes from glucose). Blood flow concentrations are apparent in PET scans of the cortical areas being activated by these tasks. Thus, we can discover the degree of activation required of different brain areas when performing certain tasks. Studies using PET have shown that, when reading, individuals with learning disorders underactivate essential regions (such as the temporal cortex) and overactivate inappropriate areas of the brain (e.g., the prefrontal cortex) because of either inefficient processing or the brain's attempt to develop compensatory pathways (Rumsey, 1996).

A simpler blood temperature measure has also been found useful. Blood temperature measures taken at the eardrum reflect which hemisphere has been activated because, when blood flow is increased, the brain tissue cools (Meiners & Dabbs, 1977).

### Magnetic Resonance Imaging (MRI)

*Magnetic resonance images* show the brain's anatomical structure by means of low-energy radio waves generated within a magnetic field. The brain's hydrogen protons resonate in response to these pulses. The MRI measures the time it takes for the pulsing of the hydrogen protons to decay; the rate of decay varies according to the density of the hydrogen. The MRI is sensitive to alterations in white matter, water content, bone marrow, and lower brain areas (brain stem, cerebellum, upper spinal cord) that other techniques have difficulty scanning. The sensitivity to white matter lesions is particularly helpful because white matter contains rapid "superhighway" neurons that connect different brain regions and are not well imaged on CAT scans (Hynd & Willis, 1988). MRI white matter lesions correlate well with neuropsychological findings (Levin, Handel, Goldman, Eisenberg, & Guinto, 1985). Because of this technology, subcortical white matter deficiency in the connections between different brain regions is becoming an important area of study.

Several variations of the standard MRI yield the structural resolution of MRI but also highlight areas of brain activation, as do PET and average evoked potentials. *Functional MRI* (fMRI) detects radio waves given off by blood hemoglobin that vibrates when the oxygen it carries is given to an activated cell. This technique contrasts areas of deoxygenated with areas of oxygenated hemoglobin, which reflects the increased blood flow required by increased neural activity. Functional MRI has an advantage over PET scans in showing better measures of blood flow changes across short time intervals, better spatial resolution, and freedom from radiation and injections. Unlike PET, fMRI is not suited to mapping the whole brain during an activity; the technique is used for only selected image slices. *Diffusion tensor MRI* (DT-MRI) measures the white matter communication channels necessary to connect messages from different brain areas. Using this method, Klingberg et al. (2000) were able to demonstrate decreased activity in the temporoparietal white matter regions of poor readers when compared to controls. *Functional magnetic resonance spectroscopic imaging* (fMRSI) is opening a new chapter on brain imaging studies by using

*(continued)*

## RESEARCH BOX 3.1 (Continued)

emitted radio signals to identify quantities of different brain chemicals involved in neuronal activation. Using fMRI and fMRSI, underactivation in poor readers' posterior regions and overactivation in anterior regions when making phonological judgments, underactivation of left hemisphere regions and overactivation of right hemisphere regions, and other unusual patterns have been found (Corina et al., 2001; Richards, 2001; Shaywitz, et al., 1998).

### Ultrasonography

In *ultrasonography,* high-frequency sound waves are generated by a transducer and directed into the body. The resulting echoes vary according to the tissue scanned. These sound waves are then converted into an image. Ultrasound is particularly valuable for viewing the brain's ventricles (four cavities that help to circulate the cerebrospinal fluid cushioning the brain and spinal nerves) and the corpus callosum (the band of fibers connecting the two cerebral hemispheres).

music he hears. The left hemisphere carries out this type of analytical and sequential reasoning.

***Though different parts of the brain "specialize," brain regions rarely work in isolation.***

Despite the specialization of different parts of the brain, brain regions rarely work in isolation. All brain regions are highly interconnected with other regions, and any type of information processing usually activates several regions at once, each to a different degree. Complex learning is dependent on the activation of an organized, functional system of different brain regions. This is why a weakness in one brain region can decrease performance in seemingly unrelated areas as well. This is also why a child with a severe reading disability has a 50 percent chance of also being identified with some other disorder, such as attention-deficit hyperactivity disorder, depression, anxiety, conduct disorder, or a language disability. The medical world refers to this co-occurrence of apparently "different" disorders as *comorbidity;* probably the truth is that all these disorders overlap because some sharing of underlying neural systems occurs.

***Complex learning is dependent on the activation of an organized, functional system of different brain regions.***

Figure 3.3 on page 65 illustrates the intricate cooperation between several brain regions that is necessary for higher-level functions involved in school learning. It is a photograph of the brain at work first reading silently and then aloud. Reading aloud stimulates up to seven areas of the brain in each hemisphere. Note that even when a person is reading silently, the areas of the brain responsible for listening and speech are stimulated to some degree. That's why, when you've been reading all day in preparation for a test, you may find that your throat feels scratchy and your mouth and jaw feel tense. Similar photographs have shown that, even when a person is resting with eyes closed and no distractions at all, the frontal lobes will be quite active as he or she continues to think.

In addition to having normal brain asymmetry, good learners must be able to pay attention appropriately. As children pay greater attention, their brain wave amplitudes increase and the time needed for the brain to respond to a stimulus decreases.

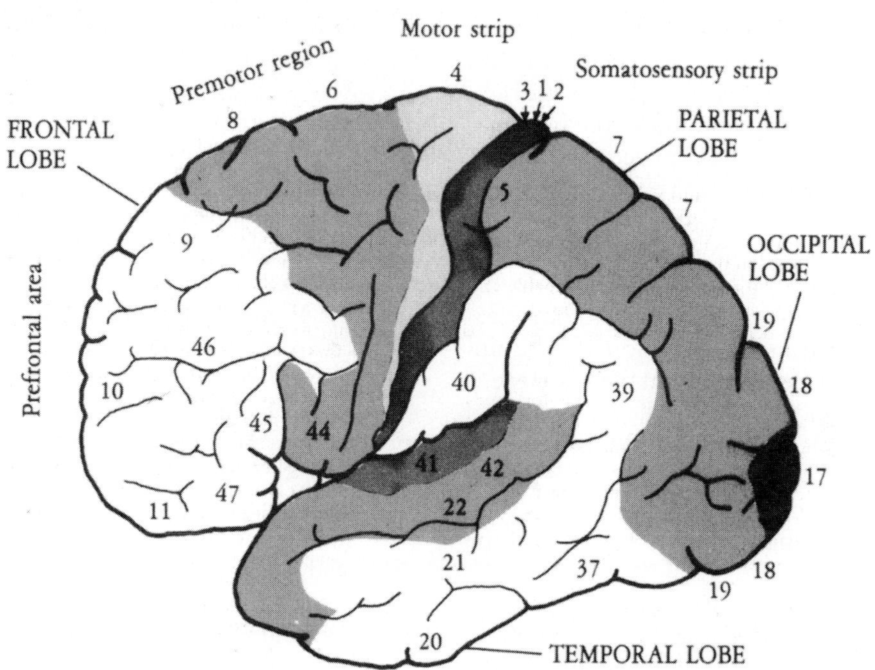


The cerebral cortex controls all conscious activity. The two halves of the cerebral cortex are almost identical in construction and metabolism but differ in function. All brain activity is controlled by the biological structure and chemical transmissions of the nervous system.

**Left Hemisphere:** In most individuals, the *left hemisphere* responds to language stimuli such as inner thought, words, symbols that have verbal meaning, and memory for verbal material (Luria, 1976). It usually contains Broca's area, an important region for speech. Over 95 percent of right-handed individuals and about 60 percent of left-handers (Segalowitz & Bryden, 1983) have speech located in the left hemisphere. The left hemisphere receives visual information from the right visual field of each eye, and movement and sensory information from the right side of the body. It specializes in information processing that involves analytical thinking, evaluating details, and sequencing. Because of the left hemisphere's use of words to reason, it plays an important role in skilled reading, mathematical analysis, and computation.

**Right Hemisphere:** The *right hemisphere* processes information as wholes (rather than details) and deals primarily with nonverbal stimuli such as body awareness (orientation in space), time sense, directional orientation (up-down), pictorial perception, mental imagery, spatial perception (Ketchum, 1967),

*(continued)*

**Figure 3.1** Brain structure–function relationships.

*Source:* Tarnopol, L., & Tarnopol, M. (1977). *Brain function and reading disabilities* (p. 9). Baltimore: University Park Press. Reprinted by permission of the authors. *General sources:* Hécaen & Albert (1978), Heilman & Valenstein (1979), Hynd & Willis (1988), Luria (1977, 1980), Tarnopol & Tarnopol (1977), Walsh (1978).

memory for visual stimuli (Luria, 1976), complex forms, color, and environmental sounds. Because of its visual-perceptual skills the right hemisphere plays an important role in appreciation of and talent in music, art, dance, sculpture, and geometrical-perspective drawing (Tarnopol & Tarnopol, 1977). The right hemisphere's role in appreciation of the overall configuration of elements—its ability to see the big picture—is important to organizational skills and social perception. If not dominant for language, the right hemisphere is still able to understand simple language and perform simple arithmetic (adding two digits). It receives visual information from the left visual field of each eye and movement and sensory information from the left side of the body.

**Temporal Lobe:** The *temporal lobe* is responsible for language reception and comprehension. Sixty percent of nerve fibers that transmit sound come from the opposite body side's ear, and 40 percent come from the same side's ear. Because language is important in learning, the hemisphere that contains these skills is called *dominant,* even when one's writing hand is controlled by the opposite cerebral hemisphere. The temporal lobe also plays an important role in emotions and behavior because of its proximity to the limbic system.

Area 41: primary auditory reception field.

Area 42: also receives auditory input; together with area 41, it contains Heschl's gyrus, which analyzes sound frequencies, lower frequencies being more centrally located.

Areas 21, 22: auditory association area capable of higher-order auditory analysis because of connections with other regions; works with area 42.

Areas 21, 37: controls auditory memory and sequencing, word meaning, retrieval of words.

**Frontal Lobe:** The *frontal lobe* is active in focusing attention, integrating awareness of the whole with the component elements, and organizing output. It is active in judgment, controlling impulsivity, assessment of risks and consequences of behaviors, and appropriateness of emotional reactions. The *primary motor strip* (area 4) in the right hemisphere controls voluntary muscular movements of the left side of the body. The left hemisphere's motor strip controls right side voluntary muscular movements. Each hemisphere contains some nerve fibers that control minor movements of the same side hand and arm.

Areas 6, 8, 44: These are the secondary or "premotor" regions that coordinate, organize, stop, or change movement that has already begun. They formulate complex motor activities through interconnections with the sensory association regions, primary motor strip, and somatosensory strip. Area 44 is called *Broca's area.* For most people this region in the left hemisphere controls speech movements and, if damaged, results in articulation difficulties. The same region in the right hemisphere is involved with speech rhythm and voice intonation.

Area 4 + premotor + sensory connections: Permit visual-motor, auditory-motor, and tactile, kinesthetic-motor associations.

Prefrontal Areas (9, 10, 45, 46, 47): Control judgment, reasoning, abstract thinking, motives, planning, perseveration, following plans, vigilance, and restraint of emotional impulses and impulsivity; appropriateness of emotional reactions; organization of goal-directed, selective behavior; regulation of states of attention or activity; activation of motor, speech, and intellectual acts as well as consciousness and affective states; orga-

**Figure 3.1** *Continued*

nization of information with respect to time and sequences.

**Parietal Lobe:** In contrast to the frontal lobe, which prefers a sequential strategy for surveying information, the parietal and occipital lobes take a more simultaneous approach, surveying stimuli in a unitary, holistic fashion. The *somatosensory strip* (areas 1, 2, 3) in the right hemisphere receives feelings of touch, texture, pain, movement, weight, and temperature from the left side of the body. The left hemisphere's strip receives sensations from the right side. Lesions on the strip result in a loss of sensation for specific body parts (see Figure 3.2).

Areas 5, 7: These are the secondary association areas which, through their connections with other regions, can analyze and synthesize more complex tactile-kinesthetic information. Lesions in these areas result in partial loss of sensitivity.

**Angular Gyrus:** The *angular gyrus* (area 39) is located in the dominant cerebral hemisphere and works together with area 40. Visual, auditory, and kinesthetic areas of the brain are connected here. If it is damaged, the individual will have deficits in reading, writing, spelling, understanding language, and body image.

**Occipital Lobe:** The *occipital lobe* processes visual stimuli. The right occipital lobe processes information from the left visual field of each eye. The left occipital lobe processes information from each eye's right visual field.

Area 17: Responds to simple visual stimuli (lines and edges).

Areas 18 and 19: Secondary visual areas with connections to other areas that permit higher-order visual functions: analyzing angles, movements, figure-ground discriminations; recognizing objects; synthesizing parts of objects into wholes; eye tracking; visual-auditory, visual-motor, and visual-sensory associations.

**Figure 3.1** *Continued*

Interestingly, it takes more neural energy to stop paying attention to an activity than to begin responding in the first place. Think about the last time you were about to blurt out a secret to a friend. You could almost feel the words rise up from your throat, and it took a significant amount of conscious effort to suppress that juicy bit of gossip. There are specific brain cells that were telling you to "stop."

*It takes more effort to stop attending to something than to have it catch your attention in the first place. This explains why many children with LD are helpless in the face of distractions.*

Because it takes more effort to stop attending to something that has caught your attention than to actually have it catch your attention, this explains why many children with learning disabilities who have underactive brain regions are helpless in the face of distractions. They can't help being sidetracked by noise in the hallway, even when they are trying hard to focus only on their work.

The functioning of the various regions of the brain is so precise and intricate that analysis of the complexity, frequency, and reaction time of brain waves from different brain regions can distinguish females from males; left-handers from right-handers; different levels of mental maturity; verbal and visual-motor competency levels; higher from lower scoring children on reading, math, and spelling tests; children with and without attention problems; good learners from learning-impaired children; and age. As we learn more about the typical student's brain development, we also gain a better understanding of the atypical patterns of children with learning disabilities.

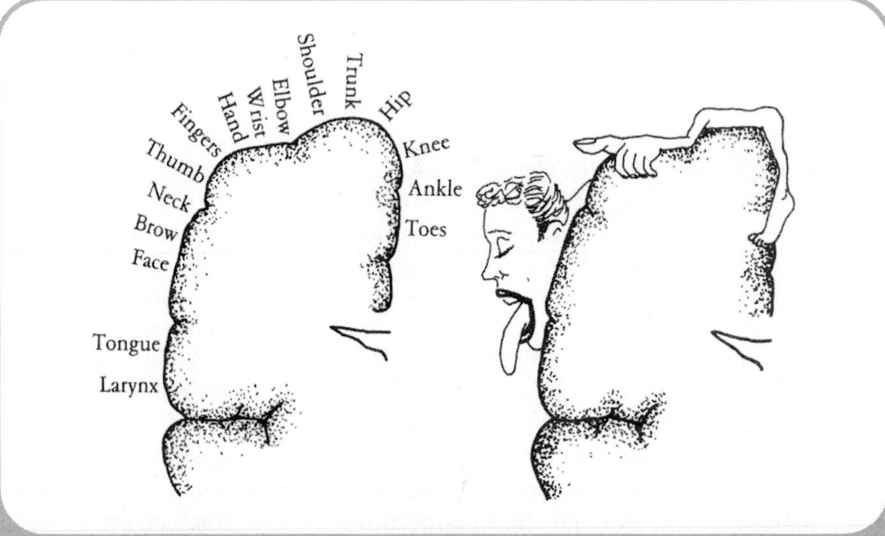


**Figure 3.2** The homunculus. The human body is represented in each hemisphere's motor strip (area 4 of the frontal lobe) and somatosensory strip (areas 1, 2, 3 of the parietal lobe) as an inverted fetus, a "homunculus." A relatively large brain area is devoted to the face, tongue, thumb, and fingers. These body parts, in turn, are able to move in more specialized fashions and to sense more acutely than are other body parts.

*Source:* Tarnopol, L., & Tarnopol, M. (1977). *Brain function and reading disabilities* (p. 222). Baltimore: University Park Press. Reprinted by permission of the authors.

## Patterns of Poor Learners

There are clear patterns of differences between good and poor learners. Some patterns are true of the majority of children with learning disabilities, whereas other patterns differentiate one LD subgroup from another.

**Patterns Common to Poor Learners.** Ask a teacher to describe her poor learners and she is very likely to say, "They seem less mature than the rest of my students academically and otherwise. They are very distractible, impulsive, and disorganized and must work extra hard to pay attention. It takes them forever to finish their work."

Researchers are now discovering why this is true. Studies find that the brain wave patterns of children who learn and behave immaturely are very much like those of younger, normally developing children. While the resting brain wave patterns of normal learners are very symmetrical in shape and amplitude, like the consistent wave action of the ocean on a calm day, the underachievers' brain wave patterns are far more uneven. In addition, while for normal learners one cerebral hemisphere is a bit more active than the other during a certain activity, poor learners seem to overuse one hemisphere and not adequately activate the weaker one.

*Poor learners seem to overuse one cerebral hemisphere and not adequately activate the weaker one.*

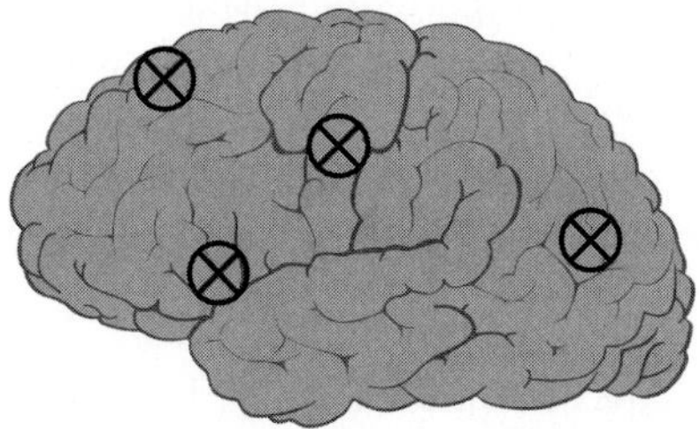

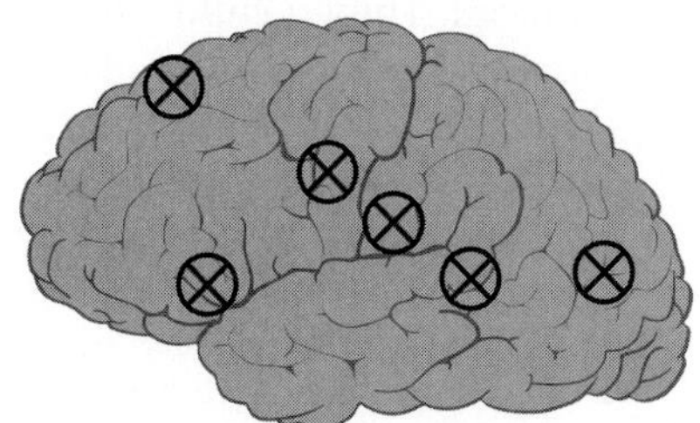

Normal brain cell activity during reading was revealed by measuring regional blood flow, which is closely related to metabolic rate and therefore to functional activity. Tomographic images show that reading silently and reading aloud involve different patterns of activity in the cortex. Reading silently (left) creates most activation in four areas: the visual association area (toward the rear of the brain), the premotor area (in the frontal lobe), the frontal eye field, and Broca's speech center in the lower part of the frontal lobe. Reading aloud (right) activates two more centers: the mouth area and the auditory cortex. The left hemisphere is shown in both cases, but similar results have been obtained from the right hemisphere. Adding the primary visual cortex, which is not reached by the radioactive isotope, the act of reading aloud calls for simultaneous activity in seven discrete cortical centers in each hemisphere.

**Figure 3.3** Brain structure-function relationships revealed through positron emission tomography.

*Source:* Adapted from Lassen, N. A., Ingvar, D. H., & Skinhøj, E. (1978). Brain function and blood flow. *Scientific American, 239*, 62–71.

Brain waves that represent attention and active mental processing often are lower in amplitude in students with LD than in average achievers. Thus, many children with learning disabilities must exert far greater than normal effort to simply stay on task or process information.

*Because of weaknesses in brain waves that represent attention, many children with LD must exert far greater than normal effort to simply stay on task or process information.*

The nervous systems of individuals with learning disabilities also respond more slowly than normal. These children take longer to process information, such as recognizing that someone is talking to them, and to perform even simple tasks such as beginning to cross a street when the light turns green. In one study, children with LD were nearly one-third of a second slower than their classmates in even starting to pronounce words they could easily read. Not only did they read slower than their classmates, but they were even slower than younger children who read at the same level. One-third of a second may not sound like a great lag, but it adds up rapidly; students quickly fall behind and often give up in frustration. This slower information-processing time tends to persist into adulthood, even if the person has made good academic progress.

*The nervous systems of individuals with LD respond more slowly than normal.*

Finally, children with learning disabilities are generally less coordinated than their peers because smooth, well-planned motor movements depend on a brain that can efficiently connect incoming and stored information with the

*Children with LD are generally less coordinated than their peers.*

motor activity. A weakness at any point along this chain results in uncoordinated output. Thus, a child who has difficulty judging the speed of an oncoming baseball will bat and miss. The child who can't remember how letters look or how words are spelled will have poorer handwriting.

**Patterns among LD Subgroups.** Three major patterns of brain functioning among the learning disabled have emerged from neuropsychological studies:

1. Overusing the right hemisphere and underusing the left
2. Overusing the left hemisphere and underusing the right
3. Frontally located brain inefficiencies that interfere with attention, motor control, organization, and planning

*Children who overuse the right hemisphere of the brain and underuse the left hemisphere are at risk on tasks requiring language and analytical proficiency.*

Children who overuse the right hemisphere of the brain and underuse the left hemisphere are at risk on tasks requiring language and analytical proficiency. These tasks include problems with reading, spelling, paying attention to and memorizing facts, mathematical calculations, writing essays, sequencing details and thoughts, and engaging in social conversation. The right hemisphere interferes with these activities because its style is to attend to wholes—word shapes and the main idea, for example—and not to analyze sounds in words or the sequence of sentences that make stories meaningful, both of which are necessary for good reading and writing skills. In short, children in this subgroup can't see the trees for the forest. Recent neuroimaging studies of children with severe reading delays find that these children's left hemispheres are underengaged during language processing tasks, and that they rely on the right hemisphere and frontal lobes to compensate for their left hemisphere inactivity.

*Children who overuse the left hemisphere and underuse the right hemisphere are at risk for difficulty with tasks that require visual-perceptual skills and the ability to get the big picture.*

The second LD subgroup does just the opposite—they overuse the left hemisphere and underuse the right hemisphere. Because the left hemisphere has a preference for language skills and analysis of details, these children are at risk for difficulty with many tasks that require visual-perceptual skills and the ability to get the big picture (which are right hemisphere activities). They can't see the forest for the trees. They have trouble with recognizing words on sight, spelling irregular words that must be remembered by how they look, nonverbal problem solving (puzzles, mazes), grasping the main idea or moral, inferential reasoning, organizing the tasks of note taking and outlining, planning essays, picking up on social cues (such as facial expressions and how close to stand to someone), mathematical reasoning that involves mentally maneuvering quantities in space, fine- and gross-motor coordination that involves spatial judgment (such as judging the distance from the car to the curb), and time concepts ("Can I beat the light?").

Although the patterns just described might be due to underdevelopment of the weaker hemisphere such that its inefficiency causes the opposite hemisphere to take charge, the converse also can be true. That is, one hemisphere might be so strong that it doesn't allow the other to do its part in helping out on a task. In either case, the least efficient strategies are activated to tackle particular tasks (recall that the right hemisphere prefers holistic strategies whereas the left is more analytical). Yet a third possibility relates to how a person goes about paying attention; in some circumstances the student's learning style results in too much or too little activation in certain hemispheres, thereby again bringing inappropriate strategies to the task at hand.

The third group of students with learning disabilities is composed of those with poor functioning of the frontal brain regions. They have particular trouble with planning, organizing, articulating, planning fine- and gross-motor movements, focusing attention, coordinating the whole picture with its parts, and modulating their behavior.

*Children with weaknesses in the frontal brain regions have trouble with planning and organizing actions, focusing attention, coordinating the whole picture with its parts, and modulating behavior.*

The research that led to the discovery of these brain pattern differences has also led to the development of teaching materials and methods designed to stimulate left- or right-hemisphere processing efficiency in the hopes of improving academic performance. Research Box 3.2 on page 68 reviews the growing number of studies suggesting that the nervous system can indeed change its wiring in response to specific kinds of practice and sensory input. In other words, neurons will wire together when we encourage them to fire together. The more a brain region is stimulated through practice, the more responsive it becomes to future input. We all have witnessed the truth of this statement at the other end of life, when older people actively learn new skills. Someone who has never played bridge, for example, but who determines to learn the game at age 70 will actually activate a portion of his or her brain that did not function as efficiently before. Use it or lose it, as the saying goes. Hence, the need for targeted, intensive, and quality teaching that addresses learning strengths and weaknesses as soon as possible after children's developmental delays are noted.

## Brain Injury

Although injury to brain tissue can and often does lead to delays in a child's development and ultimately problems with school learning, the fact of a brain injury does not automatically mean learning disabilities will follow. This is because of the brain's ability to compensate. In fact, as described later, there are many normal and advanced learners who have sustained some sort of brain injury. Most parents can attest to frightening falls their children have taken that have even included a brief period of unconsciousness. Certainly, coaches of all kinds of athletic teams can tell you of collisions between athletes and between an athlete and a very hard object. Yet most of these accident victims walk away virtually unscathed and very able to learn.

Even when we do diagnose a brain injury in a student with a learning disability, the diagnosis tells us very little about exactly what and how to teach that individual. It is far more instructive to understand the types of unique neuropsychological patterns, such as those described earlier, that can make a student's learning so difficult. Nevertheless, because brain injury is at the root of some children's learning disabilities, let us explore its causes, how often it affects learning, and whether diagnosing it is worth the trouble.

### Causes of Brain Injury

The areas of the brain that are the last to develop play the greatest role in high-level cognitive and academic reasoning abilities. These areas can be injured by carbon monoxide during suffocation or unconsciousness, nutrient and oxygen deprivation

RESEARCH BOX 3.2

## Enhancing the Efficiency of the Brain's Neural Networks through Practice

As our knowledge grows regarding the ways in which the brains of individuals with learning disabilities may be electroneurologically unique, so does our potential to use this information to target more powerful teaching strategies for students with LD. Some preliminary evidence has emerged, for example, regarding the potential for augmenting weak abilities by direct stimulation of various brain regions. Zihl (1981) trained brain-damaged adults with visual-field defects to move their eyes toward lights flashed into the defective field. This practice restored not only a portion of the visual field but also helped related visual functions. Similarly, Liepert et al. (2000), working with stroke victims, has demonstrated a 100 percent increase in the area of the cerebral cortex devoted to generating contractions in hand muscles by using a magnetic stream to penetrate a particular region of the skull to stimulate a muscle response.

These results are typical of a growing body of evidence that sensory input can expand the brain area dealing with specific functions. The more a specific brain region gets used, the more its neural circuits will enlarge. For example, we have found that pianists have enlarged left-hand representation in the brain compared to nonpianists, an expansion directly correlated with their increased left-hand dexterity and with the number of years of musical training (Amunts et al., 1997). Elbert et al. (1995) found the same results for string players. Karni et al.'s (1995) studies of brain activation with motor practice show that resting—giving time off from practice—in itself helps consolidate and strengthen the brain's activation patterns. Other investigators found that Braille readers, who use their right index fingertip to read, have a larger brain area devoted to this finger compared to their left index finger or the right index finger of non-Braille readers (Pascual-Leone & Torres, 1993). It is fascinating that even mentally imagining yourself rehearsing a simple five-finger piano routine is enough to influence the neuron network to be more active in supporting that activity (Pascual-Leone et al., 1995). We've all experienced the better follow-through in our golf swing or tennis stroke after watching the sports stars on TV, listening to commentators' critiques of their strokes, and then mentally imagining ourselves imitating Tiger Woods or Venus Williams. Well, we now know that if we put in sufficient mental practice, our subsequent improvement when actually playing may relate to very real changes in the involvement of specific brain neurons in the activity. Pascual-Leone et al. suggest that existing inactive neural connections become activated with such practice, or that synapses learn to make more effective use of existing neural circuits. This is pretty amazing research.

On a more school-related note, Tzavaras, Kaprinis, and Gatzoyas (1981) showed that when one identical twin was taught to read but the other wasn't, these functional differences actually were observable on brain-activation studies. John et al. (1977) were among the pioneering researchers in this area, showing that the intellectual decrements

such as when blood vessels are constricted or blocked, free-flowing blood such as occurs during a stroke or as a result of concussion, and pressure as from a tumor or infection. Brain injuries can happen before birth, during birth, and in the growing years; they are also more likely to be found among students identified as learning disabled than among average students.

## RESEARCH BOX 3.2 (Continued)

associated with being reared in impoverished environments were evident on brain-imaging studies. Bakker's research group has run particularly fascinating studies that have implications for different kinds of interventions for different kinds of learners (Bakker, 1984; Bakker & Vinke, 1985). Bakker et al. (1981) found that children's reading ability improved much faster if they practiced reading through the visual half-field that projected to their weaker hemisphere. Electroencephalographic (EEG) changes after brief periods of practice were striking. Teaching materials designed to stimulate processing in the underactive hemisphere also positively affected reading accuracy, speed, and EEG changes (Bakker, 1984; Bakker, Bouma, & Gardien, 1990; Bakker & Vinke, 1985). Similarly, Richards et al. (2002) found that dyslexic children with abnormally elevated lactate levels in their left frontal brain regions and abnormal activation patterns in parietal and occipital regions shifted to normal brain activation patterns after 1 to 2 months of reading intervention. In their study, Simos et al. (2002) found that children with severe word recognition and phonological difficulties, and underactive left hemisphere regions involved in phonological processing, improved markedly in both reading ability and left hemisphere activation after 80 hours of intensive remediation over a 2-month period. Equally exciting research in this area is being conducted by Benita Blachman at Syracuse University in conjunction with Yale University colleagues. These investigators are finding significant changes in functional magnetic resonance imaging patterns after exposing nonreaders to an intense phonologically based reading program. Areas of the brain that at first appeared too inefficient to support reading development, after reading intervention became more active and capable of contributing to the reading process. These brain changes are reflected in significant increases in these children's reading ability.

We have long known that stimulation facilitates brain development (Greenough, 1976). What is new, however, is evidence that the nervous system can actually change its preestablished wiring in response to specific kinds of practice or sensory input. It seems that neurons will in fact wire together if we encourage them to fire together (Sporns, 1994). The more a brain region is stimulated through practice, the more responsive it becomes to future input (Elbert et al., 1995). This is wonderful news to special educators, in particular, because their work is premised on the belief that their intense interventions will create permanent changes in children's abilities and increased potential for future learning.

The question that neuroscience must now deal with is exactly what type of stimulation is best for whom. Because researchers are just now learning which factors to investigate and how to study them, many studies are still methodologically weak, and results are contradictory. Recognizing that research on how to match intervention techniques with specific brain patterns is still in its infancy, our school programs must continue to be broad in scope, using students' stronger information-processing skills to facilitate new learning, while also trying to remediate the weaknesses that seem to be interfering with progress.

**Prenatal Factors.** A variety of prebirth problems can cause brain injury. These include RH factor incompatibility; maternal diabetes and hypothyroidism; x-rays; maternal measles; maternal drug, alcohol, and tobacco use; the mother's age (too young or too old for pregnancy); many prior pregnancies; medications that cause oxygen deprivation; maternal kidney malfunction or bleeding; and fetal infections such as rubella, cytomegalovirus, or the herpes simplex virus. Children born prematurely with a weight of 5.5 pounds or less are more likely to have a brain injury. In fact, prematurity by itself correlates significantly with later learning and behavior problems. There are also some minor physical anomalies, such as facial asymmetry, unusually long index fingers, short or curved fifth finger, atypical placement of ears or tear ducts, skin covering the tear ducts, tongue furrows, malformation of teeth, a high arch in the mouth, large gaps between toes, or unusual length of toes that are associated with learning disabilities or with lowered intelligence.

**Birth Injuries.** Babies' brains can be injured during labor and delivery because of oxygen shortage, prolonged or precipitous labor, premature separation of the placenta, or a difficult birth. Some 9 to 12 percent of full-term infants have had an intracranial hemorrhage (bleeding under the skull) during birth. That figure rises to over 40 percent for premature babies whose heads are less developed and are therefore more vulnerable to injury during the rigors of birth.

**Postnatal Factors.** A number of events after birth can injure the brain. These include serious accidents, strokes, high fevers, dehydration, brain tumors, and diseases such as encephalitis and meningitis. In fact, studies find that by age 6 as many as 20 percent of all children may have suffered a significant insult to the brain. About 1 in 3 high school students have sustained mild head injuries; 15 percent of these included a period of unconsciousness, and 12 percent of students reported multiple head injuries.

Because only about 11 percent of children are identified with handicapping conditions and because we know that brain injury is one of many factors that can cause such disabilities, why isn't there a greater correlation between head injuries and learning problems? Why, if all these children are getting bumped or worse on the head, aren't there more cases of learning disabilities? The answer is that there isn't a one-to-one, cause-and-effect relationship between a brain injury and later problems with learning. The next section tells us why.

## Effects of Brain Injury

People who have cerebral palsy or seizure disorders, as well as many of those who are blind, deaf, or learning disabled, have had a brain injury. Yet all of these individuals have different abilities, behaviors, and instructional needs. Some have very severe learning problems, while others have very few. What's the difference?

The relationship between a brain injury and a learning disability depends on answers to many questions. What caused the damage? Where in the brain is the damage located? How extensive is the damage? What was the person's developmental maturity at the time of the injury? How long has the damage been progressing? How much time has passed since the injury? What has been done to help the person retrain his or her cognitive abilities since the damage occurred?

*Although brain cells don't regenerate or repair themselves after injury, new neural connections often are formed between nondamaged cells so that learning progress continues.*

Human beings are very lucky to have "plastic" or pliable brains. Although brain cells don't regenerate or repair themselves after injury, new neural connections often are formed between nondamaged cells so that learning progress continues. This means that brain areas that are malfunctioning, but not totally destroyed, may be able to recover with stimulation. Some cells may give up their original function in order to take over the lost function. In other cases, cells that were dormant when the now damaged tissue was active may decide to adopt that function. Moreover, some existing cell systems can re-organize to handle the old function in a new way. Because all this can happen after brain injury, precise predictions of the outcome of an injury are very difficult to make.

Brain "plasticity" does decline with age. Nevertheless, injuries that happen in infancy may cause greater long-term losses in function than the same injury in older children and adults. Research Box 3.3 explains why this is so.

Just as knowing that a brain injury has happened doesn't help us predict either the existence or the extent of a learning disability, this diagnosis tells us little about the right instructional strategies for that person. Knowing about the brain's plasticity does, however, help professionals retain hope when they see that children are developing very slowly. Because of the brain's modifiability, patience and persistence in quality, intensive teaching is likely to pay off, as it did for Teddy (page 76).

## Diagnosing Brain Injury

When experts try to determine whether a person who is learning disabled has suffered a brain injury, they examine prenatal, birth, and postnatal indicators, electroencephalograms, and hard and soft neurological signs. At one time, when indicators for brain injury were found, it was automatically assumed that a brain insult had caused the learning problem. Or, if a learning problem was not yet apparent, it was predicted that a learning problem would develop in time. Today, however, we know that there are many other factors that cause learning disabilities, that positive brain injury indicators are very common among normal learners (their brains have compensated for the adverse consequences of the injury), and that brain injury indicators do not tap the functional neural systems important to high-level academic reasoning.

So, even if a child does test positive on brain injury indicators, we can't conclude that this abnormality has caused or will cause a learning problem. Coleman and Sandhu's (1967) data illustrate this point. When testing 7- to 15-year-old children, they found that the percentage of children with birth difficulties and serious brain injury indicators increased as reading achievement decreased. Nevertheless, as many as 19 percent of children who were one year ahead in reading also had notable birth difficulties, and 15 percent had serious brain injury indicators. The chart of Coleman and Sandhu's data indicates that the presence of brain injury indicators is far from a life sentence for learning problems:

***If a child tests positive on brain injury indicators, we can't conclude that this abnormality definitely caused or will cause a learning problem because these indicators don't reflect processes essential to higher-level learning.***

| 2 or more years behind in reading | 1–2 years behind in reading | Less than 1 year behind in reading | Over 1 year ahead in reading |
|---|---|---|---|
| **Birth difficulties** | | | |
| 30% | 23% | 17% | 19% |
| **Serious brain injury indicators** 26% | 23% | 11% | 15% |

RESEARCH BOX 3.3

## Brain Plasticity

Damage to a specific brain site reduces the ability of the individual to perform the function usually assumed by that area. However, this functional loss may not be permanent. The human brain has approximately 100 billion neurons and, depending on one's age, each connects through anywhere from 10,000 to 100,000 synapses to thousands of other neurons (Huttenlocher, 1979). Therefore, neurons from adjacent or distant areas often are capable of stepping up to the plate and forming connections that take over the functions of the damaged regions. The brain is fairly adaptable in this way provided that the primary, densely inervated, receptive (visual, auditory, tactile) and expressive (motor, speech) areas are not totally destroyed and provided that the dysfunction is in the more sparsely inervated secondary areas that analyze and integrate this information or in the tertiary areas where interaction and integration of neurons from various primary sites occur (Alajouanine & Lhermitte, 1965; Lenneberg, 1967). For example, before age 2 a child's right hemisphere will take over many of the left hemisphere's language functions when the latter is damaged. Between ages 2 and 5, language zones will shift within the left hemisphere in response to left hemisphere injury. The tradeoff is that the functions slated for the brain areas doing the compensatory work may decline severely because that region is pinch-hitting for more than it was meant to do. With this brain area "crowded out" of its original purpose, and the damaged area functioning inefficiently, overall language and cognitive capacities usually show some decline (Fletcher, Levin, & Landry, 1984; Kolb, 1989; Riccio & Hynd, 1996; Searleman, 1977; Springer & Deutch, 1997).

Animal studies indicate that neuronal recovery after brain injury may occur in several ways, with the best news of all being the ability of the adult primate brain to add brand new neurons, axons, and synapses throughout life (Finger & Almli, 1984; Gould et al., 1999; Greenough & Black, 1992; Huttenlocher, 1979; Kolb, 1989; Rodier, 1984):

1. Inactive, intact *axons* (nerves that send messages) take over for the inability of cut axons to repair themselves.
2. New connections sprout from the axons of undamaged neurons to repair damaged circuits; at times this sprouting may result in aberrant connections. In essence, one abnormality may be traded for another.
3. *Synapses* (areas where nerve endings meet) that had been vacated by other axon terminals are a growth stimulus for new neuronal sprouting; the sprouting pattern is not similar to the original normal connections.
4. Groups of *dendrite* branchings (nerves that receive messages) may form new circuits if stimulated appropriately, especially between ages 2 and adulthood. At times dendrites will expand in response to a loss of input.
5. *Glial* (connecting) cells regenerate and make contact with neurons so that transmission can occur.
6. The outer membrane of neurons near the site of injury may become more responsive to neurotransmitters, thereby improving recovery.
7. Better conduction may occur because of changes in synapse density after stimulation, or a gain in numbers of synapses.

RESEARCH BOX 3.3 (Continued)

8. If injury occurs before birth, the brain may respond shortly after injury by producing new cells of the correct type; however, permanent reductions in the total numbers of neurons is still likely.
9. Some brain regions are "neurogenic." That is, they can add new nerve cells throughout life from cells that originate in the subventricular zone and migrate through the white matter to the cortex, where they extend axons.
10. Enriched environments may result in positive changes in brain structure (e.g., increase in glial/neuronal ratio, enzyme activity, nucleic acid concentration, cortical and subcortical size and weight, synapse numbers per neuron, dendritic field size, blood vessels). During learning there is selective strengthening of preexisting synapses and neuron connections and active formation of new synapses and neuron connections.
11. Carefully focused stimulation of learning skills encourages growth in synapses and neural connectivity. Simply being active—as in rats exercising extensively but not learning specific new motor skills—increases the density of blood vessels but this doesn't help support greater performance ability.
12. Early overproduction of neurons and synapses, followed by a period of cell death, creates more efficient neural circuits and reduces unnecessary redundancy. Animal studies show that if too few neurons are produced initially, the brain may respond by reducing the subsequent rate of cell death.

These findings from animal studies are promising for people. Only in recent years have we developed the technical sophistication to begin to explore whether these kinds of processes are also operative in humans.

What we do know is that the human's central nervous system recovery ability varies with the nature and location of the damage, the size of the damage, the age at which the injury occurred, as well as the intensity, length, and type of retraining efforts (Reitan, 1974). Often the child's injured brain reorganizes so that old problems can be solved in new ways (Rourke et al., 1983). With significant exposure to particular stimuli and practice of particular skills, new dendritic connections sprout, new synapses are formed, preexisting neural pathways are strengthened, unused connections are weakened, and the strength of a synapse's contribution to an activity is shifted. The human central nervous system is a rapidly adapting, dynamically changing system in which modifications are driven by incoming environmental and behavioral stimuli, the brain activity that supports outgoing behaviors, and the functional significance of these stimuli and activities (Pascual-Leone et al., 1999).

In the 1970s and 1980s we already were aware that, as a result of the very young child's experience, neuron interconections and synapses are shaped and proliferate, then are fine-tuned, and finally are winnowed if unused or unnecessary to support behavior. A massive overproduction of neural connections occurs until about 1 year of age, followed by "pruning," which helps the brain function more efficiently. The elimination of redundant synapses supporting visual processing continues until about 10 years of age, while the same processes for language are completed by the onset of adolescence. The myelination of axons—the building of a protective sheath that increases the speed of

*(continued)*

**RESEARCH BOX 3.3 (Continued)**

electric impulses traveling down axons—continues for some brain regions into the adult years, as does dendrite growth (Huttenlocher, 1979; Wilson, 1988; Yakovlev & Lecours, 1967). Only recently, however, have we discovered that the human brain actually has the ability to generate brand new neurons in some brain regions throughout life (Erikkson et al., 1998; Gould et al., 1999). Research in the last decade is showing that the brain can form new neuronal connections in many brain regions throughout much of the life span (Thompson & Nelson, 2001). Because the human brain is "plastic" over much longer periods of time than previously thought, the adage "old brains can't learn new tricks" has been definitively debunked.

No data on brain plasticity are more astounding than the remarkable relearning that takes place after an entire cerebral hemisphere or lobe has been surgically removed because of epilepsy, tumor, or trauma; however, overall functioning is nevertheless compromised, with some new learning occurring with ease while other more naturally developing abilities remain underdeveloped (Bigler, 1992; Dennis & Whitaker, 1976; Fletcher et al., 1984; Kolb, 1989).

Despite the good news about the brain's plasticity, complete recovery after injury is the exception rather than the rule. Most research finds that verbal abilities are better spared after left hemisphere damage than are visual-spatial abilities after right hemisphere damage, but the sparing is incomplete (Rourke et al., 1983; Taylor, 1984). That is, even if a brain insult has produced no obvious diminution in function, when problem-solving demands require greater neurological maturity, the deficit may very well become apparent.

It had been a general belief that the adult recovers less function after equivalent brain injury than the child because (1) neuron regeneration is less efficient the older one gets, and (2) there is less room for one area of the brain to take over the activities of another because the former has already specialized for a specific function. More recently, however, evidence has accumulated indicating that young children may demonstrate as much or even more cognitive impairment when suffering from the same severity of brain injury as older children and adults (Hartlage & Telzrow, 1986; Kolb, 1989; Lord-Maes & Obrzut, 1996). Hynd and Willis (1988) explain that at birth the primary cortical zones appear mature, in contrast to the secondary and tertiary zones, which require months and years to mature (Luria, 1980). Therefore, lesions in early childhood to primary regions may deleteriously affect higher-order cognitive processes because the necessary foundations for this learning have been disturbed. Similar lesions during adulthood would have a more limited effect because the functional system for higher-order cognitive processing already has been formed. An alternative explanation for more devastating effects from early brain injury considers the fact that injury to brain tissue also produces secondary cell loss or reorganization in areas with which the tissue anatomically or functionally interrelates, even if remote from the area of damage (Rosenzweig, Bennett, & Alberti, 1984). Therefore, early brain damage in one area may alter the neuroanatomy, function, neurochemistry, and growth patterns of remaining brain systems (Isaacson & Spear, 1984). Even if the effects of the damage are not evident on simple sensory, perceptual, or motor tasks, their adverse effects may be quite apparent in higher cognitive functions (O'Leary & Boll, 1984).

Once damage and recovery have occurred, the reserve power of the brain is limited in the event of further damage (Lehrer, 1974). Nevertheless, the reserve is usually large

**RESEARCH BOX 3.3 (Continued)**

enough to help develop some compensatory skills, a finding that is critical to the success of our special education efforts. See Research Box 3.2 on page 68 for a summary of very exciting studies regarding how environmental interventions are actually beginning to grow the brain's circuitry.

*The fact that a child's brain has been injured raises red flags, but it does not automatically mean that learning disabilities will follow. The brain is plastic and often can compensate for losses.*

A similar study found no correlation between prenatal and birth-related brain injury indicators and whether teenagers had been identified as disabled. Clearly, having had a brain injury may raise red flags, but it is not an automatic predictor for learning disabilities.

The *electroencephalogram* (EEG) has also been unreliable as a predictor of learning problems. This test uses electrodes to measure electrical activity at many points near the outer surface of the brain. At one time, experts believed that, because EEGs are useful in detecting brain tumors, malformations, convulsive disorders, and coma, they might also shed light on the reasons for learning disabilities. Studies, however, found little difference in the number of average and poor learners whose EEG graphs are irregular. In four different studies, anywhere from 10 to 32 percent of average learners had abnormal EEGs. Clearly, the human brain has a great ability to compensate for abnormalities so that a person can continue to learn effectively. Indeed, the brain's compensatory ability is such that at times children with known brain injuries have entirely normal EEGs.

Examining hard and soft neurological signs also has been fruitless in predicting or explaining learning problems. *Hard neurological signs* always indicate a brain injury. They include seizures, cerebral palsy, cranial nerve abnormalities that cause blindness or deafness, and microcephaly (very small head). *Soft neurological signs* are developmental lags in gross- and fine-motor development, such as poor balance or coordination difficulties. A soft sign is demonstrated in a child who isn't walking at all or walking with difficulty well past the point when most children are running everywhere and grabbing for objects faster than they can be removed from sight. Soft signs are abnormal relative to the child's age, but they are quite normal at younger ages.

Studies have found that underachievers who have no obvious brain injuries (such as cerebral palsy), on average do not have more hard or soft signs than average learners. It is not uncommon to find that over half of good learners in a study have hard or soft signs. The largest of these studies, Nichols and Chen's National Collaborative Perinatal Project, determined that the relationship between neurological signs and learning disabilities in 7-year-olds accounted for only 1 percent of their learning problems.

Like the other brain injury indicators, hard and soft signs do not appear to reflect the brain processes necessary for high-level academic engagement. In fact, we now know that hard and soft signs can be caused by factors other than brain injury: inherited traits, maturational patterns that will be outgrown, or environmental influences such as poor health care or nutrition.

### Teddy

*A child with severe brain injury.*

Teddy was adored by his parents and four older sisters, and it was not hard to see why. At 2 years old, he was a handsome, affectionate child who responded to all the attention given him with hugs, smiles, and laughter. He was tall for his age and obviously bright: he had learned to talk early, spoke in clear three- and four-word sentences, and already recognized some letters of the alphabet. Teddy loved to watch *Sesame Street* and to look at picture books, and he also loved the playground. He was so graceful on the slide and jungle gym that his father boasted Teddy was certainly slated for athletic stardom.

Teddy's life changed, however, after a routine DPT immunization. Doctors say it was a coincidence, but the evening that he received his injection Teddy developed a high fever, had seizures, and was rushed to the local emergency room. He was hospitalized, but it was several days before the fever and seizures abated. By the end of the week it was clear that Teddy had sustained brain damage: the little boy could walk only with assistance, and he couldn't speak at all.

Over the next six months Teddy's ability to walk and talk returned, but he wasn't the same child. Instead of sitting quietly absorbed with crayons or a picture book, he became a human tornado. His coordination was poor, and he tried to stomp through things rather than move around them. He was impulsive and easily frustrated. He could not be taken to the supermarket without climbing and grabbing things off the shelves. When his parents tried to restrain him he would kick, bite, and throw tantrums. Even worse, Teddy continued to have seizures, which required frequent trials with different doses of medication.

Teddy's "out of control" behavior caused him to be dismissed by several nursery schools. Teachers complained that he knocked down other children's block towers, spoke out during story time, and splattered paint everywhere. He grabbed other children's toys and helped himself from other children's lunches. The teachers agreed that Teddy was bright enough, but they cautioned that he would have trouble in kindergarten if he could not control himself and learn to stick with tasks. Unfortunately, the teachers' predictions proved correct. Teddy's first years in school were a disaster; he couldn't attend to his lessons for long, and he was the last in his class to master basic skills. By the end of the second grade, it was obvious that read-

Despite the fact that indicators for brain injury have proved nearly useless in definitely predicting or explaining learning problems, many professionals are quick to scare parents when they note these signs. Instead they should be highlighting the brain's ability to compensate, and focusing on the neuropsychological patterns of brain functioning that are far more relevant to strengths and weaknesses in students' learning abilities and styles.

## Structural Brain Differences

Some children are born with atypical brains because of maldevelopment of the brain's tissue, neuronal circuitry, or brain organization in fetal life. This can be

## Teddy (Continued)

ing and writing were both going to be very difficult for him. Teddy's skills always continued to develop, but his progress was so slow that the gap between him and the other students in his class got wider every year. By the time he finished sixth grade, Teddy was reading and writing like a fourth grader. His seizures were largely under control and he had stopped having temper tantrums, but he remained an active, angry boy who was unpopular with other students and teachers alike.

During junior high school, continued low achievement and social isolation ate away at Teddy's feelings of self-worth. He became so angry and depressed that his parents became truly alarmed. After lengthy discussions, they decided to try placing Teddy in a private boarding school for students with learning disabilities. Teddy left home at the beginning of ninth grade.

Teddy's parents reported that by their first Parents' Day visit, they could see a change in their son. Teddy seemed heartened by the discovery that he was not the only student of his kind. He had made some friends, and he played on the school's soccer team. Teddy's teachers helped him complete tasks by allowing him to work in short sessions that were spread throughout the day. The school stressed learning through doing whenever possible, and Teddy found many of the projects he was assigned enjoyable and interesting. He had discovered that he could be a good student if he was allowed to do things his own way. For the first time since he was two, Teddy was thinking of himself as a success.

In twelfth grade, Teddy passed all of his state competency tests and declared he wanted to go on to college. Initially his parents panicked, afraid that demands at the college level would resurrect old patterns of frustration and failure. Several sessions with the school's guidance counselor, however, produced an ideal solution: following graduation, Teddy enrolled in a two-year culinary arts institute. He excelled in this training, earned an associate's degree, and rapidly found a job as a pastry chef in an exclusive resort. He recently became engaged to a vivacious young woman employed in resort management. Teddy's fiancé does all the driving because of his seizure disorder; Teddy does all the cooking, which his wife-to-be declares is a more than acceptable trade. Teddy is also designing the cake for his wedding, planned for June.

*Source:* Reprinted with the permission of The Free Press, a Division of Simon & Schuster Adult Publishing Group, from *Learning Disabilities A to Z: A Parent's Complete Guide to Learning Disabilities from Preschool to Adulthood* by Corinne R. Smith and Lisa W. Strick. Copyright © 1997 by Corrine R. Smith and Lisa W. Strick.

the result of genetic predisposition, or it can result if the fetus is subjected to stroke, drugs, hormones, toxins, malnutrition, infections, maternal stress, and more.

Evidence suggests that some people with learning disabilities are born with abnormalities in the size of their right or left hemispheres. In about two-thirds of normal individuals, the upper portion of the left temporal lobe, which is important to reading, is larger than the corresponding area in the right hemisphere. Eleven percent show larger right lobes, and 24 percent are equal in size. Given this data, it is striking that on CAT scan or magnetic resonance images (see Research Box 3.1) of brain areas involved in reading, a greater than expected number of people with reading disabilities show either larger right than left regions, or equality of both regions.

*Some people with LD are born with abnormalities in the size and cell structure of different brain regions.*

Several researchers' autopsies of eight brains of individuals with learning disabilities suggest that their brain anomalies occurred in the fifth to seventh month of pregnancy, when cells migrate upward from the base of the skull and interconnect to form gray matter. This migration seemed incomplete, with islands of nerve cells that were misplaced and never reached the cortex. The anomalies were most apparent in the left hemisphere, especially its language areas (unusually small, abnormal arrangement of neurons and cell connections), though anomalies also appeared in the right hemisphere, frontal lobe, and subcortical regions.

Unfortunately, lack of development of or damage to the cerebral cortex in intrauterine life may lead to lifelong diminishment of the function controlled by that portion of the brain. Had the same area of the brain been damaged postnatally, undamaged areas would compensate by taking over the lost ability. In fetal life, however, the corresponding healthy brain region in the opposite hemisphere appears to react by developing a more extensive than normal pattern of connections. Connections are also sent to the brain regions with which the damaged areas would have connected. Essentially, instead of taking over the lost function, the healthy brain region overdevelops its own abilities and the lost ability remains lost. Current research suggests this scenario in at least some individuals with learning disabilities—the left hemisphere isn't wired to do its job efficiently, and its efficiency is further distorted when rivaled by an overactive right hemisphere. No wonder learning problems result.

## Hereditary Factors

There is much evidence that learning disabilities, just like other disorders that affect learning and behavior (such as schizophrenia, major depression, panic disorders, attention-deficit hyperactivity disorder, alcoholism, or antisocial personality), can be inherited. Different brain structures, patterns of brain maturation, biochemical irregularities, and susceptibility to brain diseases may be passed on through families. If one child has a reading disability, there is about a 40 percent chance that a sibling or parent will also have a reading disability. Different studies report about a 30 to 50 percent chance that a child will have a reading disorder if the parent has one. The risk and severity of reading delay rises when the father, rather than the mother, has reading disorders, or if both parents are affected. Boys appear twice as likely as girls to inherit a learning disability from a parent. Jimmy's story is revealing in this regard.

*There is a 30 to 50 percent chance that a child will have a reading disorder if the parent has one, with the risk being greatest for boys.*

Given this high rate of "passing on" learning disorders, researchers have argued that learning problems that "run in families" could be the result of the shared environment in the family, and not necessarily inherited genetically. How many times have you been told that you look or act just like your sister or brother? Is this a genetic fact? Or is it the result of your being brought up in the same household?

These questions are more readily answered with studies that control for genetic and environmental influences, for example, comparing twins with their siblings and parents. Such studies have examined the heritability of learning disorders, intelligence, and handedness.

## Jimmy

*A child with a strong family history of learning disorders.*

When Jimmy's mother called the clinic to refer her son for an evaluation, the first hint that Jimmy's learning difficulties might be hereditary came over the phone. Jimmy's mother expressed her deep "flustration" in obtaining adequate services for her son's "dilekia." For a woman with a Ph.D., who was the director of a counseling center, such mispronunciations were unexpected. The mother's worst fear was that he had inherited "dilekia" from both sides of the family.

Jimmy's mother had two siblings, neither of whom had learned to read until adolescence. One now writes books, but remains a terrible speller. One child of the other sibling has been identified as learning disabled, and her younger child, a preschooler, is receiving speech and language therapy.

Jimmy's father has a master's degree in social work, a Ph.D. in philosophy, and now spends all his time back in law school. He is never satisfied with his accomplishments and keeps trying to prove his competence in new ways. Jimmy's father was very late in learning to read and still reads, in his words, "a word an hour." What he reads he remembers, however, and he is an excellent student. His professors have always allowed him to use a spell-checker on exams.

Jimmy's father comes from a family of five children, and every one has a reading disability. All but one sibling, who suffers from severe depression, have become successful vocationally. One of his brothers stutters, and a sister gets stuck on very simple words when speaking. Her conversations are punctuated by referring to objects as "thing" and elaborating when recounting an event by adding "or some such thing." Another brother is described as extremely disorganized; he gets lost in supermarkets and shopping malls and panics at the idea of traveling through a strange city.

Jimmy's mother had reason to believe that her 10-year-old son may not have been lucky enough to escape his genetic history. Take a look at his spelling in Figure 6.6 on page 168 and judge for yourself the outcome of his assessment.

## Heritability of Learning Disabilities

Studies of twins have found a genetic link to psychological and physiological characteristics that can influence learning such as hyperactivity, body responses that underlie emotionality (pulse, blood pressure, perspiring), and personality type. They have revealed a powerful role in learning disabilities as well. In the Colorado Reading Project, one of the largest studies of this type, De Fries, Pennington, Olson and their colleagues found that the likelihood of identical twins both having reading disorders was much greater (71 percent) than that for fraternal twins (49 percent); the figures for sharing of math disorders were 58 percent and 39 percent, respectively. Although fraternal twins share the same family environment, genetically they are no more alike than siblings. Identical twins, however, are even more alike in their learning because they share not only the same environment, but also the same genes. When examining reading specifically, it appears that roughly 45 percent of the traits contributing to reading are inherited, with the rest of learning being influenced by the environment. Spelling and analyzing the order of sounds in words have higher heritabilities (spelling is 60 percent, phonological awareness

*The likelihood of identical twins both having reading disorders is much greater (71 percent) than for fraternal twins (49 percent).*

is 75 percent) than learning weaknesses caused by poor visual recall of letter sequences in words (30 percent). Clearly, we need to be especially vigilant when we suspect that our students' parents may themselves have learning difficulties. Early intervention can do much to prevent further delays, and strategies that worked for the parents may prove helpful to their children.

Not surprisingly, studies of precise types of reading disabilities show some consistency among siblings. Even spelling patterns, such as whether misspellings are phonetic or nonphonetic (sound or don't sound like the intended word), are remarkably similar among family members.

There appear to be many genetic mechanisms responsible for the inheritance of learning disabilities. Using *linkage analysis,* a method of linking individuals with LD who share common genetic markers (e.g., Rh factor, blood type), thus far LD has been linked to at least eight different chromosomes.

Despite the evidence for genetic links in learning disorders, it's important to remember that what's been served up by the genes can be modified by the environment. Study after study finds that, even in twins, approximately 60 percent of their reading achievement is attributable to the shared environmental influences of their homes or other factors besides genes. In other words, the environment is a more powerful influence on learning and development than the genes, a fact that receives powerful support from studies on the heritability of intelligence.

***The environment is a more powerful influence on learning and development than the genes.***

## Heritability of Intelligence

Intelligence plays a significant role in academic achievement and identification of the learning disabled. We expect children to function at intellectual levels similar to those of their parents and in keeping with the kind of stimulation and support they have received at home. Studies show that children's learning aptitude is genetically predetermined, but their ultimate achievement levels are strongly influenced by environmental events.

***Children's learning aptitude is genetically predetermined, but their ultimate achievement levels are strongly influenced by environmental events.***

IQ levels correlate more strongly the closer the genetic relationship and the sharing of environments between individuals. Thus identical twins' IQs are more highly correlated than fraternal twins' IQs. Identical twins reared together have more similar IQs than do identical twins reared apart (which still are similar two-thirds to three-quarters of the time). Because fraternal twins are the same age, their IQs are more highly correlated than siblings' IQs because they share the general environment at exactly the same time.

The degree to which one's native intelligence can be developed is heavily dependent on the environment. Marjorie Honzik's classic 1957 study is a perfect example. She studied adopted children who were expected to have below average IQs because their biological mothers' average IQ was 86 (18th percentile). Honzik found that the IQs of the adopted children did indeed correlate with that of their biological mothers, and not with that of their adoptive mother. The brighter the biological mother, the brighter the child. Nevertheless, these children's IQs, when reared in a more stimulating environment, rose to an average of 106, above the 66th percentile. Studies repeatedly have found that IQs of adopted children rise significantly above that of their biological siblings who continued to live with their natural parents. The most astounding increases in IQ, however, from retarded to normal, are found in studies of children raised in orphanages who subsequently are placed in more nurturing environments.

It is obvious that even if genetic endowment does predict lower intellectual ability, this ability can be altered immensely through good parenting and teaching. Heredity seems to set an upper limit to intelligence, and by implication learning, but whether one reaches this limit is up to the environment.

### Inherited Handedness

Which hand you use to write with is determined to an overwhelming degree by genetic inheritance. About 8 to 12 percent of the population is left-handed, with more males in this group than females. Contrary to popular perception, there is no correlation between left-handedness and learning disabilities, intelligence, or perceptual skills, unless the preference for the left hand is the result of a brain injury or other brain abnormality. In the latter case, a child who genetically is right-handed has switched to the left hand because his or her brain cannot efficiently guide the right side's hand and finger movements. This child's left-handedness did not cause the learning problems. Instead, both the learning problems and the left-handedness are symptoms of the underlying brain dysfunction. It is the public's reaction to these children's odd behavior that has led to denigration of left-handers over the years; even the word "left" has negative connotations: in Latin, the word "left" has the same root as "sinister"; in French, the word translates as "gauche," which has come to mean awkward and inappropriate.

*There is no correlation between left-handedness and learning disabilities, intelligence, or perceptual skills, unless the preference for the left hand is the result of a brain abnormality.*

Unlike 95 percent of right-handers who have speech located in their left hemisphere, 60 percent of left-handers locate speech in the left hemisphere, 20 percent in the right hemisphere, and 20 percent in both hemispheres. Therefore left-handers are a particularly interesting group to study because their brains can locate language in the left, right, or both hemispheres. Left-handers whose language is represented in both hemispheres have an advantage following brain injury because their brains recover more rapidly than those with language located in only one hemisphere. Although some experts kid that this makes the left-hander's "two heads better than the right-hander's one," others warn that if both hemispheres must be activated for language functions, then other functions may suffer.

*Left-handers are a particularly interesting group to study because their brains can locate language in the left, right, or both hemispheres.*

## Biochemical Irregularities and Attention-Deficit Hyperactivity Disorder

Several biochemical irregularities can lead to learning disorders in children who otherwise have good potential to learn. Some of these biochemical disturbances can cause severe brain injury. Others create problems with attention and hyperactive-impulsive or hypoactive states that make it particularly hard for the child to focus and sustain attention. Although bothersome, the activity level among hyperactive-impulsive children is not really important; the real problem is that these children can't concentrate long enough on important information to learn effectively.

Many children with learning disabilities, more often girls than boys, have subtle attention deficits that are easy to overlook because the children do not cause behavioral problems in the classroom. In situations that require sustained attention and sitting still, however, children who are also hyperactive and impulsive are sure to be noticed. It might be hard to pick out a hyperactive youngster on the playground without watching carefully for the number of activity changes, problems entering and negotiating a game, and what happens when he doesn't get his way; but place the same child in the classroom and his attention shifts, overtalkativeness, and moving around are glaring.

One study revealed that hyperactive-impulsive children don't actually get up and down more often in the classroom than their peers, but they do so at inappropriate times. For example, they hop up and cross the classroom for a toy in the middle of a reading group. They can't help being distracted or dim the impulse to move toward what distracted them, even when they know it's not the right time or place. As a group these children are marked by their inappropriate activity, restlessness, impulsivity, distractibility, and poor concentration. Teachers say that the only thing consistent about them is their inconsistency.

Attention deficits seem to be at the root of these children's learning difficulties, whether the type of deficit is primarily inattentive, hyperactive-impulsive, or both. In official jargon, all are said to suffer from *attention-deficit hyperactivity disorder* (ADHD). Figure 3.4 lists the diagnostic criteria for these three types of ADHD, as put forth by the American Psychiatric Association (APA, 1994) in their popularly accepted DSM-IV diagnostic manual. The DSM-IV recommends that all the following conditions be met before a diagnosis of ADHD is confirmed:

- Many symptoms of the disorder are present
- The symptoms are severe enough to impair academic and/or social functioning
- The symptoms are inconsistent with the child's developmental level
- The symptoms have persisted six months or more
- The symptoms were present before 7 years of age
- The symptoms are observed both at school and at home
- There is no evidence of a health condition or mental illness that could cause similar problems

***Biochemical irregularities appear to be responsible for the attention difficulties and consequent hyperactive or hypoactive behavior of some students with LD.***

At least 11 different physiological hypotheses have been put forward to account for inattention and hyperactivity. This chapter concentrates on biochemical irregularity, which causes extremely short attention span, distractibility, and poor impulse control that become evident early in life and persist from year to year. Other causes of inattention and hyperactivity include genetic predisposition, brain injury, maternal smoking during pregnancy, lead poisoning, chromosomal anomalies, anxiety, emotional disturbance, stress, boredom, and temperament.

Parents of hyperactive-impulsive children with ADHD have referred to them as "unleashed tornadoes." They can't sit still, are disobedient, moody, rarely finish what they start, and have a hard time playing cooperatively for long periods of time. They run much of the time and never seem to wear themselves out, though their mothers and fathers are often worn to a frazzle. Parent tolerance for a child's activity level is influential in who does and doesn't get identified as hav-

**Attention-Deficit Hyperactivity Disorder Checklist**

According to the manual most frequently used by professionals to identify ADHD, six or more symptoms from either of the following lists suggests presence of the disorder:

**Inattention**

- often fails to give close attention to details; makes careless mistakes in schoolwork or other activities
- frequently has difficulty sustaining attention in tasks or play
- often does not seem to listen when spoken to
- often does not follow through on instructions and fails to finish schoolwork and chores
- has great difficulty getting organized
- usually dislikes and avoids tasks that require sustained mental effort (such as schoolwork or homework)
- frequently loses things (such as toys, assignments, books, and pencils)
- easily distracted by irrelevant sights and sounds
- often forgetful in daily activities

**Hyperactivity and impulsivity**

- often fidgets with hands and feet and squirms in seat
- often leaves seat in classroom or other situations where remaining seated is expected (such as at the dinner table)
- runs about or climbs excessively in situations in which it is inappropriate
- has great difficulty playing quietly
- is often "on the go" or acts as if "driven by a motor"
- talks excessively
- frequently blurts out answers before questions have been completed
- often has difficulty waiting turns
- often interrupts or intrudes on others (butts into conversations or games)

**Figure 3.4** Attention-deficit hyperactivity disorder diagnostic criteria. A child can be identified as one of three types: (1) a predominantly inattentive type, (2) a hyperactive-impulsive type, or (3) a combined type (positive for six or more symptoms from each list).

*Source:* Adapted with permission from the *Diagnostic and Statistical Manual of Mental Disorders,* Fourth Edition. Washington, DC, American Psychiatric Association, 1994.

ing ADHD. For example, the mother of Jamar, an active toddler, may see him as hyperactive if she compares him to her three relatively placid daughters. The same child born into a boisterous, always moving family is seen as just another pea in the same pod.

Teachers report that in the classroom the hyperactive-impulsive child with ADHD disrupts others, can't stay on task for any length of time, has trouble following directions, gets frustrated easily, gets distracted when working in a group, and rushes into activities without thinking. These children are immature, have poor self-esteem, don't follow class rules, impulsively hit, injure themselves and objects around them, and have temper tantrums. Teacher tolerance level and the organization of the classroom (such as seatwork vs. small group activities) have a good deal to do with which child gets referred for an ADHD evaluation.

Darrell's story is an excellent illustration of hyperactivity in the classroom. As frustrating and frustrated as he is, he is nevertheless learning. Of course, he is learning things only loosely related to the task at hand. It is not uncommon for these children to report the interesting daydreams they had during school to their parents when they get home, or mention nothing about the cafeteria that almost burned down. The symptoms of children diagnosed with ADHD are severe enough that up to two-thirds of them tend to be diagnosed with a comorbid disorder (e.g., a language, conduct, mood, or anxiety disorder).

## Darrell

*An elementary school child with extreme hyperactivity.*

At the time of evaluation, Darrell was 8 years and 7 months of age. He started school in the fall of 1966 at the age of 6 years and 2 months. His parents saw him as a bright, likeable little boy—not perfect, of course, for he seemed on the immature side. He could not dress himself and his speech was somewhat unclear. His father worried a bit about his lack of coordination; his mother was anxious that the other children might not let him play with them.

[By] February, 1969, his parents had become quite concerned about him. His rate of academic progress was slower than in the previous two years. They had had many conferences at school, always hearing that Darrell was "immature, fidgety, distractible, and unable to concentrate." The teacher said he required constant personal attention and help. They had tried seating him at the back of the room, at the front, and immediately beside the teacher, but nothing seemed to help. The parents were confused and discouraged. . . .

The following is a direct quote from the father, a nice-looking, personable, 30-year-old college graduate: "I'm concerned mainly about two things: his lack of coordination and his inability to concentrate on anything for over sixty seconds. He wants to compete and to excel in sports—he wants to so badly!—but he can't. He gets his feet mixed up and can't even kick a football. He is uncoordinated. . . ."

The mother has a warm, ready smile. She is 29 years old and has a high school education. She expresses in a healthy way her mixed feelings about her son. There was the hint of tears as she said, "It upsets me when he comes home and says the kids don't want to play with him because he's not as good as they are." Later, her irritation came through as she fumed, "He can never find anything to occupy him for longer than a few minutes. He nags me for something else to do, somewhere to go, someone to see. My patience wears out. Sometimes I feel like knocking him down."

She told us about a visit to his classroom this year. It was depressing for her. Darrell was up and down, distracting other children from their work and constantly wiggling. He got very little work done; he couldn't copy things from the board. She felt like shaking him and wondered how the teacher could abide him.

*Source:* Clements, S. D., Davis, J. S., Edgington, R., Goolsby, C. M., & Peters, J. E. (1971). Two cases of learning disabilities. In L. Tarnopol (Ed.), *Learning disorders in children: Diagnosis, medication, education.* Boston: Little, Brown. 

About 3 to 5 percent of children can be classified as having ADHD. It was once assumed that five to ten times as many boys as girls are hyperactive, but more recent evidence indicates that the ratio might be more equal. Because boys with ADHD tend to be more hyperactive, impulsive, and aggressive than girls, they more often get noticed and referred for evaluation. Among children with ADHD, various studies suggest that 20 to 40 percent have at least mild learning disabilities. Among students identified as learning disabled, various studies suggest that 15 to 30 percent can also be diagnosed with ADHD.

In contrast to the inattentive or hyperactive-impulsive child who is *underfocused,* there are children who have a problem because their attention is *overfocused.* Known as *hypoactive,* these children ponder too long, are overly attentive to details, and have a hard time making decisions. They are unmotivated, lethargic, sluggish, and need lots of sleep. Unlike their hyperactive classmates who, like it or not, occupy center stage, hypoactive children fade into the background and are often overlooked. In time, however, their slowness on assignments and difficulty with rapid responding get noticed. The Nichols and Chen National Collaborative Perinatal Project found that about 12 percent of children identified as learning disabled are hypoactive.

In the next section we discuss two types of biochemical irregularities linked to learning disorders and hyperactive or hypoactive behavior: abnormal neurochemical transmissions and endocrine disorders. Although vitamin deficiencies have been suggested as a cause of learning disabilities, there is no convincing evidence to support this notion.

## Abnormal Neurochemical Transmissions

Scientists can't measure the biochemicals that influence the brain's neural transmissions directly. Imbalances in these chemicals can be inferred, however, from reduced numbers of neurotransmitter metabolites in the urine and blood, from differences in cerebrospinal fluid, and from observing how drugs that alter brain chemistry subsequently affect attention, learning, and behavior.

***Inattention and hyperactive-impulsive behavior relate to brain underarousal rather than overarousal.***

Oddly enough, inattention and hyperactive-impulsive behavior are known to be related to brain underarousal rather than overarousal. When these children talk, read, or engage in activities that require focused attention, they don't experience the same degree of increase in blood flow or glucose utilization in the brain that normally supports these activities. Underarousal also means a diminished supply of the chemicals needed to inhibit activity. As a result, these individuals can't activate attention to high enough levels to focus attention, and they can't activate inhibitory mechanisms to screen out distractions. Once something has grabbed their attention, they can't stop themselves from paying attention or responding.

***Children with ADHD can't activate attention to high enough levels to focus attention, or inhibitory mechanisms to screen out distractions.***

If underarousal is the problem, then stimulants should be the solution. In a majority of cases, stimulants do help. Many children with any of the three forms of ADHD focus attention better, concentrate, memorize better, are less restless, and refrain from mentally, physically, or verbally responding to irrelevant diversions when they take stimulant medication. The medication seems to heighten the sensitivity of the brain's sensory and attending systems to incoming stimuli, thereby

***Stimulant medication seems to heighten the sensitivity of the brain's sensory and attending systems to incoming stimuli, thereby increasing focused attention. It also seems to energize the brains' inhibitory mechanisms so children can screen out distractions and stay on task.***

increasing focused attention. It also seems to energize the brains' inhibitory mechanisms so children can screen out distractions and stay on task. The medication has the same effect on both normal people and those with ADHD. It is effective for adults as well, though preschoolers' responses are more variable.

The most common stimulants used to deal with the symptoms of ADHD are Ritalin (methlyphenidate), Adderall (a combination of amphetamine and dextroamphetamine), Cylert (magnesium pemoline), and Dexadrine (dextroamphetamine). Seventy to 80 percent of children receiving stimulant medication appear to improve to some degree.

As beneficial as these medications are, they have side effects, including insomnia, decreased appetite, weight loss, irritability, lethargy, and abdominal pain, though these tend to diminish within a few weeks. Also observed at times are headaches, drowsiness, sadness, nausea, nightmares, pallor, increased pulse and blood pressure, apathy, a serious facial expression and hollows under the eyes, fearfulness, a dazed appearance, anxiety, and increased talkativeness. Stimulants can induce Tourette's syndrome in individuals at risk. Despite concerns expressed by parents, only one long-term study has documented a link between taking stimulants and substance abuse as an adult. Some growth and weight suppression may occur for a time, but the child does eventually reach his or her expected height and weight. Until recently, "drug holidays" were recommended during school vacations to encourage growth rebound. Because it was found that growth eventually catches up, however, many experts now recommend that children should remain on medication all the time, with drug holidays being given only to teenagers showing serious stimulant-associated growth delays. They reason that it is important for the child to be thinking and behaving as intelligently as possible, as often as possible, even when on vacation. After all, learning does not occur only in the classroom.

Not all children respond to stimulant medication; some 20 to 30 percent show no effect or actually get worse. Moreover, drug dosage is an issue. Children differ regarding the best dosage for optimal thinking. Drug dosage should be decided based on optimal school productivity and learning, even if hyperactivity and other disruptive behaviors are not quite alleviated. In general, however, both learning and behavior will improve as standard dosages increase.

Another concern about dosage is that attention, thinking, and behavior seesaw as short-acting drugs reach their peak effect within 1 or 2 hours after taking the medication, and wear off about 2 or 3 hours later. Moreover, at times these children experience a rebound effect as the stimulant wears off, becoming even more active and irritable than they were before taking the medication. If rebound occurs around bedtime, the child may require another dose to calm down enough to permit sleep. Longer-acting slow-release agents (up to 8 hours) help avoid this 4-hour up-and-down cycle, though their effectiveness may not be as powerful. When individuals do not respond favorably to stimulants, physicians have found that tricyclic antidepressants, the antihypertensive clonidine, or monoamine oxidase inhibitors can be effective for some.

***Seventy to 80 percent of hyperactive children respond to stimulants with some degree of improved attentiveness, motor performance, productivity, and speed and accuracy, as well as reduced activity in structured situations.***

The complex research process by which investigators test the efficacy of stimulant therapies is reviewed in Research Box 3.4. These studies prove that stimulant medication can significantly improve attention span, activity level, motor performance, and productivity, accuracy, and persistence in the classroom. However,

RESEARCH BOX 3.4

## Stimulant Medication Research Methods

Studies measuring the effects of stimulant medication on behavior are quite complex to design because they must control for the *placebo effect*, changes in behavior merely because people think they are on medication. In addition, these studies must not let the group data mask the individual child's response to medication. Therefore, the *double-blind, cross-over design* has been developed.

To control for placebo effects, in *double-blind* methods neither the experimenter nor the subjects know who is on drugs and who is on placebo. The *placebo* is a fake pill given to control subjects who believe they are receiving stimulants. In eight studies that used placebos, there was a 39 percent improvement rate (range = 8–67%) in hyperactivity within the placebo groups, presumably due to positive expectations fostered by taking medication (Barkley, 1977). Therefore, on average, 39 percent of the improvement in the drug groups can be attributed to positive expectancies alone. Placebo effects also can be negative. For example, Conners (1975) found that the mothers of children receiving placebos reported just as many side effects of the "drug" as did mothers of children taking Ritalin. Unfortunately, even double-blind studies aren't perfect, however; from the side effects alone, individuals may be able to guess who is on drugs (Sprague & Sleator, 1973).

Because of the individual variability in drug responses, the best studies use each child as his or her own control. This method is called a *cross-over* design because children receive the drug treatment followed by placebo, or vice versa. In addition, data on drug responders are separated from data on nonresponders to clarify differential drug effects for different people. These complex research designs help to determine exactly for whom, in which situations, and on which criteria stimulants may be helpful.

stimulant medication has been associated with only modest improvements in long-term academic achievement levels and social adjustment.

**Stimulant Medication and Attention Span.** Attention span does increase for the majority of children who take stimulants, as evidenced by physiological and behavioral measures such as greater brain wave height and frequency, greater cerebral blood flow, heightened reflectivity, reduced impulsivity, and faster reaction time and "hit rate" when required to spot things (such as number 9's flashed on a computer screen). One researcher, noting improvements in impulse control, concentration, and planning, commented that with medication hyperactive children are better able to "stop, look, and listen." Intelligence test scores have been shown to increase by about 15 percentile points in children taking these drugs because, once their attention is channeled, they can make better use of their problem-solving capabilities and past knowledge.

**Stimulant Medication and Activity Level.** Children taking stimulants are better able to sit still in structured situations that demand paying attention; their in-seat wiggling and foot wagging also decrease. By contrast, when they are not required to focus in a sustained manner on a task, such as on the playground or in the lunchroom, these children's activity level is only sometimes reduced.

**Stimulant Medication and Motor Performance.** Children show a remarkable improvement in fine- and gross-motor coordination when they take stimulant medication, including reaction time, speed and quality of copying, performing mazes, and balancing. Figure 3.5 is a dramatic illustration of penmanship without (first three lines) and with stimulant medication (last two lines). It appears that the drug has a direct effect on the metabolic and neural mechanisms that control and speed up motor responses after the brain has evaluated information, searched its memory, and decided on a course of action.

**Stimulant Medication and Academic Achievement.** On average across studies, children taking stimulant medication show about a 15 percentile point gain on standardized reading and spelling tests, though not in mathematics. In the classroom, as much as 25 to 40 percent improvement in accuracy, quantity, and speed of completing daily assignments are common, as are improvements in quiz grades. Moreover, persistence is better on frustrating tasks and on memory tasks

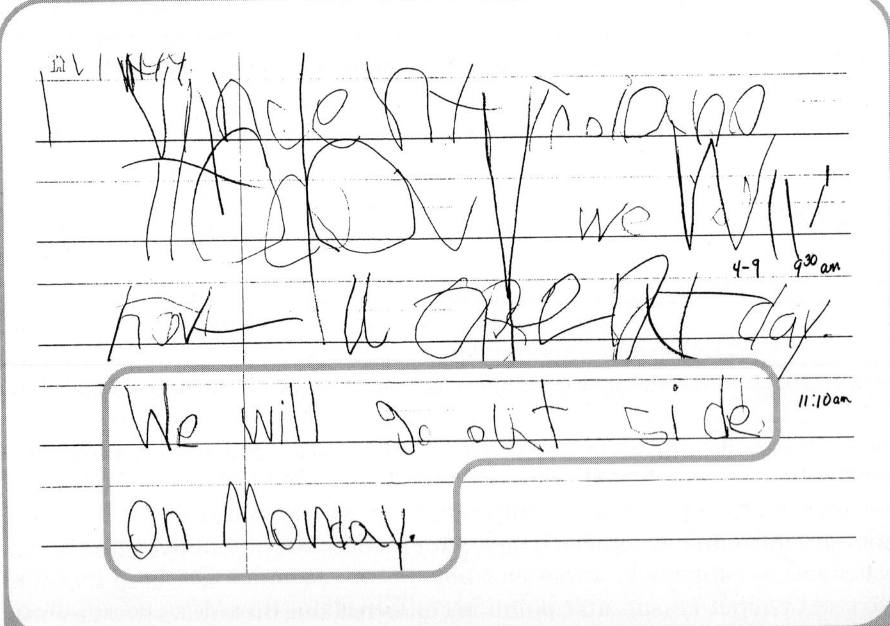


**Figure 3.5** Effects of Adderall on handwriting. This 6½-year-old copied the top three lines just before taking Adderall. One and one-half hours later he again copied the same lines, this time with much more success.

*Source:* Reprinted with permission from Rita Shuba.

(such as memorizing word pairs). The improvements in daily productivity and proficiency certainly are notable, though gains on standardized tests remain only modest.

*When taking stimulant medication, hyperactive children's improvements in daily productivity and proficiency are notable, though gains on standardized tests remain modest.*

**Stimulant Medication, Behavior, and Long-Term Adjustment.** Over time, hyperactive children do calm down. They no longer run away from their mothers in the grocery store, rip boxes off the shelf, or break grandma's best china, but their minds continue to wander. Said one adolescent, "My mind is like a television set on which someone is always changing the channels." Fidgetiness (e.g., pencil tapping), restlessness (e.g., leg wagging), impulsivity, speaking out of turn, and doing something reckless without thinking first are common.

A number of studies have shown that stimulants can suppress demanding, antisocial, aggressive, disruptive, and noncompliant behaviors, so that home and school become more manageable, less negative, and less demanding of adult supervision, guidance, admonition, and commands. Peer acceptance also improves. Despite improvements in restlessness, crying, temper outbursts, distractibility, excitability, frustration and pouting, sadly the hyperactive child's reputation for chaos sticks with him or her. Even after a few years on medication, the hyperactivity and inattention continue to set the child apart from his or her peers. These children tend to have few friends, engage in more antisocial behavior, lack ambition, are rebellious and aggressive, fail in school, have poor self-concepts, and are sad. Many are hard to discipline and end up in trouble with the law. Perhaps all those years of being told to "sit down and mind your own business" take their toll. Their reputation makes it difficult to turn around others' negative expectations, especially that of peers. It is no wonder that these youngsters continue to have difficulty negotiating their social worlds, especially when it comes to friendship and intimacy.

*Even after a few years on medication, the hyperactivity and inattention of children with ADHD continue to set them apart from their peers.*

The behavioral patterns of the hyperactive-impulsive ADHD child are particularly difficult to modify. Medication alone has more powerful effects on behavior than any other intervention. Nevertheless, no studies have shown peer relations or emotional adjustment to be any better for youngsters who have been on medication several years than for those who have never taken stimulants. It seems that stimulant medication may create greater readiness to adapt socially because adverse behaviors have diminished, yet more than medication is needed to generate long-lasting change in behavior and friendships. Studies have found that a combination of medication and behavior modification, and sometimes cognitive self-control strategy training, social skills training, or attribution training (learning to assume responsibility for the consequences of one's actions) is the most effective intervention. One example of a behavior modification intervention is for the teacher to use a remote control to add points to a monitor on the child's desk when the child is on task. The teacher and student mutually set a goal and the reward for meeting that goal. These types of interventions, about which we learn more in Chapters 7 and 11, are not nearly as effective when used alone as when used in combination with stimulant medication. The child needs to be in a more ready state to learn, and the environment needs to be appropriately structured to encourage positive change by systematically teaching these youngsters alternatives for coping with problematic situations.

*A combination of medication and behavior modification is the most effective intervention for children with ADHD.*

*Hypoactive youngsters seem to suffer from overactive central nervous system inhibitory mechanisms, which screen out stimuli that would ordinarily grab attention.*

**Overactive Inhibitory Mechanisms and Hypoactivity.** In contrast to the child with ADHD, hypoactive youngsters seem to suffer from overactive central nervous system inhibitory mechanisms. Therefore, stimuli that would usually grab a child's attention get screened out. These children's sluggishness shows improvement with sedatives, which quiet the overactive inhibitory mechanisms and allow more stimuli to come to their attention.

## Endocrine Disorders and Vitamin Deficiencies

Biochemical imbalances that result from glandular disorders, hypoglycemia, and vitamin deficiencies have been examined for possible roles in learning and behavior disorders. It's been determined that thyroid deficiencies in utero can cause intellectual decrements, and hypothyroidism in babies and toddlers can cause permanent brain damage. So too can high levels of calcium. Excess thyroid hormone can cause hyperactivity. Sugar and refined carbohydrates (white rice, white flour, potato chips)—once thought to be culprits—have for the most part escaped scientific blame for hyperactivity. Though laudable in terms of good nutrition, the vast majority of studies find that for the most part limiting intake of cake, candy, and soda do not lead to less active, restless, aggressive, or disruptive children. The number of children who respond to sugar with hyperactivity appears extremely small. Finally, there is no evidence that megadoses of vitamins have any positive impact on learning or behavior.

*For most children, limiting intake of cake, candy, and soda does not lead to less active, restless, aggressive, or disruptive behavior.*

**Thyroid Imbalances.** Although excess thyroid hormone can lead to restlessness and distractibility, insufficient thyroid hormone can create a listless individual who cannot get activated to learn. If they are not treated soon after birth, thyroid deficiencies cause severe intellectual deficits. Most of these children respond favorably to treatment, but subtle losses in intellectual and learning ability may still be apparent.

**Calcium Imbalances.** Abnormal elevation of calcium can cause personality alterations bordering on psychosis, as well as permanent intellectual deficits. Fortunately, these problems can be caught and treated early. Abnormally low calcium levels have not been associated with learning disorders.

**Hyperglycemia and Hypoglycemia.** Diabetic children experience episodes of hyperglycemia (excess sugar in the bloodstream) because their bodies don't produce enough insulin for glucose to transfer from the bloodstream into the cells, where it is utilized for energy. These episodes are often accompanied by tiredness, thirst, headaches, frequent urination, and nausea, characteristics that do not foster a child's learning potential. Even if treated with insulin, children with diabetes can suffer some loss in learning and intellectual ability, especially if disease onset is before age 5.

Hypoglycemia, or low blood sugar, can be devastating in the first two years of life when the brain is developing most rapidly. Untreated, the condition can lead to mental retardation, delayed motor development, and reduced brain size, because the brain's nerve and glial (support) cells begin to deteriorate. Severe hypoglycemia at birth is more likely among twins, newborns of low birth weight, babies of mothers who had kidney dysfunction or became diabetic, and infants who had inadequate intrauterine nutrition. The more severe a pregnant diabetic mother's hypoglycemic episodes, the lower the baby's intellectual abilities. Early treatment can help limit the central nervous system damage, though 75 percent of these children still display central nervous system abnormalities. Although episodic low blood sugar has been blamed for some older children's hyperactivity, research has not substantiated this claim.

*In infancy, untreated low blood sugar, low thyroid levels, and elevated body calcium can be devastating to learning potential.*

**Vitamin Deficiencies.** Studies of children receiving megadoses of vitamins—often over 1,000 times the usual daily requirement—have not shown that such a regimen reduces hyperactivity or improves learning potential. In fact, in one study heavy doses of vitamins made some children even more disruptive than before. Because of these findings, as well as a paucity of well-controlled studies on the topic, the American Academy of Pediatrics has declared that megavitamin therapy is unjustified as a treatment for learning disorders.

*Megadoses of vitamins have not been shown to reduce hyperactivity or improve learning potential.*

## Summary

Research on the physiology of learning difficulties has found that learning disabilities may be caused by brain injury, prenatal errors in brain development, heredity, or biochemical irregularities. Each of these can affect a student's abilities in different areas of development.

The most useful way to explore brain-behavior relationships is to identify the neuropsychological patterns that describe an individual's learning strengths and weaknesses, and to plan instruction accordingly. Family history information can also help us to understand a student's developmental patterns and the teaching approaches that have succeeded with relatives. Fortunately, the predisposition to develop a learning disability can be averted to some extent by the brain's plasticity and the powerful effects of positive home and school environments.

Biochemical irregularities appear to be responsible for the attention difficulties and hyperactive-impulsive or hypoactive behavior of some students with learning disabilities. Judging from the effects of stimulant medication, which activates neural attention and inhibitory mechanisms, it seems that many youngsters with attention deficits and/or hyperactivity need their inhibitory, attention, and sensory systems aroused so that they will be able to attend in a more focused manner and block out irrelevant information. Stimulants help 70 to 80 percent of these children, resulting in some degree of improved attentiveness, motor performance, productivity, and speed and accuracy, as well as reduced activity in structured situations. Academic gains on standardized tests are modest, however, and long-term learning and behavior gains have not yet been demonstrated.

In infancy, untreated low blood sugar, low thyroid levels, and elevated body calcium can be devastating to learning potential. Although it is a popular belief, in only a small fraction of children has it been demonstrated that excess sugar ingestion is related to hyperactive behavior—for most people sugar ingestion has no effect on behavior. Finally, megavitamin proponents have yet to support through sound research their claims that large doses of vitamins improve learning.

Although learning disabilities are physiological in origin, it is important to remember that the environment plays a major role in helping students reach the limits of their potential. Good parenting and teaching can enhance brain functioning, learning, and ultimate life adjustment far beyond what might have been expected from the child's physiological makeup alone.

## Helpful Resources

### Neuropsychological Patterns of Learning


Ackerman, P. T., Dykman, R. A., Oglesby, D. M., & Newton, J. E. O. (1994). EEG power spectra of children with dyslexia, slow learners, and normally reading children with ADD during verbal processing. *Journal of Learning Disabilities, 27*, 619–630.

Bever, T. G., & Chiarello, R. J. (1974). Cerebral dominance in musicians and nonmusicians. *Science, 185*, 537–539.

Flynn, J. M., Deering, W., Goldstein, M., & Rahbar, M. H. (1992). Electrophysiological correlates of dyslexia subtypes. *Journal of Learning Disabilities, 25*, 133–141.

Gazzaniga, M. S., Ivry, R. B., & Mangun, G. R. (1998). *Cognitive neuroscience: The biology of the mind.* New York: W. W. Norton & Co.

Habib, M. (2000). The neurological basis of developmental dyslexia: An overview and working hypothesis. *Brain, 123*, 2373–2399.

Harnadek, M. C. S., & Rourke, B. P. (1994). Principle identifying features of the syndrome of nonverbal learning disabilities in children. *Journal of Learning Disabilities, 27*, 144–154.

John, E. R., Prichep, L. S., Friedmen, J., Ahn, H., Kaye, H., & Baird, H. (1985). Neurometric evaluation of brain electrical activity in children with learning disabilities. In F. H. Duffy & N. Geschwind (Eds.), *Dyslexia: A neuroscientific approach to clinical evaluation.* Boston: Little, Brown.

Kaplan, B. J., Dewey, D. M., Crawford, S. G., & Wilson, B. N. (2001). The term *comorbidity* is of questionable value in reference to development disorders: Data and theory. *Journal of Learning Disabilities, 34*, 555–565.

Miles, T. R. (1986). On the persistence of dyslexic difficulties into adulthood. In G. Th. Pavlidis & D. F. Fisher (Eds.), *Dyslexia: Its neuropsychology and treatment.* New York: John Wiley & Sons.

Obrzut, J. E., Hynd, G. W., & Boliek, C. A. (1986). Lateral asymmetries in learning disabled children: A review. In S. J. Ceci (Ed.), *Handbook of cognitive, social, and neuropsychological aspects of learning disabilities (Vol. 1).* Hillsdale, NJ: Lawrence Erlbaum.

Pugh, K. R., Mencl, E., Jenner, A. R., Lee, J. R., Katz, L., Frost, S. J., Shaywitz, S. E., & Shaywitz, B. A. (2001). Neuroimaging studies of reading development and reading disability. *Learning Disabilities Research & Practice, 16*, 240–249.

Shaywitz, S. E., Shaywitz, B. A., Pugh, K. R., Fulbright, R. K., Constable, R. T., Mencl, W. E., Shankweiler, D. P., Liberman, A. M., Skudlarski, P., Fletcher, J. M., Katz, L., Marchione, K. E., Lacadie, C., Gatenby, C., & Gore, J. C. (1998). Functional disruption in the organization of the brain for reading in dyslexia. *Proceedings of the National Academy of Sciences of the United States of America, 95*, 2636–2641.

Springer, S. P., & Deutch, G. (1997). *Left brain, right brain: Perspectives from cognitive neuroscience (5th ed.).* New York: W. H. Freeman.


### Brain Injury


Bell, R. Q., & Waldrop, M. F. (1989). Achievement and cognition correlates of minor physical anomalies in early development. In M. H. Bornstein & N. A. Krasnegor (Eds.), *Stability and continuity in mental development: Behavioral and biological perspectives.* Hillsdale, NJ: Lawrence Erlbaum.

Cherkes-Julkowski, M. (1998). Learning disability, attention-deficit disorder, and language impairment as outcomes of prematurity; A longitudinal descriptive study. *Journal of Learning Disabilities, 31*, 294–306.

Colletti, L. F. (1979). Relationship between pregnancy and birth complications and the later development of learning disabilities. *Journal of Learning Disabilities, 12*, 659–663.

Goethe, K. E., & Levin, H. S. (1984). Behavioral manifestations during the early and long-term stages of recovery after closed head injury. *Psychiatric Annals, 14,* 540–546.

Kochanek, T. T., Kabacoff, R. I., & Lipsitt, L. P. (1990). Early identification of developmentally disabled and at-risk preschool children. *Exceptional Children, 56,* 528–538.

Matoušek, M., & Petersén, I. (1973). Frequency analysis of the EEG in normal children (1–15 years) and in normal adolescents (16–21 years). In P. Kellaway & I. Petersen (Eds.), *Automation of clinical electroencephalography.* New York: Raven Press.

McCormick, M. C. (1989). Long-term follow-up of infants discharged from neonatal intensive care units. *Journal of the American Medical Association, 261,* 1767–1772.

Nichols, P., & Chen, T. (1981). *Minimal brain dysfunction: A prospective study.* Hillsdale, NJ: Lawrence Erlbaum.

Raz, S., Lauterbach, M. D., Hopkins, T. L., Porter, C. L., Riggs, W. W., & Sander, C. J. (1995). Severity of perinatal cerebral injury and developmental outcome: A dose-response relationship. *Neuropsychology, 9,* 91–101.

Segalowitz, S. J., & Lawson, S. (1995). Subtle symptoms associated with self-reported mild head injury. *Journal of Learning Disabilities, 28,* 309–319.

Touwen, B. C. L., & Huisjes, H. J. (1984). Obstetrics, neonatal neurology, and later outcome. In C. R. Almli & S. Finger (Eds.), *Early brain damage: Vol. 1. Research orientations and clinical observations.* New York: Academic Press.

## Structural Brain Differences

Bigler, E. D. (1992). The neurobiology and neuropsychology of adult learning disorders. *Journal of Learning Disabilities, 25,* 488–506.

Brown, W. E., Eliez, S., Menon, V., Rumsey, J. M., White, C. D., & Reiss, A. L. (2001). Preliminary evidence of widespread morphological variations of the brain in dyslexia. *Neurology, 56,* 781–783.

Filipek, P. A. (1995). Neurobiologic correlates of developmental dyslexia: How do dyslexics' brains differ from those of normal readers? *Journal of Child Neurology, 10* (Suppl. 1), S62–S69.

Flowers, D. L. (1993). Brain basis for dyslexia: A summary of work in progress. *Journal of Learning Disabilities, 26,* 575–582.

Galaburda, A. M., Sherman, G. F., Rosen, G. D., Aboitiz, F., & Geschwind, N. (1985). Developmental dyslexia: Four consecutive patients with cortical anomalies. *Annals of Neurology, 18,* 222–233.

Semrud-Clikeman, M., Hynd, G., Novey, E., & Eliopulos, D. (1991). Dyslexia and brain morphology: Relationships between neuroanatomical variation and linguistic tasks. *Learning and Individual Differences, 3,* 225–242.

## Hereditary Factors

Alarecon, M., DeFries, J. C., Light, J. G., & Pennington, B. F. (1997). A twin study of mathematics disability. *Journal of Learning Disabilities, 30,* 617–623.

DeFries, J. C., & Gillis, J. J. (1991). Etiology of reading deficits in learning disabilities: Quantitative genetic analysis. In J. E. Obrzut & G. W. Hynd (Eds.), *Neuropsychological foundations of learning disabilities: A handbook of issues, methods, and practice.* San Diego: Academic Press.

Hardyck, C., & Petrinovich, L. F. (1977). Left-handedness. *Psychological Bulletin, 84,* 385–404.

Haywood, H. C., & Switzky, H. N. (1986). The malleability of intelligence: Cognitive processes as a function of polygenic-experiential interaction. *School Psychology Review, 15,* 245–255.

Honzik, M. P. (1957). Developmental studies of parent-child resemblance in intelligence. *Child Development, 28,* 215–228.

McGue, M. Bouchard, T. J., Jr., Iacono, W. G., & Lykken, D. T. (1993). Behavioral genetics of cognitive ability: A life-span perspective. In R. Plomin & G. E. McClearn (Eds.), *Nature, nurture, and psychology.* Washington, DC: American Psychological Association.

Pennington, B. F. (1995). Genetics of learning disabilities. *Journal of Child Neurology, 10* (Suppl. 1), S69–S77.

Plomin, R., DeFries, J. C., McClearn, G. E., & McGuffin, P. (2001). *Behavioral genetics* (4th ed.). New York: Worth Publishers.

Rack, J. P., & Olson, R. K. (1993). Phonological deficits, IQ, and individual differences in reading disability: Genetic and environmental influences. *Developmental Review, 13,* 269–278.

Raskind, W. H. (2001). Current understanding of the genetic basis of reading and spelling disability. *Learning Disability Quarterly, 24,* 1441–1457.

Scarr, S., Weinberg, R. A., & Waldman, I. D. (1993). IQ correlations in transracial adoptive families. *Intelligence, 17,* 541–555.

Schiff, M., Duyme, M., Dumaret, A., & Tomkiewicz, S. (1982). How much *could* we boost scholastic achievement and IQ scores? A direct answer from a French adoption study. *Cognition, 12,* 165–196.

Shalev, R. S., Manor, O., Kerem, B., Ayali, M., Badichi, N., Friedlander, Y., & Gross-Tsur, V. (2001). Developmental dyscalculia is a familial learning disability. *Journal of Learning Disabilities, 34,* 59–65.

Skeels, H. M., & Skodak, M. (1966, May). Adult status of individuals who experienced early intervention. Paper presented at the 90th annual meeting of the American Association on Mental Deficiency, Chicago, IL. In D. P. Hallahan & W. M. Cruickshank (Eds.), *Psycho-educational foundations of learning disabilities.* (1973). Englewood-Cliffs, NJ: Prentice-Hall.

Wolff, P. H., & Melngailis, I. (1994). Family patterns of developmental dyslexia. *American Journal of Medical Genetics, 54,* 122–131.

Wood, F. B., & Grigorenko, E. L. (2001). Emerging issues in the genetics of dyslexia: A methodological review. *Journal of Learning Disabilities, 34,* 503–511.

## Biochemical Irregularities and Attention-Deficit Hyperactivity Disorder

Barkley, R. A. (1998). *Attention-deficit hyperactivity disorder: A handbook for diagnosis and treatment* (2nd ed.). New York: Guilford Press.

Carlson, C. L., & Bunner, M. R. (1993). Effects of methylphenidate on the academic performance of children with attention-deficit hyperactivity disorder and learning disabilities. *School Psychology Review, 22,* 184–198.

DuPaul, G. J., Barkley, R. A., & McMurray, M. B. (1991). Therapeutic effects of medication on ADHD: Implications for school psychologists. *School Psychology Review, 20,* 203–219.

DuPaul, G. J., & Eckert, T. L. (1997). The effects of school-based interventions for attention deficit hyperactivity disorder: A meta-analysis. *School Psychology Review, 26,* 5–27.

Dykman, R. A., & Ackerman, P. T. (1991). Attention deficit disorder and specific reading disability: Separate but often overlapping disorders. *Journal of Learning Disabilities, 24,* 96–103.

Guyer, B. P. (2000). *ADHD: Achieving success in school and life.* Boston: Allyn & Bacon.

Haslam, R. H. A., Dalby, J. T., & Rademaker, A. W. (1984). Effects of megavitamin therapy on children with attention deficit disorders. *Pediatrics, 74,* 103–111.

Henker, B., & Whalen, C. K. (1989). Hyperactivity and attention deficits. *American Psychologist, 44,* 216–223.

Kavale, K. (1982). The efficacy of stimulant drug treatment for hyperactivity: A meta-analysis. *Journal of Learning Disabilities, 15,* 280–289.

Keith, R. W., & Engineer, P. (1991). Effects of methylphenidate on the auditory processing abilities of children with attention deficit-hyperactivity disorder. *Journal of Learning Disabilities, 24,* 630–636.

Klorman, R. (1991). Cognitive event-related potentials in attention deficit disorder. *Journal of Learning Disabilities, 24,* 130–140.

MTA Cooperative Group. (1999). A 14-month randomized clinical trial of treatment strategies for attention-deficit/hyperactivity disorder. *Archives of General Psychiatry, 56,* 1073–1086.

Pelham, W. E., Carlson, C., Sams, S. E., Vallano, G., Dixon, J., & Hoza, B. (1993). Separate and combined effects of methylphenidate and behavior modification on boys with attention deficit-hyperactivity disorder in the classroom. *Journal of Consulting and Clinical Psychology, 61,* 506–515.

Pelham, W. E., Wheeler, T., & Chronis, A. (1998). Empirically supported psychosocial treatments for attention deficit hyperactivity disorder. *Journal of Clinical Child Psychology, 27,* 190–205.

Porrino, L. J., Rapoport, J. L., Behar, D., Sceery, W., Ismond, D. R., & Bunney, W. E. (1983). A naturalistic assessment of the motor activity of hyperactive boys. I. Comparison with normal controls. *Archives of General Psychiatry, 40,* 681–687.

Rapport, M. D., Denney, C., DuPaul, G. J., & Gardner, M. J. (1994). Attention deficit disorder and methylphenidate: Normalization rates, clinical effectiveness, and response prediction in 76 children. *Journal of the American Academy of Child and Adolescent Psychiatry, 33,* 882–893.

Rovet, J. F., Ehrlich, R. M., Czuchta, D., & Akler, M. (1993). Psychoeducational characteristics of children and adolescents with insulin-dependent diabetes mellitus. *Journal of Learning Disabilities, 26,* 7–22.

Sandberg, D. E., & Barrick, C. (1995). Endocrine disorders in childhood: A selective survey of intellectual and educational sequelae. *School Psychology Review, 24,* 146–170.

Spencer, T., Biederman, J., Wilens, T., Harding, M., O'Donnell, D., & Griffin, S. (1996). Pharmacotherapy of attention-deficit hyperactivity disorder across the life cycle. *Journal of the American Academy of Child and Adolescent Psychiatry, 35,* 409–432.

Swanson, J. M., Cantwell, D., Lerner, M., McBurnett, K., & Hanna, G. (1991). Effects of stimulant medication on learning in children with ADHD. *Journal of Learning Disabilities, 24,* 219–230, 255.

Wilcutt, E. G., & Pennington, B. F. (2000). Comorbidity of reading disability and attention-deficit hyperactivity disorder: Differences by gender and subtype. *Journal of Learning Disabilities, 33,* 179–191.

Wolraich, M. L., Wilson, D. B., & White, J. W. (1995). The effect of sugar on behavior or cognition in children:

A meta-analysis. *Journal of the American Medical Association, 274,* 1617–1621.

Zametkin, A. J., Nordahl, T. E., Gross, M., King, A. C., Semple, W. E., Rumsey, J., Hamburger, S., & Cohen, R. M. (1990). Cerebral glucose metabolism in adults with hyperactivity of childhood onset. *New England Journal of Medicine, 323,* 1362–1366.

Zametkin, A. J., & Rapoport, J. L. (1986). The pathophysiology of attention deficit disorder with hyperactivity. A review. In B. B. Lahey & A. E. Kazdin (Eds.), *Advances in Clinical Child Psychology* (Vol. 9). New York: Plenum Press.

Children and Adults with Attention Deficit Disorders: www.chadd.org

CHAPTER FOUR

# Curricular and Environmental Contributors

**ALTHOUGH THE FEDERAL DEFINITION** of learning disabilities assumes that there is an underlying physiological cause for LD, the curriculum we require of students and the environments in which they live and learn can do much to aggravate problems or to help overcome them. In fact, a learning problem can be a minor inconvenience to children whose schools and family support them, encourage but do not push them, cheer their victories, and love them for who they are. On the other hand, a minor learning problem can become an overwhelming handicap for children who are poorly nourished, who live in a family beset by poverty, and who go to schools lacking even the most basic materials and staffed by poorly trained and overworked teachers. Children's environments in some cases can so deter their development that learning disabilities are inevitable. It is important that we pay attention to curriculum and environmental factors that contribute to learning and development so we can optimize children's growth, intercede when they are at risk, and, when possible, prevent learning difficulties from growing into chronic disabilities.

*It is important that we pay attention to curriculum and environmental factors that contribute to learning and development so we can optimize children's growth, intercede when they are at risk, and, when possible, prevent learning difficulties from growing into chronic disabilities.*

Because children with LD experience significant lags in some abilities, but have strengths in others, it's important that we match the curriculum to their uneven patterns and unique learning styles. Thus we can avoid the frustration on all sides that comes with making academic demands that students are simply unprepared to meet. If we don't adapt our school tasks—what we teach and how we teach it—to what and how these children are ready to learn, their learning problems are only aggravated.

Like curriculum factors, environmental factors that contribute to learning problems are influences beyond the child's control. They range from some schools' inability or unwillingness to accommodate a student's linguistic or cultural diversity, to poor nutrition or environmental toxins that can cause brain damage. The better we understand both the strengths and weaknesses of different students and their curricula, schools, and families, the better we can help them learn and grow.

## Curriculum Contributors

All too often, schoolwork is mismatched with the uneven abilities and unique learning styles of the learning disabled. We often teach at a level above what children with LD are ready to comprehend, and in a style that only makes learning more frustrating for them. While the rest of the class may be ready and eager to move from simple addition and subtraction to the mysteries of multiplication and division, there will be some children who are still struggling with recognizing the numerals in print. They can't catch up, even if they try harder—something their teachers and parents may be insisting they do. If no one intervenes and finds a way to assist these children to learn in a different way and at a different pace, they will give up, lose ground in their development, and perhaps become behavior problems later on.

***Very often schoolwork is mismatched with the uneven abilities and unique learning styles of the learning disabled.***

School curricula that stimulate children's development build on their strengths, remediate their weaker abilities, and find ways to work around the influence of these weaknesses on learning progress. For example, a child can be encouraged to dictate essays when penmanship problems stifle his creativity and motivation; at the same time he is taught keyboarding skills. Writing spelling words 20 times each is surely counterproductive for such a student, but dictating spellings to a partner or constructing words from Scrabble tiles work just fine to reinforce spelling skills. A third-grade nonreader can use books on tape to foster her comprehension skills and remain an active participant in class discussions, while at the same time receiving intensive reading remediation. A seventh grader whose memory is more like that of a 6-year-old—he can't remember more than 5 to 7 new pieces of information at a time—is overwhelmed by the list of 30 social studies terms he must memorize for Friday's test. Reducing the load to studying just 6 terms a day transforms the task into one at which he can now succeed; but the teacher also tries to enhance the child's memory capabilities with very direct instruction of memory tricks that most children by that age have picked up automatically. The ninth grader who is baffled by vocabulary beyond the fourth grade level will be even more baffled by the *Wives of Bath.* Although she is receiving vocabulary remediation, this should not deter her from being assigned a translation of *Wives of Bath* in order to learn about ancient British culture and enrich her knowledge base. And the high school student who can't visualize the spatial concepts in geometry will need to be supported with concrete models—just like a younger student. The bottom line in all these cases is that curriculum content and methods

***School curricula that stimulate children's development build on their strengths, remediate their weaker abilities, and find ways to work around the influence of these weaknesses on learning progress.***

*In their areas of weakness, students with LD often are taught with instructional goals and methods that are useful at younger ages. In their areas of strength, expectations and teaching approaches are for the most part the same as for their classmates.*

must be modified in order to alleviate the struggle and maximize the success of children whose learning abilities are developing unevenly. In their areas of weakness, these students often are taught with instructional goals and methods that are useful at younger ages. In their areas of strength, expectations and teaching approaches are, for the most part, the same as for their classmates.

Experts approach the problem of children's delayed and uneven abilities and learning styles from two perspectives. Maturational lag theorists tell us that the content of lessons needs to better match what students with LD are ready to learn. If Vickie hasn't yet mastered the letters *A, B,* and *C,* then why would the teacher be introducing all the letters through *X, Y,* and *Z*? Cognitive style theorists add that we need to modify our teaching to match these students' unique learning styles. Vickie, for example, gets distracted by too much to learn at one time. Thus, mastering three letters well before introducing a fourth makes sense. Both types of theorists are correct.

## Maturational Lags

We know that learning disabilities result from slower maturing of visual-perceptual, motor, language, and attention processes that make higher-cognitive problem solving and learning possible. Each child who is learning disabled passes through the various stages of development at his or her own rate and often with a unique cognitive style. The maturational lag perspective assumes that these developmental stages will follow a predictable sequence; however, unlike the typical student's smooth progression in learning abilities, the learning disabled's mental maturation proceeds by fits and starts. Adam, for example, is a bright third grader who draws superbly and is well ahead of many of his classmates in math. But he reads and follows directions like a first grader. His classmate, Tracy is an excellent reader and storyteller, but she can't put together more than 3 or 4 sentences in writing, and even then only Tracy can decipher her mangled penmanship.

Both Adam and Tracy have particular learning skills that have developed at normal rates. Other skills, however, have developed more slowly, and mimic those of typical younger children. These lags reflect a delay in the maturation of specific portions of their brains. Whether the lags are the result of brain injury, genetic predisposition, or any one of a number of possible causes is unimportant to maturational lag theorists. The treatment is always the same: gear teaching to what a child functioning at that level would be ready to learn. In other words, even if Dave is in second grade, if he still hasn't mastered the alphabet sounds, then focus on teaching letter sounds rather than forcing Dave to try to compensate by recognizing words only by sight.

Maturational lag theorists view the weaker, more immature skills of children with learning disabilities as qualitatively similar to the skills expected of normal but younger children. Once the child's skills are located on the normal continuum of development, the teacher knows exactly what to teach next, because that's the next skill children usually acquire. Some researchers have countered, however, that this isn't always so for children with LD; their learning and behavior patterns can vary considerably from what we would consider normal at an earlier stage of development. Six-year-old Jonah, for example, is incapable of paying attention for more than a few minutes at a time. When his mind flits to the first-grade guinea pig cage, he knocks over chairs and piles of papers as he makes his way to that end of the classroom. In contrast, a 1-year-old with the same level of distractibility would likely walk around the chairs and then be fascinated with the piles of papers. Jonah is oblivious to the path of destruction he's created. Similarly, Richard's story in Chapter 8 (page 296) is the tale of a person whose reading development is totally arrested—he can't even recognize his name in print—even though he's a college graduate. This kind of severe delay is not known in normal development.

Because the school curriculum is geared above the uneven learning readiness of children like Adam, Tracy, and Jonah, they are at risk for school failure. Casey's story on page 100 illustrates how very astute some children can be in figuring out ways to work around their weaknesses. If parents and teachers do not pay attention to their struggle, and appropriate intervention is not offered, more serious learning problems are bound to develop.

Larry's story (page 101) illustrates the maturational lag theorists' preference for retaining children at a grade level rather than pushing them forward into still more curricular demands they can't meet. If they are "promoted" prematurely, these children will tend to grasp only fragments of necessary skills, and they will make errors that grow into habits. If Chanequa is forced to read words before she can sound them out, for example, she will misread them and, having made the mistake once, she will likely repeat it the next time she encounters those words. Chanequa's learning process has been complicated because she not only has to learn basic decoding skills, but she also needs to unlearn the mistakes to which she's grown accustomed. We've all experienced the same phenomenon when we continue to turn at the wrong corner as we drive to our friend's house, because we originally made that mistake. Maturational lag theorists believe that when children are not ready for the work of the grade, their learning will be spotty because they grasp only portions of the curriculum. This inaccurate and incomplete understanding of concepts gives them a very shaky foundation for future learning.

***When children are not ready for the work of the grade, they will grasp only portions of the curriculum. This inaccurate and incomplete understanding of concepts creates a very shaky foundation for future learning.***

While maturational lag theorists deal with this problem through grade retention, other experts prefer that a child who is learning disabled stay with his or her class while at the same time benefiting from a curriculum that presents objectives as he or she is ready to learn them. Given the variety of maturational lags of children with learning disabilities, this means that the teacher develops an individualized teaching approach and curriculum for each child.

**Maturational Lag Patterns.** Children with learning disabilities often have more than one area in which they are developing immaturely. These areas may become noticeable in different ways at different ages as both the cognitive demands of the curriculum and the child's strengths and weaknesses change. Isaiah, for example, was slow to talk as a baby, but by the time he entered school he spoke well. He was his kindergarten teacher's favorite because he excelled at eye-hand coordination tasks such as coloring, pasting, and printing. But when reading was introduced, Isaiah again showed his weakness with language symbols. He did eventually learn to read, but in ninth grade he found French class impossible—the language weakness crept up all over again. Justin had a different profile of strengths and weaknesses. He

***Children with LD often have more than one area in which they are developing immaturely. These areas may become noticeable in different ways at different ages as both the cognitive demands of the curriculum and the child's strengths and weaknesses change.***

## Casey

*A resourceful second grader who masked his math weakness.*

Casey's mother insisted he did not know his addition and subtraction facts. His second-grade teacher was surprised to hear this. Casey had been slow to learn to read and was a poor speller, but he had always done quite well in arithmetic. Even on pop quizzes he usually got at least 80 percent of the problems right.

Alerted by his mother's concerns, however, the teacher observed Casey during the next two weekly math tests. She noticed that Casey attacked the tests in an unusual manner. He answered questions out of order, starting in the middle and then jumping around until all the problems were done. As usual, his scores were in the B to B-plus range.

Intrigued, the teacher took Casey aside and asked him why he did his tests this way. Somewhat embarrassed, Casey admitted that he had not succeeded in memorizing addition and subtraction facts like the other children in the class, but he had worked out a system for timed math quizzes. "First I find the easiest problem," he explained. "Like here, it's 7 + 1, which is easy to figure out: 8. Then I know that 7 + 2 has to be one more than 8, so I look for 7 + 2 and write 9. Then I find 7 + 3 and write 10, and next I look for 7 + 4 and write 11, and I go on like that until the time runs out."

Casey had figured out that subtraction facts also followed a sequence, so he used the same method for subtraction tests. When quizzed orally on math facts, however, it was obvious he had not memorized any of them—although he could add and subtract in his head well enough to produce correct answers if he was given a little time.

Casey was obviously a bright and resourceful lad. The fact that he was not retaining math facts, however, combined with his other academic difficulties, suggested to his teacher that he might have a learning disability. Casey's mother agreed to an evaluation. As it turned out, Casey did indeed have visual perception deficits that made it hard for him to remember many kinds of information. Casey was unable to picture things in his mind, which made tasks involving rote memorization very difficult. Imagining the spelling of irregular words was also beyond him. Casey read slowly because he had to sound words out as he went along: because he did not carry images of words in his head, he did not easily recognize words that he had seen before. Although he used his superior intelligence to compensate for these problems and was passing all his subjects, Casey's evaluation suggested that with special education support he could do much better than the B's and C's he was earning.

*Source:* Reprinted with the permission of The Free Press, a Division of Simon & Schuster Adult Publishing Group, from *Learning Disabilities A to Z: A Parent's Complete Guide to Learning Disabilities from Preschool to Adulthood* by Corinne R. Smith and Lisa W. Strick. 

was perplexed by puzzles and drawing. Even more worrisome was his poor ability to memorize sight words—words that don't follow regular phonetic patterns. Reading progress was slow. He got through with the help of his good phonetic skills, and he went on to become an accurate reader. Even though he is now a practicing lawyer, Justin is still a plodding reader, has very poor penmanship, and has trouble spelling irregular words.

Maturational lags in attention, language, visual-perceptual, or coordination skills cause problems at predictable academic stress points in the curriculum.

## Larry

*A little boy whose academic failure stemmed from immaturity and unreadiness for the work of the grade.*

Larry was examined in June 1981, at the age of 5 years 8 months shortly after the close of his kindergarten year, which had not been successful. Larry was a mid-October boy, which meant that he had started kindergarten just before his fifth birthday. Because school had been a disaster, he was referred to us to find out just what his academic and personal potentials actually were.

He was a delightful child to examine. Though small and immature-looking for his age, he was attractive, friendly, and cooperative. Findings on the Gesell Developmental Examination showed that he ranged in behavior from 3½ years to around 5½. . . . Printing any letters or numbers was cumbersome and difficult for this boy, and his copies of square and triangle were not up to his age. His intelligence quotient was in the bright normal range, and there were no outstanding visual difficulties.

Larry showed himself, in our opinion, to be [a] good candidate for kindergarten in the coming fall when he would be five years eleven months old. That a whole year of overplacement had not caused him to fall apart or to lose his enthusiasm for school was remarkable.

Larry's parents had come to us in a state of considerable anxiety. They had been told by the school psychologist that their son was a trifle "backward" and that his failure to succeed in kindergarten was due to a clear-cut learning disability. The school's recommendation was that he proceed to first grade but be given special help in the coming year . . .

It was fortunate for Larry that his parents questioned what the school had told them. It is sad to think of the all too many children in this country whose parents . . . regretfully accept the diagnosis of learning disability without at least pursuing the possibility that their child's poor school adjustment may be due simply to immaturity and unreadiness for the work of the grade in which the school has placed him or her.

*Source:* Ames, L. B. (1983). Learning disability: Truth or trap? *Journal of Learning Disabilities, 16,* pp. 19–20.

Kindergarten's "getting set" to learn, for example, requires the child to pay attention, organize, sit, and try. First grade's reading decoding and fourth grade's reading comprehension emphases require the ability to sequence sounds in words and understand complex language. Junior high's demand for an organized approach to learning and understanding complex geometric and algebraic principles requires visual-perceptual competencies. And high school's expectation for independent learning requires good coordination for note taking and essay writing, and excellent planning skills.

The adverse effects of some lags diminish with time. "Catch-up" occurs on those skills in which all children reach high enough levels of sophistication at younger ages. These earlier-maturing skills need to be just "good enough" to no longer interfere to any significant extent with learning. For example, by age 9 most children no longer have trouble with reversing letters (*b–p, b–d*) because

*Children whose developmental immaturities are in areas that tend to mature early, such as copying, may stumble through the first few years of school but then succeed.*

they have such a good conception of up from down, and left from right. They can get on with acquiring reading and writing skills. Copying is another skill that becomes good enough relatively soon, certainly by age 12 or 13. When children encounter difficulties in these early-maturing skills, their school progress tends to "lag and then leap" once their brain matures sufficiently. Their prognosis for high-level learning is excellent after they stumble through the first few years of school.

But catch-up doesn't occur in more complex, late-emerging skills such as spelling or word retrieval from memory. This is because verbal deficits are not likely to improve as rapidly as visual-spatial weaknesses, given that the educational and social demands on language abilities continue to grow as one gets older. Even if a student's reading skills do approach the level of his or her peers over time, the gap in spelling abilities tends to remain wide. Another example, word finding, is a skill important for higher-level learning because we tend to memorize information by naming and then silently rehearsing this material. When children can't quickly find the words to name what they've seen (as on an overhead projector or on a computer screen), they won't rehearse it and store it away in memory. It's gone. This "naming" lag persists into adulthood and is incredibly frustrating because these adults have so much trouble even retrieving facts they know well, such as their sister-in-law's name—a big mistake with big consequences. Calling to mind facts on a professional licensing exam clearly is an even bigger problem. We all experience this problem from time to time. Recall the last time you were trying to tell a friend about the star in a popular movie but couldn't for the life of you recall the actress's name. It was right "on the tip of your tongue" but you couldn't retrieve it. People with verbal deficits of this type experience that maddening lack of recall very frequently. Naturally, this makes higher-level learning extremely difficult.

*For children with lags in more complex information-processing skills, such as language comprehension or word retrieval, the achievement gap tends to get larger from year to year.*

When children experience persistent lags in more complex information-processing skills, their academic achievement often doesn't catch up with that of their peers. In fact, the achievement gap tends to get larger from year to year. Many students who have learning disabilities make less academic progress than even their less intelligent peers who, though they are achieving behind their classmates, are progressing as well as can be expected. It's not uncommon for children with LD to take longer to learn new tasks than equally bright peers or even younger children who read at similar levels. When compared with low-achieving children who are not learning disabled but read at the same level, the reading of children with LD tends to be qualitatively different: they read and speak slower, make slower reading progress, and their spelling errors include very odd combinations of letters.

Developmental lags are far more prevalent among boys than girls. It is not uncommon for boys to be about six months behind their female counterparts at school entry. Typical boys' language and reading skills tend to reach maturity at the end of elementary school, whereas these skills mature in girls two years earlier. When observing any typical class of 13-year-olds, it is evident that the social behavior of boys also matures later than that of girls.

*Academic tasks must be geared to what students are ready to master. Children should not be forced to fit themselves to the timing set by the curriculum.*

**Matching the Curriculum to Student Readiness Levels.** Maturational lag theorists urge us to gear academic tasks to what students are ready to master and not try to force all students to fit themselves to the timing set by the curriculum. They emphasize that there is no known way of hurrying the brain's maturation on its way, so it is the teachers who need to do the slowing down. As in the case of the second-grade nonreader, when we slow the pace of instruction so that children are taught precisely what they are ready to learn, we often find that we in fact don't need to use extraordinary teaching techniques to achieve success.

Maturational lag theorists warn us not to teach too much, too soon, too fast. As we noted earlier, a student who is forced to read before he or she is ready will make too many mistakes, pick up bad habits, and learn to hate reading. All the faulty learning will only need to be unlearned later on. By pushing, we've turned a transitory problem into a permanent deficit that will require hours and perhaps years of specialized teaching to undo.

***We must not teach too much, too soon, too fast.***

It's very important to intervene when lags become evident, as opposed to sitting back and waiting for development to take its course. Too often parents are counseled by medical or education professionals not to worry: "Be patient, your child will outgrow it." However, these children often don't outgrow learning delays, and they find themselves out of place in a culture that rewards swift progress and fast answers. Rather, we must find out precisely what these children are ready to learn in their stronger and weaker areas—and then teach it. At times intervention requires typical learning materials and strategies used with younger children who have the same skill levels. At other times, unique, intensive teaching strategies are needed.

***It's very important to intervene when lags become evident, as opposed to taking a "wait-and-see attitude," in hopes that the child will outgrow it.***

Maturational lag theorists complain that the common practice of setting a fixed curriculum and automatically promoting children from grade to grade aggravates LD. Numerous studies have shown that children who enter kindergarten ready for the school's curriculum remain among the top students from grade to grade. Children who are only partially prepared for kindergarten are just average learners six years later. Children who are completely unprepared to learn the kindergarten curriculum are at the bottom of their classes years later or have been dropped to a lower grade. Based on such findings, maturational lag theorists believe that delaying school entry, or not promoting children unready for the work of the next grade, creates a better match between the curriculum and the readiness skills of children with developmental delays.

***Children who enter school unprepared for the kindergarten curriculum are far more likely to lag behind academically and develop learning difficulties.***

It's estimated that more than 50 percent of children entering kindergarten are not ready for the curriculum. Louise Bates Ames, the most influential of the maturational lag theorists, suggested that children should enter school not by age criteria but when their behavioral and learning maturity show that they are ready for the curriculum. Boys usually should reach 6½ by September of their first-grade year to be mature enough in behavior and learning skills; for girls, it's 6 years old. One study of over 30,000 children found that children who enter school too young for their grade are far more likely than those who are older at school entry to lag behind academically and develop learning difficulties.

Teaching at levels beyond the capacity of a student with developmental lags creates multiple problems: daily failure at school leads to lowered self-image, giving up, depression, withdrawal, or acting out. Parents are disappointed, teachers frustrated, and retention may be considered because the curriculum just doesn't give children time to catch up.

The influence of maturational lag theories, along with recent stricter promotion standards and high-stakes testing to hold schools accountable, have caused many more schools to advise delaying entry by a year to give children time to catch up. Some states now require a child to be 6 years of age by September of first grade. Transition classes between kindergarten and first grade also have been implemented to give children's learning skills time to mature. Research suggests that, with this extra time, some children still achieve behind their younger classmates but others perform as well as these classmates; many slip again academically in subsequent years. What happens to the children who are advanced in school because their parents refused the delayed entry or transition class options? Many of these children meet the achievement expectations of the class they are promoted into, but for others the original achievement gap remains or widens. So, there are no easy answers.

In recent years retention rates have risen to 15 to 23 percent, depending on the locale. Males and minority children are retained more often than white females. Research suggests that retaining children can be helpful academically and socially up through second grade only under very particular circumstances: the child has average intelligence, normal emotional and social adjustment, no serious academic deficits, he or she doesn't oppose retention, and the child's parents support the retention. This represents about 5 of every 100 children who are retained. These children fit in well with the curriculum's pace. They just needed more time, which the retention provided. Retained children who do not fit these characteristics may do better for the retained year, but this temporary benefit is deceptive. Over the years, half end up no better off than similar children who had been promoted, and half lag even further behind academically. Often they are retained a second time, which seldom leads to positive academic or behavior changes. Retention is generally ineffective in middle school and high school, leading to a loss of self-image, behavior problems, and excessive absences. The fact that about 20 percent of retained students later drop out of school, compared with about 9 percent of those never retained, has been linked to the stress, stigma, and loss in esteem associated with the failure of retention and being older than one's classmates. Not surprisingly, children with learning disabilities are 2½ to 4 times more likely to be retained than their typical peers.

*Most retained children do better for the retained year but subsequently face a 50-50 chance of ending up no better off or even further behind than similar children who were promoted.*

Retention by itself isn't the answer. Repeating the same curriculum in which the child already failed just doesn't make sense for most children. Often both the teacher's and the child's expectations are lowered once retention has been chosen. Whether retained or not, children need high-quality instruction offered right away rather than waiting and hoping that an extra year will heal the developmental lags.

*Repeating the same curriculum in which the child already failed just doesn't make sense for most children.*

*Children need high quality instruction offered right away rather than hoping that an extra year will help the developmental lags go away.*

Good schools find a way to maintain strict academic standards and simultaneously offer a number of options that permit students to remain with their same-age peers while learning at their own pace. These options include adapting the grade-level curriculum, flexibly advancing through levels of instruction as set objectives are met, daily tutoring, after-school and summer programs, learning laboratories, multiage grouping, cooperative learning strategies in which children work in teams, remedial reading and math classes, and special education services.

Another interesting option that shows promise is "looping" the same teacher into accompanying his or her class to the next grade. Because the teacher is familiar with the needs of children with LD, instruction can be appropriately geared from the start, behavior management issues are reduced, parents and teachers are satisfied, and grade retention and later dropout is reduced. All of these options help build flexibility and special services into the class framework so that the rigid school curriculum is less likely to exacerbate learning problems.

## Cognitive Styles

Cognitive style theorists stress that school tasks can contribute to learning disabilities when they require students to use problem-solving strategies that they find unnatural. A person's *cognitive style* (his or her preferred way of looking at and interacting with the world) tends to remain stable throughout life and is influenced by such factors as personality, heredity, and brain injury.

***Good schools find a way to maintain academic standards while students remain with their peers and learn at their own pace.***

Recall Jonah, the hyperactive first grader. His teacher asks him to find an educational game to play quietly while she works with a reading group. He flits from game to game, never finishes any of them, and he gains little from the experience. His classmate Juli, given the same instructions, chooses one game and plays it over and over, intrigued by its details and trying to get a better score each time. Time is up long before she even thinks about trying a different game. When the teacher asks these two children to tell the reading group which games are available, Jonah's hand flies into the air because he's tried them all. But when she asks them to demonstrate a game, Juli is the one ready with an answer.

Is one child a better learner? In general, our society favors Juli's reflective approach. She's more task oriented, takes more time to arrive at solutions, and likes to analyze and memorize details. School tasks are more compatible with Juli's disposition than Jonah's. But Jonah's impulsive style has benefits too. When the teacher asks the children to find her pen in the classroom, Jonah's ability to scan the environment rapidly works well. Ask Jonah to find the movie theater listings in the newspaper, and he locates them quicker than Juli, who methodically goes through each page one at a time.

Cognitive style theorists presume that in many cases students who are experiencing learning problems have intact learning abilities, but their styles of learning are inappropriate for the classroom demands. This leads to underachievement and cumulative information deficits. On the other hand, when curricular demands match students' preferred learning styles and when students are taught more effective learning strategies, these students can learn well.

***In many cases students who are experiencing learning problems have intact learning abilities, but their styles of learning are inappropriate for the classroom demands.***

The next section discusses the most common learning styles found among students with learning disabilities.

**Impulsive and Reflective Learners.** Impulsive learners are more highly represented among students with LD than among average students. Their style is characterized by underfocused attention, distractibility, and premature decision making. They are restless, can't concentrate for long, forge ahead before understanding directions, and have social difficulties because they don't stop to consider the consequences of their actions. Overly reflective learners, at the other end of the continuum, are overfocused, delay decision making for what seems like forever, concentrate so long on bits of information that they miss the main point.

Jerome Kagan and his colleagues used the Matching Familiar Figures Test (see Figure 4.1) to study impulsive and reflective styles. Kagan and others believed that reflective children are slower, and correct, because they fear being wrong. Impulsive children, on the other hand, get through tasks fast because they aren't concerned enough to take the time to avoid errors. Other researchers countered that these children are fast or slow because of differences in their information-processing approaches. Reflective children prefer to analyze fine details, which takes time. In contrast, impulsive children prefer to focus on the overall picture, which takes less time. They claimed that reflective children are superior to impulsive children only when analyzing details. On items requiring more global analysis,

***Reflective children prefer to analyze details, while impulsive children prefer focusing on the overall picture.***

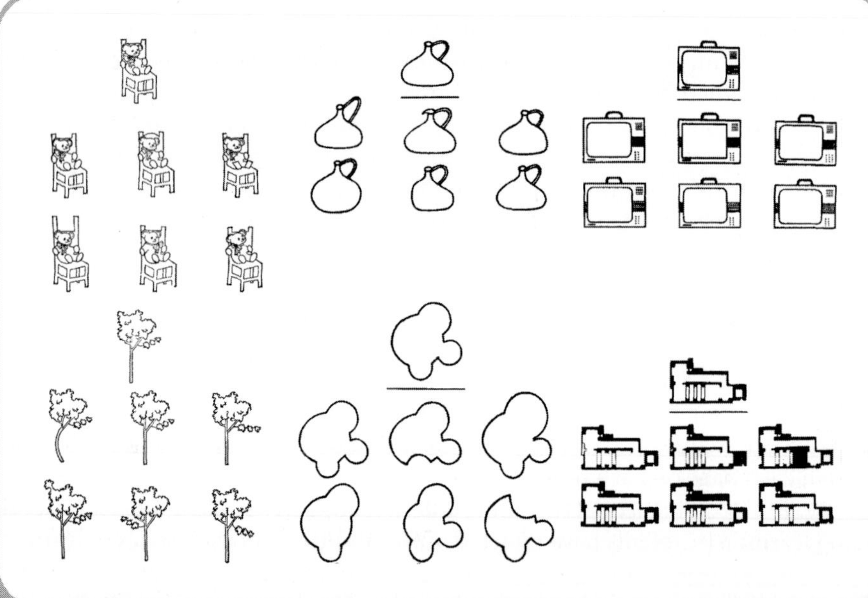

**Figure 4.1** Kagan's Matching Familiar Figures Test items that measure reflective and implusive cognitive styles. The task is to match the top figure with one of the lower six figures. Some items require studying details, while others require attending to the overall configuration.

*Sources:* Kagan, J. (1965). Reflection-impulsivity and reading ability in primary grade children. *Child Development, 36,* 613. © 1965 The Society for Research in Child Development; and Zelniker, T., & Jeffrey, W. E. (1976). Reflective and impulsive children: Strategies of information processing underlying differences in problem solving. *Monographs of the Society for Research in Child Development, 41* (5), Serial No. 168. © 1976 The Society for Research in Child Development. Reprinted by permission.

such as recognizing outlines and themes, impulsive children are equal, if not superior, to reflective children—and faster. These important studies are described in Research Box 4.1.

In a very clever study of hyperactive 4- to 6-year-old low achievers and typical learners of equal intelligence, Zentall and Gohs gave children blocks with drawings of abstract designs. The children had to decide which block to place on a stand after being given either a global cue ("it looks like a ray gun or a man's shirt")—or a detail cue ("it has a hole in the middle"). When the children had trouble making up their minds and needed an additional cue, they would sound a buzzer. If a global cue had been given first, they would get a detail cue next, and vice versa. Hyperactive children sounded the buzzer more often after a detail cue; the average learners did the opposite, needing more information when given a global cue. In other words, global information seems to be more meaningful to the hyperactive, poor learner than detailed information. These

***Global information seems to be more meaningful to the hyperactive, poor learner than detailed information.***

RESEARCH BOX 4.1

## Zelniker and Jeffrey's Study of Impulsive and Reflective Cognitive Styles

Zelniker and Jeffrey (1976) conducted four studies to test their hypothesis that impulsive children and reflective children differ in the styles with which they search information.

In the first study they analyzed MFFT items (see Figure 4.1) by whether the correct answers required attention to global (the contour, overview) or detail features. Findings indicated that reflective children were consistently superior to impulsive children on items requiring attention to detail. Although both groups performed equally well on global items, the impulsive children arrived at the solution faster.

In the second study, Zelniker and Jeffrey found that impulsive children gave more nonanalytical (looking at wholes) than analytical (looking at details) responses on the Conceptual Style Test. Reflective children showed the opposite pattern. This test requires the child to describe similarities between line drawings. The children are specifically told to be analytical and nonanalytical in responding. Impulsive children made more errors when told to be analytical than nonanalytical. Reflective children made more errors when told to be nonanalytical.

Children in the third study listened to sentences or looked at pictures. Impulsive children recalled themes rather than details. Reflective children recalled details rather than themes.

The fourth study used Bruner's Concept-Attainment Task, which required descriptions of stimulus similarities by shape, color, and size. The impulsive children named more dimensions than did the reflective children, who preferred to scan parts.

Zelniker and Jeffrey's findings suggest that impulsive and reflective children differ in information-processing strategies. These strategies then influence their response speeds and accuracy.

children don't know how to go about analyzing material that is detailed (the preponderence of schoolwork) even if they do take more time. It doesn't work to simply tell impulsive students to "slow down and you'll get it": They need to be shown how to focus on details when scanning material and why such a strategy is helpful.

*School tasks favor the reflective learner because schoolwork most often demands attention to details and taking time to think through answers.*

The school curriculum favors the reflective learner because schoolwork most often demands attention to details and taking time to think through an answer. Although impulsive children do have an advantage when it comes to getting an overview of a situation quickly, being sensitive to social cues, solving problems that don't contain the answers, and absorbing incidental information, unfortunately the demands of the school curriculum for the most part are not suited to this global learning style. Therefore, these children's failure is aggravated.

**Low Conceptual and High Conceptual Learners.** David Hunt described *low conceptual learners* as categorical thinkers who depend on rules and have trouble generating their own concepts or weighing a number of alternatives. They have a hard time directing their own learning. He described *high conceptual learners,* on the other hand, as students who generate their own concepts, provide their own rules, consider different viewpoints, and flexibly shift among alternative strategies when solving problems. They are more inquiring, self-assertive, and capable of independently handling complex conceptual material. The majority of students with learning disabilities are low conceptual thinkers.

*Low conceptual students need to be told all the information that requires attention and the exact point being illustrated by examples.*

Studies find that low conceptual students learn better from highly teacher-directed instruction than from a discovery approach, and when a rule is presented before rather than after an example so that the student knows what to be looking for. The low conceptual student needs to be told all the information that requires attention and the exact point being illustrated by examples. High conceptual learners can learn equally well no matter what the method, but they prefer discovery approaches that give them more freedom in learning.

On a simple "memorize the story" task, one researcher found that good learners preferred to be asked questions after they had heard a folk tale because they liked to organize the information in their own way. Poor learners, however, could retell the tale only if they heard the questions right before the story was read, so they could be more focused in listening for the appropriate information.

*School tasks generally favor high conceptual learners who like to discover relationships for themselves, generate their own concepts, consider different viewpoints, and are flexible in their problem solving approaches.*

School tasks generally favor the high conceptual learner. Teachers frequently encourage students to discover relationships for themselves with questions like "How could we solve this problem?" or "Why did that happen?" They less often directly provide key concepts or precise choices to ponder, yet this is just what the poor learner needs—an orderly approach to learning that provides focus and reduces confusion by coming right out and telling the child the pertinent facts and ideas. For many students with LD teaching approaches that are more structured and explicit are just what they need to promote greater integration and generalization of information. The teacher's lower-level questions (e.g., fact and sequence) will build the foundation for higher-level inferences. We must be prepared to adapt our teaching approaches to match these students' preferred instructional styles.

**Simultaneous and Successive Learners.** Imagine that you and your 10-year-old nephew Ken have just arrived at a busy airport. You head to the hotel van pickup board where 50 hotel pictures and logos line the wall. While you're still searching for your hotel, Ken shouts "There it is!" Why did he come up with the answer so fast while you were still scanning the wall, up one column of logos and down the next? You used a *successive* (analytical) approach, which takes time, while Ken used a *simultaneous* (global) approach, which is faster. For Ken, the logo just jumped out at him as in a 3-D movie.

Youngsters who prefer a simultaneous processing strategy do better on spatial-conceptual tasks such as deciding whether two different-shaped beakers contain the same amount of liquid, or whether two lines are still the same length when the distance between them increases. They readily grasp spatial language concepts such as "taller than," "below," or "inside," and they can see the big picture when organizing compositions. Successive learners, in contrast, are better at understanding the sequencing of language and sound, and thus are better at learning to read and comprehend.

*Youngsters who prefer a simultaneous processing strategy do better on spatial-conceptual tasks and on tasks where they can see the big picture.*

*Successive learners are better at understanding the sequencing of language and sound, and thus are good at learning to read and comprehend.*

Problems arise when students bring inappropriate successive or simultaneous styles to a task. Children who learn well typically use a simultaneous approach to visual and motor tasks, but successive approaches to auditory and verbal tasks. Unfortunately, children with LD may approach these tasks with the least-suited strategy. Even if they eventually solve a problem, it takes longer and is more effortful, thereby depleting enjoyment in the accomplishment and leaving little room for higher-level reasoning. If the child looks at the world in an overly global way, he or she will miss important details. On the other hand, if the child's approach to learning is always analytical, details will cloud the overall meaning. The detail-bound child is also more likely to miss social cues that could help the child fit in better.

*If the child looks at the world in an overly global way, he or she will miss important details. If the approach is always analytical, details will cloud the overall meaning.*

The stories of Ariel and JJ (page 110) illustrate how overly rigid styles, either successive or simultaneous, can interfere with learning. Although both of their teachers adapted their methods to suit each child's preferred learning strategy, these children still needed to be shown how to be more flexible in their styles. Ariel's boring, overly successive style was helped when her teacher asked her to first tell her classmates her conclusion before she launched into the endless details of a story—"where is this leading?" The teacher shifted copying from the board to the beginning of class to give Ariel more time to copy and alleviate her stress about finishing on time. Brainstorming sessions helped Ariel outline her work better. JJ, who leaps to conclusions, was helped when his teacher drew sticks next to numerals so he could count out the math answers rather than guess. The teacher also asked JJ to forecast what would happen in a story to help him focus on details and time sequences. Task modifications like these adapt to children's conceptual styles and are exactly what students with LD who are overly rigid in their approaches need to help them succeed.

**Efficient and Inefficient Learner Strategies.** Many students with learning disabilities are inefficient, inactive, and disorganized learners. They don't know how to go about learning nor do they know how to figure out what the task demands. They

## Ariel and JJ

*Children whose overly rigid successive and simultaneous cognitive styles interfere with learning.*

**Ariel**

Ariel, a 12-year-old who preferred a successive cognitive style, illustrates what can happen when a youngster is overly bound to one style. Instead of switching between strategies or letting them complement one another, Ariel stuck to a successive strategy on all tasks. When looking at the teacher's concept map of continents, for example, Ariel focused on the countries within the various bubbles, but she did not notice that each bubble represented a different continent. Copying from the board was a very slow process for Ariel. She proceeded letter by letter despite her ability to read these as sight words; therefore, she continually lagged behind the rest of the class. When Ariel was recounting an incident, the listener had no idea what point she was trying to make because she rambled off sequences of events and ideas without connecting them to any major point. Although she read and spelled at high school levels, Ariel's written compositions were a series of disconnected statements. Even when scanning a picture for the most important missing part, Ariel would list many parts but have difficulty distinguishing the one whose absence was most critical (she would overlook the minute hand on a wristwatch, for example, and say that the absent wristband was most important). Despite high grades in school, Ariel was very unhappy because she took longer than everyone else to complete homework, and often missed the main point being presented by the teacher. The disconnectedness of her conversations caused problems with her friends. Squabbles and misperceptions about what others had said to her were daily occurrences.

**JJ**

In contrast to Ariel, JJ took a simultaneous approach to most tasks. When he was shown a worksheet in first grade with a picture of 2 pigs connected by a plus sign, and the teacher asked "If there are 3 pigs and 5 more pigs come along, how many will there be all together?," JJ responded "2." He became visually bound by the pictures and could no longer attend to the teacher's words. When told to work the problem 3 + 5, JJ would randomly record a sum that "looked right" instead of counting up the answer. In stories, JJ would recognize the main ideas but could recall few of the details and seldom in the correct sequence. As a friend, however, he was empathic and great. Catching on to the rules of games was not a strength, but his friends somehow knew to actually show him how to play rather than to bother telling him the rules.

*Many students with LD have trouble figuring out task demands, put little energy into learning, and seem to be unaware that memory is possible or desirable.*

seem to have little awareness that they are to put energy into learning. Their efforts are not sustained or organized, and they seem to be unaware that memory is possible or desirable. Typical problem-solving difficulties of students with LD include

1. They fail to use a systematic plan to approach a problem. When they play 20 questions, for example, they come up with disjointed, wild-guess questions rather than questions geared toward isolating categories.
2. They fail to distinguish critical elements from those that are irrelevant in a problem.

3. They don't make use of feedback to check their accuracy, so they will abandon a right answer or return to a wrong one.
4. They can't generate new inferences or make use of new data to revise their actions and plans.
5. They fail to draw specific conclusions and remain overly general.

Left to their own devices, students with LD are more dependent in their intellectual activities, don't work as hard, are more impulsive, and are less capable of understanding directions than are average achievers. They have no notion of strategies that might help them learn, such as studying difficult material more thoroughly than easy material. When studying, poor readers ask themselves fewer questions to help comprehension, take fewer notes, look for fewer main ideas, are less exhaustive in contemplating alternative ideas, and are less effective in elaborating on information in order to remember it better. It is common for these students to ignore the fact that they don't know the meaning of certain words and phrases, nor will they look them up.

In many cases, students with LD do not have serious deficits in their actual ability to learn. Rather, their inefficient learning strategies prevent them from using their basic abilities to their best advantage. They seem to have "performance deficits" rather than "ability deficits."

*In many cases, students with LD do not have serious deficits in their actual ability to learn. Rather, their inefficient learning strategies prevent them from using their basic abilities to their best advantage.*

Often these students are helped when we use teaching methods to circumvent their inefficiencies, or we teach them better strategies. A classic study by Joseph Torgesen illustrates this point. Torgesen asked good and poor readers to push one button at a time to reveal each of seven pictures. The goal was to remember the pictures in order. As expected, poor readers had worse recall than good readers. But they also had little insight into a strategy to use for learning. Some didn't rehearse at all, others pushed the buttons in reverse order, and others rehearsed in random order. Good readers, on the other hand, systematically named the pictures and rehearsed in sequence from left to right. When Torgesen adapted the task by actually pushing the buttons in sequence for the poor readers, their recall became equal to that of good readers.

Torgesen next asked the children to memorize 24 cards belonging in 4 categories. Good readers were initially superior to poor readers. They more often named the cards and grouped them into categories, spent more time moving the cards around, and had less off-task behavior than did the poor readers. But when the poor readers were instructed to name the cards and actively sort them into categories, trained to look for categories, or to use mnemonic memory tricks, their off-task behavior dropped and their memory became equal to that of the good readers.

Because many youngsters with LD underachieve due to inappropriate, inactive, and inefficient learning strategies, we need to teach them more efficient ways to go about learning. *Metacognitive strategies* have been developed to teach these children more appropriate approaches to learning. These methods teach students to stop and think before responding, to verbalize and rehearse what they have seen, to monitor their attention and what they are to do, to visually image what they are to remember, to preplan task approaches, to use memory tricks, to

*When teaching methods circumvent inefficient cognitive styles, or we teach children better learning strategies, achievement can improve dramatically. What were thought to be basic ability deficits may actually disappear.*

reinforce their own appropriate behavior, and to organize their time. If you've ever taken a "how to succeed at college" minicourse, you'll recognize many of these points. When these students take a more systematic approach to their learning, achievement can improve dramatically and what were thought to be basic ability deficits may actually disappear.

## Family and School Environment Contributors

Many environmental factors can create learning disorders in perfectly normal children or aggravate weaknesses that already exist. Society itself contributes to the problem through a value system which states that one way of thinking and behaving is acceptable and all others are deviant. LD children are branded as handicapped because they don't meet society's standards for academic success. Many of these students could acquire knowledge well if reading were not the primary vehicle for learning. As a result, often their particular strengths and talents are overlooked, devalued, and undeveloped as the unrelenting pursuit of reading skills continues. The story of the Unlettered is a graphic and sad illustration of what happens when one can't "walk in obedience to the written word."

This section explores the many ways in which environmental contributors can reduce learning opportunities, motivation, and the child's ability to learn to his or her full potential.

### Insufficient Nutrition and Stimulation

Because insufficient nutrition and stimulation can contribute to learning disabilities, intervention is necessary to avoid any compromise of a child's learning potential. The presence of school breakfast and lunch programs attests to an understanding of the effect of nutrition on learning. We know that a hungry child or one who is in poor physical health isn't likely to have the motivation or energy for schoolwork. This is true when children live in poverty or when middle-income children—girls, mostly—become obsessed with thinness and drastically reduce their caloric intake.

*Malnutrition interferes with brain cell production, reduces brain weight, and is particularly damaging during the first 6 months of life. The result is lower than expected IQ and learning ability.*

Malnutrition interferes with brain cell production, reduces brain weight, and is particularly damaging during the first 6 months of life when the brain's nerve cells grow larger and the majority of synapses are formed. The result is lower than expected IQ and learning ability, poorer social adaptation, and reduced initiative. Fortunately, studies find that some reversal of the negative effects of poor nutrition is possible after several years of adequate nutrition and enriched care giving.

*Early sensory deprivation adversely affects brain maturation and learning. Even milder losses in stimulation, such as intermittent school attendance or dropping out, can affect intelligence.*

Early sensory deprivation also adversely affects brain maturation and learning. Even milder losses in stimulation, such as late entry into school, intermittent attendance at school, and dropping out can negatively affect intelligence.

Numerous animal studies since the 1960s have demonstrated how reduced learning opportunities affect brain development. Conversely, enriched environments and learning opportunities result in thicker gray matter, more glial cells, higher brain metabolic activity, and more chemicals needed for neural transmission. Likewise in humans, learning experiences "pump the

### The Unlettered

*The sad story of a 13-year-old who died merely because he couldn't read.*

"Although sharp at all other things," the boy could not read. He was 13 years old: at 13 years a boy's reading lessons should be over and done. Yet he could not read: or, if he might read at all, it was only such words as "cat" and "rat."

Therefore he died, which seems heavy punishment for being dull at his reading. The tramway which runs on Southend Pier is an electric tramway. It is fenced about with railings. What are railings that they should keep a boy from climbing over them? But, besides the railings, there were placards warning all who should approach of the dangers of the live rail.

If the boy could have read the placards he would not have climbed the railing. But the placards told him nothing, he being able to spell out only the simplest of words. So he climbed and took his death from the current.

The world is like that, a perilous world for those who cannot learn to read. It must be so. We cannot fence every peril so that the unlettered may take no harm from it. There is free and compulsory education: at least everybody has his chance of learning his lessons in school. The world's business is ordered on the understanding that everybody can at least spell out words.

We walk in obedience to the written word. All about us are boards and placards, telling us to do this thing or to keep from doing that other thing. Keep to the Right, we are bidden, or else we are to Keep to the Left. By this stairway we are to descend to enter the train that goes Westward; by that we go to the Eastward train. Way Out and Way In; Private; Trespassers will be Prosecuted; Pit Entrance; the street's name and the name of the railway station—all of these things are cried out to us by that wonderful device of letters, a babble of voices which make no sound.

It is hard for us to understand the case of those to whom these many signs and warnings say nothing. They must move as though bewildered, as though they were blind and deaf. No warning touches them, not even that of the board which, like the board of the Southend tramway, cries Danger and Beware.

For such as he is, the days of school-time must be long days and weary days. I will not say that all the time is mis-spent: life nowadays is safer for the boy who can read the warning board, although painfully. But the case of the boy who could read only "cat" and "rat," although he was "sharp at other things," should have its lesson for those who are taken by the strong delusion that we may see a world of book-learned men and women if we will spend the money handsomely. For it is not so: there will always be those who cannot get beyond "cat" and "rat," even some who cannot get so far.

*Source:* Critchley, M. (1970). *The dyslexic child* (pp. xiii–xv). Springfield, IL: Charles C. Thomas. Reprinted by permission.

brain" (Bakker, 1984, p. 1) such that "the brain after learning is a different one than the brain before learning" (Merzenich & Jenkins, 1995, p. 249). Parents and teachers can do much to "help the brain remake itself" because "the life we lead leaves its mark in the complex circuitry of the brain—footprints of the experiences we have had, the thoughts we have thought, the actions we have taken" (Begley, 2002, p. B4).

## Multicultural and Linguistic Diversity

*Linguistic and cultural differences often create a mismatch with the predominant white, middle-income expectations and values of our schools.*

We live in a society enriched by the traditions and values of people from different national origins, different languages, customs, knowledge, ways of thinking and styles of behavior, different parts of the country, different sexual orientations, and so on. With such diversity comes the reality that some children's backgrounds may not match the white, middle-income expectations of our schools for English to be spoken and for certain types of behaviors and knowledge to be valued above others.

How disappointing it must be to an African American child to study slavery, but not the contributions of great African American writers, musicians, and thinkers. How humiliating to a Native American child to read about how the "Indians" were "conquered," but not about the rich heritage that was nearly obliterated in the process. How frustrating for a newly immigrated Russian, Italian, or Castilian Spanish child, in whose language nearly every letter represents a single sound, to find that in English the same sounds can be represented by different letters, and the same letter can have several sounds. No wonder that some students feel alienated, unappreciated, unwelcome, unmotivated, and confused. This clash between cultures and backgrounds can contribute to learning disabilities.

Consider, for example, Native American and Asian children who may hesitate to initiate interaction with their teachers or respond to questions in class because, in their cultures, many are taught that it is impolite to set oneself apart from the group. These children have been acculturated to blend in, even if it means denying that they are knowledgeable about the subject matter. This behavior doesn't work well in our classrooms. Likewise, many Native Americans have been taught that it's disrespectful to make eye contact or to give a firm handshake, to ask direct questions, to share personal information unless the other person also shares, or to deviate from the ways of the elders. Anonymity and submissiveness are preferable to asserting their individuality and competence. Completing tasks may not be important to some Native American children because the reliance on community in their culture leads them to expect that others will complete the task in due time. The teacher's irritation grows as parents miss conferences because, for many Native Americans, time moves with the flow of events and tasks, not the hands of the clock. Although these teachings have enriched the lives of those who share this heritage, they are at odds with the individualism, competitive display of knowledge, and punctuality of our typical classrooms.

Hawaiian students sometimes report feeling picked on when asked a question in class because adults rarely interact with children that way in their culture. African American students may simply not respond when a teacher asks them a question because in many of their homes no adult would seek information they already know. The school's stress on competition, working on one's own, and staying in one's seat conflicts with a common African American cultural emphasis on harmony, movement, and working communally.

Sometimes Hispanic students are misunderstood when, out of respect, they might look away from the teacher when spoken to. To be polite, they also may avoid disagreeing with a directive by simply not following through. Many Hispanic children come from a less time-bound culture, so if they do follow through, it might be tomorrow, not today. Moreover, interrupting the teacher in order to comment is common because listening passively isn't a behavior that is encouraged in their culture. Teachers often misunderstand Mexican American students as being dishonest or lazy when they copy class work from another student, yet sharing knowledge and responsibilities is highly valued in their homes. In their families, everyone participates in even the simplest activities—such as taking out the garbage or going to the train station to greet a visitor. Relying on oneself and competing are truly foreign concepts.

Language differences can also create a significant mismatch with school expectations. In the year 2000, approximately 15 percent of schoolchildren were non-native English speakers. Close to 40 percent came from sociocultural minority groups. Because teaching is verbally based in both content and methods, this presents a major problem and handicaps these children's learning.

Consider the difficulty of phonics instruction for a Chinese student whose language is missing many of the consonant sounds of English. How frustrating our phonics method must be to the Korean student who cannot formulate the *f, r, th, v,* and *z* sounds. Even when they do master conversational English, it will be years before these students can fully absorb the vocabulary of books and the classroom. Research Box 4.2 on page 116 explores why teachers cannot assume that their students look at the world in the same way they do. Because language and culture are so closely intertwined, a concept that exists in this country may be totally meaningless to a child who speaks another language.

***Because language and culture are so closely intertwined, a concept that exists in this country may be totally meaningless to a child who speaks another language.***

It is essential that teachers be responsive to the multicultural and linguistic diversity among our students, so students don't begin to see themselves as failures and give up the will to succeed. Curricula, teacher attitudes, and teaching approaches must be modified to foster these students' self-respect and motivation by affirming their native language and knowledge and giving them opportunities to contribute to the culture of the classroom. Children will make more rapid academic and social gains when the richness of their language and culture are used as sources of learning and when their cultural differences are accommodated.

***Children make more rapid academic and social gains when the richness of their language and culture are used as sources of learning and when their cultural differences are accommodated.***

## Poverty

Poverty is clearly associated with learning disabilities, and, among children with LD, progress is more limited for those who live in poverty. Despite the fact that 77 percent of their families work (37 percent full-time), 1 in 6 American children (16 percent) still live in poverty. The poverty figure rises to about 30 percent among African American and Hispanic children. This compares with 13 to 14 percent of white, Asian, or Pacific Island children. A single parent, usually the mother, heads approximately 25 percent of white families, 64 percent of African American families, and 36 percent of Hispanic families. Forty percent of poor families are headed by a single mother, and only 1 in 4 of these children receives any child support from their father—on average $2,000 a year. In contrast, only 8 percent of children in married families lives below the poverty line.

***Academic progress is more limited for those who live in poverty.***

The greater the number of poor children in a school, the lower their overall achievement. Today's fourth graders from low socioeconomic backgrounds are

RESEARCH BOX 4.2

## The Influence of Language on What We See and Think

The idea that language has a fundamental influence on thought itself was advanced by Benjamin Whorf (1956). Whorf's early work pointed out that Eskimos have hundreds of terms to differentiate one type of snow from another. Because non-Eskimos have very few names for different types of snow, they find it difficult to imagine the varieties that the Eskimos say exist. If these varieties are pointed out, the non-Eskimo fails to recognize the characteristics that the Eskimo finds so meaningful. On the other hand, Eskimos have only one name for what we label as blue, purple, and violet; therefore, they do not interpret these hues with the same complexity that we do. Likewise, Eskimos and Navajos label red, orange, and yellow as only two colors (Collier & Hoover, 1987). Eskimos also have no word for bread, so they would not understand "let's break bread." The Hopi, who have no word for time, describe it as an experience of subjective length—which can wreak havoc with scheduled school meetings and getting children to school on time.

To the average American, a camel is a camel, but to the average Arab, the conception of camels is far richer, with over 50 words to describe these animals. For the American, rhyming games are important precursors to reading. In contrast, in most Asian languages rhymes do not exist, so the Asian American has difficulty appreciating the importance of preschool rhyming activities, and nursery rhymes hold little appeal (Welton, 1990). Interestingly, the Korean language often omits nouns and emphasizes verbs, but English emphasizes nouns. A correlate of these language differences appears to be that young Korean children are more advanced than English speakers with "means-end" abilities (as in using a stick to obtain an object that is out of reach), but delayed in ability to conceptualize categories of objects (Gopnik, Choi, & Baumberger, 1996). On a more personal note, being of Hungarian origin I now understand why my parents brooded over the fact that my American husband was extremely rude when he greeted them with "hello." In Hungarian, "hello" translates into "I kiss you"—and, with Hungarian having several "kiss" words, the implication of Hungarian's "hello" kiss was a big fat one planted on the cheek. (I finally solved the problem by teaching my husband the Hungarian word for "hello," but I never told him the literal translation!)

Clearly, language and culture are so tied to one another that teachers cannot assume that pupils from different cultural and linguistic backgrounds will see the world as they do. These children do not have the same starting points. Because of their culture and language heritage, they interpret classroom events and what teachers say differently than what was intended. Their behavior and language, in turn, are interpreted differently than they had intended by their teachers and peers. These students' differences must not only be understood in order to enrich their learning experience, but the differences must also be welcomed, explored, and shared in order to enrich the cultural and conceptual experiences of all students in the classroom.

already over two years behind in basic reading and math skills compared with students who are not poor. By twelfth grade they are nearly four years behind their more advantaged peers. The high school dropout rate in low-income families is 25 percent compared to the national average of 11 percent. Only 3.5

percent of students in the highest quartile of family income dropout. White students drop out at a rate of approximately 7 percent, while African Americans and Hispanics, who are overrepresented in the lowest income brackets, drop out at a rate of about 13 and 28 percent, respectively. When students do graduate high school, about 67 percent of white graduates enroll immediately in postsecondary education, in comparison with only 56 percent of African American graduates and 41 percent of Hispanic graduates. This difference has long-lasting implications for future employment and earnings. College graduates have more than twice the earnings of high school dropouts and 75 percent greater earnings than high school graduates.

The poor achievement of some low-income students is due in part to poor nutrition and medical care from the very beginning of life, which can compromise brain development. Complications of prenatal life, delivery, childhood diseases, and accidents that can harm the brain of the developing child are disproportionately higher among the poor. Those living in poverty are also less likely to eat healthy diets and get sufficient exercise. They are more likely to smoke, abuse alcohol and drugs, become depressed, and suffer psychological stress, all of which doesn't bode well for learning.

Children born to poor families are less likely to be fully immunized and more often suffer from lead poisoning and encephalitis. They acquire language and reading readiness skills later, in part because there is less parental stimulation at home in the form of language, toys, and books that foster language development. They more often arrive at school impulsive, hyperactive, with a limited fund of information and problem-solving skills, and minimal encouragement of scholastic success. They may suffer from simply coming from a very large family in which individual attention is a rare thing. The National Assessment of Educational Progress data shows that when these children begin school deficient in literacy skills, they are likely to remain behind even through high school graduation.

*When children begin school deficient in literacy skills, they are likely to remain behind even through high school graduation.*

It is important to remember, though, that not all children of poverty are at risk for achieving less than their more economically advantaged peers. Chapter 13 discusses the factors that help children raised in poverty to overcome tremendous odds and go on to success and lives of contribution.

*Not all children of poverty are at risk for achieving less than their more economically advantaged peers.*

Because what is learned in the home, school, and general environment neurochemically alters the brain's general capacities, this learning is likely to affect future achievement. Therefore, it is essential that we offer parent education programs pertaining to health and child rearing, as well as job training and continuing education, to fight the adverse effects of poverty on learning potential. Learning to read, high school graduation, and home encouragement of learning are critical to breaking the cycle of underemployment and poverty.

*Because what is learned in the home, school, and general environment neurochemically alters the brain's general capacities, this learning affects future achievement.*

## Adverse Emotional Climate

Children who have fled war, torture, and famine only to face a new culture without one of their parents or as orphans carry scars that delay their school achievement or make it nearly impossible. Children who live in "urban war zones" where shootings and other forms of violence are nearly daily occurrences are hard-pressed to concentrate in class. How can they when they are so anxious, depressed, withdrawn, and sleepless? The nearly 1 million children who are among the homeless have few resources to support their learning. The growing numbers of abused and neglected children—over 3 million reports to authorities each year—are understandably poorly prepared to learn.

A number of seemingly less catastrophic events can disrupt a child's learning. These include family disorganization; divorce and emotional instability; maternal stress during pregnancy; harsh, critical, and neglectful mothering; parental job loss; difficult parental temperaments; and parental reinforcement of negative behaviors.

*Children with LD tend to be more depressed than others, and their negative mood reduces the amount of energy they can put into learning.*

Emotional stress can develop because of school frustrations as well. Children with LD tend to be more depressed than others, and their negative mood reduces the amount of energy they can put into learning. Irrelevant thoughts sidetrack their attention, and sadness, poor self-esteem, and anxiety can subtly influence their cognitive activities. There is some evidence that when teachers make a concerted effort to cheer these students up by creating pleasing environments and inducing positive thoughts, they learn more and faster.

*Because any type of stress activates the brain through increased blood flow, emotional states actually produce unique brain states that in turn can affect learning.*

At the very simplest level, emotion drives what we pay attention to, which in turn drives our learning and memory. However, emotional states also can alter neuroendocrine and immune responses that increase the risk of illness (e.g., gastrointestinal disorders, headaches, seizures, infections), which, of course, affects the ability to learn. Because any type of stress activates the brain through increased blood flow, emotional states actually produce unique brain states that in turn can affect learning. The more we alleviate negative stresses in the classroom, the more we prevent their contributing to learning disabilities.

## Environmental Toxins

*Environmental toxins can predispose children before or after birth to severe learning and health problems.*

Environmental toxins can predispose children before or after birth to severe learning and health problems. Most of the over 80,000 chemicals in pesticides, herbicides, drugs, cosmetics, food additives, fertilizers, and industrial substances have not been tested for their neurotoxic effects. To date, occupational standards have been set for only about 600 chemicals. Of these, about one-third are known to have negative effects on the central nervous system. Educators need to be aware of these hazards and help children and families avoid exposures that may deter learning.

**Prenatal Toxic Effects.** The brain in utero generates neurons at the rate of 250,000 per minute. Yet the fetus has neither a placental barrier against toxic substances nor the capacity to detoxify them. Consequently, prenatal toxic exposures can have significant effects on later health and cognitive status. Mercury exposure, for example, arrests the division of neurons, cadmium can cause brain hemorrhages, and inhalant anesthetics can interfere with cell proliferation. Lead, a long-known offender, affects the brain's blood vessels and reduces the number of neurons and dendrite connections. Low-dose prenatal lead exposure can result in preterm delivery, and higher doses can lead to spontaneous abortions. Prenatal polychlorinated biphenyl (PCB) exposure is related to IQ and attention deficits, hyperactivity, and learning disabilities years later.

Recreational drugs such as marijuana and cocaine also have known adverse prenatal effects. Maternal marijuana smoking increases the risk for premature delivery and subsequent learning problems. Cocaine causes malformation of the brain because of oxygen deprivation, intrauterine growth retardation, increased rate of preterm delivery, and genitourinary tract abnormalities. The 1,000 "crack babies" born each day in the United States face an increased risk of seizures, strokes, abnormal reflexes, poor or absent visual and auditory orientation, marked hyperactivity, irritability, distractability, delayed language and fine-motor development, and poor interactive ability later on. As infants, they are easily overstimulated. They are most calm and alert when left alone—not a very good way to encourage cognitive development.

Maternal cigarette smoking has been associated with attention deficits and hyperactivity, and mild intellectual, language, and academic delays in children. Excessive maternal alcohol consumption may lead to neurological and physical abnormalities, significant cognitive delays, hyperactivity, attention and memory problems, fine- and gross-motor delays, language deficits, difficulty with organization and problem solving, and emotional problems. As little as one drink a day during pregnancy can be harmful.

The harmful effects of the toxins mentioned are evident in both mothers and their babies. Other toxins affect the developing fetus but not the mother. These include the sleeping pill thalidomide (babies are born with missing limbs), the acne medicine Accutane (babies have severe heart deformities, abnormally small heads and eyes, and absent ears), and the antimiscarriage drug diethylstilbestrol, or DES (adult daughters have greater rates of premature birth, miscarriage, and vaginal cancer).

**Postnatal Toxic Effects.** The neurological, psychological, intellectual, learning, and behavioral effects of environmental toxins after birth have been well documented. Among these toxins are lead, arsenic, aluminum, cadmium, carbon monoxide, mercury, radiation, chemotherapy, illicit drugs, and solvents used in paint, glue, and cleaning solutions. Parents carry home some of these toxins on their clothing, from work or hobbies (such as stained glass work or furniture refinishing). Other toxins contaminate children through such means as pesticides, air pollution, and drugs. There has been many a heartbreak as children permanently damage their brains with licit or illicit drugs, and they are no longer the same individuals they once were. As educators, we must be aware of how toxins can impair students' development and work with parents, students, and the community to reduce the dangers that result from drug abuse, industrial hazards, and environmental pollution.

**Food Allergies.** It's estimated that 60 to 80 percent of individuals are allergic to at least one food. Reactions to the food may range from a mild stomachache or headache to hives and a full-blown asthma attack. Food additives (artificial colorings, flavors, preservatives), in particular, have been scrutinized as allergens related to learning disorders, especially hyperactivity. There also are reports of hyperactivity after ingesting aspirin and salicylates (natural aspirinlike compounds in fruits and vegetables). Benjamin Feingold's diet, which eliminates all food additives and

*Only a very small group of hyperactive preschool children respond to food additives and salicylates with deteriorations in learning, behavior, and eye-hand coordination.*

salicylates, has been recommended to reduce hyperactivity in children sensitive to these substances. Well-controlled studies, however, have concluded that only a very small group of hyperactive preschool children appear to respond to food additives with deteriorations in learning, behavior, and eye-hand coordination. Most children show no improvement in attention or learning when on Feingold's diet, and behavioral improvements are only slightly better than what might be expected by chance. The research concludes that although a very small group of hyperactive preschoolers can be helped by eliminating food additives and salicylates from their diets, the favorable effects reported by parents for other children are probably due to heightened expectations, increased attention to the child, and better nutritional status.

*Allergies aggravate but do not cause learning disabilities.*

**Nonfood Allergies.** Despite case reports linking nonfood allergies to learning disabilities, well-designed studies have not found that more youngsters with LD suffer from allergies. Most experts conclude that allergies aggravate rather than cause learning disabilities. After all, it's hard to concentrate and do your best work when you are coughing, itching, sniffling, wheezing, didn't get a good night's sleep, and your ears are stuffed due to pollen, dust, or animal dander in the air. Ironically, the side effects of some allergy medicines may themselves complicate learning by making the child inattentive, dizzy, restless, lethargic, irritable, or hyperactive. Evidence supports the use of desensitization therapies to help students become sufficiently comfortable to attend to instruction, but the learning disability won't disappear as a result of the therapy.

## Poor Teaching

Poor teaching involves far more than an inappropriate match between the school's curriculum and the students' needs. It also involves the kind of expectations that the teacher communicates to students, the teacher's ability to deal with special needs in the classroom, his or her knowledge of normal child development, sensitivity to students' different learning and behavioral styles, and understanding that when English is the child's second language, conversational fluency doesn't equate to academic language proficiency. Moreover, when teachers do not personalize instruction to accommodate individual differences, the number of children identified as LD increases.

*Poor teaching not only aggravates existing learning problems, but it can also increase the number of children erroneously identified as LD.*

Poor teaching not only aggravates existing learning problems, but it can also increase the number of children erroneously identified as learning disabled. This can happen when some children fall behind because they haven't had the right learning opportunities. The discrepancy between their intellectual ability and achievement is really a pseudodiscrepancy that wouldn't have occurred if teaching had been personalized and effective. Researchers who are demonstrating that instruction helps establish and strengthen specific neural networks point out that poor instruction leaves a child without the necessary neural substrate to support academic progress.

The poor showing of our schoolchildren on the National Assessment of Educational Progress tests is an indictment of the overall quality of education in the United States. When 38 percent of fourth graders read below a "basic" comprehen-

## Mancele

*An adult with learning disabilities who was cheated of an education.*

My disability in reading, writing, and spelling affected me in two ways. first I had no confidents in myself and the second is the fear I had inside of me.

My fear was and still is so grete [great] that if someone asked me to read, spell, or write down directions, I would break out in a sweat. The fear was divercateing [devastating] to me. About school I don't remember my early years because I don't thing I was taught anything to remember anything about school. However, from the sixth or seven grade, I new I had a problem. I was tested and put into what was called an opportunity class, they call it.

They sed that it would be a special class to help me. Most of the "opportunity" class was made up of young black men. We had the "opportunity" of running movies all day for other classes in our school. This was our opportunity for learning. The classes were taught by one teacher. He was subpose to teach us in all subjects, math sceance [science] and Enlish, Histery, etc. The movies were fun to show, however the only thing I learned was showing movies. So my seventh and eighth grade Education was a lost, too. Most of our tests in class were motobowt [multiple] chosuis [choice]. I got good marks some B, too. I became putty [pretty] good in taking tests. Even on my spelling lists I got 75% or 80% carick [correct]. I could menerize [memorize] anything for a short time, but in two weeks after I forget it all. Because I menorize it. It did not matter what order it was in or giving it to me. I learn the sound of each word, then the letters. But didn't know the words themself. I graduated from High school knowing I could not read or spell afbulb [above] third grade. When I had to write a book reported, the pain in my head would come and I would pannick. I would pick out key words in some books I knew, and picked out key sentence, then put them together for my book report. "So now they say I have a learning disability. I say I wasn't taught."

*Source:* Reprinted by permission of Mancele W. Simmons Jr.

sion level, and only 23 percent score at or above a "proficient level" in writing, something is very wrong. The data are as grim for eighth and twelfth graders in this national assessment program, with 25 to 30 percent reading below grade level. Almost one-third of seniors lack a basic grasp of the structure and operations of American government. More than half of white twelfth graders can read a complicated text, but fewer than 20 to 25 percent of Hispanic and African American students can do so. In math, 1 in 10 white seniors, but only 1 in 30 Hispanic and 1 in 100 African American seniors can easily solve an elementary algebra problem. Only 28 percent of high school seniors find their schoolwork "often or always meaningful," and only 21 percent characterize their courses as "quite or very interesting." Only 39 percent of seniors feel that their school learning will be "quite or very important" in later life.

Given the large percentage of children who are functioning below grade level and unmotivated by the curriculum, many educators and politicians are focusing on the inadequacies of teachers' skills and the teaching environment, especially the resource inequities and lowered expectations in poorer schools. As a result, some researchers recommend that we eliminate the term "learning disabilities" in favor of *teaching disabilities.* Mancele's sad story illustrates the long-term intensive intervention needed by many individuals with LD, and the lost potential when appropriate intervention isn't available or offered.

***If students are to change, it is largely because teachers and parents have been willing to make changes in the curriculum, school, and home environments that promote learning.***

Clearly the problem and the solution is not in the child alone. If students are to change, it is largely because teachers and parents have been willing to make changes in the curriculum, school, and home environments that promote learning. Indeed, the story of learning disabilities is full of parents and teachers who refused to accept the status quo, believed in their children, and fought long and hard to fix the schools so their students would succeed.

## Summary

Students with LD enter the classroom with unique patterns of strengths and weaknesses. Some information-processing abilities important to academic achievement are well developed, whereas others are immature. In addition, these youngsters often have fairly stable styles in approaching learning tasks. Whether any of these students' uneven ability patterns and unique learning styles become liabilities depends on the nature of the school tasks they are expected to accomplish and the environments in which they study, live, and play.

***When the positive attributes of the youngster's unique learning and personality characteristics, the curriculum, and environments are combined, the effects of the learning disability can be moderated, and the chances for academic and behavioral progress are enhanced.***

Learning success is facilitated when the school curriculum is well matched to what students are ready to learn and to their learning styles. Maturational lag theorists note that the immaturities of students with LD make them unready for the work of their grade. Because they learn much like younger, normally developing children, teaching approaches and content that work at younger ages often can be employed. They warn that if we teach beyond these students' capabilities, then distorted learning results, leading to more severe deficits. Cognitive style theorists note that students' unique learning styles are advantageous to learning in some circumstances, but detrimental in others. A detail-oriented curriculum and discovery-oriented teaching methods are particularly mismatched with the cognitive styles and learning strategies of many students with LD, thereby aggravating their learning problems.

Besides appropriately matching the curriculum to students' learning needs, intervention is necessary to avoid learning delays associated with inadequate nutrition and stimulation, poverty, adverse emotional climate, environmental toxins, and poor teaching. In addition, it is very important for teachers to be sensitive to the multicultural and linguistic diversity in their classrooms, and to modify the curriculum to welcome these students, affirm their cultural backgrounds, and accommodate their academic needs.

Much of the responsibility for learning success falls on the home and school influences that affect the development and competence of the child. Consequently, when we explore the contributors to a student's learning problems, we must consider how specific curricular expectations and environmental factors are interacting with the youngster's unique learning and personality characteristics.

When the positive attributes of each are combined, the effects of the learning disability can be moderated, and the chances for academic and behavioral progress are enhanced.

## Helpful Resources

### Curriculum Contributors


Ames, L. B. (1968). Learning disabilities: The developmental point of view. In H. R. Myklebust (Ed.), *Progress in learning disabilities* (Vol. 1). New York: Grune & Stratton.

Carlton, M. P., & Winsler, A. (1999). School readiness: The need for a paradigm shift. *School Psychology Review, 28*, 338–352.

Cunningham, A. E., & Stanovich, K. E. (1997). Early reading acquisition and its relation to reading experience and ability 10 years later. *Developmental Psychology, 33*, 934–945.

Das, J. P., Kirby, J. R., & Jarman, R. F. (1979). *Simultaneous and successive cognitive processes.* Orlando, FL: Academic Press.

Denckla, M. B. (1979). Childhood learning disabilities. In K. M. Heilman & E. Valenstein (Eds.), *Clinical neuropsychology.* New York: Oxford University Press.

Francis, D. J., Shaywitz, S. E., Stuebing, K. K., Shaywitz, B. A., & Fletcher, J. M. (1996). Developmental lag versus deficit models of reading disability: A longitudinal, individual growth curves analysis. *Journal of Educational Psychology, 88*, 3–17.

Holmes, J. M. (1987). Natural histories in learning disabilities: Neuropsychological difference/environmental demand. In S. J. Ceci (Ed.), *Handbook of cognitive, social and neuropsychological aspects of learning disabilities* (Vol. 2). Hillsdale, NJ: Lawrence Erlbaum.

Hunt, D. E. (1974). Learning styles and teaching strategies. *High School Behavioral Science, 2*, 22–34.

Jimerson, S. R. (2001). Meta-analysis of grade retention research: Implications for practice in the 21st century. *School Psychology Review, 30*, 420–437.

Juel, C. (1988). Learning to read and write: A longitudinal study of 54 children from first through fourth grades. *Journal of Educational Psychology, 80*, 437–447.

Keogh, B. K. (1973). Perceptual and cognitive styles: Implications for special education. In L. Mann & D. A. Sabatino (Eds.), *The first review of special education.* Philadelphia: JSE Press.

Kinsbourne, M., & Caplan, P. (1979). *Children's learning and attention problems.* Boston, MA: Little, Brown.

Korhonen, T. T. (1995). The persistence of rapid naming problems in children with reading disabilities: A nine year follow-up. *Journal of Learning Disabilities, 28*, 232–239.

LaBuda, M. C., & DeFries, J. C. (1988). Cognitive abilities in children with reading disabilities and controls: A follow-up study. *Journal of Learning Disabilities, 21*, 562–566.

Maier, A. S. (1980). The effect of focusing on the cognitive processes of learning disabled children. *Journal of Learning Disabilities, 13*, 143–147.

McKinney, J. D., Osborne, S. S., & Schulte, A. C. (1993). Academic consequences of learning disability: Longitudinal prediction of outcomes at 11 years of age. *Learning Disabilities Research & Practice, 8*, 19–27.

Medway, F. J., & Rose, J. S. (1986). Grade retention. In T. R. Kratochwill (Ed.), *Advances in school psychology* (Vol. 5), pp. 141–175. Hillsdale, NJ: Lawrence Erlbaum.

Roth, M., McCaul, E., & Barnes, K. (1993). Who becomes an "at-risk" student? The predictive value of a kindergarten screening battery. *Exceptional Children, 59*, 348–358.

Shaywitz, S. E., Fletcher, J. M., Holahan, J. M., Shneider, A. E., Marchione, K. E., Stuebing, K. K., Francis, D. J., Pugh, K. R., & Shaywitz, B. A. (1999). Persistence of dyslexia: The Connecticut Longitudinal Study at adolescence. *Pediatrics, 104*, 1351–1359.

Shinn, M. R., Ysseldyke, J. E., Deno, S. L., & Tindal, G. A. (1986). A comparison of differences between students labeled learning disabled and low achieving on measures of classroom performance. *Journal of Learning Disabilities, 19*, 545–552.

Stone, A., & Michals, D. (1986). Problem-solving skills in learning disabled children. In S. J. Ceci (Ed.), *Handbook of cognitive, social, and neuropsychological aspects of learning disabilities* (Vol. 1). Hillsdale, NJ: Lawrence Erlbaum.

Torgesen, J. K. (1977). Memorization processes in reading-disabled children. *Journal of Educational Psychology, 69*, 571–578.

Weintraub, S., & Mesulam, M. M. (1983). Developmental learning disabilities of the right hemisphere: Emotional, interpersonal, and cognitive components. *Archives of Neurology, 40*, 463–468.

Wolf, M., & Obregón, M. (1992). Early naming deficits, developmental dyslexia, and a specific deficit hypothesis. *Brain and Language, 42,* 219–247.

Zentall, S. S., & Gohs, D. E. (1984). Hyperactive and comparison children's response to detailed vs. global cues in communication tasks. *Learning Disability Quarterly, 7,* 77–87.

National Center for Education Statistics dropout rates in the U.S.: http://www.nces.ed.gov/pubs2001/dropout

## Family and Environment Contributors

Adler, N. E., Boyce, T., Chesney, M. A., Cohen, S., Folkman, S., Kahn, R. L., & Syme, S. L. (1994). Socioeconomic status and health: The challenge of the gradient. *American Psychologist, 49,* 15–24.

Bender, B. G. (1999). Learning disorders associated with asthma and allergies. *School Psychology Review, 28,* 204–214.

Bigsby, R., Chapin, R. E., Daston, G. P., Davis, B. J., Gorski, J., Gray, L. E., Howdeshell, K. L., Zoeller, R. T., & Vom Saal, F. S. (1999). Evaluating the effects of endocrine disruptors on endocrine function during development. *Environmental Health Perspectives, 107 (Suppl. 4),* 613–618.

Brucker-Davis, F. (1998). Effects of environmental synthetic chemicals on thyroid function. *Thyroid 8(9),* 827–856.

Ceci, S. J. (1991). How much does schooling influence general intelligence and its cognitive components? A reassessment of the evidence. *Developmental Psychology, 27,* 703–722.

Chasnoff, I. J., Griffith, D. R., MacGregor, S., Dirkes, K., & Burnes, K. A. (1989). Temporal patterns of cocaine use in pregnancy. *Journal of the American Medical Association, 261,* 1741–1744.

Collier, C., & Hoover, J. J. (1987). Sociocultural considerations when referring minority children for learning disabilities. *Learning Disabilities Focus, 3,* 39–45.

Cravioto, J. (1972). Nutrition and learning in children. In N. S. Springer (Ed.), *Nutrition and mental retardation.* Ann Arbor, MI: Institute for the Study of Mental Retardation and Related Disabilities.

Delgado-Gaitan, C., & Trueba, H. T. (1985). Ethnographic study of participant structures in task completion: Reinterpretation of "handicaps" in Mexican children. *Learning Disability Quarterly, 8,* 67–75.

Dennis, W. (1960). Causes of retardation among institutional children: Iran. *Journal of Genetic Psychology, 96,* 47–59.

Feingold, B. F. (1976). Hyperkinesis and learning disabilities linked to the ingestion of artificial food colors and flavors. *Journal of Learning Disabilities, 9,* 551–559.

Langdon, H. W. (1992). *Hispanic children and adults with communication disorders: Assessment and intervention.* Gaithersburg, MD: Aspen.

Lewis, M., Worobey, J., Ramsay, D. S., & McCormak, M. K. (1992). Prenatal exposure to heavy metals: Effect on childhood cognitive skills and health status. *Pediatrics, 89,* 1010–1015.

McLoughlin, J. A., Nall, M., & Petrosko, J. (1985). Allergies and learning disabilities. *Learning Disability Quarterly, 8,* 255–260.

McLoyd, V. (1998). Socioeconomic disadvantage and child development. *American Psychologist, 53,* 185–204.

Nichols, P., & Chen, T. (1981). *Minimal brain dysfunction: A prospective study.* Hillsdale, NJ: Lawrence Erlbaum.

Nieto, S. (1992). *Affirming diversity: The sociopolitical context of multicultural education.* New York: Longman.

Osofsky, J. D. (1995). The effects of exposure to violence on young children. *American Psychologist, 50,* 782–788.

Phelps, L. (1995). Psychoeducational outcomes of fetal alcohol syndrome. *School Psychology Review, 24,* 200–212.

Phelps, L. (1999). Low-level lead exposure: Implications for research and practice. *School Psychology Review, 3,* 477–492.

Phelps, L., & Cox, D. (1993). Children with perinatal cocaine exposure: Resilient or handicapped? *School Psychology Review, 22,* 710–724.

Pocock, S. J., Smith, M., & Baghurst, P. (1994). Environmental lead and children's intelligence: A systematic review of the epidemiological evidence. *British Medical Journal, 309,* 1189–1197.

Pollitt, E., Gorman, K. S., Engle, P. L., Martorell, R., & Rivera, J. (1993). Early supplementary feeding and cognition: Effects over two decades. *Monographs of the Society for Research in Child Development, 58* (serial No. 235).

Porterfield, S. P., & Hendry, L. B. (1998). Impact of PCBs on thyroid hormone directed brain development. *Toxicology and Industrial Health, 14,* (Nos. 1&2), 103–120.

Rodier, P. M. (1984). Exogenous sources of malformations in development: CNS malformations and developmental repair processes. In E. S. Gollin (Ed.), *Malformations of development.* New York: Academic Press.

Rosenstock, L., Keifer, M., Daniell, W. E., McConnell, R., Claypoole, K., & The Pesticide Health Effects Study Group. (1991). Chronic central nervous system effects of acute organophosphate pesticide intoxication. *Lancet, 338,* 223–227.

Salovey, P., Rothman, A. J., Detweiler, J. B., & Steward, W. T. (2000). Emotional states and physical health. *American Psychologist, 55,* 110–121.

Schettler, T., Solomon, G., Valenti, M., & Huddle, A. (2000). *Generations at risk: Reproductive health and the environment.* Cambridge, MA: MIT Press.

Sonderegger, T. B. (Ed). (1992). *Perinatal substance abuse: Research findings and clinical implications.* Baltimore: Johns Hopkins University Press.

Spitz, R. A. (1945). Hospitalism: An inquiry into the genesis of psychiatric conditions in early childhood. *Psychoanalytic Study of the Child, 1,* 53–74.

Weiss, B., Williams, J. H., Margen, S., et al. (1980). Behavioral responses to artificial food colors. *Science, 207,* 1487.

Werner, E. E. (1989, April). Children of the Garden Island. *Scientific American, 260,* 106–111.

Yasutake, D., & Bryan, T. (1995). The influence of induced positive affect on middle school children with and without learning disabilities. *Learning Disabilities Research & Practice, 10,* 38–45.

Children's Defense Fund Poverty figures: http://www.childrensdefense.org

National Assessment of Education Progress: http://www.nceds.ed.gov/nationsreportcard

National Center for Education statistics: http://www.nces.ed.gov

CHAPTER FIVE

# Information-Processing Patterns in Learning Disabilities

**THIS CHAPTER ANSWERS** the question "When a physiological, curricular, or environmental factor contributes to a learning disability, what exactly has happened?" We know that any of these factors can make it difficult for some students to cope with a school's curriculum. We also know that problems arise when the curriculum isn't adapted to exactly what a student is ready to learn, and to his or her particular learning style. But why is this so?

The answer is that learning is a challenge for students with learning disabilities because one or more of their information-processing abilities are underdeveloped and immature. Their ability to process information is inadequate for the task of attending to, making meaning of, storing, and applying the knowledge taught in school.

By definition, students who are learning disabled have trouble remembering information that average learners can easily retain. In this chapter, we explore the ways in which information-processing weaknesses contribute to these memory difficulties. The information-processing patterns of students with LD interact with their cognitive abilities, learning styles, current knowledge, social skills, and motivation, to determine exactly what they will pay attention to, learn, and remember.

There are four information-processing abilities that affect learning and memory: (1) visual-perceptual skills, (2) language and phonological processing skills, (3) attention, and (4) motor skills. Visual-perceptual processes are important to reading and math achievement at young ages, and they play a subtle role later on in some aspects of spelling and writing, and math, conceptual, and social reasoning. Motor difficulties make expression, particularly through writing, problematic. Ultimately, however, language weaknesses, phonological processing difficulties, and attention deficits play the greatest role in the most severe, long-lasting learning problems.

*Visual-perceptual processes are important to reading and math achievement at young ages, and motor difficulties make expression problematic.*

*Language weaknesses, phonological-processing difficulties, and attention deficits play the greatest role in the most severe, long-lasting learning problems.*

## Visual-Perceptual Skills

Despite the popular belief 50 years ago that the eye itself is to blame for reading disorders, there is no difference between the peripheral visual functions of good and poor readers. Poor vision and uncoordinated eye movements don't seem to be at the root of children's reading disorders. Children with visual impairments scan visual material with the same efficiency as do children with no visual problems.

It is not eye functioning, but the ability to process visual information at a perceptual and cognitive level that's important to reading. The skill of reading requires us to mentally translate the visual symbols we see into language. It is the translation process that is difficult for children with weaknesses in this area. Indeed, poor readers have just as much trouble with Braille and Morse code, which translates nonvisual symbol systems into language, as they do with reading.

*It is not eye functioning, but the ability to process visual information at a perceptual and cognitive level that is important to reading.*

When we read, our eyes proceed through a succession of pauses (fixations), each followed by a smooth, fast jump (saccade). The eyes fixate between 87 to 95 percent of the time. Good as well as poor readers who encounter unfamiliar or difficult material either slow down to take time for analysis or make their eyes regress to reread a word or phrase. Because the tasks of decoding and comprehending are so much more difficult for students with reading disabilities, they need more fixations, longer fixations, and more regressions than better readers. The complexity of dealing with written words and their meaning causes these irregular eye movements; irregular eye movements do not cause reading disabilities. In fact, when visual tasks are not taxing, such as scanning pictures or reading very easy material, the eye movements of poor readers are quite normal.

Although peripheral-visual problems, such as farsightedness, can aggravate reading disorders by causing discomfort, fatigue, and confusion, studies have concluded that training only these visual functions does not improve reading skills. Visual training can help with wandering eyes and focusing, making it more comfortable for children to look at print, but only reading remediation can teach the skills necessary for reading.

Instead of peripheral-visual functions, we should be focusing on visual perception, the brain's ability to take in visual information, interpret what is seen, organize the information, and store and transmit it. All of these processes happen in a matter of milliseconds for the majority of readers.

Visual-perceptual difficulties are most likely to cause problems in kindergarten and first grade. For some individuals, though, these problems persist in a

*Visual-perceptual difficulties are most likely to cause problems in kindergarten and first grade. For some individuals these problems persist in a mild to moderate form into adulthood.*

mild to moderate form into adulthood, as Joseph's story illustrates. Joseph, and others like him, have inefficient visual processing that is related to difficulty in focusing on words as wholes (they sound them out) or to slower pickup of information from visual images. Thus these individuals have less information, or more confusing information, to store in memory. Just as you might have difficulty finding the correct image in Figure 5.1, as adults people like Joseph continue to have trouble recognizing words at a glance, remembering common English spelling patterns, or remembering how to spell irregular words that can't be sounded out. Related math and social reasoning difficulties are also common.

Figure 5.2 on page 130 lists some of the visual-perceptual weaknesses commonly associated with reading problems. Because many of these abilities also in-

## Joseph

*A law student whose learning progress has been slowed by visual-perceptual weaknesses.*

Despite his subtle visual-perceptual difficulties, Joseph graduated from college and earned a master's degree in political science. Now, at age 23, he is applying to law school.

Joseph's accomplishments did not come easily. They required determination and hard work. He had to drop some advanced math and business statistics courses because he could not envision how two-dimensional circles became three-dimensional, how planes intersected, and how graphs were constructed. He could not perceive where certain numbers fell along a continuum, as in estimating the height of an average woman or the temperature at which water would feel hot. Because Joseph cannot conjure up mental images, his spelling of phonetically irregular words has remained poor. Although a slow reader, Joseph learned to read at a satisfactory level because he could analyze the words' sounds, and he could use his good language comprehension to detect reading errors that made no sense.

Joseph generally overanalyzes and must force himself to attend to the overall concepts being conveyed. Typically, he will memorize all the details in an assignment, understand the ideas to which they relate, yet be unable to list the main ideas in an organized fashion. For example, if Joseph is shown two circles (one red, one blue) that transformed into two squares (one black, one green) and asked how the two sets differ, he will say the red circle turned into a black square and the blue circle turned into a green square. When asked for the overall principle that transformed one set into another, Joseph will repeat his analysis of the details. However, when then given a choice of categorical concepts (color, size, number, or shape), he will immediately recognize "shape" as the correct concept. It is typical for Joseph to know the answer all along, yet the big picture is not automatically prominent in his awareness.

Because he has excellent language abilities, Joseph did make it through law school, but he had to work hard to overcome his detail-bound style. He needed the help of an advanced student in each course to guide him in looking at the big picture. "Canned briefs" were very helpful in alerting him to what is important and what is irrelevant. Joseph also dictated his examinations to compensate for his spelling difficulties, and he requested extra time to fulfill required reading assignments.

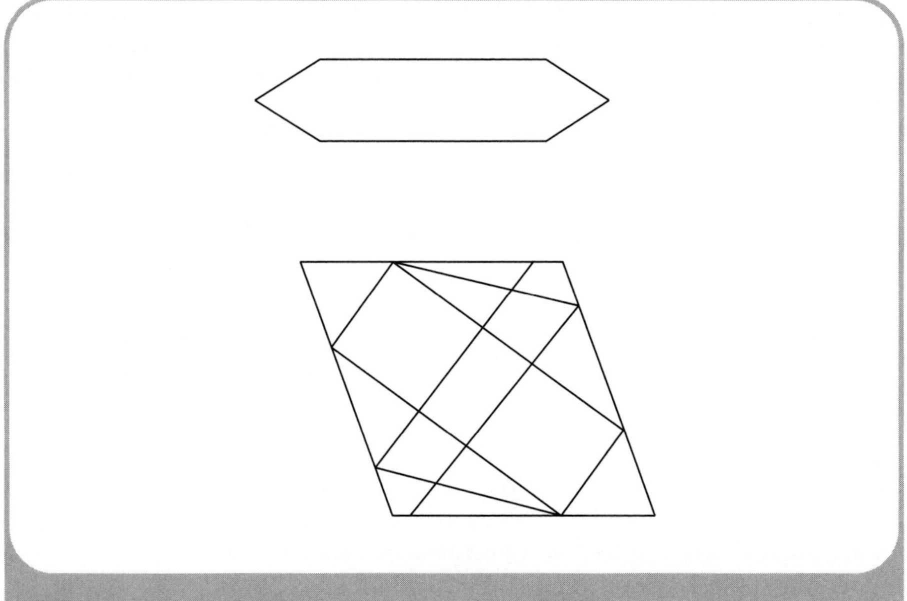

**Figure 5.1** Simulation of a visual-perceptual weakness. Instructions: Find the design on the top within the drawing below. Children with visual-perceptual difficulties are likely to have difficulty on this task, as well as on analogous tasks such as locating words in a dictionary and skimming reading material for specific information.

*Source:* Unknown.

volve language, motor, attention, and memory skills, many weaknesses that appear at first glance to be visual-perceptual in origin may actually be problems with these other skills.

## Visual Perception and Reading

As previously mentioned, visual-perceptual ability correlates highly with reading achievement in kindergarten and first grade. By second and third grades, however, the visual-perceptual role in reading is greatly overshadowed by the need for efficient language and phonological-processing abilities. Language and phonological-processing abilities are far more highly related to reading success because higher-level reading relies more on the comprehension of a language system and matching sounds to letters than on the visual analysis of the symbols themselves. Witness the fact that blind people read and comprehend, even though they can't see the print.

Therefore, visual-perceptual weaknesses are not major contributors to the most persistent, severe reading disabilities. Nevertheless, a few very subtle visual processing differences do distinguish some poor readers from good readers.

**Visual-Perceptual Weaknesses**

- Slow to discriminate shapes, as in trying to put a circle into a square hole (*visual discrimination* problem)
- Confuses left and right
- Poor spatial judgment, as in discriminating bigger from smaller objects or the right screw to fit into a hole
- Difficulty estimating time, being on time
- Poor sense of direction (takes forever to learn one's way around a new place; gets lost in a new house)
- Difficulty judging speed and distance (as in athletic activities, driving a car)
- Poor visual imagery; can't perceive the end product in puzzles and mazes, or becomes confused with computer game graphics
- Difficulty conceptualizing higher-level math concepts
- Trouble interpreting maps, graphs, charts, and diagrams
- Trouble perceiving the body language and subtleties in social communication; doesn't pick up on others' moods and feelings
- Trouble getting the main idea or focusing on the whole; focuses on details instead
- A busy background interferes with focusing on the most important stimulus, as in busy worksheets or spotting one's friend in a crowd (*figure-ground* problem)
- Trouble finding embedded figures, as in a word search or spotting a keyword in a paragraph
- Poor visual memory for shapes and sequences of objects, letters, and numbers
- Trouble choosing a missing piece to complete a figure or design (as in a puzzle) or spotting a critical element in a story
- Trouble perceiving which pieces fit together to make a whole, as in a model or developing a story line
- Often loses things, cannot spot objects "in plain sight"
- Difficulty spotting errors in one's own work
- Difficulty planning and organizing one's day or work
- Difficulty perceiving strategies for success in games

**Motor Functions That Can Be Affected by Visual-Perceptual Weaknesses**

- Delays in learning to copy designs and letters; many inaccuracies
- Slow and poorly executed handwriting; dislikes and avoids writing
- Papers are messy and incomplete; many cross-outs and erasures
- Difficulty remembering shapes of letters and numbers, and which way they face when writing (reversals and rotations)
- Uneven spacing between letters and words
- Plans space poorly when drawing, doing projects, copying
- Omits letters from words and words from sentences when writing or copying
- Poor spelling because can't remember how words should look (spells phonetically)
- Poor alignment of math problems results in computation errors
- Poor drawing of human figures
- Poor manual skills and sloppy work
- Clumsy gait and body movements (bumps into furniture and doorways)
- Slow reaction time (as in slowness reacting to a traffic signal change or yelling "bingo")
- Poor balance due to spatial judgment problems
- Awkward finer-motor movements, as in typing
- Performance IQ lower than Verbal IQ

**Figure 5.2** Visual-perceptual weaknesses associated with academic delays.

**Language Functions That Can Be Affected by Visual-Perceptual Weaknesses**

- Misreads similar-looking letters and words (*b* and *d, m* and *w, bread* and *beard*)
- Reversal of letter sequences in reading and spelling (*was* and *saw; on* and *no*)
- Difficulty recognizing and remembering sight words, but can sound out words phonetically
- Loses place when reading
- Has trouble finding letters in words or words in sentences
- Poor memory for printed words, number sequences, diagrams, maps, illustrations
- Poor comprehension of main ideas and themes
- Confuses "right" and "left"
- Difficulty memorizing math facts, formulas, equations
- Trouble "getting to the point" (becomes bogged down in details; can describe portico of a building but not the building's overall style and shape)

**Figure 5.2** *Continued*

These weaknesses present long-term mild to moderate obstacles to learning and adjustment.

Research suggests that weaknesses in right hemisphere visual-perceptual strategies may result in poor recognition of words at a glance, poor memory for typical spelling patterns, difficulty remembering irregular spellings, and poor comprehension of main ideas. Slow visual information processing may also cause problems remembering what has been seen.

*Weaknesses in right hemisphere visual-perceptual strategies may result in poor recognition of words at a glance, poor memory for typical spelling patterns, difficulty remembering irregular spellings, and poor comprehension of main ideas.*

**Right Hemisphere Strategy Weaknesses.** The right hemisphere of the brain appears to specialize in functions involving perception of visual forms and the overall arrangement of these forms in their allotted space *(visuospatial functions)*. The left hemisphere usually specializes in language skills and the analysis and sequencing of details. You can remember this by keeping in mind the axiom that artists, who specialize in helping us see things in a special way, are "right-brained" and that professors, who help us examine every nuance that makes up the whole, are "left-brained." Research suggests that we learn to read by first using the artist's visual-perceptual strengths, but later switch to using more of the professor's analytical and language talents.

The right hemisphere does best with novel and complex visual information. This, together with its visuospatial talents, is why it comes into play as a child begins to understand that letters are important. He or she pays attention first to the letters themselves, their shapes and directions. With practice, the letters and words are no longer new to the child, so perceptual analysis is less necessary and the right hemisphere becomes less important in processing. Now the child begins to analyze words phonetically and to comprehend sentence meanings, so the left hemisphere takes on a greater role in reading. Although the brain's right and left hemispheres contribute with different activation levels to the reading process at

*The brain's right and left hemispheres contribute with different activation levels to the reading process at different ages, but efficient reading depends on both hemispheres interacting during the reading process.*

different ages, efficient reading depends on both hemispheres interacting dynamically during the reading process.

The initial visual reliance on attributes such as colors, logos, and the global shapes of words explains why Deneva can recognize her own name in print at the age of 3 and why she can zero in on words like McDonald's and Coca-Cola with astonishing speed from the back seat of the car. This ability develops long before children know their letter sounds, can sound out letters in words, or blend them together.

Unfortunately, some children never develop a strong visual-perceptual strategy in beginning reading. They underuse right hemisphere strategies, preferring to approach reading in an overanalytical, language-based manner. Because they don't develop the ability to quickly scan words as a whole, they painstakingly sound out each word or try to guess the word from its context in the sentence.

With their left hemisphere analytical-linguistic strengths, these children can sound out and spell words that sound exactly as they look (e.g., *park*). Their language skills also help them to manage high-level comprehension. However, their ability to recognize words at a glance is compromised, and they have lifelong trouble remembering typical spelling patterns (e.g., which words end in *le* vs. *el*) and in spelling words that can't be sounded out (e.g., *knight* or *precious*). All these spelling words need to be remembered as a mental image or by analogy to known words having the same spelling patterns. These individuals also have trouble coming up with the main idea of a paragraph or story because they can't focus on and grasp the big picture.

*Slow visual information processing interferes with remembering what has been seen.*

**Slow Visual Information Processing.** Some individuals' difficulty with recognizing words on sight or calling visual images to mind (as in irregular spellings) is due to picking up and transmitting visual information at a much slower rate than is typical. Their brains need a longer time without any interference from a new stimulus to interpret what they have seen—often one-tenth of a second more than the typical child. Several studies have shown that these children's first image is still being processed when a new image intrudes and overlaps with it; the result is total confusion.

Imagine the beginning reader whose zealous teacher points to the first letter in a word, then the second letter, the third, and so forth. If the child needs more time to process than the teacher allows, images can overlap. For example, when a *c* is followed by an *l*, the child may see a *d* instead.

Visual information processing, from attending to an image to storing it away in memory, occurs extremely rapidly in the average student. Apparently, visual information can persist as an image in our minds for at best one-third to one-half of a second. During this time, we code what we just saw and transmit it to short-term storage. This short-term storage can last for only a few seconds longer. If we don't figure out some way to remember what we have seen (naming the letter or word, for example, or conjuring up its image again, thinking of a rhyme, using an association trick), then we won't remember it.

*The faster information can be processed, the more time will remain for comprehension, interpretation, and storage.*

Thus the person who processes visual information slowly is at a real disadvantage. The faster information can be processed, the more time will be left over for comprehension, interpretation, and storage. This also is why slow visual information processors have trouble learning common letter sequences in reading and spelling; if it takes too long to register the first letter, it will have dissipated from memory by the time the second letter is registered, making it difficult to learn the two as a team (e.g., *br* or *ing*).

## Visual Perception and Mathematics

*Visual-perceptual skills contribute to math achievement, but good language skills are critical to handling the verbal reasoning of more complex mathematical problem solving.*

As with reading, visual-perceptual abilities do play a role in math achievement, but good language skills are critical to handling the verbal reasoning of more complex mathematical problem solving. Children whose math deficits persist into adolescence and adulthood, despite having adequate language, reading, and spelling skills, often have right hemisphere weaknesses. These right hemisphere weaknesses with global reasoning are accompanied by such nonverbal learning problems as perceptual and coordination weaknesses, social imperceptiveness (they don't get the subtleties of what's going on), and difficulty reasoning about the big picture.

Young children will do well in arithmetic if they are skilled at visual discrimination (noting differences between figures), visuospatial organization, visual-motor coordination, and memory for visual sequences. For example, when Jake, who is a kindergartner, counts ten blocks, he helps himself by spacing them in an orderly fashion. To leave them scattered randomly on the table might mean he'll count the same block twice or skip one altogether. Jake must also coordinate his visual-motor movements by touching and counting only one block at a time. Later on, he'll have to know how to align columns of numbers, in which direction to add or borrow, and pay attention to visual details such as plus or minus signs and decimal points.

The ability to mentally manipulate spatial relationships is also important to math success. Jasmine, a third grader, can "push together" 3 and 2 dots in her mind or 4 and 1 oranges because she recognizes "fiveness" in all its visual combinations. She can easily in her mind link 4 more oranges to the 5 already pictured. This type of reasoning helps her judge whether the size of an answer "seems" right.

Despite the connection of visual-perceptual skills to early math reasoning, studies show that in the long run only 10 percent of the skills assessed on visual-perceptual tasks appear to be related to arithmetic achievement. As in reading, strong verbal abilities are even more essential to math success. Try solving the third math problem in Figure 5.3 on page 134, and you'll see that visual-perception skills take you only so far. You can't solve the problem without talking it through. When dealing with such concepts as money, time, and measurement, language skills are critical to analyzing the problem, sequencing thoughts, and reasoning.

Given the strong role of language in most learning, experts agree that the student with visual-perceptual deficits but strong language abilities generally has a good chance of making up his or her deficits. Nevertheless, when visual-perceptual deficits are severe, mathematical and other more subtle weaknesses are likely to linger (such as problems with irregular spellings, letter formation, social imperceptiveness, catching the gist of conversations or the author's arguments).

*The student with visual-perceptual deficits but strong language abilities generally has a good chance of making up his or her deficits.*

**Figure 5.3** Simulation of a math problem. Requiring a good deal of "self-talk" to solve, this problem illustrates the critical involvement of language skills in mathematics.

## Language and Phonological Processing Skills

*The majority of people with reading disorders have problems processing, storing, retrieving, or expressing language and phonological information.*

*The poorer one's language skills, the more severe a learning disability is likely to be.*

The majority of people with reading disorders have problems processing, storing, retrieving, or expressing language and *phonological* (the order of sounds in words) information. Many were slow to speak as very young children, and their reading delays became evident soon after their language finally began to improve. Even when they eventually become proficient readers, these children's continuing language weaknesses often interfere with their reading comprehension and written expression. Later on in their schooling, they may face trouble with poetry and foreign languages. And the poorer one's language skills, the more severe a learning disability is likely to be. Conversely, the higher these children's verbal skills, the faster their progress in reading tends to be.

Many children with learning disabilities have multiple language weaknesses like those of Peter. Many of the language weaknesses associated with learning difficulties are listed in Figure 5.4 on page 136. Unlike the diminishing relationship between visual-perceptual weaknesses and reading as children get older, the negative impact of language and phonological delays persists throughout the school years and beyond. The language-related delays that contribute most directly to reading disorders are left hemisphere strategy weaknesses, immature phonological awareness, poor phonological and verbal coding in working memory, difficulty retrieving phonological and verbal codes, and linguistic weaknesses.

### Left Hemisphere Strategy Weaknesses

In the normal process of development, the left hemisphere of the brain for most individuals becomes more specialized for language processing than does the

## Peter

*A second grader with severe learning disabilities due to phonological processing, language, and word-finding weaknesses.*

Peter is now in second grade and has had a terrible time learning to read. He is a cute fellow and is well liked by his peers. On the playground, or in physical education and art classes, he's as much a member of the in-group as anyone else. But in music class, reading group, and class discussion he is on the periphery. Peter has a terrible time in music class because he can't say the words in a song fast enough to keep up with the beat. It is not uncommon for the group to pause at the completion of a phrase of music and for all heads to suddenly turn. Giggles are heard as Peter trails the rest with the final phrase.

In his reading group, Peter takes so long to think of which sound goes with which letter in a word that he's forgotten the beginning sounds by the time he gets to the end of the word. Often the word he comes up with is utter nonsense. He can't even guess at words well because he doesn't understand the grammatical structure of the sentences and word meanings well enough to guess correctly. In class discussions Peter raises his hand eagerly when he knows the answer. But when he is called on, the light fades from his eyes as he struggles to pull the right words out of his head. He finally gives up as his classmates echo "call on me, I know."

Peter has severe deficits in several aspects of language: awareness of the phonological segments that make up words, learning phonetic rules, learning meanings of words, and being able to quickly retrieve sounds and words from memory. Because all these abilities are involved in reading, he has significant reading difficulties.

corresponding area of the right hemisphere. Some children with learning disabilities follow this pattern, but many others do not. Instead, they may have no language-dominance differences between hemispheres, have right hemisphere preferences, or process one type of material (e.g., digits) with one hemisphere and another type (e.g., words) with the other.

Typically, the reading process in children is believed to involve a shift from right to left hemisphere processing preferences, which seems to happen around the second or third grade. Instead of concentrating on the visual configurations of words, children now sound out words or predict them from the grammar and context of the passage.

In the previous section on visual-perceptual skills, we described children with learning disabilities who seem not to have mastered the right hemisphere phase, and therefore apply an overly left hemisphere style to reading. In this section we discuss the opposite scenario, the child who prefers right hemisphere strategies in reading and does not shift preference to the left hemisphere's more analytical language-processing mode. Reading is severely delayed for this type of student because the right hemisphere's holistic information-processing style is not well suited to the higher-level, analytical language demands of more complex reading and comprehension.

**Language Comprehension and Production**

- Delayed rate of early language development; trouble naming objects or people
- Weak auditory memory (recalling digits, words, or sentences)
- Poor memory for idea units in a dictated story
- Difficulty with auditory closure (combining sound fragments into whole words)
- Poor verbal-coding ability (translating nonverbal events into words to aid recall)
- Poor auditory discrimination of sounds and words; confuses words with similar sounds (*frustrate* for *fluctuate;* produces hybrids such as *flustrate*)
- Difficulty identifying words masked by background noise (*auditory figure-ground* problem)
- Poor story retelling: includes fewer words and ideas, events, grammatically complex sentences, descriptions of internal (seeing, feeling) responses, gerunds and participles; less use of pronouns and conjunctions to make stories cohesive; less mature plot elements (major character, motivating conflict, appropriate sequence); uses pronouns for which referents haven't been specified
- Less mature verbal associations (such as responding *red* goes with *bird* vs. *red* goes with *blue*)
- Trouble understanding ambiguous sentences, proverbs, jokes
- Poor ability to differentiate statements of information from questions
- Poor comprehension of long, complex sentences, semantics, and sentence structures
- Small speaking vocabulary (uses vague and imprecise language); uses simple sentence types and immature linguistic patterns
- Speech is slow or halting; uses verbal "stalling" mechanisms (*uh, um, you know*)
- Poor knowledge of grammatical rules
- Weak ability to define words, provide verbal opposites, formulate sentences and converse (conveying directions, elaborate), give logical reasons for common events, classify and compare
- Poor sequencing of verbal information, as in telling a story from beginning to end
- Poor understanding of the verbal categories of space and time
- Poor comprehension and learning of puns, synonyms, homonyms
- Cluttered and disorganized speech; poor sentence formation
- Inefficient use of prosodic cues (stress, pitch, pauses) to aid comprehension
- Minor articulation difficulties
- Weak comprehension of rapidly spoken language
- Doesn't modulate tone of voice appropriately; speaks in monotone, or too loud
- Lower Verbal IQ than Performance IQ

**Reading Readiness**

- Mispronounces words (such as *aluminum, specific*) and phonologically complex phrases (*the brown and blue plaid pants*)
- Can't rapidly name pictured objects, colors, shapes, letters, numerals, or events (as in *birthday party*)
- Wrong labels given for common objects, people, letters, numerals
- Insensitive to rhymes and alliterations
- Doesn't understand Pig Latin game
- Poor analysis of the order of sounds in words: identifying which words have a common sound at the beginning, end, or in the middle
- Trouble segmenting words into syllables and sounds
- Trouble deleting and substituting sounds in words
- Trouble blending sounds in words
- Poor listening comprehension

**Figure 5.4** Language weaknesses associated with academic delays.

- Uses hand gestures and body language to help convey messages
- Does not understand or remember instructions

**Reading Decoding**

- Problem associating letters with sounds
- Makes sound-sequencing errors, as in reading *snug* for *sung*
- Sound-sequencing problems cause word analysis problems in reading
- Slow reading (due to slow sound retrieval and sequencing)
- Oral reading deteriorates within a few sentences (due to declining ability to retrieve sounds from memory)
- Poor comprehension of what has been read due to language comprehension weaknesses

**Writing**

- Spelling can be bizarre (not phonetic)
- Short and incomplete written assignments; brief sentences and limited vocabulary
- Poorly organized ideas in written assignments; not logically presented
- Little theme development; writes bare lists of facts or events rather than developing ideas, characters, or plot

**Math**

- Slow on math fact drills due to retrieval problems (*word-finding* problem)
- Difficulty with word problems due to poor language comprehension
- Problems with higher-level math due to difficulties with analysis and logical reasoning

**Figure 5.4** *Continued*

Young children who underuse the left hemisphere and overuse right hemisphere information-processing styles tend to be more severely reading disabled than those who do the opposite. They try to read by fixating on the visual configuration of words, rather than on their sound patterns. Their phonetic analysis is a slow, laborious process moving along syllable by syllable. Their spelling is very unorthodox and often results in completely incomprehensible words because the wrong sounds are inserted, some sounds are omitted, and letter order is confused. Jimmy's spelling and that of adults with LD on pages 168 and 203 (Figures 6.6 and 6.17) are good illustrations of the severity of this problem. Because of their language weaknesses, these children also have trouble getting past the main idea in their comprehension and writing; details are ignored and ideas aren't developed in a logical order.

***Young children who underuse the left hemisphere and overuse right hemisphere information-processing styles tend to be more severely reading disabled than those who do the opposite.***

## Phonological Awareness

Data from numerous studies show that the ability to analyze, sequence, and remember sounds in words is second only to intelligence in contributing to reading achievement. The more proficient a student is in *phonological awareness*—the ability to segment words into their individual sounds—the better he or she is likely to read, and the faster the reading progress.

***The ability to analyze, sequence, and remember sounds in words is second only to intelligence in contributing to reading achievement.***

Many students with learning disabilities are far less aware of the sound structure of spoken language than are typical students. It's not that they can't discriminate the sounds of letters from one another—a *b* versus an *f*, for example. If they couldn't do that they'd be unable to speak understandably. Rather, they run into trouble when they have to discriminate at a finer perceptual and cognitive level, such as breaking apart the order of individual sounds in words. For example, if you asked a child with weaknesses in this area the question, "What sound do you hear at the beginning of the word *mail*?" he or she would have trouble picking out the *mmm* sound.

***Children with LD often have difficulty breaking down sentences into words, words into syllables, and syllables into their individual sounds.***

Children with learning disabilities often have difficulty breaking down sentences into words, words into syllables, and syllables into their individual sounds. One study found that these children even had difficulty repeating unfamiliar words—for example, *kerpinnular*—that require a good deal of phonemic processing to perceive correctly; younger children who read at the same level had no problem with this task. Getting the order of sounds confused in words is evident in the speech of those with learning disabilities even as adults. Another study found that poor readers had difficulty figuring out which word in a series didn't belong—*weed, peel, need, and deed,* for example. Children four years younger who read at an equivalent level could do this easily. Yet another study found that elementary school children with LD had much more trouble than good readers telling whether words rhymed. Children with LD were also much slower than non-LD children in indicating whether the "names" of two letters that were shown to them were the same (for example, *A* and *a*). Interestingly, both groups performed equally well in indicating whether two letters, numbers, or geometric figures *looked* alike. Hundreds of such studies highlight phonological awareness weaknesses as the basis of many children's learning disabilities.

The ability of older preschoolers and kindergartners to group words based on rhyme or a shared initial sound is highly related to subsequent reading and spelling progress. Often the young child's understanding of how words are broken down into smaller units or sounds is a more powerful predictor of reading and spelling acquisition than even his or her IQ. The relationship of phonological awareness to reading makes sense because reading involves analyzing the sounds of letters and sequencing them together in the right order to form a word.

***Just as with visual processing, some children with LD appear to need a significantly longer time to process auditory stimuli.***

What seems to be at the root of this problem? Just as with visual processing, some children with LD appear to need a significantly longer time to process auditory stimuli. Paula Tallal found that when two syllables or sounds are presented too close in succession (less than 150 milliseconds apart), some children couldn't tell which came first. They couldn't even tell whether the two sounds were the same in pitch. In contrast, average achievers can do these tasks well, even with only 8 milliseconds separating stimuli. The more difficulty that Tallal's students had with this rapid acoustic analysis, the more errors they made in sounding out nonsense words. When the interval between the sounds is made longer, or the sounds last longer (one-quarter of a second or more), then students with reading impairments can perform as well on these acoustical tasks as children who read well.

Children who process auditory information slowly have the most trouble with "stop" consonant sounds like *b, t,* or *p* because these sounds can't be sustained long enough for them to process. Vowel sounds, on the other hand, can be sustained and therefore are more readily processed. Tallal believes that problems in this area may

| Key Word | Response |
|---|---|
| study | sludn, setdid, staddy, sduey, shaen, stied, sitd |
| kitchen | chin, kinl, kengun, ckin |
| city | stiy, ciedy, deit, caiy |
| black | billk, blane, ballk |

**Figure 5.5** Spelling errors of adults with phonological processing disorders.

*Source:* Frauenheim, J. G. (1978). Academic achievement characteristics of adult males who were diagnosed as dyslexic in childhood. *Journal of Learning Disabilities, 11*, p. 480.

contribute to comprehension weaknesses because the consonant sounds, not vowels, carry the meaning in English. In speech, those consonants may pass by before the student with a learning disability can even register what's been heard.

This slowed auditory processing implies underactivation of related regions in the left hemisphere. This in fact has been demonstrated with brain imaging studies in both children and adults with severe reading disabilities. In one study the adults could correctly indicate if two dictated words rhymed, but their processing was remarkably slow and inefficient. Figure 5.5 illustrates the spellings of adults whose reading disabilities are due to severe phonological-awareness weaknesses; their spellings are largely indecipherable because the letters do not approximate the correct order of sounds in the words.

## Phonological and Verbal Coding in Working Memory

When we see or hear information, our *working memory* (processes during short-term memory that help store the information) allows us just 250 milliseconds to 25 seconds to think of a way to remember it. After that, the information is lost. Most of us use verbal labeling to increase the chance we'll remember what we've seen or heard. For example, many people store visual images of letters, words, and objects as sounds. Having seen the picture of the animal "bat," for instance, they usually store it in its sound rather than visual form. A month later, when asked to recall the image, they run the risk of replying that they actually saw a *baseball bat.* Similarly, when we sound out words, it is the sounds rather than the images that are held in memory. Therefore, reading reversal errors that appear to be visual misperceptions (e.g., *pen/den, top/pot,* or *sung/snug*) often are really related to difficulty in analyzing and holding onto the sequence of the individual sounds in working memory.

*Memory abilities are strongly tied to how automatically and efficiently we use language to label what is seen. Labels help us attend to, organize, rehearse, store, and recall the information.*

Because working-memory time is so short after information is presented, it makes sense that our memory abilities are strongly tied to how automatically and efficiently we use language to label what we have seen. Labels help us attend to, give meaning to, organize, rehearse, store, and recall the information. The labeling process is called *phonological coding* when we are referring to the analysis of sound sequences in words, or *verbal mediation* when referring to the analysis of meaningful words in sentences. Students who label what they see are making good use of their working memory time, and therefore remember much more than those who don't.

Some children with LD have trouble decoding words and remembering what they have read because they don't use their working-memory time to phonologically or verbally code the information. Some are inefficient at doing this even when given a verbal prompt—"Remember this shape: it looks like a *house.*"

As indicated in Figure 5.2, poor readers commonly have trouble remembering what they have seen. Although for some this can be due to weak visual-perceptual strategies and slow visual information processing, more often these children don't remember because of phonological-awareness problems or failure to use verbal labeling to aid memory. Proficiency in verbal labeling is critical to academic success because reading is a "meaningful language" task—that is, it's not a matter of simply being able to recognize letters or words; we must also interpret and remember what those words mean. To illustrate further the power of labeling what we see, many studies have found that poor readers can perform just as well as good readers at remembering visual information that none of the children can name—such as strange words written in Hebrew, designs and doodles, unfamiliar faces, sequences of block designs. However, when what is looked at can be named (such as three-letter nonwords, numbers, strings of words), the poor reader's performance falls markedly compared with the good reader.

The term *auditory-sequential memory difficulties* is sometimes used to describe the working-memory weaknesses of children who cannot remember verbal items in a sequence, such as letters, numbers, words, and sounds. If children can't retain sounds in a sequence, then they'll have trouble reading from the beginning to the end of a word. They'll also have trouble when one word reminds them of another they already know, but they must decode the new word by substituting a sound in a specific place—for example, /*c*/at for /*p*/at or cu/*b*/ for cu/*t*/. Beginning readers must learn to analyze, omit, substitute, and retain sounds in a sequence in order to succeed. Much of this depends on their ability to hold these sounds in memory for a short time.

George Miller's landmark studies nearly one-half century ago suggested that for any of us to hold onto and remember more than 5 or 6 letters in a sequence, we need to recode them into more manageable chunks (e.g., *ex- peri- ment,* as opposed to *experiment*). This is the theory on which our "chunking" of telephone numbers is based. Imagine how difficult reading would be if you had to approach each word letter by letter. Yet this is what some children with LD must do, because their phonological-coding weaknesses make it difficult for them to master syllable patterns and commit them to memory.

## Retrieval of Phonological and Verbal Codes

Students with reading disabilities, despite knowing the names of objects, colors, numbers, letters, letter sounds, and words, are much slower and less accurate at naming them than average readers. We all have times when we can't grasp the right word in conversation, even though it seems to be on the tip of our tongues. For some children with LD it is the norm to have unusually long silences between words, choose the wrong word, describe the word they're groping for, name another object in the same category, mispronounce words, put syllables in the wrong sequence, use fillers like *thing, uh,* or *you know,* or talk around a topic. This auditory retrieval difficulty is called a *naming* or *word-finding problem.* Try the exercise in Figure 5.6 to get a sense of the helpless feeling one can get when you know you know something but have no cues to help you retrieve this information.

Children with word-finding difficulties have trouble retrieving words and letter sounds even though they know them well. For them, sounding out words is arduous and often unsuccessful because they forget the sounds of previous letters by the time they struggle to recall the sound of the next letter in a word. Although they might misread a word, they often are able to find it quickly on a page when it is dictated to them because they didn't have to retrieve the sounds themselves. Because of their phonological retrieval problems, they are much slower to pronounce even words they can read. Moreover, the retrieval struggle is so taxing that, even when the child can read a word in the first line of a passage, he or she can't sound it out again 20 lines later—the retrieval energy is simply used up. As they struggle to decode each word, these children's capacity to remember and integrate the information they read is reduced, and their comprehension suffers.

Spring and Capps's classic study found that when children don't reach a naming rate of one object per second, they don't even attempt to use verbal mediation

*INSTRUCTIONS:* Complete the missing word that begins with each initial.

| | |
|---|---|
| *EXAMPLE:* 16 O. in a P. | 16 ounces in a pound |
| **1.** 26 L. in the A. | ____________ |
| **2.** 7 W. of the A. W. | ____________ |
| **3.** 54 C. in a D. (WITH THE J.) | ____________ |
| **4.** 88 P. K. | ____________ |
| **5.** 32 D. F. at which W. F. | ____________ |
| **6.** 200 D. for P. G. in M. | ____________ |
| **7.** 3 B. M. (S. H. T. R.) | ____________ |
| **8.** 11 P. on a F. T. | ____________ |

**Figure 5.6** Simulation of word-finding difficulties. Readers can't recall the right words from memory despite knowing the information.

*Source:* Unknown.

as a memory aid. They tested this notion by showing children eight cards, which were then laid face down in a row. Children were then asked to match a ninth card to one on the table. Good readers named each card before it was laid down, but poor readers didn't. Since overt (speaking aloud) or covert (speaking to oneself) naming increases the ability to remember, it is obvious why the poor readers didn't remember.

*Word-finding problems may remain a lifelong source of reading, learning, and expressive difficulties for the learning disabled. Their naming ability may never catch up.*

Studies find that children typically become faster namers with age and better at remembering because they have stored more related words and knowledge that help cue retrieval, such as synonyms, words in the same category, and related ideas. Unfortunately, however, word-finding problems may remain a lifelong source of reading, learning, and expressive difficulties for the learning disabled—their naming ability may never catch up. It may plateau as early as 8 to 10 years of age, whereas those without learning disabilities continue to increase their naming speeds throughout their junior high school years. Jason's story illustrates how naming difficulties can affect many aspects of life far beyond the ability to read well.

## Jason

*A successful engineer and businessman with word-finding problems.*

Jason, an engineering college graduate who owns his own heating repair business, explains how his naming difficulties have affected his life. Jason always did well at remembering concepts but could never remember names, places, dates, baseball batting averages, and so forth. Consequently, he came to believe that he could contribute little to conversations. He says that today he enters conversations "from the perimeter," waiting for people to get beyond the exchange of facts to the idea level.

A 6-foot-tall, brawny, handsome fellow, Jason's reticence began in elementary school when classmates in the lunchroom would outargue him with more accurate facts, no matter what the topic of conversation. He soon learned to retreat socially. An exceptional tennis player, Jason never calls the score because he fears making verbal errors. When he returned to his tenth-year high school reunion, no one remembered him.

Jason's reading and spelling difficulties have continued into adulthood. He has read one novel in his entire life and never reads the newspaper. TV is his source of information. When writing, Jason can only catch his misspellings after he finishes each word and inspects whether it "looks right." Number reversals occur occasionally on his order sheets, but he catches them when the sums don't make sense and the order numbers don't match those in the catalog. Jason has learned to check and double-check any written work.

Jason is a sympathetic, pleasant fellow for whom finding business partners is easy. He has always sought partners who could be the up-front salespeople, good at making small talk. Jason, on the other hand, is the mechanical genius on whose skills everyone relies, and without whom there could be no business. He describes himself as an accommodating, honest, dependable person who is always on time and always helping others out. "Since I can't teach people anything new besides engineering, I've become the nice guy. When I was 16, I was the first person to get my license, and so I drove everyone around. What else could I do? I want to be liked."

Children who cannot word-find efficiently not only have trouble decoding but they also have difficulty with using language as a comprehension and memory aid. Normal readers generally pause about every two seconds to interpret what they've read, and then store it in memory. If they don't do this, the information will be lost. But students who have inefficient access to stored sounds and words, and thus read very slowly, won't be able to comprehend what they've read or remember it because they have to spend too much time with the decoding process. Two seconds have passed before a message that makes any sense can be read or understood.

*Poor naming causes trouble with both spoken and written language because sounds can't be retrieved to read words, words can't be retrieved to express ideas, and language can't be used as a comprehension and memory aid.*

It is not surprising that the speed of naming objects, letters, colors, and the like is an excellent predictor of reading success. And the faster one can name, the faster one can calculate simple math facts. Students with learning disabilities are slower on both tasks. Poor naming causes trouble with both spoken and written language because it means that sounds can't be retrieved to read words and words can't be retrieved to express ideas. Research Box 5.1 on page 144 reviews several hypotheses regarding the origins of these word-finding difficulties.

## Linguistic Weaknesses

*The ability to understand and to express oneself in language are significant factors in the processes of decoding, comprehending, writing, and social interaction.*

The ability to understand and to express oneself in language are significant factors in the processes of decoding, comprehending, writing, and social interaction. Go back to the story of Peter on page 135 and try to imagine what his reaction would be to the following instructions: "Set the oven to 350 degrees and after you stir in the ingredients one at a time, bake the brownies for 30 minutes in a greased pan." The steps are out of sequence, but most people can reorder them and produce some tasty snacks. In contrast, many children with learning disabilities are unable to comprehend such basic grammatical relations. Therefore, their ability to understand and infer from oral language or reading material suffers.

These children's language weaknesses make it difficult for them to use grammar or context to help decode difficult words. For example, a child with average reading skills looks at a story about a camping trip that took place last week and quickly infers that the verbs should be in the past tense. In other words, his or her eyes pick up the letters "hik" and their brain automatically supplies the "ed." Delays in acquiring vocabulary and understanding idioms and metaphors further complicate reading, comprehension, and writing. Some children with LD are fortunate that their linguistic weaknesses become apparent only when expressing themselves, because their comprehension of language concepts has developed normally. These children need remedial help and accommodations in order to improve and work around their oral language and writing problems.

In order to read, comprehend, and compose accurately and rapidly, we must translate the written symbol into sound, grammar, and meaning in a parallel fashion. If the student can't access any one of these automatically, reading and composition abilities are delayed. Fisher and Athey poignantly illustrated the contribution of linguistic weaknesses to reading and writing delays in a clever study. Using designs to represent words, the investigators found that children with reading disabilities learned to "read" these designs as quickly as good readers. But, when these

RESEARCH BOX 5.1

## Hypotheses for the Origin of Word-Finding Difficulties

A number of hypotheses have been put forward to explain the origin of word-finding difficulties and its correlation with reading disorders. Early on, investigators reasoned that word-finding difficulties were directly related to children's phonological awareness weaknesses, that is, a structural brain deficit was hypothesized to keep students from accessing the verbal and phonological cues that could help them perform phonological awareness tasks and also remember stored verbal information (Swanson, 1983; Torgesen & Houck, 1980). Alternatively, Wiig and Semel (1980) reasoned that the slow word finding is due to the child's perceptual confusion between similar-sounding words (which causes the wrong word to be called up), or to the child's poor use of grammatical cues to aid recall.

Because phonological awareness difficulties and slow word finding do not always go hand in hand, however (children with reading disorders can have one, both, or neither), other investigators have suggested that slow detection of visual stimuli or a slow articulation rate may hamper rehearsing the information to be memorized in the first place, so that connections between visual and verbal information are compromised and weak (Ackerman, Dykman, and Gardner, 1990; Baddeley, 1986; Chase, 1996; Wolf, Bowers, & Biddle, 2000). This results in slow word-finding. The slow visual pickup argument has received experimental support. However, most studies have failed to support the slow articulation rate theory (Ackerman & Dykman, 1993; Wolf et al., 2000).

Kail and Leonard (1986) propose that the problem is at the word-knowledge end, caused by the fact that these children do not have a rich enough base of information about

designs were used to form sentences, the children with reading disabilities read at a slower pace because their language inefficiencies hampered predictions of the words to come. When asked to use the designs to compose sentences, these children's sentences were brief, included many grammatical errors, and used designs that made no logical sense. Try the exercise in Figure 5.7 on page 146 to get some sense of the frustration and loss of self-confidence when a person has the basic knowledge called for but encounters vocabulary in conversations or textbooks that is well beyond his or her reach.

## Attention

Imagine you are caring for a 5-year-old niece who's tackling a chocolate ice cream cone on a hot day. When she's done and thoroughly covered in chocolate mess, you tell her to run to the bathroom and wash up. She strolls back two minutes later, still a mess. She looks at you in all innocence and asks, "What did you tell me to do?" In all likelihood, you'd smile, repeat your instructions, pat her on the head, and send her on her way.

**RESEARCH BOX 5.1 (Continued)**

a word's meaning (e.g., synonyms, related ideas and words) to facilitate rapid retrieval of the word for use in a variety of grammatical forms or contexts. Even though words are known, they are less distinct in the children's memories and less easily recalled. To a lesser degree, Kail and Leonard also found some of the problem to be due to these children's inefficient and inappropriate retrieval strategies (e.g., not using category or initial sound cues to help them recall).

Farmer and Klein (1995) propose that it simply takes more time for the neural pathways of the child with word-finding difficulties to process the incoming information and choose the correct response. Besides remembering the sounds and connecting these with the visual stimuli, the neurological processes of scanning stimuli, searching one's memory, preparing to respond, sequencing the response, and planning the motor movements required for the response are quite complicated, and problems can occur at any of these junctures (Denckla & Cutting, 1999; Snyder & Downey, 1995). Kail, Hall, and Caskey (1999) in fact found that many students with reading disabilities have processing-speed problems in all modalities.

Further research on this issue is likely to discover, as with most everything in the LD field, that multiple sources of breakdown are at play in these children's slow word-finding speeds. What this literature teaches us thus far is that we should try to "deepen" children's verbal knowledge with synonyms and elaborations, so that if a particular word can't be called to mind a substitute can be easily found.

Now imagine the same scene with a 10-year-old niece. If she wandered back a mess, you'd start to wonder about the child's hearing or her ability to understand, pay attention, remember, obey, or even practice simple hygiene. And it's likely that you'd be annoyed.

If your 10-year-old niece is learning disabled, her trouble following directions may be related to her inability to focus and sustain attention long enough to absorb information. For children with LD, attention seems to cause a problem in the initial storage of information. When they do attend to and practice information long enough to learn it, they have no more problem remembering than do average achievers. Even with sufficient time and practice, however, many of these students' recall difficulties appear to get worse relative to their classmates because their peers begin to use sophisticated strategies to increase their memory capacities (such as mnemonic devices, association tricks, and visual imagery). But the learning disabled usually do not try these strategies. Moreover, their storage inefficiencies might be complicated by inefficiencies in retrieving the information once learned because of word-finding difficulties. As previously mentioned, word finding may not mature with age in the learning disabled, as it does for the average achievers.

***For children with LD, attention seems to cause a problem in the initial storage of information. When they do attend to and practice information long enough to learn it, they most often have no more problem remembering than do average achievers.***

*INSTRUCTIONS:* Translate the following common sayings.

*EXAMPLE:* Scintillate, scintillate, asteroid minific. (Twinkle, twinkle, little star.)

1. Members of an avian species of identical plumage congregate.
2. Pulchritude possesses solely cutaneous profundity.
3. It is fruitless to become lachrymose over precipitately departed lactic fluid.
4. Freedom from the incrustation of grime is contiguous to rectitude.
5. The stylus is more potent than the claymore.
6. It is fruitless to try to indoctrinate a superannuated canine with innovate maneuvers.
7. The temperature of the aqueous content of an unremittingly ogled vessel does not attain 671.4 degrees Kelvin.
8. All articles that coruscate with resplendence, are not truly aurific.

**Figure 5.7** Simulation of linguistic weaknesses. It is very frustrating to know information but be blocked from demonstrating this knowledge by vocabulary well beyond one's capabilities.

*Source:* Unknown.

A fundamental contributor to the poor learning of students with LD is immature attending ability. Good attending includes the ability to be alert to a stimulus, decide on a goal, get ready to respond, focus on the right stimuli, sustain attention long enough, delay responding while considering alternatives, and then decide on an answer or action. Attending to the essential information and then organizing it for storage are critical if information is to be remembered.

***It's fairly easy to catch the attention of students with LD, but focusing their attention long enough and critically enough to allow learning to happen is much more difficult.***

Studies show that it's fairly easy to catch the attention of students who are learning disabled, but focusing their attention long enough and critically enough to allow learning to happen is much more difficult. Here's the difference between caught and focused attention. You are very tired and distracted, but you go ahead and read your little brother a bedtime story as you promised. You read all the words correctly and in the right sequence. You know this because now your brother is asking a lot of "but why did" questions. He understood you. But why are you clueless about the answers to his questions? Your attention was "caught" long enough to read the story, but obviously not "focused" enough for the material to be comprehended or stored in your memory.

Similarly, for many students with LD, difficulty focusing and sustaining selective attention is at the root of their learning problems. Several reasons for this weakness have been proposed: physiological difficulties, cognitive styles incompatible with selective attention, and poor use of verbal mediation to aid attention and memory.

## Physiological Difficulties

*For many students with LD, difficulty with focusing and sustaining attention has a physiological basis.*

For many students with LD difficulty with focusing and sustaining attention has a physiological basis. This is particularly true of those diagnosed with attention-deficit hyperactivity disorder. These children have trouble maintaining high attention levels, take longer to react to stimuli, and do not have the typical physiological indices associated with attention. They have lower electroencephalogram (EEG) amplitudes, slower EEG response rates to stimuli, and their EEGs remain at a peak for less time. They also show less left hemisphere activation than expected, lower metabolic activity in their frontal lobe white matter, lower cerebral glucose metabolism, and lower heart rate changes. These inefficient attention processes may interfere with learning to such a degree that over time visual- and auditory-processing abilities become compromised. For example, when a child can't sit still long enough to hear a story, he or she misses out on the chance to learn sophisticated vocabulary and grammar that are part of our conversational and written language worlds. When this happens day in and day out, this may in turn lead to cumulative language deficits where there were none to begin with.

Have you ever heard someone refer to a clumsy person by saying "He (or she) can't chew gum and walk at the same time"? For the learning disabled, this is a fact of life. It seems that while their right or left hemispheres are engaged in one activity, they have difficulty allotting energy to another activity that is mediated by the same hemisphere—tapping a pencil rapidly with the right hand while talking, for example. When this interference occurs in typical learners, they tend to continue to process verbal information and diminish the motor activity. Children who are learning disabled, however, may do the opposite. If language efficiency and learning are sacrificed when a student is required to do too many competing things at once, his or her achievement will suffer even further.

High school and college students are notorious for watching television and studying at the same time, or talking on the cell phone while listening to their favorite music and playing a video game. This dual tasking is impossible for many individuals with a learning disability, and, because of this difficulty allocating cognitive energy to two tasks at once, they miss out on things that others simply absorb without trying. Ceci and Baker's clever research illustrates this point. These researchers had children play a computer game in which they were to land a spaceship on as many planets as possible and avoid being blown up by antiaircraft rocket launchers. Of course, the spaceships were programmed to blow up at specified times. As the spaceship disintegrated amid a loud crashing sound, the child (who had been told to ignore lists of words being read through earphones) heard the word *black*. Within 9 to 15 trials children's skin conductance indicated that they had become physiologically conditioned to the word *black* (because of the excitement accompanying the blowups), even if no blowup was occurring. Then children stopped playing the game. Next, the children repeated words that were presented so rapidly to one ear that they were unaware that competing words were

*Because it is difficult for some students with LD to allocate cognitive energy to two tasks at once, they miss out on things that others simply absorb without trying.*

being presented simultaneously to the other ear. Incredibly, the skin conductance of children without LD showed the conditioned response to *black,* even though they were totally unaware that the word had been presented to the unattended ear. In contrast, the children with LD had far less of a response. Non-LD children even reacted to a rhyming word (*back*) and synonyms (*dark, brown*); the children with LD showed less of a reaction.

*The attention of students with LD may be impaired at an automatic level that requires no purposeful awareness.*

This research suggests that the attention of students with LD may be impaired at an automatic level that requires no purposeful awareness. Teachers frequently complain that, for some of their students, "sound goes in one ear and out the other." More than once, they've found themselves waving a hand in front of a student's face and asking "Are you in there?" Once the student "comes to," he or she is mystified by the teacher's reaction.

*Children with attention deficits need to put inordinate and exhausting effort into actively processing information.*

Parents, too, report that all too often their child seems to be totally unaware of the call to dinner or the signal "it's time to go," especially if he or she is engrossed in some activity. Given the many physiological indices reflecting poor attention, it appears that these children need to put inordinate and exhausting effort into actively processing information, a task that children without learning problems do automatically.

## Cognitive Style and Attention

*Unique cognitive styles may predispose a child to poor attention either by deterring attention from what's important or encouraging inappropriate task strategies.*

Unique cognitive styles may predispose a child to poor attention either by deterring attention from what's important or encouraging inappropriate task strategies. For example, distractible children may take in all the stimuli around them and therefore not be able to focus on the task's most important features. A beautifully illustrated book may actually hinder their ability to read the text rather than enhance understanding of the story.

Impulsive response styles go hand in hand with poor attention. An impulsive child will jump in with the answer long before he or she has considered all the information and all the possible responses. The good news is that these children can be helped to learn to focus, sustain, and organize their attention. As their selective attention gets better, their tendency to respond quickly and make mistakes diminishes, and their memory improves.

Likewise, when we help the student with a simultaneous processing style to focus on critical details instead of only the main idea, learning improves. When we draw attention to the main idea for a child with an overly successive processing style, we help him or her learn, too.

## Verbal Mediation and Attention

When a person does not use verbal labeling to help focus attention, the information that caught attention is not likely to be organized for storage, and therefore not recalled. By overtly or covertly speaking to themselves about what was just heard or read, children can markedly increase their ability to abstract and generalize from this information. However, verbal mediation doesn't come easily to the learning disabled because of their language weaknesses and nonstrategic approaches to learning. Research has shown that even when verbal cues are offered to help these children retrieve an object's name, for example, or organize information into categories, they ignore these cues. In other words, even when given useful verbal information, children with learning disabilities may not recognize how it can be helpful.

Because students with LD can increase their problem-solving and memory skills by literally talking to themselves as they work, many may appear to have memory deficiencies when in fact they don't—they simply do not spontaneously use verbal mediation to help themselves remember. Fortunately, these children can be taught to use verbal mediation effectively, so that their attention and memory improve. Helpful strategies are reviewed in Chapter 7.

***Students with LD may appear to have memory deficiencies when in fact they don't—they simply do not spontaneously use verbal mediation to help themselves remember.***

## Motor Skills

Students with LD often have trouble with their gross-motor, hand, and oral movements. Disturbances in gaining information through touch and movement also are common. Slow motor speed is typical of the learning disabled, just as they are slow to find words when speaking, read words that they already know, or pick up on visual cues. Allison, a law school graduate, has severe motor difficulties that have plagued her throughout her life. See more of her story below.

***Slow motor speed is typical of children with LD.***

As many as 75 to 90 percent of all poor readers seem to have motor difficulties; copying, handwriting, directing the computer mouse, and other eye-hand

***As many as 75 to 90 percent of all poor readers seem to have motor difficulties.***

### Allison

*A successful law school graduate plagued with severe motor difficulties.*

As a youngster, Allison always had a difficult time with recess, physical education class, youth-group dances, and summer camp sports activities. Her coordination has not improved with time. At the age of 23, Allison cannot walk a straight line, or touch her nose when her eyes are closed. She skips and jumps with difficulty.

When Allison is unsure of what she wants to say, her speech becomes slurred. Because she has difficulty visualizing symbols in her mind, she still reverses letters and numbers when she writes. At her supervisor's house she once reached into a bowl of plastic cherries, didn't feel anything wrong, and put some in her mouth. Allison's handwriting is illegible.

Fortunately, these weaknesses need not deter Allison's career as a lawyer. She can dictate her work and delegate proofreading to someone else. Furthermore, her coordination difficulties need not affect her social life. Given the enthusiasm of Americans for spectator sports, Allison fits in nicely. In fact, Allison is quite popular among amateur ice skaters because she's developed a Web page to raise funds for their training. Allison did, however, encounter a problem at her wedding, where she knocked over a candelabra on the way down the aisle, and, despite months of practicing, appeared very awkward when the band leader invited the happy couple to dance their first dance.

**When Nathan Colors**

When Nathan colors, his crayon
becomes a weapon against the white paper.
It is his mission to color in every bit of
available background.
His coloring brain comes from his toes
and grips his entire body driving its power
down into his he-man fingers.
He sucks in drool as his concentration grows.

When Nathan colors, his crayons
make a popping sound as weapon after weapon
is broken by the paper enemy.
On December 26th, Nathan's coloring can
is filled with new, smooth shiny soldiers.
By January, his army is broken into small
midget fighters.
His mother watches as he pushes 1/4" nubs
into the paper with his he-man thumb ends.

When Nathan colors, his world is
lost in the mission of wiping out white.
This is no calming, passive playtime
like it might be for other children.
Coloring is exhausting and sometimes,
it must be followed by a snack break
or, on rainy days,
a doze on the couch.

**Figure 5.8** Nathan's coloring. Nathan's anger and frustration with his fine-motor difficulties is evident in his drawing and his mother's commentary.

*Source:* Reprinted by permission of Debra L. Morse-Little (1989).

coordination tasks are troublesome. In nearly three-quarters of these students their motor weaknesses are unrelated to underlying visual-perceptual deficits. For example, if they are asked to point out errors in how they copied complex designs, these children usually can do this quite well, despite being unable to copy the figures themselves. Likewise, their articulation difficulties seldom are due to inability to hear sounds accurately; usually the problem is specific to oral movements.

***Motor difficulties by themselves don't cause learning problems; rather they make it more difficult for students to show what they've learned.***

Motor difficulties by themselves don't cause learning problems. Rather they make it more difficult for students to show what they've learned. For example, a child may make mistakes trying to repeat what's been heard or avoid essays because the act of writing is so difficult. Keeping up with the worksheets and finishing timed tests is a problem because of these children's slowness.

It seems that coordination difficulties frequently accompany learning disorders because a very large area of the sensorimotor and motor cortex handles hand, finger, body, and oral sensations and movements. When there is a dysfunction in adjacent brain regions that are essential to higher-level cognitive and academic performance, things can also go wrong in the nearby sensorimotor and motor regions. In addition, any messages about how to feel, speak, or move coming from higher-level brain areas that are not attending to, organizing, storing, or retrieving information well will be reflected in motor and verbal inefficiencies. This is why you can't bat effectively if you don't watch the ball or why you may stammer if you can't think of the word you want to use.

Coordination problems can lead to sloppy or illegible handwriting, awkward pencil grip, reluctance to complete lengthy written assignments, trouble with keyboarding, and math errors because of illegibility or poor alignment of numerals. These children may also have articulation difficulties, marked motor slowness, immature coloring and artwork, and difficulty with scissors and other tools. Their social standing is often diminished by their poor athletic skills, clumsiness on the playground, and sloppiness in dressing (buttons and zippers open, shoes untied). They often drop, spill, and knock things over. These problems make it tough to find friends. These youngsters are often frustrated at understanding much more than they can express orally or in writing. Such anger and frustration is evident in Nathan's coloring and his mother's commentary (see Figure 5.8 on page 150). Nathan is now in third grade and very proud of how well he reads. Because his handwriting problems continue, he dictates compositions, uses a computer, tape-records homework assignments, and works with a peer who records the math computations. If a student's problems are only motor related, and he or she can withstand the lower grades that will come from written work, then the outlook for eventual success is good.

***If a student's problems are only motor related, then the outlook for eventual success is good.***

## Summary

One or more information-processing weaknesses can underlie learning disabilities. Peripheral visual factors, such as poor eyesight and inefficient eye movements, do not cause learning disabilities. Nevertheless, they can make the use of the eyes when reading uncomfortable, possibly aggravating existing learning difficulties. Visual-perceptual factors influence learning at young ages and continue to do so in subtle ways at older ages. The most frequent and powerful contributors to academic achievement, however, are language, phonological-processing skills, and attention abilities. All are complexly interrelated and greatly influence what information is attended to, and how it is understood, organized for storage, rehearsed, and recalled. Although motor disabilities often accompany the visual-perceptual, language, and attention weaknesses of students with learning disabilities, they do not contribute to the learning difficulty. Rather, they make it difficult for these youngsters to express what they know.

Although patterns of information-processing weaknesses in students with LD have been identified, each child with a learning disability differs from the other in specific characteristics and needs. Even two individuals with the same type of weakness will differ in exactly how the learning disability plays itself out. The intervention strategies may also differ. So many factors impact learning that information processing weakness is not a certain predictor of learning disabilities. It is, however, a risk factor that warrants close monitoring and immediate intervention if learning or social problems develop.

## Helpful Resources

### Visual-Perceptual Skills

Bakker, D. J. (1983). Hemispheric specialization and specific reading retardation. In M. Rutter (Ed.), *Developmental neuropsychiatry.* New York: Guilford Press.

Boden, C., & Brodeur, D. A. (1999). Visual processing of verbal and nonverbal stimuli in adolescents with reading disabilities. *Journal of Learning Disabilities, 32,* 58–71.

Fletcher, J. (1991). Qualitative descriptions of error recovery patterns across reading level and sentence type: An eye movement analysis. *Journal of Learning Disabilities, 24,* 568–575.

Galaburda, A., & Livingstone, M. (1993). Evidence for a magnocellular defect in developmental dyslexia. *Annals of the New York Academy of Sciences, 682,* 70–82.

Harnadek, M. C. S., & Rourke, B. P. (1994). Principal identifying features of the syndrome of nonverbal learning disabilities in children. *Journal of Learning Disabilities, 27,* 144–154.

Helveston, E. M., Weber, J. C., Miller, K., Robertson, K., Hohberger, G., Estes, R., Ellis, F. D., Pick, N., & Helveston, B. H. (1985). Visual function and academic performance. *American Journal of Ophthalmology, 99,* 346–355.

Knowlton, M. (1997). Efficiency in visual scanning of children with and without visual disabilities. *Exceptional Children, 63,* 557–565.

Larsen, S. C., & Hammill, D. D. (1975). The relationship of selected visual-perceptual abilities to school learning. *Journal of Special Education, 9,* 281–291.

Lehmkuhle, S., Garzia, R. P., Turner, L., Hash, T., & Baro, J. A. (1993). A defective visual pathway in children with reading disability. *New England Journal of Medicine, 328,* 989–996.

Markee, T., Brown, W. S., Moore, L. H., & Theberge, D. C. (1996). Callosal function in dyslexia: Evoked potential interhemisphere transfer time and bilateral field advantage. *Developmental Neuropsychology, 12,* 409–428.

Rourke, B. P., Bakker, D. J., Fisk, J. L., & Strang, J. D. (1983). *Child neuropsychology: An introduction to theory, research, and clinical practice.* New York: Guilford Press.

Shafrir, U., & Siegel, L. S. (1994). Subtypes of learning disabilities in adolescents and adults. *Journal of Learning Disabilities, 27,* 123–134.

Solan, H. A., & Mozlin, R. (1986). The correlations of perceptual-motor maturation to readiness and reading in kindergarten and the primary grades. *Journal of the American Optometric Association, 57,* 28–35.

Stanley, G., & Hall, R. (1973). Short-term visual information processing in dyslexics. *Child Development, 44,* 841–844.

### Language and Phonological Processing Skills

Allor, J. H. (2002). The relationships of phonemic awareness and rapid naming to reading development. *Learning Disability Quarterly, 25,* 47–57.

Baddeley, A. D. (1986). *Working memory.* London: Oxford University Press.

Bakker, D. J., & Licht, P., (1986). Learning to read: Changing horses in mid-stream. In G. Th. Pavlidis & D. F. Fisher (Eds.), *Dyslexia: Its neuropsychology and treatment.* New York: John Wiley & Sons.

Blachman, B. A. (1991). Early intervention for children's reading problems: Clinical applications of the research in phonological awareness. *Topics in Language Disorders, 12,* 51–65.

Bradley, L., & Bryant, P. (1985). *Rhyme and reason in reading and spelling.* Ann Arbor, MI: University of Michigan Press.

Cermak, L. S. (1983). Information processing deficits in children with learning disabilities. *Journal of Learning Disabilities, 16,* 599–605.

Fisher, D. F., & Athey, I. (1986). Methodological issues in research with the learning disabled: Establishing true controls. In G. T. Pavlidis & D. F. Fisher (Eds.), *Dyslexia: Its neuropsychology and treatment.* New York: John Wiley.

Hier, D. B., LeMay, M., Rosenberger, P. B., & Perlo, V. P. (1978). Developmental dyslexia: Evidence for a subgroup with a reversal of cerebral asymmetry. *Archives of Neurology, 35,* 90–92.

Kavale, K. (1981). The relationship between auditory perceptual skills and reading ability: A meta-analysis. *Journal of Learning Disabilities, 14,* 539–546.

Kuder, S. J. (1991). Language abilities and progress in a direct instruction reading program for students with learning disabilities. *Journal of Learning Disabilities, 24,* 124–127.

Liberman, I. Y., & Shankweiler, D. (1985). Phonology and the problems of learning to read and write. *Remedial and Special Education, 6(6),* 8–17.

MacDonald, G. W., & Cornwall, A. (1995). The relationship between phonological awareness and reading and spelling achievement eleven years later. *Journal of Learning Disabilities, 28,* 523–527.

Meyer, M. S., Wood, F. B., Hart, L. A., & Felton, R. H. (1998). Selective predictive value of rapid automatized naming in poor readers. *Journal of Learning Disabilities, 31,* 106–117.

Miller, G. A. (1956). The magical number seven, plus or minus two: Some limits on our capacity for processing information. *The Psychological Review, 63,* 81–97.

Rumsey, J. M. Andreason, P., Zametkin, A. J., Aquino, T., King, C., Hamburger, S. D., Pikus, A., Rapoport, J. L., & Cohen, R. M. (1992). Failure to activate left temporoparietal cortex in dyslexia: An oxygen 15 positron emission tomographic study. *Archives of Neurology, 49,* 527–534.

Shaywitz, S. E., Fletcher, J. M., Holahan, J. M., Shneider, A. E., Marchione, K. E., Stuebing, K. K., Francis, D. J., Pugh, K. R., & Shaywitz, B. A. (1999). Persistence of dyslexia: The Connecticut Longitudinal Study at adolescence. *Pediatrics, 104,* 1351–1359.

Snowling, M. J. (1981). Phonemic deficits in developmental dyslexia. *Psychological Research, 43,* 219–234.

Spring, C., & Capps, C. (1974). Encoding speed, rehearsal, and probed recall of dyslexic boys. *Journal of Educational Psychology, 66,* 780–786.

Tallal, P., Miller, S., & Fitch, R. H. (1996). Neurobiological basics of speech: A case for the preeminence of temporal processing. In C. H. Chase, G. D. Rosen, & G. F. Sherman (Eds.), *Developmental dyslexia: Neural, cognitive, and genetic mechanisms* (pp. 159–184). Baltimore: York Press.

Tallal, P., Miller, S. L., Jenkins, W. M., & Merzenich, M. M. (1997). The role of temporal processing in developmental language-based learning disorders: Research and clinical implications. In B. Blachman (Ed.), *Foundations of reading acquisition and dyslexia: Implications for early intervention* (pp. 49–66). Mahwah, NJ: Lawrence Erlbaum.

Torgesen, J. K. (1988). Studies of children with learning disabilities who perform poorly on memory span tasks. *Journal of Learning Disabilities, 21,* 605–612.

Torgesen, J. K., Wagner, R. K., & Rashotte, C. A. (1994). Longitudinal studies of phonological processing and reading. *Journal of Learning Disabilities, 27,* 276–286.

Wolf, M., & Bowers, P. G. (1999). The "double-deficit hypothesis" for the developmental dyslexias. *Journal of Educational Psychology, 91,* 415–438.

## Attention

Brainerd, C. J., Kingma, J., & Howe, M. L. (1986). Long-term memory development and learning disability: Storage and retrieval loci of disabled/nondisabled differences. In S. J. Ceci (Ed.), *Handbook of cognitive, social, and neuropsychological aspects of learning disabilities* (Vol. 1). Hillsdale, NJ: Lawrence Erlbaum.

Ceci, S. J. (1983). Automatic and purposive semantic processing characteristics of normal and language/learning-disabled children. *Developmental Psychology, 19,* 427–439.

Ceci, S. J., & Baker, J. G. (1989). On learning . . . more or less: A knowledge × process × context view of learning disabilities. *Journal of Learning Disabilities, 22,* 90–99.

Keogh, B. K. (1973). Perceptual and cognitive styles: Implications for special education. In L. Mann & D. A. Sabatino (Eds.), *The first review of special education.* Philadelphia: JSE Press.

Keogh, B. K., & Margolis, J. (1976). Learn to labor and to wait: Attentional problems of children with learning disorders. *Journal of Learning Disabilities, 9,* 276–286.

Mann, C. A., Lubar, J. F., Zimmerman, A. W., Miller, C. A., & Muenchen, R. A., (1992). Quantitative analysis of EEG in boys with attention-deficit-hyperactivity disorder: Controlled study with clinical implications. *Pediatric Neurology, 8,* 30–36.

Richards, G. P., Samuels, S. J., Turnure, J. E., & Ysseldyke, J. E. (1990). Sustained and selective attention in children with learning disabilities. *Journal of Learning Disabilities, 23,* 129–136.

Swanson, H. L. (1988). Memory subtypes in learning disabled readers. *Learning Disability Quarterly, 11,* 342–357.

Torgesen, J., & Goldman, T. (1977). Verbal rehearsal and short-term memory in reading disabled children. *Child Development, 48,* 56–60.

Zametkin, A. J., Nordahl, T. E., Gross, M., King, A. C., Semple, W. E., Rumsey, J., Hamburger, S., & Cohen, R. M. (1990). Cerebral glucose metabolism in adults with hyperactivity of childhood onset. *New England Journal of Medicine, 323,* 1362–1366.

## Motor Skills

Benton, A. L., & Pearl, D. (1978). *Dyslexia: An appraisal of current knowledge.* New York: Oxford University Press.

Critchley, M. (1970). *The dyslexic child.* Springfield, IL: Charles C. Thomas.

Kavale, K. (1982). Meta-analysis of the relationship between visual perceptual skills and reading achievement. *Journal of Learning Disabilities, 15,* 42–51.

Keogh, B. K., & Smith, C. E. (1967). Visuo-motor ability for school prediction: A seven-year study. *Perceptual and Motor Skills, 25,* 101–110.

Larsen, S. C., & Hammill, D. D. (1975). The relationship of selected visual-perceptual abilities to school learning. *Journal of Special Education, 9,* 281–291.

CHAPTER SIX

# Academic Development

**TO FULLY UNDERSTAND** the academic problems faced by students who are learning disabled—how to plan their curriculum and how to choose the most appropriate teaching strategies—it is important first to learn what is considered normal academic development. How do average students acquire reading, writing, and math skills, and how do they learn in content areas? How do children identified as learning disabled differ? This chapter explores academic development from both perspectives in the elementary grades, junior high and high school years, and the transition to adult life. The variety of interventions available to address academic weaknesses in these areas are examined in Chapters 10 through 14.

Unfortunately, the learning problems of many students with LD tend not to disappear with time, despite extensive elementary school interventions. Although students who are learning disabled do make progress, they generally continue to achieve significantly lower than their age and grade expectations. National testing indicates that gaps between the reading and math achievement levels of students with learning disabilities and their peers generally widen over the years, as do their gaps in subject area knowledge. It is not unusual for high school seniors with learning disabilities to score on average below the 20th percentile in basic skills and content knowledge when compared with their classmates.

*With intervention, students with LD do make progress, but they generally continue to achieve significantly lower than their age and grade expectations.*

For some children with LD, disabilities that seem to have been outgrown after intensive intervention reappear when they encounter new and harder cognitive or environmental demands. Still other children appear to be keeping up in the early grades only to fall significantly behind in high school when learning becomes a much more complex process. Some children also have excellent compensatory skills that can mask the great learning struggle they are actually experiencing.

*Many students with LD have areas of talent and strength that can serve them well in school and into adulthood.*

Although areas of weakness often persist, at the same time many students with LD have areas of talent and strength that can serve them well in school and into adulthood. Therefore we must address these students' needs in both their areas of strength and weakness through appropriate general and special education programming, tutoring, learning strategy training, intensified vocational preparation programs, and transition planning aimed at maximizing postsecondary educational opportunities, employment, and life satisfaction.

## The Elementary School Years

Robert Fulghum's wonderful way of capturing the life lessons that children absorb in their first few months of school is now legendary (see page 157). It's a time when children learn how to work and play cooperatively and, most importantly, when the foundation gets laid for all the learning to come. In kindergarten, teachers reinforce the cognitive and information-processing skills that most directly support academic progress. Children learn how to organize their approach to tasks, monitor their attention and physical activity, work on their own and in a group, and get along. Long-lasting attitudes toward oneself as a learner and toward school begin to take shape.

*In kindergarten, teachers reinforce the cognitive and information-processing skills that most directly support academic progress.*

Skills that increase kindergarteners' readiness to progress academically include knowing the alphabet and numbers; how to rhyme words; how to segment words into syllables and sounds; naming common colors, objects, and designs; copying designs; writing their name; vocabulary comprehension; following directions; and simple number concepts. Many children enter school with several of these skills already established. For them, progress is a matter of elaborating on this knowledge. Kindergarten is another matter for children with learning disabilities, however, who have yet to master these foundation skills. Their inefficient information-processing and unique cognitive styles keep them on the sidelines while their peers forge ahead. For them learning is a struggle that leaves them confused, overwhelmed, and questioning their worth as individuals.

*Kindergarten children with LD enter school with inefficient information-processing skills, unique cognitive styles, and delays in foundation skills that are needed to support academic progress.*

Children with LD can succeed, however. How much they learn depends on individual, curriculum, and environmental factors, such as the rate at which their cognitive and information-processing abilities mature, their motivation and perseverance, their attitude toward education, the fund of knowledge they bring from home, their teachers' skills and attitudes, and the characteristics of their classroom and classmates.

Kindergarten is spent developing a child's readiness for formal instruction in the basic reading, writing, and math skills essential to support higher-level learning. First and second grades emphasize building a strong foundation in these three areas. A dramatic shift in school expectations, however, begins when a child enters the upper elementary grades. By fourth grade, and with each passing grade, children are expected to assume much more responsibility for their own learning. By this time their reading, comprehension, and learning strategies have matured suf-

## All I Really Need to Know I Learned in Kindergarten

All I really need to know about how to live and what to do and how to be I learned in kindergarten. Wisdom was not at the top of the graduate-school mountain, but there in the sandpile at Sunday School. These are the things I learned:

Share everything.
Play fair.
Don't hit people.
Put things back where you found them.
Clean up your own mess.
Don't take things that aren't yours.
Say you're sorry when you hurt somebody.
Wash your hands before you eat.
Flush.
Warm cookies and cold milk are good for you.

Live a balanced life—learn some and think some and draw and paint and sing and dance and play and work every day some.

Take a nap every afternoon.
When you go out into the world, watch out for traffic, hold hands, and stick together.
Be aware of wonder. Remember the little seed in the Styrofoam cup: The roots go down and the plant goes up and nobody really knows how or why, but we are all like that.
Goldfish and hamsters and white mice and even the little seed in the Styrofoam cup—they all die. So do we.
And then remember the Dick-and-Jane books and the first word you learned—the biggest word of all—LOOK.

Everything you need to know is in there somewhere. The Golden Rule and love and basic sanitation. Ecology and politics and equality and sane living.

Take any one of those items and extrapolate it into sophisticated adult terms and apply it to your family life or your work or your government or your world and it holds true and clear and firm. Think what a better world it would be if we all—the whole world—had cookies and milk about three o'clock every afternoon and then lay down with our blankies for a nap. Or if all governments had a basic policy to always put things back where they found them and to clean up their own mess.

And it is still true, no matter how old you are—when you go out into the world, it is best to hold hands and stick together.

*Source:* Fulghum, R. (1988). *All I really need to know I learned in kindergarten: Uncommon thoughts on common things* (pp. 6–8). New York: Villard Books. Copyright © 1986, 1988 by Robert Fulghum. Reprinted by permission of Villard Books, a division of Random House, Inc.

ficiently to handle independent reading and research requiring long-term planning and organization. Children's growing skills in spelling, handwriting, and written expression allow a shift to more complex written tests and short essays to assess their knowledge. The typical student's strong basic skills, developed during the early elementary grades, form the foundation for building much more complex comprehension and written expression skills in the later elementary school years. These more complex skills, in turn, are used to tackle learning in content area subjects such as social studies and science.

***By fourth grade, the average student's reading, comprehension, and learning strategies have matured sufficiently to handle independent reading and research requiring long-term planning and organization.***

In the wake of this great leap forward in learning, a child with a learning disability is at a terrible disadvantage. Still trying to master the basics, the student with LD is ill-prepared to handle higher-level content area instruction. It comes as no surprise that one-third to one-half or more of children with LD have disabilities in multiple academic areas, though the severity in each area may differ. The individual's information-processing weaknesses carry through all academic subjects because competency in all subjects relies on language, basic perceptual skills, and attention skills. It's not uncommon to see intellectual ability begin to decline in the later elementary school years as students with LD find it difficult to remain motivated and are hampered by cumulative underexposure to reading content, vocabulary, and concepts that could have augmented their reasoning abilities.

*One-third to one-half or more of children with LD have disabilities in multiple academic areas.*

*Often intellectual ability begins to decline in the later elementary years due to cumulative underexposure to reading content, vocabulary, and concepts that could have augmented reasoning abilities.*

Some children emerge for the first time as learning disabled in the later elementary grades. They may have muddled through at the back of the pack in the early grades, only to falter significantly when faced with the more complex comprehension, written expression, and math requirements of the later elementary grades. By this time also, these students have failed often enough to lower their self-confidence and zeal to achieve. Many have also been ignored and experienced rejection from their higher-achieving peers, which further damages their often weak social skills. These emotional jolts are often more damaging to future adjustment than the academic weaknesses themselves.

## Reading Decoding

Critical to all learning is the ability to read for understanding. The first step in this process is learning to decode, which involves cracking the alphabetical code. Typically children begin learning to decode by attending to selected visual aspects of words, and then they progress to analyzing and sequencing the individual sounds. This is followed by internalization of the commonly occurring patterns of letters in words, and finally they master reading for meaning with little conscious attention to decoding.

Some children with learning disabilities follow the same path, albeit in a slower fashion. For them, a curriculum adjusted to their maturational readiness levels may be all that's needed for success. For others, reading is a major problem because they overuse either the visual or the phonological strategies, and underuse the alternate approach. For the most severely learning disabled, reading is blocked because they are weak in both processes, and highly specialized teaching approaches are necessary.

*Reading progress becomes problematic when children overuse either the visual or the phonological strategies, and underuse the alternate approach. For the most severely learning disabled, reading is blocked because they are weak in both processes.*

**Acquisition of Decoding Skills.** Many aspects of learning to read are still being debated among experts. There is growing consensus, however, that learning to read involves a gradual shift from a primarily visual processing task to one that involves analyzing and sequencing sounds, becoming aware of common letter sequences, and finally assigning meaning to the written language. Brain imaging studies show that the proficient reader has integrated the visual and phonetic aspects, and he or she can merely glance at words and instantly recognize them. Experts generally agree upon three broad, overlapping stages in the process of reading development:

- *Stage one: Global visual attention.* Children rely on clues from the visual attributes of selected word parts, or the words' context. Preschoolers will quickly recognize *Dunkin' Donuts* from the logo's orange and hot pink colors, *McDonald's* from its golden arches, or their own name from the pattern of shapes they see in the word and word length. In one study, for example, young children easily learned to "read" a word from a flash card that had a thumbprint on it. When shown the word again without the thumbprint, they couldn't read it. But when shown another word, accompanied by the same thumbprint, the children "read" it as the first word!

- *Stage two: Systematic visual and alphabetic attention to parts*
  *Initial phase.* The child begins to see that separate words make up a phrase. Word shape and length are important clues to meaning. For example, the child sees that there are two words in *Burger King* and that there is an up-then-down shape to the word *King.*
  *Secondary phase.* The child attends to the details within each word. He or she can see the difference between the words *king* and *wing,* for example, though all the letter sounds are not familiar. Eventually the child masters those sounds, attends to their order in words—beginning with the first and last letters—and finally can sound out unfamiliar words letter by letter. At the same time, he or she is absorbing the visual sequences of common multi-letter units in words (such as *tion, est*), thereby becoming familiar with common English spelling patterns. The more practiced children become at pronouncing chunks of letters, the better they can read new words by analogy to the words they already know (for example, reading *fountain* by analogy to *mountain,* or *brother* by analogy to *mother*). The child's letter-sound knowledge and growing knowledge of how to pronounce common letter patterns eventually secures the word in memory.

- *Stage three: Reading for comprehension.* The child is able to read with greater and greater ease by looking at words and paying less attention to letter cues. Because the visual, *orthographic* (common spelling patterns), and phonetic aspects of words are processed with such little effort, the child can now concentrate on meaning.

***Typically children begin learning to decode by attending to selected visual aspects of words, and then they learn to analyze and sequence individual sounds in words. Finally they internalize common letter patterns in words and read for meaning with little conscious attention to decoding.***

Research suggests that what's happening is that as the child matures a shift in strategy preference from the right to the left hemisphere of the brain takes place during stage two. By stage three, the left hemisphere's phonological/analytical strategies (to a greater extent) and the right hemisphere's visual/holistic strategies (to a lesser extent) have learned to cooperate in such an automatic fashion that word recognition is instant. The eye merely glances at words' letter patterns to get a clue to familiar words, and the child's phonetic knowledge effortlessly helps out on unfamiliar words. Orthographic awareness matures at this stage as the child understands the conventional combinations of letters in English, those combinations that can't possibly be English (*fz* for example, or *hg,* or *ck* as the beginning of a word), and those that sound different in combination than in isolation (*ight,* for example, or *kn*). The left hemisphere language centers are active in making meaning out of what has been read. The interplay between visual and phonological

*Accomplished readers recognize familiar words instantly by using their efficient visual channels, which focus on whole words and familiar letter patterns within words. They decode unfamiliar words through the phonological channel, which analyzes and sequences sound patterns.*

processes in reading development and the role of anticipation of grammar and meaning in this process have been the subject of much reading research.

**Visual and Phonological Processes.** Accomplished readers recognize familiar words instantly by using their efficient visual channels, which focus on whole words and familiar letter patterns (*orthographic recognition*) within words. They decode unfamiliar words through the phonological channel, which analyzes and sequences sound patterns according to what has been learned about letter order in the English language. This process is rapid, because good readers are efficient at dealing with word parts that have inconsistent pronunciations—such as *aid* in "said" or "maid" or *ove* in "love" or "stove"—as well as pronunciation rules (vowels are "short" in a consonant-vowel-consonant word, but "long" when a silent *e* is added: *cap* and *cape,* for example).

The orthographic route—recognizing conventional spelling patterns—turns out to be the faster way to derive meaning than the phonological route of sounding out words. Phonology requires the three steps of print, sound, and meaning, but orthographic recognition requires only two steps: recognition and meaning. Orthographic recognition develops after many successful encounters with print using the phonological route.

*Orthographic recognition of letter patterns in words develops after many successful encounters with print using the phonological route.*

The interplay between the visual and phonological processes just described becomes automatic in normal reading. No one process is entirely responsible because fluent reading requires multiple cognitive abilities to come together simultaneously and successively. At each stage of reading acquisition, the child benefits from the assistance of the cognitive systems active during the previous stages. In essence, the eye instantly recognizes a word from prior exposures, but the other word reading processes are at work to confirm the identity of the word: phonetic knowledge confirms that the pronunciation fits the spelling, knowledge of common spelling patterns and analogies to other known words confirms the pronunciation, and language comprehension confirms that the word is consistent with the text's meaning. The redundancy between all these processes helps maintain reading accuracy, sensitizes the reader to errors, and provides a way to self-correct.

*Even when the eye instantly recognizes a familiar word, phonetic and spelling-pattern knowledge confirms the pronunciation, while language comprehension confirms that the word is consistent with the text's meaning.*

**Anticipation of Grammar and Meaning.** Anticipation of the grammar and meaning in a reading passage is helpful to the reading process. Although the efficient reader favors the orthographic route to decoding, there is evidence that he or she switches as needed between orthographic, phonological, grammar, and meaning cues, using only a few at a time. Context is a big help when difficult or novel words are encountered. It is common for fluent readers to miscall words that fit according to the meaning and grammar of the sentence. For example, a third grader might read the sentence "Mother told Father to go to the grocery store to buy meat" as "Mom told Dad to stop by the market and get meat." This misreading is not considered problematic, because the meaning of the sentence is preserved; the child has used good linguistic skills to anticipate what the passage is saying. In other words, he's reading for meaning rather than meaninglessly pronouncing words.

Look at the passage in Figure 6.1. What does it say? Now look at it again. Did you notice that the word "to" is repeated? Probably not, since the grammar and

FORBIDDEN TO
TO ENTER THE DUNES

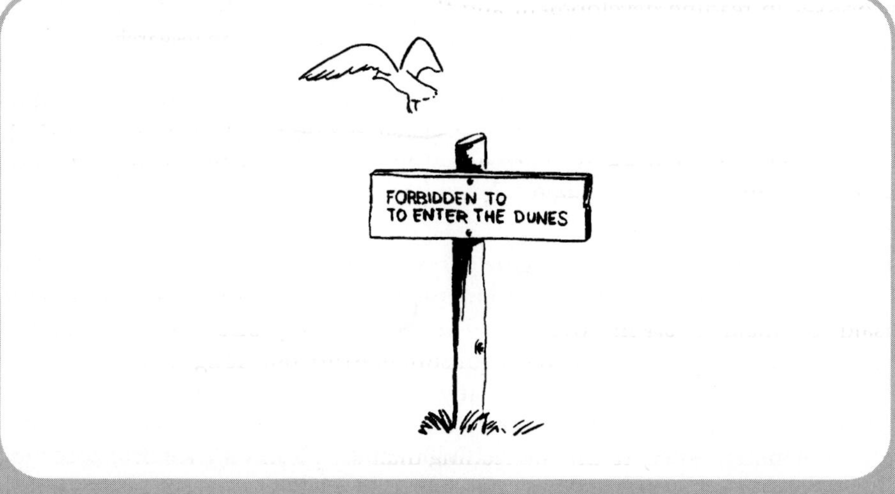

**Figure 6.1** Passage grammar and meaning help guide decoding.

*Source:* Bakker, D. J., & Licht, R. (1986). Learning to read: Changing horses in midstream. In G. Th. Pavlidis & D. F. Fisher (Eds.), *Dyslexia: Its neuropsychology and treatment* (p. 88). New York: John Wiley & Sons. © 1986 by John Wiley & Sons. Reprinted by permission.

meaning of the passage guided your reading, causing you to neglect the perceptual features of the words. Now look at Figure 6.2. Although the penmanship in the underlined words looks identical, you correctly read the word as "event" in the first sentence but "went" in the second sentence. Again, you've used your language skills and context to determine meaning. The same skills enable you to read, "Did you notice how content Judy was when she found out the content of her birthday

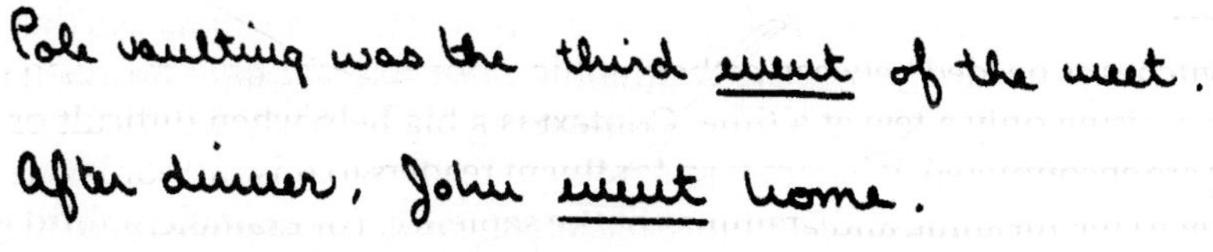

Pole vaulting was the third event of the meet.
After dinner, John went home.

**Figure 6.2** Linguistic skills help guide decoding when the orthographic information is vague.

*Source:* Nash-Webber, B. (1975). The role of semantics in automatic speech understanding. In D. G. Bobrow & A. Collins (Eds.), *Representation and understanding.* New York: Academic Press. Reprinted by permission of Daniel G. Bobrow.

package?" without mispronouncing the two meanings of the word "content." Or, "When the photographer got too close, the dove dove into the bushes."

*Efficient readers recognize most words so rapidly using their visual and phonological competencies that comprehension cues have little time to be processed and influence decoding. Poor readers, on the other hand, rely more often on context to supplement their weak decoding abilities.*

Efficient readers recognize most words so rapidly using their visual and phonological competencies that comprehension cues have little time to be processed and influence decoding. Poor readers, on the other hand, because decoding is such a struggle, rely more often on context to supplement their slow, nonsystematic decoding abilities.

**Typical Decoding Patterns.** Figure 6.3 presents the typical sequence of decoding and reading comprehension development. By second grade, children are usually in stage two of reading acquisition and by third grade they are entering stage three. By fourth grade children usually stop "learning to read" and are expected to "read to learn." It's at this stage that many children become avid readers for fun, as attested to by the Harry Potter phenomenon.

When they enter school, most children already know a great deal about the alphabet, its sounds, and the order of sounds in words. In fact, 3-year-olds are already aware that a sentence consists of discrete words. The ability of 3- and 4-year-olds to detect rhymes predicts their readiness to begin reading.

Kindergarteners can usually match letters and short words visually, discriminate among at least three stimuli at once (seeing the difference between "rat" and "tar," for example, or detecting the common sound in three rhyming words), and scan a line of print from left to right. About half of kindergarteners can split words into syllables. They are correct half the time when asked to identify and provide rhymes, blend a phoneme with a stem (for example, *d-og*), and tell whether two words begin or end with the same sound. Breaking a word into its individual sounds, or telling how many sounds they hear in a word, are beyond the capacity of most kindergarteners—less than 20 percent are able to do this.

*By age 6 approximately 90 percent of children can segment a word into syllables and 70 percent can segment a word into individual sounds.*

By age 6, approximately 90 percent of children can segment a word into its syllables and 70 percent can segment a word into its *phonemes* (individual sounds). By the end of first grade, most children can count the phonemes they hear in words and delete initial phonemes to make new words (for example, *cup–up*). The average first grader requires two visual fixations per word, but by the upper elementary grades he or she needs less than one fixation per word. Fixations last 200 to 250 milliseconds, after which the eye jumps roughly 8 spaces to the right. Half of 5- and 6-year-olds are weak in their fixation ability, so they complain that letters tend to "move around." While fixating on a word, the first grader's span extends about 11 letters/spaces to the right. Adults typically scan about 15 characters/spaces to the right on each fixation. About 10 to 15 percent of the time, the fluent reader's eyes move back in the text to comprehend material already read.

By age 7, 75 percent of children can substitute phonemes to form new words (and 95 percent by fifth grade). For example, *c*up easily shifts to *p*up, and sp*i*t to sp*o*t. They also are less likely to be confused by the orientation of reversible letters. More reading errors appear to be made with the letter *b* than with the letters *d* or *p*; very few errors are made with the letter *g*. By second grade, 70 percent of children are stable in their visual fixations (and 90 percent by age 10). They no longer complain that the letters are moving.

| | |
|---|---|
| *Middle School* | Understands paradoxes; appreciates elements of style (e.g., imagery/foreshadowing/flashback/symbolism/irony/mood); recognizes biased writings and propaganda; uses appendices, *Readers Guide to Periodicals,* atlas, almanac, appropriate reference sources; recognizes figures of speech such as personification (e.g., *the computer yawned and spit out the disk*), hyperbole (intentional exaggeration, e.g., *waiting for an eternity*), onomatopoeia (word that imitates sounds, e.g., *cuckoo*); can read many adult level books |
| *Fifth Grade* | Makes generalizations; recognizes theme; uses copyright page, preface, cross-references; familiar with more literary forms (e.g., autobiography, fable, legend); reasons using syllogisms (e.g., if a=b and b=c, then a=c); can read many popular magazines |
| *Fourth Grade* | Begins to develop different reading styles/rates for different purposes (e.g., skimming); locates and uses references; increases silent reading rate; expands vocabulary; recognizes plot and implied main idea; understands idioms/multiple meanings; paraphrases or summarizes a story or article; selects/evaluates/organizes study materials; discriminates different forms of writing (e.g., folk tale, science fiction, biography); appreciates author's point of view; considerable independent reading expected; can read newspaper, restaurant menu |
| *Third Grade* | Reading focus shifts from decoding to comprehension; rapid expansion of sight vocabulary and word-analysis skills (e.g., igh, eight); interprets homophones (e.g., way, weigh) and homographs (e.g., grizzly *bear,* to *bear* arms); reversals of letters and words generally disappear; reads selectively to locate information; reading speed increases with development of silent reading skills; distinguishes fiction/nonfiction, fact/opinion, synonym/antonym; recalls prior knowledge and relates to new text; recognizes author's purpose; uses index, captions, subheadings, margin notes; uses encyclopedia, telephone directory; interprets diagrams; reads for both knowledge and recreation |
| *Second Grade* | Mastery of harder phonetic skills (e.g., kn, wr, gh, ck, lk, ir, ur, oi, au, oa); sounds out unfamiliar words based on individual letter sounds, familiar spelling patterns, root words, endings; identifies words from contextual clues; less confusion with reversible letters; varies in pitch, stress, volume when reading aloud; aware of syllabication rules, prefixes/suffixes, changing y to i or f/fe to v before adding ending; compares/evaluates information; recognizes character, setting, motive, resolution of a story; uses library for simple research purposes; interprets graphs; uses dictionary |
| *First Grade* | Identifies consonants in all positions in a word; reads long and short vowels, some vowel teams (e.g., ee, ae) and consonant diagraphs (e.g., ch, sh, th); growing ability to break dictated words into individual sounds; reads word families (e.g., cat, hat, rat); growing sight vocabulary; aware of root words, endings, compound words, contractions; recognizes main idea and cause/effect in story; draws conclusions; follows simple written directions; aware of author, title, table of contents, alphabetical order; recognizes a play; interprets maps and globes |
| *Kindergarten* | Points to/names upper and lowercase alphabet letters; recognizes some commonly seen words (e.g., STOP, McDonald's, Sesame Street); begins to associate letters with their sounds; matches simple words to corresponding pictures; rhymes; growing awareness of whether words begin or end with the same sound; developing ability to break spoken words into syllables; blends dictated sounds to make a word; recognizes that reading proceeds from left to right and from top to bottom on a page; interprets picture stories; recognizes/compares/contrasts facts in a story; aware of time sequence in a story and predicts outcome; recognizes poetry; distinguishes reality from fantasy |

**Figure 6.3** Typical curriculum sequence for developing reading skills.

*The faster and more accurately children decode, the more their attention is freed to comprehend what has been read.*

By third grade (age 8), reading reversals tend to disappear. Children are generally adept at analyzing words based on their sounds, orthography, grammar (e.g., roots and prefixes), and clues gained from context. The faster and more accurately children decode, the more their attention is freed to comprehend what has been read. Naturally the most automatic decoders will tend to be the ones who comprehend the most.

In terms of actual reading of words, researchers find that in the fall of first grade, beginning readers can read about 5 words correctly in one minute. Soon after, progress occurs by leaps and bounds. By the end of the year, the average student has progressed to accurately reading about 40 to 60 words in a minute. The rate doubles again by the end of second grade (about 80 to 100 words per minute). Third grade is another year of rapid gain, after which the reading rate levels off to 100 to 180 words per minute. Truly skilled readers eventually read more than 300 words per minute—that's 5 words per second.

Beginning readers generally read more words incorrectly (on average 10 words incorrect per minute) than correctly. The number of errors decreases to 1 to 2 words read incorrectly per minute by sixth grade. Reading errors typical of elementary school children include

- Omitting letters or syllables in a word
- Omitting words in a sentence
- Omitting or inserting word endings
- Inserting extra sounds in words, or extra words in sentences
- Substituting words that look, sound, or have meanings similar to the printed word
- Mispronouncing initial, final, and medial letters; vowels pose greater difficulties than consonants
- Reversing whole words and the order of letters or syllables in a word (these usually are due to phonological sequencing or attention factors rather than to visual confusion)
- Transposing the order of words in a sentence
- Repeating words
- Using the wrong inflection, or ignoring punctuation

By third grade, teachers seldom listen to children read aloud anymore. Although most children are reading silently, many still subvocalize—move their lips—as they read.

*While some children with LD may progress slowly through the reading stages in the expected way, others show patterns that are qualitatively different from even younger typical learners.*

**Decoding Patterns of Students with Learning Disabilities.** Because of their information-processing immaturities, most children with LD lag behind their classmates in reading. While some may progress slowly through the reading stages in the expected way, others show patterns that are qualitatively different from even younger typical learners. Many never get beyond stage two reading because they get stuck overusing the visual/holistic or the phonological/analytical information-processing strategy and underusing the alternate strategy, or they underuse both strategies. Thus, the normal interplay between visual and phonological processes never gets established.

Children with visual-processing weaknesses have trouble recognizing and remembering how letter patterns and whole-word configurations look. They seem to attend only to partial cues in words, overlooking systematic analysis of English orthography. Children with phonological-processing weaknesses seem to be unaware that spoken language is segmented. They have trouble remembering letter sounds, analyzing the individual sounds in words, and blending these into words in the correct order. The most severely learning disabled have both weaknesses.

*Children with visual-processing weaknesses have trouble recognizing and remembering how letter patterns and whole-word configurations look.*

*Children with phonological-processing weaknesses, 60 percent of children with LD, have trouble remembering letter sounds, analyzing the individual sounds in words, and blending these into words. The most severely learning disabled have both weaknesses.*

Figures 6.4 and 6.5 list the decoding and spelling patterns of children with these information-processing weaknesses. Figure 6.6 illustrates through spelling how these students' processing preferences tend to persist into the upper grades, even though their reading ability has improved.

Studies have shown that, of students with learning disabilities, 60 percent generally have a phonological weakness, less than 10 percent have a predominant visual-processing weakness, and approximately 20 percent have both patterns at once. Children who have either a phonological- or a visual-processing weakness have more favorable prognoses than those with both weaknesses.

Phonological-processing weaknesses and language delays contribute more severely to reading disorders than do visual-processing deficits. Children with

- Confusion with letters that differ in orientation (*b–d, p–q*)
- Confusion with words whose parts can be reversed (*was–saw; bread–beard*)
- Very limited sight vocabulary; few words are instantly recognized from their familiar orthographic patterns—they need to be sounded out laboriously, as though being seen for the first time
- Losing the place because one doesn't instantly recognize what had already been read, as when switching one's gaze from the end of one line to the beginning of the next
- Omitting letters and words because they weren't noticed
- Masking the image of one letter, by moving the eye too rapidly to the next letter, may result in omission of the first letter when reading
- Difficulty learning irregular words that can't be sounded out (e.g., *yacht, pneumonia*)
- Difficulty with rapid retrieval of words when spelling due to revisualization weaknesses
- Visual stimuli when reading prove so confusing that it is easier for the child to learn to read by first spelling the words orally and then putting them in print
- Insertions, omissions, and substitutions, when the meaning of the passage is guiding reading
- Strengths in left hemisphere language-processing, analytical and sequential abilities, and detail analysis; can sound out phonetically regular words even up to grade level
- Difficulty recalling the shape of a letter when writing
- Spells phonetically but not bizarrely (*laf–laugh; bisnis–business*)
- Can spell difficult phonetic words but not simple irregular words

**Figure 6.4** Decoding and spelling patterns of children with visual-processing weaknesses.

- Difficulty discriminating between individual sounds (occurs very seldom)
- Difficulty processing rapid auditory inputs: if the teacher models a word but the child does not perceive consonant sounds that cannot be sustained (e.g., *p–b*), these may then be omitted in reading and spelling
- Poor ability to analyze the sequence of sounds and syllables in words; leads to reversals in reading; analysis and sequencing errors when speaking are common (e.g., "lead a snot into temptation" and "Harold be thy name" in the Lord's Prayer, or "elmenopee" being one lumped cluster in the alphabet song
- Poor ability to remember individual sounds or combinations of sounds
- Difficulty blending individual sounds into words
- Difficulty listening to words and omitting one sound and substituting another (say *cat;* now take off the /c/ and put on a /f/); such abilities are essential to word analysis, during which children decode by matching the new word to known words, and making the appropriate substitutions; skill with initial consonants develops first, then final consonants, and then medial vowels and consonants
- Difficulty remembering the sounds of letters and letter combinations
- Difficulty with rapid retrieval of letter sounds, so that the beginning of a word is forgotten by the time the last letter sound is recalled (word-finding problem)
- Difficulty analyzing new words because of poor knowledge of phonetic rules
- Vowel sounds are particularly troublesome
- Word substitutions may be conceptually (*person, human*) or visually (*horse, house*) related
- Limited sight vocabulary because phonetic cues can't aid memory
- Guessing at unfamiliar words rather than employing word-analysis skills
- Spelling is extremely poor because it is attempted by sight rather than by ear
- Correct spellings occur primarily on words that the child has encountered repeatedly and can revisualize
- Bizarre spellings that seldom can be identified, even by the child, because they do not follow phonetic patterns
- Extraneous letters and omitted syllables in spelling

**Figure 6.5** Decoding and spelling patterns of children with phonological-processing weaknesses.

*Phonological-processing weaknesses and language delays contribute more severely to reading disorders than do visual-processing deficits.*

phonological-processing problems have trouble sounding out unfamiliar words. If they also have language delays, they have trouble using predictions of grammar or meaning to aid in decoding. Children with visual-processing weaknesses but phonological-processing strengths, on the other hand, can at least sound out unfamiliar words, though their reading is labored because they can't quickly recognize words from their orthographic patterns. Because reading is the translation of language into a new symbol system, the better a child's language skills, the more rapid his or her reading progress is likely to be.

*Because reading is the translation of language into a new symbol system, the better a child's language skills, the more rapid reading progress is likely to be.*

Very often poor readers are hampered by poor attending abilities. Sometimes this inattention masquerades as a visual- or phonological-processing weakness. The inattentive child guesses wildly at words using the first or last letters, doesn't

ADMISSION $1.50

SOLD OUT

however

despite her anger

*Transcription:* *I'm sorry your to late for this show, however next week we will have the same sale*
*Despite her anger, she refrained from nocking his block off with the reminents of the lamp*

Maxine is a 15-year-old ninth grader of above average intelligence. When asked to compose sentences using specific words, Maxine's spellings all sound the way they should. Because of her perceptual disability, however, she does not recognize how these words should look. Likewise, she overlooks periods.

| Known Words | Unknown Words |
|---|---|
| friendship | badge |
| remember | democrat |
| important | quotation |
| comb | source |
| unless | justice |
| flower | honorable |
| whole | hasten |

A gifted seventh grader, Ethan earned over 500 on both the verbal and quantitative Scholastic Achievement Tests administered orally in seventh grade. He can spell "known" words within his sight vocabulary by remembering how they look but, unlike average achievers, he has difficulty phonetically approximating the spellings of "unknown" words that he has not yet learned to read.

**Figure 6.6** *(Top)* Spelling patterns of a student with visual-processing weaknesses. *(Bottom)* Spelling patterns of a student with phonological-processing weaknesses.

*(continued)*

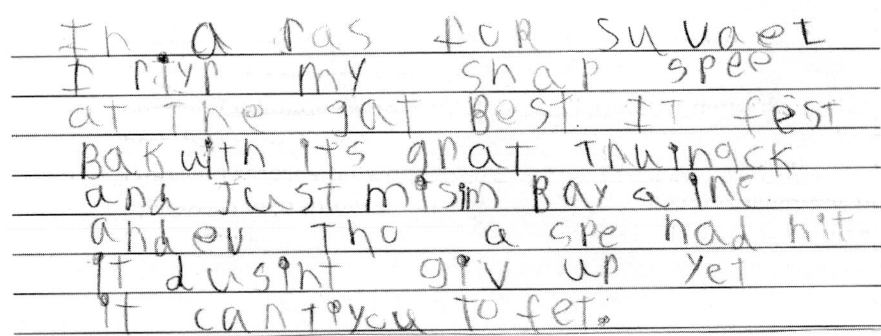

*Transcription:* *In a race for survival I raised my sharp spear at the great beast. It fought back with its great trunk and just missed him by an inch and even though a spear had hit it doesn't give up yet it can tire you to fight.*

Jimmy is a 10-year-old of high average intelligence whose parents and seven aunts and uncles have severe reading disabilities. His older sister is an honor student. Jimmy does not spell with good phonetic equivalents, and he can spell very few words in his limited sight vocabulary.

**Figure 6.6** *Continued.* Spelling patterns of a student with both visual- and phonological-processing weaknesses.

take the time to sound out, and doesn't pay attention to the order of letters in a word or the way words are ordered in a sentence. He or she also misses the orientation of reversible letters. Errors increase as reading continues because the child's attentional resources wane rapidly. Fortunately, when teachers help these students systematically focus their attention on the important features of words and passages, they often find that the child has some very good basic abilities to bring to the task of reading.

Careful analysis of whether a child's reading error patterns are visual, phonological, or language confusions is very helpful when planning which weaknesses to remediate and which strengths to capitalize on in teaching. A careful analysis can show that children's errors usually are not random mistakes. Their mistakes are due to miscues generated by the child's information-processing style or past learning. Miscues that change the meaning of a passage (reading *pit* for *pet,* for example) are more serious than those that do not interfere with comprehension (as in substituting *mom* for *mother*). Teachers are advised not to pay too much attention to word omissions or insertions because they seldom alter the passage's meaning.

***Children's reading errors generally are not random mistakes. They are due to miscues generated by the child's information-processing style or past learning.***

The tendency to reverse letters when reading or spelling has troubled parents and professionals ever since reading disabilities were first recognized. The majority of these reversals are related to poor use of knowledge about letter sounds and the order of sounds to assist in distinguishing letters and words whose orientation can be reversed. As reading skills improve, reversal errors diminish. Figure 6.7 and Research Box 6.1 on page 170 explain why these reversals deserve far less attention in the teaching process than does fostering children's phonetic analysis skills.

When reading, children with reading disabilities often hold the book too close to the face (because of the effort being expended), fidget, refuse to read, read slowly word by word, use an unnatural voice quality, and ignore words they can't read. They read accurately only one-third to one-half of the words their classmates can read. After such a struggle, it's no wonder these children have trouble understanding or remembering much of what they've read.

***Children with reading disabilities read accurately only one-third to one-half of the words their classmates can read. After this struggle, these children have trouble understanding or remembering much of what they've read.***

In writing, as in his reading, this 10-year-old student has far more difficulty approximating the phonetic equivalent of words (9 errors) than he does with reversal of letter orientation (2 errors) or with transposing the order of sounds in words (1 error).

**Figure 6.7** The writing of students with LD shows a low frequency of letter reversals compared to other errors.

RESEARCH BOX 6.1

## Letter Reversals in Reading and Spelling

As a proportion of total errors, reversals of letter and word orientation are no greater for poor readers than for good readers (Stanovich, 1982). Reversals seem to occur more often for poor readers, however, because these students' overall error rates are greater. When writing (see Figure 6.7 on page 169, for example), only 15 percent of the errors of children with reading disabilities tend to be reversals of letter orientation, a visual error (Liberman, 1985). In contrast, Liberman found that consonant sounds accounted for 32 percent of errors; vowel sounds, 43 percent; and transpositions of the order of sounds in words, 10 percent (which is responsible for *dynamic reversals,* as in *pit* for *tip*).

By age 8 to 8½ reversals disappear in average readers, but the reversal tendency can persist longer for children with LD. As children's reading skills improve, their reversal errors diminish, and by age ten the difference between the number of reversals made by children with and without reading disabilities becomes negligible (Wolff & Melngailis, 1996). Although increasing a child's attention to letter orientation and reversal errors is important and useful, exercises in this area should not be allowed to overshadow sharpening of a child's phonetic analysis abilities.

Intensive reading intervention is critical the moment reading decoding delays become apparent. Considering that the average child in the elementary grades learns about 3,000 new words per year, there is no time to waste. If the child with a learning disability continues to struggle with the basic decoding process, comprehension will suffer as well. When comprehension suffers, so does exposure to information and ideas meant to spur a child's intellectual development.

## Reading Comprehension

*Once past the decoding stage of reading, children can make use of their reading skills as tools for learning.*

Once past the decoding stage of reading, children can make use of their reading skills as tools for learning. In the earlier grades, they become attuned to story elements such as the main character, sequence of events, inferences, motivations and feelings, and sentence order. As they get older, they become more efficient at recognizing and recalling facts, main themes and relationships, drawing conclusions, making judgments and generalizations, predicting outcomes, applying what they've learned, and following directions. Instruction shifts from decoding to helping children develop strategies for extracting meaning from their reading and for independent study such as skimming, using reference materials, outlining, summarizing, altering reading rate with the purpose of reading, using headings, note taking, and so on.

*Students with LD expend so much energy decoding that they have little energy left for comprehension.*

Unfortunately, students who are learning disabled are often still struggling to decode. They expend so much energy in this effort that they have little energy left for comprehension. This problem is aggravated by the fact that their poor decoding skills have inhibited growth in comprehension and memory strategies that average readers develop as they gain skills in reading.

Lectures and tapes as aids to learning assist poor readers a great deal with their comprehension, but they are not sufficient. The vocabulary used when teachers lecture is rarely as rich and varied as that used in written material. Moreover, detailed information conveyed orally is harder to recall. Although tapes can be replayed (which students seldom do), unrecorded lectures and class discussion cannot, which prevents students from reviewing harder material. Consequently, over time students who rely on oral material only may not develop a rich enough knowledge base and vocabulary to support comprehension of increasingly complex content in the upper grades.

*Over time students who rely on oral material only (lectures, tapes) may not develop a rich enough knowledge base and vocabulary to support comprehension of increasingly complex content in the upper grades.*

For other students with learning disabilities, the comprehension problem goes far beyond simply decoding weaknesses. Their comprehension is compromised because they don't understand the language of instruction or they use inefficient learner strategies. Thus, learning is problematic through both reading and listening.

**Linguistic Deficits.** A number of language weaknesses make comprehension difficult. Children may not understand the vocabulary and grammar they are reading. Moreover, the sheer number of words in a sentence may overwhelm them. These are serious problems in the face of expectations in the upper elementary grades to read long passages with high-level vocabulary and language embellishments such as antonyms, metaphors, idioms, proverbs, and poetry.

*Children with LD may not understand the vocabulary and grammar they are reading, and the sheer number of words in a sentence may overwhelm them.*

Children with language weaknesses don't automatically pick up meaning from what they read. Nor do they find it easy to convey what they do understand if they are hampered by poor grammar, articulation, or word-finding problems. These language weaknesses require extensive intervention by both the speech-language pathologist and the teacher, and major accommodations are required in the language of the curriculum.

**Inefficient Learner Strategies.** Some students with LD have good learning abilities, but they approach learning tasks inefficiently. Others have inefficient strategies because they have information-processing weaknesses such as inadequate selective attention, weak visual and holistic processing strategies, or weak language-processing, analysis, and sequencing strategies. Yet other students' preferred cognitive styles (preferring big ideas to details, for example) don't match the demands of the curriculum. Because inefficient learner strategies can interfere with every aspect of the learning process, it's important not only to match teaching approaches to students' preferred learning strategies but also to directly teach a student with LD how to pay attention, think, memorize, and retrieve information more effectively. The way that "knowing how to know" typically evolves, and the metacognitive training that can help students become aware of what they need to do to learn more effectively, are explored in Chapter 7.

*Because inefficient learner strategies can interfere with every aspect of the learning process, it's important to match teaching approaches to students' preferred learning strategies but also to directly teach a student with LD how to pay attention, think, memorize, and retrieve information more effectively.*

## Written Expression

Written expression is the highest form of language accomplishment. Writing requires the child to translate his or her comprehension, reasoning, and expression skills into the symbol system we use for reading. Students with learning disabilities frequently experience lifelong difficulties in this area.

*Written expression is the highest form of language accomplishment, requiring children to translate their comprehension, reasoning, and expression skills into the symbol system used for reading.*

**Acquisition of Written Language.** Figure 6.8 outlines the typical curriculum sequence for developing written expression skills. Although children have been writing with "invented" spellings (spelling words as they sound) and telling stories since their preschool days, in the upper elementary grades they hone their spelling and handwriting skills while developing a greater understanding of the mechanical rules (capitalization, punctuation, grammar) and ideational aspects of writing. The ideational aspect can be divided into five categories.

1. *Story.* The child names and describes the objects, characters, time and setting; presents a plot, action, and ending; addresses abstract issues such as a theme, morality, causation, goals, and personal reactions of characters.
2. *Fluency.* The child's stories have longer sentences and more words as he or she gets older. The average number of words written about a picture jumps from about 85 words in third grade to 200 words in sixth grade.
3. *Cohesion.* The child writes stories that are easy to understand because he or she has supplied logical transitions between sentences, ideas, and events.
4. *Reality.* The story is believable given the author's perceptions, even if a fantasy.
5. *Style.* A unique style can be discerned, which includes appropriate use of different sentence forms, tone, and choice of vocabulary to express thoughts.

By the time they enter school, most children already have a well-developed idea of how to create stories. With maturity their stories include more inferences, critical evaluation, and abstract language (such as metaphors and plays on words). Students also are able to proofread their work more critically and to make modifications where appropriate. The ability to plan and revise using notes is usually established by the time the child enters middle school. Before age 10, children tend to think of planning as writing, so "planning" consists simply of producing a first draft.

**Written Language Patterns of Students with Learning Disabilities.** We expect children with reading and spelling disorders to have a difficult time with writing. The same problems that delay reading and spelling acquisition interfere with the quality of their written expression. These children's stories often are limited in vocabulary, idea generation, and maturity of themes. They tend to get bogged down in descriptions of characters or settings, or they use free associations rather than action sequences. Their stories may not have a beginning, middle, or ending; they may not state a problem to be resolved. They neglect the characters' motives, thoughts, feelings, and relationships. They may not set the scene at a specific location, provide a sense of time, or deal with causation. Their work is complicated further by poor spelling, grammar, organization, or cohesion. They use fewer words, ideas, pertinent details, descriptions, and comparison-contrast. Capitalization, punctuation, revising, irrelevancies, and redundancies are typical problems.

The stories of students with LD may be a string of "and thens" without relationship to major and minor ideas. These students tend to be most concerned with what to say next rather than with how their ideas relate to an overall premise. And they spend virtually no time planning their writing or revising the finished product.

|  |  |
|---|---|
| *Middle School* | Develops increasing sophistication in ideas and expression; accurate/effective/appropriate choice of words and phrases; edits to improve style and effect; avoids wordiness and unnecessary repetition; uses complex sentences; avoids vagueness and omissions; develops paragraphs with details/reasons/examples/comparisons; checks for accuracy of statements; connects ideas with transition words; develops paragraphs with topic sentences; adds introduction and conclusion; checks reasoning; uses several sources to prepare a report; makes a bibliography; capitalizes first word of a quote/adjectives of race and nationality; punctuates appropriately; learns to use footnotes; learns note taking skills |
| *Fifth Grade* | Varies type of sentences, including imperative; subjects and verbs agree; uses compound subjects and predicates; ideas are clearly stated in more than one paragraph; keeps to the topic; uses antonyms/prefixes/suffixes/contractions/compound words/ words with sensory images/rhyme and rhythm; greater precision in choice of words; uses dictionary for definitions/syllables/pronunciation; capitalizes names of streets/places/persons/countries/oceans/trade names/beginning items in outlines/titles with a name (e.g., President Roosevelt); uses quotation marks or underlining for titles; classifies words by parts of speech; uses subheads in outlines; writes from outline; writes dialogue; recognizes topic sentences; enjoys writing/receiving letters; keeps a diary |
| *Fourth Grade* | Writes in cursive; develops interesting paragraphs and a sense of the writing process (outline first, write, revise); chooses words that appeal to the senses or that precisely explain a point; capitalizes names of cities/states/organizations; uses apostrophe to show possession, hyphen to divide word at end of line, exclamation point, colon after salutation, quotation marks, comma before quotation in a sentence, period after outline items or Roman numerals; uses command sentences; avoids sentence fragments; selects appropriate title; makes simple outline; writes/tells stories that have character and plot |
| *Third Grade* | Writes with both printing and cursive; writes short passages expressing a central idea; sequences ideas well and uses expanded vocabulary; identifies/uses various sentence forms (e.g., declarative, interrogative/exclamatory); combines short, choppy sentences into longer ones; uses interesting beginning and ending sentences; avoids run-on sentences; uses synonyms; distinguishes meaning and spelling of homonyms; uses the prefix "un" and the suffix "less"; capitalizes month/day/common holidays/first word in a line of verse/"Dear"/"Sincerely;" adds period after abbreviations/initials; uses apostrophe in common contractions (e.g., isn't); adds commas in a list; indents; spells many words in sight vocabulary (including irregular words such as "eight"); proofreads own and others' work |
| *Second Grade* | Writes letters legibly and uses appropriate size; understands how writing should be laid out (e.g., margins); combines short sentences into paragraphs; spelling and grammatical expression continue to improve; uses words with similar and opposite meanings in writing; alphabetizes; capitalizes important words in book titles, proper names, Mr./Mrs./Miss/Ms.; adds question mark at the end of a question; adds comma after salutation and closing of a letter; adds comma between the month/year and city/state; avoids running sentences together with "and"; begins to use cursive; begins to develop proofreading skills |
| *First Grade* | Uses traditional as well as invented spellings; works on copying letters and words; writes simple sentences; begins to write short poems, invitations, compositions; tries to use words that describe what the child sees, hears, feels as well as how things look, act, feel; capitalizes the first word of a sentence, first and last names, names of streets/towns/the school, and I; adds a period at the end of sentences and after numbers in a list; prints on the line |
| *K* | Develops ability to hold and use pencils; traces/copies/writes letters, name, and simple sight words; writes short "stories" using dashes for words or invented spellings |

**Figure 6.8** Typical curriculum sequence for developing written expression skills.

Students with visual-processing difficulties but good language abilities may be good writers but poor spellers. Those with motor-production problems can often compose well if allowed to dictate or use a tape recorder.

*Students with language disturbances are the most severely disabled when it comes to writing.*

Students with language disturbances are the most severely disabled when it comes to writing. If they can't develop ideas orally, how can they be expected to do so in writing? When a 12-year-old's grammar is like that of a 5- or 6-year-old, or when word comprehension is equal to a 7- or 8-year-old, he or she has only a slim chance of mastering high-level writing skills without explicit and intense language remediation.

If their written expression is problematic because of attention deficits or unique cognitive styles, children can succeed when they are made aware of their styles and are taught systematic methods to follow for writing, including brainstorming and editing checklists. The impulsive child (who writes a few short paragraphs and thinks he or she has said it all) can be encouraged to support main ideas by elaborating with relevant details. The overly reflective child (who writes page after page but never comes to the point) may be helped by learning to create outlines that build the theme.

*The best kind of writing remediation focuses on idea generation rather than spelling, handwriting, and other mechanics. Without good ideas to write about, the rest is useless.*

The best kind of writing remediation focuses on idea generation rather than spelling, handwriting, and other mechanics. Without good ideas to write about, the rest is useless. Writing is important not only as an avenue for creativity and a way for students to develop thinking ability, but it is also the major means by which they are evaluated in the upper grades.

## Handwriting

*Visual-perceptual difficulties, motor incoordination, and attention weaknesses make writing legibly and correctly a real trial for some children with LD.*

Handwriting is often the Achilles heel of the learning disabled. Their visual-perceptual difficulties, motor incoordination, and attention weaknesses make writing legibly and correctly a real trial. Unfortunately, handwriting problems often mask children's more competent underlying knowledge. And there's no escape. In spite of the nearly universal availability of word processors, young children still handwrite the majority of their homework, in-class assignments, and tests. That 30 to 60 percent of the school day is spent in paper-pencil and other fine-motor activities (cutting, pasting, drawing) poses quite an obstacle for the 75 to 90 percent of students with learning disabilities who have fine-motor difficulties.

**Acquisition of Handwriting Skills.** By the time most children enter first grade, they can hold a pencil comfortably in the typical three-finger grasp, print letters from memory, and copy 3- to 4-letter words. They know that printing moves from left to right, and they can stay reasonably close to the line. Their letters may vary in size, spacing, alignment, proportion, slant, pencil pressure (heavy, light), and form. Reversals of letter orientation and sequence are common when children in the early grades write, though far less common than form errors. For most children, reversals tend to disappear by age 8 to 8½.

*Reversals of letter orientation and sequence are common when children in the early grades write, though far less common than form errors. Reversals tend to disappear by age 8 to 8½.*

Figure 6.9 shows handwriting samples of weak, average, and strong writers at different grades. The quality of these children's samples differs sharply from the handwriting of children with learning disabilities shown in the same figure and elsewhere in this text. As you can see, by the end of third grade, children have made

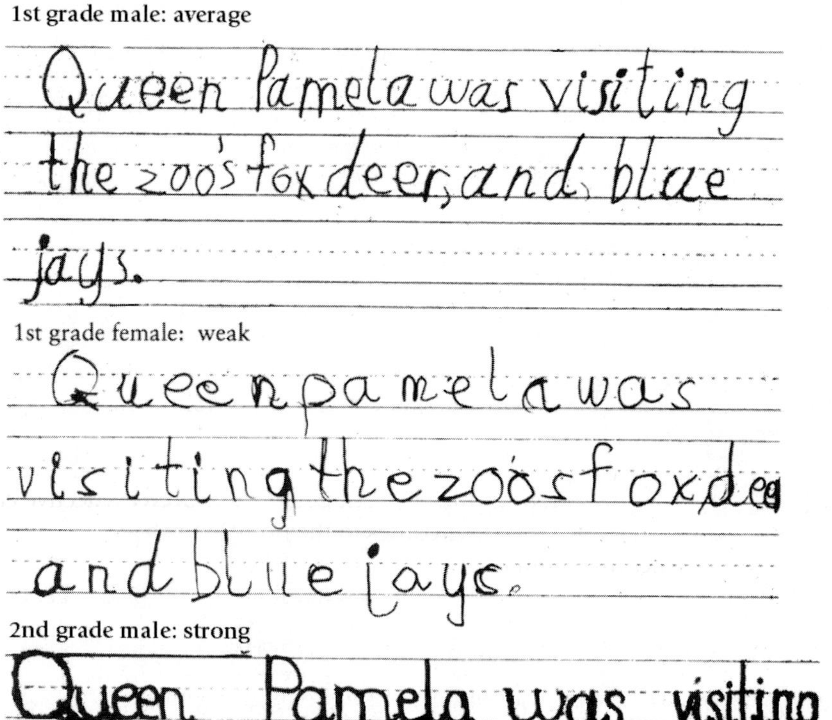

1st grade male: average

Queen Pamela was visiting
the zoo's fox deer, and blue
jays.

1st grade female: weak

Queenpamelawas
visitingthezoo'sfoxdee
andbluejays.

2nd grade male: strong

Queen Pamela was visiting
the zoo's fox, deer, and blue
jays.

2nd grade female: average

Queen Pamela was visiting
The zoo's fox, deer, and
blue jays.

**Figure 6.9** Handwriting samples of weak, average, and strong writers as well as students with learning disabilities. The samples were collected by having each student in a suburban elementary school copy the same sentence. The samples were sorted by sex into weak, average, and strong piles at each grade level. The middlemost sample in each pile is what has been reproduced here.

*(continued)*

3rd grade male: weak

Queen Pamela was visiting the soo's fox deer and blue jays.

3rd grade male: average

Queen Pamela was visiting the zoo's fox deer and blue jays.

4th grade male: average

Queen Pamela was visiting the zoo's fox, deer, and blue jays.

4th grade male: weak

Queen Pamela was visiting the zoo's fox, deer and blue jays.

4th grade male: strong

Queen Pamela was visiting the zoo's fox, deer, and blue jays.

3rd grade female: strong

Queen Pamela was visiting the zoo's fox, deer and bluejays.

3rd grade female: weak

Queen Pamela was visit the zoo fox, deer and blue-jays

4th grade female: strong

Queen Pamela was visiting the zoo's fox, deer, and blue jays.

4th grade female: average

Queen Pamela was visiting the zoo's fox, deer, and blue jays.

4th grade female: weak

Queen Pamela was iting the zoo's fox, deer and blue jays.

**Figure 6.9** *Continued*

**1st grade female with a learning disability: age 7**

**6th grade female with a learning disability: age 14**

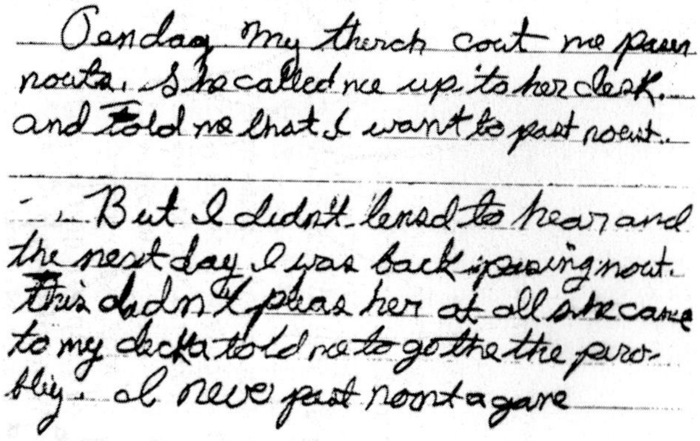

**3rd grade male with a learning disability: age 9**

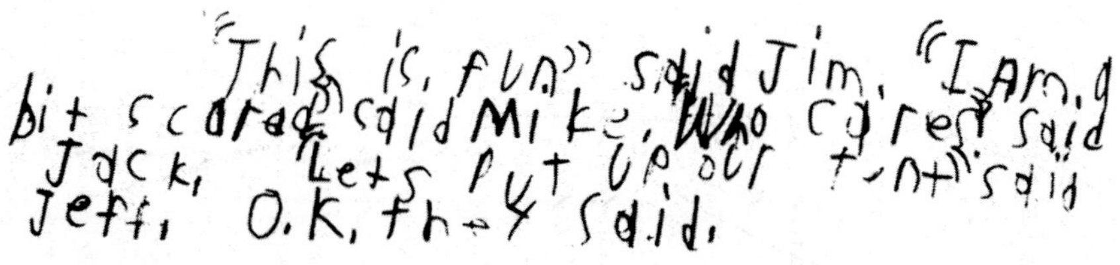

**Figure 6.9** *Continued*

the transition to cursive writing, which refines itself in subsequent grades. By sixth grade, children (especially girls) have experimented with many handwriting styles and usually have adopted one style that will remain their own with minor variations throughout their lives. Left-handers have no more trouble writing than right-handers, though they need to slant their paper in the opposite direction to prevent the characteristic "hook."

**Handwriting Patterns of Students with Learning Disabilities.** Children with handwriting difficulties tend to write slowly and in a labored fashion. The end product is often sloppy and illegible. They seldom develop a distinct style of handwriting. Written tests and essays pose difficulties because the painstaking process of directing their pencils to form letters impedes their thought processes; sustaining energy long enough to put their thoughts on paper is extremely difficult. The slow writing speed impedes the quality and quantity of what is written. When children can access letter forms rapidly in memory and produce them automatically without conscious effort, their attentional resources are freed up to plan the writing content and generate text.

*The learning disabled write on average 30 percent slower than children without disabilities.*

Though there is considerable variability, from the upper elementary years onward the average students easily can write about 70 characters per minute. The learning disabled are on average 30 percent slower. Though they can increase their writing speed to equal that of their peers, legibility suffers. By contrast, when their classmates are asked to speed up, their speed increases almost twice as much as the increase of the learning disabled, but legibility is preserved.

Many children with weaknesses in this area grip their pencils awkwardly and too tightly. Their writing postures are uncomfortable, and they exert too much pressure on the paper. As shown in Figure 6.10, their letters often don't meet the line. Poor handwriters have difficulty with letter size, slant, formation, and spac-

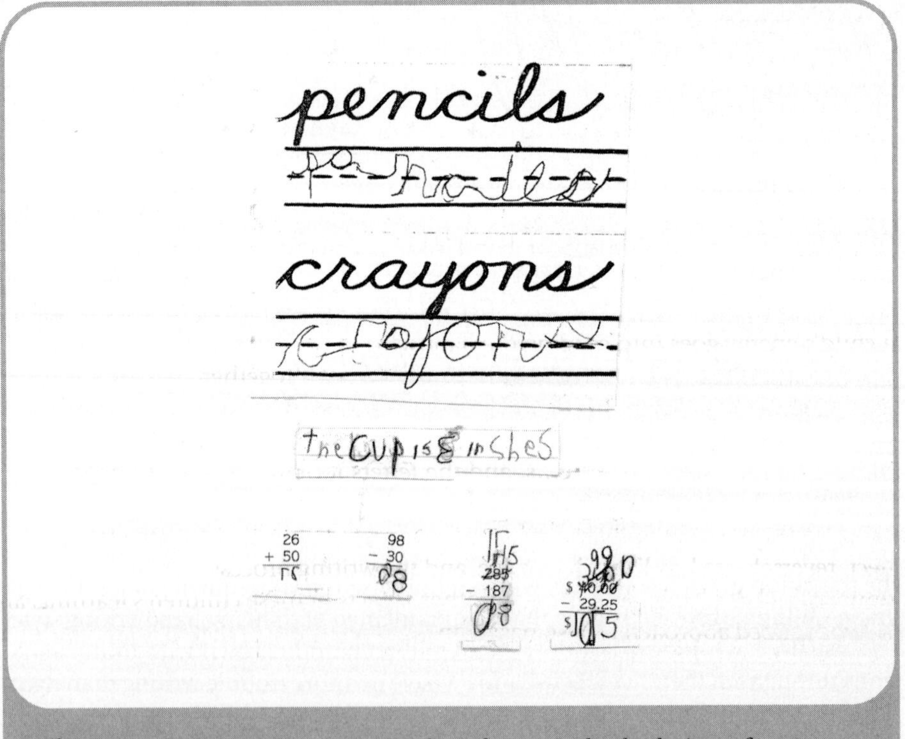


**Figure 6.10** Cursive copying and mathematical calculation of an 8-year-old boy with average intelligence who has learning disabilities.

ing. Forming letters made up of verticals and horizontal strokes *(T, L, F)* present less of a problem than those containing diagonals *(K)* or curves that meet lines *(R)*. Interspersing capital and small letters is common.

As seen in Figure 6.10, writing reversals continue longer than customary in these children. This is especially true for boys. Reversals seem to occur because these children don't allocate sufficient attention to the features that distinguish one letter or number from another, especially the direction in which a letter or number faces. Typical readers use their knowledge of letter sounds to help sharpen these distinctions, but children with reading delays do not have this advantage. Reversals tend to resolve themselves as children learn to use their visual, language, and cognitive competencies to distinguish "up" from "down" *(p–b, u–n, m–w)* and "left" from "right" *(b–d, E–3)*. Reversals of numbers tend to be resolved before letter reversals, perhaps because there are fewer to confuse. The handwriting problems of students with LD have been related to underlying visual-perceptual difficulties, motor incoordination, or attention weaknesses.

***Visual-Perceptual Difficulties.*** The child with visual-perceptual difficulties may pause while writing because he or she can't recall how a letter looks, or stop while copying because he or she can't hold in mind the images of the letters. Poor spatial judgment also compromises handwriting quality. Only about 25 percent of children with learning disabilities have this kind of problem related to handwriting.

***Uncoordinated Motor Movements.*** The application of uncoordinated motor movements to the writing space is the most common cause of handwriting problems. These children's hands don't seem to write "automatically," so they must consciously plan and direct their hand's movements. In contrast, the typical child without LD, having memorized a piano piece, simply relaxes and lets his or her hands play away. Try sticking your hand into ice water for one minute, and then try to write. Like the learning disabled, you'll see how much energy you have to divert from what you're writing to instruct your hand on how to move. When so much of a child's energy goes into guiding the handwriting itself, it's no wonder that ideas become muddled, abbreviated, disorganized, or lost altogether.

***When so much of a child's energy goes into guiding the handwriting itself, ideas become muddled, abbreviated, disorganized, or lost altogether.***

There is debate about whether young children with handwriting difficulties should use printing or switch to cursive writing. Printing has the advantage of requiring less complex movements, and the letters look like those in books. Some say that it is better to learn one system well than to be confused about two. On the other hand, cursive writing makes spatial judgments easier because the letters connect, reversals are less likely in cursive, and the writing process is more rapid, continuous, and rhythmic. As with many other aspects of these children's learning, an individualized approach is best, based on what seems to work best for a particular child.

***Inattention.*** Inattention can have an impact at the input and output stages of handwriting. Children miss details of letters and words and don't plan their space and motor movements. Their inattention causes them to drift off in midstream, having produced very little. The child with LD hands in a paper that looks like it's gone through a war. Impulsive as he is, he'll simply write over errors in bolder print. If she bothers to erase, she'll often do so incompletely, turning the paper into a black smudge. Homework is returned folded haphazardly or torn—if it gets returned at all. The inattentive child can do far better when attention is appropriately focused and sustained.

## Spelling

*For most individuals with LD, spelling is a much more difficult task than reading, and difficulties persist long after reading problems have been resolved.*

Children's spelling reflects their ability to hear positions of sounds in spoken words as well as their ability to store and recall the orthographic patterns in words they have read. For most individuals with learning disabilities, spelling is a much more difficult task than reading, and difficulties persist long after reading problems have been resolved.

**Acquisition of Spelling Skills.** Spelling instruction usually doesn't begin in earnest until the middle of second grade. This gives children time to become familiar with the visual and *phonic* (letter sounds) elements of reading words. In the meantime, "invented" spellings—that is, spelling words the way they sound, such as *blt* for *built*—is encouraged. Children can point to correct spellings of words long before they can spell these same words from memory (this is true of adults also: even though you can spot if the word *conscientious* "looks right," try spelling it!).

*Children seem to approach spelling first with phonological strategies and then add visual strategies gained from familiarity with print conventions.*

The spelling acquisition process is the reverse of stages one and two in reading acquisition. Children seem to approach spelling first with phonological strategies and then add visual strategies gained from familiarity with print conventions. Preschoolers and young elementary school children often will represent a whole syllable or word with one letter. They invent their spellings around the consonants they hear in words (e.g., *quick* becomes KWK). Subvocalizing while spelling highlights these phonetic elements and helps reduce errors. Accuracy is greatest on the first sound in a word, and second best with the last sound. Medial sounds are difficult, as are vowels (which often appear in the medial position). By third grade, vowel knowledge improves and children are more aware of predictable arrangements of strings of English letters. Therefore, their spellings of words begin to approximate conventional spelling patterns and rules. Students typically continue to spell by this orthographic route, imagining the possible letter combinations. When that fails, they fall back on phonetic analysis.

English is particularly challenging to the would-be speller. Only 50 percent of English words follow regular phonetic rules. The only way to remember the irregular words is to revisualize them or deduce their spellings from derivations (roots, prefixes, suffixes), from syntax (a past tense signals an "ed" ending for the word *walk,* rather than a "t" as in *walkt*), or from familiar words that might follow a similar orthographic pattern. In English, one orthographic form can have multiple pronunciations (*cough, through, dough; height, weight*), and different patterns can have the same pronunciations (*weigh, way; threw, through*). Mastery of these patterns (e.g., that *ite* goes with *bite,* but *ight* goes with *sight*) develops later than phonetic spelling ability. Here are some other peculiarities of English spelling (just for fun . . . though the learning disabled wouldn't agree):

- The bandage was wound too tightly around the wound.
- The Bedouin stopped in the desert to eat his dessert.
- My jaw got number after the number of injections.
- I shed a tear when I noticed the tear in my stocking.

Given its complexity, it is understandable that spelling often remains a lifelong challenge for individuals with learning disabilities. Figure 6.11 shows the spelling of an average second grader who can analyze and sequence sounds in words and is beginning to take note of irregular spellings.

Invented spellings of young elementary school children are often good approximations and can convey meaning effectively. By the intermediate grades, however, children are usually able to spell more than 80 percent of the words they recognize by sight, even those that are phonetically irregular.

***By the intermediate grades, children are usually able to spell more than 80 percent of words they recognize by sight, even those that are phonetically irregular.***

**Spelling Patterns of Students with Learning Disabilities.** Children with learning disabilities often can spell less than half of their sight vocabularies. Their spelling errors include inserting unnecessary letters (*umberella* for *umbrella*), omitting letters (*famly* for *family*), substituting letters (*kast* for *cast*), phonetic spelling of irregular words (*sed* for *said*), directional confusion (*was* for *saw*), vowel-consonant order changes (*tabel* for *table*), vowel substitutions (*doller* for *dollar*), letter orientation confusion (*d–b, p–q, n–u,* etc.), and reversed letter sequences (*aminals* for *animals*).

***Children with LD often can spell less than half of their sight vocabularies.***

Figure 6.6 illustrated the difficulty that children who are learning disabled have with the phonetic elements of spelling, the revisualization/orthographic awareness elements, or with both. These children typically show the same types of errors in spelling as they do in reading. Consider Avery, for example, who has a phonological-processing problem and has trouble analyzing the sound sequences in words. Although she is able to spell irregular words with which she is familiar, Avery can't spell easier phonetically regular words with which she is unfamiliar. Because she also has language delays, Avery does not use language cues to guess at spellings (e.g., that a past tense must be indicated by "ed"—*spilled* not *spilt*). Malcolm, on the other hand, has visual-processing and orthographic awareness weaknesses. He can spell phonetically regular words he's never seen, yet has trouble revisualizing the conventional letter sequences in familiar irregular words. Of the two, Avery will be the more impaired in both reading and spelling. After all, she can't rely on her phonological skills and there is a limit to the number of words anyone can store as visual images. When visual recall fails, we need to rely on phonetic analysis to aid our spelling.

***Children with LD show the same types of errors in spelling as they do in reading, with phonological-processing weaknesses creating greater delays than visual-processing weaknesses.***

Figure 6.12 shows the spelling of 10-year-old Joe, who is trying to apply orthographic and visualization strategies to recall spellings. His phonics skills are progressing, but you can still see the underlying language and phonological difficulties in his grammatical errors and phoneme omissions and substitutions.

Finally, as in reading, attention deficits too can influence spelling quality. When the inattentive child is prompted to think about whether he or she has seen the word before, which familiar words sound similar, and the different possible spellings, spelling often improves.

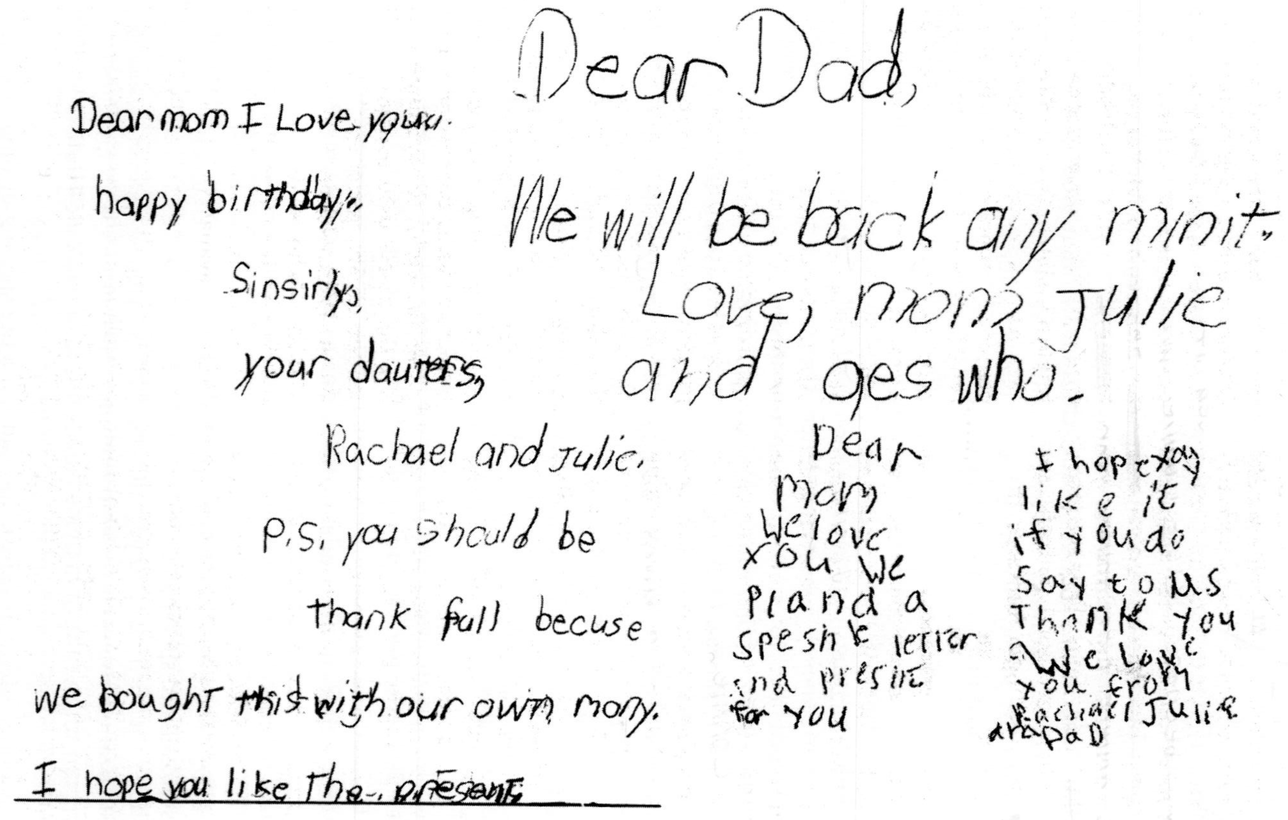

Dear mom I Love you.

happy birthday.

Sinsirly,

your dauters,

Rachael and Julie.

P.S. you should be

thank full becuse

we bought this with our own mony.

I hope you like the present

Dear Dad,

We will be back any minit.

Love, mom Julie

and ges who.

Dear

mom

We love

you We

pland a

speshle letter

and presint

for you

I hope you

like it

if you do

Say to us

Thank you

We love

you from

Rachael Julie

and Dad

Figure 6.11 Phonetic spelling of an average second grader.

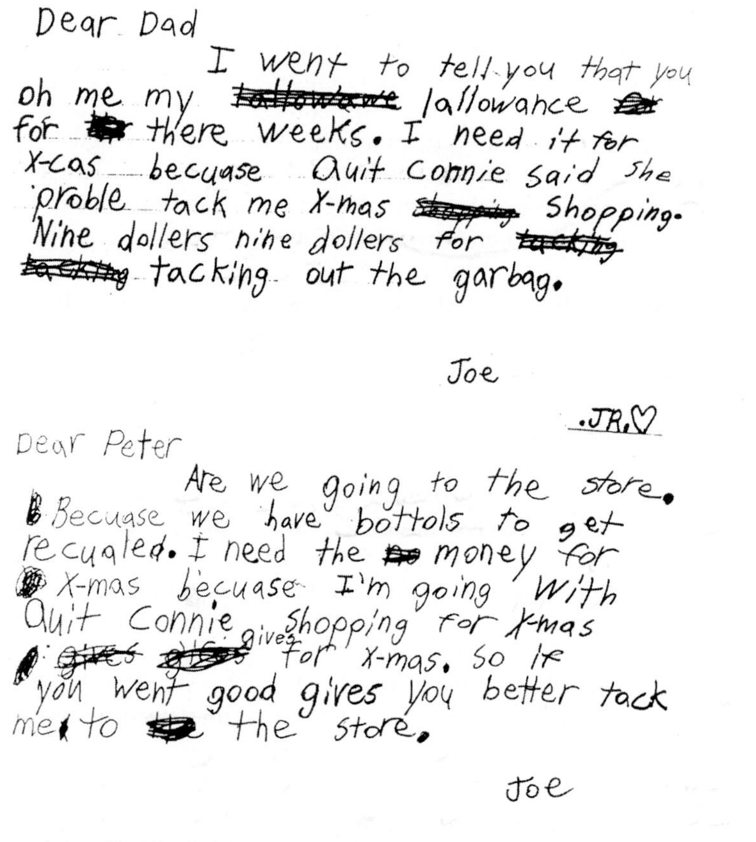

Dear Dad
I went to tell you that you
oh me my lallowance
for there weeks. I need it for
X-cas becuase Auit Connie said she
proble tack me X-mas Shopping.
Nine dollers nine dollers for
tacking out the garbag.

Joe

.JR.♡

Dear Peter
Are we going to the store.
Becuase we have bottols to get
recualed. I need the money for
X-mas becuase I'm going With
Auit Connie shopping for X-mas
gives for X-mas. So if
you went good gives you better tack
me to the store.

Joe

**Figure 6.12** Correspondence of Joe, a 10-year-old boy with learning disabilities.

## Mathematics

In spite of the computer revolution and the rapid calculations now available with the click of a mouse, math skills still matter, even in relatively low-skilled jobs. The grocery clerk still needs to judge whether the register's reading of the cost of oranges makes sense given the number the customer has bought, or whether a coupon can't be doubled because the sum would be greater than the cost of the item, or whether the advertised percentage off an item has actually been entered into the computer.

Like reading and spelling, mathematics involves the integration of important cognitive and information-processing abilities. Visual-spatial abilities, for example, allow us to imagine and rearrange objects in our minds and thereby help us mentally add and subtract. Fine-motor coordination helps us to keep track of objects counted, to write numerals, and to align them correctly while calculating. Focused attention is essential for learning math concepts and also to determine what information is and is not important in a word problem. Language skills are highly related to math success because mathematical symbols (+, –, ×) are just another way of symbolizing numerical language concepts. Word problems must be read and understood (the vocabulary, grammar, and sentence length often are quite complex), and math reasoning depends on a good deal of language flexibility when, for example, we search our minds for a number fact while holding another in abeyance—as we do when borrowing in subtraction.

**Acquisition of Mathematics Skills.** Children enter school with a good deal of quantitative reasoning ability and experience. As early as 4 months of age, infants anticipate that when one object is added to another this should result in two, and that if one object is taken away from a set of two, one object should remain. As toddlers they can pick out piles that represent *lots* and *a little,* and they can nonverbally calculate how many items they had just seen (e.g., putting out two disks to match two that had been hidden). They can also nonverbally add and subtract in this same scenario, as they see a disk being added to or subtracted from the hidden pile. Between ages 2 and 3 children finally begin to count using number words.

*By age 3, most children have established accurate one-to-one correspondence while counting objects. By age 4, they understand that the last number "word" reached when counting indicates the total items in the set.*

By age 3, most children have established accurate one-to-one correspondence while counting objects. Within the next year, they come to understand that the last number "word" reached when counting indicates the total items in the set—known as the principle of cardinality. They also understand that if two groups of objects match up (every plate has a cupcake), then each set must contain the same number of items. Children's ability to solve concrete addition and subtraction problems—as in combining two piles to show "how many altogether"—remains superior to their ability to add with numbers alone (without objects) until they are about 5½ to 6½ years old. If a child is transitioned too soon to working with numerals, this important nonverbal reasoning process seems to be suppressed and math acquisition is disrupted.

*School exercises that force children to memorize numerals and use numerals to calculate before their intuitive sense of quantities is firmly established only exacerbate children's math weaknesses.*

School exercises that force children to memorize numerals and use numerals to calculate before their nonverbal, intuitive sense of quantities is firmly established only exacerbate children's math weaknesses. Such instruction suppresses children's "counting up and down" and usually includes limited discussion and concrete demonstration of quantitative concepts. In fact, research finds that encouraging counting, including on the fingers (!), actually speeds up eventual memorization of number facts because the child has generated and practiced the answer so often—and fully understands its logic.

For formal math instruction to proceed smoothly, a child needs to be able to do the following:

- Match objects by size, shape, and color
- Sort objects by size, shape, and color names
- Compare sets of objects by quantity (more/most, lots/little) and size (bigger/smaller, taller/shorter)

- Recognize that additional items result in more than one had before, and that removing items results in less than before
- Recognize that if nothing has been added or taken away, the same amount remains
- Recognize that parts can come together to make a whole
- Arrange a series of objects by size
- Match each item of one kind with a single item of another kind (e.g., one napkin per person)
- Recognize the amount of "one"
- Match sets of objects by amount
- Model the adding or subtracting of one or two objects from a set
- Match a spoken number with the correct number of objects
- Recognize that the last number in a counting sequence names the quantity in the whole set
- Point to the correct numeral when named
- Name written numerals
- Count to ten
- Recall the number of objects seen by naming the number, or choosing the correct number of objects
- Imitate and recall the spatial arrangement of objects
- Copy numerals accurately

Math calculation skills progress faster once a child has mastered this list and once his or her cognitive abilities mature enough to reason flexibly about several pieces of information at once. Most important for math progress, the child must conceptually be mature enough to recognize that:

1. *When things look different, they can still be the same.* The addition problem 2 + 4 is the same as 3 + 3, for example. A dime is the same as two nickels, even though the nickels look larger. A half-gallon milk carton holds the same amount as a half-gallon jug of cider. Eighty floor tiles cover the floor, whether an 8 × 10 foot bedroom or 5 × 16 foot hallway.
2. *Things may look the same but still be different.* A 4 may represent four objects, or one-quarter of the objects as in ¼, four 10s as in 40, or four 100s as in 400.

*Even at age 10 or 12 children with LD often do not grasp the basic math concept that when things look different they can still be the same, and when they look the same they may be different.*

Piaget observed that children become able to engage in this type of flexible cognitive reasoning by ages 6 to 7. Children with learning disabilities are generally two or more years delayed in making this transition, often not grasping these basic math concepts even at age 10 or 12. Even when they do, they may remain less flexible in this reasoning than their average achieving peers.

The typical pace of the math curricula through middle school is depicted in Figure 6.13. Addition and subtraction usually begin by counting objects, including the trusty fingers. When adding, the child begins by creating and counting two

| | |
|---|---|
| *Middle School* | Masters order of operations in complex problems; multiplies/divides two fractions; adds, subtracts, multiplies divides decimals to the thousandth; understands real, rational, irrational numbers and different number bases; calculates square and cube roots; estimates percentages/proportions; calculates discount, sales tax, restaurant tip; understands markup, commission, simple interest, compound interest, percent increase/decrease; understands angles (complementary, supplementary, adjacent, straight, congruent . . .); calculates volume of a cylinder; calculates arc/circumference of circle; understands equilateral, isosceles, scalene, obtuse figures; organizes sets of data; graphs coordinates, transformations, reflections, rotations, equations with two variables; solves equations by substitution; begins to learn about conditional probability, permutations, factorial notation, relative frequency, normal curve, pythagorean theorem; deepens understanding of previously taught skills and concepts |
| *Fifth Grade* | Multiplies three digit numbers (962 × 334); can work harder division problems (102 ÷ 32); adds, subtracts, multiplies mixed numbers; divides a whole number by a fraction; represents fractions as decimals, ratios, percents; adds, subtracts, multiplies, with decimals; understands use of equations, formulas, "working backward"; estimates products/quotients; begins to learn about exponents, greatest common factor, bases, prime factors, composite numbers, integers; understands percent, ratios; understands mean, median, mode; measures area/circumference of a circle, perimeter/areas of triangles and parallelograms, volume of cube; performs metric conversions; uses compass, protractor; reads scale drawings |
| *Fourth Grade* | Adds columns of 3 or more numbers; multiplies three digit by two digit numbers (348 × 34); performs simple division (44/22); reduces fractions to lowest terms; adds/subtracts fractions with different denominators (3/4 + 2/3); adds/subtracts decimals; converts decimals to percents; counts/makes change for up to $20.00; estimates time; can measure time in hours, minutes, seconds; understands acute, obtuse, right angles; computes area of rectangles; identifies parallel, perpendicular, intersecting lines; calculates weight in tons, length in meters, volume in cubic centimeters |
| *Third Grade* | Understands place value to thousands; adds and subtracts four digit numbers (e.g., 1,017 – 978); learns multiplication facts to 9 × 9; solves simple multiplication and division problems (642 × or ÷ 2); relates division to repeated subtractions; counts by 4s, 1000s; learns harder Roman numerals; introduction to fractions (adds/estimates/orders simple fractions; understands mixed numbers; reads fractions of an inch) and geometry (identifies hexagon, pentagon); understands diameter, radius, volume, area; understands decimals; begins to learn about negative numbers, probability, percentage, ratio; solves harder number story problems |
| *Second Grade* | Identifies/writes numbers to 999; Adds/subtracts two and three digit numbers with and without regrouping (e.g., 223 + 88, 124 – 16); multiplies by 2, 3, 4, 5; counts by 3s, 100s; reads/writes Roman numerals to XII; counts money and makes change up to $10.00; recognizes days of the week, months, and seasons of the year on a calendar; tells time to five minutes on a clock with hands; learns basic measurements (inch, foot, pint, pound); recognizes equivalents (e.g., two quarters = one half; four quarts = one gallon); divides area into 2/3, 3/4, 10ths; graphs simple data |
| *First Grade* | Counts/reads/writes/orders numbers to 99; begins learning addition and subtraction facts to 20; performs simple addition/subtraction problems (e.g., 23 + 11); understands multiplication as repeated addition; counts by 2s, 5s and 10s; identifies odd/even numbers; estimates answers; understands 1/2, 1/3, 1/4; gains elementary knowledge of calendar (e.g., counts how many days to birthday), time (tells time to half hour; understands schedules; reads digital clock), measurement (cup, pint, quart, liter, inch, cm, kg, lb), and money (knows value of quarter; compares prices); solves simple number story problems; reads bar graphs and charts. |
| *Kindergarten* | Matches/sorts/names objects by size, color and shape; recites and recognizes numbers 1–20; one-to-one correspondence; counts/adds up to nine objects; knows addition/subtraction facts to six; evaluates objects by quantity, dimensions, size (e.g., more/less, longer/shorter, tall/tallest, bigger/same); writes numbers 1–10; understands concepts of addition and subtraction; knows symbols +, –, =; recognizes whole vs. half; understands ordinals (first, 5th); learns beginning concepts of weight, time (e.g., before/after; understands lunch is at 12:00; tells time to the hour), money (knows value of pennies, nickels, dimes), and temperature (hotter/colder); aware of locations (e.g., above/below, left/right, nearest/farthest); interprets simple maps, graphs and tallies. |

**Figure 6.13** Typical curriculum sequence for developing math skills.

separate sets (4 apples here and 2 apples there) and then recounting the combined set. Beginning subtractors start with the full set (6 apples), take away the required number of items (2 apples), and recount the remainder (4 apples left).

By age 6 or 7, these simple math operations can be done mentally. Children add by starting with one addend (e.g., 5) and then "count on" by ones to add the second addend. To solve 5 + 3, for example, the child starts with "5," and counts on "6, 7, 8." Not until 9 years old can children subtract mentally by counting up from the smaller number (9 – 2 is solved by counting 3, 4, 5, 6, 7, 8, 9) or counting down from the larger quantity (9 – 2 is solved as 9, 8, 7, 6, 5, 4, 3). When calculating mentally, older children will automatically convert problems to require fewer counts (e.g., 5 + 3 rather than 3 + 5). When they encounter multiplication, they approach it as a repeated addition problem (5 × 3 is solved by counting 5 books + 5 books + 5 books).

Third grade is the time when children begin to transition from "counting up" math facts to recalling number facts automatically—half count up and half know math facts automatically. Between fourth and sixth grades, children's ability to retrieve math facts automatically becomes equal to that of adults. This enables children to calculate in their heads with speed. It is normal for children to apply math fact knowledge and sophisticated calculation strategies at some times, but to apply lower-level strategies at other times (how often do you find yourself touching *your* fingers to count up?).

***Third grade is the time when children begin to transition from "counting up" math facts to recalling number facts automatically.***

The word problems that children encounter in school rely heavily on language reasoning. Their aim is to help children learn to sort out the relevant information from the irrelevant in everyday practical situations. Addition and subtraction word problems are easiest when the story describes an increase or decrease in quantity that corresponds with the mathematical operation the child is to do (add or subtract). By age 9, children learn to interpret problems in which the language may indicate a decrease (suggests subtraction) but the opposite is true (they must add). Resnick (1989) offers this example:

***The word problems children encounter in school rely heavily on language reasoning. They aim to help children learn to sort out the relevant information from the irrelevant in everyday practical situations.***

> Ana went shopping. She spent $3.50 and then counted her money when she got home. She had $2.35 left. How much did Ana have when she started out? (p. 165)

Combining problems, in which items (apples and oranges) get renamed into a new category (how much "fruit" is there altogether?) also are difficult in the early elementary grades. Good math students help themselves solve word problems by paraphrasing them in their own words, visualizing the problems using illustrations or mental imaging, estimating the answers, and evaluating the logic of their answers.

Girls tend to be more proficient than boys in computation and number fact memorization. Boys, on the other hand, tend to be superior on more complex math reasoning taught in high school and word problems involving multiple steps. Although there is some evidence for a genetic link to male math reasoning superiority, researchers suggest that gender-stereotyping is at least partially to blame. Society tends to perceive math as more valuable to boys, so expectations for boys are higher and they get more encouragement to enroll in higher-level math courses and math-related classes such as chemistry and physics. This results in lower math achievement and confidence among females. The fact that the male

***Girls tend to be more proficient than boys in computation and number fact memorization, but boys are more proficient in more complex math reasoning. Societal expectations may play a role here.***

superiority gap is moderate and closing suggests that girls may have good math potential if only their parents and teachers adjust their expectations.

**Mathematics Patterns of Students with Learning Disabilities.** Rourke and other investigators have identified nine arithmetic disabilities that implicate a variety of information-processing weaknesses:

1. *Spatial organization:* misaligning numbers in columns; confusing directionality, as in wondering which way a 6 faces and misreading numbers (71 for 17), or subtracting the minuend from the subtrahend:

$$\begin{array}{r} 36 \\ -\ 18 \\ \hline 22 \end{array}$$

2. *Alertness to visual detail:* misreading mathematical signs, omitting a necessary detail (dollar sign, decimal)
3. *Procedural errors:* missing or adding a step; applying steps in the wrong order, as in adding a carried number before multiplying:

$$18 \times 8 = \begin{array}{r} {\scriptstyle 6} \\ 18 \\ \times\ 8 \\ \hline 4 \end{array} = \begin{array}{r} 78 \\ \times\ 8 \\ \hline 564 \end{array}$$

4. *Failure to shift psychological set:* continuing to apply a previous procedure (e.g., addition) when the problem calls for a shift to another procedure (e.g., subtraction)
5. *Graphomotor:* numbers are printed large, crowded, and poorly formed so that children can't read their writing while calculating; at an earlier age this might manifest as disorganized one-to-one correspondence when counting objects
6. *Memory:* poor recall of number facts
7. *Mathematical judgment and reasoning:* giving unreasonable answers and being unaware of the incongruity (10 + 9 = 109); not generalizing a known skill to a new, slightly different problem
8. *Language:* Poor ability to verbally express and reason about math terms and relationships—numerals, operational symbols, operations
9. *Reading:* Poor ability to read numerals and operational symbols

Many of these math difficulties are illustrated in the math calculations of 9-year-old Greg, in Figure 6.14. Greg is so confused by numerical operations that he inappropriately applies strategies from one type of solution to another. Sometimes he's correct. At other times he gets the answer but for the wrong reason. For example, in problem 5, Greg borrows 10 from the 3 in the tens column, adds it to the 2 in the ones column, and then carries the 1 once he adds 12 + 7. The answer is correct, but he set it up as a subtraction problem. In problem 9, he began adding with the left-hand column, recording the 2 for 12 (8 + 4), and carrying the 1. In problem 11

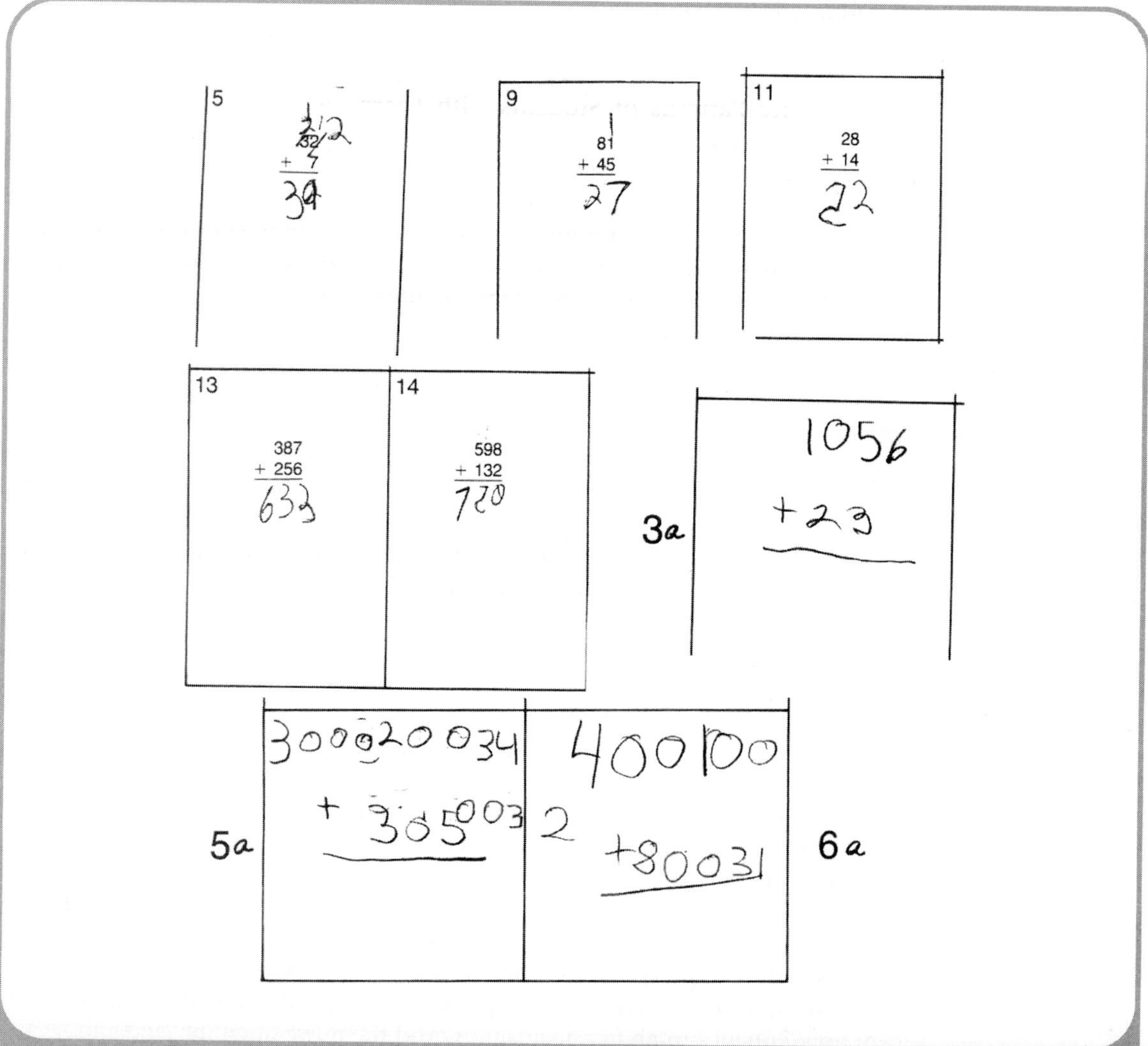


**Figure 6.14** Mathematical calculations of a 9-year-old student with learning disabilities.

he forgets to carry the 1 and demonstrates his confusion about how 3s and 5s are formed. The same thing recurs in problem 14, but this time he carries. Greg's poor comprehension of numerical concepts is illustrated in how he recorded dictated numbers (problems 3a, 5a, 6a): "one hundred and fifty-six plus twenty-three," "three thousand, two hundred and thirty-four," and "four thousand one hundred."

We need to remember that seemingly simple math calculations involve an incredible number of steps. For example, simply solving 62 × 96 involves 33 steps, beginning with interpreting the sign and remembering to start at the right.

It is obvious that efficient language skills are critical to systematizing a child's recall and application of the large numbers of steps, rules, and math facts involved.

Unfortunately, due in part to their information-processing weaknesses, many students with LD never achieve a high level of math proficiency. A recent developmental study found that while students with LD mastered addition of a 1-digit with a 2-digit number by age 9, and three 1-digit numbers by age 10, 9-year-old nonLD students had already mastered addition of three 2-digit numbers. Students with LD mastered subtracting a 1-digit number from another 1-digit number by age 13, a skill that average students performed easily by age 9. By age 12 average students had mastered subtracting one 4-digit number from another, and multiplication of two 1-digit numbers; 2-digit by 3-digit multiplication was mastered by age 14, and dividing a 3-digit by a 2-digit number by age 13. Children with LD, however, lagged behind about two years in attaining these skills, and the gap in skills increased with each year.

*In addition to calculation challenges, the judgments and reading involved in word problems prove particularly troublesome to youngsters with LD.*

Besides the calculation challenges, the judgments involved in word problems prove particularly troublesome to youngsters with learning disabilities, especially as the problems increasingly tax a child's reading abilities. Irrelevant numerical information in these problems has been found to cause these students even more confusion than does irrelevant linguistic information.

In the intermediate grades students face a math curriculum that has become conceptually more difficult, with even more word problems and more written instructions to follow. In addition, math concepts are relied on to a greater extent than in prior years for mastery of the social studies and science curricula.

Whereas some students with LD eventually discover aspects of the reading process for themselves, this type of discovery is harder with math calculations. Students must be explicitly taught how and why they calculate as they do. And they must commit number facts to memory in a conscious way.

The more automatic a child's number facts, the more energy he or she can focus on mathematical reasoning when solving problems. Nevertheless, many children have such difficulty learning math facts that experts advise concentrating on basic mathematical relationships and problem-solving approaches, and leaving the actual computing to charts or calculators. They argue that a better number sense will itself enhance math fact acquisition. And the more often the student sees the correct math fact on a chart or calculator, the more his or her math fact knowledge will improve. If, instead of a calculator, children must rely on their faulty math fact knowledge, they will only practice errors and add to their math fact confusion.

*Developing number sense is far more important than number fact knowledge.*

Number sense is far more important than number fact knowledge. If you are thinking about buying the family-size package, you need to be able to judge whether it really is a bargain when compared to the smaller package. Computers as well are making it increasingly important for students to first and foremost comprehend math relationships so they can better judge the accuracy of their computer calculations. If you are buying an item over the Internet, for instance, you need to know whether the cost plus shipping would be more than if you purchased it at the local mall.

Children who have significant problems with math relationships often also have *nonverbal learning disabilities.* They have trouble with time and spatial relationships. They get lost, come late to class, or can't figure out the number of months until their next birthday. They may have trouble keeping time to music or mastering social dancing. Social difficulties are common since they have trouble interpreting the moods, feelings, and nonverbal cues from those around them, and communicating their own feelings with the appropriate affect—for example, they might say they're angry but sport a smile. The give and take of social interactions stupefies these children. Their poor social perception and judgment often are accompanied by motor incoordination, marked slowness in most activities, attention and visual-spatial deficits, tactile perception problems, as well as poor nonverbal reasoning and difficulty in "getting the big picture."

*Children who have significant problems with math relationships often also have nonverbal learning disabilities with time, spatial, and social judgments.*

### Content-Area Learning

When linguistic skills and learner strategies are weak, comprehension suffers—whether when reading or listening—and achievement in content areas such as science and social studies becomes problematic. A youngster's ability to attend to, understand, and remember content area information is further influenced by the cultural background, vocabulary, and prior knowledge he or she brings to reading and listening. We refer to this background as the child's *schema.* New information enriches an existing schema (e.g., a child's fund of knowledge about dinosaurs), and if there is no existing schema for the topic (e.g., black holes), a new schema is created. The richer the student's background schema, the easier it will be for new information to be linked with the old and be understood. That's why a child with parents who read aloud story after story, who patiently answer the thousands of questions asked, who encourage experimentation, who broaden the child's experience through excursions, and who praise learning accomplishments is at a distinct advantage in school and in life.

*The richer the student's background knowledge and vocabulary, the easier it will be for new information to be linked with the old, understood, and remembered.*

Knowledge does beget knowledge. The richer the child's vocabulary and store of knowledge, the better will be his or her reading and listening comprehension. For students with learning disabilities, unfortunately, their poverty of vocabulary and knowledge base limits how much sense they can make of new information. Moreover, without a strong base for adding new information, not much is remembered. Even if a schema for the information does exist, it seems that, instead of letting the new information modify the old, students with learning disabilities tend to use the old information to distort the new. The end result is further confusion in learning.

Modifying the language of instruction, teaching appropriate learning strategies, and exposing children to essential vocabulary and background knowledge prior to more detailed coverage of a topic are important if students with LD are to progress in content-area learning. When this is not done, these students become less and less knowledgeable in relation to their peers and perhaps also less socially interesting because they share less in common.

*Modifying the language of instruction, teaching appropriate learning strategies, and exposing children to essential vocabulary and background knowledge prior to more detailed coverage of a topic are important if students with LD are to progress in content-area learning.*

## The Middle and High School Years

Despite years of intense individualized instruction, many adolescents with learning disabilities still lag behind their peers academically. Delays of up to four years on reading and writing achievement tests are not unusual—and the gap continues to grow year by year. Whatever the reading level is in seventh grade, it is unlikely to change much thereafter. Because reading and writing are the keys to the curriculum at this stage, substandard performance and/or failure in content-area courses are common. As with reading and writing, the gap in math skills between students with LD and their peers tends to widen over time.

Basic skill remediation does make sense for this age group, particularly if students have just recently been identified as learning disabled or if they have experienced poor-quality remediation. Such instruction also takes advantage of the sudden acceleration in learning ability that some students experience in adolescence. On the other hand, a one-sided emphasis on basic skills may deprive teenagers of opportunities to acquire important content-area knowledge and to prepare for postsecondary education, a vocation, and independent living. Tutoring in content areas can achieve both aims by stressing basic skills while also helping students gain important knowledge.

***Basic skill remediation is important for teenagers, but so are opportunities to acquire important content-area knowledge and to prepare for postsecondary education, a vocation, and independent living.***

Consider the situation of Kristin, age 12, whose learning disabilities are caused by very severe language delays. Figure 6.15 illustrates the linguistic delays of this girl, who charms people with her outgoing social skills and who competently runs a good deal of her parents' dairy farm. Her Performance IQ (perceptual and motor skills) is over 30 points higher than her Verbal IQ (language skills), which is in the retarded ranges. She speaks as she writes, and her academic achievement has peaked at a second-grade level. Kristin's severe language delays preclude her understanding the standard vocabulary of the middle school science and social studies content matter.

For students like Kristin, some experts believe that by ages 14 to 16 the educational focus should shift to helping them live with their disabilities by developing ways to compensate for their weaknesses, sharpening learning strategies, enhancing their strengths, and selecting realistic educational and vocational goals that capitalize on areas of competence and reduce the impact of the learning disability. These students need extensive tutorial and learning strategy assistance in academics, but they also need to learn how to get organized, work independently, use time wisely, and plan ahead. Work on these competencies must occur within a context that emphasizes transition planning toward adult vocational and social independence.

***The curriculum of the secondary school years must emphasize skills needed for transition planning toward adult vocational and social independence.***

## Academic Competency

Academic competency has implications for students with LD not only in terms of their persistence to graduation but also in light of a relatively recent national emphasis on minimum competencies for all high school graduates. Planning for the high school years is doomed to failure without the cooperation and input of the students themselves, whether learning disabled or not. This planning must remain sensitive to the universal adolescent need to be as much like their peers as possible. Isolating or publicly marking them as different always poses a threat and limits success for students with a learning disability, for example, by requiring them to leave the room for extended time on a test. By planning together as a team with these students, school staff can establish rapport, engage cooperation, build personal responsibility and independence, and convey confidence in these students' ability to exercise good judgment and control over their lives.

June 29

Dear Alicia,

Did you get my letter? I'm start backing for my trip to bayouca for camping with my friend. I write you next week befor I leave for camp. Did you like my turtle picter. My pumpkins are under water from the rain. Can you write your phone number to me.

P.S. Have a great Summer and worldful Summer too.

Sincerely,
Kristin

**Figure 6.15** Letter written by a 12-year-old with severe language disabilities whose academic skills peaked at a second-grade level.

Unfortunately, students with learning disabilities are often not included in this planning process. This omission may influence the alarming dropout rate in this population—27 percent as compared to an overall dropout rate of 11 percent. For students with LD who were held back a grade, the dropout rate rises to over 40 percent. Other factors contributing to leaving high school before graduation include continued academic frustration, inappropriate courses, insufficient remedial and counseling services, and, if there had been a retention, the fact that the student is older than his or her peers.

*Factors contributing to leaving high school before graduation include continued academic frustration, inappropriate courses, insufficient remedial and counseling services, and, if there had been a retention, the fact that the student is older than his or her peers.*

Dropping out is almost never a good choice for a student who is learning disabled. The unemployment rate for dropouts is one and a half times that of high school graduates, and dropouts earn just two-thirds the salary of high school graduates. Research suggests that the reading and math achievement levels of students with LD at the end of ninth grade are critical predictors of whether they will continue in high school.

*For students with LD, their reading and math achievement levels at the end of ninth grade are critical predictors of whether they will continue in high school.*

Most teenagers with learning disabilities attend general education classes and receive support services from special education teachers and consultants. But their regular teachers, who are responsible for teaching more than 100 students a day, often find it difficult to modify content-area instruction and devise testing and grading options tailored to the individual needs of these students.

Frequently, the special education staff also is stretched too thin to meet these students' needs. LD teachers see their roles as providing instruction in basic skills

*LD teachers see their roles as providing instruction in basic skills and learning strategies. Under pressure from state competency requirements, however, these teachers are often forced to devote more time than they would like to content-area tutoring.*

and learning strategies. When they are under pressure from state competency requirements, however, these teachers are often forced to devote more time than they would like to content-area tutoring. In doing so, they forgo important basic skills and strategy instruction on how to learn, which in the end would help their students with LD become more independent learners. Special education teachers often compromise by using content-area material to reinforce basic skills. Although students are more likely to apply these new skills when taught in context, it is also true that LD teachers are unfamiliar with the regular class content and teach too many students to prepare lessons effectively.

Because of growing national concern over the poor basic skill competencies of high school graduates in general, many states have instituted more rigorous coursework requirements for graduation. Some have dropped basic courses, assuming students with academic delays can be accommodated in regular classes. In addition, minimum competency testing (MCT) for grade-to-grade promotion or graduation has been established in over half of states.

In order to ensure accountability for students with special needs, the 1997 reauthorization of the Individuals with Disabilities Education Act (IDEA) mandated that children with disabilities be included in state and district assessment programs. This has been hailed as a way to hold schools and teachers accountable for solid teaching and to ensure funding for special services to these children. Nevertheless, there is concern that higher standards and high-stakes competency testing will increase the number of students with learning disabilities who face grade retention and the possibility of not graduating or, worse, dropping out of school. If students can't earn the same high school diploma as their peers, or even a modified diploma, this severely impacts their future educational and vocational opportunities. Currently only one-third of students with learning disabilities earn the standard high school diploma.

*Higher standards and high-stakes competency testing could increase the number of students with LD who face grade retention and the possibility of not graduating or dropping out of school. Currently only one-third of students with LD earn the standard high school diploma.*

MCT programs grew out of the alarm generated by several commissions that faulted the national education system for the country's declining economic and political status in the world. The best known of these was the National Commission on Excellence in Education which released its report, *A Nation at Risk,* in 1983. The report emphasized that our nation could prosper and be secure only if business, university faculties, and the military had an expanded supply of well-educated young people:

> Our Nation is at risk. Our once unchallenged preeminence in commerce, industry, science, and technological innovation is being overtaken by competitors throughout the world. . . . the educational foundations of our society are presently being eroded by a rising tide of mediocrity that threatens our very future as a Nation and a people. (p. 5)

There was plenty of data to support this alarm. National testing in the 1980s showed that the average 17-year-old could not understand moderately complicated reading information. Just 65 percent could write a clear paragraph for a job application; well-reasoned compositions were impossible for most. The National Assessment of Educational Progress (NAEP) revealed that the average 17-year-old could answer only about half of basic questions about United States democratic principles and history. Almost two decades later NAEP results are little better:

Fewer than half of high school seniors understand decimals, percents, and fractions; just 5 percent understand basic algebra and geometry; 93 percent of 17-year-olds can't solve multistep math problems, and 59 percent can't understand or summarize more complex reading material.

Declining SAT scores and the poor showing by African Americans and Hispanics on all tests have further fueled the public's outrage. The laxity of our high schools was reflected in a national survey that showed that high school seniors put in just three hours a week on homework. Yet their average grade was close to a B. Even low-ability seniors who reported doing no homework at all earned better than a C average.

In response to these concerns, in 1994 Congress allocated major funding to a Goals 2000 program that encouraged states to adopt strict educational content and performance standards. Among its objectives were that all children will start school ready to learn; that students will demonstrate competence in challenging subject matter in grades 4, 8, and 12; and that 90 percent of high school students will graduate by the year 2000. The latest such legislation, the No Child Left Behind Act of 2001, provides federal funds to low-achieving schools for supplemental remedial assistance to students beyond the regular school day and year. The law also requires that schools permit parents to transfer their children to better-performing schools when the home school has shown no increase in overall student achievement over a two-year period. Major federal allocations to boost educational quality continue, but the NAEP research indicates that nationally the average student is only marginally better educated than two decades earlier. Apparent gains are due primarily to the narrowing of the black-white gap in achievement—a hopeful forecast.

The overall effect of high stakes competency tests appears to be a narrowing of the curriculum as teachers teach to the test. While state competency test scores may rise a bit, in turn SAT, ACT, NAEP, and AP scores tend to decline due to the limits imposed on students' exposure to a broader range of information and problem-solving.

Some states that have instituted MCTs have used these tests to identify students in need of remedial instruction, to provide an early warning of problems, and to gauge school progress. When used as criteria for high school graduation, the MCT standard tends to be set at a seventh- to ninth-grade knowledge and skill level.

This growing reliance on passing high-stakes tests to earn the high school diploma has alarmed those who advocate for the learning disabled. Students with LD may need more comprehensive curricula or alternative paths to a diploma in order to avoid being shut out of postschool employment and educational opportunities, and finding themselves in the lowest-paying jobs and least advantaged sector of society. The Council for Exceptional Children (CEC) has taken issue with the drive to establish common standards for every student:

***Students with LD may need more comprehensive curricula or alternative paths to a diploma in order to avoid being shut out of postschool employment and educational opportunities, and finding themselves in the lowest-paying jobs and least advantaged sector of society.***

> [W]e strongly oppose singular standards to measure achievement. The abilities of our students vary greatly, and curricula and assessment must relate to such variability. . . . Singular criteria for curricula and assessment to determine competence, graduation, or program evaluation is immoral, poor educational practice, a violation of student and societal needs, and contrary to the fundamental tenets of

> our society. . . . Measures of achievement and competency must reflect individually determined curricula. . . . Graduation, including a diploma, should be granted to all students who satisfactorily complete their individually determined curricula. (Cain et al., 1984, pp. 488–489)

The CEC's statement stressed that schools must develop a student's individual aspirations and talents, even when they don't match the curriculum. It also called for the development of students' personal and social skills so they can be better prepared to become contributing citizens.

Most states using MCTs allow test modifications for students with learning disabilities, such as reading content-area tests aloud to the student and permitting oral responses (to work around reading and writing difficulties), extended time (to allow for slow information processing), and modifying the test format (e.g., ordering items from easiest to hardest, marking answers in the test booklet rather than the confusing "bubble" sheet, spreading test administration over several sessions, using a quieter room, writing on the computer). The 1997 IDEA reauthorization requires that the student's individualized education program (IEP) specify any modifications necessary for the administration of state or district assessments of student achievement. If by the IEP it is determined that a student will not participate in a particular assessment, the IEP must state why that achievement assessment is inappropriate and how the student will be assessed.

When special education students do not meet MCT requirements, they can still receive a modified high school diploma certifying that they have attended school and met the requirements for their IEP. These include special education diplomas, certificates of completion, and occupational diplomas. In the following pages we explore the reading, writing, and math competencies of students with LD at the middle and high school levels.

**Reading.** Although middle and high school students typically read at a variety of grade levels, most have sufficient decoding and comprehension skills to engage actively and independently in the more complex and greater volume of reading required in high school. They can compare and evaluate information from a variety of sources, synthesize that information, form hypotheses, and critically evaluate literature. Faced with challenging information, secondary level students learn to monitor and evaluate their understanding automatically as they read. They make use of the text's structure to facilitate understanding by differentiating main idea sentences from supporting material and identifying different levels of importance of ideas. They activate their background knowledge to help make sense of and remember what they are reading. When they have difficulty understanding, they know how to compensate for it by re-reading, scanning forward for clarification, using the dictionary, and asking the teacher for help.

*Many students with LD plateau at fourth- or fifth-grade reading levels early in high school and show little further progress.*

By contrast, many adolescents with learning disabilities are still acquiring reading skills. They may still be having problems with basic sight vocabulary, word-attack skills, reading rate, and ability to gain meaning from longer sentences and paragraphs. Many students who are learning disabled plateau at fourth- or fifth-grade reading levels early in high school and show little further progress. The level of reading proficiency attained in third grade seems to be particularly predictive of whether significant gains can be expected in the future.

Even if they have learned to decode well, many students with LD tend not to monitor their reading for comprehension. They are less efficient at scanning the text for specific information, don't notice inconsistencies, don't use the text's organization to help them understand (e.g., headings, tables, captions, and summaries), and don't self-question or activate prior knowledge as they read in order to make the information more meaningful. Many do not think it unusual at all when a passage has made no sense. They might not even notice the discontinuity when they inadvertently flip two pages at once while reading.

***Even if they have learned to decode well, many students with LD tend not to monitor their reading for comprehension.***

Experts point out that schools actually promote reading problems among the learning disabled when they overemphasize literal comprehension, provide poorly organized and poorly written teaching materials, offer inadequate diagnostic and instructional techniques, and lack comprehensive planning for teaching reading at the secondary level. Perhaps most devastating is the assumption that if students haven't learned to read by now, they never will. All students can learn something, particularly when provided with intensive training at the proper instructional level, and in a different way from prior instructional efforts. As one group of researchers put it, "most dyslexia is only terminal if you believe it is" (Cunningham, Cunningham, & Arthur, 1981, p. 13).

A critical element in reading remediation at the adolescent stage is student cooperation. If they are motivated, research finds that students with little prior special education help can increase at least two grade levels in reading in high school, with half of this gain occurring in the first year of help. In addition, special educators must help students learn to listen in class more effectively, to develop study skills such as note taking and outlining, to acquire research skills such as conducting computer searches, and to learn test-taking strategies.

***If they are motivated, research finds that students with little prior special education help can increase at least two grade levels in reading in high school.***

Accommodations for the student with LD also are critical to maximize learning opportunities in content areas. This may involve listening to tapes, to a computer-synthesized voice, or to a human reader. Curriculum materials can be rewritten at lower readability levels, with unnecessary detail eliminated. Easier versions of classics (e.g., *Romeo and Juliet*) and science and social studies texts can be arranged.

***Accommodations for the student with LD are critical to maximize learning opportunities in the content areas.***

Encouraging reading, any kind of reading, is very important in order to practice basic skills and build the foundation for new learning. If students don't read, they tend to become less and less knowledgeable and capable of absorbing knowledge as time passes. Unfortunately, teachers contribute to this cumulative knowledge deficit because too often they feel unprepared to address in class issues of pressing social concern such as racism, world hunger, women's rights, privacy rights—unless these come up spontaneously during current events discussions or in response to student questions. Yet these are the very subjects that, due to personal relevancy, might prompt students to read more and think more intelligently. In any case, if students are not exposed to these issues, they are being denied access to the rich historical, cultural, and political background that is every citizen's concern and responsibility.

***Encouragement of reading, any kind of reading, is very important in order to practice basic skills and build the foundation for new learning. Students who don't read tend to become less and less knowledgeable and capable of absorbing knowledge as time passes.***

**Written Language.** Writing is critical to the way students demonstrate what they have learned, and it is also an essential aid in organizing thought. For those who lack the capacity and confidence to express themselves this way, the experience of writing can be highly frustrating.

***Writing problems are prevalent and difficult to remediate because proficiency depends on students' expanding experiential and knowledge base and on their developing language, reading, and self-monitoring skills.***

Writing problems are prevalent and difficult to remediate because proficiency depends on students' expanding experiential and knowledge base and on their developing language, reading, and self-monitoring skills, all of which may be concerns for the learning disabled. Compared with their peers, adolescents with LD often write at a slower pace, have a more limited vocabulary, and make a higher frequency of mechanical errors. They omit information related to time, goals, reactions of characters, and endings. Ideas are not elaborated, creative, organized, or connected with transitional words that signal relationships (such as *although, however*). These students are also less competent at monitoring and revising their writing errors. When they do make corrections, it's usually to fix their handwriting or to make minor word or phrase changes that have no effect on the meaning. If they add information, seldom is there an attempt to reorganize, improve beginnings and endings, or delete insignificant details.

***Writing weaknesses are exacerbated by remediation that focuses insufficiently on generation and development of ideas.***

The writing weaknesses of students with learning disabilities are often exacerbated by earlier remedial efforts that focused too narrowly on reading and spelling, instead of the generation and development of ideas. Despite these interventions, spelling usually continues to lag behind the reading skills of children with LD, as samples of Craig's work in Figure 6.16 show. Craig is a bright 13-year-old who has had difficulty mastering the visual and orthographic aspects of spelling. When given a second-grade word list, he spells it with less than 40 percent accuracy. His phonological strengths are evident in his errors, which are all good phonetic equivalents. Note how Craig spelled *come, said, we,* and *went,* words he has encountered no doubt thousands of times.

Experts recommend that in efforts to improve writing skills the focus should first be on building students' motivation to write, giving them confidence that they know a great deal to write about and that their thoughts are worthy of communication. Most of these students require modifications on tests so that their writing weaknesses don't hamper communicating what they've learned. These modifications include extended time (due to slow writing speed), oral exams, multiple-choice rather than short-answer formats, or permission to answer in outline form.

**Mathematics.** Despite the ready availability of handheld calculators, we still need to understand basic arithmetic operations, if only to check answers to see if they make sense. Besides, a calculator isn't very helpful unless we can tell it which operations to perform and in what order.

Adolescents with learning disabilities often reach somewhat higher levels of achievement in math than in reading. Although some become more able to handle abstract, less memory-related high school math after having struggled with signs and number facts in the earlier grades, for many others achievement peaks at around the fifth-grade level. Generally, the better developed a student's language and perceptual skills, the greater math progress is likely to be.

Like the elementary school child, the teenager with LD continues to have difficulty with computational operations, choice of math rules, ignoring of extraneous

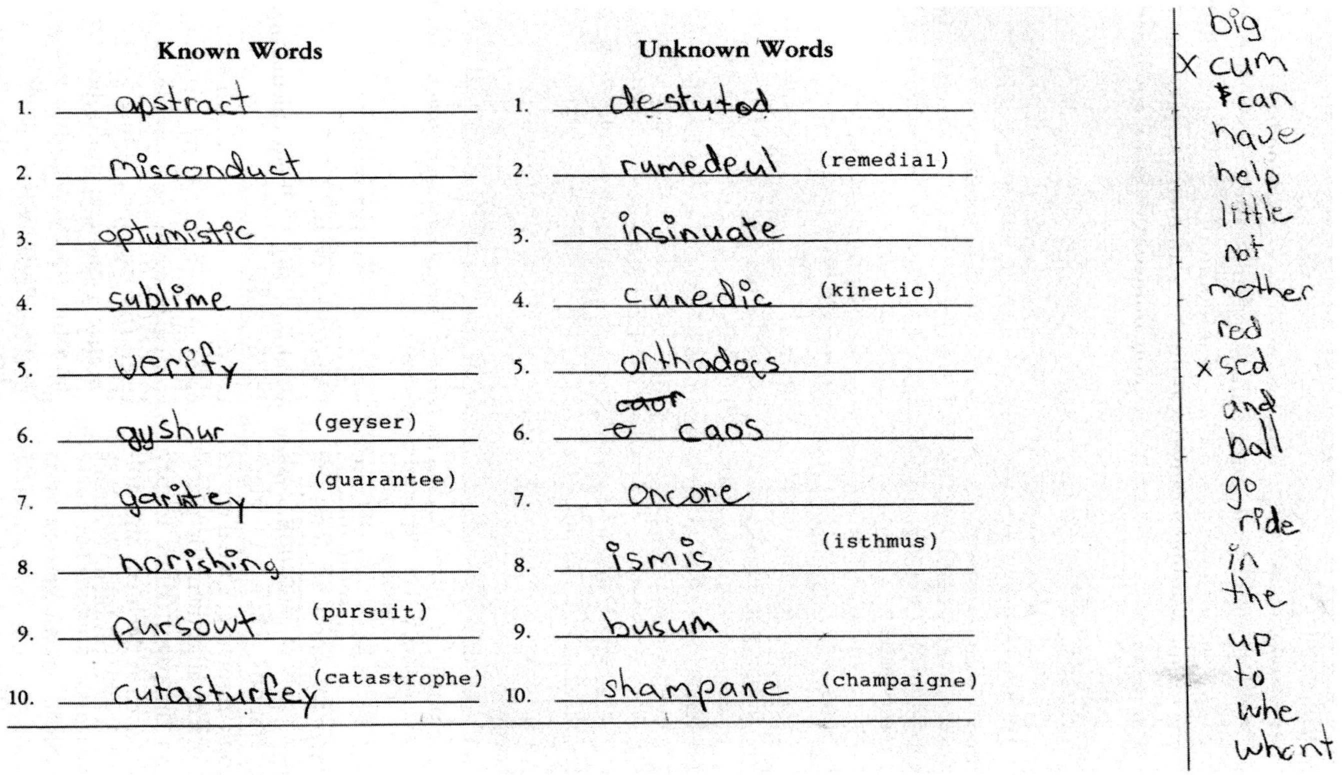

| | Known Words | | Unknown Words |
|---|---|---|---|
| 1. | apstract | 1. | destutod |
| 2. | misconduct | 2. | rumedeul (remedial) |
| 3. | optumistic | 3. | insinuate |
| 4. | sublime | 4. | cunedic (kinetic) |
| 5. | verify | 5. | orthadocs |
| 6. | gyshur (geyser) | 6. | ~~caor~~ caos |
| 7. | garitey (guarantee) | 7. | oncore |
| 8. | norishing | 8. | ismis (isthmus) |
| 9. | pursowt (pursuit) | 9. | busum |
| 10. | cutasturfey (catastrophe) | 10. | shampane (champaigne) |

big
X cum
can
have
help
little
not
mother
red
X sed
and
ball
go
ride
in
the
up
to
whe
whent

**Figure 6.16** Good phonetic equivalents of Craig, a bright, 13-year-old with learning disabilities. Craig was asked to spell "known" words (words he could read instantly by sight) as well as "unknown" words that he couldn't read or had to sound out. The spellings on the far right are of some second-grade-level words that Craig could easily read.

information in word problems, solving problems with multiple steps and mixed operations, using more efficient strategies (such as multiplying instead of adding the same number a few times), computing at a reasonable speed, incorrect alignment of figures on a page, ignoring details such as decimal points and dollar signs, and subtraction problem reversals, such as

$$\begin{array}{r} 25 \\ -16 \\ \hline 11 \end{array}$$

*Although students with LD can compensate for math fact weaknesses with a calculator, they must develop mathematical understanding and logical reasoning to use the calculator in the first place and to function in everyday life.*

Experts still argue over whether we should emphasize memorizing math facts in secondary school, and thus make quantitative reasoning easier, or stress the reasoning component, which in itself will encourage learning of math facts. The second argument usually wins because, although students with LD can compensate for math fact weaknesses with a calculator, they must develop mathematical understanding and logical reasoning to use the calculator in the first place and to function in everyday life.

Because the math abilities of many students who are learning disabled reach a ceiling at a fourth- or fifth-grade level, learning functional mathematical life skills is essential. This includes learning to follow measurements in recipes, using the Dewey decimal system in the library, budgeting, making change, figuring tax and interest, computing sale prices, calculating payroll deductions and hours worked, reading charts and maps, planning quantities of food to buy, timing medication, keeping score in a game, and so on.

## Transition Planning

*By age 16 a transition plan must be implemented that addresses the student's postsecondary education plans, job placement and community living skills.*

The 1997 reauthorization of IDEA requires that, beginning at age 14 and annually thereafter, the teenagers' IEP address the course of study that will meet his or her transition needs. By age 16 a transition plan must be implemented that addresses the student's postsecondary education plans, job placement and evaluation, community living plans, interagency responsibilities, as well as such everyday concerns as shopping, leisure time activities, cooperation with coworkers, community travel, and money management. The plan must be as comprehensive as possible given the fact that students with learning disabilities, particularly those who don't continue their education after high school, are likely to be unemployed or underemployed young adults who live at home with their parents.

*Students with LD are often caught between narrow and insufficient vocational training programs geared toward students with less potential, and the reading, writing, and coping challenges of career exploration programs made available to their average achieving peers.*

With the passage of the Educational Amendments of 1974 (PL 93-380) came the idea of *career education,* a continuous process that begins in early childhood and prepares a person for a wide variety of social, personal, leisure time, and vocational roles in life. *Vocational education,* preparing students for specific jobs, is just one subset of career education and, as currently offered, usually provides little for the teenager with learning disabilities. These students are often caught between narrow and insufficient vocational training programs geared toward students with less potential, and the reading, writing, and coping challenges of career exploration programs made available to their average achieving peers.

When special care is taken to ensure a good match between career education efforts and student needs, many students avoid dropping out and benefit from gaining skills that employers will value. Research finds that adolescents with LD may do just as well as their peers in many job seeking/keeping skills, such as finding and following up on leads to a job, telephoning an employer to ask for an interview, accepting suggestions from an employer, and complimenting a coworker. However, other behaviors important to vocational success may elude them, including how to write a request for an interview letter, act energetic and interested during an interview, write a follow-up letter after an interview, accept criticism from an employer, provide constructive criticism to a coworker, or explain a problem to a supervisor.

In a nationwide survey of high school seniors, those with learning disabilities expressed significantly lower expectations for their careers than did others. Clearly, broader programs are needed to stretch these students' aspirations by helping them explore various career options, improve their communication skills, brush up on survival reading, writing, and math skills (reading want ads, completing job applications, writing a resumé, balancing a checkbook, reading a bus schedule), and build self-confidence, positive work habits, and attitudes. Such broad training makes even more sense today when rapidly changing technology means that people will change jobs, and often careers, several times before retirement.

Because employment success depends on the ability to acquire new skills independently and to adapt to changing work situations, it's critical that students be taught to make job-related decisions, learn new tasks independently, evaluate their job performance, and decide on necessary adjustments. In addition, they need to develop the social skills that will help them work cooperatively with others. Jobs are lost more often because of poor interpersonal and social skills than technical skill deficiencies. One of the best ways to teach these skills is by building job-shadowing, volunteer work, supervised apprenticeships, and paid work opportunities into the high school curriculum. Such work-study programs lower dropout rates, positively affect school and work attitudes, augment achievement, and improve employment rates after graduation.

***Jobs are lost more often because of poor interpersonal and social skills than technical skill deficiencies. One of the best ways to teach these skills is by building job shadowing, volunteer work, supervised apprenticeships, and paid work opportunities into the high school curriculum.***

In addition to career planning, counselors should be ready to help students with learning disabilities consider higher education opportunities. With curriculum modifications and good support, many can and do succeed in college.

## The Adult Years

Success is most likely to come to those adults whose learning disabilities are less severe; who have the highest intelligence; who come from enriched, supportive homes; and who benefited from intensive intervention. These advantages have helped them to remediate some weaknesses, compensate for others, and develop alternate routes to success.

***Success is most likely to come to those adults whose learning disabilities are less severe, who have the highest intelligence, who come from enriched, supportive homes, and who benefited from intensive intervention.***

Several studies have reported the outlook for adults with LD to be quite favorable. One study of middle to high socioeconomic status LD graduates of a boarding school who were average to high intelligence showed that 50 percent had earned at least a bachelor's degree and approximately 8 percent had graduate degrees; another 38 percent had some college or technical training beyond high school. A high percentage of the college students had majored in business and had gone on to managerial and sales positions. Interestingly, nearly half still struggled with their spelling and more than a third were reluctant readers. Only 18 percent had entered professional or technical fields (usually teachers, designers, computer specialists), in comparison with 53 percent of the control group (usually physicians and lawyers).

Another study of learning disabled young adults of middle socioeconomic status found that 80 percent had graduated from high school, 58 percent had entered college, and 31 percent had gone on to graduate school. Only 11 percent were unemployed. Likewise, in a follow-up study of average-intelligence young adults who had severe reading disorders as children, 83 percent had graduated from high school, over half had gone on to college or vocational school, and all were vocationally successful. All had achieved an average adult reading level. Nevertheless, they reported that they had not liked school, did not read for pleasure, and didn't feel they were masters of their own destinies. In a study of college students, in spite of lower reading levels than their peers, these students could comprehend just as well when given at least 25 percent extra time.

These largely positive outcomes, however, are the exception rather than the rule for adults with learning disabilities, particularly those who have not had the intellectual, socioeconomic, and educational advantages of the adults described above. For many, learning weaknesses appear to become even more pronounced in adulthood, because of the large discrepancy between the individual's abilities and adult job and schooling demands.

The great heterogeneity of the adult LD population means that some can read only a few words and still can't identify the order of sounds in words, while others can read at the twelfth-grade level. Even in those who read at higher levels, however, the residuals of the learning disability are still evident when we look closely enough: they may still tend to guess and make errors on third- and fourth-grade words, identify words by guessing from context and first/last letter cues, make many errors on vowels and medial portions of words, still find phoneme segmentation difficult, read slowly, and spell bizarrely with syllables and sounds omitted (Figure 6.17 presents an example). Slow response times, word-finding problems, and comprehension difficulties are not unusual. Despite having graduated high school, one study found that at the average age of 27, these individuals still read at about second-grade levels. Reversals when reading letters and words continued *(on-no, saw-was)*. Another study reported on college students with learning disabilities who still read at only the sixth-grade level; their reading speed was slower than that of typical sixth graders. Other college students read at eleventh-grade levels, but their spelling remained inferior to that of sixth graders who read equivalently. Persistent difficulties like these can erode one's confidence, motivation to persist and try on a job, and lead to serious adjustment difficulties.

***Persistent academic difficulties are the norm for adults with LD. These can erode self-confidence and motivation, and lead to serious adjustment difficulties.***

Clearly, even with years of intervention many youngsters with learning disabilities don't outgrow their language, perceptual, attention, and academic problems. Despite this, their vocational and personal adjustment can be enhanced a great deal if they are encouraged to participate in postsecondary educational opportunities.

Dictation of: "The yellow pig saw the little baby" to adults who were reading disabled as children

| John | AGE | 19 |
|---|---|---|
| Performance | IQ | 111 |
| Verbal | IQ | 91 |

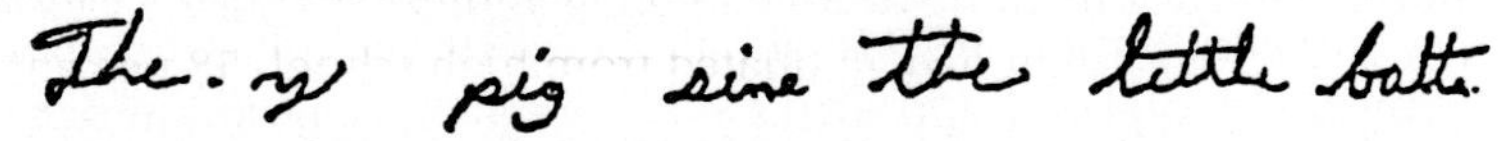

The. y pig sine the little batt.

| Fred | AGE | 26 |
|---|---|---|
| Performance | IQ | 101 |
| Verbal | IQ | 83 |

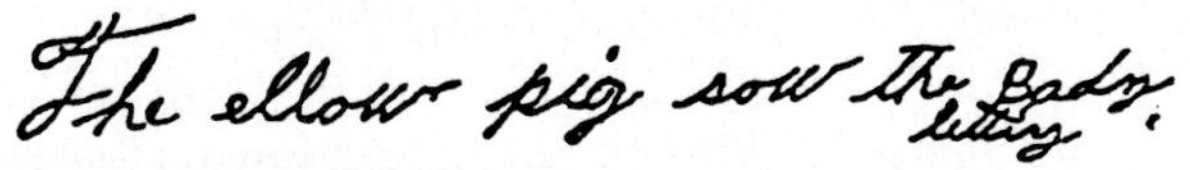

The ellow pig sow the Bady litty.

| Alan | AGE | 20 |
|---|---|---|
| Performance | IQ | 100 |
| Verbal | IQ | 87 |

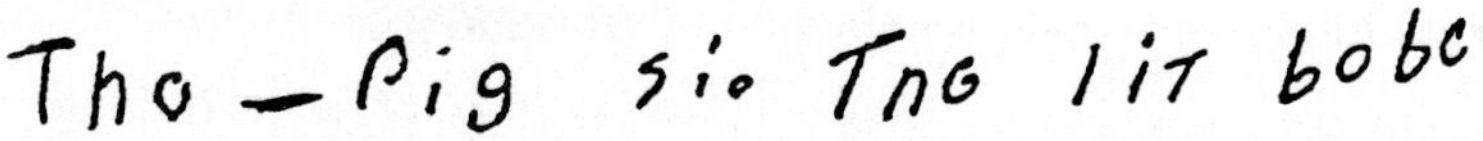

Tho – Pig si. Tno lit bobc

**Figure 6.17** The spelling errors of adults who were reading disabled as youngsters reflect difficulty with phonological awareness of sound sequences.

*Source:* Adapted from Frauenheim, J. G. Academic achievement characteristics of adult males who were diagnosed as dyslexic in childhood. © 1978 The Professional Press, Inc. Reprinted with permission of the publisher from *Journal of Learning Disabilities,* 8700 Shoal Creek Blvd., Austin, TX 78758, vol. 11, pp. 480–481.

## Postsecondary Educational Opportunities

All states permit students with disabilities to remain enrolled in school to age 21, thus allowing extra time for degree completion. After high school, one way to significantly improve students' career potential is through postsecondary education. One of the goals of the mandated IEP transition plan is to increase the chances that students who are learning disabled will take advantage of this opportunity. The more schooling one has, the greater one's chances for higher-level employment and the lower the chances of living in poverty.

*The more schooling one has, the greater one's chances for higher-level employment and the lower the chance of living in poverty.*

Students with learning disabilities who do pursue higher education tend to be those with higher intellectual, reading, and math capabilities; those who had the social skills and confidence to participate in high school extracurricular activities; and those who used community resources for job assistance and information. Currently, 28 percent of high school graduates with LD move on to study at a four-year college, in comparison with 62 percent of their nondisabled peers. Options for further education besides a four-year college include schooling through military enlistment; technical schools (one-year business school, cosmetology); government-funded transition programs; and two-year private and community colleges. If a high school diploma hasn't been earned, then enrolling in a GED (General Educational Development certificate) class should be a priority in order to earn a high school equivalency diploma and increase employment opportunities. Currently, one out of seven high school diplomas issued each year is based on passing a GED test.

The law supports evaluation, counseling, and vocational training for adults whose severe learning disabilities pose a substantial impediment to employment (through the Office of Vocational and Educational Services for Individuals with Disabilities; PL 95-602, Rehabilitation, Comprehensive Services, and Developmental Disabilities Amendments of 1978), as well as postsecondary educational and transition programs (PL 98-199, the Education of the Handicapped Act Amendments of 1983). Even with these resources, only 58 percent of individuals with learning disabilities enroll in some form of postsecondary education within five years of leaving high school. This contrasts with 72 percent of students without disabilities. Reasons given for this low enrollment include the lower educational and occupational aspirations among the learning disabled; inadequate collaboration between vocational rehabilitation and special education personnel; and the need for more remedial, vocational, independent living, counseling, and social-skills training programs.

***Only 58 percent of students with LD enroll in some form of post-secondary education within five years of leaving high school. This contrasts with 72 percent of students without disabilities.***

At the college level, admissions have increased markedly for the learning disabled, in part because of nondiscriminatory policies dictated by Section 504 of the Rehabilitation Act of 1973 (PL 93-112), and in part because these students can now take untimed SATs. Scores increase on SATs the more time that students with LD can spend on the test. These increases average over 30 points per section above what would be expected from simply retaking the test. SAT scores of nondisabled students do not improve to any significant extent with extra time.

Services at the college level also have increased, in part as a result of the right to reasonable accommodations afforded by the 1990 Americans with Disabilities Act (ADA). Colleges now have special offices and trained staff to support the advising, tutoring, and counseling needs of students with LD. Accommodations that can be made to help these students succeed in the classroom include offering specially designed courses and even separate academic tracks that emphasize basic skills, substitutions for required courses (e.g., substituting a multicultural course for the foreign language requirement, or statistics for math), taped texts, taped lectures, and note taking services. Professors can offer untimed tests, different exam formats (multiple-choice or essay), take-home and oral exams, use of a word processor, and quieter, less distracting test locations. Proofreaders can check for spelling and grammatical errors on research papers. Students may get advance copies of syllabi to get a head start on the readings, or attend several sections of a class in order to get exposed to the same message in different ways. Students can

***Colleges now have special offices and trained staff to support the advising, tutoring, and counseling needs of students with LD.***

also enroll in summer courses to reduce their academic year load, or stretch the typical 4-year program to 5 or 6 years.

Those who work with college students with learning disabilities are often struck by their disorganization, inability to plan time, difficulty with stress management, lack of self-awareness of their learning needs, poor self-advocacy, social difficulties, and disabling anxiety about failure. Many do not study in more than a cursory way, nor do they take advantage of opportunities to make learning easier for themselves (such as using tutoring services, buying highlighted used texts that already pinpoint the important information, asking for copies of the professor's lectures notes, tape-recording lectures, auditing a class before taking it). Their poor self-concepts, the hope that their problems will disappear, fearfulness about disclosing their disabilities, and lack of assertiveness make it very hard for them to ask professors for the accommodations that might help them succeed.

Given the long, hard struggle and all the failures along the way, it's a wonder that any students who are learning disabled make it as far as college. But they do, and many succeed. They tend to be independent, motivated self-advocates who accept their need for more time and energy for studying, are able to plan study time, can evaluate their progress realistically, can handle frustration, seek out mentors, and can match their strengths with course requirements when selecting a course of study. It has been said that students who thrive at the most competitive colleges exhibit an "extraordinary drive and determination . . . together with their exceptional intelligence [that] enables them to accomplish more with their disability than others for whom things have come easier. Such proven resiliency becomes a critical factor in meeting future challenges successfully" (Shaywitz & Shaw, 1988, p. 84).

*Given the long, hard struggle and all the failures along the way, it's a wonder that any students with LD make it as far as college. But they do, and many succeed. They tend to be independent, motivated self-advocates who accept their need for more time and energy for studying, can handle frustration, seek out mentors, and select a course of study that matches their strengths.*

## Summary

Learning disabilities present lifelong learning challenges. Although academic development is the primary focus of schooling, by the high school years transition planning for adult life becomes equally important. In order to maximize success as an adult, whether vocationally or in independent living, postsecondary education is critical.

Though improvement is the rule, particularly when the student has received extensive remediation in the elementary grades, many adolescents with LD still lag behind academically, and further progress is slow. Variability between these students in achievement levels and strength/weakness patterns is great.

While implementation of more rigorous standards for graduation and minimum competency testing help the learning disabled by increasing program quality, at the same time they may diminish the chances for these youngsters to earn the same academic diploma as their peers. This in turn affects their future educational and vocational opportunities.

Because learning disabilities follow teenagers into adulthood, adults may curtail their postsecondary education, which unfortunately hampers their vocational options and life adjustment. Those adults with the most favorable outcomes have less severe learning disabilities, choose vocations that capitalize on their strengths, have high intelligence levels that help them compensate for weaknesses, and have benefited from supportive and stimulating home and school environments that nurtured their motivation, persistence, and belief in themselves.

## Helpful Resources

### The Elementary School Years


Adams, M. J. (1990). *Beginning to read: Thinking and learning about print.* Cambridge, MA: MIT Press.

Berninger, V. W. (1990). Multiple orthographic codes: Key to alternative instructional methodologies for developing the orthographic-phonological connections underlying word identification. *School Psychology Review, 19,* 518–533.

Byrne, B., Freebody, P., & Gates, A. (1992). Longitudinal data on the relations of word-reading strategies to comprehension, reading time, and phonemic awareness. *Reading Research Quarterly, 27,* 141–151.

Chall, J. (1983). *Stages of reading development.* New York: McGraw-Hill.

Chase, C. H., & Tallal, P. (1991). Cognitive models of developmental reading disorders. In J. E. Obrzut & G. W. Hynd (Eds.), *Neuropsychological foundations of learning disabilities: A handbook of issues, methods, and practice.* New York: Academic Press.

Das, J. P., Kirby, J., & Jarman, R. F. (1975). Simultaneous and successive syntheses: An alternative model for cognitive abilities. *Psychological Bulletin, 82,* 87–103.

Denckla, M. B. (1991). Academic and extracurricular aspects of nonverbal learning disabilities. *Psychiatric Annals, 21,* 717–724.

Deuel, R. K. (1995). Developmental dysgraphia and motor skills disorders. *Journal of Child Neurology, 10,* S6–S8.

Ehri, L. C. (1989). The development of spelling knowledge and its role in reading acquisition and reading disability. *Journal of Learning Disabilities, 22,* 356–365.

Ehri, L. C. (1997). Sight word learning in normal readers and dyslexics. In B. Blachman (Ed.), *Foundations of reading acquisition and dyslexia: Implications for early intervention* (pp. 163–189). Mahwah, NJ: Lawrence Erlbaum.

Englert, C. S., Culatta, B. E., & Horn, D. G. (1987). Influence of irrelevant information in addition word problems on problem solving. *Learning Disability Quarterly, 10,* 29–36.

Frith, U. (1985). Beneath the surface of developmental dyslexia. In K. E. Patterson, J. C. Marshall, & M. Coltheart (Eds.), *Surface dyslexia: Neuropsychological and cognitive studies of phonological reading.* Hillsdale, NJ: Lawrence Erlbaum.

Fuson, K. C. (1988). *Children's counting and concepts of number.* New York: Springer-Verlag.

Goodman, K. S., & Goodman, Y. M. (1977). Learning about psycholinguistic processes by analyzing oral reading. *Harvard Educational Review, 47,* 317–333.

Graham, S. (1990). The role of production factors in learning disabled students' composition. *Journal of Educational Psychology, 82,* 781–791.

Graham, S., Berninger, V. W., Abbott, R. D., Abbott, S. P., & Whitaker, D. (1997). Role of mechanics in composing of elementary school students: A new methodological approach. *Journal of Educational Psychology, 89,* 170–182.

Gregg, N., & Mather, N. (2002). School is fun at recess: Informal analyses of written language for students with learning disabilities. *Journal of Learning Disabilities, 35,* 7–22.

Griffith, P. L. (1991). Phonemic awareness helps first graders invent spellings and third graders remember correct spellings. *Journal of Reading Behavior, 23,* 215–233.

Gross-Tsur, V., Shalev, R. S., Manor, O., & Amir, N. (1995). Developmental right-hemisphere syndrome: Clinical spectrum of the nonverbal learning disability. *Journal of Learning Disabilities, 28,* 80–86.

Harnadek, M. C. S., & Rourke, B. P. (1994). Principle identifying features of the syndrome of nonverbal learning disabilities in children. *Journal of Learning Disabilities, 27,* 144–154.

Hedges, L. V., & Nowell, A. (1995). Sex differences in mental test scores, variability, and numbers of high-scoring individuals. *Science, 269,* 41–45.

Henderson, E. H., & Beers, J. W. (Eds.). (1980). *Developmental and cognitive aspects of learning to spell: A reflection of word knowledge.* Newark, DE: International Reading Association.

Huttenlocher, J., Jordan, N. C., & Levine, S. C. (1994). A mental model for early arithmetic. *Journal of Experimental Psychology: General, 123,* 284–296.

Hyde, J. S., Fennema, E., & Lamon, S. J. (1990). Gender differences in mathematics performance: A meta-analysis. *Psychological Bulletin, 107,* 139–155.

Jacklin, C. N. (1989). Female and male: Issues of gender. *American Psychologist, 44,* 127–133.

Jordan, N. C., & Hanich, L. B. (2000). Mathematical thinking in second-grade children with different forms of LD. *Journal of Learning Disabilities, 33,* 567–578.

Laughton, J., & Morris, N. C. (1989). Story grammar knowledge of learning disabled students. *Learning Disabilities Research, 4,* 87–95.

Levine, S. C., Jordan, N. C., and Huttenlocher, J. (1992). Development of calculation abilities in young children. *Journal of Experimental Child Psychology, 53,* 72–103.

Liberman, I. Y., Shankweiler, D., Fischer, F. W., & Carter, B. (1974). Reading and the awareness of linguistic segments. *Journal of Experimental Child Psychology, 18,* 201–212.

Manis, F. R., Szeszulski, P. A., Holt, L. K., & Graves, K. (1988). A developmental perspective on dyslexic subtypes. *Annals of Dyslexia, 38,* 139–153.

Mann, V. A. (1993). Phoneme awareness and future reading ability. *Journal of Learning Disabilities, 26,* 259–269.

McHale, K., & Cermak, S. A. (1992). Fine motor activities in elementary school: Preliminary findings and provisional implications for children with fine motor problems. *American Journal of Occupational Therapy, 46,* 898–903.

McKinney, J. D., Osborne, S. S., and Schulte, A. C. (1993). Academic consequences of learning disability: Longitudinal prediction of outcomes at 11 years of age. *Learning Disabilities Research & Practice, 8,* 19–27.

Metsala, J. L., & Ehri, L. C. (Eds.) (1998). *Word recognition in beginning literacy.* Mahwah, NJ: Lawrence Erlbaum.

Montague, M. (1992). The effects of cognitive and metacognitive strategy instruction on the mathematical problem solving of middle school students with learning disabilities. *Journal of Learning Disabilities, 25,* 230–248.

Montague, M., Graves, A., & Leavell, A. (1991). Planning, procedural facilitation, and narrative composition of junior high students with learning disabilities. *Learning Disabilities Research & Practice, 6,* 219–224.

Montague, M., Maddox, C. D., & Dereshiwsky, M. I. (1990). Story grammar and comprehension and production of narrative prose by students with learning disabilities. *Journal of Learning Disabilities, 23,* 190–197.

Morrison, F. J. (1987). The nature of reading disability: Toward an integrative framework. In S. J. Ceci (Ed.), *Handbook of cognitive, social, and neuropsychological aspects of learning disabilities* (Vol. 2). Hillsdale, NJ: Lawrence Erlbaum.

Nodine, B. F., Barenbaum, E., & Newcomer, P. (1985). Story composition by learning disabled, reading disabled, and normal children. *Learning Disability Quarterly, 8,* 167–179.

Piaget, J. (1976). Piaget's theory. In B. Inhelder, H. H. Chipman, & C. Zwingmann (Eds.), *Piaget and his school: A reader in developmental psychology.* New York: Springer-Verlag.

Poteet, J. A. (1980). Informal assessment of written expression. *Learning Disability Quarterly, 3*(4), 88–98.

Rayner, K. (1996). What we can learn about reading processes from eye movements. In C. H. Chase, G. D. Rosen, & G. F. Sherman (Eds.), *Developmental dyslexia: Neural, cognitive, and genetic mechanisms.* Baltimore: York Press.

Resnick, L. B. (1989). Developing mathematical knowledge. *American Psychologist, 44,* 162–169.

Riccio, C. A., & Hynd, G. W. (1995). Contributions of neuropsychology to our understanding of developmental reading problems. *School Psychology Review, 24,* 415–425.

Riley, N. J. (1989). Piagetian cognitive functioning in students with learning disabilities. *Journal of Learning Disabilities, 22,* 444–451.

Rourke, B. P. (1993). Arithmetic disabilities specific and otherwise: A neuropsychological perspective. *Journal of Learning Disabilities, 26,* 214–226.

Rourke, B. P., & Conway, J. A. (1997). Disabilities of arithmetical reasoning: Perspectives from neurology and neuropsychology. *Journal of Learning Disabilities, 30,* 34–46.

Share, D. L., & Stanovich, K. E. (1995). Cognitive processes in early reading development: Accommodating individual differences into a model of acquisition. *Issues in Education: Contributions from Educational Psychology, 1,* 1–57.

Shinn, M. R., Good, R. H., Knutson, N., Tilly, W. D., & Collins, V. L. (1992). Curriculum-based measurement of oral reading fluency: A confirmatory analysis of its relation to reading. *School Psychology Review, 21,* 459–479.

Snider, V. E., & Tarver, S. G. (1987). The effect of early reading failure on acquisition of knowledge among students with learning disabilities. *Journal of Learning Disabilities, 20,* 351–356, 373.

Spear-Swerling, L., & Sternberg, R. J. (1994). The road not taken: An integrative theoretical model of reading disability. *Journal of Learning Disabilities, 27,* 91–103, 122.

Speece, D. L., McKinney, J. D., & Appelbaum, M. I. (1986). Longitudinal development of conservation skills in learning disabled children. *Journal of Learning Disabilities, 19,* 302–307.

Stage, S. A., & Wagner, R. K. (1992). Development of young children's phonological and orthographic knowledge as revealed by their spellings. *Developmental Psychology, 28,* 287–296.

Stanovich, K. E. (1982). Individual differences in the cognitive processes of reading: I. word decoding. *Journal of Learning Disabilities, 15,* 485–493.

Stanovich, K. E. (1986). Explaining the variance in reading ability in terms of psychological processes: What have we learned? *Annals of Dyslexia, 35,* 67–96.

Stanovich, K. E. (1988). Explaining the differences between the dyslexic and the garden-variety poor reader: The phonological-core variable-difference model. *Journal of Learning Disabilities, 21,* 590–604.

Sweeney, J. E., & Rourke, B. P. (1985). Spelling disability subtypes. In B. P. Rourke (Ed.), *Neuropsychology of learning disabilities.* New York: Guilford Press.

Treiman, R. (1997). Spelling in normal children and dyslexics. In B. Blachman (Ed.), *Foundations of reading acquisition and dyslexia: Implications for early intervention* (pp. 191–218). Mahwah, NJ: Lawrence Erlbaum.

Weisberg, R. (1988). 1980s: A change in focus of reading comprehension research—A review of reading/learning disabilities research based on an interactive model of reading. *Learning Disability Quarterly, 11,* 149–159.

No Child Left Behind Act of 2001: http://www.nclb.gov

## The Middle and High School Years

Algozzine, B., O'Shea, D. J., Crews, W. B., & Stoddard, K. (1987). Analysis of mathematics competence of learning disabled adolescents. *Journal of Special Education, 21,* 97–107.

Badian, N. A. (1988). The prediction of good and poor reading before kindergarten entry: A nine-year follow-up. *Journal of Learning Disabilities, 21,* 98–103, 123.

Bassett, D. S., & Smith, T. E. C. (1996). Transition in an era of reform. *Journal of Learning Disabilities, 29,* 161–166.

Bos, C. S., & Filip, D. (1984). Comprehension monitoring in learning disabled and average students. *Journal of Learning Disabilities, 17,* 229–233.

Bransford, J. D., Stein, B. S., & Vye, N. J. (1982). Helping students learn how to learn from written texts. In M. H. Singer (Ed.), *Competent reader, disabled reader.* Hillsdale, NJ: Lawrence Erlbaum.

Cawley, J. F., Parmar, R. S., Fan Yan, W., & Miller, J. H. (1998). Arithmetic computation abilities of students with learning disabilities: Implications for curriculum. *Learning Disabilities Research & Practice, 13,* 68–74.

Edgar, E. (1987). Secondary programs in special education: Are many of them justifiable? *Exceptional Children, 53,* 555–561.

Evers, R. B. (1996). The positive force of vocational education: Transition outcomes for youth with learning disabilities. *Journal of Learning Disabilities, 29,* 69–78.

Evers, R. B., & Bursuck, W. (1993). Teacher ratings of instructional and setting demands in vocational education classes. *Learning Disability Quarterly, 16,* 82–92.

Forell, E. R., & Hood, J. (1985). A longitudinal study of two groups of children with early reading problems. *Annals of Dyslexia, 35,* 97–116.

Garnett, K. (1992). Developing fluency with basic number facts: Intervention for students with learning disabilities. *Learning Disabilities Research & Practice, 7,* 210–216.

Hodgkinson, H. L. (1986, May 14). Here they come, ready or not. *Education Week,* pp. 13–87.

Horn, W. F., O'Donnell, J. P., & Vitulano, L. A. (1983). Long-term follow-up studies of learning disabled persons. *Journal of Learning Disabilities, 16,* 542–555.

Keith, T. Z., & Page, E. B. (1985). Homework works at school: National evidence for policy changes. *School Psychology Review, 14,* 351–359.

Korhonen, T. T. (1995). The persistence of rapid naming problems in children with reading disabilities: A nine year follow-up. *Journal of Learning Disabilities, 28,* 232–239.

Levin, E. K., Zigmond, N., & Birch, J. W. (1985). A follow-up study of 52 learning disabled adolescents. *Journal of Learning Disabilities, 18,* 2–7.

MacArthur, C. S., Graham, S., & Schwartz, S. (1991). Knowledge of revision and revising behavior among students with learning disabilities. *Learning Disabilities Quarterly, 14,* 61–73.

Mithaug, D. E., Martin, J. E., & Agran, M. (1987). Adaptability instruction: The goal of transitional programming. *Exceptional Children, 53,* 500–505.

Okolo, C. M., & Sitlington, P. (1986). The role of special education in LD adolescents' transition from school to work. *Learning Disability Quarterly, 9,* 141–155.

Roessler, R. T., & Johnson, V. A. (1987). Developing job maintenance skills in learning disabled youth. *Journal of Learning Disabilities, 20,* 428–432.

Rusch, F. R., & Phelps, L. A. (1987). Secondary special education and transition from school to work: A national policy. *Exceptional Children, 53,* 487–492.

Shapiro, E. S., & Lentz, F. E. (1991). Vocational-technical programs: Follow-up of students with learning disabilities. *Exceptional Children, 58,* 47–59.

Taylor, B. M., & Samuels, S. J. (1983). Children's use of text structure in the recall of expository material. *American Educational Research Journal, 20,* 517–528.

Vallecorsa, A. L., & Garriss, E. (1990). Story composition skills of middle-grade students with learning disabilities. *Exceptional Children, 57*, 48–54.

Zentall, S. S., & Ferkis, M. A. (1993). Mathematical problem solving for youth with ADHD, with and without learning disabilities. *Learning Disability Quarterly, 16*, 6–18.

National Assessment of Educational Progress: http://www.nceds.ed.gov/nationsreportcard

National Center on Educational Outcomes: http://www.education.umn.edu/nceo

National Education Longitudinal Study: http://www.nces.ed.gov/surveys/nels88

Closing the Achievement Gap, National Central Regional Educational Laboratory: http://www.ncrel.org

## The Adult Years

Blackorby, J., & Wagner, M. (1996). Longitudinal postschool outcomes of youth with disabilities: Findings from the National Longitudinal Transition Study. *Exceptional Children, 62*, 399–413.

Bruck, M. (1985). The adult functioning of children with specific learning disabilities: A follow-up study. In I. E. Siegel (Ed.), *Advances in applied developmental psychology* (Vol. 1). Norwood, NJ: Ablex.

Bruck, M. (1993). Word recognition and component phonological processing skills of adults with childhood diagnoses of dyslexia. *Developmental Review, 13*, 258–268.

Centra, J. A. (1986). Handicapped student performance on the Scholastic Aptitude Test. *Journal of Learning Disabilities, 19*, 324–327.

Denckla, M. B. (1993). The child with developmental disabilities grown up: Adult residua of childhood disorders. *Neurologic Clinics, 11*, 105–125.

Dowdy, C. A. (1996). Vocational rehabilitation and special education: Partners in transition for individuals with learning disabilities. *Journal of Learning Disabilities, 29*, 137–147.

Felton, R. H., Naylor, C. E., & Wood, F. B. (1990). Neuropsychological profile of adult dyslexics. *Brain and Language, 39*, 485–497.

Finucci, J. M. (1986). Follow-up studies of developmental dyslexia and other learning disabilities. In S. D. Smith (Ed.), *Genetics and learning disabilities.* San Diego: College-Hill Press.

Hoffman, F. J., Sheldon, K. L., Minskoff, E. H., Sautter, S. W., Steidle, E. F., Baker, D. P., Bailey, M. B., & Echols, L. D. (1987). Needs of learning disabled adults. *Journal of Learning Disabilities, 20*, 43–52.

Liberman, I. Y., Rubin, H., Duques, S., & Carlisle, J. (1985). Linguistic abilities and spelling proficiency in kindergarteners and adult poor spellers. In D. B. Gray & J. F. Kavanaugh (Eds.), *Biobehavioral measures of dyslexia.* Parkton, MD: York Press.

Miller, R. J., Snider, B., & Rzonca, C. (1990). Variables related to the decision of young adults with learning disabilities to participate in postsecondary education. *Journal of Learning Disabilities, 23*, 349–354.

Mosberg, L., & Johns, D. (1994). Reading and listening comprehension in college students with developmental dyslexia. *Learning Disabilities Research & Practice, 9*, 130–135.

Pennington, B. F., Van Orden, G. C., Smith, S. D., Green, P. A., & Haith, M. M. (1990). Phonological processing skills and deficits in adult dyslexics. *Child Development, 61*, 1753–1778.

Rojewski, J. W. (1999). Occupational and education aspirations and attainment of young adults with and without LD 2 years after high school completion. *Journal of Learning Disabilities, 32*, 533–552.

Wilson, A. M., & Lesaux, N. K. (2001). Persistence of phonological processing deficits in college students with dyslexia who have age-appropriate reading skills. *Journal of Learning Disabilities, 34*, 394–400.

American Council on Education: http://www.acenet.edu

Americans with Disabilities Information Hotline, Disability Rights Section, Civil Rights Division, U.S. Department of Justice: http://www.usdoj.gov/crt/ada

Transition to Employment or Postsecondary Education, Heath Resource Center: http://www.heath-resource-center.org

CHAPTER SEVEN

# Learning Strategy and Information-Processing Development

**STUDENTS WITH LEARNING DISABILITIES** are bright enough to have learned the basic skills and information required by their schools. Yet their achievement in one or more academic areas lags behind what is expected. Despite adequate learning opportunities, these students fail to remember the information they have been exposed to. We can attribute their memory difficulties to one of several factors: an insufficient knowledge base to which new knowledge can be anchored, poor use of strategies to help store and recall information, and various information-processing weaknesses that interfere with information storage and retrieval.

The learning strategies and information-processing skills of most individuals with LD develop in the order typically expected, but they do so at a much slower pace. Not only are these children's learning patterns immature for their age, but many of their patterns are also qualitatively unusual when compared to the patterns of younger, average students who are achieving at the same level. For example, when reading easy material, ninth-grader Tony reads as many words correctly in a minute as the average fourth grader Lissy, yet Lissy instantaneously sounds out words she has never seen before. Tony can't do that. He attacks new words haltingly or he simply skips them, hoping he'll be able to understand what he's reading anyhow. Tony still reverses letter order in his spelling—*gril* for *girl*. Only 40 percent of the words in his essays are spelled correctly, and the rest don't phonetically approximate the sounds in the word. By contrast, Lissy spells 80 percent of the words she can read correctly, and what she does misspell at least looks similar to what the word sounds like (e.g., *brue* for *brew*). Adena is another student with a learning disability. She is a tenth grader whose language skills are more like that of a sixth grader. This lag has affected her reading comprehension, writing, and reasoning abilities. When memorizing science and social studies content, she just can't seem to implant the long lists of information in her brain. Zoly, like most sixth graders, also has trouble remembering these lists, but Zoly responds to association, first letter, or rhyming hints offered by the teacher and quickly pulls out the information, commenting "Oh yes! The word is ______." Such cues don't help Adena at all because of her language weaknesses. Like Tony, some of Adena's learning skills are much like that of younger students, but they are also qualitatively different.

***The learning patterns of children with LD are immature for their age, and many patterns are qualitatively unusual when compared to younger, average students achieving at the same level.***

This chapter describes the normal course of development for attention and memory; learning strategies; and perceptual, motor, and language abilities from preschool to adulthood. Delays in these abilities can affect a student's capacity to process and remember knowledge, and the ability to communicate what he or she knows. Knowing typical developmental processes helps us to detect delays and intervene as soon as possible.

***An insufficient knowledge base to which new knowledge can be anchored, and delays in learning strategies and information processing abilities can affect a student's capacity to process and remember knowledge.***

## Attention, Memory, and Learning Strategies

As mentioned previously, attention weaknesses can be major contributors to learning disabilities. It makes sense that if children's attention is not fully engaged in their learning, they will have less information to commit to memory and as a result they may be less able to reason logically about that information and to solve related problems. Therefore, teachers need to be alert to their students' inefficient attention processes so that they can modify either the attention-getting aspects of instruction or the way that students interact with the learning task.

Each time a student's attention is not engaged and maintained, an opportunity to learn is lost. When many such opportunities are lost, wide gaps in knowledge and skills are to be expected. These gaps, in turn, make new knowledge less meaningful and therefore less memorable.

***Each time a student's attention is not engaged an opportunity to learn is lost.***

Try the mind challengers in Figure 7.1 (*hint:* the first answer is "touchdown"). To solve these, you had to simultaneously attend to, read, reason about, and hold in memory both the figural aspects and word meanings, while you searched for familiar sayings. When one approach didn't work, you tried another. For students with LD, this would be extremely difficult, if not impossible. They have trouble combining new information with the old, coordinating perceptual and verbal problem solving, and trying various paths toward a solution. In the following pages we explore how attention, problem-solving, memory, and learning strategies typically develop, and the differences often found among the learning disabled.

Instructions: determine the word or phrase represented by the symbols and letters below.

| T<br>O<br>U<br>C<br>H | CYCLE<br>CYCLE<br>CYCLE | R<br>O<br>ROADS<br>D<br>S | DEATH/LIFE |
|---|---|---|---|
| MAN / BOARD | SAND (in a box) | STAND / I | ECNALG |

**Figure 7.1** Mind challengers.

*Source:* Unknown.

## Attention and Problem Solving

Preschoolers are attracted to bright, colorful, and eye-catching novel objects. They examine certain features of such objects over and over again with great care, but ignore other features. Their attention can easily be distracted by anything more interesting that comes along. When they pay attention, they flit from feature to feature without consistent organization or direction. It is at ages 4 or 5, that familiar objects begin to arouse more attention than novel ones—witness the favorite teddy bear that never leaves the child's arms.

*Preschoolers attend and learn better when color, shape, or novelty attributes attract their attention, when handling objects, when the material is three-dimensional, and when important features are accentuated.*

Preschoolers attend and learn better when color or shape attributes of tasks are used to attract their attention, when they can handle objects, when the position of objects is shifted, when tasks are systematically explained, when the material is three-dimensional (a toy train vs. a picture of a train), when important features are accentuated, and when recognition rather than recall is required (e.g., telling a child to "point to the cow" vs. asking "what do we call this animal?"). Don't expect a toddler to work with you for long, however. Not until they reach age 5 can children attend to a single activity for about seven minutes when playing.

*A preschooler who has a difficult time paying attention usually also is highly active. Activity levels begin to decrease at age 3 and continue to decline into adolescence.*

Usually a preschooler who has a difficult time paying attention is also highly active. At age 3 activity levels begin to decline somewhat, and this trend continues into adolescence, first because the ability to focus and sustain attention is maturing and second because adults and peers tend to be less indulgent of annoying behavior as time goes by. Nevertheless, although the highly active older child may have learned to stop leaping up and dashing around the classroom, he or she may still be prone to finger or pencil tapping, leg wagging, chair rocking, overexcitability, and poorly focused attention and sustained effort.

Attention matures much more slowly for children with learning disabilities than for their average-achieving classmates. With weak attention comes weak problem-solving strategies. Even after years of maturation and schooling, teenagers with LD most often continue to be more distractible and impulsive than their peers. They also use fewer mental control processes—known as *executive functions*—to direct their learning. These include setting a goal, decision making regarding which information to attend to, inhibiting responding to distractions while engaging in problem solving, trying new strategies when old ones don't work, or simply asking for clarification. Thus their comprehension and recall suffer.

***Teenagers with LD tend to be more distractible and impulsive than their peers and they use fewer mental control processes to direct their learning.***

Students with learning disabilities tend not to use strategies to increase their comprehension, such as critical evaluation; trying a new tack when they don't understand; using headings, captions, and summaries to get an overview; summarizing; narrowing a problem to manageable proportions; rereading when they haven't understood a passage; locating related sources of information; using a table of contents or an index; scanning a passage; sorting relevant from irrelevant details; underlining and note taking; and keeping an open mind for additional evidence that could modify their solution to a problem.

They are often unaware of logical inconsistencies in a reading passage or even that a page is missing. They may try to play a game without knowing all the rules, and they are less able than their peers at detecting errors in their own work (e.g., spelling errors). When they do see errors, they may not bother to correct them, and they don't study longer when the work is more difficult to learn. These students also tend to use immature strategies in mathematics, such as counting all the items in two sets rather than counting on from one set, or trying alternative approaches when stuck on a math fact (such as tallies or counting subvocally). A trial-and-error approach to math is common, but paraphrasing to help understand a word problem or drawing a picture of the problem seldom happens. Overall, these students are less conceptually mature about what academics are all about. For example, when asked by one researcher, "What is good writing," an answer like "good posture, sit up straight," is not uncommon (Graham, Schwartz, & MacArthur, 1993).

***Problem solving inefficiencies of students with LD carry over into everyday life—into juggling homework, home responsibilities, social relationships, and more.***

These inefficiencies carry over into everyday life—into juggling homework, home responsibilities, social relationships, and more. Mindy's story (page 214) illustrates how the psychological aspects of a learning disability only further complicate the child's attempt to focus on what's important in the task at hand.

Deficient reading skills, and lags in attention, logical reasoning, and abstract thinking, in combination with school programs that overemphasize remediation of deficits instead of also developing areas of strength, mean that over time students with LD are underexposed to a broad array of information, language, and ideas that could stimulate their cognitive development. Declining scores on intelligence tests in adolescence should come as no surprise; academic failures further exacerbate their declining motivation to grow and develop.

***Due to their weaknesses and an overemphasis on remediation of deficits, students often are underexposed to a broad array of information, language, and ideas that could stimulate their cognitive development.***

Figure 7.2 on page 215 lists many thinking skills that need to be encouraged in students with learning disabilities, beginning with fostering the easiest of these skills in the early school years. Having a prior knowledge base before entering school creates an important foundation for applying these skills. Prior knowledge isn't enough, however. Thinking means being able to find that prior knowledge in memory and connect it with the new information. The thinker "prepares to think, thinks, rethinks, checks, rechecks, and concludes" (French & Rhoder, 1992, p. 15).

## Mindy

*The psychological aspects of LD complicate her learning.*

On October 24, 1974, I was born with birth complications. These problems resulted in me becoming epileptic and learning disabled.

I didn't know anything was "wrong" with me until I reached school age. In kindergarten, I had further difficulties and needed to have my head shaved. This is when I really began to feel different than the other kids. Even my teacher labeled me as a problem child, ridiculed me and accused me of not paying attention (when I actually was having petite mal seizures). Thankfully, I repeated kindergarten and had a teacher that was more understanding of my behaviors. She encouraged me to focus on my strengths rather than my weaknesses. Unfortunately, repeating this grade and a fall birthday, makes me two years older than my peers.

As I progressed in school, the kids started to tease and make fun of me. In fifth grade, I was becoming depressed over how I was being treated until I wrote a letter to my classmates, explaining the story of my life. This seemed to help them understand why it took me longer to learn and needed special help.

As a teenager I had to struggle with being accepted. I just couldn't seem to find my place among the other students. Nobody wanted me to participate in their study groups, teams or social gatherings. My teachers saw me as a burden to have in their classrooms. Successes were few for me at that time.

My low self-esteem makes me susceptible to the influence of other students. I find myself doing things that I wouldn't do normally just to have some friends that will accept me.

Another difficult issue of my disorder is my exaggerated emotions. I seem be overly sensitive to most people and take on their problems as my own. These feelings keep me from focusing on my own tasks. I become overwhelmed and distracted when it comes to life's daily routines.

Even though I have been labeled as having learning disabilities, I think in some ways I have greater learning abilities than people who are nondisabled. I am able to accept other people and see them as who they are rather than what their obstacles are. Because of problems in my life, I have been able to develop a strong and supportive group of individuals who are helping me to learn to accept myself. The non-acceptance of myself is the greatest disability I need to over come.

*Source:* Reprinted by permission of Mindy Quinn Buchtel.

The thinker also considers different perspectives on an issue, believes that he or she can come to understand the matter at hand, learns from talking with others, and has confidence that his or her opinions are important.

*Teachers should focus on developing thinking skills from day one of a child's school career; the teenage years can be a time of rapid cognitive growth in this area.*

Teachers should be focused on developing thinking skills from day one of a child's school career. For the child who is markedly delayed, the teenage years become a critical period for improving these skills. For some teenagers this can be a time of rapid cognitive growth. If they do not improve, these students' attention, reasoning, and problem-solving weaknesses will continue to adversely affect learning, performance, and social interactions into adulthood. A major problem also faced by many adults with LD is continued slow information processing, whether being slow to start crossing a street when the light turns green, slow to move a computer's mouse, slow to give the waiter their order, or slow to make a simple decision.

1. Observing
2. Describing
3. Developing concepts
4. Interpreting concepts
5. Differentiating and defining
6. Questioning
7. Hypothesizing
8. Comparing and contrasting
9. Evaluating
10. Testing and making judgments
11. Forming supportive arguments
12. Persuading
13. Generating new ideas
14. Transforming/recombining old and new ideas
15. Generalizing
16. Predicting and explaining
17. Organizing materials, ideas, and tasks
18. Problem solving
    - identifying the problem
    - analyzing the problem
    - developing options
    - decision making
    - executing the decision
    - evaluating the decision
19. Deciding how to go about remembering
20. Deciding time management

**Figure 7.2** Thinking skills.

*Source:* Adapted from Alley, G., & Deshler, D. (1979). *Teaching the learning disabled adolescent: Strategies and methods.* Denver: Love Publishing Company; French, J. N., & Rhoder, C. (1992). *Teaching thinking skills: Theory and practice.* New York: Garland.

Because many students with LD are too immature to use strategies to interact intellectually with material in an intensive, planful, and goal-directed manner, teachers need to be very explicit in directing them to what is important to focus on and how to go about problem solving. Knowledge of the normal sequence in which attention, memory, and problem solving develops is of great value to the teacher in guiding instruction.

*Because many students with LD are too immature to use strategies to interact with material in an intensive and planful manner, teachers need to direct them to what is important to focus on and how to go about problem solving.*

## Short- and Long-Term Memory

The beginning of memory development is already evident soon after birth, when infants show that they recognize stimuli to which they've been exposed. Within the first year, recall of this information becomes evident. This accumulating knowledge will influence what continues to be learned, and memory strategies will enhance learning even further.

The passive process of accumulating and holding onto segments of information as they arrive in the central nervous system for processing is called *short-term memory.* Most interestingly, older preschoolers and adults are virtually identical in the amount and quality of information they can momentarily hold onto when the information is seen or heard. Their capacity is the same, as is the decay rate for this information. Auditory information persists slightly longer than does visual information.

*Older preschoolers and adults are virtually identical in the amount and quality of information they can momentarily hold onto when the information is seen or heard.*

Generally, short-term memory lasts only one-quarter of a second to 25 seconds, and it is limited to 3 to 15 chunks of meaningful data. In order for this short-term

*In order for short-term information to be understood and preserved, it must be transformed in some way to make it memorable, such as by association or repetition.*

information to be understood and preserved, it must be transformed in some way to make it memorable, such as by association or repetition. The simultaneous processing and transformation of short-term information in order to preserve it is referred to as *working memory.*

Working memory has only a limited capacity of attentional resources. Think about the time when you were learning to drive a car. You had a "limited capacity" to take in the scenery as you drove because you were so engrossed in making sure you were driving in the right lane, at the right speed, and avoiding pedestrians or other cars. Later on, when driving became automatic and required less active attentional resources, you could take in more detail, carry on a conversation with your passenger, and change the radio station, all the while driving safely.

As in the driving example, the more past knowledge and practice we have (such as automatically steering the car), the more related new information we can attend to and absorb. And this is where adults differ from preschoolers, despite both being able to hold the same amount of short-term information. Adults are able to absorb more because of their past knowledge, which gets associated with the new information and makes it more meaningful. Past knowledge helps adults more automatically conceptualize and organize the new information, so that more time can be spent deploying strategies to remember what is new. Put differently, because adults can make meaning of information faster than children, they have time to process more items and even rehearse them before the information decays. Adults also are more resistant to interference and distraction, which focuses their working memory time more efficiently. The combination of this greater knowledge base and strategy use permits more abstract, effective, and efficient thought in adults, which again frees up working memory for other purposes. This ability to increase the capacity of our working memory to consider more information—especially when we engage in automatic tasks—is supported by brain imaging studies showing an actual reduction in brain metabolic activity in areas that are well practiced. This in turn seems to free the brain to reallocate energy to other activities or information.

*Adults are quicker than children at deploying strategies to help them remember information, and their fund of knowledge makes related new information more memorable.*

To eventually store information in *long-term memory,* a person needs to activate multiple cognitive abilities such as perception, language, thought, prior knowledge, and strategies to process the information meaningfully. Because older people can do all this at once, and better than younger people, they remember better—despite equivalent short-term memory spans. The frustration Nancy expresses in Figure 7.3 is typical of so many students with LD who can't get all these processes going in synchrony in order to remember. At least Nancy knows she has a "high voltage" brain. But many children with LD simply give up on school—and worse, on themselves.

## Recognition and Recall

*The basic memory processes of recognition and recall mature during the first two years of life.*

The basic memory processes of *recognition* and *recall* mature during the first 2 years of life. Young infants show us *recognition* of familiar objects through their *orienting reactions*—increased alertness, decreased sucking, and decreased heart rate. Infants as young as 2 months retain for a few days the memory that they can make a mobile shake by kicking their leg (which is connected to the mobile via a ribbon). Six-month-olds can recall this for an interval of 2 to 3 weeks. Before 1 year of age, the

**Figure 7.3** Children with learning difficulties often have problems with memory.

*Source:* NANCY Reprinted by permission of United Feature Syndicate, Inc.

ability to *recall* a thought from memory emerges. For example, a baby will remember that she left her favorite toy in the kitchen and retrieve it. Recall is more difficult than recognition. Ask an 18-month-old to point to a picture of a doggy in a book and he'll usually do it without fail. But ask him to tell you "What is this?" and he is likely to stumble.

At around 11 months of age, children can imitate a 2-step event right after seeing it, for example, they can unhook a toy gate and release a toy car to roll down a track. By 13 months children can actually remember about half of such activities 1 week later, and some activities for as long as 8 months. By 20 months, children can repeat a 3-step event after seeing and imitating it just once. This progresses to 5 steps at 24 months and 8 steps at 30 months. Recall improves as the child has more experience with producing the steps in the same order, and as more reminder cues are available. Once infants can recall events, ideas, and objects, even when they're absent, their basic recognition and recall processes are established.

## Knowledge

*What we already know influences what we will pay attention to, helps it to be stored, and cues its retrieval.*

What we already know influences what we will pay attention to, store, and retrieve. We've all experienced the fact that the way we remember a situation may not really be the way it happened. This is because, after the passage of time, our new knowledge will alter and reshape our memory of an event or piece of information. Moreover, when new information comes along, we evaluate it in terms of what we already know. This makes it hard to entirely displace old information in memory with new information. For example, let's say you've heard a nasty rumor about a friend. Even though eventually you learn that the rumor had no basis in fact, your memory will hold on to the old, false information for a long time to come—and color new interactions with that friend. We continually alter new knowledge to which we are exposed by changing its meaning, embellishing, fitting it to previous knowledge, rehearsing some but not other aspects, and reorganizing it.

This continuous reshaping of our memory for events and information not only influences what we will consider meaningful enough to learn, it also results in memory representations that are conceptually simpler, easier to label, and consistent with our attitudes, temperaments, characters, developmental abilities, social backgrounds, and historical information. Brainerd and Reyna's *fuzzy trace theory* suggests that we recall vague gists about information over time but lose the verbatim details. The more deeply and complexly we process information to begin with, the longer it will be remembered. In fact, research shows that most often when children fail to remember, the problem is *not* because of a retrieval failure. Instead, memory fails because the information wasn't stored richly to begin with. Therefore, most recall weaknesses in children occur because knowledge is not processed deeply enough in their working memories, and then stored deeply enough in long-term memory.

*The more deeply and complexly we process information to begin with, the longer it will be remembered. Memory usually fails because the information wasn't stored richly to begin with.*

To acquire knowledge and file it away in an organized way so that it enriches and augments our store of knowledge, we must be able to *categorize* it—see the similarities in objects or events. When children can categorize, they can link new vocabulary to known meanings, generalize grammar from one phrase to a new phrase, and even judge whether what they are about to do is likely to have the same consequences as other actions that they already know are "good" or "bad" or "safe" or "unsafe." Understanding new concepts is far better when they can be linked with categories of knowledge that are already organized in ways that make sense. Memory is also better as a result. Categorization ability is evident as early as 1 year of age, and continues to develop through the elementary school years.

Clearly, memory is not a passive process of absorbing information. It is a complex combination of a person's information-processing abilities, personality, experiences, and knowledge. Information already stored is very influential in guiding attention, giving meaning to, and ultimately storing, transforming, and retrieving new information. Therefore, the more knowledge a child has, the more he or she can learn. Exposure to a broad range of knowledge, and practice with categorization skills, can help make new information more attention getting, meaningful, and memorable.

In summary, the inefficient memories of students with LD are due in part to a poor fund of knowledge and their difficulty activating this knowledge and integrating it with new information. Mary Anne's story is a humorous reminder that we can never assume that students have the necessary background information for a lesson. For students with LD to remember school lessons, we must first activate any relevant background information they may have.

*The more knowledge a child has, the more he or she can learn. The inefficient memories of students with LD are due in part to their difficulty activating stored knowledge and linking it to new information.*

## Learning Strategies

Preschoolers can describe good learning strategies to us, but they seldom actually use these strategies to remember something. When learning a sequence, such as the alphabet or a song, they find it easier to remember what comes later in the series; the earlier items are more difficult because rehearsal is needed to hold them in short-term memory and keep the information from fading. Knowing this, teachers try to shorten sequences for these children in order to help them remember: for example, they teach counting to 5, and then 6 through 10—not 1 to 10 at once.

## Mary Anne

*Humorous tales that warn us to include background information in lessons.*

In the 25 years I have taught children with learning disabilities, I have learned to always expect the unexpected and never, NEVER assume a student has prior knowledge of a subject, no matter how old, how intelligent, or how "streetwise" he or she is.

I can recall junior high students who didn't know the difference between the white and yellow pages of the phone book because they have never had the opportunity to use one. (If you can't read, you call the operator for a phone number.)

I remember the high school dropout who was learning how to plan and prepare a meal in a life-skills class. After the class selected burgers and fries as their main course, they had to construct a grocery list—rolls, ground hamburger, potatoes. . . . "Potatoes?" one young man inquired. "What do you need potatoes for?"

"The fries!" came the response.

"No kidding! Fries are made out of potatoes?"

But my favorite story came from a 17-year-old student, deficient in both auditory and visual processing, who shared his experience at his sister's wedding with me: "My Ma says to me to stop by the drug store on the way to the reception and pick up a card for my sister. So I did, and I picked out this card with lots of pretty flowers on it cause I thought she'd like it. But when I got to the wedding reception, and my sister opened up the card, she started laughing, and she passes it around, and everybody starts laughing. So I says, 'What's so funny!'. . . . How was I supposed to know it was a "symphony" card! . . . But my ma said it was o.k. cause my sister only stayed married for six months anyway."

*Source:* Reprinted by permission of Mary Anne Coppola.

Efficient long-term storage of information requires use of memory strategies such as visualization and verbal rehearsal. Preschoolers are too immature to benefit from these strategies, but by age 8 children discover a good deal about memory strategies, and by age 10 they actually use these strategies on their own. It's not until the middle school and high school years, however, that these strategies become highly developed. Research Box 7.1 summarizes the order in which these memory strategies mature.

***Efficient long-term storage of information requires memory strategies such as visualization and verbal rehearsal, which mature in the middle school and high school years.***

Flavell coined the term *metacognition* for the process of knowing how to go about learning and in fact trying to do so. Metacognition includes both knowing of memory strategies that can be helpful, and selecting among and modifying strategies in order to solve problems. Children get better at this through the years.

Average achievers vary greatly in the way they choose to use strategies, and in when and how they use them. Students with LD generally are far less mature than their peers in their repertoire, awareness, and use of memory strategies. They don't tend to use spontaneous verbal rehearsal efficiently, organize information for recall, use memory cues unless they are prompted, or begin to use all of the available cues. In short, they seem to be unaware that memory can be facilitated and that different strategies can help on different types of tasks. Students with LD tend to spend

***Many students with LD seem unaware that memory can be facilitated and that different strategies can help on different types of tasks.***

*(text continues on page 224)*

RESEARCH BOX 7.1

## The Maturation of Metacognitive Abilities

There is evidence that the short-term memory storage capabilities of a 6-year-old are very much like that of an adult. But we all know that adults' memories are much stronger than that of little children. This is because what we call "memory" is for the most part the result of our purposeful deployment of strategic "control processes" that help us remember. These "metacognitive strategies" augment the learning of adults far beyond that of little children, despite both having equivalent short-term storage capabilities. Elementary school children are already beginning to develop these control processes, and by the teenage years children use these quite effectively to help themselves memorize.

As children mature, they automatically store, retain, and retrieve information better and differently than younger children because their knowledge base, conceptual systems, and strategic processing become more highly developed. When they encode information, children who are 7 to 8 years old are already more selective and more exhaustive than younger children in attending to the relevant features. The fund of basic knowledge they have internalized helps them to interpret new situations as analogous to familiar situations, thereby enhancing their reasoning about the information and their ability to store and recall it. Younger children (ages 4 to 6), on the other hand, need to literally see or be shown the similarities between objects to draw the analogies (Siegler, 1989). The older child's knowledge and conceptual advantages make information more memorable because it is more familiar, meaningful, conceptually interrelated, and subject to the child's inferential ability and elaboration ability (Flavell & Wellman, 1977). Consequently, more and varied cues are available to aid the older child's recall. In other words, memory ability increases through a combination of improvements in mental capacities, strategies, and ever-expanding and connected content knowledge.

Before age 5, children seldom use intentional plans to remember. When told to memorize, they perceive the information in an idle, purposeless fashion. The 5-year-old might set a goal to remember, but he or she doesn't know how to go about doing it. As children mature, they begin to recognize that intensive, persistent, planned, goal-directed, intellectual interaction with the information aids memory and retrieval (Paris & Lindauer, 1977). The younger elementary school child can be "trapped" into adopting appropriate memory strategies by the nature of the task, by the type of question, quality of pretraining, and by heightening motivation that counteracts fatigue, boredom, and distractibility. Nevertheless, these children do not automatically seek out the best strategy for learning. The young child may not even use the same strategy on successive problems of the same type. The child may apply a strategy perfectly under one set of conditions but show no evidence of using that same strategy, or any strategy, under another set of conditions (Spiker & Cantor, 1983). For example, even when elementary and middle school students notice that they do not remember information they have read, many do not intentionally reinspect those portions of the text that could provide the information; when asked about this, some claim that it takes too much time or that "it is illegal" (Garner & Alexander, 1989, p. 145).

Because of their increasing knowledge base, more rapid information processing, and growing strategy use, the immediate recall ability of children increases steeply between ages 7 and 11, and plateaus during the teenage years. After age 5 and through the teenage years, the automatic use and efficiency of memory strategies increase (Paris & Lin-

**RESEARCH BOX 7.1 (Continued)**

dauer, 1977). Children's use of cognitive strategies has been likened to the ebb and flow of "overlapping waves," each wave being a different strategy (Siegler, 2000). Instead of progressing stepwise from one strategy to a more effective strategy as a child gets older, children use overlapping strategies for prolonged periods of time. With experience, old strategies gradually are replaced with more useful ones, but the old, less efficient ones persist as well. Overall, there is enormous variability and overlap in children's strategy "waves" from day to day, year to year, and even within a single trial. Discovery of new strategies is abrupt, but changes in strategy use are gradual because children often abandon the superior strategies for a time and regress to less sophisticated approaches. Therefore, it may take quite some time before the discovery of a new strategy provides substantial benefit to the child's problem solving. Novel strategies are generated by children when their existing approaches have been successful on a task, but also when they have led to failure. Their growing conceptual understanding guides these discoveries—it is not a matter of blind trial and error. Research has found that the more variability there is in a child's strategy repertoire, the faster he or she will learn. Older children are more likely than younger ones to try alternate strategies when their initial strategy does not produce correct performance (Siegler, 1989, 2000). These strategies combine with a child's maturing knowledge base, conceptual abilities, and awareness of how memory works to increase memory abilities with age. Berk (1997), Schneider & Pressley (1997), and Smith (1994) have summarized how children's awareness and use of memory strategies mature over time:

#### Naming and Verbal Rehearsal

Few preschoolers spontaneously use verbal rehearsal. When instructed to rehearse, this activity does little to aid memory until about 6 years of age. By first grade, children are transitioning toward spontaneous rehearsal; those who do rehearse are better at recalling items such as picture sequences. Although nonrehearsers can be induced to rehearse with minimal instruction and demonstration, and their memory will then equal that of rehearsers, over half of these children revert to nonrehearsing on other tasks. Spontaneous verbal rehearsal during memory tasks increases noticeably until age 10. Younger children verbalize stimulus names only while the stimuli are present, but older children verbalize them even in their absence. Up to age 10 children tend to rehearse one item at a time, but by sixth grade children rehearse words several times using grouping, thereby getting markedly better at remembering lists of related information.

#### Categorizing in Order to Organize Material

Grouping information in order to aid recall has only a small effect on the memory ability of 4-year-olds. Children discover the grouping strategy at different ages over the next few years, such that by 10 years of age memory is significantly enhanced by such grouping for most children. Four-year-olds group objects in order to help them remember (e.g., which cans are hiding M&Ms vs. pegs). However, they do not spontaneously categorize more abstract, verbal information, such as plants or transportation vehicles. When they are instructed to group such information into categories, 4-year-olds can generate the categories

*(continued)*

RESEARCH BOX 7.1 (Continued)

and their recall improves. Nevertheless, they abandon this strategy when no longer directed to do so because it is so effortful for them. By second grade, categorizing helps more than repetition when learning lists of information. Until third grade, children's inclination is to use functional associations as memory aids (e.g., linking *monkey* with *banana*), instead of studying same-category information together (e.g., recalling all *animals* as a category and *foods* as another category). By 8 years of age and older, children automatically think categorically, especially when the information is highly familiar. The older child, for example, asks category questions in the game Twenty Questions ("Is it fruit?"); 6-year-olds, on the other hand, ask questions that confirm or eliminate one hypothesis at a time ("Is it a banana?" "Is it an apple?").

**Elaborating through Associations**

Compared to rehearsal and categorization, elaboration is a later-developing metacognitive ability. Elaboration can take many forms, including describing an interaction between two unrelated items ("the *cattle* swam in the *bay*"); identifying an attribute such as color, shape, or location that two items share in common ("Sidney, Australia is located about where Georgia is in the U.S."); a shared owner ("the farmer has cattle and a bay on his land"); keyword mnemonic associations, and others. Even at the end of high school many students fail to purposely generate elaborations to make information more memorable, although at all ages—even preschool ages—memory improves if an elaboration is told to the student.

As 6- through 12-year-old children get better at inferring about and elaborating on the meaning of stories, their memory for the content shows improvement because they are processing this information more deeply. Recall also improves during these years because children become able to use implied cues to retrieve prior knowledge; at younger ages the cues need to be present in order to spur recall (e.g., an empty cage to cue an animal name), yet the cue might be ignored or even named instead of the word to be recalled. Spontaneous elaboration accelerates after age 11 and gradually continues to develop until adulthood. The richer the quality of associations students create with the information, the more they will rehearse this information as a chunk while studying and develop multiple ways to cue their memory.

**Visual Imagery**

Preschoolers can generate images to help them remember only with a great deal of prompting and when using concrete objects. While 6- and 7-year-olds can generate these images with less prompting, they are inefficient at using them to memorize information. By age 8, however, children can apply self-generated images to help themselves learn things such as object and picture names. Mental imagery increases in effectiveness until age 11, when it becomes an effective strategy for recalling both verbal and visual material.

**Monitoring Comprehension**

First and second graders are less adept than third graders at judging whether they have understood incomplete directions for a game. Only by watching a partial demonstration or trying the task themselves can younger children evaluate whether they need more information. Even sixth graders may not automatically recognize inconsistencies in a text

## RESEARCH BOX 7.1 (Continued)

they read; detection does increase by age 12, if children are forewarned of the inconsistencies. An increase can be noted from second to fifth grade in children's ability to attend to the context if it will help memory, and to ignore the context when it is not helpful. Sixth graders also will reduce their reading speed and look back through material that is unclear to a greater extent than third graders; younger children may show puzzled expressions, but they have trouble explaining what is wrong. Interestingly, incidental learning rises until age 11 but declines thereafter because children get better at keeping their attention from being drawn to irrelevant aspects of tasks.

### Highlighting and Recording Information

Children at all ages are able to distinguish the most important material in a story or text, provided the material is appropriate for their age and maturity level. When told that they can do anything they wish to improve recall of a passage, however, elementary school students are far less likely to underline or take notes when compared to middle school and high school students. When these strategies are used automatically, they aid recall far more than when directed by an adult. Older students are more likely to paraphrase and reorganize the text as they underline or take notes, and they have more foresight about keeping written records of past problem-solving attempts so as to skip possible solutions or not repeat others.

### Awareness of How Memory Works

Three- and 4-year-old children understand that noise, lack of interest, and thinking about other things can hinder attentiveness to a task. It is not until 4 years of age that children have a general grasp of what it means to "remember" or "forget." For the most part, they believe that "looking at" something is the best way to remember it. By ages 5 and 6, children are aware that their memory is limited, and that the number of items to be learned will determine whether the task is easy or difficult, as will the familiarity of the items, the amount of study time available, and whether recognition or recall is required. At about this time children recognize that optimal learning involves concentration, motivation, and avoidance of distractions. They recognize that categorization, rehearsal, and naming of items help them to memorize. Not until sixth grade do children understand that the categorization strategy is superior to the others. The ability to sense when they have studied well enough to remember a set of items improves noticeably through the elementary years, as does recognition that categorizing items, opposites, or linking information through a story makes information more memorable than trying to recall unrelated items. Similar improvements are seen in children's recognition that information too similar to the target information can interfere with memory, and that it is easier to recall something in one's own words than in others' words.

Kindergarteners can come up with at least one strategy to remember (e.g., to take skates to school). As children become older, they can think of multiple ways to remember, and these usually rely on self-responsibility ("I'll write it down") rather than external aids ("I'll ask mom to remind me"). It is not unusual for kindergarten and first-grade children to be convinced that they always remember well and never forget anything. By 9 to 11 years old, children recognize that memorization skills vary from person to person and

*(continued)*

**RESEARCH BOX 7.1 (Continued)**

from situation to situation. By this time, children are aware that they do not have an equally good memory in all situations, and that others might remember better. Older students have a more realistic and accurate picture of their memory abilities and limitations than do younger children. They are more aware of and sensitive to the need to memorize; for example, they recognize that items not recalled on tests need more study than ones that were recalled. They also learn much better when they report using cognitive strategies.

**Retrieval Strategies**

Retrieval processes become more efficient between ages 4 and 12. Kindergartners spontaneously apply simple retrieval strategies such as association cues. But complex retrieval strategies such as exhaustively searching one's memory, evaluating the information, or reorganizing it does not emerge until the late elementary and early adolescent years. Searching one's long-term memory intelligently requires evaluating the task at hand and then proceeding in a systematic, flexible, exhaustive, and selective fashion, skills which require greater maturity. Younger children can be helped to remember if given a cue at the time of memorizing (e.g., asking "Are these weapons?" when presenting *knife-ax*), and again when retrieval is required ("What weapon goes with knife?"). Teenagers, on the other hand, are aware of numerous resources at their disposal for helping them recall information, and actively deploy them.

less time studying information before they believe they are ready to recall it, and then they recall it less well than their peers. They often aren't aware that the longer is the list to memorize, the longer they should take to study it. They study at a constant rate, no matter what the task. Often they don't monitor their understanding of incoming information or actively reason about the material. In fact, they tend to approach a text as though it were just random details to be memorized. A frequent response to a comprehension question is to apply no line of reasoning at all, and college students with LD will describe their memorization strategy for tests as simply "rereading the book."

Piaget believed, and research has confirmed, that the more aware that students are of their reasoning processes, the more knowledge they will be able to gain and then generalize to new situations. For example, Alec is able to memorize better if he understands why it benefits him to rehearse the states and capitals a few at a time, over and over again, rather than just telling him to do so.

Teachers can help their students with LD employ more effective learning strategies by providing specific *metacognitive training.* Metacognitive strategies include knowing that you are forgetful and therefore sticking Post-It reminders where you're likely to see them, recognizing your strengths and weaknesses and choosing college courses or a vocation accordingly, knowing that studying for an essay versus multiple-choice exam requires different approaches, knowing to think about all alternatives before choosing an answer, and deciding when note taking is useful and when it doesn't work.

The average student becomes savvy about what a particular teacher wants and will plan his or her studying accordingly. Some teachers are detail oriented and seem to delight in putting the most obscure information on tests; others are "big picture" instructors who favor broad essay questions that test students' ability to connect chunks of information and make inferences. All students at one time or another have raised the plaintive cry in class, "Will this be on the test?" Average-achieving students know how much studying is enough in order to do well, how to figure out difficult material, how to break down large tasks, how new information fits with what is already known, and whether prior information should be altered in light of the new information—or the information rejected.

*Teachers can teach metacognitive lessons to help students gain self-awareness of their knowledge how they think, and how they can remember.*

Basically, metacognitive lessons translate into teaching students how to gain self-awareness of their knowledge and how they think, so they can decide what they learn and remember, as well as how and when they learn and remember it. As students age, their metacognitive skills become more effective because older children are more active, flexible, organized, and efficient in learning and retrieval skills.

Students with learning disabilities who receive metacognitive training often perform at higher-skill levels and learn more intelligently. The hope is that the strategies will become automatic and effortless, thereby freeing cognitive energy for understanding and storing information. The most effective strategies are those that are self-generated, because they match the student's learning style. Even if students don't self-generate these approaches as they get older, they still need to be taught metacognitive skills. Early adolescence is a prime time for such instruction because students are mature enough not only to benefit from this training, but also to apply what they've learned to new circumstances.

*The most effective memory strategies are those that are self-generated, because they match the student's learning style.*

Teachers should train students in these strategies extensively, and the strategies should remain as simple as possible in order to help students eventually "own" their strategies and use them automatically. Until a strategy becomes automatic, it can divert attention from the academic content. Experts suggest teaching no more than 3 to 4 new strategies a year. More difficult strategies, such as those depicted in Figure 7.4, require at least a fourth- to fifth-grade reading ability to be used effectively. As with all learning strategies, these work best when students know why they work and receive feedback as they employ them.

Another approach is to incorporate memory strategies directly into classroom lessons. These improve learning for all children, but the learning disabled make particularly marked gains. One study, for example, showed that the passing rates of students with LD on a social studies test increased from 11 to 77 percent when the teacher incorporated memory strategies into the lesson. Simply repeating the information didn't help.

Visual imagery, verbal mediation, self-monitoring, and modeling are among the methods that have helped youngsters with LD learn to attend to the important elements of their assignments, organize them for recall, and be able to retrieve them from memory. Teaching these strategies are critical because research suggests that students with LD can remember just as well as their peers, provided the information has been stored meaningfully and deeply in the first place.

*Teaching learning strategies is critical because students with LD can remember as well as their peers, provided the information has been stored in the first place.*

**Visual Imagery.** Teaching youngsters to mentally imagine the material they are studying has been very helpful in aiding language acquisition, reading comprehension,

**RIDER: A Visual Imagery Strategy for Reading Comprehension**

R = Read (the sentence)
I = Image (make an image or picture in your mind)
D = Describe (describe how the new image is different from the last sentence)
E = Evaluate (as you make the image, check to make sure it contains everything necessary)
R = Repeat (as you read the next sentence repeat the steps to RIDE)

**DEFENDS: A Writing Strategy for Defending a Position**

D = Decide on exact position
E = Examine the reasons for the position
F = Form a list of points that explain each reason
E = Expose position in the first sentence
N = Note each reason and supporting points
D = Drive home the position in the last sentence
S = SEARCH for errors and correct
- S = See if it makes sense
- E = Eject incomplete sentences
- A = Ask if it's convincing
- R = Reveal COPS errors & correct
  - C = Capitalization
  - O = Overall appearance
  - P = Punctuation
  - S = Spelling
- C = Copy over neatly
- H = Have a last look

**Figure 7.4** Mnemonic learning strategies.

*Source:* Ellis, E. S., & Lenz, B. K. (1987). A component analysis of effective learning strategies for LD students. *Learning Disabilities Focus, 2,* 97–101. Reprinted by permission of the Division of Learning Disabilities.

*Teaching youngsters to mentally imagine the material they are studying facilitates learning.*

and memory for quotes, among other things. One effective technique to enhance reading comprehension, for example, is for children to think of a picture to associate with each sentence in a passage. Because children below the age of 8 have difficulty creating images to mirror what they've read, this technique is most effective for older children.

Picture cues apparently help children formulate inferences, which later serve as useful retrieval cues. When students describe these images to themselves and store this verbal information, they then have both visual and verbal cues to call on for recall. Figure 7.5 illustrates the type of visual images that students can create for themselves to help remember social studies content. Teacher-prepared aids that simplify text into images also facilitate attention, comprehension, and learning.

**Verbal Mediation.** Self-verbalization is a powerful aid to learning. In Bandura's classic study, as children observed a scene they either verbalized the model's actions, just watched, or verbalized irrelevant material. Verbalizing the actions was clearly the most effective way for the children to recall and imitate the scene they had observed. Verbal self-instruction, self-questioning techniques, and mnemonics (verbal memory aids) have since proved to be powerful mediators for learning.

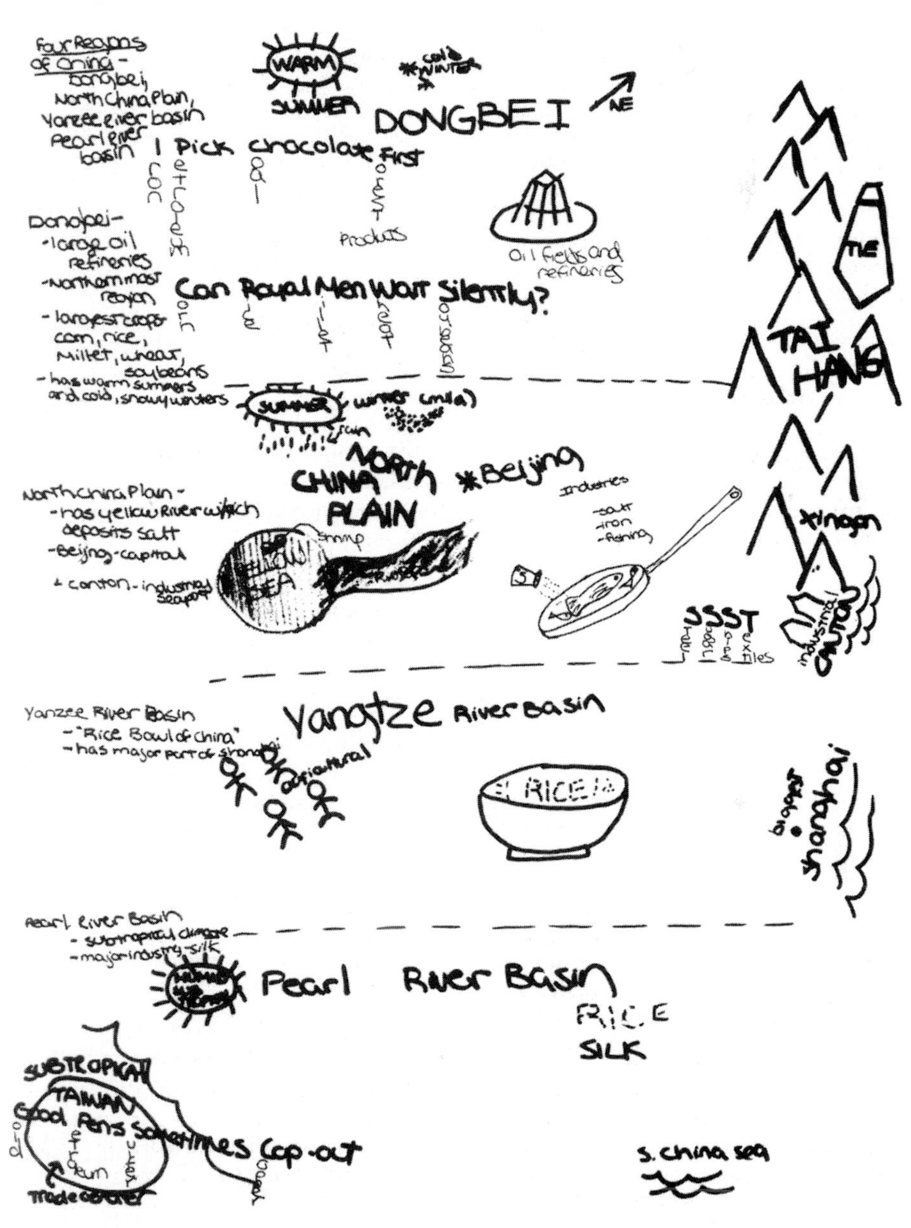


**Figure 7.5** Images of China. This ninth grader has arranged the geographical regions of China from north to south along the page. Pictures are used to aid recall (e.g., a bowl of rice to represent "Rice Bowl of China"; stick figures of farmers to depict an agricultural society; fish being salted in a frying pan to depict the salt, fishing, and iron industries). Frequent use has been made of mnemonics (e.g., first letters of words in sentences spur recall of industrial products; a drawing of a necktie helps to recall the name of the "Tai" Hang mountain region).

***Verbal self-instruction, self-questioning techniques, and mnemonics are powerful strategies for learning.***

*Verbal Self-Instruction.* Researcher Donald Meichenbaum applied the principles of the self-regulatory function of speech to help students focus attention on task-relevant stimuli and behaviors in a mature, organized, and self-guided fashion. First he had students observe the instructor modeling such behaviors as sizing up the problem, focusing on relevant aspects, doing the task, self-evaluating performance, and correcting errors. Next the students went through three stages of performing the task:

1. Using the instructor's verbal directions,
2. On their own while self-instructing aloud or in a whisper, and
3. On their own while self-instructing silently.

By literally talking to themselves in this manner, impulsive children have improved their problem-solving skills dramatically. This method has also improved the attention to task and math accuracy and productivity of children with LD. Children who use verbal self-instruction make more and better revisions in their written work, their essays are longer, they find and correct more mechanical errors, and they comprehend their reading better. Success also increases as students talk themselves through a task with encouraging self-statements. Meichenbaum's method is most useful to youngsters who don't spontaneously analyze their experience in verbal terms and therefore don't plan their problem solving approaches.

With one exception, as overt or inner speech increases, so does task success. The exception is when a 3-year-old or younger child tries to use self-commands to inhibit a motor activity; often these self-commands call attention to and generate the very activity the child wants to inhibit. Robin, for example, may be repeating out loud her mother's warning, "Don't touch! Don't touch!" as she approaches Aunt Fritzie's precious glass figurines; but she will go ahead and touch them anyway. It's only when she reaches age 4 to 4½ that words inhibit the compulsion to touch. Until then, it's best to put the treasures out of harm's way.

Often parents find their preschoolers self-instructing aloud as they solve problems during play, and by age 5 these instructions become inaudible to others. The more the 5-year-old verbalizes to himself or herself, the better is the child's overall ability to memorize. By the early elementary years, this technique becomes a reliable tool for aiding memory.

Self-instruction also is an effective way to teach students cognitive strategies to monitor their inappropriate behavior tendencies. The behavior is broken down into small units, and the student is made aware of the sequence of events that have triggered his or her negative reactions. Cindy, for example, is upset because "every time I walk past Charlie's desk to sharpen my pencil I end up doing something stupid because I don't like how he looks at me." Verbal self-instruction can help Cindy to interrupt the chain of events early (she can take a different path to the pencil sharpener) or to change her responses ("I'll ignore Charlie").

Verbal self-instruction can also turn around the negative self-statements students who are learning disabled tend to make when they approach a task—"I'll never be able to do that!" Substituting positive statements such as "Now I'm getting it!" or "I can handle this" is often very effective in augmenting performance and building a "can do" attitude.

***Self-Questioning Techniques.*** Self-questions, such as those shown in Figure 7.6, have improved math word problem solutions and comprehension in content-area subject matter. An example of a self-questioning comprehension strategy is RAM:

R Read the passage.
A Ask the "wh" questions (who, what, where, when, why) while reading, and predict the answer.
M Mark the answers to the "wh" words as I come across them in the passage.

CAPS, another self-questioning strategy, has been effective in helping students locate information in a story:

C Who are the characters?
A What is the aim or purpose?
P What problem or situation occurs in the story?
S How is the problem solved?

These types of strategies work by helping students survey the task, clarify the purpose, summarize the main idea and details, clarify ambiguities (by rereading or asking for help), recite important facts, and stimulate interest and evaluation by predicting what might happen next.

***Mnemonics.*** Mnemonic strategies have helped many students who are learning disabled. Many of us rely on them in the form of acronyms—for example, PEAR could stand for popcorn, eggs, applesauce, and raisins as a reminder of what to buy at the supermarket. One researcher illustrated the helpfulness of this "first-letter" method for students with LD when memorizing material like the major fatal diseases in the early twentieth century: *STRIP + D* = syphilis, typhoid, rabies, influenza, polio, diabetes. The related sentence "If you got any of these diseases in

**Self-Questions for Representing Algebra Word Problems**

1. Have I read and understood each sentence? Are there any words whose meaning I have to ask?
2. Have I got the whole picture, a representation, for this problem?
3. Have I written down my representation on the worksheet? (goal; unknown(s); known(s); type of problem; equation)
4. What should I look for in a new problem to see if it is the same kind of problem?

**Figure 7.6** Self-questions on prompt cards.

*Source:* Hutchinson, N. L. (1993). Effects of cognitive strategy instruction on algebra problem solving of adolescents with learning disabilities. *Learning Disability Quarterly, 16,* p. 39.

1900, you had to go and *STRIP* at the *D*octor's" helped facilitate recall (Ellis & Lenz, 1987). Figure 7.4 illustrates some of the acronyms that can help organize a student's approach to learning. Another example, the PLEASE strategy, has helped sixth graders with LD improve the quality of their compositions in just half a school year (Welch, 1992):

P = Pick a topic
L = List your ideas about the topic
E = Evaluate your list
A = Activate the paragraph with the topic sentence
S = Supply supporting sentences
E = End with a concluding sentence, and
Evaluate your work.

Another mnemonic device is the *keyword method* illustrated in Figures 7.7, 7.8, and 7.9. In one study, the recall of students with LD who were given keyword cues was nearly 80 percent, compared with 31 percent for those who studied the same pictures but weren't given the mnemonic cues. This method has helped students with LD to master high school science and history facts and math, English, and foreign language vocabulary (e.g., the Italian word *fonda,* meaning "bag," is depicted as a *phone in a bag*). In one study, for example, the students' memory for the natural resources, technological advances, wealth, and population growth in the town of *Fostoria* (keyword *frost*) was aided by illustrating oil pumps, comput-

**Figure 7.7** Pictorial mnemonic keyword vocabulary illustration. The word *ranid,* which means "frog," is recalled by associating a similar-looking keyword, *rain,* with a scene of a frog enjoying the rain.

*Source:* Mastropieri, M. A., Scruggs, T. E., Levin, J. R., Gaffney, J., & McLoone, B. (1985). Mnemonic vocabulary instruction for learning disabled students. *Learning Disability Quarterly,* 8, 57–63, p. 58. Reprinted by permission of the Division of Learning Disabilities.

**Figure 7.8** Mnemonic illustration depicting Madison as capital of Wisconsin. Wisconsin is recalled by associating it with the keyword *whisk broom,* and Madison with the keyword *maid.*

*Source:* Mastropieri, M. A., Scruggs, T. E., Bakken, J. P., & Brigham, F. J. (1992). A complex mnemonic strategy for teaching states and their capitals: Comparing forward and backward associations. *Learning Disabilities Research & Practice, 7,* p. 97. Reprinted by permission of the Division of Learning Disabilities.

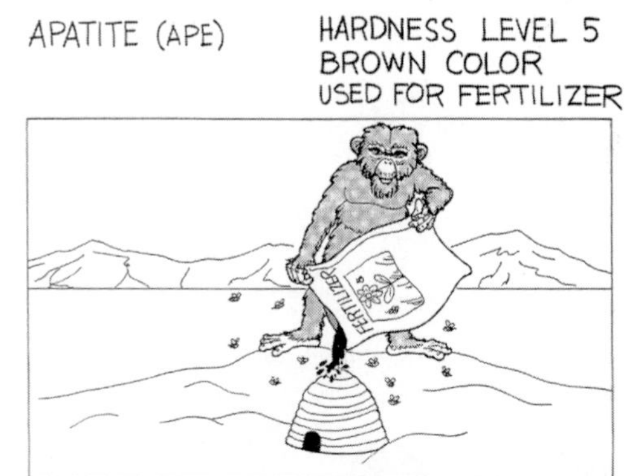


**Figure 7.9** Mnemonic instruction. The properties of the mineral *apatite* are learned with this mnemonic: *ape,* both the ape and apatite are brown; the hardness level of apatite is *five,* which rhymes with hive; and it is used for *fertilizer.*

*Source:* Scruggs, T. E., Mastropieri, M. A., Levin, J. R., McLoone, B., Gaffney, J. S., & Prater, M. A. (1985). Increasing content-area learning: A comparison of mnemonic and visual-spatial direct instruction. *Learning Disabilities Research, 1,* p. 20. Reprinted by permission.

ers, scattered money, and crowds of people—all covered with frost. In another study, memorizing states and capitals (e.g., "Concord is the capital of New Hampshire") was facilitated by a sentence and drawing that cued recall: "The old man walked his *ham*ster down the street with a *cord* around its neck." When a similar method was used to teach middle school students eighteenth-century North American battle sites, the mnemonic condition resulted in significantly better ability to locate specific battles on a map and whether the British (sites colored red) or Americans (sites colored blue) had won (see Figure 7.10). Results using these approaches appear to be best when the teacher provides the mnemonic rather than when students are asked to figure out how the keyword relates or to generate their own keyword and illustration. Even though students enjoy coming up with keywords and illustrations, the process is so difficult and time-consuming that valuable time is sacrificed that could have been devoted to learning content.

*Acrostics* support recall by creating an entire sentence, such that the first letter of each word represents the information to be memorized. Our piano teachers used this method when they drilled into us "Every Good Boy Does Fine" as an aid for recalling the names of the lines in the treble clef. Finally, the *pegword method* involves choosing a word that relates to each item in a numbered list so as to rhyme

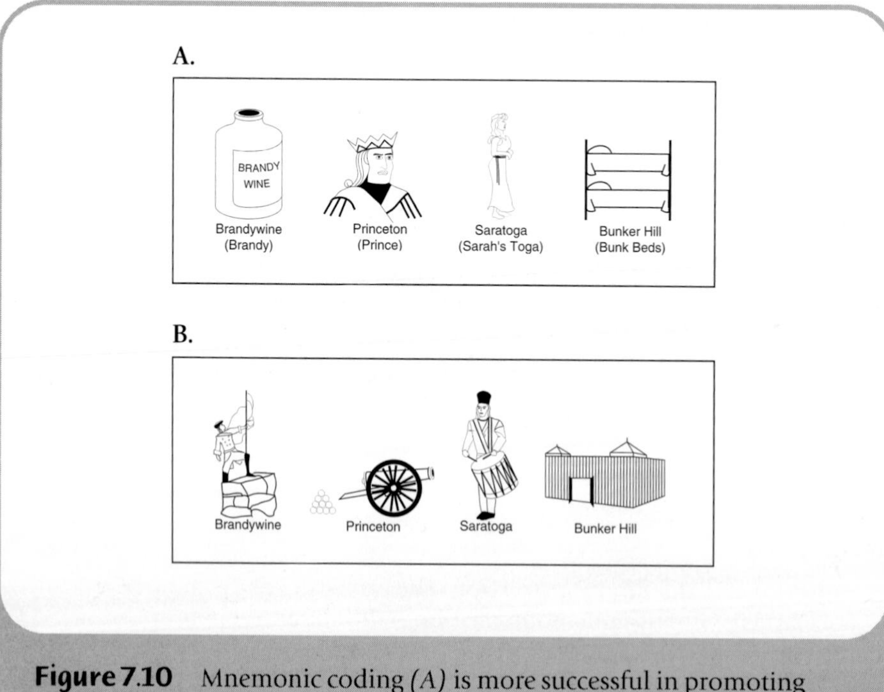


**Figure 7.10** Mnemonic coding *(A)* is more successful in promoting learning than noncoded *(B)* material.

*Source:* Scruggs, T. E., Mastropieri, M. A., Brigham, F. J., & Sullivan, G. S. (1992). Effects of mnemonic reconstructions on the spatial learning of adolescents with learning disabilities. *Learning Disability Quarterly, 15,* 157–158.

with the designated number, such as hive with five in Figure 7.9. In one study, students with LD were taught the names and numbers of eight U.S. presidents. Those who used a traditional method of rehearsing the name and number while looking at a picture of the president recalled an average of 3.8 names and 5 numbers. Those who used mnemonics (e.g., the fourteenth president Franklin Pierce is depicted as a *purse* being *pierced* by a fork) recalled 11 names and 9.6 numbers. This method has resulted in excellent recall of the first ten amendments to the U.S. Constitution, the order of admission of states to the union, and much more.

**Self-Monitoring.** Many metacognitive training studies have taught students how to monitor their classroom behavior and scan material appropriately before deciding on answers. One approach used the visual prompt and self-monitoring sheet shown in Figure 7.11 to increase on-task behavior of teenagers with LD. The students heard a recorded, random tone at 1- to 2½-minute intervals. They were instructed to place a check on their self-monitoring sheets at the prompt. Their attention, and that of children in other studies, improved 50 to 100 percent. In addition to on-task behavior, this method has proved effective in math, reading, and spelling to improve task accuracy, assignment completion, breaking tasks down into parts, recall of details, delay of responding while examining alternatives, and looking for similarities and differences. Self-monitoring methods have

*Self-monitoring cue cards of on-task behavior, productivity, and accuracy, especially when combined with graphing performance, have been very effective learning aids.*

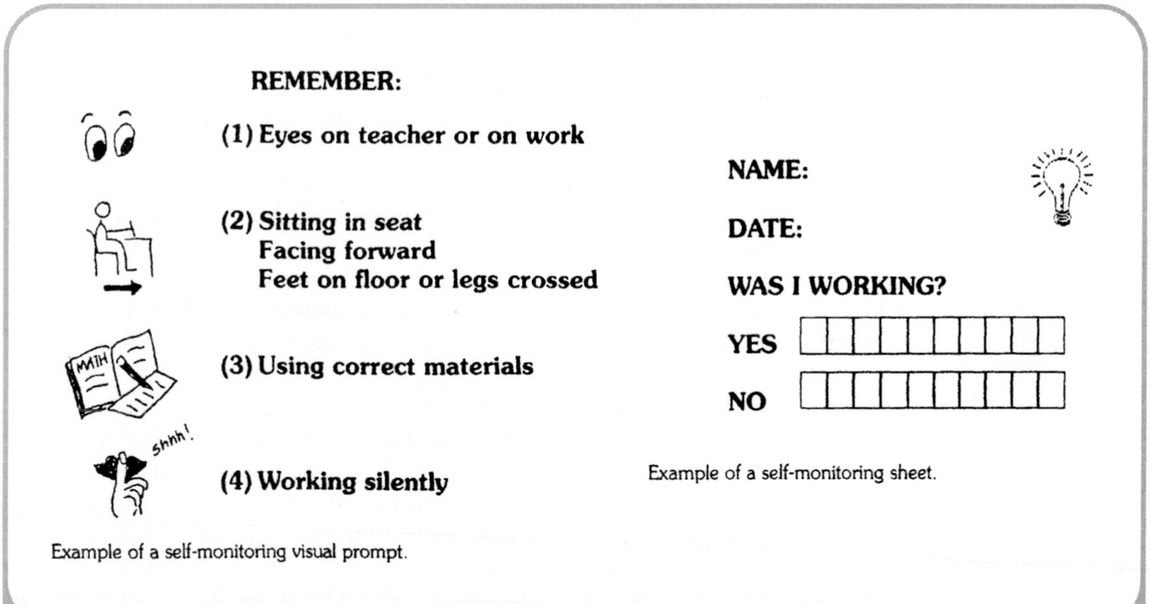

**REMEMBER:**

**(1) Eyes on teacher or on work**

**(2) Sitting in seat**
**Facing forward**
**Feet on floor or legs crossed**

**(3) Using correct materials**

**(4) Working silently**

Example of a self-monitoring visual prompt.

**NAME:**

**DATE:**

**WAS I WORKING?**

| | | | | | | | | | |
|---|---|---|---|---|---|---|---|---|---|
| **YES** | | | | | | | | | |
| **NO** | | | | | | | | | |

Example of a self-monitoring sheet.

**Figure 7.11** Example of an effective self-monitoring aid.

*Source:* Prater, M. A., Chilman, R. J. B., Temple, J., & Miller, S. R. (1991). Self-monitoring of on-task behavior by adolescents with learning disabilities. *Learning Disability Quarterly, 14*, p. 169. Reprinted by permission of the Council for Learning Disabilities.

also been effective in helping students to detect their own errors, decrease inappropriate verbalization, and improve reading comprehension, the quality of written compositions, handwriting, and more. The additional act of graphing their on-task behavior after using self-monitoring cards has been very helpful in increasing on-task behavior, productivity, and accuracy. Teaching students with LD exactly how to monitor their own strategies has resulted in more long-lasting effects than merely cautioning them to take more time before answering.

*Modeling, or imitating others performing correctly, has a strong vicarious effect on learning strategies.*

**Modeling.** Most metacognitive training incorporates some form of modeling. Watching others perform correctly can have a strong vicarious effect on learning strategies. Imitating after watching is even more powerful. Modeling seems to work because it draws attention to aspects of tasks that students ordinarily would not have noticed. For this same reason, working in groups is particularly helpful for youngsters with LD because attention is drawn to the kinds of strategies and reasoning used by peers. A particularly powerful form of modeling with respect to encouraging behavioral changes is watching carefully edited videotapes of oneself acting appropriately in a given situation, followed by discussion, role play, and teacher feedback. Modeling has been effective in enhancing reflectivity in impulsive children, reading comprehension, computational accuracy, question-asking and answering, problem solving, and much more.

### Other Metacognitive Approaches

1. Elaborating on ideas in a personally meaningful way (such as relating drip irrigation methods in Ecuador to how the flowers could have been displayed at Uncle Steve's wedding instead of burying the roots in dirt); students with LD tend not to generate these associations spontaneously.
2. Chunking (as in telephone numbers: 610-649-3989); students with LD need to have their attention drawn to the separate "chunks" in order to actually use them to aid memory.
3. Paraphrasing material in one's own words.
4. Developing uniquely personal approaches to material, no matter how roundabout and odd. The student's own approach often works better than teacher suggestions.
5. Reviewing material at distributed intervals.
6. Using associations with attention-getting information (e.g., in associating the dangers of potential chemical weapons with the September 11th tragedies).
7. Reviewing relevant old knowledge before beginning to study new information.
8. Highlighting and charting relationships in the material (such as similarities and differences, cause and effect).
9. Generating overall principles and inferences that are linked with specific content.
10. Stopping to draw conclusions.
11. Creating new ideas.
12. Making judgments.
13. Distinguishing between different requirements for multiple-choice versus essay exams and studying accordingly.

*No matter how roundabout and odd, the student's own special approach to learning often works better than teacher suggestions.*

Unfortunately, in spite of great enthusiasm for metacognitive training approaches, transfer of these learning strategies to novel tasks on which strategy training has not occurred has been disappointing. Chapter 12 presents more specific strategies for developing study skills, test-taking skills, and transfer of school knowledge to survival skills that are important for employment and independent living.

*In spite of great enthusiasm for metacognitive approaches, transfer of these learning strategies to new tasks has been disappointing.*

## Visual-Perceptual, Motor, and Language Development

Because a learning strategies approach can improve attention and learning, it's believed that many students with learning disabilities may have strategy impairments rather than information-processing impairments in their basic capacity to learn. All of us have used inefficient strategies from time to time. Think about the last time you were introduced to a guy at a party and then forgot his name seconds later. You had made no effort to repeat his name, associate a distinguishing facial characteristic with his name, or in any other way act on the information so that you would recall it later. Your memory lapse was due to your failure to invoke a strategy to help you remember, rather than an information-processing weakness.

*Because learning strategies improve attention and learning, many students with LD may have strategy impairments rather than information-processing impairments in their basic capacity to learn.*

Unfortunately, many students with LD aren't lucky enough to be underachieving only because they are inefficient in how they go about learning. Many have basic delays in attention, visual-perception, motor, and language development that make it difficult to absorb new information, pull stored information from memory, and demonstrate knowledge and thoughts to others. Their academic achievement suffers because their poor information-processing skills don't support higher-level learning. In addition, because their information-processing skills aren't automatic, the processing effort competes with incoming information for attentional resources in the students' working memories. As a result, memory suffers.

*Other students with LD aren't lucky enough to be underachieving only because they are inefficient in how they go about learning. Many have basic delays in attention, visual-perception, motor, and language development that make it difficult to absorb new information, pull information from memory, and demonstrate knowledge to others.*

Youngsters who underachieve in all academic areas tend to have both visual-perceptual and language impairments. Those with language weaknesses but perceptual strengths are better at math than at reading and spelling. Those with perceptual weaknesses but language strengths are better at reading but poorer at math. Children with perceptual weaknesses often experience greater social and emotional difficulties than do students with perceptual strengths because they aren't sensitive to the "big picture." Their difficulties with social perception and interaction are commonly referred to as *nonverbal learning disabilities.*

There is a great deal of variability among students within each type of learning disability, and the strength/weakness patterns of individual children often are not as clear-cut as described above. In addition, with maturation and time for compensation, cognitive and information-processing weaknesses may show up in more subtle ways in teenagers and adults. Patterns can change.

It's important not to simply sit back and wait for development to take its course when we notice lags in information-processing skills essential for learning. There are many good ways to remediate and develop compensations for information-processing inefficiencies and thus improve students' chances for academic success. For example, when a child's spelling difficulty is caused by poor perception of the order of sounds in words, we can help him or her develop phoneme segmentation skills through phonological awareness training, while also providing phonetic instruction in reading and spelling. A child who has trouble grasping a pencil can be shown a better way and thus improve his or her handwriting. Children with poor social communication can learn to respond appropriately to friendly greetings and normal kidding. When a novel is linguistically too difficult, an easier version can be provided while the more complex vocabulary is being taught.

When persistent information-processing problems interfere with learning, teachers must modify tasks that prove troublesome in order to provide the student maximum access to the curriculum. For example, a student might be offered a version of Shakespeare's *Romeo and Juliet* in simpler English rather than the more challenging Elizabethan original. A student with persistent language delays might take American Sign Language in place of foreign language courses. For a student who has trouble maintaining attention, shorter lectures, a study carrel, and activity-oriented instruction might be the answer. A student whose handwriting is nearly illegible because of fine-motor deficiencies could be permitted to type assignments on a computer or dictate them using voice recognition software.

*Train only those information-processing skills that have immediate, direct transfer value to obvious skills needed for academic progress.*

Some professionals have tried to remediate information-processing weaknesses without directly tying the activities and skills to academic tasks. Not uncommon have been exercises in crawling, trampolining, eye movements, puzzles, solving mazes, repeating strings of sounds, and "crossing the midline" by drawing large X's on a board. These approaches have not resulted in academic gains because the skills trained have little in common with those needed for higher-level reasoning in academics. A good rule of thumb for teachers is to train only those information-processing skills that have immediate, direct transfer value to obvious skills needed for academic progress—such as word searches to train children to spot words quickly, practicing drawing the lines and curves that make up individual letters, and breaking apart the order of sounds in words.

*Children's information-processing abilities don't develop in a smooth, linear fashion—spurts and plateaus are to be expected.*

It is important to recognize that children's information-processing abilities don't develop in a smooth, linear fashion, whether they're average learners or learning disabled. One day, 1½-year-old Elana has just 10 words in her vocabulary; the next day she awakens with 15 more. One week, 4-year-old Henry thinks a deck of cards is for tossing around the living room; the next week he's a champion Old Maid player. One evening, 6½-year-old Leah struggles to read a book and gives up in tearful frustration. The next night she reads it with ease. Although Elana is making enormous language strides, her motor development may stand still. While Henry's attending ability is mushrooming, his toileting skills may slip. All these spurts and plateaus are to be expected.

*Children with LD who are maturing slowly in information-processing skills tend to resolve their lags in a way that follows the normal continuum of development. Familiarity with typical development helps identify the next most appropriate developmental objective.*

Spurts in young children's development—veritable cognitive explosions—are especially evident at ages 2 and 6. This enormous growth in language, perception, thought, attention, and coordination corresponds with natural spurts in brain development. Sudden increases in attention, judgment, planning, and organization continue at periodic intervals, but especially at ages 14 and 16 and in early adulthood.

Familiarity with the typical development of information-processing skills helps us to plan remediation, because students with LD will benefit from being exposed to the next-more-difficult task in the developmental continuum. It also gives us ideas on how to identify and capitalize on students' strengths during instruction. The remainder of this chapter contrasts the normal development of information-processing skills with that of students with LD.

## Visual Perception Development

The sequence in which visual-perceptual skills are acquired is important to know because children with LD who are maturing slowly in these areas tend to resolve their lags in a way that follows the normal continuum of development. Understanding the order, then, helps us direct our assessments and guide remedial planning. For instance, we know that preschoolers match objects by shape before they match them by color. Therefore, we'll have more success if we first have children with visual-perceptual lags gather together all the fruits that are round before we ask them to match all the fruits that are red.

Knowledge of the order of visual-perceptual development tells us that we should help students discriminate verticals, perpendiculars, up-down, and asymmetrical figures before left-right reversal figures, diagonals, or symmetrical figures; this has clear implications for the order of introducing letters and numbers to children who have difficulty discriminating one from another. We should draw children's attention to the outlines of designs (as in a *narrow and tall* vs. *short and wide* house) and letters first (as in letters that are *straight* vs. *curved*), then to the internal elements (windows, doorknobs, a *t* is made up of two crossed lines), and then to both combined. Three-dimensional objects draw much more attention than two-dimensional ones. Position in space is also a very important dimension to young children. The next time you're with a 1-year-old, pick up any object and place it to his or her left. Then move it to the right. Then to the center. The child is delighted. Knowing this, with older preschoolers we often play games of concentration that use position as a key to reinforcing basic concepts.

*Students distinguish verticals, perpendiculars, and up-down figures before right-left reversal figures or diagonals. Children's attention is drawn to outlines before internal elements, three-dimensional objects before two-dimensional figures, and position in space.*

Newborns and young infants have a great deal of visual-perceptual ability. At 2 months they can discriminate colors; at 3 months, they can identify familiar and unfamiliar faces; by 4 months, they can distinguish simple shapes and small sets containing different numbers of objects.

By ages 3 to 4 children can tell that numbers and letters are different from scribbles and pictures. Letter discrimination begins by distinguishing letters with straight lines from those with curves. By age 6 children can discriminate well among letters, and it is at age 7 that discrimination among forms that differ in rotation, reversal, and perspective becomes easy for children. At this age, 85 percent of children can accurately point to their left and right sides. These developmental trends explain why young children find letters that look similar so confusing. They frequently miscall reversible letters such as *b* and *d,* and write letters backward. Left-right transformations (*b–d; p–g*) resolve themselves later than up-down transformations (*b–p; m–w*), up-down being an easier concept for young children. It also has been suggested that the concept of left-right presents a greater challenge because this is not an important dimension in young children's worlds. Although it doesn't matter which way a toy truck faces when a child is playing, it certainly does matter whether the cup of milk is held right side up or upside down. Both kinds of reversals normally disappear by the mid-elementary school years, though they persist longer in children with learning disabilities.

*Until age 7, many children find letters that look similar confusing, with left-right transformations being harder than up-down transformations.*

*Handling draws the preschooler's attention to features of an object that the child might have ignored, and movement helps grab and sustain the child's attention.*

In the 1950s and 1960s, teachers were urged to incorporate movement into learning tasks because feedback from touch and movement was presumed to sharpen children's visual perception of objects and letters. However, research has shown that simple visual perceptions are learned well before an infant can even move around or hold onto objects. The reason that handling and movement are helpful, and still recommended, is because handling draws the child's attention to features of an object that the child might have ignored, and movement helps grab and sustain the child's attention.

Because visual perception of form and space develops so early in life, simple types of visual processing don't appear at fault when preschoolers with learning disabilities can't match colors and shapes or differentiate between letter shapes. If these simple visual perceptions had not already developed, a preschooler hardly could realize where a step is, avoid walking into a wall, or discriminate a cup from a plate. Even if a child is delayed in these perceptual abilities, he or she has plenty of time to catch up before school begins and in the early elementary years. Therefore, a lag in simple visual processing of letter forms is not a serious deterrent to reading progress. It is the more complex visual-perceptual weaknesses described in Chapter 5, such as right-hemisphere strategy weaknesses and slow visual information processing, that contribute to learning disabilities. Though these weaknesses tend to persist through the adult years, they have only a mild to moderate impact on learning. Because visual-perceptual skills tend to reach "good enough" thresholds during the primary grades, children can make learning progress despite continued perceptual interferences with sight vocabulary, irregular spellings, grasping main ideas, and mathematics concepts.

*Because visual-perceptual skills tend to reach "good enough" thresholds during the primary grades, children can make learning progress despite continued perceptual interferences with sight vocabulary, irregular spellings, grasping main ideas, and mathematics concepts.*

## Motor Development

Many children with LD have fine- and gross-motor coordination difficulties. As preschoolers, they had trouble with puzzles, stacking blocks, drawing people, or copying designs. In elementary school, these difficulties showed in their handwriting, art class, gym, and playground activities. The biggest problem caused by motor weaknesses is the limit it places on demonstrating what one knows through drawing or writing. After speech, writing is the second major way children have to show us what they know.

*Fine-motor coordination difficulties often persist into adolescence and adulthood in the form of illegible handwriting and poor spacing of written work.*

Although fine-motor coordination generally improves with age, difficulties often persist into adolescence and adulthood in the form of illegible handwriting and poor spacing of written work. Fortunately, tape recorders and computers are effective tools to bypass such problems.

**Fine-Motor Development.** Fine-motor function traditionally refers to the use of the muscles of the hand. However, when a child draws, he or she brings many more muscles into play, including those of the upper trunk and legs to maintain balance in the chair and those of the upper arm to position the hand. Just to pick up a pencil a child must engage the motor system as well as sensations about the position of joints and limbs, and where the pencil is touching the skin. To guide drawing, the child must engage his or her conceptual, visual-perceptual, and language skills. Table 7.1 traces the development of manipulatory and drawing skills from the time an infant's eye tracking becomes smooth at 4 to 8 weeks through

**TABLE 7.1 Development of Manipulatory and Drawing Skills**

| *Age* | *Manipulatory Skill* | *Drawing Skill* |
|---|---|---|
| 8–12 weeks | • Moves extremities in response to rattle | |
| 12 weeks | • Looks at own hand and holds it aloft while sweeping at an object<br>Glances back and forth from hand to object | |
| 24 weeks | • Grasps and lifts objects in a palm grasp | |
| 28 weeks | • Is able to reach with both hands<br>Transfers an object from hand to hand<br>Resecures an object after dropping it | |
| 40 weeks | • Holds objects between finger and thumb, replacing the palm grasp | |
| 48 weeks | • Reaching is well coordinated | |
| 12 months | | • Uses crayons to make marks on paper |
| 15 months | • Makes a tower of 2 cubes<br>Takes 6 cubes in and out of cup<br>Manipulates and drinks from a cup<br>Takes off shoes<br>Throws and retrieves objects<br>Opens doors<br>Imitates sweeping, combing hair | • Imitates a horizontal scribble (~~) |
| 18 months | • Makes a tower of 3 to 4 cubes<br>Turns pages of a book, several at a time | • Scribbles spontaneously<br>Makes strokes imitatively |
| 18–21 months | • Strings beads | • Imitates a vertical stroke (\|) |
| 2 years | • Places circle, triangle, and square in formboard puzzle<br>Makes a tower of 6 to 7 cubes<br>Aligns 2 or more cubes to make a train<br>Puts on and takes off pants<br>Removes coat or dress unassisted<br>Throws ball overhand | • Imitates V stroke<br>Imitates circular stroke |
| 2¼ years | | • Imitates horizontal strokes |
| 2½ years | • Obtains own drink of water with cup<br>Dries own hands<br>Stacks 5 rings on peg by size | • Imitates H strokes<br>Copies vertical line |
| 3 years | • Makes a tower of 9 cubes<br>Imitates a cube bridge<br>Dresses self | • Copies circle<br>Copies horizontal lines<br>Imitates cross |

*(continued)*

**TABLE 7.1 (Continued)**

| *Age* | *Manipulatory Skill* | *Drawing Skill* |
|---|---|---|
| 3½ years | | • Imitates X |
| 4 years | • Puts 10 or more pellets into a bottle in 2 to 5 seconds | • Draws person with two parts<br>Copies cross<br>Copies diagonal line |
| 4½ years | • Buttons<br>Cuts, pastes | • Copies square<br>20 percent of children print letters |
| 5 years | • Ties shoes | • Copies X<br>Copies triangle |
| 6 years | | • Copies diamond<br>Copies rectangle with embedded diagonals |

*Source:* Adapted from Gard, A., Gilman, L., & Gorman, J. (1980). *Speech and language development chart:* Salt Lake City, UT: Word Making Publications; Gesell, A. (1940). *The first five years of life.* New York: Harper & Row; Hynd, G. W., & Willis, W. G. (1988). *Pediatric neuropsychology.* New York: Grune & Stratton; Knobloch, H., & Pasamanick, B. (1974). *Gesell and Amatruda's developmental diagnosis.* New York: Harper & Row; Telzrow, C. F., & Hartlage, L. C. (1983). Evaluation and programming for infants and preschoolers with neurological and neuropsychological impairments. In C. R. Reynolds & J. H. Clark (Eds.), *Assessment and programming for young children with low-incidence handicaps.* New York: Plenum Press.

the time the child enters school. Typical handwriting samples are illustrated in Chapter 6.

***Preschoolers master copying verticals first, then horizontals, followed by circles, diagonals, squares, and triangles.***

Children start drawing by scribbling dots, zigzags, loops, circles, and lines. Once they start to copy figures, they master verticals first, then horizontals, followed by circles, diagonals, squares, and triangles. This parallels the same pattern as the visual discrimination development of preschoolers.

As children mature, they begin to draw pictures of people. Their products are generally good reflections of their overall cognitive awareness, visual-motor development, and social maturity, as well as their attitudes about themselves and those close to them. The first step in drawing people is the scribble at about age 2, followed by an oval or circle with markings to represent facial features at age 3. At the same time, children begin to make drawings that look like suns—a big circle with rays that resemble arms and legs. Children next combine these two forms, resulting in a sun containing facial features and rays for arms and legs. As they mature, children add one more feature about every three months—ears, for example, then feet, and so on. By the time the child enters kindergarten, his or her "people" are fairly sophisticated, containing detail, proportion, and two-dimensional parts. Most five-year-olds draw people with heads, eyes, a nose, mouth, body, and legs. Also common are arms, hair, feet, fingers, and one item of clothing. Next children add two-dimensional arms and legs, a neck, hands, ears, eyebrows, pupils, five fingers, arms extending down rather than outward, and more clothing. With age, the last items to be added tend to be two-dimensional feet, arms attached at the shoulder, nostrils, elbows, knees, two lips, greater proportionality, and a profile drawing.

By kindergarten age, children can typically copy the individual lines that make up letters and short words. With time the print becomes smaller, the spacing uniform, and letters stay on the line. In third grade comes the transition to cursive writing followed by a distinct handwriting style, usually developed by sixth grade.

***By kindergarten age, children can typically copy the individual lines that make up letters and short words.***

**Gross-Motor Development.** Gross-motor function is the earliest developmental ability we can evaluate at birth. Although abnormalities at this time may reflect some brain dysfunction, academic learning is affected only if high-level reasoning areas of the brain have also been impaired. Because the brain areas essential to cognitive performance are located near the areas of the brain involved in motor function, an injury or delay in any area important to higher-level cognitive processes could affect nearby motor areas as well. Moreover, inefficiency in information processing often is reflected in awkward movements because the body is given insufficient information about exactly how, when, and where to move. For these reasons, we need to be alert to motor delays that may signal potential difficulties in higher-level cognitive functions as well.

***An injury or delay in an area important to higher-level cognitive processes could affect nearby motor areas as well. Moreover, information processing inefficiencies often are reflected in awkward movements because the body is given insufficient information about exactly how, when, and where to move.***

Despite the fact that poor motor coordination does not itself cause a learning disability, it certainly can make demonstrating knowledge difficult, and makes life in school and at home frustrating. A child whose blocks always fall down before the house is built or whose handmade valentines always look scraggly certainly is frustrated. When Maya trips over a friend playing on the floor, inadvertently knocks over someone's block tower, paints streaks on the easel when classmates are drawing houses and flowers, or is so slow that she's always "it" in games of tag, her self-concept suffers. Social interaction on the playground is cut off because activities that Maya's peers delight in—jungle gyms, sliding boards—are frightful to her and even make her nauseated. Although these difficulties improve with age, continued clumsiness and poor athletic ability make social life and social status particularly problematic for teenagers with gross-motor weaknesses. Their incoordination follows the teenagers into adulthood; fortunately, however, the American penchant for spectator sports makes living with these weaknesses as an adult much easier.

***Poor motor coordination does not itself cause a learning disability, but it makes demonstrating knowledge difficult and can influence the social status of some youngsters.***

The earliest assessment of motor functions in infants is the evaluation of *primitive reflexes,* those involuntary motor responses elicited by outside stimulation. An example is the tonic neck reflex. When a baby is laid on his or her back with the head turned to one side, the arm and leg will extend on the side the baby is facing. The other arm and leg will flex. Physicians assess the primitive reflexes, along with motor strength and muscle tone, to predict future neuromotor development. If these reflexes persist too long and don't become incorporated into more complex motor patterns such as grasping, controlling the head and trunk, and coordinating movements of different body parts, the maturation of voluntary motor movements will be disrupted.

Even if the above scenario does happen, these types of neurological abnormalities at birth generally don't mean that learning disabilities will follow. Gross-motor neurological indicators don't reflect the brain areas involved in higher-level academic reasoning, and the brain's higher-level reasoning areas can be modified greatly through an enriched home and school environment.

Table 7.2 lists the ages at which approximately 50 percent of children reach specific motor milestones. In the 1950s to 1970s there was much discussion about whether the side of the body one prefers to use has anything to do with learning disabilities. Although it was once believed that failure to develop a consistent body side with which to kick, catch, write, or peek through a keyhole—known as *laterality* or *dominance*—was related to the brain's failure to develop the superiority of one hemisphere over another for visual perception and language functions, this has not proven to be true. Good learners often display *mixed laterality* or *mixed dominance.* Nor does left- or right-handedness bear any relationship to learning disabilities. Left- and right-handedness appear related to learning disabilities only when the choice of hand has been forced by a brain injury that affected higher-cognitive abilities as well.

*Good learners often display mixed dominance.*

Before handedness is fully established, the normal child switches back and forth between right and left hands. Right-handedness generally becomes predominant by age 4, but it can be established as late as 10 years of age. Not until age 8 or 9 does a child use the right hand for all purposes. In contrast to the right-hander, the majority of left-handed children exhibit varying degrees of ambidexterity throughout life, in part because of society's encouragement and the fact that the world is geared toward the right-hander: just look at how guitars, carving knives, and potato peelers are made.

*Right-handedness generally becomes predominant by age 4.*

*The majority of left-handed children exhibit varying degrees of ambidexterity throughout life.*

Although gross-motor function develops largely with neurological maturity, some aspects can be influenced through teaching. Therefore, remediation of motor delays warrants the attention of parents, teachers, and occupational and physical therapists. Familiarity with the sequence of normal motor development helps us choose the most appropriate and least frustrating teaching objectives for children with delays in this area. Any gains made in motor coordination can help children to demonstrate what they know, whether it be drawing shapes on a blackboard or assembling a model, and to interrelate more effectively when playing. If a hand preference is slow to develop, it is recommended that motor activities with both hands be encouraged, until a natural preference becomes apparent.

## Language Development

*Because words are symbols for concepts, any trouble processing these symbols affects a person's thinking, comprehension, speaking, and social interactions. Delays in this area tend to persist, so that language cannot be used effectively to facilitate learning.*

Because words are symbols for concepts and ideas, any trouble processing these symbols affects a person's thinking, problem-solving, listening comprehension, speaking, and social interactions. Moreover, any activity in which we use speech to direct ourselves as to what to look at, remember, or how to move also is affected. Unfortunately, for children with language difficulties, their delays tend to persist into the elementary years and beyond, so that language cannot be used effectively to facilitate learning.

Although the vocabulary of the average student generally doubles between the third and seventh grades, this doesn't happen for children with LD who have language weaknesses. Their limited vocabulary means they have a harder time understanding what they read or hear, and more difficulty communicating what they know when speaking or writing. These difficulties in turn limit opportunities for

## TABLE 7.2 Gross-Motor Landmarks

| *Age* | |
|---|---|
| ***Prone and Upright Posture*** | |
| 16 weeks | • Raises head when lying on stomach; head is almost perpendicular to surface |
| 20 weeks | • Makes compensatory head movements when pulled from lying on back to a sitting posture |
| 24 weeks | • Rolls over<br>Supports self on extended arms in the prone position |
| 28 weeks | • In a sitting position, holds trunk erect momentarily |
| 36 weeks | • Holds trunk erect indefinitely |
| 40 weeks | • Holds trunk erect and maintains balance as turns to side to pick up an object |
| 44 weeks | • Goes from sitting to prone to sitting positions |
| ***Sitting, Crawling, Standing, Walking, and Running*** | |
| 12 weeks | • Supports much of weight on legs when held vertically |
| 28 weeks | • Sits alone<br>Crawls with abdomen in contact with floor<br>Supports full weight when held vertically |
| 36 weeks | • In creeping position, supports weight on toes<br>Pulls self into a standing position but has insufficient motor control to lower self |
| 48 weeks | • Pulls to standing and is able to walk holding on to furniture |
| 12–18 months | • Walks alone with elevation of arms; feet are wide-based for support |
| 18 months | • Walks sideways and backward |
| 21 months | • Walks up three steps alone |
| 2 years | • Runs<br>Goes up and down stairs placing both feet on each step |
| 2–3 years | • Kicks a ball on the floor<br>Balances on one foot for one second<br>Imitates crossing of the feet |
| 3 years | • Walks up stairs using alternating feet, but comes down stairs placing both feet on each step<br>Rides tricycle<br>Balances on each foot for 2 seconds |
| 4 years | • Somersaults<br>Balances well on toes<br>Walks a straight line 3 meters long<br>Hops on one foot<br>Touches fingers to thumb in succession<br>Balances on one foot for up to 10 seconds<br>Walks up and down stairs one step per foot |
| 4–5 years | • Skips<br>Catches a bounced ball |

*Sources:* Adapted from Gesell, A. (1940). *The first five years of life.* New York: Harper & Row; Hynd, G. W., & Willis, W. G. (1988). *Pediatric neuropsychology.* New York: Grune & Stratton; Knobloch, H., & Pasamanick, B. (1974). *Gesell and Amatruda's developmental diagnosis.* New York: Harper & Row; Telzrow, C. F., & Hartlage, L. C. (1983). Evaluation and programming for infants and preschoolers with neurological and neuropsychological impairments. In C. R. Reynolds & G. H. Clark (Eds.), *Assessment and programming for young children with low-incidence handicaps.* New York: Plenum Press.

higher-level learning. Word-finding and phonological awareness difficulties are still evident in teenagers with LD, as are problems with comprehending difficult grammar, distorting words (such as *bucker* for *buckle*), and using incomplete and less sophisticated sentences.

***Language weaknesses of as many as half of affected children are still evident in adulthood and often relate to lower adult functioning.***

Language weaknesses of as many as half of affected children are still evident in adulthood and often relate to lower adult functioning. The deficits can be subtle or they can be very obvious, as when a person fails to find the right word to express himself or herself, can't follow directions, or has trouble participating in conversations or even getting the joke in normal, everyday kidding. Rex's letter to me critiquing my parent book on learning disabilities illustrates the way language delays persist with time.

Because of the critical impact of language skills on thought, learning, and social adjustment, it is essential for teachers, other professionals, and parents to monitor students' language acquisition, to assess whether language delays are creating other delays, and to intervene as soon as possible.

Although theorists still disagree about how we actually acquire language, most LD experts have adopted the *interactionist* view. This view states that children choose words from the environment to reflect their thoughts, and in turn generate new word combinations that they've never heard before. For example, a toddler, understanding that his mother wants to put him to bed, selects the words "no" and "night" from vocabulary he's heard before, and in expressing himself creates "no night night." It is believed that language and thought develop both independently and simultaneously, each influencing the other's continued development.

According to Piaget and others, language becomes possible when children can represent their thoughts in language, typically at about 1½ to 2 years of age. This is the time when, because they can use language to hold onto ideas, youngsters can easily imagine people or objects even when they are absent, play "pretend," scribble images from memory, try to communicate something that happened before, and initiate a past trick such as delightedly flinging food from the high chair, in anticipation of the adult's reaction. Basically, without thought as a prerequisite, children can't develop meaningful language. And once they start to talk, speech further develops their thinking.

***Without thought as a prerequisite, children can't develop meaningful language. And once they start to talk, speech further develops their thinking.***

Helmer Myklebust, one of the pioneers in learning disabilities, proposed that infants can't comprehend the spoken word (*receptive language*) until they have enough meaningful experience to be reflected in thought (*inner language*). In other words, because a baby has the concept of a warm, nurturing relationship with his female parent who refers to herself as "Mama," the baby can connect the sound *Ma Ma* with this wonderful person in his life and eventually call her by name (*expressive language*).

The infant's inner language eventually evolves into thinking in words, using mental trial and error to problem-solve, classifying experiences (such as "happy," "fun"), and talking to himself or herself. Enhancement of either the inner, receptive, or expressive phases of language enhances the others as well.

Inner language disturbances are the most debilitating of all language disorders. Children with such a disturbance don't gain meaning from experience, and therefore, even if they acquire some language, they can't use it to represent thoughts. Receptive disorders always cause expressive disorders because children

## Rex

*A 40-year-old with persistent, severe language disabilities.*

Corrine,

I Did phone you as asked · Mid Sunday, no answer Machine or answer found at you residence.

Thus With pen in hand i can offer only a brief Summery of your Book in General.

as soon as i opened the book i became Glued to the pages in mind

Brian · Aisha · Frank · Joel · told of a Mirror reflection of My youth, i felt a weird Sence of Closeness to my fellow Self.

The First and Second of and Third of Part one, I had to read Twice,

Part Two, and the Rest of the book Drew me away from its Contents as Boring. or Non Stimutating. For I learned of ADHD.

Which took me to arresting My 81-year old

*(continued)*

**Rex** (Continued from preceding page)

aunt, what Did i miss in Knowing
about my birth? My aunt stated i
was a Mercurial Baby, 1st in N.Y.S.
Based on 5 1/4 months. Left in incubator Longer
then Expected, and Lived.

Thus causing Underlying Neurological
Impairments, Like Bethhoven and
einstein,

and lead me to Chadd to a book by
Edward Hallowell M.D, Driven to Distraction

thus allowing me to understand the Concept
of What makes Rex, "Rex."

and that is where i am now,
with 40 years Left in my Life.

Thank you for Letting me Share
The Conflict, I Have lived With
for 40.

Rex,

P.S. College. RIT or Cornell.

Despite continuing disabilities, Rex has utilized his perceptual and coordination strengths to build a successful "handyman" business. This is part of Rex's critique of my parenting book, *Learning Disabilities: A to Z.* Motivated by his mother's support, and spurred by his business success, at age 40 Rex responded to "What's next Rex?" with "College. RIT or Cornell." Reprinted with permission.

can't meaningfully respond when they don't understand what's been said. Even when the disorder is limited to only expressive language, the limited conversational practice eventually diminishes receptive language as well.

The interactionist view that language and thought are intimately intertwined suggests several ways in which we can help children who don't think or express themselves as intelligently as possible. We can, for example, specifically teach them language to help them reason and express themselves. We can also make experiences more meaningful, so that related words can be better understood and they, in turn, can be used to convey meaning. Consider how much more meaningful it must be for a child to pet sheep at a petting zoo, hear the real "baa-baa," and learn about the origins of his or her wool sweater while feeling the sheep's fur, than just looking at pictures of sheep in picture books, repeating "baa-baa," and learning in the abstract about how wool is made.

Language acquisition, whether receptive or expressive, has five components: *phonology,* the individual sounds; *morphology,* the meaningful units within words; *syntax,* the grammatical sentence rules; *semantics,* the meaningful connection of words and phrases, and *pragmatics,* the ability to engage in conversational speech. A weakness in any one of these may affect proficiency in another. For example, if Nadine has trouble formulating the /s/ phoneme, she won't be able to express the plural morpheme, even if she understands it. If she can't understand the semantics of the idiom "go jump in a lake" or "drop dead," she will have pragmatic problems conversing with others.

Children with language delays tend to acquire language skills in the same order as children without such delays, though at a slower pace. Phonetic and morphological weaknesses tend to resolve themselves within the elementary school years. Syntax takes longer to acquire, and semantics and pragmatics may present lifelong difficulties.

***Children with language delays tend to acquire language skills in the same order as children without such delays, though at a slower pace.***

**Phonology.** *Phonemes* are the smallest units of sound that form words. By themselves they have no meaning. For instance, the three phonemes—/c/ /a/ /t/—mean nothing unless they are combined into the word for feline. By 6 years of age, most children can pronounce all the phonemes of the English language. Often children who are slow at picking up prereading skills also were delayed as infants in vocalization, auditory discrimination, and articulation.

***Vocalization.*** One of the first signs of a potential language disorder may be a subtle abnormality and annoying quality in a child's voice and patterns while crying. Babies typically begin vocalizing one or two sounds during the first month after birth. At about 3 to 4 months, they smile and vocalize to an adult's smile, and vocalize back when talked to. You can hear pleasure, displeasure, eagerness, satisfaction, and anger in these vocalizations. Laughing out loud begins at 4 to 6 months, as does babbling repeated syllables and sounds. By about 8 months, the babbling begins to have adult inflections, and by 9 to 10 months babies can vocalize all the sounds and imitate a number of syllables.

***One of the first signs of a potential language disorder may be a subtle abnormality and annoying quality in a child's voice and patterns while crying.***

***Auditory Discrimination.*** Remarkably, within a few days after birth babies can discriminate not only speech sounds (e.g., /b/ from /g/) but also their own native

*Event-related potentials just days after birth can predict preschool language development and reading development at age 8.*

language from other languages. Their left hemispheres are already actively responding to syllables and words, while music and noise create more activation of the right hemisphere. It is amazing that left and right hemisphere event-related potentials recorded at this very young age can predict language development at ages 3 and 5 with considerable accuracy, and reading development at age 8. Amplitude and latency measures at birth can discriminate with 92 percent accuracy children who later require reading intervention.

By 2 months, infants can recognize words they've heard in rhythmical phrases, such as words in nursery rhymes. By 3 to 4 months, they attend to speech better, and soon after they can discriminate strangers' voices, find the source of sounds, play purposefully with noise-making toys, and respond appropriately to friendly or angry voices. By 4½ months, babies listen longer to their own names than to other names.

By 3 years of age, children's growing phonological awareness is evident as they recite nursery rhymes and play with words (enjoying saying *deanut dutter dandwich,* for example.) This sensitivity to rhyme predicts the emergence of phonological segmentation skills (e.g., awareness of beginning, middle, and ending sounds heard in words) and the ability to read simple words over the next 15 months. Rhyming and segmentation skills also correlate strongly with vocabulary and grammatical development during preschool, and with first-grade reading ability.

*Breaking apart the individual sounds in words is difficult because these sounds fold into one another when we speak. This phonological segmentation skill and rhyming correlate strongly with preschool vocabulary and grammatical development, and with first-grade reading ability.*

Breaking apart the individual sounds in words is difficult because these sounds fold into one another when we speak. Several studies have shown how weaknesses in this area disrupt not only decoding and spelling progress at early ages, but also social communication later on, as in understanding plays on words—for example, "What did the judge say when the skunk entered the courtroom? Odor in the court." Yet these same children may be able to "get" more cognitively challenging jokes, such as "Why did the farmer name his hog Ink? Because he kept running out of the pen," or "What did the newscaster say after he announced that the world had come to an end? Stay tuned, news at eleven" (Bruno, Johnson, & Simon, 1987, 1988). Paula Tallal has tied some children's difficulty discriminating the sounds they hear in words to their slow information processing. These children have an easier time when sounds persist longer, such as /s/ and /m/, than when they stop right after they begin, as in /b/ and /t/.

*Articulation.* Children's speech is largely unintelligible at 1 year of age; but by age 2, 65 percent of their speech can be understood; by age 3, 80 percent; and by age 4½, it is usually fully intelligible. The hardest sounds to master are f (mastered at age 5 to 6), *v, th, l, zh, sh* (at age 6½), *z, s, th, r,* and *w* (at age 7½).

Persistent articulation difficulties tend to resolve themselves by adolescence. When they are not accompanied by other delays, they're not highly related to learning disabilities. This is because articulation disorders represent a motor-movement or motor-planning difficulty and do not involve higher-level perceptual and cognitive abilities. Naturally, poor articulation can make communicating with others frustrating. One of the first signs of a potential motor problem with articulation can be sucking problems at birth. If a child has difficulty discriminating sounds, this also affects articulation.

Many children have no trouble discriminating and articulating individual sounds, but they have difficulty detecting and imitating transitions from one phoneme to another in consonant clusters, syllables, and words (e.g., *saw* is easy but *straw* is harder). Similarly, some children can pronounce single words well but make distortions on these same words when in sentences. Poor perception of sound sequences and the rhythmical patterns of speech can result in a number of articulation weaknesses: unintelligible speech; stuttering; sound reversals (e.g., *aminal* for *animal*); jerky, irregular speech; difficulty monitoring one's own or interpreting another's pitch and loudness; and rhyming difficulty. The preschooler whose articulation disorder is caused by this type of conceptual inability to analyze the order of sounds in words is at high risk for developing a learning disability.

**Morphology.** *Morphemes* are the smallest meaningful units in words. For instance, *cats* consists of two morphemes /cat/ and the /s/ that makes it plural. Other morphemes are prefixes, verb tense forms (walk*ed*), person (*he* walks), and so on. Only when the child understands the meanings of morphemes can he or she string several together to make meaningful sentences.

Children can understand language well before they can express themselves in words. Around 4 to 6 months of age, babies will look in response to their names. By 9 months, they can respond to requests like "give me" and directions like "put the spoon in the cup" and the all too frequent "no-no."

Baby's first true word is uttered between 10 and 18 months of age. Soon after their first birthday, most children can say 10 words; by age 1½, 30 to 50 words. Vocabulary nearly doubles every 6 months thereafter, so that by age 4 a child has a speaking vocabulary of 1,000 to 1,500 words. Among children's first words are those conveying common actions (*bye-bye*), objects they do something with (*bottle, sock*), and words based on perceptions meaningful to the baby (*up* for movement; *mmm* for tasty food). Table 7.3 on page 250 details the typical progression of a child's *receptive language* (understanding language) and *expressive language* (speaking) from 1 to 7 years of age. Table 7.4 on page 254 describes the course of morphological and syntactic acquisition from age 1½ years onward.

Many children with learning disabilities have significant delays understanding or expressing such morphological rules as third-person verb forms, verb tenses, possessives, singular/plural, irregular plurals, past-tense forms, comparatives/superlatives, and prefixes. The fact that many parts of words are unstressed (e.g., endings) or not very meaningful (articles, prepositions) only complicates acquisition of these skills. Problems with comprehension always result in expressive difficulties using certain word forms to convey meaning.

*The weak vocabularies of many youngsters with LD provide a limited foundation on which new vocabulary and knowledge can be built.*

Unfortunately the weak vocabularies of many youngsters with learning disabilities provide a limited foundation on which new vocabulary and knowledge can be built. They often benefit when texts are rewritten in easier vocabulary, when shorter sentences are used, and when unimportant details are eliminated. Learning a new symbol system, such as a foreign language or geometry, is understandably difficult given that their native language itself was so hard to master.

**Syntax.** *Syntax* refers to the way in which words are strung together into meaningful sentences. This grammatical structure is critical to meaning. For instance, "Will you go with daddy?" means something very different than "You will go with daddy."

## TABLE 7.3 Emergence of Language Skills from One to Seven Years of Age

| *Age* | *Receptive Skills* | *Expressive Skills* |
|---|---|---|
| 1–1½ years | • Comprehends approximately 50 words<br>Recognizes own name<br>Recognizes familiar sounds (telephone, doorbell)<br>Stops activity in response to "no"<br>Follows simple 1-step commands<br>Points to objects when named<br>Understands most simple questions<br>Points to own nose, eyes, and other body parts on request | • Says *mama* or *dada* or other first word (usually an animal, food, or toy)<br>Imitates words such as *baby, more, apple, up*<br>Tries to sing simple tunes such as "Jack and Jill"<br>Says 2 words in a single utterance<br>Uses meaningful gestures such as pointing to make wants known<br>Extensive vocalization and echoing responses<br>Identifies 2 or more objects or pictures when asked "what's this"<br>Uses 3 to 20 words including *all gone, more*<br>Uses 2-word phrases and short sentences<br>Uses jargon<br>Clearly pronounces 4 to 7 words |
| 1½–2 years | • Comprehends approximately 300 words<br>Responds to play requests such as "Put the doll in the chair," "Wipe the doll's nose"<br>Listens to simple, short stories<br>Shakes head yes/no appropriately<br>Points to 5 parts of a doll such as *hand, mouth,* and *eyes* on request<br>Points to 2 to 5 pictures of objects on request (*dog, shoe*)<br>Discriminates between 2 related requests such as "Give me the cup; Give me the plate"<br>Responds to simple requests for actions such as "Pick up the hat," "Give daddy the cup" | • Uses approximately 50 recognizable words<br>Combines 2 words to describe ideas or events such as "Daddy bye-bye"<br>Verbalizes "no"<br>Uses words to make wants known ("cookie," "milk")<br>Speaks 10 words with clear pronunciation<br>Verbalizes immediate experiences<br>Names 1 to 3 pictured objects (*car, doll*)<br>Attempts to describe past experiences<br>Marked decrease in sound and word repetition; has discarded jargon<br>Names 3 related objects such as socks, shoes, pants<br>Responds to basic questions such as "What is your name?" and "What does the doggie say?" |

**TABLE 7.3 (Continued)**

| *Age* | *Receptive Skills* | *Expressive Skills* |
|---|---|---|
| 2–2½ years | • Comprehends approximately 500 words<br>Listens to 5- to 10-minute story<br>Identifies pictured objects on request when their function is indicated as in "Show me the one that you wear" or "Show me the one that you eat"<br>Carries out series of 2 related commands<br>Has concept of *one* and *all* | • Uses 200 intelligible words<br>Combines 3 to 4 words in sentences<br>Indicates age by holding up fingers<br>Tells how common objects such as *fork, cup, shoe,* are used<br>Names 6 objects by use<br>Answers "where," "what . . . doing," and "what do you (hear) with" questions<br>Verbalizes toilet needs<br>Counts to 3<br>Tells own sex |
| 2½–3 years | • Comprehends approximately 900 words<br>Points to pictures of 10 objects described by their use<br>Listens to 20-minute story<br>Knows *in/on/under/big/little* | • Uses 500 intelligible words<br>Answers "what (runs)" questions<br>Answers simple "who," "why," "where," "how many" questions<br>Answers one of three questions: "What do you do when you're hungry, sleepy, cold?" (2 by age 3½; 3 by age 4)<br>Asks simple questions: "What's that?"<br>Asks yes/no questions: ("Is he sleeping?") |
| 3–3½ years | • Comprehends 1,200 words<br>Knows *in front of, behind, hard/soft, rough/smooth, circle/square*<br>Responds to commands involving 3 actions or objects | • Combines 4 to 5 words in sentences<br>Uses 800 words<br>Responds to "How . . . " questions<br>Names 8 to 10 pictures<br>States action<br>Supplies last word ("Stoves are. . . .")<br>Counts 3 objects and points to each |
| 3½–4 years | • Comprehends 1,500 to 2,000 words<br>Recognizes one color | • Uses 1000 to 1500 words<br>Can do simple verbal analogies ("Daddy is a man, mommy is a . . . ")<br>Responds to "how much," "how long," and "what if" questions<br>Relates two events in correct sequence<br>Tells story mixing real and unreal<br>Long, detailed conversations<br>Repeats 12 to 13 syllable sentences<br>Asks "how," "why," "when" questions and expects detailed explanations |

*(continued)*

**TABLE 7.3 (Continued)**

| *Age* | *Receptive Skills* | *Expressive Skills* |
|---|---|---|
| 4–4½ years | • Understands concept of number 3<br>Knows *between, above, below, top, bottom*<br>Points to 9 shapes when named | • Combines 4 to 7 words in sentences<br>Responds to "how far" questions<br>Defines simple words<br>Counts 4 objects<br>Rote counts to 10 |
| 4½–5 years | • Comprehends 2,500 to 2,800 words<br>Recognizes 2 to 3 primary colors<br>Knows *heavy/light, loud/soft, like/unlike, long/short* | • Combines 5 to 8 words in sentences<br>Uses 1,500 to 2,000 words<br>Names 1 color<br>Answers complex comprehension questions<br>Answers simple "when," "how often" questions<br>Asks meaning of words<br>Tells long story accurately<br>Counts 10 objects<br>Can name objects as *first/middle/last*<br>Repeats days of week in sequence |
| 5–6 years | • Comprehends 13,000 words<br>Understands *opposite of,* A.M./P.M., *yesterday/tomorrow, more/less, some/many, several/few, most/least, before/after, now/later, across*<br>Comprehends number concepts to 10<br>Points to penny, nickel, dime, quarter<br>Points to half, whole, right, left<br>Points to numerals 1 to 25<br>Can classify same objects by shape and color | • Can answer "what happens if" questions<br>Counts 12 objects<br>Rote counts to 30<br>Names basic colors<br>Names 5 letters of alphabet<br>States similarities and differences of objects<br>Describes location or movement: *through, away, from, toward, over*<br>Names positions of objects: *first, second, third*<br>Names days of week in order |
| 6–7 years | • Comprehends 20,000 to 26,000 words<br>Understands rough time intervals and seasons<br>Aware of others' speech errors | • Uses 10,000 words<br>States preceding and following numbers and days of week<br>Tells address<br>Recites the alphabet<br>Rote counts to 100 |

*Sources:* Adapted from Berk, L. E. (1997). *Child development* (4th ed.). Boston: Allyn & Bacon; Gard, A., Gilman, L., & Gorman, J. (1980). *Speech and language development chart.* Salt Lake City, UT: Word Making Productions; Wiig, E. H., & Semel, E. M. (1980). *Language assessment and intervention for the learning disabled* (pp. 15–17). Columbus, OH: Charles E. Merrill.

## TABLE 7.4 Order of Morphological and Syntactic Development

| *Skill* | *Approximate Age of Acquisition* |
|---|---|
| • Negation ("no bed"); possessive emerging ("daddy car")<br>Uses pronoun and name for self ("me Tommy")<br>33% of utterances are nouns | 1½–2 years |
| • Articles *a, the; in/on*<br>Present progressive "ing" on verbs<br>Regular plural form emerging (*cat/cats*); irregular past tense emerging<br>Some contractions in habitual phrases (*don't, can't, it's, that's*)<br>25% of utterances are nouns, 25% verbs | 2–2½ years |
| • Auxiliary *is/am* + "ing" ("boy *is* runn*ing*")<br>*Is* + adjective ("bell is red"); *'s* for possession ("daddy*'s* car")<br>Regular past tense verbs (*walk/walked*); future tense emerging (*do, can, will*)<br>Pronouns (*I, me, you, mine*); contracted form of is (*he's running*)<br>Imperatives (*go, get it, don't*); *not* emerging<br>Adverbs of location emerging (*here, there*) | 2½–3 years |
| • *Is* at beginning of questions<br>*Won't, can't; and* as a conjunction; superlative "est" (*fattest*)<br>Present progressive *are* + "ing" ("boys are running")<br>Regular plurals (*cat/cats*); irregular plurals emerging (*child/children*) | 3–3½ years |
| • Pronouns (*he, she*); *myself* emerging<br>*Got* ("I got it"); conjunction *because* emerging<br>*Was, were* questions emerging (was he there?) | 3½–4 years |
| • *If, so; our, they, their; could, would*<br>Irregular plurals (*child/children*); comparative "er" emerging (*smaller*)<br>Passive voice emerging ("The dog was killed by the boy.") | 4–4½ years |
| • Adjective/noun agreement; noun derivation "-er" (*painter, farmer*) | 4½–5 years |
| • Adverbial endings emerging | 5–6 years |
| • Noun derivation "ist" (*bicyclist*); homonyms emerging<br>Perfect tense emerging (*have, had*)<br>Consistently correct morphology (including passive voice, irregular past tense, comparatives (*bigger*), adverbial endings (*slowly*) | 6–7 years |

*Sources:* Adapted from Gard, A., Gilman, L., & Gorman, J. (1980). *Speech and language development chart.* Salt Lake City, UT: Word Making Productions; Wiig, E. H., & Semel, E. M. (1980). *Language assessment and intervention for the learning disabled.* Columbus, OH: Charles E. Merrill.

At 18 to 24 months of age children begin to understand basic grammatical relations and they can combine two words at a time. Toddlers at first reduce adult speech into high-information nouns and verbs, so that the question "Do you see the milk?," for example, is imitated as "See milk?" By age 2 to 2½ children begin to use subjects and predicates—"Mommy going" or "Bottle fall down." At 3½ to 4 years of age, subjects and verbs agree. And by kindergarten, the typical child has mastered many of the complex grammatical rules of adult language.

***By kindergarten, the typical child has mastered many of the complex grammatical rules of adult language.***

Some students with learning disabilities have *surface structure language difficulties;* that is, they understand the meanings of words but get confused by the number or order of words in a sentence. The syntax comprehension difficulties of these children is reflected in their expressive language. They omit words, add inappropriate words, use incorrect grammar, and distort the order of words and phrases. As preschoolers they often use only 2- and 3-word sentences and have a very difficult time expressing their thoughts or using language to aid their thinking process.

***Some students with learning disabilities understand the meanings of words but get confused by the number or order of words in a sentence.***

**Semantics.** *Semantics* provides the meaningful connection between words and sentences and other ideas and events. Unless a child has some system of meaning, language is useless. Toddlers start by expressing semantic content through single words and letting context supply the meaning. "Cookie" could mean "I want a cookie" or "There is a cookie" or "The cookie crashed to the floor." They learn quickly to describe the events happening in the present and by early elementary school, they can express very complex ideas about past and future events.

Children with learning disabilities often have a number of semantic difficulties, including understanding and remembering words that sound alike (*two, too*), words that have dual meanings (*draw a check* vs. *draw a picture*), adjectives that are difficult to describe (shape and time concepts), comparative relations (*smaller than*), prepositions (*on account of, despite*), and interpreting idioms, metaphors, morals, proverbs, negative and "wh" (who, what, where, when, why) questions. These are known as *deep structure language difficulties,* and they often persist throughout life. Understanding poetry, colloquial language, and symbolic literature eludes the student with this type of language weakness.

Word-finding problems, a common characteristic of LD, limits a person's verbal fluency and creativity in elaborating on concepts. Semantic problems are a significant cause of word-finding problems because they limit the richness of or access to stored knowledge about words. A narrow vocabulary with imprecise meaning limits the ability to call up the right word on a moment's notice. These individuals erroneously associate words with others in the same semantic category (*tiger* for *lion; paper fork* for *plastic fork*), opposites (*aunt* for *uncle*), words with similar phonemes (*cake* for *steak*), or repeat the same word over and over. They substitute imprecise ("thing") or inappropriate words; resort to synonyms, gesture, or stall ("uhm," "you know"); or talk around and around a topic until the listener is thoroughly annoyed. When all else fails, they change the topic.

***Word-finding difficulties and LD often go hand in hand because both require accurate retrieval of words. Slow retrieval impairs reading comprehension and the use of verbal rehearsal to aid planning and memory.***

Word-finding difficulties and LD often go hand in hand because in both children are required to accurately retrieve words. Slow word-finding affects reading and calculation accuracy and speed. The slower the reading speed, the fewer words students can read before they need to pause to assimilate the information. Because this breaks up the language into unnatural units that do not convey a whole thought, comprehension suffers. In addition, slow word-finding interferes with verbal rehearsal, which ordinarily is a great aid to memory and to planfully following through with tasks.

**Pragmatics.** *Pragmatics* refers to competence in interpersonal communication. Pragmatics combines all the previous skills so that one's words are adjusted to the particular person being spoken to, what was just said, the topic and goal of the discussion, and the time and setting. Early signs of pragmatic competence are evident when babies respond to facial expressions, understand parents' gestures, and, at 7 to 9 months, look at other family members when they are named (as in "Mommy better hurry or she'll be late"). At 9 months, babies can interact in games of pat-a-cake and peek-a-boo. By 1 to 1½ years, it is clear that they can perceive others' emotions.

***Weak pragmatic speech is a major contributor to the social problems of children with LD.***

Weak pragmatic speech is a major contributor to the social problems of the learning disabled. Children with weaknesses in this area tend not to attribute meaning to a speaker's style—or *prosody* —such as speed, pitch, stress patterns, duration of words, intonation, and pauses between words; nor do they take context into account to help them understand. By age 10 average learners both hear and understand such fine distinctions as "She showed *her* baby pictures" versus "She showed her *baby* pictures," or "big green house" versus "big greenhouse." Although some children with LD can perceive these prosodic cues, they often are poor at interpreting what they mean.

Problems interpreting prosodic cues can grow when the student gets into high school and lectures become a primary means for conveying information, or in the adult work environment where listening is critical. Because of reading disabilities, many individuals with LD have to rely more heavily on listening to learn, but this avenue for gaining information may prove problematic for them as well.

Listening is a complicated procedure that requires processing through many different channels:

1. The *linguistic channel:* comprehending single and multiple meanings of words (e.g., "*what a trip*").
2. The *paralinguistic channel:* understanding a speaker's tone, quality, loudness, speed, and pauses.
3. The *visual channel:* gaining information from a speaker's appearance.
4. The *kinesic channel:* comprehending nonverbal cues such as posture, facial expression, eye contact, and gestures.

As might be expected, many students with pragmatic difficulties also have trouble interpreting nonverbal communication. A hand on the shoulder, meant to convey a friendly greeting, may be perceived as a threat. Diane may not see the intent in her mother's eyes when she says to her daughter "Can you clear your place?" Diane responds cheerfully, "Yes, I can!" while her plate and glass remain right where they were. These students may also stare at others, stand too close when speaking, have a hard time understanding another's perspective, and not recognize when a listener needs more explicit information to understand what is being discussed. They often are "out of sync" with others, lost, and frustrated.

When this occurs on a regular basis, it is understandable that self-doubt builds and self-confidence erodes.

To complicate matters, nonverbal communication patterns differ from culture to culture. For example, Japanese people tend to smile as an accompaniment to any social act, not as a way to indicate agreement. For them and for other people of Asian origin, direct eye contact when speaking often is considered rude, so looking away is actually being polite. The person with pragmatic weaknesses has difficulty being sensitive to these nuances and interpreting them appropriately.

***Poor listening skills, trouble interpreting nonverbal communication, and poor oral communication can affect peer acceptance, teacher evaluation, social-emotional development, and future job adjustment.***

Clearly, poor listening skills, trouble interpreting nonverbal communication, and poor oral communication can have an impact on peer acceptance, teacher evaluation, social-emotional development, and future job adjustment. Therefore, intervention and instructional modifications are critical. For example, children can be taught to whisper in the movie theater, add inflection and energy to their speaking voices, or to read body language to determine whether a hug would be welcome or not. Teenagers can learn to set a goal for the conversation, avoid a monologue, take turns, stand at an appropriate distance, and stop interrupting.

Certainly, the help of a speech-language pathologist is warranted to help remediate these language disabilities, thereby augmenting the student's chances for academic and social success. The language of textbooks must be adapted when necessary, and teachers who rely on lecturing need to think about the clarity of their instructions and examples, the amount of time they spend introducing new vocabulary, the way they elicit background schema to make new information more meaningful and memorable, how they organize their material and ask questions to test for comprehension, their pacing, their use of concrete examples, and so on. Many students with LD require this type of careful teaching in order to access the language of instruction.

## Summary

Despite adequate intellectual resources and learning opportunities, students with LD have difficulty learning basic skills and retaining information. These memory difficulties relate to an insufficient knowledge base to which new information can be anchored, poor use of strategies to aid storage and retrieval, and the interference of various information-processing inefficiencies with the processing of information. For the most part these students' learning strategies and information-processing skills develop in the same order as would typically be expected, although at a slower rate. When compared with younger students who are achieving at similar levels, the learning patterns of the learning disabled often tend to be qualitatively less mature.

The first signs of learning disabilities frequently become apparent in the preschool years. Delays in attention, memory, learning strategies, visual-perception, motor, or language abilities contrast with pockets of strength. These uneven patterns continue into elementary school and beyond, interfering in subtle or more pervasive ways with achievement and adjustment.

It is important to be aware of the normal sequence of learning strategy and information-processing development, so that we can detect weaknesses that need to be strengthened and design appropriate learning objectives and remedial strategies. Attention and memory also will improve as we help students to gain more knowledge and store this knowledge in a deeper, more meaningful way; in this way the old information can guide attention to the new information, give it meaning, help it to be stored, and cue its retrieval. The more knowledge a student has, the more the student can learn. Likewise, the more strategically the student approaches learning and the more automatic the information-processing skills, the better the learning outcome.

## Helpful Resources

### Attention, Memory, and Learning Strategies

Ashbaker, M. H., & Swanson, H. L. (1996). Short-term memory and working memory operations and their contribution to reading in adolescents with and without learning disabilities. *Learning Disabilities Research & Practice, 11*, 206–213.

Baddeley, A. (1994). The magical number seven: Still magic after all these years? *Psychological Review, 101*, 353–356.

Baddeley, A. D. (1986). *Working memory.* London: Oxford University Press.

Bandura, A., Grusec, J. E., & Menlove, F. L. (1966). Observational learning as a function of symbolization and incentive set. *Child Development, 37*, 499–506.

Bauer, R. H. (1987). Control processes as a way of understanding, diagnosing, and remediating learning disabilities. In H. L. Swanson (Ed.), *Advances in learning and behavioral disabilities: Memory and learning disabilities.* Greenwich, CT: JAI Press.

Bauer, P. J. (1996). What do infants recall of their lives? Memory for specific events by one to two year olds. *American Psychologist, 51*, 29–41.

Bos, C. S., & Filip, D. (1984). Comprehension monitoring in learning disabled and average students. *Journal of Learning Disabilities, 17*, 229–233.

Brainerd, C. J., Kingma, J., & Howe, M. L. (1986). Long-term memory development and learning disability: Storage and retrieval loci of disabled/nondisabled differences. In S. J. Ceci (Ed.), *Handbook of cognitive, social, and neuropsychological aspects of learning disabilities* (Vol. 1). Hillsdale, NJ: Lawrence Erlbaum.

Brainerd, C. J., & Reyna, V. F. (1993). Memory independence and memory interference in cognitive development. *Psychological Review, 100*, 42–67.

Brown, R. T., & Alford, N. (1984). Ameliorating attentional deficits and concomitant academic deficiencies in learning disabled children through cognitive training. *Journal of Learning Disabilities, 17*, 20–26.

Bulgren, J. A., Schumaker, J. B., & Deshler, D. D. (1994). The effects of a recall enhancement routine on the test performance of secondary students with and without learning disabilities. *Learning Disabilities Research & Practice, 9*, 2–11.

Clark, E., Kehle, T. J., Jenson, W. R., & Beck, D. E. (1992). Evaluation of the parameters of self-modeling interventions. *School Psychology Review, 21*, 246–254.

Digangi, S. A., Maag, J. W., & Rutherford, R. B., Jr. (1991). Self-graphing of on-task behavior: Enhancing the reactive effects of self-monitoring on on-task behavior and academic performance. *Learning Disability Quarterly, 14*, 221–230.

Ellis, E. S. (1996). Reading strategy instruction. In D. D. Deshler, E. S. Ellis, & B. K. Lenz (Eds.), *Teaching adolescents with learning disabilities: Strategies and methods* (2nd ed.). Denver: Love Publishing.

Epstein, M. H., Bursuck, W., & Cullinan, D. (1985). Patterns of behavior problems among the learning disabled: Boys aged 12–18, girls aged 6–11, and girls aged 12–18. *Journal of Learning Disabilities, 8*, 123–129.

Ferro, S. C., & Pressley, M. G. (1991). Imagery generation by learning disabled and average-achieving 11- to 13-year-olds. *Learning Disability Quarterly, 14*, 231–239.

Flavell, J. H. (1971). What is memory development the development of? *Human Development, 14*, 272–278.

Flavell, J. H. (1976). Metacognitive aspects of problem solving. In L. B. Resnick (Ed.), *The nature of intelligence.* Hillsdale, NJ: Lawrence Erlbaum.

Greeno, J. G. (1989). A perspective on thinking. *American Psychologist, 44*, 134–141.

Hagen, J. W., Jongeward, R. H., & Kail, R. V. (1975). Cognitive perspectives on the development of memory. In H. W. Reese (Ed.), *Advances in child development and behavior* (Vol. 10). New York: Academic Press.

Hughes, A. (1996). Memory and test-taking strategies. In D. D. Deshler, E. S. Ellis, & B. K. Lenz (Eds.), *Teaching adolescents with learning disabilities: Strategies and methods* (2nd ed.). Denver: Love Publishing.

Kamann, M. P., & Wong, B. Y. L. (1993). Inducing adaptive coping self-statements in children with learning disabilities through self-instruction training. *Journal of Learning Disabilities, 26,* 630–638.

Kar, B. C., Dash, U. N., Das, J. P., & Carlson, J. (1993). Two experiments on the dynamic assessment of planning. *Learning and Individual Differences, 5,* 13–29.

King-Sears, M. E., Mercer, C. D., & Sindelar, P. T. (1992). Toward independence with keyword mnemonics: A strategy for science vocabulary instruction. *Remedial and Special Education, 13* (5), 22–33.

Larson, K. A., & Gerber, M. M. (1987). Effects of social metacognitive training for enhancing overt behavior in learning disabled and low achieving delinquents. *Exceptional Children, 54,* 201–211.

Lloyd, J. W., & Loper, A. B, (1986). Measurement and evaluation of task-related learning behaviors: Attention to task and metacognition. *School Psychology Review, 15,* 336–345.

Lucangeli, D., Galderisi, D., & Cornoldi, D. (1995). Specific and general transfer effects following metamemory training. *Learning Disabilities Research & Practice, 10,* 11–21.

Mastropieri, M. A., Scruggs, T. E., & Whedon, C. (1997). Using mnemonic strategies to teach information about U.S. presidents: A classroom-based investigation. *Learning Disability Quarterly, 20,* 13–21.

Meichenbaum, D. (1977). *Cognitive-behavior modification: An integrative approach.* New York: Plenum Press.

Miles, T. R. (1986). On the persistence of dyslexic difficulties into adulthood. In G. Th. Pavlidis & D. F. Fisher (Eds.), *Dyslexia: Its neuropsychology and treatment.* New York: John Wiley & Sons.

Montague, M., Applegate, B., & Marquard, K. (1993). Cognitive strategy instruction and mathematical problem-solving performance of students with learning disabilities. *Learning Disabilities Research & Practice, 8,* 223–232.

Niedelman, M. (1991). Problem solving and transfer. *Journal of Learning Disabilities, 24,* 322–329.

Owings, R. A., Petersen, G. A., Bransford, J. D., Morris, C. D., & Stein, B. S. (1980). Spontaneous monitoring and regulation of learning: A comparison of successful and less successful fifth graders. *Journal of Educational Psychology, 72,* 250–256.

Palincsar, A. S. (1986). Metacognitive strategy instruction. *Exceptional Children, 53,* 118–124.

Paris, S. G., & Lindauer, B. K. (1977). Constructive aspects of children's comprehension and memory. In R. V. Kail & J. W. Hagen (Eds.), *Perspectives on the development of memory and cognition.* Hillsdale, NJ: Lawrence Erlbaum.

Parker, T. B., Freston, C. W., & Drew, C. J. (1975). Comparison of verbal performance of normal and learning disabled children as a function of input organization. *Journal of Learning Disabilities, 8,* 386–393.

Reid, R. (1996). Research in self-monitoring with students with learning disabilities: The present, the prospects, the pitfalls. *Journal of Learning Disabilities, 29,* 317–331.

Ridberg, E. H., Parke, R. D., & Hetherington, E. M. (1971). Modification of impulsive and reflective cognitive styles through observation of film-mediated models. *Developmental Psychology, 5,* 369–377.

Ryan, E. B., Short, E. J., & Weed, K. A. (1986). The role of cognitive strategy training in improving the academic performance of learning disabled children. *Journal of Learning Disabilities, 19,* 521–529.

Samuels, S. J. (1986). Why children fail to learn and what to do about it. *Exceptional Children, 53,* 7–16.

Schunk, D. H., & Rice, J. M. (1993). Strategy fading and progress feedback: Effects on self-efficacy and comprehension among students receiving remedial reading services. *The Journal of Special Education, 27,* 257–276.

Scruggs, T. E., & Mastropieri, M. A. (1990). Mnemonic instruction for students with learning disabilities: What it is and what it does. *Learning Disability Quarterly, 13,* 271–280.

Scruggs, T. E., & Mastropieri, M. A. (1992). Classroom applications of mnemonic instruction: Acquisition, maintenance and generalization. *Exceptional Children, 58,* 219–229.

Swanson, H. L. (1999). Reading comprehension and working memory in learning-disabled readers: Is the phonological loop more important than the executive system? *Journal of Experimental Child Psychology, 72,* 1–31.

Wong, B. Y. L., & Jones, W. (1982). Increasing metacomprehension in learning disabled and normally achieving students through self-questioning training. *Learning Disability Quarterly, 5,* 228–240.

## Visual-Perceptual, Motor, and Language Development

Akshoomoff, N. A., & Stiles, J. (1995). Developmental trends in visuospatial analysis and planning: I.

Copying a complex figure. *Neuropsychology, 9,* 364–377.

Belmont, L., & Birch, H. G. (1963). Lateral dominance and right-left awareness in normal children. *Child Development, 34,* 257–270.

Berk, L. E. (2002). *Child development* (6th ed). Boston: Allyn & Bacon.

Bloom, L. (1970). *Language development: Form and function in emerging grammars.* Cambridge, MA: MIT Press.

Bryan, T. (1977). Learning disabled children's comprehension of nonverbal communication. *Journal of Learning Disabilities, 10,* 501–506.

Clark, E. (1973). What's in a word? On the child's acquisition of semantics in his first language. In T. E. Moore (Ed.), *Cognitive development and the acquisition of language.* New York: Academic Press.

Conderman, G. (1995). Social-status of sixth- and seventh-grade students with learning disabilities. *Learning Disability Quarterly, 18,* 13–24.

Felton, R. H., Naylor, C. E., & Wood, F. B. (1990). Neuropsychological profile of adult dyslexics. *Brain and Language, 39,* 485–497.

Fletcher, J. M., & Satz, P. (1985). Cluster analysis and the search for learning disability subtypes. In B. P. Rourke (Ed.), *Neuropsychology of learning disabilities.* New York: Guilford Press.

Gibson, E. J., Gibson, J. J., Pick, A. D., & Osser, H. A. (1962). Developmental study of the discrimination of letter-like forms. *Journal of Comparative and Physiological Psychology, 55,* 897–906.

Hall, P. K., & Tomblin, J. B. (1978). A follow-up study of children with articulation and language disorders. *Journal of Speech and Hearing Disorders, 43,* 227–241.

Hicks, R. E., & Kinsbourne, M. (1978). Human handedness. In M. Kinsbourne (Ed.), *The asymmetrical function of the brain.* New York: Cambridge University Press.

Johnson, D. J., & Blalock, J. W. (Eds.). (1987). *Adults with learning disabilities: Clinical studies.* Orlando, FL: Grune & Stratton.

Kellogg, R., & O'Dell, S. (1969). *Analyzing children's art.* Palo Alto, CA: National Press Books.

Koppitz, E. M. (1968). *Psychological evaluation of children's human figure drawings.* New York: Grune & Stratton.

Lapadat, J. C. (1991). Pragmatic language skills of students with language and/or learning disabilities: A quantitative synthesis. *Journal of Learning Disabilities, 24,* 147–158.

Lester, B. M. (1987). Developmental outcome prediction from acoustic cry analysis in term and preterm infants. *Pediatrics, 80,* 529–534.

Lewis, B. A., Freebairn, L. A., & Taylor, H. G. (2000). Follow-up of children with early expressive phonology disorders. *Journal of Learning Disabilities, 33,* 433–444.

Maclean, M., Bryant, P., & Bradley, L. (1987). Rhymes, nursery rhymes, and reading in early childhood. *Merrill-Palmer Quarterly, 33,* 255–281.

MacNamara, J. (1972). Cognitive basis of language learning in infants. *Psychological Review, 79,* 1–13.

Mann, V. A., Cowin, E., & Schoenheimer, J. (1989). Phonological processing, language comprehension, and reading ability. *Journal of Learning Disabilities, 22,* 76–89.

Mathinos, D. A. (1991). Conversational engagement of children with learning disabilities. *Journal of Learning Disabilities, 24,* 439–445.

Molfese, D. (2000). Predicting dyslexia at 8 years of age using neonatal brain responses. *Brain and Language, 72,* 238–245.

Molfese, D. L., & Molfese, V. J. (1985). Electrophysiological indices of auditory discrimination in newborn infants: The bases for predicting later language development? *Infant Behavior and Development, 8,* 197–211.

Morrison, D. C. (1986). Neurobehavioral dysfunction and learning disabilities in children. In S. J. Ceci (Ed.), *Handbook of cognitive, social, and neuropsychological aspects of learning disabilities* (Vol. 1). Hillsdale, NJ: Lawrence Erlbaum.

Nelson, K. (1973). Structure and strategy in learning to talk. *Monographs of the Society for Research in Child Development, 38*(1–2, Serial No. 149).

Nichols, P., & Chen, T. (1981). *Minimal brain dysfunction: A prospective study.* Hillsdale, NJ: Lawrence Erlbaum.

Piaget, J. (1962). *The language and thought of the child.* New York: World Publishing.

Pick, A. D., Frankel, D. G., & Hess, V. L. (1975). Childrens' attention: The development of selectivity. *Review of Child Development Research, 5,* 325–383.

Rourke, B. P. (1987). Syndrome of nonverbal learning disabilities: The final common pathway of white-matter disease/dysfunction? *Clinical Neuropsychologist, 1,* 209–234.

Shafrir, U., & Siegel, L. S. (1994). Subtypes of learning disabilities in adolescents and adults. *Journal of Learning Disabilities, 27,* 123–134.

Spreen, O., & Haaf, R. G. (1986). Empirically derived learning disability subtypes: A replication attempt and longitudinal patterns over 15 years. *Journal of Learning Disabilities, 19,* 170–180.

Stirling, E. G., & Miles, T. R. (1988). Naming ability and oral fluency in dyslexic adolescents. *Annals of Dyslexia, 38,* 50–72.

Wade, J., & Kass, C. E. (1987). Component deficit and academic remediation of learning disabilities. *Journal of Learning Disabilities, 20,* 441–447.

Wiig, E. H., & Semel, E. M. (1976). *Language disabilities in children and adolescents.* Columbus, OH: Charles E. Merrill.

Wilkinson, A., Stratta, L., & Dudley, P. (1974). *The quality of listening.* London: Macmillan Education.

Wynn, K. (1992). Addition and subtraction by human infants. *Nature, 358,* 749–750.

Young, G. (1977). Manual specialization in infancy: Implications for lateralization of brain function. In S. J. Segalowitz & F. A. Gruber (Eds.), *Language development and neurological theory.* New York: Academic Press.

Zaporozhets, A. V. (1965). The development of perception in the preschool child. In P. Mussen (Ed.), European research in cognitive development. *Monographs of the Society for Research in Child Development, 30*(2, Serial No. 100).

Child Development Institute: http://www.childdevelopmentinfo.com

National Institute of Child Health & Development: http://www.nichd.nih.gov

CHAPTER EIGHT

# Social-Emotional Development

**SUCCESS IN LIFE** often has much more to do with how a person feels about himself or herself than it does with academic achievement or intellectual level. Nowhere is this more true than with the learning disabled. In fact, those among the learning disabled population who have learned to persevere, to make and maintain positive relationships, and to make use of the skills employers value most—honesty, cheerfulness, and dependability—have the best chance to be successful in life. This is true in spite of severe learning deficits and a lifetime of struggle to achieve academically. Therefore, parents and teachers have a special responsibility to focus just as intensively on the social side of learning disabilities as on the academic side.

*Success in life has much more to do with how people feel about themselves than it does with academic achievement or intellectual level. Those among the learning disabled who have learned to persevere, to maintain positive relationships, and to be honest, cheerful, and dependable on the job have the best chance to be successful in life, despite severe learning deficits.*

It is true that many students with learning disabilities are less accepted by peers, interact awkwardly with others, have trouble perceiving social cues, and tend to give up in the face of challenge. Behavioral disturbances are more frequent among these students—especially males—than among their nondisabled peers. Although it is frustrating to work with some of these children, being the one who is learning disabled is even more frustrating—the child with LD can't walk away from it. Recognizing that a few children consume the majority of a teacher's energy, Lavoie (1998) assures us that this is exactly as it should be: "The squeaky wheel *needs* the grease"; those who make the most demands on our attention *need* our attention the most because "the pain a troubled child causes is never greater than the pain that (s)he feels." These are the children we focus on in this chapter. Teachers and others who work with children who are learning disabled need to

*Teachers and others who work with children with LD need to make special efforts to help them develop their personal strengths, take pride in themselves, persist when things are difficult, find the motivation to succeed, and develop satisfying interpersonal relationships.*

make special efforts to help them develop their personal strengths, learn to take pride in themselves, persist when their lives at school and home become intolerable, find the motivation to succeed, and develop satisfying interpersonal relationships. These things don't come naturally to many of these children, but they can be learned.

*Although about 75 percent of children with LD suffer social skills weaknesses and/or have low self-images, many have well-adjusted personalities, are well liked by peers, and believe they can succeed.*

Joe's story paints a sad picture of a youngster who entered school eager to learn but whose social-emotional problems, coupled with his learning disability, slowly but surely pushed him to the edge of his peer group. As graphic as his story is, it's important to remember that not every student who is learning disabled faces such a fate. Although about 75 percent of this population suffer social skills weaknesses and/or have low self-images, the parents of 1 out of every 2 children nonetheless see them as having balanced, well-adjusted personalities. Many are as well liked as their peers, and some in fact are popular. Many carry on mature, considerate, and persuasive conversations, cope well with conflict, and are attuned to others' feelings and thoughts. Some may not be the most popular students in school or have as many friends as their peers, but they do have at least one good friend and they participate in a variety of social activities with gusto and enjoyment. Most important, despite fully recognizing their academic struggle, they like themselves and believe they can succeed, even when they have to work twice as hard as their peers.

Many personal, family, teacher, and peer factors influence whether children develop social and emotional adjustment difficulties. If people important to Elizabeth treat her differently or avoid her because of her disabilities, they deprive her of opportunities to develop important social skills such as trust, humor, understanding different perspectives, resolving conflicts, competing, and understanding and managing her own feelings. Without these social skills, the chances for rejection and isolation grow. The need for early and effective intervention is critical.

## The Preschooler

In order to recognize when a child is in trouble emotionally or socially, it's important to know what's normal in these areas at various points in life. From a very young age children's temperaments and the feedback they get from parents, teachers, and peers begin to shape attitudes and behavior patterns that can exacerbate their learning disabilities or enable them to persevere in spite of adversity and frustration.

*The quality of the parent-child relationship is key to social-emotional adjustment later in life.*

The process of becoming content with oneself and with others begins at birth. The quality of the parent-child relationship is key to social-emotional adjustment later in life. From birth to 1½ years, children learn to trust their parents' abilities to meet their needs. This is a "vertical" relationship. Mothers and fathers have greater knowledge and power, and children depend on parental control and nurturance.

The earliest development of social skills is apparent at 5 to 14 weeks of age as babies respond to other babies by gazing at some length. By 3 months of age, infants "take turns" in conversation with their mother by cooing in response to her loving words. This reciprocity is evident again in games of peek-a-boo and pat-a-cake at about 9 months of age.

## Joe

*A learning disability mushroomed into severe problems coping with everyday living.*

I like to call it an adventure because that's what living with a learning disability feels like to me today. It's an adventure like living one of the *Raiders of the Lost Ark* movies. I never know what's going to happen until it does (p. 7).

The day that changed my life happened in spelling class. Since spelling was one of my most defeating subjects I had taken to getting sick the day of spelling tests and that was that. After missing several spelling test days, my friends started teasing me. I started getting embarrassed and very uncomfortable. . . .

I always tried to study for tests, but it seemed like I never made any headway. I just couldn't get the words, and even the ones I knew how to spell regularly came hard for me in a test (p. 13).

Edith, the girl who sat in front of me, looked around and stuck out her tongue at me. I don't know why she did that, but she did it all the time. Spelling was the first thing we did on that morning. That was fine with me—get it over with.

I pulled my tablet of paper towards me and numbered one through ten on a piece of paper. My hand started to sweat so I wiped it on my pants. Mrs. Pendelton called out the first word and the pencils around me started scratching away. I spelled the word. We went on down the list. After she called out the last word and everyone had finished she told us to pass our papers to the person in front of us. I passed mine to Edith and the guy from the front seat came back and dropped his paper off with me. We started correcting each other's papers. The tenth word was *themselves.* Mrs. Pendelton spelled it out and after she was finished she asked if anyone in class had gotten that word right.

Some hands went up, but not Edith's. Mrs. Pendelton congratulated the two or three who had gotten the word right. Then Edith's hand went up.

"Mrs. Pendelton, guess what? Joe didn't use any vowels in *themselves.*"

Edith held up my paper for the teacher to see and looked back and laughed at me. I died. Then I looked around and the whole class was looking at me and they were all laughing. And things changed forever right then and there. . . .

The day of that defeat marked a turning point where I took my first step into a downward spiral (p. 14).

I was sitting in school and I couldn't convince anyone that I was able to do anything. And the harder I tried, the worse it got.

It was in the fifth grade that I first realized that I was being overlooked because I was labeled lazy or lacking incentive. I was able to see that, as I was watching my friends leave me behind and it hurt. When the pain and fear became overwhelming, I reached out to my friends the only way I could think of, I became a clown. I could disrupt a classroom at any moment. The teachers hated it, but my classmates loved it and I started getting some status. Even Kevin started leaving me alone most of the time. He even stopped kicking me in the back. It was great (pp. 16–17).

In the classroom a lot of my behavior is very learning disabled. I have a limited attention span and have a hard time keeping quiet. I wiggle and fidget, I chew gum, I daydream, sometimes I'll say things out loud inappropriately, responding to a half-heard phrase the teachers said, and I'm often entirely out of context. It's very embarrassing (p. 70).

Study halls were nothing but social situations for me. I didn't understand what I was supposed to do in a study hall. I could not grasp how to study and study halls were so quiet they drove me crazy. Quiet is a form of deprivation for me. A

*(continued)*

**Joe** (Continued)

study hall was like being in a deprivation tank (p. 111).

I always would end up in the bonehead reading section . . . All of my friends were over on the other side and I was over with those "others." I hated being over with the other kids. They were the ones the "cool" kids picked on. It was a pain to be with them. I was really scared about something rubbing off on me. And I am sure now that they all felt the same about me. . . .

It was funny. I always knew I had a problem learning like everyone else but I always knew I wasn't dumb. I was scared all the time of being thought dumb but in my heart I knew I wasn't. I hated being set apart. It made every day so tense for me (p. 17).

So, like a lot of learning disabled kids, I was beginning a career of sticking out, being different. I was noisy, not because I wanted the negative attention it got me, but because I needed and wanted acceptance from my peers and couldn't figure out how to be one of them. With no built in road-map, unable to understand the strange land I was in, things seemed to be getting worse and worse (p. 29).

I felt different enough from my classmates that stress began piling upon stress. Soon I couldn't trust anything. If a teacher were to ask me what county I lived in I could be thinking "Gallatin County" but out might pop, "America."

This began to happen often. The classroom would be disrupted and the teacher would be mad. I would be embarrassed but the students thought I was great. This could happen to me everyday and countless times in a day. I didn't want to be a smart Alec but the teacher thought I did and my classmates thought I did. If the principal became involved he thought I did, and heck, even my parents began to think I did.

I literally, by then, had little control over my tongue. I still don't today. I hear things and I respond with an inability to screen what I'll say. I don't want to do this and I do my utmost to safeguard myself but I have no protection. Given enough time something inane will always pop out. I've even stopped going to certain business meetings because of a fear of making an ass of myself. This is painful, but this is a fact and I have to accept it. . . . I don't know where the wires are crossed, but crossed they are (p. 20).

[There were] times when I would do or say something and my friends would look at me like I was from another planet. It would mostly happen to me when I would come upon a group of my friends somewhere and try to join into the conversation. . . . I would listen in a group and then give the group my ideas. When I did that, the conversation would die and they would all look at me.

I'd die a thousand deaths. . . .

I thought people were starting to laugh at me and maybe even call me dumb, stupid or retarded. I was never sure, but to me it felt that way, and I started to react to these feelings. What I started doing was going totally nuts every time the word dumb or any synonym of it was associated with me. I beat up people for even thinking I was dumb.

A close friend took me aside one day and talked to me about how many people were scared of me and asked me if that was what I wanted. The answer was easy, "No, I don't want anyone scared of me." So I came up with another answer and that was the one I stayed with for a long time. I just went quiet, and just didn't join into things as much . . . I hated the part of me that I couldn't seem to control (pp. 21–22).

When I was a little kid I loved telling jokes more than anything in the whole world. I loved to make people laugh. It was a pleasure to me to make people laugh. As I was growing up I was pretty good at it, too. I was like everyone else in the world. I loved to make people laugh, but if they were laughing at me it wasn't funny.

As I moved into my eighth grade year I became something to laugh at. I was becoming

**Joe** (Continued)

goofy. I was watching my friends start to relate to the teachers in an adult way and I would try to talk to teachers in the same way. It just didn't work.

I would crack a joke in class and instead of getting my friends to laugh they were starting to tell me to be quiet. My jokes weren't getting the response I was wanting anymore. I was really getting scared about what to do with myself. I had cruised for a long time on my ability to get people to laugh. It was scary to think that it wasn't working anymore.

I started to try to keep my mouth shut in class and it worked sometimes. I was able to be quiet. My problem started coming from the teachers. If I was quiet they would start asking me questions again. For instance, I would be sitting in math class and the teacher would ask me a question. I hadn't spouted off to him in [a] couple of months so he thought it was probably safe to ask me [a] question. So he asked me to answer a question. I had no idea how to answer it. Not one clue.

Now I was in trouble as far as I was concerned and the class was waiting for my answer. I was screwed. I was going to look stupid. I was looking stupid right now!

"Joe, do you know the answer? We've gone over it twice now during class, how about an answer."

Great, we've gone over it twice. Now I really feel stupid. I was in the batter's box and I was striking out. The teacher looked at me and I think he saw and smelled the fear coming out of me. He heaved a sigh and called on the dumbest person in the class. The one person we all picked on in the hallway and the lunch room.

"Richard, tell me the answer?" Richard knew the answer. I slid down in my chair and died. I was humiliated Richard had known the answer and he had made me look stupid. . . .

The thing that was scaring me the most was watching my friends talking to adults and seeing the adults relate right back to them on the same level. When I would try and talk with adults or teachers, all I got was weird looks. . . .

I'd start quoting facts no one wanted to hear. I'd make up facts a lot of times. I'd lie to get accepted, and the sad thing was that everyone knew it. I could see it in their faces.

I don't know why I talked like I did. It made me sound even more immature than I was, but even though I knew it sounded wrong I couldn't stop. I just wanted to be accepted and I thought that was the way to sound grown up. I heard my folks talking facts and figures all the time. I thought I sounded just like them. I didn't. (pp. 34–35).

I wanted to be with my friends who were on the other side of the building. It just didn't seem fair . . . even in the shop classes I was having trouble. It was seeming harder for me than the regular classes. I wasn't able to follow the directions that the teacher was giving.

Verbal directions have always been hard for me. I just can't seem to filter out the information from the spoken word. It usually seems like a different language to me. I hear it and then have to take it to the translation department inside of my brain. In that process something is always lost and I only get part of the information . . .

I was desperately trying to find some way to fit in and all I was doing was getting egg on my face. I would go and find my friends at a party and try to hang out with them. I was not welcomed any more. They were talking about things and classes that I was no longer a part of.

I was totally lost. I was going farther and farther down a road that I didn't like and I was getting into more and more trouble. I was starting to get caught skipping classes and my parents weren't happy with me. I was feeling angrier and I wasn't having much luck expressing it.

I would be in class, trying to listen to the teacher and not be a nuisance and something, anything, would happen and I'd get mad. I would be in the hall walking just after class and rage

*(continued)*

**Joe** (Continued)

would start welling up in me. I would reach over and smack a locker and bust up my knuckles.

The people around me would look at me like I was a totally freaked out person. The sad fact was that I was feeling freaked out. . . .

The school part of me was in the toilet and home was going down fast. I was pulling farther away from everybody around me and I wasn't talking to people anymore. Not talking was driving me crazy, but I was scared to open up.

There were people who were reaching out to me and trying to help me, but I'd just blow them off as fast as I could (pp. 37–39). . . .

Getting through the "friendship minefield" seemed too dangerous to even try. It still does, sometimes, today . . .

One day in high school I was sitting bored with another lecture from one of the older teachers. I'd gotten totally spaced out and my mind was off in orbit visiting the spaceship Enterprise.

I guess I was really out there because the guy behind had to hit me twice on the shoulder to get my attention. I jerked myself back up in the seat and looked at the teacher. The teacher always reminded me of TOUCHÉ TURTLE one of my favorite cartoon characters. He had a skinny face, no neck, and a jutting upper lip that looked like a snapping turtle.

"Ahh, Mr. Lair has rejoined us, how nice."

"What, turtle face?"

I waited for the class to start laughing and it didn't happen (p. 41).

My inappropriate social behavior has always been the thing that has brought me the most pain and the thing I always get defensive about first. Living life is my biggest problem (p. 43).

I just don't read the cues other people can read, like body language, facial expression, tension in the air (p. 51).

My brain and following directions just don't agree. . . . Whenever my brain gets information it slows down . . .

It was probably the reason I lost some of the jobs I lost. In the restaurant when I was a cook the boss would start calling out orders and my brain was slowing down with each order. What my boss needed was me acknowledging each order given. What was going on with me was I felt like I was a prize fighter and each order was a punch coming in. I was punch drunk within ten minutes of being up on the line (p. 58).

Wherever I went I brought my mess with me. That mess, I was learning, was my perpetually low self-esteem. I viewed life as a continuing battle and I was always losing. I would wake up in the morning, put on my bulls-eye and people would shoot at it, of course. Then I'd sit back and say to myself, "See I was right, they were out to get me." I was the one who did this to myself—all I had to do was take off the bulls-eye. . . .

A few people tried to tell me I wasn't wearing the right clothes but I didn't believe them mainly because I'd dressed that way for a long time, it was security for me, and I wasn't ready to give it up. For me to give up dressing the way I did would entail change, and that was unacceptable because it terrified me . . .

Change was death, they were one and the same. . . . I love familiarity, I find comfort in it. I can drive the same way to work forever and not find anything wrong with it. I love having things at home in the same place. I love consistency (p. 50).

. . . living is what is kicking my butt, and I struggle with it every day (p. 23).

I'm still learning that as a learning disabled person I spend so much energy protecting myself. I still live in such fear of being thought stupid most of the time, and it strongly influences everything I do and all of my decisions (p. 25).

[Time] is something that I just don't get and I wish I really did. It would make life much easier. . . . I expect the help to be on time and I think I should set the example, but it hasn't worked out

**Joe** (Continued)

yet. I'm still usually ten or fifteen minutes late and it's a problem. I've tried the same games with my clock that everyone uses. I've made solemn vows not to be late again and they only last three or four days. I've come to work to find a shivering employee who has no key waiting for me to let her in. I've lost jobs because of this.

Another problem is orderliness. I don't pick up things around the store. I pick up things when it's overwhelming, but I just don't see how messy it is until it's reached overwhelming proportions . . .

Anger is another problem. It's been a part of me since I was little kid. I can be doing almost anything and all of a sudden I'm angry. I can't for the life of me tell you why, but one second I'm fine and the next I'm angry. I've tried all my life to control this, I work on it every day. When it's the worst is when I'm doing something and become frustrated. Watch out! I'm a stick of dynamite waiting to blow up.

I couldn't even find one thing in a grocery store. No one believed me when I said I didn't know how to shop, but I really didn't. It's almost impossible to convince people you can't do something that they take for granted. . . . There's too much for me to take in when I'm in the big places. They have so much to choose from that it almost kills me to make a decision. . . .

In order to stay relaxed I've had to see that some things that I do in life are not age appropriate. I've made the conscious decision to continue doing them because they're a part of who I am—like blowing bubbles or playing with my yoyo at work. I have a friend who's just like me. . . .

This is one part of being LD. I love being this child-like way. It makes it all worthwhile. I hope this part of me never grows up. And I hope I can continue to stay loose and relaxed about being this way (pp. 55–56).

My mentor Jerry and I often talk about how getting out of bed in the morning is an incredibly hard thing for us. When we wake up in the morning we both have to laugh at how our day immediately assails us and then paralyzes us. We have had to learn to cope by breaking it into simple things. The process starts with, "Okay, reach over and turn the alarm off. Into the bathroom, take a shower, brush your teeth. Keep going, don't let your mind run away. Start getting positive thoughts going through your brain. You're okay. You're okay". . .

It's real simple for me to see how unmanageable my life is. I can't keep a checkbook balanced. I always have to wear something on my left hand to know what way is right or left. I'm daily apologizing at least a dozen times for making LD inappropriate comments. I have a total inability to structure my time (p. 115).

"For what I am today shame on a lot of things. If I stay that way, shame on me" (p. 47).

*Source:* Lair, J. T. (1992). *Cookie and me.* Bozeman, MT. Reprinted by permission.

Around 7 months of age, babies develop *object permanence.* That is, they know something exists, even if it is out of sight. Because mother is such an important figure, infants at around this age put up a tremendous fuss when she leaves. Well before age 2, babies display caring behaviors such as hugging, kissing, patting, and offering words of comfort to someone who is crying, ill, or injured.

Also at around 2 years of age, children can keep at least two pieces of information in mind at once and can imitate activities they have witnessed—pretending to stir food in a bowl and then lick the spoon, for example. They connect two words in speech and their reasoning abilities evolve rapidly. With greater use of language and symbolic play comes more frequent and longer play with other children and less flitting from activity to activity. For the most part though, 2-year-olds tend to play *next* to each other absorbed in their own activities rather than *with* each other. Two-year-olds make choices about what they want to do, can exercise some self-restraint, and show obvious pride in accomplishing what they set out to do, even if it's grabbing an ink marker and scribbling on the wall.

From age 2 on, children gradually begin to play in a more complementary fashion. Though "parallel play" is still the norm, they do begin to exchange roles, play games, "pretend," actively direct and organize their play, and even suggest new twists to a game in order to be invited to join in with those already playing. The young child's ability to play well with others is a good predictor of his or her social competence in later years.

*The young child's ability to play well with others is a good predictor of his or her social competence in later years.*

Initiative and autonomy continue to develop as the child's cognitive, language, and motor skills mature. The 2½-year-old ventures out of mother's watchful presence, knowing that mother will be there when she's needed. This exercise in greater autonomy sometimes gets expressed as the tantrums that mark the "terrible twos" when children resist parental authority, often at inconvenient times and in highly public places.

*From age 3 onward, children's cooperative play increases, and they begin to have friends. Through these friendship relationships social skills mature and develop.*

From age 3 onward, children's cooperative play increases, and they begin to have friends. Eighty percent of children express a strong preference for at least one peer, and 30 percent of their play involves reciprocal interactions. These friendships are "horizontal" relationships through which social skills mature and develop. Children who approach others in a positive way are more likely to receive positive responses in return. In the preschooler, these positive approaches include sharing, showing affection, offering assistance, suggesting a play idea, and joining in rough-and-tumble play. Research shows that preschool friends disagree with each other more often than children who aren't friends, but they also disengage from the conflict (walk away, switch to a new game) more often and more rapidly. Their conflicts are less aggressive, angry, or rejecting than with nonfriends, and the children usually end with staying near each other and playing, rather than one child "winning."

The quality of the very young child's vertical and horizontal relationships affects his or her long-term social competence. These are the experiences that show children what kinds of behavior are appropriate, how to anticipate good or bad consequences, when to trust, and so on. A securely attached child is likely to have a positive outlook, be attentive, motivated, and open to learning. It is this type of attitude that helps a child when the going gets rough.

*A securely attached child is likely to have a positive outlook, be attentive, motivated, and open to learning.*

## Temperament

Parents' ability to adapt to their child's temperament is critical to the social and emotional adjustment of the child with learning disabilities. Often these children have unique and challenging temperaments.

We now know that children come into the world with a distinct temperament, which tends to persist to a greater or lesser degree throughout life. Research using the nine categories listed in Figure 8.1 has classified infants into three temperament styles: the easy child who sleeps and eats on a regular schedule, has a re-

1. *Activity.* The amount of physical motion during such activities as eating, playing, and studying.
2. *Rhythmicity.* The regularity of such physiologic functions as hunger, sleep, and elimination.
3. *Approach/Withdrawal.* The tendency to initially approach or withdraw from a new stimulus, be it, for example, a new person, classroom, food, toy, or teaching method.
4. *Adaptability.* The ease with which a child adjusts over time to new or altered situations, such as a new school, schedule, or altered rules in a game.
5. *Intensity.* The level of emotional energy expressed in both positive and negative circumstances.
6. *Mood.* The amount of joyful and friendly versus unhappy and unpleasant behavior in a variety of situations.
7. *Persistence.* The length of time a child pursues an activity despite obstacles such as a difficult task or more desirable options.
8. *Distractibility.* The extent to which extraneous stimuli divert the attention and behavior of the child.
9. *Threshold.* The intensity level of stimulation before a child will indicate sensitivity to such changes as lighting, sound, texture of clothing, odors, people's moods, and pain.

**Figure 8.1** Nine categories of temperament and their definitions.

*Source:* Adapted from Thomas, A., & Chess, S. (1977). *Temperament and development.* New York: Brunner/Mazel. Reprinted by permission.

liably sunny personality, and who adapts easily to change (e.g., loves his or her first bath and can fall asleep in unfamiliar places); the difficult child who is unpredictable in his or her sleeping and eating, who reacts negatively to change, and is frequently irritable and unhappy; and the slow-to-warm-up child whose reactions, whether positive or negative, are tentative and mild in intensity.

*Temperament traits do modify over time, but when difficult temperament traits persist, these frequently are associated with learning, emotional, and social difficulties.*

The difficult young child is at greater risk for future behavior problems, though this is by no means certain. Traits can and do modify over time given the interaction between the child's temperament, a child's abilities and desires, and environmental influences. When difficult temperament traits persist, however, they frequently are associated with learning, emotional, and social difficulties. As babies, difficult children are not easy to comfort, less likely to cuddle, and less friendly to strangers. As preschoolers, they wrestle, hit, jump, push, beat, fuss, cling, and disobey more often than others. They are much more likely to be chastened by their parents and preschool teachers. Not surprisingly, they are not popular among their classmates and feel lonely. Sadly, although these preschoolers do attempt to form friendships, their approaches are frequently rebuffed. The beginning of lowered self-confidence and loss of feelings of control are evident.

Parents of many students with learning disabilities describe their children as having been difficult infants and preschoolers. Hyperactive children in particular are trying from day one. Parents are exhausted from rocking their colicky baby

*It's not easy for parents to feel as attached to children with difficult temperaments as to their siblings. Parents feel worn down and out of control much of the time.*

*It takes a very special parent to remain accepting, peaceful, and encouraging while at the same time setting firm limits and a structure that promotes the child's personal comfort and acceptable behavior.*

who sleeps little, cries constantly, and resists most efforts to be calmed. Parents react by feeling helpless and incompetent when nothing can make their infant happy. They worry when they're gone about what catastrophe has happened with the babysitter. They can't go to a restaurant for fear that their child will race pell-mell among the diners. A trip to the supermarket or the shopping mall can turn into havoc because of full-tilt temper tantrums and other disasters (getting lost, running ahead to an escalator). Reading a book or watching a video together is filled with interruption. Plans shift constantly to accommodate the child. Unfortunately, it's not easy for parents to feel as attached to these children as to their siblings. Parents feel worn down and out of control much of the time. Siblings complain because their lives are disrupted. And grandparents are quick to blame the parents. It takes a very special parent to remain accepting, peaceful, and encouraging while setting firm limits and a structure that promotes greater personal comfort and more acceptable behavior.

Children who were born prematurely often are among those with difficult temperaments. As babies, they tend to be highly sensitive. They overreact to stimuli and are easily stressed. Like hyperactive children, they need parents to structure their interactions with the environment and with people and to help them when they feel disorganized and overwhelmed.

*Parents of a neurologically immature or difficult baby often interpret the baby's responses as their failure to care for their own child; they may think that the baby doesn't love them and is rebuffing them.*

Unfortunately, parents of a neurologically immature or difficult baby often interpret the baby's withdrawal, crying, flailing, or limp responses as their failure to care for their own child. Worse, they often think that the baby doesn't love them and is rebuffing them. These parents need help understanding that the problem is caused by different levels of neurological organization or by different temperaments, not a lack of love. The child is doing the best he or she can. Parents need to know that with patient guidance and well-structured environments their children can be more at ease and achieve more harmonious interactions. Parents also need to turn attention to their own temperaments and adapt them to better match their child's. For example, although a parent loves reading for hours, she should restrain herself from even attempting to read a book cover to cover with her difficult toddler; three pages at a sitting keeps everyone on an even keel—and looking forward to the next good time they have together while reading.

## The Elementary School Student

By the time they are school age, children place a very high value on their friends. Six- to 8-year-olds tell you that they like friends who play nicely and are willing to share. Nine- to 11-year-olds want friends who will be there for them for understanding, companionship, and help.

*Seventy percent of children's friendships are made in school. In first grade about one-third of children have at least one mutual friend, and three by sixth grade.*

School is a critical environment for children in terms of honing their socialization skills and learning from peer feedback "who am I?" This is where 70 percent of children's friendships are made. In first grade about one-third of children have at least one mutual friend. By fifth and sixth grade the average child has three mutual friends. The older elementary student nominates on average 11 children as "good friends," although only 3 of these nominations are reciprocated. Half of these "friends" are from within the same classroom, and another 25 percent or so from elsewhere in the school. Thirty percent of "good friends" are contacts made outside of school.

As the elementary school years continue, mutual friendships persist over longer periods, and the children spend more and more time together. From preschool through adolescence, these close friendships rarely cross sexes. Good friendships are powerful predictors of future social-emotional adjustment and motivation to succeed academically. The way these children get along with peers is a strong predictor of adolescent and adult adjustment, including school dropout, emotional problems, and trouble with the law.

*Good friendships and the way children get along with peers are strong predictors of adolescent and adult adjustment.*

The social status of children among their peers relates to their ability to be helpful, to follow the rules, and to be friendly to others. Those who are rejected by peers are those who are more aggressive and engage in inappropriate social interactions such as being disruptive and uncooperative.

*The social status of children among their peers relates to their ability to be helpful, to follow the rules, and to be friendly to others.*

The learning disabled often are at a disadvantage in their social relationships. A number of factors can work against their being able to make and keep friends, including their information-processing inefficiencies, inattentiveness, restlessness, unique cognitive styles and temperaments, immaturity, reactions to failure, and poor quality of social learning opportunities. Their articulation and motor problems often make conversation and joining in sports and games difficult. They may stand out from others because they're oblivious to the latest styles (e.g., jeans cinched above the waist instead of resting on the hips). Their hyperactivity, anxiety, moodiness, brooding, impulsivity, poor task persistence, and slowness at doing most anything doesn't help them win friends. These children also have difficulty accepting and helping others, and expressing their feelings. Moreover, the label "learning disabled" in itself can deplete academic confidence. Add to this their poor self-concept about their intellectual, physical, and social abilities, and it's understandable that maintaining a positive attitude is not one of their strong points. It 's no wonder that 1 out of 3 or 4 children with LD report feeling depressed.

In the classroom, children with learning disabilities, when compared with their peers, are more often ignored or judged negatively by their teachers and peers. They more often are the objects of teachers' negative statements, criticisms, warnings, behavioral corrections, and negative nonverbal reactions such as sighs and rolled eyes. As Jeff's story on page 272 indicates, these students are well aware of when they are being patronized or dealt with unfairly or dishonestly by teachers, which only increases their anger and behavior problems. Teachers are also more likely to rate students with LD as distractible, hyperactive, anxious, shy, withdrawn, and less self-confident, persistent, cooperative, assertive, self-controlled, adaptable to new situations, or socially outgoing. When asked questions like "whom would you like/not like to sit beside or invite to a party?" classmates' responses indicate that the learning disabled often are less popular, less accepted, more ignored and rejected, and more likely to play alone. By the time children burst onto the playground for recess, they've already made agreements about whom they will play with and what they will play. The learning disabled tend to have no clue that that's how things work—they're left out before they even leave the classroom. On the positive side, the more that classmates admire a child with a learning disability, whether because of a special talent, good looks, or athletic

*Children with LD, when compared with their peers, are more often ignored or judged negatively by their teachers and peers.*

*Just one mutual friend is enough for students with LD to prevent loneliness and view their social acceptance favorably.*

ability, the higher the child's social status is among his or her peers. Studies show that just one mutual friend is enough for students with LD to prevent loneliness and have favorable views of their social acceptance.

Life outside school also is different for the learning disabled. They tend to engage in fewer extracurricular activities and only infrequently socialize with

## Jeff

*A software designer with LD complains about being patronized by teachers.*

My mother remembers me coming home from school and saying "I am so much smarter than those guys. Why are they so dumb and they can read and I can't?" I always had a little of that constructive arrogance, you know. I never really thought I was stupid, and I think that's fortunate for me. But I remember being overwhelmed, and just downright obstinate about the way I wanted to do things . . . One thing I was very sensitive about throughout my elementary education was, you know, just evaluate me on what I do; don't say "Well, you misspelled nine out of ten words, but you did a great job on this one word so we'll give you 100 with two smiley faces at the top." I mean, don't lie to me in terms of my performance. I was always really aware of how I was doing, and I was also aware of how everybody else in the class was doing. I was quite on top of that . . .

I remember in fifth grade we had to do a report. The subject I chose was "Arms and Armor in the Middle Ages." My dad took me to the Metropolitan Museum in New York City and I pawed over every single piece of armor in their collection. We bought tons of books and my father read all these books to me. Then I basically created my own book. I cut up all the books Dad bought me—I cut pictures out and I cut words out and I created this report. I didn't really type anything or write anything but I took all the things I wanted to say out of all the different books and I pasted them together. It was a great report, and it was obvious that for me to accomplish this had taken enormous effort—I mean, I can't begin to tell you, hours and hours. So I handed in this report like it was nothing, like everybody hands in their report, and that's how I wanted it treated. I mean I just wanted to know if I really worked hard and did my best, how would I do? In this particular school the grades were E for excellent, then B,C,D and F I don't know why they didn't use A, but they didn't. Everybody in the class who got an E on their reports got an E for excellent, except me. The teacher gave me an E for *effort.* I was so irate about this particular event; I mean—irate is an understatement. My parents had this medication to give me when I got out of control and after school that day I had everybody piling on top of me to get one of these pills down my throat. But I was behaving this way because of these tremendous *injustices.* It was just the most incredibly offensive thing to me at the time. I would have been happy with a B or a C, but instead I got an E for *effort* . . .

After that I decided I was not going to let this thing and these people run my life. So I began to run everybody else's life. I was very, very intrusive on other people, to the point where my sixth-grade teacher—one day early in the fall he left the classroom without saying a word. I found out later he went to my parents' home and he broke into tears and said, "I can't have this kid in my classroom. He has to go."

Interview by Jennifer Kagan

classmates. Even strangers judge these children more negatively after merely observing their nonverbal behaviors.

*Some mothers of students with LD expect even less of their children with learning disabilities than the children expect of themselves. They may downplay their children's successes by attributing them to luck and compound their failures by blaming them on poor ability.*

Often parents too regard their children with learning disabilities differently. They may express less affection for them than for their siblings, something that may have already become apparent in infancy if mothers demonstrated less responsiveness to this baby's needs. Some parents expect even less of their children with LD than the children expect of themselves. One study found that mothers of these children downplayed their children's successes by attributing them to luck and compounded their failures by blaming them on poor ability. Mothers of average achievers did just the opposite; for them success was due to the child's abilities, and failure to bad luck.

Fortunately, some students with learning disabilities never develop emotional or social problems, and others outgrow their difficulties. But for many others they persist. Three factors tend to perpetuate these difficulties: language disabilities, social imperceptiveness, and learned helplessness.

## Language Disabilities and Social Relationships

*The speech of many students with LD contrasts sharply with the excellent conversational skills of their peers, thereby contributing to their social isolation and emotional difficulties.*

The speech of many students with learning disabilities contrasts sharply with the excellent conversational skills of their peers. For example, one study asked children to teach the experimenter how to play checkers. The learning disabled used more sentences than the control children but conveyed less information. Their vocabulary was smaller, repetitive, and less meaningful, and their sentences were shorter and grammatically simpler. They had difficulty describing the game's objectives and strategies, often isolating one aspect of the game to highlight. When the experimenter asked for clarification, the children frequently simply repeated what they had just said, instead of expanding on it. On the whole, these children preferred to demonstrate the game rather than to verbalize strategies. Frequently they got sidetracked and played checkers by themselves, totally ignoring the person they were supposed to instruct.

Youngsters who are learning disabled often can't adjust their language to the age level of the person they are speaking to—using baby talk with an adult, for example. Nor can they adapt to what's just been said or to the topic, often interjecting non sequitors or saying the same thing over and over again. They have trouble interpreting and inferring from what others say, taking turns in conversation, and taking another's perspective. Their sentences are shorter and less grammatically complex, and they don't use intonation, eye contact, or body language effectively to convey meaning. They have a hard time with idioms (e.g., "keep your nose clean"), humor, and ambiguous sentences (e.g., "They fed her dog biscuits"). Those with word-finding problems are slow to choose their words and as a result have a problem maintaining conversations. Given these difficulties, it is not surprising that the conversations of children with LD are characterized by a high proportion of silence.

As listeners, children with learning disabilities are less likely to recognize that a situation calls for clarification, so they don't ask questions. When they do ask, their questions often don't achieve their purpose or they don't give the speaker a chance to respond: " . . . and the substitute teacher we have—do you like her?—I don't—I mean, I really can't stand her because . . . " (Mathinos, 1988, p. 442).

These students are well aware of their comprehension and conversational problems. As a result, they overestimate the speaker's ability to make sense. They shift responsibility for successful conversation to the speaker, whether with peers, adults, or even their own parents. As you might expect, they are not as persuasive as their peers and tend to give up their own viewpoints in favor of others'. It's easy to see how language disabilities can interfere with building friendships, peer acceptance, and self-image.

## Social Imperceptiveness

*Students with LD, especially those with visual-perceptual weaknesses, often lack insight into the affect, attitudes, intentions, and expectations others communicate verbally and nonverbally.*

Students with learning disabilities, especially those with visual-perceptual weaknesses, often lack insight into the affect, attitudes, intentions, and expectations others communicate verbally and nonverbally. This ability to take others' perspectives is called *decentering*. This skill typically develops from 5 to 7 years of age and shows marked increases between ages 8 and 11 to 13. At the same time, children naturally transition from being impulsive to being more reflective and able to consider more than one side of an issue. Considering several hypotheses and choosing the best solution becomes easier for them. All this cognitive and strategy growth helps them with their social relationships.

Owing to their various immaturities, students with learning disabilities often take longer to make the shift to understanding another's perspective. Their poor comprehension of social rules naturally exacerbates their isolation and withdrawal. Studies have shown that these children can be less accurate than their peers at analyzing a social problem; foreseeing the possible consequences of various solutions; interpreting nonverbal cues of affection, gratitude, and anger; asking forgiveness; interpreting facial expressions, gestures, or posture; and describing another's feelings. Even interpreting humor in cartoons can present problems. These difficulties are often referred to as *nonverbal learning disabilities.*

Students with nonverbal learning disabilities have less insight into what's going on socially or how they are faring in groups. This is one reason why they tend to make more negative or competitive statements than their peers, laugh inappropriately, generate fewer options for resolving conflicts, not use eye contact and smiling to convey interest in another speaker, and have a hard time adjusting to new or complex situations. Sometimes these children are well aware of their lower status and functioning among peers, but at other times they unrealistically overestimate this status. It makes sense that poor social perception leads to poor peer acceptance. The learning disabled often try hard to fit in and can't understand the reactions and rebuffs they get from others.

*Poor social perception leads to poor peer acceptance. Children with LD often try hard to fit in and can't understand the reactions and rebuffs they get from others.*

The social imperceptiveness of many youngsters with learning disabilities may reflect immature development rather than a true deficiency. When they interact with younger children or when they are explicitly told what the social expectations are, their behavior can become indistinguishable from their peers. Many have a good repertoire of social skills, but because of their immaturity they need to be taught how to assess the right times to use the right skills. This points to the importance of teaching children not only social skills but also how to better understand the demands of various social situations so that they can apply the skills they have more appropriately.

*Many children with LD have a good repertoire of social skills, but because of their immaturity they need to be taught how to assess the right times to use the right skills.*

## Learned Helplessness

By first or second grade children begin to connect their successes and failures to the amount of personal *effort* they put into a task. They're confident that they can do well if they try. As they get older, however, they add *ability* into the equation and begin comparing their performance with others. It does not take long before the string of failures of the child with a learning disability inevitably leads to distrusting his or her abilities and giving up: "Why bother, I'm so dumb."

Table 8.1 traces how such children come to adopt a *"learned helpless"* attitude toward achievement, an attitude that it's just not worth trying to do better. Studies have shown that as many as 70 percent of students who are learning disabled believe that they have little control over success. They are no longer motivated to prove that they are competent and are defeated even before they begin because they believe they are "too stupid," or that something external to them will prevent success (such as "the teacher is too picky").

*Many children with LD adopt the attitude that their poor ability makes it not worth trying to achieve.*

*Turning around this negative self-evaluation is very important, because self-concept is a far more powerful predictor of academic progress than IQ for students with LD.*

The lower the child's self-concept is, the more that he or she points to poor ability to explain failures and the less persistent he or she is likely to be, even when the outcome could have been positive. Turning around this negative self-evaluation is a very important goal for teachers, because self-concept has been found to be a far more powerful predictor of academic progress than IQ for students with LD.

Unlike poor achievers, good achievers are internally motivated. They have learned that success is related to personal effort and that it's always worth trying because success is likely. When they fail, they might blame bad luck or external factors, or admit that they didn't put in enough effort ("I deserved a D since I chose to go to the movies rather than study").

Students with learning disabilities understand that lack of effort contributes to failure, but they are much more likely to chalk up their failures to their poor abilities. When they do succeed, they credit good luck or some other external factor, such as "the teacher was just being nice to me." They find it extremely difficult to take personal credit for success. As a result, they see no purpose in struggling with difficult tasks, putting time into studying, trying to be organized, or watching others' successful strategies and copying them. Tanis Bryan explains, "Not expecting to be in control of learning, the learning disabled may wait to be rescued" (1986, p. 227). (This kind of helplessness is not limited to those with LD. Average achievers, too, may stare blankly at a teacher who has posed a question, waiting and hoping that the teacher will provide the answer and spare them the effort of even trying. Sometimes even the best of teachers tend to oblige).

*When students with LD do succeed, many credit good luck or some other external factor, which only reinforces the attitude that there's no purpose in trying.*

When we discuss with students their beliefs about what causes success and failure, help them make choices about what to achieve and how they will achieve it, let them know we're there to support them, help them break tasks into more manageable parts, and attribute their successes to very specific abilities and efforts rather than to luck, these students stand a chance to regain their interest, enthusiasm, and motivation to put energy into learning. Specific praise—"Good try at sounding out"—is better than saying simply, "You're great." Because these children do not believe they are capable, general praise means little. When we instead praise a concrete effort, we've shifted their attention to what they can do to meet the curriculum's challenges.

**TABLE 8.1 The Development of Motivated versus Learned Helpless Attitudes toward Achievement**

| | *Type of Achievement Related to Expectations of Society and Schools* | *Type of Adult Feedback* / *Attribution Made by Child* | *Type of Affect Associated with Internal Evaluation of Performance* | *Child's Understanding of His or Her Role in Cause-Effect Relationships* | *Expectations and Probability of Subsequent Behavior* |
|---|---|---|---|---|---|
| High achiever | Success is positively valued by our society. Success is defined by schools as desirable | Positive feedback from adults. The child receives positive labels such as smart, gifted, etc. Child accepts and internalizes positive labels. / The cause of success is attributed by the child to ability and effort. | The positive effects of pride, accomplishment, and competence are associated with successful performance. The child self-reinforces his or her performance with internal positive self-statements. The child's self-concept is enhanced. | The child perceives that his or her effort determines positive outcome. Energy is seen as a means of solving problem. | The child has expectancy of success for future performance. Increased probability of future success serves as an incentive to work harder. |
| Low achiever | Failure is negatively valued by our society. Failure is defined by schools as undesirable. | Negative feedback from adults. The child receives negative labels such as slow, learning problems, etc. Child accepts and internalizes negative labels. / The cause of failure by the child is attributed to lack of ability. | The negative effects of frustration, shame, indifference are associated with failure. Internal statements of the child are primarily negative, reflecting his or her lack of ability. The child's self-concept is decreased. | No causal relationship is perceived between effort and outcome by the child. Therefore, the child considers effort a waste of energy. Energy is spent on avoiding the task. | The child has expectancy of failure in future. Increased probability of failure, therefore, no incentive to expend effort. |

*Source:* Grimes, L. (1981). Learned helplessness and attribution theory: Redefining children's learning problems. *Learning Disability Quarterly, 4*(1), p. 92. Reprinted by permission.

***When students with LD begin to understand the relationship between effort and success, they persist longer on difficult tasks and are more strategic in their learning.***

The good news is that when students with LD begin to understand the relationship between effort and success, they do persist longer on difficult tasks and are more strategic at going about learning. They begin to see themselves as more able and responsible for successes. In addition, because their initial performance is so diminished by low motivation, extrinsic and intrinsic motivational techniques produce great increases in performance for the learning disabled, even greater than those for their average achieving classmates.

**Extrinsic Motivation.** After years of academic struggle, children can't be expected to bring energy and enthusiasm to the table. So teachers must provide it by communicating with confidence, enthusiasm, and energy that the child can and will make gains, and also by using reinforcers wisely. Extrinsic incentives can help children who avoid challenges to put in more effort, but only if the desired goal is within the child's reach. In one study, boys with learning disabilities who performed poorly on sit-ups and relay runs improved to average performance levels when told that they were the kinds of children who did well on such tasks or that the apple juice they drank had given them the extra energy to do well. Building extrinsic motivators like these into our teaching can be very effective, but the goal should ultimately be to help students develop the inner desire to do well.

***Extrinsic motivators can help children who avoid challenges to put in more effort, but only if the desired goal is within the child's reach. The ultimate goal is to help students develop the inner desire to do well.***

Examples of additional external motivators include praise, charting successes, and earning rewards such as stars, a treat, time to play tapes or computer games, or more recess time. Point systems that reward children for improved attention, learning, accuracy, productivity, and behavior have particularly powerful effects on their learning rates and spontaneous use of learning strategies. For example, a teacher can award points for meeting each of four class rules: stay on task, speak nicely, follow directions, complete assignments. These points accumulate toward a prize or privilege. *Responses cost systems* also are very effective. Students are given points or concrete rewards, but lose a few whenever they show certain behaviors, such as being off task or not completing a certain percentage of problems.

*Contracting* is another useful motivator because the child actually makes decisions about what he or she wants to achieve and what the consequences will be, in negotiation with the teacher. The child could contract to complete specific academic objectives, meet personal goals, or improve a certain percentage (as in 85 percent accuracy on homework). The success of contracting is attributed to the *Premack principle,* which states that a less favored activity (such as doing homework) will take on greater value when followed by a more highly valued activity (such as watching TV). The positive consequence becomes a strong incentive for the student to put effort into less favored activities.

External reinforcement can also come from classroom materials and assignments that are of high interest or that value a student's linguistic and cultural background. Possibilities include collecting stories from a student's elderly relatives or doing research on famous people who share the student's language or heritage.

A student's response to extrinsic motivators is a very individual thing. What works for one student won't work for another. Once a powerful motivator is found, it should be maintained for a time and then withdrawn gradually in order to prevent reversal of the behavior change. After years of failure, any short period of extrinsic reinforcement by itself won't cause a youngster to appreciate his or her capabilities and value learning for learning's sake. Turning learned helplessness around is a long process.

***Once a powerful extrinsic motivator is found, it should be maintained for a time and then withdrawn gradually.***

***Type and Frequency of Incentives.*** Rewards work, but it's important to use the right type and frequency of these incentives for maximum benefit. With hyperactive children, for example, rewards at times can be very distracting. Also, in some circumstances, incentives actually reduce motivation. Research Box 8.1 presents several hypotheses for this unintended consequence.

*Praise as an incentive is very useful, but it should be used sparingly, be well-timed, and targeted to a specific behavior.*

Praise as an incentive is very useful, but it should be used sparingly, especially at the secondary school level where no more than 5 to 10 percent of a student's efforts should be praised. When it is used, praise should be well-timed and targeted to a specific behavior. Saying, "You did a good job today" as the student leaves class is less effective than looking at a test when handed in and saying, "Ten out of 15 spelling words correct! You're really paying attention to the order of letters today!"

To prevent rewards and praise from being counterproductive, experts suggest the following:

*Don't use rewards or much praise when students are already excited about a task.*

*Use the least obvious and attention-getting reward that is effective.*

*Focus on what the child accomplished rather than on what he or she gets as a reward.*

1. Don't use rewards or much praise when students are excited about a new task. They are already motivated and this sincere interest in their work is enough.
2. Use the least obvious and attention-getting reward that is effective. Using bigger rewards may cause students to work for the incentive only, stopping when the reward is withdrawn—as so often happens when parents promise "I'll buy you a car if you get all A's." The A's surely happen that term, but never again. Applying this principle, encouragement of on-task behavior in the classroom by breaking the assignment into parts, followed by your smile when each part is submitted, may be incentive enough.
3. Focus on what the child accomplished rather than on what he or she gets as a reward. This fosters self-perceptions of competence, independence, and task enjoyment. If rewards are related to the content of the tasks—a handmade journal of bound sheets of paper for completing writing assignments, for instance—then students are more likely to see the reward as inherent in doing the task.

*Grading Systems.* Competition for grades is the classic form of external reinforcement used in school. The theory is that competing for good grades will enhance performance. But the truth is that this kind of competition is only fun for the best students. Because students who are learning disabled don't believe they can win at this game, they aren't motivated to compete. Richard Lavoie explains the problem this way:

> Many well-intentioned teachers emphasize competition in their classroom in the mistaken belief that they are preparing the child for the intense competition that he will face in society. In their zeal to replicate the "big, bad world" these teachers have created classroom environments wherein the level and intensity of competition far exceeds that of the adult world. Our society does require competition in order to achieve success but this competition has two fundamental components: (a) adults do not compete unless they elect to and (b) we compete only against our peers and equals. Most classroom competitive activities (for example, spelling bees, mathematics games) do not meet those criteria. (1986, p. 63)

In addition to feeling ill-equipped in the first place to compete academically, tests only induce even more anxiety for students with LD and actually reduce performance. For this and other reasons, it's important that we find ways besides tests to

RESEARCH BOX 8.1

## Why Rewards at Times May Reduce Motivation

Rewards at times may produce a disincentive toward engaging in a certain behavior, such as reading, rather than enhancing a child's motivation to do so. Ryan and Deci (2000) point out that self-motivation is high when people feel that they are competent to do a task, make the choice to do it, and have others' support to pursue this goal. When tangible rewards are added to this mix, however, the person's feelings of autonomy can be squelched. The external incentive has become the motivator—the cause for engaging in the task. Internal motivation then declines. The same deflation of motivation is true when students are given directives and deadlines ("I did it because I was told I had to"). Eisenberger and Cameron (1996) also find a decline in motivation when people are told to expect a tangible reward for simply engaging in an activity, rather than being rewarded only if the activity is completed or if the performance is of high quality. Malouf (1983) explains why tangible rewards can be counterproductive to high motivation:

1. Self-Perception and Attributions
   - If a person is already intrinsically motivated, offering a reward will decrease the individual's incentive to engage in that behavior when the reward is no longer delivered ("I got an ice cream cone last time I sat still at McDonald's. Why not now? If I don't get the ice cream, I guess I don't need to behave").
   - People value a behavior more highly if they perceive that it is their own choice rather than being influenced by external factors. Adelman and Taylor (1990) explain that if students perceive a reward to be coercing compliance, thereby limiting personal control, this can result in psychological reactance against the behavior being reinforced ("I hate helping the child with a disability in our class—the teacher makes me do it").
   - If the rewards bear no relationship to the activity (e.g., money for practicing drawing versus more crayons and markers), then the target behavior (enjoying drawing) may be reduced because the child will attribute his or her engagement in that behavior to the consequences ("I drew because I got money" vs. "I had fun drawing a picture—I got to use some neat colored pens"). When a goal becomes construed as only a means to an end, that goal loses some of its value. Worse, it can undermine a student's intrinsic motivation because learning is directed away from learning for learning's sake and toward getting rewards (stars, grades).
2. Competing Responses
   - Rewards may elicit competing responses that are incompatible with task motivation. For example, if Terry is frustrated because she can't delay gratification until the reward is received, then she experiences the task as unpleasant, which will reduce her motivation to engage in it again. Alternatively, if the reward becomes a distraction for Terry or its anticipation engenders much excitement, then this may impair her task performance, which in turn reduces motivation. In addition, because learning is dependent on rewards, Terry may focus primarily on getting the reward in the easiest way possible and not do the best she can. Obviously the more attention-getting and desirable the extrinsic reward, the more likely it will interfere with Terry's learning.

*(continued)*

## RESEARCH BOX 8.1 (Continued)

3. Reinforcement Contrast
   - Rewards may be compared with one's previous reward history, so that a particular reward may not be perceived as a reward and behavior may be suppressed ("Last year's teacher gave me computer time for reading a whole book. This year's teacher will give me 15 minutes of free time. No thank you!").

Certainly this research cautions us to be more aware of the types of rewards we establish at home and in the classroom, so that they are in fact motivation enhancers rather than deterrents to performance. If tangible rewards are used, it is best if they are unexpected, not salient enough to distract the child from the task at hand, and awarded contingent on completing a task or doing it well (e.g., finishing a whole story or reading a few pages with good-quality performance, vs. simply staring at and flipping pages) (Eisenberger & Cameron, 1996).

***It's important that we find ways besides tests to assess student learning. Because students with LD don't believe they can win at this game, they aren't motivated to compete.***

assess student learning. Cooperative learning (described in Chapter 14), in which students work together to accomplish a goal, alleviates some of the evaluation stress experienced by students with LD and promotes motivation and performance. Portfolio assessment is another useful alternative. Portfolio items can consist of written products, projects, oral reports, demonstrations, and performances. The student's and teacher's written statements regarding the strategies, progress, and proficiency represented by the portfolio contents stress progress toward concrete, thoughtful, creative, and meaningful goals. Depending on the purpose, several types of portfolios can be compiled: showcase portfolios, which collect the student's best work for the purpose of gaining admission to a job or program; reflective portfolios, in which the purpose of the contents is to reflect a child's effort and use of various strategies; cumulative portfolios, which collect a series of items illustrating change in learning over time; goal-based portfolios, which showcase the final products that meet preestablished goals; and process portfolios, which document the steps a child used to complete a piece, such as the steps in a research project.

Narrative evaluations have become increasingly popular, as have progress notes on effort and achievement since the last marking period. There are also many options for grading adaptations beyond grading the child's mastery in comparison to that of classmates: marking "achieved" or "progressing" on a checklist of specific curriculum objectives; pass-fail options such as honor pass, high pass, pass, low pass, or fail; giving level-specific grades such as 3B (performing B work at the third-grade level); and grading based on adjusted length or components of assignments (the transcript can reflect a different course title to differentiate a much lower level of responsibility than the standard course). Figure 8.2 illustrates a grading rubric in which a checklist is created that represents a project's components. The grade is based on points earned on each item. All students in the class are graded using the same rubric, but the components can be modified based on an individual student's needs.

Name Jonathan Smith Date 1-2-98

**Checklist for the Business Letter**

| Requirements (Components) | possible points | points earned | Comments |
|---|---|---|---|
| Heading | 4 | 4 | |
| Inside Address | 4 | 4 | |
| Greeting | 2 | 2 | |
| Spacing | 3 | 3 | |
| Body: 2 ~~3~~ Support ~ Statements | ~~8~~ 6 | 6 | 2 required supports |
| Complete Sentences | ~~10~~ | / | Not graded. Need to work on punctuation. Capitals look good! |
| Correct Spelling | ~~3~~ | / | Not graded. Practice editing on Computer. |
| Written in Pen | 2 | 2 | |
| Readable | 5 | 5 | |
| Closing | 2 | 2 | |
| Signature | 1 | 1 | |
| **TOTAL** | ~~42~~ 29 | 29 | |

Grade A 100%

Attachments: rough copy
final copy

Student Signature

Parent Signature

**Figure 8.2** Sample grading rubric for individualizing project components.

*Source:* Bradley, D. F., & Calvin, M. B. (1998). Grading modified assignments: Equity or compromise? *Teaching Exceptional Children, 31*, p. 27. Copyright © 1998 by The Council for Exceptional Children. Reprinted with permission.

Another interesting grading option, suggested by Larry Lieberman, calls for the student, teacher, and parents to decide which of three levels of tests is most appropriate given the course content and competition from peers:

Level one: Regular test
Level two: Somewhat less abstract, requiring fill-ins and short answers

Level three: Most concrete—true-false, multiple choice (requires recognition versus recall)

The highest grade for a level-three test would be a C+; for level two, a B+; and for level one, an A. If students do well on one level, they can choose to try the next, with the best grade being the final grade. Lieberman comments:

> Think about it—if a kid has the option to either make a C+ on a level-three test or to fail a level-one test, what choice do you think he will make? (1986, p. 423)

Contracting can also be used to award grades based on specific agreed-upon goals: for example, a written term paper earns an A, an annotated outline earns a B, an organized folder of research materials on the topic earns a C. Another option is to give students opportunities to raise their grades by doing more homework, correcting errors, or completing extra projects. Teachers can also hold grading conferences with individual students at the end of each quarter. Students present their own estimate of their grades on a self-assessment sheet such as the one shown in Figure 8.3. This gives them a feeling of ownership and a greater understanding of what they need to do to earn a better grade next time.

**Intrinsic Motivation.** The very best form of motivation comes from within. Anyone observing healthy and well-attached infants knows that children are naturally curious and interested in learning, exploring, and mastering challenges. Youngsters with less innate talent but who gain satisfaction from engaging in tasks with responsibility, creativity, and effort can equal the performance of students with IQs 20 points higher. Persistence and task orientation make very significant contributions to achievement, sometimes over twice that made by IQ. Nowhere is this phenomenon more evident than in tracking the occupational success of mid-1960s Asian American high school graduates who were of average intelligence. Nevertheless, disproportionate to their numbers, they were working in high-level managerial, professional, and technical positions usually occupied by individuals testing above the 90th percentile on IQ tests. These people benefited from being raised by families that valued education above all else and instilled this drive in their children.

*Persistence and task orientation make very significant contributions to achievement, sometimes over twice that made by IQ.*

Students with learning disabilities who, despite competing against the odds, have maintained high internal motivation also can achieve significantly beyond the expectations set by their intellectual or information-processing weaknesses. Unfortunately, when such a student's high motivation results in grade-level achievement, the fact that the child has a learning disability may be missed altogether. Ironically, the child's motivation can mask his or her constant struggle, frustration, and effort to keep up.

*Students with LD who have maintained high internal motivation can achieve far beyond the expectations set by their intellectual or information-processing weaknesses.*

The very best support for internal motivation is the family. When children see their parents and other family members work hard to achieve, they tend to do likewise. And after a while, they don't need hugs, praise, or treats for doing well. Achievement has become a highly valued motivator in its own right.

*The very best support for internal motivation is the family.*

To be intrinsically motivated to achieve an objective, the child needs to be interested in the task. But interest isn't enough. A sense of competence ("I can do

English 9 **Self-Assessment**

Name ______________________________ Date _____

WRITING / READING (circle one)

A) Write your quarter goals here.

1. ______________________________
2. ______________________________
3. ______________________________
4. ______________________________
5. ______________________________

For each goal, tell what % you believe you've achieved and state why. (e.g., If you were to receive credit for 4 pieces of writing and you did 3, you achieved 75% of that goal.)

1. __________% ______________________________
2. __________% ______________________________
3. __________% ______________________________
4. __________% ______________________________
5. __________% ______________________________

B) Write down, in a sentence, your assessment of your effort and attitude this quarter.

______________________________

______________________________

______________________________

C) On a scale of 1–10, assess the Quality of your work.

______________________________

D) Select your best writing/reading and explain why it's your best.

______________________________

______________________________

E) GRADE DESIRED FOR WRITING/READING (circle one)

______________________________

F) Set two goals for yourself next quarter.

1. ______________________________
2. ______________________________

**Figure 8.3** Grading conference worksheet.

*Source:* Ryan, D. (1991, Winter). Management and evaluation revisited. *The School Psychologist, 9* (1), p. 19. Reprinted by permission.

this"), autonomy ("I am making the decision to do this"), and relatedness ("I feel secure and supported in doing this") supports this intrinsic motivation. In other words, the higher Serena's feelings of competence and the more she sees her family and school as supporting independence in learning and behavior, the higher Serena's achievement is likely to be. As Figure 8.4 illustrates, this process begins by taking pride in even the smallest of victories. It is important to recognize and reward moves in the right direction—not to expect perfection.

*It is important to recognize and reward moves in the right direction—do not expect perfection.*

For teachers, there is no better way to build intrinsic motivation than by creating rewarding learning experiences that capitalize on students' strengths; encouraging students' talents; building identification and satisfaction by incorporating meaningful ethnic, cultural, and native-language material into the curriculum; and accommodating to a child's weaknesses so that the regular curriculum becomes more accessible. Howard Adelman and Linda Taylor comment:

> Schools have the responsibility not only to help individuals overcome learning problems but also to facilitate ongoing development and provide opportunities for creative growth through enrichment activity. The fact that a person has a problem learning to read doesn't alter the fact that he or she can learn a variety of other things—and undoubtedly wants to. To find the time for remediation, it may be tempting to set aside enrichment and even some developmental learning opportunities; to do so, however, deprives individuals of other important experiences. It may also negatively affect their attitude toward the school, toward the teacher, and toward overcoming their problems. At the very least, school programs that overstress problem remediation risk becoming tedious and disheartening. (1986, p. 604)

*Students' abilities and talents need just as much nurturing as their learning weaknesses require help. These abilities form the foundation on which students build their future work and interpersonal lives.*

Students' abilities and talents need just as much nurturing as their learning weaknesses require help. It is on the foundation of these abilities, not on their disabilities, that students will build their future work and interpersonal lives.

**Figure 8.4** Learn to recognize little victories.

*Source:* PEANUTS is reprinted by permission of the United Feature Syndicate, Inc.

## The Secondary School Student

Even if a child who is learning disabled has done reasonably well academically and socially through the elementary years, by adolescence learning disabilities have a greater chance of negatively affecting self-concept and motivation. Seldom does a student grow up in America with a disability and emerge unscathed from the experience.

Adolescence is a time of great challenge for the soon-to-be adult. He or she is dealing with physical changes, emerging sexuality, new social roles, school transitions, vocational planning, extracurricular interests, preparing for independent living, examination of values, and a growing desire for autonomy and control in decision making. The continued and positive development of social skills is a particularly important priority because social aptitude is highly related to a person's satisfaction in all aspects of life.

Although unique and different in many ways, adolescence does not wholly transform a person's personality from what it was as a child. Those with LD who were socially savvy as children tend to remain that way through the teenage years. Some use their social skills very effectively to compensate for deficits in other areas. But for those who never developed these skills in childhood or for those who are slow to adapt, overreactive, distractible, or moody, adolescence can be a trial. These teens are tackling important personal issues without the tools to help them learn or ease the transition.

*Although unique and different in many ways, adolescence does not wholly transform a person's personality from what it was as a child.*

Adolescence's reputation as a time of storm and stress is true only for some teenagers. Less than 20 percent of teenagers experience such turmoil, and the numbers of family conflicts do not increase dramatically; rather, it is the focus of conflicts that changes to adolescent issues—dating, driving, appearance, sexuality, curfews, substance use. The greater mood swings and risk-taking behavior in adolescence contribute to conflicts with parents, but for the most part, teenagers and parents agree on more serious issues such as the value of honesty and the importance of education. Teenagers still love and depend on their families, even as they take the steps necessary to transition to being independent adults. In most families, adolescence does not seriously breach the parent-child relationship. Figure 8.5 is a poignant plea for the continued support and direction teenagers want and need from their parents while they struggle to grow up.

*Adolescence's reputation as a time of storm and stress is true for less than 20 percent of teenagers. In most families, the number of family conflicts do not increase dramatically in adolescence.*

With the physical, social, and emotional changes of adolescence comes a cognitive leap in reasoning ability. Teenagers become sensitive to the differences in feelings between themselves and others and more often can take another's perspective. They think about possibilities and alternatives, values, and family issues from a more objective stance. Because of their newly developed capacities for abstract reasoning, they are better able to see the difference between what is really happening and what a person thinks or says is happening. They become alert to the symbolic as well as literal meaning of events, and are disappointed to learn that people don't always mean what they say. They also become aware that adults are not always right, and in fact often work hard to cover up their mistakes. Because they can now see beneath the surface of situations, they can perceive hidden threats to their well-being (as when parents' insistence on not dating a person, or insistence on a curfew, really is a hidden statement about what and

**Memo from a Child to: Parents**

1. Don't spoil me. I know quite well that I ought not to have all I ask for—I'm only testing you.
2. Don't be afraid to be firm with me. I prefer it, it makes me feel secure.
3. Don't let me form bad habits. I have to rely on you to detect them in the early stages.
4. Don't make me feel smaller than I am. It only makes me behave stupidly "big."
5. Don't correct me in front of people if you can help it. I'll take much more notice if you talk quietly with me in private.
6. Don't make me feel that my mistakes are sins. It upsets my sense of values.
7. Don't protect me from consequences. I need to learn the painful way sometimes.
8. Don't be too upset when I say "I hate you." Sometimes it isn't you I hate but your power to thwart me.
9. Don't take too much notice of my small ailments. Sometimes they get me the attention I need.
10. Don't nag. If you do, I shall have to protect myself by appearing deaf.
11. Don't forget that I cannot explain myself as well as I should like. That is why I am not always accurate.
12. Don't put me off when I ask questions. If you do, you will find that I stop asking and seek my information elsewhere.
13. Don't be inconsistent. That completely confuses me and makes me lose faith in you.
14. Don't tell me my fears are silly. They are terribly real and you can do much to reassure me if you try to understand.
15. Don't ever suggest that you are perfect or infallible. It gives me too great a shock when I discover that you are neither.
16. Don't ever think that it is beneath your dignity to apologize to me. An honest apology makes me feel surprisingly warm towards you.
17. Don't forget I love experimenting. I couldn't get along without it, so please put up with it.
18. Don't forget how quickly I am growing up. It must be very difficult for you to keep pace with me, but please do try.
19. Don't forget that I don't thrive without lots of love and understanding, but I don't need to tell you, do I?
20. Please keep yourself fit and healthy. I need you.

**Figure 8.5** A teenager's message. This list, which appeared in *New York Magazine* in a health club ad, describes what one teenager wanted from his or her parents.

*Source: New York Magazine,* April 11, 1988, p. 114. Reprinted by permission.

who is sexually permissible). With this maturing of reasoning skills comes a time of sorting out to discover who the teenager is relative to all these new perspectives on the world.

For a while, teenagers' thinking is understandably egocentric. With all their new "revelations," they are convinced that they are entirely unique. They develop a strong desire for independence not only because of Western society's push toward autonomy, but also because they are learning to depend on the one reality they can trust—themselves.

The perception of teenagers that they are so unique convinces them that everyone is watching their every move closely. Self-consciousness, embarrassment, nervousness, and a decline in time experienced as "very happy" follow suit. All this questioning and focus on what the world is doing and thinking results in an unusual vulnerability to peer influence. Amid all these changes, most adolescents nevertheless still take pleasure in most aspects of their lives and are satisfied with most of their relationships most of the time.

It is in the safety of close friendships that teenagers explore their individuality—first as part of, and then separate from, the group. But teenagers with LD frequently haven't formed these peer group attachments in the first place. Thus they are deprived of the chance to explore new roles and new relationships, as well as having the buffer of a peer group to ease their transition to a new adult identity. Often they make one of two debilitating decisions: they remain excessively attached to and dependent on their parents' support and authority, or they separate prematurely from their families. They set themselves adrift, without having come to grips with the questions of "Who am I?" and "Where am I going?"

Just as with the elementary school student, these teenagers' problems with interpersonal relationships are related to their behavioral difficulties, learned helplessness, and social imperceptiveness.

## Behavioral Difficulties

Despite the litany of negative characteristics reported by many studies, they are not true for all teenagers who are learning disabled—not even for the majority. Many students with LD are popular, well-adjusted, self-confident, admired by their teachers, and well loved by their families. They have just as many mutual friends as their nondisabled peers, and hang out and talk on the phone with them just as often. They feel as satisfied with themselves and as accepted as their peers, despite low feelings of academic competence.

*Many teenagers with LD are well-adjusted, popular, and self-confident; they feel satisfied with themselves and accepted by their peers, despite low feelings of academic competence.*

Nevertheless, teenagers with learning disabilities are at a greater risk for personal maladjustment and antisocial behavior than their nondisabled peers. These difficulties are greatest for those with the most severe learning disabilities and neurological involvement. These students are bright enough to see that they are different from their peers, and this hurts. Frequently they will disguise their feelings by claiming that an assignment was "too dumb" to do; by purposely doing sloppy work; by becoming the class clown; by avoiding challenges for fear of failure; by becoming an "expert" in an area of personal strength to sidetrack attention from a disability (such as knowing everything about baseball records); and by projecting weaknesses onto the shortcomings of the school, teacher, or parent. Given the great effort required to cope with school, family, and social relationships, they naturally tend to be more depressed than their peers.

*Given the great effort required to cope with school, family, and social relationships, teenagers with LD tend to be more depressed than their peers.*

Teachers report that these teenagers are more likely than their classmates to be defiant, resistant, prone to unethical behavior, have poor emotional control, be hyperactive, and unable to delay gratification. They are often passively off task (such as not looking at the book). Parents rate their teenagers with LD as being unusually immature, anxious, hostile, withdrawn, aggressive, cruel, uncommunicative, and hyperactive. They note that their children are rigid, unimaginative, unfriendly, distant, ashamed, unpopular, and lack self-confidence. Many are moody, brood, self-blame, complain of headaches and stomachaches, are fatigued, and show antisocial behavior such as lying, stealing, tantrums, or destroying property. In at least one study, students with LD reported greater victimization by classmates, including being threatened, assaulted, or having possessions taken. Studies are split on whether the learning disabled are more likely to abuse alcohol or other drugs.

*Teenagers with LD tend to have more behavioral problems than their peers, participate less in extracurricular activities, have fewer social contacts with friends, report more loneliness, and are less liked by classmates.*

Not surprisingly, teenagers with LD participate less in organized extracurricular activities, have fewer social contacts with friends, turn less often to peers for help, report more loneliness, and are less well liked by classmates, especially if they are aggressive and disruptive.

## Learned Helplessness

When teenagers go through the slow process of discovering who they are and deciding where they want to go, their new understandings grow from a sense of competence and mastery. But the learning disabled don't have the positive experiences that help them form a picture of themselves. Many tend to be unusually dependent on others and are more likely than their peers to question their intelligence.

*Many teens with LD see themselves as academically less competent and view their chances for academic success as bleak; anticipating failure, many just won't try.*

Like the elementary students described earlier, teenagers with LD tend to attribute their failures to basic inability and chalk their successes up to luck or some other external factor beyond their control, such as easy test questions. They see themselves as academically less competent and view their chances for academic success as bleak. Even when they do succeed, they worry that they won't be able to handle the next challenge. Anticipating failure, many just won't try. Failing because they didn't do the work is easier for them to handle emotionally than failing because they tried and proved themselves incompetent. Sadly, often their parents and teachers have equally low academic expectations for them. A survey of high school seniors with LD clearly reflected their learned helplessness. They responded more positively than their nondisabled peers to the following statements:

1. Good luck is more important than hard work for success.
2. Every time I try to get ahead, something or somebody stops me.
3. Planning only makes a person unhappy, since plans hardly ever work out anyway.
4. People who accept their condition in life are happier than those who try to change things (Gregory, Shanahan, & Walberg, 1986).

Whereas schools should be encouraging these students' talents—and often they are extraordinary entrepreneurs, artists, musicians, computer technicians, or athletes—schools instead focus on their weaknesses. Worse, unless countermanded in the individualized education program (IEP), teenagers with LD may be excluded from the very extracurricular activities in which they could excel by some schools' "no pass–no play" rule. If their sense of cognitive incompetence generalizes to these talents, they may ultimately pursue them halfheartedly or not at all. The same can happen with social interactions.

In our efforts to help teenagers with "learned helplessness," we must be careful not to go overboard in offering so much support and help that we endanger their developing independence, their ability to cope under pressure, their desire to strive for goals, and their belief in their abilities. Experts, for example, have urged us not to change the nature of a student's homework unless absolutely necessary. Given that homework is a major stimulus for phone calls to collaborate after school, we need to be careful not to cut the student with LD out of this important social loop. Assigning the same homework increases the probability for students to be perceived as valued members of their learning communities, and sends the message that they can contribute and succeed. Likewise, high schools are urged not to lower curriculum requirements or modify standard materials unless absolutely necessary. After all, future employers won't modify work materials and expectations or judge these individuals' contributions by a different standard. These students, just as all others, need to work hard to succeed at requirements that are within their capabilities.

*We must be careful not to offer so much support and help that we endanger students' developing independence and their ability to cope under pressure.*

*High schools should not lower curriculum requirements or modify standard materials unless absolutely necessary.*

## Social Imperceptiveness

Social perception does increase with age. But many teenagers with learning disabilities, particularly those with visual-perceptual weaknesses, continue to lag behind. They have particular trouble understanding subtle facial and behavioral cues, often misinterpreting negative cues as positive and vice versa. In one study, when teenagers rated how well others liked them, only 6 of 28 teenagers who were learning disabled accurately perceived their social status. Often these students do things that attract negative attention and then wonder what went wrong. Their feelings of inadequacy are only reinforced.

Because social perception is such an integral part of all human interaction, these nonverbal learning disabilities can be among the most debilitating of all learning disabilities. Teachers and others sensitive to these issues can help by establishing mentoring relationships, and by offering group counseling and social skills training. Experts, for example, have developed lessons around the 50 basic social skills listed in Figure 8.6 on page 290, which are taught through modeling, role playing, immediate feedback, and real-life practice. Similar techniques are used to teach anger control, moral reasoning, problem solving, stress management, empathy, cooperation, and other social skills. There is a high degree of detail involved in this type of training. For example, in Schumaker's (1992) program, students are taught to ask for help using the following steps: face the person, make eye contact, use serious voice tone and facial expression, keep a straight body posture, say the person's name, ask if he or she has time to help, explain the problem, ask for advice, listen carefully, ask questions, if possible do the task immediately and ask for feedback, and say "thank you."

*Nonverbal learning disabilities can be among the most debilitating of all learning disabilities.*

Equally important is to teach students with LD to praise others when appropriate and show interest, in effect making others feel that they matter. This is so important because research has shown that those who most easily become accepted socially are the ones who enhance the self-esteem of the people with whom they associate. Finally, grooming, clean and neat clothing (if in style!), posture, and

*Those who most easily become accepted socially are the ones who enhance the self-esteem of the people with whom they associate—an important lesson for students with LD.*

**Group I. Beginning Social Skills**

1. Listening
2. Starting a conversation
3. Having a conversation
4. Asking a question
5. Saying thank you
6. Introducing yourself
7. Introducing other people
8. Giving a compliment

**Group II. Advanced Social Skills**

9. Asking for help
10. Joining in
11. Giving instructions
12. Following instructions
13. Apologizing
14. Convincing others

**Group III. Skills for Dealing with Feelings**

15. Knowing your feelings
16. Expressing your feelings
17. Understanding the feelings of others
18. Dealing with someone else's anger
19. Expressing affection
20. Dealing with fear
21. Rewarding yourself

**Group IV. Skill Alternatives to Aggression**

22. Asking permission
23. Sharing something
24. Helping others
25. Negotiation
26. Using self-control
27. Standing up for your rights
28. Responding to teasing
29. Avoiding trouble with others
30. Keeping out of fights

**Group V. Skills for Dealing with Stress**

31. Making a complaint
32. Answering a complaint
33. Sportsmanship after the game
34. Dealing with embarrassment
35. Dealing with being left out
36. Standing up for a friend
37. Responding to persuasion
38. Responding to failure
39. Dealing with contradictory messages
40. Dealing with an accusation
41. Getting ready for a difficult conversation
42. Dealing with group pressure

**Group VI. Planning Skills**

43. Deciding on something to do
44. Deciding what caused a problem
45. Setting a goal
46. Deciding on your abilities
47. Gathering information
48. Arranging problems by importance
49. Making a decision
50. Concentrating on a task

**Figure 8.6** Sample objectives included in social skills programs.

*Source:* Goldstein, A., Sprafkin, R., Gershaw, N., & Klein, P. (1980). *Skill-streaming the adolescent: A structured learning approach to teaching prosocial skills,* pp. 84–85. Champaign, IL: Research Press. Reprinted by permission.

general attractiveness, all of which contribute to popularity, are important objectives not to be overlooked. The greater cooperativeness and understanding of others developed through these various means should help enhance the social acceptance of the learning disabled.

## Learning Disabilities and Juvenile Delinquency

Poor academic achievement, lack of motivation, and short attention span are some of the descriptors that appear in the folders of both juvenile delinquents and adolescents with learning disabilities. Other similarities include low frustration tolerance, negative self-concept, less skill in social problem solving, poor perspective taking, poor impulse control, trouble sizing up a problem, inability to generate multiple and effective solutions, evaluate consequences, or monitor performance. Several studies have shown that severe hyperactivity and conduct problems such as aggressive-defiant behaviors in childhood are important predictors of antisocial behavior in adolescence and adulthood.

Various studies report that some 18 to 55 percent of students labeled as juvenile delinquents have LD. Teens with learning disabilities, especially those with attention-deficit hyperactivity disorder, report more arrests, convictions, and incarcerations than do their nondisabled peers. Once they are found guilty of a crime, the learning disabled tend to have greater recidivism and parole failure than those without learning disabilities.

*Teens with LD, especially those with attention-deficit hyperactivity disorder, report more arrests, convictions, and incarcerations than do their nondisabled peers.*

The link between learning disabilities and juvenile delinquency is stronger when there are severe family problems such as divorce, separation, alcoholism, economic hardships, physical and mental abuse, and criminal behavior. This is also true when the teenager has received little remedial attention or has attended school irregularly.

Three hypotheses have been put forward to explain the higher incidence of juvenile delinquency among the learning disabled: school failure, differential treatment, and increased susceptibility.

**School Failure.** This rationale proposes that failure at school erodes social acceptance, which in turn erodes self-confidence to the point that, given the right psychological and environmental incentives, the teenager with LD may indulge in delinquent behavior. School failure increases the chances of school dropout, another strong correlate of delinquency. In support of the school failure/delinquency rationale, data indicate that white youth from high socioeconomic status families engage in more delinquent behavior than do youth from low-income families. This may reflect the frustration and disappointment of youngsters from higher socioeconomic families at not living up to the expectations set for them by their families and social milieu.

Some experts believe that students failing academically may turn to delinquency in part because it gives them at least one peer group in which they can be recognized. Teenagers don't want to be different, and those with learning disabilities are smart enough to realize that they are—and it lasts for life. At any moment, most teenagers would prefer to be viewed as a bad kid, rather than a dumb kid.

*Some experts believe that students failing academically may turn to delinquency because it gives them at least one peer group in which they can be recognized. Most teenagers would prefer to be viewed as a bad kid, rather than a dumb kid.*

**Differential Treatment.** Several studies have shown that, for comparable offenses, adolescents with LD and/or hyperactivity are arrested or brought before judges more often than their nondisabled peers. The causes are believed to be related both to the youths' weaknesses (such as poor expressive capabilities, ineptness at presenting oneself in a positive manner, or inability to reason abstractly—such as about the protection afforded by the right of silence) and to factors inherent in the judicial system itself, which is a highly cognitive, verbal, strategy-oriented procedure. Once in court, the disposition of the cases for teenagers with LD generally is no more severe than for nondisabled delinquents.

*For comparable offenses, adolescents with LD and/or hyperactivity are more often arrested or brought before judges, but disposition of their cases is no more severe than for nondisabled delinquents.*

**Increased Susceptibility.** Because of their linguistic differences, social imperceptiveness, poor learning from experience, and impulsivity, factors that might restrain a nondisabled peer from committing an antisocial act simply don't have the same effect on a person with learning disabilities. Trouble with the law can stem from immaturity in interpreting others' moods or messages, interpreting situations and choosing the best solution, negotiating, dealing with anger, showing concern with wrongdoing, anticipating consequences, taking others' perspectives, controlling impulsivity, accepting and giving negative feedback, resisting peer pressure, and standing up for what one thinks is right.

***Linguistic differences, social imperceptiveness, poor learning from experience, impulsivity, and immaturity in moral reasoning combine to make teenagers with LD more susceptible to delinquent behavior.***

Susceptibility to delinquent behavior may also come from immaturity in moral reasoning. Elementary school children judge right from wrong based on whether their needs will be met or whether they will be rewarded, or caught and punished. As they become older, they become less egocentric and more sensitive to group norms for behavior, the need for fairness, and the need to obey rules to protect society's welfare. This involves judging right from wrong by considering others' circumstances and perspectives, and taking responsibility for maintaining relationships even if this means violating societal rules (e.g., a husband without insurance stealing an expensive drug in order to save his wife's life). This also involves speaking up about societal rules that are harmful to society's development, as many did during the civil rights marches. Unfortunately, many teenagers with learning disabilities are not yet ready to judge rightness according to loyalty to others and a commitment to contribute to society.

Classroom discussions about moral dilemmas have proved successful in increasing the level of moral reasoning of students and decreasing their egocentric following of rules only when these meet their own needs and desires—the "what's in it for me" attitude. Recidivism has been reduced through mentoring and developing strong adult relationships, encouraging youths' talents, vocational education, and Outward Bound type programs that focus on fellowship and leadership.

The link between learning disabilities and juvenile delinquency makes preventive measures incumbent upon our schools. Nevertheless, it's important not to rush to judgment. In most cases, youth who are learning disabled do not get into trouble with the law. These teenagers already have a difficult enough time functioning and being accepted without being earmarked as potential delinquents.

## The Adult

Learning disabilities, as we have learned, tend not to disappear with age and often continue into adulthood. Exactly how vocational and social adjustment will be affected depends on the adult's strengths and weaknesses; his or her past academic, social, and emotional experiences; and the expectations of the settings in which the adult lives, works, and plays.

***Despite persistent weaknesses, many adults with LD do go on to postsecondary education, get good jobs, and positively contributed to their families and communities.***

Despite persistent weaknesses, many adults with LD do go on to postsecondary education, get good jobs, raise their children well, get along with their spouses and friends, and contribute to their communities. These tend to be the individuals who have compensated for their learning difficulties through intellectual and motivational resources, and adequate instructional and emotional support. They are in tune with their strengths and weaknesses and have made a conscious choice to take charge of their lives, set realistic goals, work hard, and choose educational and work environments that optimize their strengths. Most important, they surrounded themselves with supportive friends, family, and mentors, and they learned to accept their experience with LD and take on new challenges with confidence that odds can be overcome.

*Successful adults with LD surround themselves with supportive friends, family, and mentors, learn to accept their experience with LD, take advantage of instructional opportunities, and take on challenges with confidence that odds can be overcome.*

Unfortunately, more often than not adults with LD have not had the advantage of adequate schooling and emotional support. Many tend to forego postsecondary schooling, have less vocational success, and less satisfying interpersonal relationships.

Understanding the difficulties faced by adults with learning disabilities is important so that we can intervene preventively in schools, as well as intensify adult services. Fortunately, today's adult with LD has many more vocational and independent living options than in the past.

## Vocational Adjustment

The type of job and level of income you achieve touches all aspects of your life: the home you can have, the vacations you can take, the schooling you can provide your children, your personal satisfaction, and much more. Job success is more highly correlated with the number of years of schooling one pursues than any other factor, more even than IQ or achievement level, socioeconomic status, and life stressors. IQ correlations with occupational status indicate that the two share only 20 to 25 percent of attributes in common, leaving much room for other influences such as persistence in school. The more years of education that adults with LD complete, the more satisfied they tend to be with their employment and with life in general, no matter the severity of their learning disability.

As many as 27 percent of individuals with learning disabilities drop out of high school; 63 percent of students with LD earn a "certificate" or high school diplomas. Only 58 percent of graduates with LD continue some form of education after high school, compared with 72 percent of the general population. In the general population, 62 percent of high school graduates go on to college; but only 28 percent of graduates with LD follow this course. The rest opt for lower level two-year and vocational schools. The high school dropout with LD is employed at about 40 percent lower rates than high school graduates with LD. Dropouts earn about one-third less than graduates. Students with some college experience earn 20 percent more than a high school graduate and 75 percent more once they graduate from college. Those who persist in school learn to "keep on keeping on" and thus develop the skills most valued by employers: dependability, task persistence, and good attitudes. These qualities are much more important to job success than level of academic achievement.

*Job success is more highly correlated with the number of years of schooling one pursues than any other factor.*

*Those who persist in school learn to "keep on keeping on" and thus develop the skills most valued by employers: dependability, task persistence, and good attitudes. These qualities are much more important than level of academic achievement to job success.*

Because the high school diploma is fast becoming the minimum requirement for just about any kind of job, it is predicted that high school dropouts will soon be 60 percent less likely to be employed than graduates. Unskilled work opportunities now constitute only 5 percent of jobs, and success on skilled jobs, whether blue or white collar, depends in part on quite sophisticated reading, comprehension, and computation abilities.

It's understandable that many young adults with learning disabilities, especially those who were hyperactive, severely language or reading disabled, or more seriously involved neurologically, end up in lower-level jobs than would be expected from their intelligence and parental occupations. These disabilities limited their academic aspirations, slackened their pace through school, and narrowed vocational options. When compared with nondisabled adults, adults with LD tend to have significantly lower job status. They set their expectations lower than their peers, and are influenced by the doubts of teachers and parents regarding their ability to pursue more challenging careers. In the end many find themselves in entry-level and part-time positions, plagued by frequent job changes and periods of unemployment.

***Adults with LD tend to have significantly lower job aspirations and status than nondisabled adults.***

Many of these adults express disappointment with themselves. They aren't happy with their employment, lack the zeal to achieve, and feel inadequate, guilty, and embarrassed. They often fear that their employer will find out about their disabilities, when in fact employers express the wish that the learning disabled would identify themselves so that they can be informed about what employees with LD need to be successful.

***Barriers to vocational success for adults with LD include untrained vocational counselors and the reading skills and work speed emphasized in vocational training programs, vocational aptitude tests, and job applications.***

Besides their lack of belief in themselves, another continuing barrier remains the fact that vocational training programs, employment bureaus, vocational aptitude tests, and job applications heavily emphasize reading skills and fast work speed, even if these are not skills needed on the job. Added to these obstacles is the relatively small number of educators and vocational counselors familiar with the special needs of adults with learning disabilities. Nevertheless, opportunities to find jobs that capitalize on the strengths of adults with LD are increasing. This is due to high school transition planning that begins at age 14, transition programs that begin at age 16 and can last through age 21, increased postsecondary educational options and government-funded vocational education programs, and fewer employment barriers for the disabled. It is also true that discrimination in the employment of individuals with disabilities who are otherwise qualified for the job is prohibited by any program receiving federal financial assistance (Section 504, The Rehabilitation Act of 1973; PL 93-112).

The Americans with Disabilities Act of 1990 (ADA) states that employers of more than 15 people are required to provide reasonable accommodations to qualified persons with disabilities. The ADA broadly defines a person with disabilities as someone who has a physical or mental impairment that substantially limits one or more major life activity—this refers to *learning* in the case of the learning disabled—or who may be discriminated against because of a record of such impairment. Employers cannot ask applicants if they have a disability or give tests to screen out people with disabilities. An employer can only ask if an applicant needs accommodations to meet job requirements. Those accommodations cannot impose an undue hardship on the employer. Examples of reasonable accommodations include use of a spell-checker, editing help on written work, taped instructions, a nondistracting work area, and allowing for frequent breaks, all of which could be of assistance to people with learning disabilities.

Despite the ADA, there is the real issue of employer bias against hiring the learning disabled. For this reason it is unusual for applicants with LD to disclose their disability. In making this choice, they also choose to forego the accommodations that might have promoted success at a job. Without disclosure, difficulties encountered at the interview or on the job may be misinterpreted as laziness, incompetence, or worse. Certainly, much work remains to be done in the public sensitivity arena so that the learning disabled don't fear asking for what they need.

*Much work remains to be done in the public sensitivity arena so that the learning disabled don't fear asking for accomodations on the job.*

Now that the school age student with LD is better understood, it is important for the field of learning disabilities to increase attention to the adults with LD who need help. To maximize adult vocational success, there is a need for a much earlier and more intense emphasis on vocational preparation at the secondary level, including apprenticeships and work-study programs. Curriculum modifications that encourage students to pursue their passions, foster areas of talent, and support high school graduation and aspirations for postsecondary education are critical.

Much more work also needs to be done after the high school years to help adults make a successful transition to work life, including greater opportunities for job coaching, and establishing transition work settings where supervision is intensified. These interventions are important because research shows that adults who become vocationally successful in early adulthood are likely to continue to meet with success throughout their lives. An important component of this success that can't be ignored is very prescribed support at the high school and adult levels for the self-concept, motivation, self-awareness, self-advocacy, independence, and responsibility of the learning disabled, all of which are essential for more favorable vocational forecasts.

*Apprenticeships, work-study programs, coaching, and supervised work settings assist in the transition to work life; adults who become vocationally successful in early adulthood are likely to continue to meet with success throughout life.*

## Social-Emotional Adjustment

The correlation between intellectual ability and adult everyday life performance and satisfaction is no more than about 20 percent. Far more important are such qualities as ambition, integrity, leadership, responsibility, dependability, extraversion, willingness to try hard, emotional stability, sensitivity, and knowing how to ask for and use help. One expert summarizes all these "ego strength" qualities needed by the learning disabled in one word—"guts."

Unfortunately, many adults with learning disabilities are particularly handicapped in the emotional-social realm. Like the adolescent with similar deficits, these adults have trouble interpreting the emotions, attitudes, and intentions that others communicate through language, facial expression, or body posture. Thus, they tend to respond inappropriately—even to expressions of affection or approval—and risk rejection by others. This in turn leads to feelings of insecurity and low self-worth. As a result, the adult is less able to call on positive emotional strengths to support continued education, to become vocationally successful, to live independently, and to have meaningful leisure time activities.

Follow-up studies of children with learning disabilities find that nearly half have social-emotional difficulties and loneliness that persist into adulthood. The more severe the childhood adjustment difficulties, emotional instability, and poor frustration tolerance were, the more likely that social and emotional problems will persist. It is not unusual for adults with LD to report continued trouble with controlling tempers, dealing with frustration, dependence, social isolation, loneliness, depression, extreme shyness, organizational skills, and dealing with finances.

*Nearly 50 percent of children with LD have social-emotional difficulties and loneliness that persist into adulthood.*

They report being worried and unhappy a good deal of the time. Involvement in recreational activities and social organizations are limited in part because there is little time left after the strain of needing to take more time to accomplish work and daily living tasks. These adults tend to be less satisfied with contacts with relatives, use more prescription drugs, and have fewer plans for future education and vocational training. Many have trouble breaking away from home, and over half still live with their parents into their late twenties. In time, over three-quarters do move out and live independently.

Even if many of the individual's learning delays have been resolved by adulthood, the residuals of the earlier emotional pressures may still create personality abnormalities, and disrupt a marriage and family. A study conducted by the Learning Disabilities Association of America found that despite the fact that nearly half the adults surveyed were unemployed and many of those who did have jobs were not satisfied with their work, the respondents ranked social relationships as the area in which they most needed assistance.

Follow-up studies of children who had been hyperactive are similar, showing that, as adults, one-third to one-half continue to underachieve, be socially and emotionally immature, have poor self-esteem, be restless and impulsive, nervous and quick-tempered, and have trouble paying attention. Hyperactive young adults tend to be less successful than their peers and family members; they have more job changes, greater debt, more residential moves, problems with aggression, more car accidents, more suicide attempts and psychiatric symptoms, and a generally more impulsive lifestyle. The lower the socioeconomic status of these adults and the more troubled their families had been, the higher is the involvement with police and drugs. Most studies find that having taken stimulant medication in childhood is unrelated to adult drug or alcohol abuse, long-term academic and work achievement, and antisocial and personality disorders.

Adults' stories of their journeys as learning disabled individuals are telling. They drive home the need for great empathy and sensitivity on our part because most individuals with LD have had a much more difficult life course emotionally. Richard Devine, a talented goldsmith and college graduate who can barely read, has this to say of the emotional toll:

> I have experienced first-hand the anguish, anger, despair and utter frustration of the inarticulate child who cannot tell the literate person that literacy is not the only level on which he exists; that he is a whole person with many ways of giving and receiving information other than by reading and writing; and that the social environment's demand for functional literacy tends to overshadow all the other potentials an individual may possess. . . . Functional literacy is not the only measure of an individual and never was. My argument is with the world of education which tends sometimes to forget the relative narrowness of its focus and thereby does many of us a grave disservice. . . . It is possible to achieve a successful, fulfilling life even without the ability to read. . . . The educational system could deal with the dyslexic child by working with the strengths and talents of that individual child instead of concentrating on his or her inability to read and thus destroying the child's faith in him/herself. [I] successfully completed high school and obtained a college degree even though [I am] functionally illiterate. [I] learned with [my] heart, my hands, my mind, and my will,

## Sarah and Marc

*Law students whose differences in self-esteem affect their life decisions.*

Sarah never read until she was 11 years old. Her one and only dream in life was to become a lawyer. But she almost did not make it to law school because her self-concept was so poor that she could not admit to others that she was learning disabled.

Sarah had taken the academic route of the intellectual, hoping that her bank of facts would prove her worth and intelligence and see her through any social encounters. She seldom dated, had few friends, and felt comfortable only among adults with whom she was assured of no ridicule or rebuffs. Sarah never asked for help in college and made it through with a low B average. Her law boards too were only average. Although she was exceptionally bright in verbal conceptual abilities, she was hampered on all tests and assignments by a very slow reading speed and spelling and handwriting no better than a seventh grader's. Because of her overanalytic, detail-bound conceptual style, she often missed the main themes and could not organize major, relative to minor, points. She always depersonalized conversations and turned them into intellectual, political discussions. For example, when asked to write an essay about how the saying "no man is an island" applied to her life, Sarah wrote about Locke's philosophy of a state.

At Sarah's law school interview, she was told in no uncertain terms that she was too dumb to either apply to law school or become a lawyer. Her college grades and law boards were given as examples. When Sarah then explained her learning disability, no one believed her—it had been a secret for too long. To counter the law school's rejection, Sarah's parents begged her to ask for recommendations from all the politicians and lawyers with whom she had interned over the years. They had all evaluated her contributions highly, in spite of her weaknesses. Sarah was afraid to ask them for recommendations, feeling that she would lose the esteem of the few people who made her feel competent. She decided not to pursue law school any further. She would give up her dream because she could risk no more deprecation.

Sarah's parents finally prevailed on her to consider her future before her pride. She confided in her former employers. She found that they had known all along that something was wrong with her; she had required more tutelage in her apprenticeships than had any of her predecessors. Nevertheless, her dedication was outstanding, and her work showed progress. Therefore, they wrote Sarah her recommendations and she was admitted to law school. She also began intense reading, spelling, and written language remediation.

Unlike Sarah, Marc, who had a very similar learning disability, learned early in life that others would always note his weaknesses. There was no escaping it, so he made no attempt to hide his disability. He conferenced with college professors before beginning each course; he worked out compensatory exam writing and grading systems. He did not leave anything to chance. When he wrote an exam, he sprawled in big letters at the top: "Dr. _______, please remember that I am a dyslexic. You agreed to grade me as follows. . . . If you have any questions please contact me at . . ." Well Marc, like Sarah, got Bs, but he was a personality-plus person. In his junior year of college he was elected president of the Student Senate. He was admitted to law school and negotiated for extended time for briefs, oral exams, and a four- instead of three-year schedule. He even made Law Review. Today Marc is a successful lawyer. He says he would "die" without the spellchecker on his computer. Marc feels like a valued individual in spite of his continuing disabilities, and he never hesitates to ask for help. Sarah is just finishing law school. She does not plan to venture out on her own. She has a place waiting for her in her father's law firm.

> and not through literacy. . . . everyone has skills and talents, even if they are not those which our society and its educational machinery traditionally values. . . . There is a person inside the person the school and society is trying to teach. We must learn to respect and re-value that person. It is only because the system's view of literacy is so inflexible that dyslexia is regarded as a "learning disability" at all. What an incredibly narrow view of learning this is, and what an incredibly limiting view of the human potential! (Devine & Rose, 1981)

Sarah and Marc's stories (page 297), though both made it through law school, are interesting because they present contrasting views of a lifetime of learning disability. The difference between Sarah and Marc is directly related to their feelings of self-worth—not their intellectual or academic competency levels. Their stories as well as Joe's drive home the point that it is incumbent on educators to do all they can to support the emotional and social development of individuals with LD so that they enter adulthood not only with the attitude that they can accomplish anything they set their minds to, but also with the remarkable resilience, coping skills, and unique panache that led to the triumphs of other adults whose stories you have read throughout this book.

Fortunately, federal, state, and local nonprofit programs that help young adults make the transition to independent living are increasing. These include supervision and counseling in group homes or special apartment complexes that help the adult with LD learn how to take responsibility for daily living needs such as cooking, cleaning, and shopping; leisure time activities such as clubs or sports; and developing a social network. These programs reinforce important habits such as punctuality, respect for property, following rules, and grooming; they also help the young adult set appropriate personal and social goals. In addition, high school special educators increasingly are assuming the role of transition specialists, actively developing interagency relationships that can facilitate the adjustment of graduates with LD.

***Social and emotional adjustment, more so than the learning disability itself, means the difference between success or failure in postsecondary education, on the job, and in managing the important personal, family, and community responsibilities of adulthood.***

The importance of social-emotional concerns in making the transition to adulthood is drawing more attention and intervention efforts. Often these attributes, more so than the learning disability itself, mean the difference between success or failure in postsecondary education, on the job, and in managing the important personal, family, and community responsibilities of adulthood. Not only can the personality and behavior styles of adults with LD make the difference between success and failure in life, they can influence another generation as these adults pass on a healthy outlook and appropriate habits to their own children.

## Summary

The uneven academic development of the school-age child often is accompanied by uneven development in social and emotional areas as well. Precursors to later social and emotional adjustment difficulties are apparent as early as the preschool years, when some children's difficult temperaments, inattention, and high activity levels require the moderating influence of very patient, structured, and understanding parenting. By the elementary school years, the uneven development of many children with LD, together with their disappointment in not living up to their own, their parents', or their schools' expectations, frequently results in poor self-esteem, poor motivation, unhappiness, and limited friendships. When these students constantly fail, are perceived negatively by others, are awkward in social relationships, and give up, their chances for successful life adjustment are diminished. Parents and teachers must help these children to become more conversationally appropriate, more socially insightful, and more trusting that effort is likely to lead to success. This involves maximizing opportunities for social learning and positive personal-social adjustment, offering social skills training programs, encouraging talents, modifying grading systems, developing cooperative learning systems, using extrinsic motivators where necessary, and encouraging intrinsic motivation.

Many students with learning disabilities have personal, family, and school resources that help support their self-esteem and motivation. But others do not, and the social and emotional problems of the elementary school years only compound themselves in adolescence. How these adolescents feel about themselves and relate to others colors not only their academic performance and interpersonal interactions but also their potential for personal and vocational satisfaction. Given the link between LD and juvenile delinquency in some students, continued efforts must be made to implement effective prevention and treatment programs. Developing the social repertoires of adolescents with LD is critical so that they will avoid delinquency; adjust favorably to adult work, family, and social situations; and not find themselves treated differentially by employers, peers, and authorities.

*Learning disabilities last a lifetime. But with good schooling, motivation, intelligence, and family support, adults with LD can succeed in employee, family, and friendship roles.*

Learning disabilities last a lifetime. Many of these adults, because of excellent schooling, motivation, intelligence, and family support, succeed very well in employee, spouse, parent, and friendship roles. For others, however, despite substantial gains, the residuals of the learning disability are still apparent in less than optimal adult vocational, social, and independent living adjustment. Because of increasing attention to social and emotional concomitants of LD during the school years, as well as a fuller range of postsecondary educational, independent living, career planning, and vocational opportunities, there is growing optimism that these individuals in the future may more successfully meet life's challenges as adults.

## Helpful Resources

### The Preschooler

Als, H. (1985). Patterns of infant behavior: Analogues of later organizational difficulties? In F. H. Duffy & N. Geschwind (Eds.), *Dyslexia: A neuroscientific approach to clinical evaluation.* Boston: Little, Brown.

Berk, L. E. (2002). *Child development* (6th ed). Boston: Allyn & Bacon.

Erikson, E. H. (1963). *Childhood and society.* New York: W. W. Norton.

Hartup, W. W. (1989). Social relationships and their developmental significance. *American Psychologist, 44,* 120–126.

Hartup, W. W., Laursen, B., Stewart, M. I., & Eastenson, A. (1988). Conflict and the friendship relations of young children. *Child Development, 59,* 1590–1600.

Keogh, B. K., & Burstein, N. D. (1988). Relationship of temperament to preschoolers' interactions with peers and teachers. *Exceptional Children, 54*, 456–461.

Lee, C. L., & Bates, J. E. (1985). Mother-child interaction at age 2 years and perceived difficult temperament. *Child Development, 56*, 1314–1325.

Margalit, M. (1998). Loneliness and coherence among preschool children with learning disabilities. *Journal of Learning Disabilities, 31*, 173–180.

Martin, R. P., Drew, K. D., Gaddis, L. R., & Moseley, M. (1988). Prediction of elementary school achievement from preschool temperament: Three studies. *School Psychology Review, 17*, 125–137.

Matheny, A. P., Jr., Wilson, R. S., & Nuss, S. M. (1984). Toddler temperament: Stability across settings and over ages. *Child Development, 55*, 1200–1211.

Odom, S. L., McConnell, S. R., & McEvoy, M. A. (1992). *Social competence of young children with disabilities: Issues and strategies for intervention*. Baltimore: Paul H. Brookes.

Perlmutter, B. F. (1986). Personality variables and peer relations of children and adolescents with learning disabilities. In S. J. Ceci (Ed.), *Handbook of cognitive, social, and neuropsychological aspects of learning disabilities* (Vol. 1). Hillsdale, NJ: Lawrence Erlbaum.

Sroufe, L. A., & Fleeson, J. (1986). Attachment and the construction of relationships. In W. W. Hartup & Z. Rubin (Eds.), *Relationships and development*. Hillsdale, NJ: Lawrence Erlbaum.

Thomas, A., & Chess, S. (1977). *Temperament and development*. New York: Brunner/Mazel.

Zahn-Waxler, C., Radke-Yarrow, M., Wagner, E., & Chapman, M. (1992). Development of concern for others. *Developmental Psychology, 28*, 126–136.

## The Elementary School Student

Adelman, H. S., & Chaney, L. A. (1982). Impact of motivation on task performance of children with and without psychoeducational problems. *Journal of Learning Disabilities, 15*, 242–244.

Bear, G. G., Juvonen, J., & McInerney, F. (1993). Self-perceptions and peer relations of boys with and boys without learning disabilities in an integrated setting: A longitudinal study. *Learning Disability Quarterly, 16*, 127–136.

Bear, G. G., & Minke, K. M. (1996). Positive bias in maintenance of self-worth among children with LD. *Learning Disability Quarterly, 19*, 23–32.

Borkowski, J. G., Weyhing, R. S., & Turner, L. A. (1986). Attributional retraining and the teaching of strategies. *Exceptional Children, 53*, 130–137.

Boucher, C. R. (1986). Pragmatics: The meaning of verbal language in learning disabled and nondisabled boys. *Learning Disability Quarterly, 9*, 285–294.

Brophy, J. (1981). Teacher praise: A functional analysis. *Review of Educational Research, 51*, 5–32.

Bruck, M., & Hébert, M. (1982). Correlates of learning disabled students' peer-interaction patterns. *Learning Disability Quarterly, 5*, 353–362.

Bruininks, V. L. (1978). Actual and perceived peer status of learning disabled students in mainstream programs. *Journal of Special Education, 12*, 51–58.

Bryan, J. H., Sonnefeld, L. J., & Grabowski, B. (1983). The relationship between fear of failure and learning disabilities. *Learning Disability Quarterly, 6*, 217–222.

Bryan, T. (1978). Social relationships and verbal interactions of learning disabled children. *Journal of Learning Disabilities, 11*, 107–115.

Bryan, T. (1986). Personality and situational factors in learning disabilities. In G. Th. Pavlidis & D. F. Fisher (Eds.), *Dyslexia: Its neurology and treatment*. New York: John Wiley.

Bursuck, W., Polloway, E. A., Plante, L., Epstein, M. H., Jayanthi, M., & McConeghy, J. (1996). Report and grading and adaptations: A national survey of classroom practices. *Exceptional Children, 62*, 301–318.

Bursuck, W. D. (1989). A comparison of students with learning disabilities to low achieving and higher achieving students on three dimensions of social competence. *Journal of Learning Disabilities, 22*, 188–194.

Carlson, C. L. (1987). Social interaction goals and strategies of children with learning disabilities. *Journal of Learning Disabilities, 20*, 306–311.

Carlson, C. L., & Tamm, L. (2000). Responsiveness of children with attention-deficit/hyperactivity disorder to reward and response cost: Differential impact on performance and motivation. *Journal of Consulting and Clinical Psychology, 68*, 73–83.

Cartledge, G., Stupay, D., & Kaczala, C. (1986). Social skills and social perception of LD and nonhandicapped elementary-school students. *Learning Disability Quarterly, 9*, 226–234.

Chapman, R. B., Larsen, S. C., & Parker, R. M. (1979). Interactions of first-grade teachers with learning disordered children. *Journal of Learning Disabilities, 12*, 225-230.

Coleman, J. M., & Minnett, A. M. (1993). Learning disabilities and social competence: A social ecological perspective. *Exceptional Children, 59*, 234–246.

Cooley, E. J., & Ayres, R. R. (1988). Self-concept and success-failure attributions of nonhandicapped students and students with learning disabilities. *Journal of Learning Disabilities, 21*, 174–178.

Deci, E. L., Hodges, R., Pierson, L., & Tomassone, J. (1992). Autonomy and competence as motivational factors in students with learning disabilities and emotional handicaps. *Journal of Learning Disabilities, 25*, 457–471.

Dimitrovsky, L., Spector, H., Levy-Shiff, R., & Vaki, E. (1998). Interpretation of facial expressions of affect in children with learning disabilities with verbal or nonverbal deficits. *Journal of Learning Disabilities, 31*, 286–292, 312.

Doll, B. (1996). Children without friends: Implications for practice and policy. *School Psychology Review, 25*, 165–183.

Donahoe, K., & Zigmond, N. (1990). Academic grades of ninth-grade urban learning-disabled students and low-achieving peers. *Exceptionality, 1*, 17–27.

Donahue, M. (1986). Linguistic and communicative development in learning-disabled children. In S. J. Ceci (Ed.), *Handbook of cognitive, social, and neuropsychological aspects of learning disabilities* (Vol. 1). Hillsdale, NJ: Lawrence Erlbaum.

Dorval, B., McKinney, J. D., & Feagans, L. (1982). Teacher interaction with learning disabled children and average achievers. *Journal of Pediatric Psychology, 7*, 317–330.

Douglas, V. I., & Parry, P. A. (1983). Effects of reward on delayed reaction time task performance of hyperactive children. *Journal of Abnormal Child Psychology, 11*, 313–326.

Durrant, J. E. (1993). Attributions for achievement outcomes among behavioral subgroups of children with learning disabilities. *The Journal of Special Education, 27*, 306–320.

Dweck, C. S. (1975). The role of expectations and attributions in the alleviation of learned helplessness. *Journal of Personality and Social Psychology, 31*, 674–685.

Dweck, C. S., & Leggett, E. L. (1988). A social-cognitive approach to motivation and personality. *Psychological Review, 95*, 256–273.

Epstein, M. H., Cullinan, D., & Nieminen, G. (1984). Social behavior problems of learning disabled and normal girls. *Journal of Learning Disabilities, 17*, 609–611.

Farmer, T. W., & Farmer, E. M. Z. (1996). Social relationships of students with exceptionalities in mainstream classrooms: Social networks and homophily. *Exceptional Children, 62*, 431–450.

Fisher, B. L., Allen, R., & Kose, G. (1996). The relationship between anxiety and problem-solving skills in children with and without learning disabilities. *Journal of Learning Disabilities, 29*, 439–446.

Flavell, J. H., Botkin, P. T., Fry, C. L., Wright, J. W., & Jarvis, P. E. (1968). *The development of role-taking and communication skills in childhood.* New York: John Wiley & Sons.

Flynn, J. R. (1991). *Asian Americans: Achievement beyond IQ.* Hillsdale, NJ: Erlbaum.

Fuerst, D. R., Fisk, J. L., & Rourke, B. P. (1989). Psychosocial functioning of learning-disabled children: Replicability of statistically derived subtypes. *Journal of Consulting and Clinical Psychology, 57*, 275–280.

George, T. P., & Hartmann, D. P. (1996). Friendship networks of unpopular, average, and popular children. *Child Development, 67*, 2301–2316.

Gerber, P. J., & Zinkgraf, S. A. (1982). A comparative study of social-perceptual ability in learning disabled and nonhandicapped students. *Learning Disability Quarterly, 5*, 374–378.

Gottlieb, B. W., Gottlieb, J., Berkell, D., & Levy, L. (1986). Sociometric status and solitary play of LD boys and girls. *Journal of Learning Disabilities, 19*, 619–622.

Gresham, F. M., & Reschly, D. J. (1986). Social skill deficits and low peer acceptance of mainstreamed learning disabled children. *Learning Disability Quarterly, 9*, 23–32.

Gross-Tsur, V., Shalev, R. S., Manor, O., & Amir, N. (1995). Developmental right-hemisphere syndrome: Clinical spectrum of the nonverbal learning disability. *Journal of Learning Disabilities, 28*, 80–86.

Haager, D., & Vaughn, S. (1995). Parent, teacher, peer, and self-reports of the social competence of students with learning disabilities. *Journal of Learning Disabilities, 28*, 205–215, 231.

Hallahan, D. P., Tarver, S. G., Kauffman, J. M., & Graybeal, N. L. (1978). A comparison of the effect of reinforcement and response cost on the selective attention of learning disabled children. *Journal of Learning Disabilities, 11*, 430–438.

Halmhuber, N. L., & Paris, S. G. (1993). Perceptions of competence and control and the use of coping strategies by children with disabilities. *Learning Disability Quarterly, 16*, 93–111.

Harnadek, M. C. S., & Rourke, B. P. (1994). Principal identifying features of the syndrome of nonverbal learning disabilities in children. *Journal of Learning Disabilities, 27*, 144–154.

Hartup, W. W. (1996). The company they keep: Friendships and their developmental significance. *Child Development, 67*, 1–13.

Horowitz, E. C. (1981). Popularity, decentering ability, and role-taking skills in learning disabled and normal children. *Learning Disability Quarterly, 4 (1)*, 23–30.

Hoyle, S. G., & Serafica, F. C. (1988). Peer status of children with and without learning disabilities—A multimethod study. *Learning Disability Quarterly, 11,* 322–332.

Kavale, K. A., & Forness, S. R. (1996). Social skill deficits and learning disabilities: A meta-analysis. *Journal of Learning Disabilities, 29,* 226–237.

Keogh, B. K. (1982). Children's temperament and teachers' decisions. In R. Porter & G. M. Collins (Eds.), *Temperamental differences in infants and young children* (CIBA Foundation Symposium 89). London: Pitman.

Kershner, J. R. (1990). Self-concept and IQ as predictors of remedial success in children with learning disabilities. *Journal of Learning Disabilities, 23,* 368–374.

Lewis, S. K., & Lawrence-Patterson, E. (1989). Locus of control of children with learning disabilities and perceived locus of control by significant others. *Journal of Learning Disabilities, 22,* 255–257.

Licht, B. G., Kistner, J. A., Ozkaragoz, T., Shapiro, S., & Clausen, L. (1985). Causal attributions of learning disabled children: Individual differences and their implications for persistence. *Journal of Educational Psychology, 77,* 208–216.

Kloomok, S., & Cosden, M. (1994). Self-concept in children with learning disabilities: The relationship between global self-concept, academic "discounting," nonacademic self-concept, and perceived social support. *Learning Disability Quarterly, 17,* 140–153.

Knight-Arest, I. (1984). Communicative effectiveness of learning disabled and normally achieving 10- to 13-year-old boys. *Learning Disability Quarterly, 7,* 237–245.

LaGreca, A. M., & Stone, W. L. (1990). LD status and achievement: Confounding variables in the study of children's social status, self-esteem, and behavioral functioning. *Journal of Learning Disabilities, 23,* 483–490.

Markoski, B. D. (1983). Conversational interactions of the learning disabled and nondisabled child. *Journal of Learning Disabilities, 16,* 606–609.

Mathinos, D. A. (1988). Communicative competence of children with learning disabilities. *Journal of Learning Disabilities, 21,* 437–443.

Mevarech, Z. R. (1985). The relationships between temperament characteristics, intelligence, task-engagement, and mathematics achievement. *British Journal of Educational Psychology, 55,* 156–163.

Michaels, C. R., & Lewandowski, L. J. (1990). Psychological adjustment and family functioning of boys with learning disabilities. *Journal of Learning Disabilities, 23,* 446–450.

Nabuzoka, D., & Smith, P. K. (1995). Identification of expressions of emotions by children with and without learning disabilities. *Learning Disabilities Research & Practice, 10,* 91–101.

Olsen, J. L., Wong, B. Y. L., & Marx, R. W. (1983). Linguistic and metacognitive aspects of normally achieving and learning disabled children's communication process. *Learning Disability Quarterly, 6,* 289–304.

Owen, F. W., Adams, P. A., Forrest, T., Stolz, L. M., & Fisher, S. (1971). Learning disorders in children: Sibling studies. *Monographs of the Society for Research in Child Development, 36* (4, Serial No. 144).

Parker, J. G., & Asher, S. R. (1987). Peer relations and later personal adjustment: Are low-accepted children at risk? *Psychological Bulletin, 102,* 357–389.

Pearl, R. (1982). LD children's attributions for success and failure: A replication with a labeled LD sample. *Learning Disability Quarterly, 5,* 173–176.

Pearl, R., & Bryan, T. (1982). Mothers' attributions for their learning disabled child's successes and failures. *Learning Disability Quarterly, 5*(1), 53–57.

Perlmutter, B. F., & Bryan, J. H. (1984). First impressions, ingratiation, and the learning disabled child. *Journal of Learning Disabilities, 17,* 157–161.

Pickering, E., Pickering, A., & Buchanan, M. L. (1987). LD and nonhandicapped boys' comprehension of cartoon humor. *Learning Disability Quarterly, 10,* 45–51.

Polloway, E. A., Epstein, M. H., Bursuck, W. D., Roderique, T. W., McConeghy, J. L., & Jayanthi, M. (1994). Classroom grading: A national survey of policies. *Remedial and Special Education, 15,* 162–170.

Pullis, M., & Cadwell, J. (1982). The influence of children's temperament characteristics on teachers' decision strategies. *American Educational Research Journal, 19,* 165–181.

Sabornie, E. J., Marshall, K. J., & Ellis, E. S. (1990). Restructuring of mainstream sociometry with learning disabled and nonhandicapped students. *Exceptional Children, 56,* 314–323.

Salend, S. (1998). Using portfolios to assess student performance. *Teaching Exceptional Children, 31,* 36–43.

Sainato, D. M., Zigmond, N., & Strain, P. S. (1983). Social status and initiations of interaction by learning disabled students in a regular education setting. *Analysis and Intervention in Developmental Disabilities, 3,* 71–87.

Sale, P., & Carey, D. M. (1995). The sociometric status of students with disabilities in a full-inclusion school. *Exceptional Children, 62,* 6–19.

Schunk, D. H., & Cox, P. D. (1986). Strategy training and attributional feedback with learning disabled students. *Journal of Educational Psychology, 78,* 201–209.

Shondrick, D. D., Serafica, F. C., Clark, P., & Miller, K. G. (1992). Interpersonal problem solving and creativity in boys with and boys without learning disabilities. *Learning Disability Quarterly, 15*, 95–102.

Siperstein, G. N., & Goding, M. J. (1985). Teachers' behavior toward LD and non-LD children: A strategy for change. *Journal of Learning Disabilities, 18*, 139–144.

Smith, D. S., & Nagle, R. J. (1995). Self-perceptions and social comparisons among children with learning disabilities. *Journal of Learning Disabilities, 28*, 364–371.

Stiliadis, K., & Wiener, J. (1989). Relationship between social perception and peer status in children with learning disabilities. *Journal of Learning Disabilities, 22*, 624–629.

Stone, W. L., & LaGreca, A. M. (1990). The social status of children with learning disabilities: A reexamination. *Journal of Learning Disabilities, 23*, 32–37.

Thorne, B. (1986). Girls and boys together . . . but mostly apart: Gender arrangements in elementary schools. In W. W. Hartup & Z. Rubin (Eds.), *Relationships and development.* Hillsdale, NJ: Erlbaum.

Vallance, D. D., Cummings, R. L., & Humphries, T. (1998). Mediators of the risk for problem behavior in children with language learning disabilities. *Journal of Learning Disabilities, 31*, 160–171.

Vaughn, S., & Haager, D. (1994). Social competence as a multifaceted construct: How do students with learning disabilities fare? *Learning Disability Quarterly, 17*, 253–266.

Wright-Strawderman, C., & Watson, B. L. (1992). The prevalence of depressive symptoms in children with learning disabilities. *Journal of Learning Disabilities, 25*, 258–264.

## The Secondary School Student

Aponik, D. A., & Dembo, M. H. (1983). LD and normal adolescents' causal attributions of success and failure at different levels of task difficulty. *Learning Disability Quarterly, 6*, 31–39.

Arnett, J. J. (1999). Adolescent storm and stress, reconsidered. *American Psychologist, 54*, 317–326.

Bender, W. N. (1987). Secondary personality and behavioral problems in adolescents with learning disabilities. *Journal of Learning Disabilities, 20*, 280–285.

Bender, W. N., & Smith, J. F. (1990). Classroom behavior of children and adolescents with learning disabilities: A meta-analysis. *Journal of Learning Disabilities, 23*, 298–305.

Brier, N. (1994). Targeted treatment for adjudicated youth with learning disabilities: Effects on recidivism. *Journal of Learning Disabilities, 27*, 215–222.

Bryan, T., Pearl, R., & Fallon, P. (1989). Conformity to peer pressure by students with learning disabilities: A replication. *Journal of Learning Disabilities, 22*, 458–459.

Bryan, T., Pearl, R., & Herzog, A. (1989). Learning disabled adolescents' vulnerability to crime: Attitudes, anxieties, experiences. *Learning Disability Quarterly, 5*, 51–60.

Conderman, G. (1995). Social-status of sixth- and seventh-grade students with learning disabilities. *Learning Disability Quarterly, 18*, 13–24.

Dalley, M. B., Bolocofsky, D. N., Alcorn, M. B., & Baker, C. (1992). Depressive symptomatology, attributional style, dysfunctional attitude, and social competency in adolescents with and without learning disabilities. *School Psychology Review, 21*, 444–458.

Derr, A. M. (1986). How learning disabled adolescent boys make moral judgments. *Journal of Learning Disabilities, 19*, 160–164.

Forness, S. R., & Kavale, K. A. (1996). Treating social skill deficits in children with learning disabilities: A meta-analysis of the research. *Learning Disability Quarterly, 19*, 2–13.

Geisthardt, C., & Munsch, J. (1996). Coping with school stress: A comparison ofadolescents with and without learning disabilities. *Journal of Learning Disabilities, 29*, 287–296.

Gilligan, C. (1982). *In a different voice: Psychological theory and women's development.* Cambridge, MA: Harvard University Press.

Hayden, B., & Pickar, D. (1981). The impact of moral discussions on children's level of moral reasoning. *Journal of Moral Education, 10*(2), 131–134.

Heavey, C. L., Adelman, H. S., Nelson, P., & Smith, D. C. (1989). Learning problems, anger, perceived control, and misbehavior. *Journal of Learning Disabilities, 22*, 46–50, 59.

Hiebert, B., Wong, B., & Hunter, M. (1982). Affective influences on learning disabled adolescents. *Learning Disability Quarterly, 5*, 334–343.

Holder, H. B., & Kirkpatrick, S. W. (1990). Interpretation of emotion from facial expressions in children with and without learning disabilities. *Journal of Learning Disabilities, 24*, 170–177.

Hollander, H. E. (1986). Learning disability among seriously delinquent youths: A perspective. In G. Th. Pavlidis & D. F. Fisher (Eds.), *Dyslexia: Its neuropsychology and treatment.* New York: John Wiley & Sons.

Jackson, S. C., Enright, R. D., & Murdock, J. Y. (1987). Social perception problems in learning disabled youth: Developmental lag versus perceptual deficit. *Journal of Learning Disabilities, 20,* 361–364.

Katims, D. S., Zapata, J. T., & Yin, Z. (1996). Risk factors for substance use by Mexican American youth with and without learning disabilities. *Journal of Learning Disabilities, 29,* 213–219, 212.

Keilitz, I., & Dunivant, N. (1986). The relationship between learning disability and juvenile delinquency. Current state of knowledge. *Remedial and Special Education, 7*(3), 18–26.

Kistner, J., Haskett, M., White, K., & Robbins, F. (1987). Perceived competence and self-worth of LD and normally achieving students. *Learning Disability Quarterly, 10,* 37–44.

Kohlberg, L. (1981). *The philosophy of moral development.* San Francisco: Harper & Row.

Kolb, S. M., & Hanley-Maxwell, C. (2003). Critical social skills for adolescents with high incidence disabilities: Parental perspectives. *Exceptional Children, 69,* 163–179.

Larson, K. A. (1988). A research review and alternative hypothesis explaining the link between learning disability and delinquency. *Journal of Learning Disabilities, 21,* 357–369.

Maag, J. W., & Reid, R. (1994). The phenomenology of depression among students with and without learning disabilities: More similar than different. *Learning Disabilities Research & Practice, 9,* 91–103.

Mannuzza, S., Klein, R. G., Konig, P. H., & Giampino, T. L. (1989). Hyperactive boys almost grown up: IV. Criminality and its relationship to psychiatric status. *Archives of General Psychiatry, 46,* 1073–1079.

Margalit, M., & Shulman, S. (1986). Autonomy perceptions and anxiety expressions of learning disabled adolescents. *Journal of Learning Disabilities, 19,* 291–293.

McConaughy, S. H. (1986). Social competence and behavioral problems of learning disabled boys aged 12–16. *Journal of Learning Disabilities, 19,* 101–106.

Montgomery, M. S. (1994). Self-concept and children with learning disabilities: Observer-child concordance across six context-dependant domains. *Journal of Learning Disabilities, 27,* 254–262.

Parker, J. G., & Asher, S. R. (1993). Friendship and friendship quality in middle childhood: Links with peer group acceptance and feelings of loneliness and social dissatisfaction. *Developmental Psychology, 29,* 611–621.

Pearl, R., & Cosden, M. (1982). Sizing up a situation: LD children's understanding of social interactions. *Learning Disability Quarterly, 5,* 371–373.

Perlmutter, B. F., Crocker, J., Cordray, D., & Garstecki, D. (1983). Sociometric status and related personality characteristics of mainstreamed learning disabled adolescents. *Learning Disability Quarterly, 6,* 20–30.

Phelps, L. A., & Hanley-Maxwell, C. (1997). School-to-work transitions for youth with disabilities: A review of outcomes and practices. *Review of Educational Research, 67,* 197–226.

Porter, J. E., & Rourke, B. P. (1985). Socioemotional functioning of learning-disabled children: A subtypal analysis of personality patterns. In B. P. Rourke (Ed.), *Neuropsychology of learning disabilities.* New York: Guilford Press.

Powers, S. I., Hauser, S. T., & Kilner, L. A. (1989). Adolescent mental health. *American Psychologist, 44,* 200–208.

Raviv, D., & Stone, C. A. (1991). Individual differences in the self-image of adolescents with learning disabilities: The roles of severity, time of diagnosis, and parental perceptions. *Journal of Learning Disabilities, 24,* 602–611, 629.

Ritter, D. R. (1989). Social competence and problem behavior of adolescent girls with learning disabilities. *Journal of Learning Disabilities, 22,* 460–461.

Sabornie, E. J. (1994). Social-affective characteristics in early adolescents identified as learning disabled and nondisabled. *Learning Disability Quarterly, 17,* 268–279.

Sabornie, E. J., & Kauffman, J. M. (1986). Social acceptance of learning disabled adolescents. *Learning Disability Quarterly, 9,* 55–60.

Schumaker, J. B., Wildgen, J. S., & Sherman, J. A. (1982). Social interaction of learning disabled junior high students in their regular classrooms: An observational analysis. *Journal of Learning Disabilities, 15,* 355–358.

Silverman, R., & Zigmond, N. (1983). Self-concept in learning disabled adolescents. *Journal of Learning Disabilities, 16,* 478–482.

Sisterhen, D. H., & Gerber, P. J. (1989). Auditory, visual, and multisensory nonverbal social perception in adolescents with and without learning disabilities. *Journal of Learning Disabilities, 22,* 245–249, 257.

Stallings, J. (1975). Implementation and child effects of teaching practices in follow through classrooms. *Monographs of the Society for Research in Child Development, 40* (Serial No. 163), Nos. 7–8.

Tollefson, N., Tracy, D. B., Johnson, E. P., Buenning, M., Farmer, A., & Barke, C. R. (1982). Attribution patterns of learning disabled adolescents. *Learning Disability Quarterly, 5*(1), 14–20.

Tur-Kaspa, H., & Bryan, T. (1994). Social information-processing skills of students with learning disabilities. *Learning Disabilities Research & Practice, 9,* 12–23.

Vaughn, S., McIntosh, R., Schumm, J. S., Haager, D., & Callwood, D. (1993). Social status, peer acceptance, and reciprocal friendships revisited. *Learning Disabilities Research & Practice, 8,* 82–88.

Waldie, K., & Spreen, O. (1993). The relationship between learning disabilities and persisting delinquency. *Journal of Learning Disabilities, 26,* 417–423.

Walker, L. J. (1989). A longitudinal study of moral reasoning. *Child Development, 60,* 157–166.

National Center on Secondary Education and Transition: http://www.ncset.org

National Information Center for Children and Youth with Disabilities transition information: http://www.nichcy.org

## The Adult

Barrett, G. V., & Depinet, R. L. (1991). A reconsideration of testing for competence rather than for intelligence. *American Psychologist, 46,* 1012–1024.

Blackorby, J., & Wagner, M. (1996). Longitudinal post-school outcomes of youth with disabilities: Findings from the National Longitudinal Transition Study. *Exceptional Children, 62,* 399–413.

Bruck, M. (1985). The adult functioning of children with specific learning disabilities: A follow-up study. In I. E. Siegel (Ed.), *Advances in applied developmental psychology* (Vol. 1). Norwood, NJ: Ablex.

Evers, R. B. (1996). The positive force of vocational education: Transition outcomes for youth with learning disabilities. *Journal of Learning Disabilities, 29,* 69–78.

Gerber, P. J., Ginsberg, R., & Reiff, H. B. (1992). Identifying alterable patterns in employment success for highly successful adults with learning disabilities. *Journal of Learning Disabilities, 25,* 475–487.

Goleman, D. (1995). *Emotional intelligence.* NY: Bantam Books.

Greenbaum, B., Graham, S., & Scales, W. (1996). Adults with learning disabilities: Occupational and social status after college. *Journal of Learning Disabilities, 29,* 167–173.

Kanter, A. S. (1999). Toward equality: The ADA's accommodation of differences. In M. Jones & L. A. Basser Marks (Eds.), *Disability, divers-ability, and legal change* (pp. 227–250). Boston: M. Nijhoff.

Madaus, J. W., Foley, T. E., McGuire, J. M., & Ruban, L. M. (2002). Employment self-disclosure of postsecondary graduates with learning disabilities: Rates and rationales. *Journal of Learning Disabilities, 35,* 364–369.

Mannuzza, S., Klein, R. G., Bessler, A., Malloy, P., & LaPadula, M. (1993). Adult outcome of hyperactive boys: Education achievement, occupational rank, and psychiatric status. *Archives of General Psychiatry, 50,* 565–576.

McClelland, D. C. (1973). Testing for competence rather than for "intelligence." *American Psychologist, 28,* 1–14.

Minskoff, E. H., Sautter, S. W., Hoffman, F. J., & Hawks, R. (1987). Employer attitudes toward hiring the learning disabled. *Journal of Learning Disabilities, 20,* 53–57.

Okolo, C. M., & Sitlington, P. (1986). The role of special education in LD adolescents' transition from school to work. *Learning Disability Quarterly, 9,* 141–155.

Raskind, M. H., Goldberg, R. J., Higgins, E. L., & Herman, K. L. (1999). Patterns of change and predictors of success in individuals with learning disabilities: Results from a twenty-year longitudinal study. *Learning Disabilities Research & Practice, 14,* 35–49.

Rodis, P., Garrod, A., & Boscardin, M. L. (2001). *Learning disabilities & life stories.* Boston: Allyn & Bacon.

Rogan, L. L., & Hartman, L. D. (1990). Adult outcome of learning disabled students ten years after initial follow-up. *Learning Disabilities Focus, 5,* 91–102.

Rojewski, J. W. (1996). Educational and occupational aspirations of high school seniors with learning disabilities. *Exceptional Children, 62,* 463–476.

Sitlington, P. L., & Frank, A. R. (1993). Dropouts with learning disabilities: What happens to them as young adults? *Learning Disabilities Research & Practice, 8,* 244–252.

Sitlington, P. L., Frank, A. R., & Carson, R. (1993). Adult adjustment among high school graduates with mild disabilities. *Exceptional Children, 59,* 221–233.

Spekman, N. J., Goldberg, R. J., & Herman, K. L. (1992). Learning disabled children grow up: A search for factors related to success in the young adult years. *Learning Disabilities Research & Practice, 7,* 161–170.

Vogel, S. A., & Forness, S. R. (1992). Social functioning in adults with learning disabilities. *School Psychology Review, 21,* 375–386.

Vogel, S. A., Hruby, P. J., & Adelman, P. B. (1993). Educational and psychological factors in successful and unsuccessful college students with learning disabilities. *Learning Disabilities Research & Practice, 8,* 35–43.

Weiss, G., & Hechtman, L. (1993). Hyperactive children grown up (2nd ed.): *ADHD in children, adolescents, and adults.* New York: Guilford.

Werner, E. E. (1993). Risk and resilience in individuals with learning disabilities: Lessons learned from the Kauai longitudinal study. *Learning Disabilities Research & Practice, 8,* 28–34.

Zigmond, N., & Thornton, H. (1985). Follow-up of post-secondary-age learning disabled graduates and drop-outs. *Learning Disabilities Research & Practice, 1,* 50–55.

School dropout data, postsecondary education, vocational education, earnings:

Condition of Education: http://www.nces.ed.gov/programs/coe

Digest of Educational Statistics: http://www.nces.ed.gov/pubs2002/digest2001

ERIC Clearing House on Adult, Career, & Vocational Education: www.ericacve.org

Job accommodations Network: http://www.jan.wvu.edu

CHAPTER NINE

# Assessment

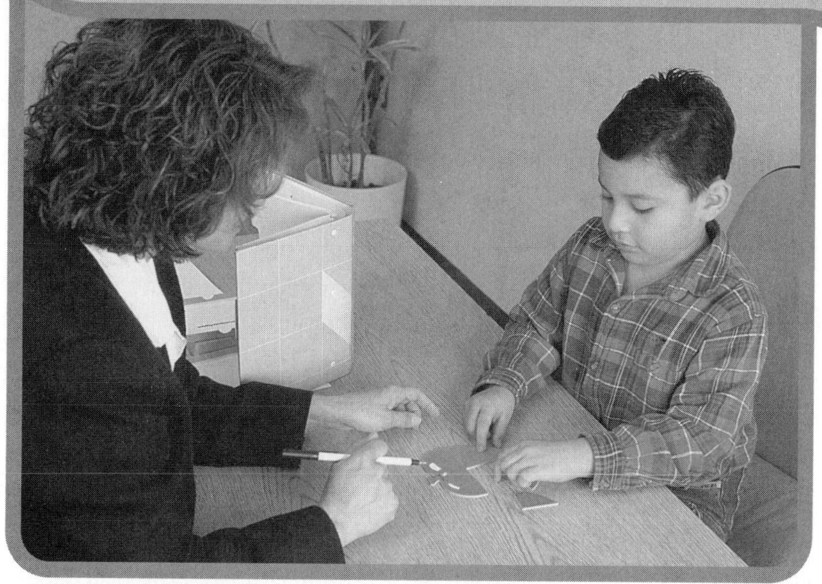

**THE NATURE AND SEVERITY** of any one person's learning disorders depend on the interaction among his or her personal characteristics, the required curriculum, and the expectations and characteristics of the environments in which the individual lives, studies, and plays. Only a multidimensional assessment framework can discover why a student is experiencing learning problems and how the student's strengths and weaknesses can be matched with the curriculum and environments in a way that will promote academic and social growth. The multiple perspectives that must be taken into account, and the technical and conceptual concerns about many of our assessment instruments, make the assessment process anything but simple.

*Assessment* is the process of gathering data to clarify students' strengths and weaknesses and to make decisions that will facilitate their educational and psychological growth. Assessment is not simply testing; testing is just one part of the process. Many other means of data collection are involved:

*Assessment is the process of gathering data to clarify students' strengths and weaknesses and to make decisions that will facilitate their educational and psychological growth.*

- Observing the student's interactions with parents, teachers, and peers
- Interviewing the student and significant others
- Examining school records and past evaluation results
- Evaluating medical and developmental histories
- Using information from checklists completed by parents, teachers, or the student

*Assessment is not simply testing.*

- Evaluating curriculum requirements and alternative options
- Evaluating the student's style and rate of learning during trial teaching
- Task-analyzing the curriculum to identify which objectives have been mastered and those that still need to be mastered
- Collecting data on peer acceptance, classroom climate, classroom teaching practices, and teacher attitudes toward the student with learning disabilities

The specific methods chosen will depend on the purpose of assessment, the assessment model followed by the evaluation team, and the specific domains of concern.

## Assessment Purposes

*Common reasons for assessment include referral, screening, identification, instructional planning, and assessing pupil progress.*

The particular purpose for assessment dictates which techniques we can use to achieve the best results. The most common reasons for assessment are referral, screening, identification, instructional planning, and assessing pupil progress. We also use assessment to develop and evaluate new assessment and intervention strategies and to conduct research that sheds new light on the characteristics and intervention needs of the learning disabled.

### Referral

Each year teachers refer 3 to 5 percent of their pupils for psychological and educational assessment. When pupils are referred for suspected reading and learning disabilities, from one-half to three-quarters ultimately are identified as requiring special education. Often as many as five different professionals are involved in the testing, which accounts for over 40 percent of the cost of educating a student with disabilities.

*Teacher assistance teams made up of experienced general and special education teachers consult with the classroom teacher prior to special education referral to suggest interventions.*

Unfortunately, the assessment process itself consumes a significant amount of time that could have been devoted to teaching these students. To address this concern, many schools have developed *prereferral* or *teacher assistance teams* made up of experienced general and special education teachers and other specialists. Team members consult with the classroom teacher on a student's difficulties, observe in the classroom, gather informal data related to the problems, hypothesize about the origins of these problems, and suggest interventions. The team's goal is to act preventively to circumvent the development of academic and behavioral problems. The team defers a decision on whether to recommend more in-depth assessment until the recommended program modifications have been implemented and their effectiveness evaluated. Essentially, the teacher takes on an action research role and systematically experiments with various intervention approaches. Currently 22 states require these instructional support teams, and 15 more recommend that they be established.

The success of teacher assistance teams has reduced referral rates for actual testing and the numbers of students ultimately identified as having LD. They have also increased the accuracy of referrals since a greater percentage of the smaller group eventually referred for evaluation does get identified as having LD and needing special education services. The success of teacher assistance teams suggests that regular classroom teachers are capable of personalizing the learning environment for students with LD so that fewer of them enter the referral process. The more constructive that regular classroom environments become, the more that special education can be reserved for those who really need it. It is for this reason that the very first step in assessment is to consult with the teacher regarding how the curriculum and setting can be adapted to better meet the needs of a student who is struggling.

***The first step in assessment is to consult with the teacher regarding how the curriculum and setting can be adapted to better meet the needs of the student who is struggling.***

## Screening

Screening is used to identify students who lag sufficiently behind their peers to warrant additional instruction or assessment. Screening usually uses norm-referenced tests administered to groups of students. *Norm-referenced tests* compare an individual with others of the same age who share similar sociocultural and experiential backgrounds. Screening tests might show that Rosa, for example, has learned less than expected for her age, grade, and years of schooling. Further assessment might be recommended to determine the factors that are contributing to her underachievement. Vision and hearing screening tests are routine first steps in schools to identify physical problems that could interfere with learning and adjustment.

## Identification

To comply with state and federal laws and regulations, pupils are assessed to identify those with LD and to develop a general framework for intervention. Once a student is identified as learning disabled, the Individuals with Disabilities Education Act 1997 reauthorization (IDEA) requires that every three years a decision be made by the Individualized Education Program (IEP) team and parents about whether reassessment is necessary to determine if the child continues to have a disability and if the student is placed in the most appropriate program. Chapter 2 discussed the assessment issues involved in identifying students as "learning disabled." Assessment practices that lead to identification of LD can help guide program choices in a general way, but they are insufficient for planning day-to-day instructional modifications.

## Instructional Planning

Assessment data are collected to assist educational personnel in planning programs that will enhance the educational achievement and psychological adjustment of students with LD. Emphasis is placed on determining precisely which academic skills students have and have not mastered and how they approach learning. The results help teachers decide both what and how to teach.

## Student Progress

Once programs are implemented, we need to measure students' progress to determine further program adjustments. IDEA mandates that the IEP be reviewed annually for this purpose. Techniques to assess progress include teacher-constructed checklists of academic objectives, standardized tests, classroom observation, measurement of success on class activities, and behavior checklists. Systematic monitoring of

*Systematic monitoring of progress and graphing the results, as often as once or twice weekly, has been associated with significantly higher rates of student learning.*

progress within the actual curriculum, as often as once or twice weekly, has been associated with significantly higher rates of student learning. This monitoring works best when actual data are collected, graphed, and discussed with the students, such as how many more words the student reads correctly in one minute this week when compared to the prior month. Instead of simply recording the data, graphs are useful because they seem to be more frequently analyzed by teachers and provide a more positive form of feedback to students. Informal observation is less effective in augmenting student learning rates. Learning rates also increase when teachers apply specific decision rules to interpret the data that they collect, rather than relying on judgment alone—for example, "if for three consecutive math calculation measurements the child falls below the target, I must change my instructional method."

Data on pupil progress are also useful for evaluating the effectiveness of different intervention programs for different types of students. A school, for example, might evaluate the effectiveness of different classroom organization patterns (individual seatwork vs. working in cooperative groups, for example) in helping children pay attention. Pupil progress evaluations also address whether a student with LD makes more progress in one versus another educational setting. Schools annually engage in pupil progress evaluations to check on basic skill and content-area gains; they then reevaluate their curriculum based on these findings. Thus, analyses of pupil progress can provide not only specific, programmatically useful information on student skills, strategies, and behaviors, but also information on necessary curriculum and setting modifications.

## Models of Assessment

There are a number of philosophical models of assessment. Some focus primarily on the student and how the development of particular skills can augment his or her success. Other models focus on the curriculum and environments, and how they can be modified to best meet a student's needs and augment progress. Each model varies in emphasis, in the measures used, and in how the results affect intervention strategies. Because a single model provides only a partial view of the student and his or her needs, we generally employ multiple assessment models to design the best, most comprehensive, and most individualized interventions for a student.

*Because each philosophical model of assessment provides only a partial view of the student and his or her needs, employing multiple assessment models is necessary.*

### Focus on the Student

In this model, the assumption is that the problem originates within the individual student. The primary concern is with identifying and remediating the student's learning deficits.

*The medical model defines a problem in terms of biological symptoms of pathology and prescribes treatment for the biological condition.*

**Medical Model.** The medical model defines a problem in terms of biological symptoms of pathology. It assumes that the cause of the student's problems is biological and not related to the student's experiential background. Brain injury resulting from oxygen deprivation at birth, for instance, can be diagnosed without taking background into consideration.

Because many biological problems can go unrecognized, screening can identify students at risk for learning problems because of medical conditions such as visual or hearing impairments, cardiac-related lethargy, or hyperactivity caused by biochemical irregularities, and then refer the students for more thorough medical or neuropsychological assessment. Interventions within the medical model treat the biological condition (e.g., prescribing eyeglasses or hearing aids, a special diet, exercises, or medications).

**Information-Processing Model.** This model defines a problem in terms of such information-processing weaknesses as visual-perceptual, motor, language, or attention and memory deficits. As in the medical model, these deficits can go undetected and result in the student being misunderstood as lazy, insolent, or of low ability when in fact an information-processing deficit is at the root of the student's underachievement.

***The information-processing model defines a problem in terms of information-processing weaknesses; these require both remediation and compensation.***

Assessment in this model, for example, may determine that Joanie does well when tasks require verbal responses but has trouble when fine-motor coordination is required. Although she has good language and mathematical reasoning abilities, Joanie is not productive at school because of her nearly illegible writing. Within this model, intervention might consist of giving Joanie lessons to strengthen her fine-motor coordination (remediation of deficit), while adapting tests and classwork to be primarily oral (compensation for deficit). Because intervention focuses on both remediation (building up deficits) and compensation (working around deficits by capitalizing on strengths), assessment in this model identifies both strengths and weaknesses.

Assessment within the information-processing model is helpful in giving us clues as to why a child is having trouble learning. Nevertheless, the model has been criticized because in most cases it's impossible to break down complex school tasks and student behavior into separate information-processing skills for the purposes of assessment, and then remediate each separately. On most tasks a number of information-processing skills will play a role, each to a different degree. Complicating the matter is the fact that the reliability and validity of information-processing measures are generally poor. Often the items on the test bear little relationship to the skills needed on actual academic tasks—mazes, puzzles, or memory for digits, for example. The result can be invalid diagnoses and educationally irrelevant remedial recommendations that divert attention from teaching more important academic skills.

As we gain sophistication in identifying the precise process deficits that impede academic performance (e.g., phonological awareness), we will be able to develop more sensitive tests and interventions targeted toward remediation of these information-processing delays. As with the medical model, assessments that focus on processing factors alone are too narrow to lead to comprehensive educational and psychological interventions. They don't, for example, tell us exactly which school skills should be taught or the best setting for instructing a child.

## Focus on the Student's Interactions with the Curriculum

This focus concerns itself with how students relate to specific aspects of academic, social, and daily living tasks that they are expected to accomplish.

**Task Analysis Model.** This model is applied to classroom tasks to discover which curriculum components are well matched to the capabilities of students with LD and which task modifications might be necessary. Because this model is based on the real curriculum, the relationship between assessment and intervention is much closer than in the information-processing model.

*Task analysis discovers which curriculum objectives a student has and hasn't mastered, and the information-processing demands of task that are easy or problematic.*

Teachers use the task analysis model to conduct *content task analysis* that determines whether a student has a sufficient knowledge base to progress in a given curriculum. When a task proves too difficult, it is analyzed into component parts to see which subskills the student has and hasn't mastered. For example, if division is problematical, we need to find out whether the student can add, subtract, and multiply. We then teach the deficient skills. As illustrated in Table 9.1, if the child can't write or name letters, we need to know whether he or she can point to letters when the teacher reads them and whether he or she can visually discriminate one letter from another, draw them, and repeat letter names accurately. Teaching then begins where the child is succeeding, and gradually moves up the developmental ladder. A teenager who is having trouble studying for tests might be asked the questions in Figure 9.1 to analyze which aspects of preparing for tests are most troublesome. Once we know what the student already knows, we can better plan the next steps in the teaching process and the skills that require remediation.

Teachers also conduct *process task analysis* to analyze the information-processing demands of tasks, from the most to least difficult processes:

1. *Expressive/receptive:* It is harder to express what we know than it is to recognize the correct material. That's why multiple-choice tests usually are easier than essay tests, and recognizing whether a word is correctly spelled is easier than actually having to spell it.

**TABLE 9.1 Task Analysis of Letter Naming**

*Easier ⟷ Harder*

| *Memory* | *Modality Input-Output* | *Task Requirements* |
|---|---|---|
| Recall | Auditory-motor | Write the letter "C" when "C" is dictated by the teacher |
| Recall | Visual-oral | Read the letter "C" when presented on a card |
| Recognition | Auditory-motor | Teacher says "C"; student points to the "C" |
| Recognition | Visual-oral | Teacher points to a "C" and asks "Is this a 'C'?"; student responds yes or no |
| *No Memory* | | |
| Discrimination | Visual-motor | Student matches the "C" with another "C" among several distractor letters |
| Discrimination | Auditory-vocal | Teacher says the sounds C—C or the words *cat—cat* *"are they the same or different?"* C—*P* or *cat—pat* "are they the same or different?"; student responds |
| Repetition | Auditory-vocal | Teacher says "C"; student repeats "C" |
| Repetition | Visual-motor | Student copies a model of "C" |

Student Name: ______________ Date: ______________ Examiner: ______________
**Type of Test:**
Multiple Choice _____ Short Answer _____ Essay _____ Standardized _____
Class Test _____ % of Grade _____
Subject: ______________________________________________

**Test Preparation**

Interview the student by asking the open-ended question first, followed by the probe question as required. Tell me how you study: ______________________________________________
______________________________________________
______________________________________________
______________________________________________
______________________________________________

Probes:

1. Do you usually study in a special place? Yes _____ No _____ Where? ______________
2. Do you have a special time for studying? Yes _____ No _____ When? ______________
3. How long can you study before you take a break? _____ hours _____ minutes
4. When you know you have a test coming up a week away, when do you start studying for it? _____
5. Do you usually find yourself having to cram the night before? Yes _____ No _____ For how long can you cram before you can't concentrate any longer? _____ hours _____ minutes
6. Do you prefer to study in a quiet place, with music playing or in front of the television set? _____ What do you normally do? ______________________________________________
7. Do you sit at a desk, in an easy chair or lie on the bed or the floor when you study? __________
8. Do you study from your notebook? _____ textbook? both? _____ Which do you like best?
______________________________________________
9. Tell me what goes through your head as you study. ______________________________________________
______________________________________________
10. When you study, do you try to figure out what information is most important? Yes _____ No _____ or to predict what questions will be on the test? Yes _____ No _____ How do you do that? ______________________________________________
______________________________________________
11. Which subjects do you find the easiest to study? ______________________________________________
______________________________________________
Why? ______________________________________________
12. Which subjects do you find the hardest to study? ______________________________________________
______________________________________________
Why? ______________________________________________

**Figure 9.1** Checklist for assessing students' test preparation and performance.

*Source:* Wiener, J. (1986). Alternatives in the assessment of the learning disabled adolescent: A learning strategies approach. *Learning Disabilities Focus, 12*, 97–107, p. 102. Reprinted by permission of the Division for Learning Disabilities.

*(continued)*

**Test-Taking Behavior**

Evaluate the student's performance in each area by marking a ✓ in the appropriate column:

| | Excellent | Adequate | Inadequate | Notes |
|---|---|---|---|---|
| • Punctuality<br>• Equipped (e.g., pen, pencil)<br>• Motivation<br>• Planning of time<br>• Checking of work<br>• Accuracy of prediction of grade | | | | |
| • Anxiety Level | High | Moderate | Low | |

**Test Product**

Analyze a recent examination or test by examining the areas listed below and questioning the student when clarification is needed. Evaluate the student's performance in each area by marking a ✓ in the appropriate column:

| | Excellent | Adequate | Inadequate | Not Applicable | Notes |
|---|---|---|---|---|---|
| Handwriting: Neatness<br>Legibility<br>Speed<br>• Accuracy of Reading of Questions<br>• Comprehension of Subtleties of Questions<br>• Spelling<br>• Grammar<br>• Punctuation<br>• Appropriateness of Vocabulary to Discipline<br>• Sequencing & Organization of Thoughts<br>• Relevance of Answers<br>• Conceptualization of Answers<br>• Elaboration of Answers | | | | | |

Comments: ______________________________

______________________________

**Figure 9.1** *Continued*

2. *Social/nonsocial:* Working in a group, with its distractions and fewer reinforcers for staying on task, is harder than maintaining attention when taught one-on-one.

3. *Abstract/concrete:* Abstract tasks are harder than concrete tasks. For example, adding numerals is harder than adding with blocks.
4. *Verbal/nonverbal:* Language tasks usually are harder than visual-motor tasks. For example, Jaqueem may be able to match the printed word *cat* with another printed word *cat,* find it among three *bat*'s because it is different, and copy the word *cat.* But he may be less able to retrieve the language to read the word, and even less able to recall both the language and visual symbols simultaneously to spell and write *"cat"* from memory.
5. *Symbolic/nonsymbolic:* Dealing with symbols or symbolic information is harder than nonsymbolic information. Understanding language that is translated into a new symbol system such as printed words, for example, is harder than understanding the same words through listening. It's easier to be directly told that an author is writing about anger and misfortune than to intuit that his or her use of "red" alludes to anger and "black" to an impending calamity.
6. *Sequential/static:* Dealing with elements in a series is more difficult than dealing with each in isolation. For example, mastering all 26 letters of the alphabet in sequence or 20 capitals of states is harder than learning 4 at a time.
7. *Long-term memory/short-term memory/no memory:* Remembering something for a long time is harder than remembering it for a few minutes. And not having to remember—as in an open-book test—is easiest of all.

## Focus on the Student's Interactions with Environments

These models assume that a student's learning problems relate to the individual's interactions with environments, such as classrooms and the home.

*In the social systems model the primary focus is on whether the individual conforms to the specific role expectations of the different settings with which he or she interacts.*

**Social Systems Model.** In the social systems model the primary focus is on whether the individual conforms to the specific role expectations of the different settings with which he or she interacts. For example, most of us know to keep quiet and shut off our cell phones once the lights dim in a movie theater, making it all the more jarring when some people carry on audible conversations during the movie. In the classroom, students are expected to work quietly at their desks most of the time, behavior that would be out of place in the school cafeteria.

In a given setting, the most powerful people set the expectations for normal behavior. Thus, in a particular classroom, the teacher's expectations for appropriate behavior and his or her tolerance level might determine whether a child is considered hyperactive. In a different setting, or with a different teacher, the child may not be considered hyperactive at all.

The social systems model looks at the role expectations for the diversity of environments with which the student is likely to interact. If a student is to function well within a social system, he or she needs to develop positive interpersonal ties with others in the system and to acquire the skills necessary to fulfill his or her role. This role difference explains many parents' confusion upon first learning of their child's academic or behavior problems in school. At home the child is seen as typical in every way, and parents can't understand why suddenly their child doesn't fit in at school. Classroom intervention under this model focuses on helping students develop good relationships with teachers and peers and on attaining those skills—paying attention, following directions, sharing—that will lead to success in that particular environment.

*The ecological model is concerned primarily with how the structural, affective, and organizational components of environments influence individual behavior, and then modifying these to promote appropriate learning and behavior.*

**Ecological Assessment Model.** This model is concerned primarily with how the structural, affective, and organizational components of different environments influence individual behavior. A basic premise is that each environment exerts dependable influences on all those within that setting. For example, participants in third-grade reading groups behave in consistent ways even though the participants change throughout the morning. The environment promotes behavior that is appropriate in this setting (such as listening when someone reads, answering questions), but a playground promotes different behaviors (such as running and screaming).

When a child misbehaves or makes many errors, the ecological model examines how the objective components of the environment may be influencing a student's behavior, such as the work load, interruptions from public address system announcements, busy bulletin boards, the curriculum, teachers, peers, support personnel, adult or peer praise and criticism, time schedules, seating arrangements, and more. It also assesses the subjective parts of the environment, such as the student's descriptions of a place as boring or fun, warm or threatening, chaotic or organized.

Intervention in this model aims at changing the structural, affective, or organizational parts of the environment. It is assumed that a change that works for one child would help almost everyone in that same setting or situation. For example, consider Noah, who suffers from a condition that makes it difficult for him to climb stairs without becoming exhausted. His last class is scheduled two flights up. He worries so much about those stairs that he can't pay attention in social studies, his next-to-last class. Placing him in another class located on the first floor solves the problem. If a class is too noisy for Sasha to concentrate, she might be given earphones to wear that play white noise. If a child is picking on José, the children's desks can be separated and cooperative learning activities instituted to enhance José's peer acceptance. What works for Noah, Sasha, or José would work for any child in that same situation.

*Behavioral assessment measures actual student, peer, and teacher behaviors in the setting of concern and then shapes a student's behavior through structured environmental manipulations.*

**Behavioral Assessment Model.** Behavioral approaches incorporate both the social systems and ecological assessment models by measuring actual student, peer, and teacher behaviors in the environment of concern. This could be the classroom, home, neighborhood, school halls, cafeteria, playground, or even church choir practice. The natural setting is critical. When a child is tested by a strange adult in a strange room with a strange set of questions and tasks that may be unrelated to the curriculum, inappropriate inferences about his or her learning problems may well result. For example, when Debbie is given one-on-one testing, this situation provides much more verbal and nonverbal reinforcement than does classroom work, with the result that Debbie performs to her peak and we end up overestimating what she is capable of accomplishing on her own in the busier classroom.

The behavioral model may also focus on cognitive (thoughts, images), affective (feelings, interpretations), physiological (heart rate prior to a test), and structural (arrangement of desks) components of the interaction between students and environments—anything that can be measured or observed. A multitude of measurement strategies fit this model including interviewing, use of rating scales, systematic observation and measurement of behavior in natural or testing situations (e.g., number of minutes on task with various teaching approaches), self-evaluation, and biofeedback monitoring. Interventions are based on an approach that aims to shape a youngster's behavior by manipulating the environment so that an event ("read this word after me") will elicit a certain behavior (the child reads correctly), followed by positive consequences (teacher praise, for example).

## Focus on the Student in a Broader Sociocultural Context

This approach focuses on being responsive to the cultural pluralism that exists in this country and others. It attempts to interpret assessment results in a way that is not biased by the dominant culture, which in the United States is the middle-class, Anglo-American tradition. The need for such an approach grew out of concerns about test discrimination and overrepresentation of sociocultural minorities in special education classes.

**Pluralistic Model.** In the pluralistic model, a student is defined as having a problem only when poor performance persists despite controlling for sociocultural bias. It assumes that the potential for learning is distributed in the same way across all racial, ethnic, and cultural groups. Therefore, differences in test performance between cultural groups are assumed to arise from biases in the tests and test procedures themselves.

*In the pluralistic model, a student is defined as having a problem only when poor performance persists despite controlling for sociocultural biases in tests and test procedures. The model assumes that the potential for learning is distributed in the same way across all racial, ethnic, and cultural groups, so any group differences in test performance are due to bias.*

Because the pluralistic model assumes that tests assess what an individual has learned about the cultural heritage represented in the test, all tests, according to this model, are culturally biased. For example, knowing who wrote *Romeo and Juliet* depends on belonging to a culture that values Shakespeare. But not knowing the answer to such a question does not mean a person has a lower learning aptitude. Assessment in the pluralistic model attempts to control for such cultural biases.

In order to deal with the issue of sociocultural bias in predicting children's learning aptitude, *culture-free tests* were developed in the 1950s. They failed as measures, however, because they did not predict school performance, which is determined by the dominant culture, and because sociocultural differences could not be eliminated entirely. Naturally, no test can be developed in a cultural vacuum. All questions and materials (even puzzles and block designs) have some cultural context.

*Culture-free, culture-fair, and culture-specific tests failed because they did not predict school performance, which is determined by the dominant culture.*

Two alternatives to these tests are *culture-fair tests* and *culture-specific tests.* The culture-fair test tries to balance items across cultural groups. But again, this test does not predict success in our predominantly white, middle-class schools. In fact, contrary to expectations, African American and lower socioeconomic status children do better on culturally loaded tests than the culture-fair tests, and on verbal tests than on nonverbal tests. This makes sense because they are learning the dominant culture's vocabulary and information in school, and the more abstract and analytical reasoning of the culture-fair test is something to which they haven't been exposed. Culture-specific tests (African American vocabulary tests, for example) also don't predict school success because the school's culture is so different from the cultural items on such tests. Moreover, constructing culture-specific tests is difficult because of the considerable heterogeneity within each ethnic or cultural group—Spanish vocabulary and pronunciation, for example, differ depending on the country and region of origin.

A comprehensive assessment that includes all the various assessment domains can effectively address the broad focus suggested by the pluralistic model. In effect, nonbiased assessment is a process rather than a set of instruments. Jessica's story is a good example of how this model can ensure fairness and effectiveness, regardless of a child's ethnicity and sociocultural background.

***Nonbiased assessment is a process rather than a set of instruments.***

Jane Mercer's System of Multicultural Pluralistic Assessment (SOMPA), though now outdated, was the most far-reaching attempt thus far to achieve non-discriminatory testing. The SOMPA focused on performance on the Wechsler Intelligence Scale for Children—Revised, which was interpreted not as measuring intelligence but rather the child's adaptation to the student role in the white, middle-class school system. After calculating the student's IQ score against the standard norms, the SOMPA then estimated the student's intelligence more fairly by comparing his or her test performance with the scores of children who shared a similar sociocultural background. This procedure made it easier to identify socioculturally diverse students as learning disabled because their IQs were adjusted upward, making discrepancies between intelligence and achievement more apparent. Research Box 9.1 on page 320 explores important issues related to testing the intellectual aptitude of children from different sociocultural backgrounds as well as methodological alternatives to traditional IQ tests.

## Assessment Methods

***Because our interventions on behalf of students with LD require modifications at the student, curriculum, and environmental levels, a multidimensional approach to assessment should focus on each.***

Because our interventions on behalf of students with LD require modifications at the student (e.g., prescribe eyeglasses), curriculum (e.g., teach at easier developmental levels), and environmental (e.g., seat children in clusters rather than rows) levels, we clearly need to take a multidimensional approach to assessment. Therefore, some of our assessment methods focus on the child, while others focus on his or her interactions with a variety of curriculum variables and environments.

Assessment tests are categorized as either *norm-referenced,* which compare the student with his or her peers, or *criterion-referenced,* which determine whether the student has learned specific skills. A test that tells us that Brett has mastered math better than 15 percent of children in the nation at his grade level is norm-referenced, whereas a test that shows he can add two-digit numbers, but not when regrouping (carrying) is required, is criterion-referenced. The norm-referenced test makes a judgment about Brett's reading achievement by sampling his knowledge of a few letters and comparing his score with the children on whom the test was standardized. By comparison, the criterion-referenced test asks Brett to name all 26 letters.

Norm-referenced tests are used for screening and identification, whereas criterion-referenced tests identify *what* skills need to be taught. *Informal evaluation strategies* help us discover *how* to teach by focusing on questions about how the student's abilities and learning styles relate to the curriculum and classroom environment. *Curriculum-based measurement,* which uses informal, criterion-referenced

## Jessica

*Nonbiased assessment recognized her as learning disabled rather than mentally retarded.*

Jessica was brought to Syracuse University's Psychoeducational Teaching Laboratory by her mother, who refused to accept the results of a school assessment that Jessica was mentally retarded. The 7-year-old had made almost no progress in first grade, and she had performed in the retarded range on a standard IQ test. In addition, the psychologist who had administered the test indicated that Jessica's responses seemed random on many tasks. It was as if she did not understand what she was expected to do.

Jessica's mother told the clinic staff that her husband had died five months earlier. He had battled cancer for five years, and during that time the family's activities had revolved around his needs. For the last year of his life, his bed had been in the middle of the living room. The family was supported by public assistance. There was barely enough income to cover the most basic necessities; there was no money for "extras" for Jessica or her two younger brothers. None of the children had attended preschool or received regular medical care.

A visit by the evaluation team to Jessica's home found it barren; there were no toys, games, or books—not even crayons. When the team arrived, they found Jessica and her brothers amusing themselves by throwing themselves against a wall and seeing who rebounded farthest.

Taking their cue from the psychologist's description of Jessica being "clueless" during testing, and considering Jessica's home background, the team wondered whether lack of familiarity with IQ-test type of tasks may have played a part in Jessica's poor IQ test performance. Consequently, the team decided to administer another intelligence test. But before doing so, they spent time playing with Jessica, using games that were similar to the tasks on the test. For example, Jessica was asked to describe similarities as she grouped pictures of vehicles, flowers, and birds because on the test she would be asked to categorize. She was asked to copy designs because on the test she would have to copy a "code." She discussed her problem-solving strategies while sequencing pictures of making a pizza, building a skyscraper, and an imminent storm. She would have to do this type of activity too on the test. Before taking the test, Jessica was reminded to approach the questions in the same way she had when playing. This time Jessica scored well within the average IQ range. The first test had tapped Jessica's relatively barren exposure to school-type learning experiences at home, not her cognitive abilities.

The discrepancy between Jessica's higher intelligence and very slow learning rate over the subsequent months eventually led to her identification as learning disabled. She was found to have language processing disabilities that required special services from the speech pathologist and a specialist in LD. With these supports, Jessica's learning rate improved. The clinic team helped Jessica's mother find free preschool programs for her two boys, and guided her to a parenting workshop where she could learn more about her children's needs and develop her own parenting skills. A pluralistic approach to assessment helped to sort out Jessica's eventual diagnosis and institute preventive action with her brothers' learning.

strategies to measure progress over time in the curriculum, is among the most useful forms of assessment for instructional planning. Also very helpful is *authentic assessment,* which measures different types of student products in daily class work (such as projects and performances) instead of relying on tests alone.

RESEARCH BOX 9.1

## Intelligence Testing of Children from Socioculturally Diverse Backgrounds

Critics have assailed intelligence tests as biased against ethnic minorities because these groups score significantly lower on IQ tests than white middle-income Americans. Studies find, however, that these tests are not biased in that they do fulfill their purpose—predicting achievement and adult success. They do this just as well for African Americans and Hispanics as they do for whites (Barrett & Depinet, 1991; Brown, Reynolds, & Whitaker, 1999; Gottfredson, 1997; Neisser et al., 1996).

African Amiercans on average score 15 points below white Americans on IQ tests. Hispanic Americans score roughly midway between these groups (Gottfredson, 1997). Because of these group differences, IQ tests have been accused of being racially and ethnically biased. However, studies of the various sources of possible bias do not confirm that these tests are biased. For example, on IQ test items often presumed to be culturally loaded and therefore unfair, there are no significant differences between African Americans and whites (Brown, 1999; Koh, Abbatiello, & McLoughlin, 1984; Sattler, 2001). Consider an item commonly thought to be culturally biased: "What is the thing to do if a boy/girl much smaller than yourself starts to fight with you?" Aftrican Americans actually answer this item correctly more often than whites. Critics had wrongly argued that the right answer for African Americans would be to fight, because avoiding the fight would reduce one's status among peers. Most items on most tests show no evidence of bias. A few items favor one or another ethnic group (whites over African Americans, and vice versa) but the overall effect on IQ scores is negligible. African American and white children actually show less of a performance gap on verbal items than on nonverbal items (puzzles, blocks) that are presumed to be less subject to cultural bias.

Other sources of presumed test bias also have not held up to scrutiny after years of research. Examiner bias, for example, is not a factor due to the race of the examiner. When African American rather than white examiners test African American students, the scores still do not increase (Jensen, 1984; Sattler, 2001). There are no differences in overall test-taking behaviors between children of different ethnic groups that would favor one group over another, and the psychological processes tapped by different items are the same across groups; the easier items are easier for all ethnic groups and the harder items are harder for all groups (Brown et al., 1999).

So how do we interpret lower scores on IQ tests for ethnic minorities when compared with white students? *Scoring low on these tests merely means that the child hasn't been exposed to or learned the information and problem-solving strategies necessary to do well. It does not mean that the child is low in "intelligence," whose definition will vary from culture to culture.*

What critics have been referring to as bias within IQ tests is in reality the confluence of several factors that serve to disadvantage children from socioculturally diverse backgrounds on these tests:

1. Ethnic minorities have been exposed in their environments to a different set of cultural knowledge, problem-solving strategies, and language conventions than the white

## RESEARCH BOX 9.1 (Continued)

middle-income information, problem-solving approaches, and language valued on IQ tests.

2. Poverty and ethnic minority status are highly linked (Natriello, Pallas, & McDill, 1990), and the pervasive influence of low socioeconomic status deters learning school-type content, limits sophistication with test-taking skills, and reduces motivation in testing situations (Sattler, 2001). Data from approximately 4500 school districts included in the 1992 Elementary and Secondary School Civil Rights Compliance Report indicate that the likelihood of being identified as mentally retarded could be predicted from five demographic variables: value of housing, household income, percentage of children in the school district "at risk," percentage of adults in the community without a high school diploma, and percentage of limited English proficient children. If the percentage of African Americans in the district is added into the equation, the predictability of mental retardation increases to 36 percent. When African American and white children of equal socioeconomic status are compared, their IQ test performance becomes more similar (5 to 8 points apart instead of 15). Although the IQ gap does close to some extent within the same income group, this still represents a significant difference (Eysenck, 1984; Williams & Ceci, 1997). These persistent discrepancies may be due to cultural differences (Neisser et al., 1996).
3. Those with enriched environments and better educational opportunities are likely to earn higher intelligence scores because of the positive effects of environmental stimulation and schooling on IQ. Because IQ tests include many achievement-related items and taps problem-solving strategies nurtured in school, better schooling and more years of schooling—which occurs more often for whites—shows itself on the IQ tests (Ceci & Williams, 1997; Frumkin, 1997).
4. The role of genetic influences in IQ test differences continues to be hotly debated (Herrnstein & Murray, 1994; Lynn, 1997; Reynolds & Brown, 1984; Rushton, 1997).
5. A referral bias and the biased interpretation of IQ tests by examiners often occurs during the assessment process. Historically, more minority children (especially males) have been referred for assessment and subsequently placed in segregated special education classes for the mentally retarded and seriously emotionally disturbed than white children with the same low scores (Harry & Anderson, 1994; Mercer, 1973). Examiners have made the mistake of not factoring into their decision making the extent to which limited experience and education decreases IQ test performance.

Because of their poor performance on IQ tests, disproportionate numbers of children from low-income and nonwhite families historically have been identified as mildly mentally retarded and placed in classes for the mentally retarded (Argulewicz, 1983; Brosnan, 1983; Dunn, 1968; National Center for Educational Statistics, 1992; Office of Civil Rights, 1992; Patrick & Reschly, 1982). When Jane Mercer (1970, 1973) tallied the races of Riverside, California special class students (IQ 79 or below), she found 3 times more Mexican American and 2½ times more African American students than would be expected from their percentage in the general population. However, when she used the American

*(continued)*

## RESEARCH BOX 9.1 (Continued)

Association on Mental Deficiency's definition of retardation, which requires both intellectual and adaptive (daily living) skills to be deficient for identification of a child as mentally retarded, the majority of the youngsters had to be declassified because their adaptive skills were normal and their IQs were within normal ranges on special test norms constructed from their own cultural group's IQ test performance (Mercer & Lewis, 1978). In another study, 67 percent of mildly retarded youngsters were declassified after adaptive behavior measurement proved that, in the nonschool world, these students functioned normally (Coulter, Morrow, & Tucker, 1978).

Unfortunately, placements in special classes for the mentally retarded are not associated with any higher academic achievement, and in fact sometimes have been associated with lower achievement, than had the children remained in regular classes (Carlberg & Kavale, 1980; Gottlieb, Rose, & Lessen, 1983). Therefore, in the *Larry P.* v. *Riles* case, October 1979, California Federal District Court Judge Robert Peckham ruled that IQ tests for placing African American children in programs for the retarded are discriminatory, and he banned their use (a statewide injunction had been in effect since 1974). In 1980, Illinois Federal District Court Judge John F. Grady upheld the use of IQ tests with African American children provided that these tests were not the sole criteria for determination of an educational program (*Parents in Action on Special Education* v. *Hannon*). Florida and Georgia had similar rulings (Reschly, Kicklighter, & McKee, 1988). On September 26, 1986, Judge Peckham barred all California public schools from administering IQ tests to African American students for any special education reason. Instead he recommended that measures of adaptive behavior, academic achievement, classroom performance, personal history, development, and instruments designed to pinpoint strengths and weaknesses in various areas be used. In response, *Crawford et al.* v. *Honic et al.* was filed in California in 1988 by African American families who claimed that their civil rights had been violated by being barred from voluntarily taking IQ tests (e.g., for determination of giftedness). This resulted in Judge Peckham reversing his ban for three specific children to take an IQ test for learning disability identification purposes (August 31, 1992). On the grounds of this reversal, the California Association of School Psychologists continues to contest the state's ban on IQ testing for African American children.

Despite reductions as a result of litigation, racial and ethnic minorities have continued to be overrepresented in classes for the retarded in many parts of the country (Artiles & Trent, 1994; Chinn & Hughes, 1987; MacMillan, Hendrick, & Watkins, 1988; Oswald et al., 1999) and treated differentially in other ways as well. In 1999–2000, 34 percent of children identified as mentally retarded and 30 percent of all students with "developmental delays" were African American, while the percentage of African Americans in the general population was only 14.5 percent (Twenty-third Annual Report to Congress, 2001). African American children are almost 2½ times more likely to be identified as mentally retarded, as are their non–African American peers (Oswald et al., 1999). Proportionally more African Americans (32 percent) and Hispanics (26 percent) than white students (15 percent) with disabilities are educated for over 60 percent of the school day outside the regular class. Conversely, while 52 percent of whites with LD currently are assigned for more than 80 percent of the school day to a regular class, the figure is 35 percent for

## RESEARCH BOX 9.1 (Continued)

African Americans and 42 percent for Hispanics with LD (Twenty-third Annual Report to Congress, 2001).

What happened to those students who were declassified by litigation as mentally retarded? Many quickly found their way into classes for the learning disabled (Gottlieb et al., 1994; Tucker, 1980; Wright & Santa Cruz, 1983). As a result of increasing cautiousness in identifying children from socioculturally diverse backgrounds as mentally retarded, there is concern about whether the label of LD has become another subtle form of discrimination that will reduce teacher, student, and parent aspirations and motivation. Reduced expectations leads to poor quality education, which in turn leads to reduced achievement, graduation rate, earnings, and postsecondary schooling.

For those declassified children who cannot demonstrate significant ability-achievement discrepancies for identification as learning disabled, the only option is regular class placement without special educational services (Forness, 1985), or Title I remedial help offered to children achieving below the 20th percentile. Unable to pass curricular minimum competency tests, a high proportion of these youngsters and those for whom English is a second language have ended up retained, dropping out, or being denied high school diplomas (Gersten & Woodward, 1994; MacMillan et al., 1988). The latest figures indicate that whereas 63 percent of white students with LD complete high school, the percentage is far lower for African Amiercans (44 percent) and Hispanics (53 percent) with LD (Twenty-third Annual Report to Congress, 2001). This is a problem across the entire country. Exacerbating this situation is the growing hesitance of educators to refer language-minority children and socioculturally diverse children of low socioeconomic status or intelligence to special education in spite of the disproportionate difficulties experienced by these groups; they do not hesitate to refer white children of similar intelligence (Flynn, 1984; Frame, Clarizio, & Porter, 1984; Gersten & Woodward, 1994; Tomlinson et al., 1977). MacMillan et al. (1988) raise the question of whether our efforts to normalize the school experiences of children from diverse cultural and linguistic backgrounds actually have reduced their educational opportunities—a de facto reverse racism.

The use of intelligence tests in identification of children with LD from diverse cultural and linguistic backgrounds is troublesome because, if these tests underestimate their intelligence, we might deny these youngsters special education opportunities from which they could benefit. Although today's IQ tests are technically sound and great care is taken that representative samples of children, stratified by region, race, socioeconomic status, and gender, are included in a test's norm group, this still doesn't solve the problem of culturally and linguistically diverse students being unprepared to do well on these tests.

The new Cognitive Assessment System purports to reduce the gap in performance between cultural groups. At one time two other measures took a very special approach to this issue and were useful, but the norms are now outdated: Mercer's (1979) Estimated Learning Potential score (which adjusts IQ upward based on urban acculturation, socioeconomic status, family structure, and size), and Kaufman and Kaufman's (1983) Kaufman Assessment Battery for Children (which provides intelligence norms for African American and white children of various socioeconomic levels, and adjusts IQ upward because highly verbal and school-related items have been moved to another scale). The

*(continued)*

**RESEARCH BOX 9.1 (Continued)**

latter two measures, however, do not predict school achievement—the whole purpose of IQ tests—as well as do standard IQ measures (Sattler, 2001).

Adaptive behavior measures provide one alternative to standardized IQ tests for estimating the expected achievement of these students, as does dynamic assessment (which evaluates changes in a child's abilities or learning rate after modification of task instructions, materials, and strategies). Syracuse University's Psychoeducational Teaching Laboratory was among the earliest pioneers of dynamic assessment approaches (Smith, 1999). Clinic staff demonstrated how, using a standardized test, modifications can be made in the assessor's behaviors, test administration, content, and interpretation to get a feel for the child's best capabilities under the most facilitating circumstances. Such modifications can help overcome biases introduced by a strange or threatening examination format, misinterpreted directions, scoring down moral judgments that fit with the student's cultural learning but not the test's expectations, language differences, test format inconsistent with the child's cognitive style, visual stimuli to which the child has not previously been exposed, the assessor's negative interpretation of behavior which is appropriate in the student's culture, and so forth (Smith, 1980, 1999). Comparison of performance under standardized versus nonstandard conditions reflects the level at which a child could potentially function if tasks were appropriately adjusted.

After reading about all these machinations, the reader probably would agree that it is a shame that whether students fit a label is what will determine whether they get the special help they need. Prereferral intervention teams offer a promising way of avoiding unnecessary testing and misclassification, and getting on with intensified teaching. Under IDEA's 1997 reauthorization, children can be identified with a "developmental delay" to receive special education through age 9. After age 9 a more intensive assessment is necessary because the law requires that a specific disability be designated.

## Norm-Referenced Measures

For a norm-referenced test to be useful, it must meet several criteria:

1. *Reliability:* Scores must be consistent from one testing time to another, such as two weeks apart.
2. *Validity:* The test measures what it's supposed to measure.
3. *Standardized administration and scoring procedures:* All examiners use similar procedures so that there is a uniform standard for comparing the child's performance with the norm group's performance.
4. *Norms:* These are based on an appropriate sociocultural and educational comparison group.

***Just because a test is published doesn't mean it's any good. Many have poor reliability, validity, and norms.***

Just because a test is published doesn't mean it's any good. A large portion of tests fail to meet some or all of the above criteria. Fortunately, there are excellent resources for checking the effectiveness of these tests, including the test manual itself, the Buros Mental Measurement Yearbook series, and Jerome Sattler (2001) and Salvia and Ysseldyke's (2001) texts.

Norm-referenced measures help us screen for students at risk for psychological or educational problems, but they sample too few skills to help us plan exactly *what* or *how* to teach. Additional approaches are necessary to address these questions, including *"testing the limits,"* which involves coaching the student on how to approach a task on the test, observing the student's learning rate, and watching for generalization of this strategy to new test items. Test items also can be task analyzed to discover exactly which component skills the child has and hasn't mastered, and why some may be particularly problematic.

*Norm-referenced measures are used for screening and identification.*

## Criterion-Referenced Measures

These measures provide information on *what* to teach. Although some of these tests are normed, norms are not critical for their purpose.

*Criterion-referenced measures identify* what *skills need to be taught.*

Students' scores on criterion-referenced measures are affected by the amount of overlap between their curriculum and the test items. More often than not, test items don't correspond to what has been taught in the classroom. On math tests, for example, more than half the content may come from topics never covered by the text. The same thing is true of reading tests, where only in first and second grades is there a large overlap with the content of the students' readers. Moreover, the problem-solving strategies called for on the test may differ from those practiced in the classroom.When this is the case, tests may underestimate the skills students actually have mastered. If, however, we want to know how well children can generalize their classroom learning to new material and problems, then the less the test and curriculum overlap, the better.

## Informal Evaluation Strategies

A variety of nonstandard assessment strategies can provide information about both *what* and *how* to teach. Figures 9.2 on page 326 and 9.3 on page 327, for example, illustrate an interview that not only identifies some aspects of a secondary school student's learning difficulties but also how to intervene effectively. Clinical interviews in which students "talk through" the process they used in arriving at answers are very helpful to teachers in finding out about children's reasoning and misunderstandings that need to be corrected.

*Task analysis,* another informal evaluation procedure, checks for mastery by breaking down complex instructional goals into their component subskills. This helps to pinpoint the student's current knowledge and the next skill to be taught. *Error analysis,* a form of task analysis, is very useful in determining whether the child's errors might be due to a misunderstanding or misapplication of some processes or procedures, for example adding the "carried" number when multiplying—as though it were an addition problem.

Another approach is *systematic observation* of the student in the classroom, which has the advantage of assessing the problem in the setting where the problem occurs rather than generalizing from a strange testing situation. Behaviors related to the problem are counted for a set number of minutes and graphed—for example, the number of 10-second intervals the child is on task in a 15-minute time block, when compared with his or her classmates.

Student Name: ________________ Date: ________________ Examiner: ________________

Text: Subject ________________________ Grade Level ________________

Select a chapter of a textbook in a content subject such as history, geography, or science. The textbook should be one currently in use in the student's program.

**Word Identification**

Ask the student to read aloud a passage of about 200 words. Note the number of words identified correctly.

_____ % of words identified correctly

If the student identified 90% or more of the words correctly, proceed with the assessment. If the student identified less than 90% of the words correctly, select an easier textbook. Hesitations and self corrections should not be counted as errors.

**Survey of Strategies**

Tell the student to show you how he/she would study the chapter in order to learn the material for a test. Ask him/her to verbalize his/her thoughts during the course of reading. Note the strategies employed by placing a ✓ in the blank space.

- Skimmed: introduction _____
  headings _____
  figures and illustrations _____
  italics _____
  conclusion _____
  prior to reading the chapter _____
- Read the chapter from beginning to end _____
- Began to read chapter, then gave up _____
- Spontaneously asked himself/herself questions while reading _____
- Used study questions as a guide for reading _____
- Picked out the main ideas or important points while reading _____
- Paraphrased main ideas or important points _____
- Looked up unknown words in the dictionary _____
- Underlined or highlighted important information _____
- Made notes _____
- Predicted questions that might be on an examination _____

Other: ________________________________________________

________________________________________________

________________________________________________

________________________________________________

________________________________________________

________________________________________________

________________________________________________

**Figure 9.2** Interview questions on gaining information from text.

*Source:* Adapted from Wiener, J. (1986). Alternatives in the assessment of the learning disabled adolescent: A learning strategies approach. *Learning Disabilities Focus, 12,* 97–107, p. 106. Reprinted by permission of the Division for Learning Disabilities.

Student Name: ________________ Date: ________________ Examiner: ________________

**The Task Environment**

1. How did you select the topic/book? ______________________________
2. Are you interested in it?
   very interested ______ somewhat interested ______ not at all interested ______
3. How did the teacher prepare you for the assignment? ______________________________

**Previous Knowledge**

4. Have you previously been taught to write essays/projects/reports?
   Yes ______ No ______ What were you taught? ______________________________
5. What did you know about the topic before you started? ______________________________

**Planning**

6. Did you have a plan for writing the essay/project/report? Yes ______ No ______
   What was it? ______________________________
7. When did you begin thinking about the topic? ______________________________
8. Did you do any research? Yes ______ No ______ What resources did you use? ______________________________
9. How much time did you have for writing (i.e. _____ between date assignment was given and assignment due)? _____ days. How did you use that time?______________________________
10. Did you make an outline? Yes ______ No ______ What kind of thinking did you do first? ___
    What was your organizational plan (outline)? ______________________________

**Translating/Reviewing**

11. How many drafts did you write? one ______ two ______ three ______
12. How long did it take to write each one?
    1. ______ hrs/mins 2. ______ hrs/mins 3. ______ hrs/mins
13. Did you write your first draft with pencil? ______ pen? ______ typewriter? ______ word processor? ______
14. Did you ask a friend or family member to read the first draft and make suggestions?
    Yes ______ No ______ What kind of suggestions did they have? ______________________________
15. Did you proof read the final draft? Yes ______ No ______

**Evaluating**

16. What grade did you think you would get? ______ Why? ______________________________
17. What was the teacher's evaluation? ______________________________

**Figure 9.3** Interview questions on essay/project/report writing.

*Source:* Adapted from Wiener, J. (1986). Alternatives in the assessment of the learning disabled adolescent: A learning strategies approach. *Learning Disabilities Focus, 12,* 97–107, p. 100. Reprinted by permission of the Division for Learning Disabilities.

*Dynamic assessment involves systematically trying a variety of materials and strategies to shed light on how a student learns best.*

*Dynamic assessment* involves systematically trying and evaluating a variety of instructional techniques, including varying materials, methods of presentation or response, and types of feedback. The goal is to learn the extent and type of supports that will help students learn best, and obstacles to avoid. These evaluation strategies are also called *direct, formative,* and *process assessment,* or simply *"trial teaching."* They help reveal the level of performance a child might reach if given appropriate help from an adult. These methods also are very useful for evaluating the effectiveness of suggested instructional adaptations over time.

In dynamic assessment, the educator observes a student's performance on various classroom tasks and makes hypotheses about task characteristics that might facilitate success. These might include having the child listen to a recorded version of the text while following the print version, "prepping" the child with cues to help him or her connect new information to prior knowledge, reducing distractions, or giving corrective feedback. Dynamic assessment might also mean finding the things that get in the way of student learning such as too-rapid presentation rate, anxiety, or writing versus dictating essays.

With hypotheses in hand, the educator can then manipulate tasks. The child might listen to the teacher read the story and then answer questions instead of reading himself or herself. The child might take an untimed math fact quiz if time pressure seems to be a problem. He or she could learn to self-verbalize as he or she studies to enhance memory. Points might be earned to increase motivation. The child's success rates are compared under various teaching approaches. Throughout this process teachers need to be aware that one instructional modification might be quite effective on one task, yet not work on another.

*By offering different types of problem-solving supports to children and observing their progress, assessors gain insight into abilities that are emerging, the child's ultimate learning aptitude, and strategies for instructional intervention.*

Vygotsky, an early twentieth century Russian self-fashioned psychologist, was a leader in promoting these informal approaches to assessment—discovering not only what children can and can't do, but what they are capable of if given appropriate "scaffolding" by the adult. By offering different types of cognitive problem-solving assistance to children and observing their progress toward solutions, assessors gain insight into abilities that are in the process of emerging and the child's ultimate learning aptitude once these mature. Most importantly, useful strategies have been uncovered for helping the child progress on the classroom's educational tasks.

A basic assumption of those who use nonstandard assessment procedures is that a student's abilities can be masked by environmental variables such as inappropriate task content, strategies, or environments. By removing task and setting barriers and adding appropriate supports, we can build bridges toward success. Though they are time-consuming, informal strategies are essential to developing a complete understanding of how children learn.

## Curriculum-Based Measurement

*Curriculum-based measurement uses the actual classroom content to assess how students are progressing in comparison to their classmates.*

*Curriculum-based measurement,* or CBM, uses the actual classroom content to assess how students are progressing in comparison to their classmates, all of whom are exposed to similar educational programming. Decoding and reading comprehension progress, for example, can be reliably and validly measured in the number of words a child reads accurately from a classroom reader in 1 minute. Spelling progress can be reliably measured by counting the number of letter-pairs (two successive letters) correctly spelled in a 2-minute test drawn from a class spelling list. In comparison to the typical spelling test, in CBM a child who has the same number of words misspelled as the prior month could still be showing progress because more consecutive letters within the words are correct. Similarly, math progress can be assessed by the number of correct digits (rather than just the number of correct problems) in a 2-minute sample of curriculum problems. Written language progress is assessed from the number of words written in 3 minutes in response to a story starter or topic sentence.

Another means of evaluating progress is tallying the day in the school year when the majority of children achieve a specific objective. For example, first-grader Christine writes all 26 letters of the alphabet correctly on the 160th day of the 180-day school year (160/180). This is considerably slower than her classmates, all of whom could do this by the 55th day.

CBM is also an excellent tool for evaluating classroom behavior. Ratings every ten seconds might tabulate how often the student distracts others vocally, is out of place, has unacceptable physical contact with a person or a person's property, or is off task. The target child's behavior is rated every odd minute, and a different classmate's behavior every even minute, until all children have been assessed. The target child's data is then compared with that of his or her classmates.

With some training, teachers are able to conduct these assessments within minutes themselves. These simple measures very easily distinguish those students who lag so far behind their peers that they need a more comprehensive evaluation for special education identification and services. CBM also distinguishes students with LD from slow learners, because the pace of progress of the child with LD is even slower. With CBM's frequent monitoring, program modifications are possible sooner rather than waiting until students fail standardized tests at the end of the year. Programs also can be revised more frequently because progress checks are occurring at regular intervals.

***With CBM's frequent monitoring, programs are revised frequently, rather than waiting until students fail end-of-year tests.***

CBM has the advantage of shifting the problem-solving focus toward program evaluation rather than being quick to pin a student's academic delays on the child alone. For example, if students read more words accurately and spend more time on task in Ms. Banach's class than they do in Mr. Brasch's room, and both classes are composed of similar kinds of students, then this suggests that Mr. Brasch's teaching materials and methods, rather than his students, should become the focus of assessment. An added advantage of CBM is that, contrary to standardized tests, it uses items from the actual classroom curriculum and uses the school's children to tabulate norms based on the experiences of students in a particular school.

CBM's objective measurement of progress is especially important because teachers tend to overestimate the amount that children have mastered. This results in moving on in the curriculum too rapidly, without first establishing the basic fundamentals. With CBM, teacher referrals for special education evaluations are reduced by as much as half, and the children ultimately referred are more likely to have a learning disability. The reduced time spent testing frees psychologists and special educators for more intense intervention with those who really need it and for collaboration with teachers on program development. With more accurate progress data from CBM, the overreferral by teachers of male students, males with

***CBM's objective measurement of progress is especially important because teachers tend to overestimate the amount that children have mastered. This results in moving on in the curriculum too rapidly, without first establishing the basic fundamentals.***

*CBM's frequent progress monitoring is associated with higher levels of student achievement.*

behavior problems, African Americans, low-income, and physically unattractive children also has been curtailed. Most importantly, the frequent progress monitoring is associated with higher levels of student achievement.

### Authentic Assessment

Authentic assessment relies on evaluation of exhibits, demonstrations, performances (art, music, plays), experiments, debates, oral reports, "reaction" papers, portfolios of work samples, and more. Student portfolios have the advantage of showing what students have done that reflects progress and evolving strategies in work that the student values, rather than assessing learning on objectives that are only of the teacher's choosing. The different types of portfolios teachers find useful were reviewed in Chapter 8.

*Authentic assessment reflects progress and evolving strategies in work that the student values.*

The variety of products students generate in authentic assessment displays the application of knowledge, initiative, creativity, specific strategies, higher-level thinking, and problem-solving skills to substantive, high-quality instructional activities. The quality of the product is evaluated against criteria developed from the consensus of expert teachers. Feedback from this method helps students self-evaluate and feel successful because the extent of their progress is recognized, no matter how their achievements compare to that of peers. Authentic assessment also helps teachers write more numerous and specific instructional recommendations than do more traditional evaluation methods.

## Multidimensional Assessment Approaches

The primary goal of assessment with students who have LD is to plan effective programs to help them develop educationally and personally. To achieve this, IDEA mandates multidimensional, nondiscriminatory assessment procedures. It also requires that multiple perspectives be represented within the assessment and planning process.

*Because learning is influenced by the student's characteristics and how these interact with the student's curriculum and learning environments, we need as much information about the student in as many domains as possible.*

Evaluators recognize that learning does not occur in isolation. It is influenced by the student's characteristics and how these interact with the student's curriculum and learning environments. Therefore, we need as much information about the student in as many domains as possible—a picture of the whole person. This necessitates a team approach, a team that includes the parents and, as much as possible, the students themselves.

### Multiple Dimensions

A thorough assessment of a learning problem requires multiple measures that span many assessment domains. It should consider the student's interactions with the curriculum and learning settings, and the student's and significant others' subjective impressions of these influences. IDEA's identification procedures require at least two measures to determine an appropriate educational program, though in practice far more than two measures are necessary.

IDEA requires that a team member other than the students' general education teacher observe their academic performance in the regular classroom. If the individual being assessed is out of school or a preschooler, observation occurs in an environment appropriate for someone that age. IDEA also requires that the testing materials not be racially or culturally biased and that they be provided and administered in the child's native language or other mode of communication (e.g., sign language), if the child is not a fluent English speaker. An assessment can be considered unbiased when it leads to effective intervention for students from ethnic and racial minority groups.

*An assessment can be considered unbiased when it leads to effective intervention for students from ethnic and racial minority groups.*

## Multiple Perspectives

IDEA's regulations require a multidisciplinary team that includes at least one member with knowledge of the suspected area of disability, the child's regular classroom teacher (if the child is not in a regular class, then a regular classroom teacher qualified to teach a child of this age), and at least one person qualified to conduct individual diagnostic examinations of children, such as a school psychologist or learning disability specialist. Most often, an even wider range of professionals are involved, including speech-language pathologists, social workers, nurses, occupational and physical therapists, and school administrators. The teacher's involvement in the assessment process is important because it offers valuable information about the student and explores the teacher's level of commitment to a variety of possible intervention suggestions.

Parent involvement is also essential for a complete assessment. IDEA gives parents a great deal of influence in the process. By law they can, for example, request timely evaluations, participate in the development of their child's IEP, request mediation or an impartial hearing if they disagree with findings, request a free and independent assessment, hire a lawyer, receive a copy of the evaluation report, and so on. Parents must consent to the initial evaluation and all subsequent reevaluations. Beyond requirements, parent perspectives are essential because they come from people who know the pupil most directly, over the longest duration, and over the widest range of settings.

*Parent perspectives in the assessment process are essential because they come from people who know the pupil most directly, over the longest duration, and over the widest range of settings.*

Students, too, should be partners in the assessment process. They can shed light on problematical aspects of their learning, which learning strategies are easiest, and which interventions are preferred. Their involvement often promotes more rapid gains in learning. IDEA mandates that teenagers must be invited to participate in their transition planning. Unfortunately, despite the helpfulness of including students, they are frequently bystanders and not invited into the discussions. This often results in unfortunate misunderstandings ("I must be stupid if all these people are worried about me") and little commitment to making interventions succeed. Barry, Rachael, and Robin's stories (pages 332 and 333) present a humorous look at what can happen when we consult with the students we are evaluating. Robin's story is familiar to many special educators.

*As partners in the assessment process, students can shed light on problematical aspects of their learning, which learning strategies are easiest, and which interventions are preferred.*

When we include teachers, parents, and students in problem identification, assessment, and decision making, each is more likely to become constructively involved in the intervention process as well. If these individuals merely receive the assessment report, the likelihood of follow-through is reduced.

The choice of examiners also is important to consider. Often the more familiar the examiner and the student are with each other, the more likely the student will perform to capacity in the assessment. The child's teacher is a likely choice, but

## Barry

*A bright eleventh grader who outsmarted the visual sequential memory test despite severe deficits in this area.*

Barry, a bright eleventh grader who read accurately but slowly and spelled no better than a second grader, was being evaluated at Syracuse University's Psychoeducational Teaching Laboratory. His teachers did not understand the nature of his learning disability and were seeking instructional direction. Barry's goal was to enroll in a technical school on graduation; this was something that disappointed his parents, who were both college graduates. Yet they could see no alternative.

Barry's major difficulty in school was with written expression. His spelling was terrible, and his teachers graded off for this. In his classes, Barry's teachers used overheads when lecturing. Unfortunately, Barry was so slow in copying these that he seldom had an accurate set of notes to study from.

Informal assessment and task analysis indicated that Barry could spell with good phonetic equivalents, but he could recall very few irregular spellings. When a word was flashed for one second, he caught only the first two letters. He was unable to recall the word as a whole.

It was hypothesized that Barry had a severe deficit in processing visual images. In fact, to his dismay, he could not even imagine in his head what his girlfriend looked like. During trial teaching in spelling, when he was asked to close his eyes and image a word, he was unable to do so.

By coincidence, on the day of Barry's last session at the laboratory, a new test of visual-perceptual skills arrived. Barry was the perfect candidate to try it out. With one exception, Barry performed below the performance expected of an 8-year-old on all subtests: matching patterns, recalling a specific figure he had just seen, finding a hidden figure, and deciding which figure when completed would look like the model. To our surprise, however, he got nearly every item correct that required recalling a sequence of up to 9 +'s and –'s (for example, + + – + – – + + –), by finding this pattern among three distractors. Given Barry's inability to recall even two letters in a word, we were taken aback and confronted Barry with "How *did* you *do* that?" He smiled sheepishly and replied, "Simple, I just looked at the last two things in the line!" And, in fact, if one looks at just the last two +'s or –'s in the row, one can be correct on all but two items! Had we not asked Barry, who knows what kind of conclusions we would have come to.

Barry began using a word processor in high school to correct his spelling, and his teachers made a separate set of their notes for him so that he wouldn't have to copy from the overhead. In addition, spelling was no longer graded in his written work. Once Barry understood his disability, he felt so much better about himself that he changed his career goals. Today Barry is a sophomore in a community college.

others, such as psychologists and learning disability specialists, can establish rapport through preparatory phone calls to the student, a visit to the home, or games and discussion prior to testing.

***A team approach is critical to ensuring that multiple perspectives on the strengths and weaknesses of the student, curriculum, and learning environments are considered.***

A team approach to assessment saves time and cost. The team decides who needs to be involved and which measures to use so that different professionals don't waste time and energy with testing the same skill in different ways. A team approach is also critical to ensuring that multiple perspectives on the strengths and weaknesses of the student, curriculum, and learning environments are considered.

## Rachael and Robin

*Stories of the importance of consulting with the students we are evaluating.*

Rachael turned 5 right before entering kindergarten. At the beginning of the year she could write her name in capitals, but she sometimes reversed letters—which is fairly common at this age. Rachael's teacher noted that her drawing ability was far beyond age expectations. It showed excellent attention to detail and appreciation of spatial relationships. Rachael understood left and right on her body as well as on objects. She was well-coordinated and was adept with scissors and putting together puzzles.

After about two months of school, Rachael began to write her name from right to left on the paper, reversing all of the letters (lɘɒʜɔɒЯ). When her teacher corrected her, Rachael would respond irritably "I know." The next day she would write her name correctly on one paper and in reverse on another. The teacher was confused and began to wonder if Rachael might have a learning disability. Yet the fact that Rachael could write her name correctly "if she wanted to," combined with her excellent drawing and fine-motor skills, led the teacher to believe there was nothing wrong with Rachael's visual perception or fine-motor abilities. Baffled, the teacher continued to monitor the situation and to remind Rachael that she should write from left to right.

Soon, Rachael began to write other words in mirror-style as well. Her teacher was most put out when she noticed yet another anomaly that reflected Rachael's excellent memory and backward sequencing skills. Rachael wrote her name on the right side of the page and reversed, but, as the teacher had directed, she began from the left with the "⅃" in the center of the page. She then continued in reverse order toward the right, ending with "Я." Exasperated, the teacher finally asked Rachael why she chose to write this way. Rachael responded quite confidently, "This is the way I'm supposed to write in Hebrew!"

A call to Rachael's parents cleared up the issue. Rachael had begun Hebrew instruction in religious school at the same time she started kindergarten. Apparently she had decided to make the English language conform to Hebrew rules, in which one writes from right to left. Because Rachael had excellent visual-perceptual skills and a keen sense of direction, it made sense to her that if you were going to reverse the direction of a word, you should reverse the directions of all the letters too!

The possibility of delaying further instruction in Hebrew until Rachael had mastered the basics of writing in English was discussed, but in the end all Rachael needed was an explanation that different languages had different rules. By April, Rachael's writing (in both English and Hebrew) was perfect. Although Rachael's case is unique, it does illustrate the worthiness of consulting with students whose thinking processes we're attempting to second-guess.

In another case, Robin, an eighth grader, did not agree with the assessment team's recommendation for resource room services. She knew she needed help but refused to leave her classroom for tutoring because she viewed it as stigmatizing. Instead, she suggested after-school tutoring; she was willing to spend extra time at the academics in order to avoid what she felt was a socially devaluing recommendation. Robin's commitment to this choice was more likely to lead to effort and progress than if she had been forced to receive instruction in the resource room. The after-school tutoring arrangement worked out well, especially because it was set up as "help tables" for which many students would stay—including those needing extended day programs because their parents worked.

## Assessment Domains

In this section we explore the various evaluation domains and the types of assessment tools employed in each. Any team member who assesses a student must have the necessary training and expertise. A particular credential, however, does not make a person an expert in assessment. Individuals who assess students must be well versed in special education, skilled in establishing rapport with students, and familiar with appropriate strategies and tools for the kinds of decisions they need to make.

Because students with LD may be able to demonstrate their capabilities when asked in one way but not another, it is particularly important that the assessment instruments selected maximize students' opportunities to demonstrate their knowledge and problem-solving abilities. The formats of typical reading comprehension and spelling tests depicted in Figures 9.4, 9.5, and 9.6 illustrate this point. The student may answer comprehension questions after orally or silently reading a passage, may point to the correct picture after reading silently, or may add the missing word in a sentence. In one spelling test the student writes dictated words. On another test he or she merely points to the one spelling among four that is correct. Clearly, each task taps different abilities, only some of which are the same as those required in the classroom. Therefore, the evaluator needs to know not only the technical aspects of test administration, scoring, interpretation, reliability, and validity but also the intelligent use of test information. It is equally important that the evaluator know how to use informal evaluation strategies that clarify how a student goes about learning. In addition, the evaluator must be sensitive to what is expected in the regular curriculum and

The student answers oral questions after reading a passage.

Mary was going downtown to watch the parade. She skipped and ran along the street because she could hardly wait to get there. She was early and found a good place to stand.

Pretty soon she could hear the music of the bands coming down the main street. The men of the first band were dressed in scarlet, with white feathers in their hats. The men of the second band were clad in dark blue, with red feathers in their caps.

1. Why did Mary go downtown? *(to see the parade)*
2. Had the parade started before she got there? *(no)*
3. What did she hear after she found a place to stand? *(music or bands)*
4. What came first in the parade? *(band)*

**Figure 9.4** Representative item from a reading comprehension test.

*Source:* From *Diagnostic Reading Scales* devised by George D. Spache. Reprinted by permission of the publisher, CTB/McGraw-Hill, Del Monte Research Park, Monterey, CA 93940. 

In the first format the student writes dictated words. In the second format the student points to the correct spelling.

| | |
|---|---|
| go | Children *go* to school. |
| cut | Mother will *cut* the cake. |
| nature | The study of *nature* is interesting. |
| reasonable | His request was *reasonable* and just. |
| appropriation | Congress made an *appropriation* for schools. |

| | |
|---|---|
| bok | boc |
| booke | book |

| | |
|---|---|
| aciletate | facilitate |
| fasilitate | facilitait |

**Figure 9.5** Representative items from spelling tests.

*Source* (top): Jastak, S., & Wilkinson, G. S. (1984). *Wide Range Achievement Test—Revised.* Wilmington, DE.: Jastak Associates, Inc. Reprinted by permission.

NOTE (bottom): Test item similar to Peabody Individual Achievement Test—Revised.

the typical variability among students. The referred student's strengths and weaknesses must be judged accordingly.

## Initial Steps

***Referral forms, records, interviews, and observation in the pupil's natural settings help us gain a perspective on reasons behind a student's weaknesses.***

When a teacher, parent, or student makes a referral for assessment, team members first examine available records, interview the student and relevant others, and observe in the pupil's natural settings. These procedures help us to evaluate past learning opportunities so as to gain a perspective on possible reasons behind a student's weaknesses. Marcus, for example, transferred school systems in the middle of second grade and experienced immediate difficulty in reading. When given the word *sand* to read he just stared at it and guessed. An analysis of Marcus's previous curriculum showed that he had been taught through a whole-language approach to read words by looking at them rather than sounding them out. Unlike other children, he did not figure out the phonics code on his own. The referral process was halted at this point so that the new teacher could intensify phonics instruction. Marcus required more practice and a more systematic approach than most of his peers, yet once he learned this material he retained it reasonably well. What initially

**Figure 9.6** Representative items from reading comprehension tests. In one format the student identifies the appropriate picture. In the second format, the student fills in the blanks.

*Source:* Dunn, L. M., & Markwardt, F. C. (1989). *Peabody Individual Achievement Test—Revised.* Circle Pines, MN: American Guidance Service. Reprinted by permission.

looked like a disability was largely a lack of opportunity to learn. No further assessment was needed.

**Referrals.** Care must be taken to develop a referral form that invites the involvement of the person making the referral in the assessment process. By requiring detailed descriptions of the problem, for example, the person making the referral is more likely to consider how the curriculum, settings, teacher, or parents have influenced the student. For example, saying "Kelly isn't liked because she's bossy" is less helpful than reporting "When Kelly is left out by her peers she becomes vocal about telling them what to do; her peers respond with even more rejection." A referral form might also focus on a student's strengths, thereby eliciting hints on how to go about teaching and helping the informant view the child in a more positive light. By asking about strategies that have and haven't worked and best guesses as to why, the form suggests that the ultimate purpose of the assessment is for all involved to develop appropriate programming, not just to be satisfied with identification of a child as having LD.

**Records.** Examining school records can provide helpful clues. Was the child absent during presentation of key material? Did the child attend other schools that taught different material or used different approaches? Are family-school relationships or sociocultural and linguistic background factors to be considered? Medical and developmental history, grades, and yearly achievement test scores can shed light on questions to examine further during the assessment process and measures to use.

**Interviews.** Interviews with teachers, parents, the student, and relevant others are extremely important to the assessment process. The interview provides a chronology of relevant events, clarifies the referral reasons and perceptions of the problem, describes strengths that could help with programming, gives insights to different individuals' beliefs and expectations, and determines the assessment goals. An interviewer's wording of questions, follow-up responses, tone of voice, body language, and personal biases can influence the interviewee's responses and subsequent behaviors and attitudes toward the child. For example, teachers are more likely to consider their own actions as affecting children's problems, and begin to change them, when interviewers ask for detailed descriptions of problematical situations rather than for more general and open-ended responses. Given that nearly 40 percent of children are ethnic minorities yet 80 percent of educators are white, interviewers must be particularly respectful of different belief systems and willing to conform their opinions to the families' cultural framework (e.g., an Asian or Hispanic family that doesn't share the interviewer's value for independence). The interviewer also must be mindful of the style and norms for social interaction, behavior, dress, and pace with which families feel most comfortable.

**Naturalistic Observation.** The use of observation early in the assessment process is important in order to provide information about how a problem manifests itself in the actual settings of concern. Often observation shows that formal assessment is not needed; the problem might be resolved instead through consultation with the teacher and others in the pupil's environment.

Observation early in the assessment process teaches the assessment team more about the perspectives and frustrations of individuals in the student's environment and creates a valuable baseline for evaluating the effectiveness of later interventions. Teachers appreciate the time taken by the team to observe in class. In addition, parents often view conclusions drawn from observation as more relevant than those drawn from standardized tests whose results are difficult to understand.

***Observation early in the assessment process teaches the assessment team about the perspectives of individuals in the student's environment and creates a baseline for evaluating the effectiveness of interventions.***

The referred student is not the only focus of observation. Extensive observation of classmates is important because it informs the team of students' typical behaviors in various settings and grades, and about teachers' expectations for these students. This information helps the team to determine whether the behavior of a student with LD is atypical and to predict how the behavior may change over time in a different classroom.

Classroom norms are easy to collect at the same time that one observes the referred student. For example, for a few minutes daily, the referred student and randomly selected nonreferred students might be rated on the number of minutes spent in and out of their seat in various classes, positive and negative comments directed toward them by teachers, the kinds of student behaviors that elicit these comments, number of math problems completed independently, minutes attending to task in different seating arrangements, and so forth.

***Developing local norms is an effective strategy for understanding the extent of an individual student's problems.***

Developing local norms is an effective strategy for understanding the extent of an individual student's problems. Dave, a bright fifth grader, is an interesting case in point. Dave was referred for evaluation because his parents believed that he was irresponsible. He was lazy about making breakfast for his parents, washing the dishes, taking out the garbage, making the beds, emptying the kitty litter, and more. Both parents worked and expected Dave to assume more than a child's share of responsibilities. When Dave's parents were disbelieving that the problem was really with their expectations, Dave's classmates were asked to list all the jobs they were expected to do. The jobs were put on a master list, and each child had to indicate whether he or she did the job never, sometimes, once a week, two to three times a week, or every day, and how often their parents needed to remind them to do the jobs. Dave's parents finally were convinced when they saw that Dave had twice as many responsibilities as the average student (an amazing 56!) and required fewer reminders than any other boys.

A variety of observational methods exist, including giving a detailed narrative description, recording the number of intervals during which a particular behavior occurred (e.g., during how many class periods did the child exit for bathroom breaks), recording the number of times a behavior was observed within a certain time period, how long the behavior continued, or the length of time between an event (e.g., teacher direction to begin a math sheet) and a behavior (the student began working). Ratings by the teacher, parent, or pupil also can be collected. All these data are very helpful to intervention planning. Malcolm's teachers, for example, rated how many minutes he was on task in each class. The average time was five minutes. Malcolm's teachers then decided to award points for every ten minutes of focused attention rather than expecting good attention for the whole period. Malcolm was delighted that his efforts were recognized, and expectations were then gradually increased. Alfonso's case was of a different nature and demonstrates the value of self-monitored observations. For a week, Alfonso marked a tally sheet every time he had a temper tantrum at home. Alfonso also rated how often he *felt* like throwing a tantrum. When they added up the tallies, Alfonso's parents realized that he was indeed showing a good deal of self-control; the suggestion that they should praise this self-control rather than punish the occasional outbursts became easier for his parents to accept.

Reliability is just as much an issue when observing as when testing. Periodic reliability checks with another observer are important because observational reliability and validity can slip with time, and the observer's biases can begin to influence what he or she sees.

**Analogue Observation.** Analogue observations provide a controlled situation outside the classroom in which the behaviors of concern are easier to observe—for example, increments in learning when students are offered incentives. In the Psychoeducational Teaching Laboratory at Syracuse University, for example, evaluators occasionally observe parent-child interactions through a sequence of free play between the parent and child, the child playing while the parent completes forms at one side of the room, the parent and child working on a cooperative task (parent turns the knob that makes a horizontal line and the child turns the knob that makes a vertical line on an Etch-A-Sketch, so as to create a triangle), cleaning up materials, or the parent tutoring the student. Dependence/independence, response to authority and demands for compliance, reward/ discipline patterns, and so forth are observed. Particularly telling are observations of parent reactions as they watch the assessment process through a one-way mirror.

## Multicultural and Linguistic Diversity

A student's language and sociocultural background will influence assessment results in all domains. Therefore, when there is considerable discrepancy between the student and the school in language and sociocultural background, the team must be especially cautious in the interpretation of assessment information.

**Primary Language.** Assessment of primary language is not only common sense but also a requirement under IDEA. When a student is non-English or limited-English speaking, assessment must be conducted in the youngster's primary language and the team should avoid norm-referenced tests of achievement and ability. Although interpreters have been suggested, there are many inherent problems with such attempts. Items do not have the same meaning in both languages, item difficulties change with translations, and translations may not be in the same dialect that the student is used to speaking. Evaluation of discrepancies between intelligence and achievement for these students is best accomplished by using their adaptive behavior as an estimate of intellectual ability. Although nonverbal intelligence tests also can be used, these are less predictive of school functioning than are verbal measures.

*When a student is non-English or limited-English speaking, assessment must be conducted in the youngster's primary language.*

When a nonnative student finally becomes conversationally proficient in English, it does not mean that the youngster has the cognitive and academic language proficiency to do well on standard tests or school tasks. Bilingual students who appear facile with English continue to score lower on verbal than nonverbal tests. This is because, although everyday conversational proficiency can be acquired in 1½ to 2 years of exposure to English, it may take 5 to 7 years to fully absorb the American cultural and language nuances.

*Although everyday conversational proficiency can be acquired in 1½ to 2 years of exposure to English, it may take 5 to 7 years to fully absorb the American cultural and language nuances. This has implications for testing.*

Evaluators also need to be sensitive to the fact that some children who have grown up in English-speaking environments have culturally related language problems as a result of exposure to learning strategies that are disadvantageous in our highly language-loaded classrooms. Collier and Hoover offer this example:

> Many Native American children are taught primarily to use kinesthetic strategies, that is, to do as the knowledgeable one does, with a minimum of oral direction. Young girls learn to weave by watching a weaver and weaving on a small scale loom.

> The oral instruction is not how to weave, but stories and information about sheep, patterns, history, and so on. These are effective strategies within the context, but will not be as effective in the highly oral/aural instruction of the American public school classroom. The teacher will need to provide direct instruction in listening to directions, in following directions, and in monitoring one's own written and oral responses without concrete or kinesthetic cues. (1987, p. 44)

Clearly, the extent of English proficiency and the degree to which this matches classroom expectations are extremely important to consider in evaluations.

*The variability among individuals within a socioeconomic, racial, or ethnically diverse group is often as large or larger than the differences between groups.*

**Sociocultural Background.** The term *sociocultural background* refers to socioeconomic status, race, and ethnicity. None of these variables alone is sufficient to explain a child's achievement because the variability among individuals within a group is often as large or larger than the differences between groups. Therefore, we must be careful to avoid unwarranted generalizations from these factors and instead focus on the specific variables that may influence a particular student's achievement, such as home language, emotional concerns, no books in the home, or the extent of prior familiarity with test-type materials. When these factors are not taken into account, assessment observations can be misinterpreted, and inappropriate identification and programming may occur. Maria's story (page 341) illustrates this point. Another example is of Navajo young children, who may not relate to tests as tasks on which they should attempt to do their best because the concept of evaluation for the purpose of demonstrating competence is unfamiliar to them. Unless the assessment team is sensitive to this cultural attribute, team members may underestimate these students' abilities and knowledge. Because the information-processing weaknesses associated with learning disabilities are far more prevalent among lower-income individuals and among racial and ethnic minorities, it is particularly important to be alert that this fact doesn't bias our assessment and lead to unwarranted identification as learning disabled. Special sensitivity also is required when recommending program modifications and transition plans, so that these interventions match the family's culturally based aspirations.

## Language Domain

*Language competence is critical to academic success, and therefore very important to assess.*

Language competence is critical to academic success and therefore very important to assess. This includes evaluating listening vocabulary, oral vocabulary, auditory discrimination, rhyming and phonological awareness, syntactic and semantic knowledge, articulation, auditory sequencing and memory, word-finding, reasoning through language, and pragmatic speech. Besides using tests to evaluate these skills, speech-language pathologists record samples of children's natural speech to evaluate their conversational abilities. Issues of reliability and validity are just as important in these informal techniques as with standardized measures.

## Educational Domain

*The better a test matches the actual curriculum the better it reflects a student's achievement.*

Schools use a wide variety of general achievement tests as screening devices. The better a test matches the actual curriculum, the better it will reflect a student's achievement. When Hannah has been instructed with concrete math materials, for

## Maria

*Sociocultural factors led to misidentification as mentally retarded.*

Five-year-old Maria had failed her kindergarten screening test and had been referred for additional testing. A school-administered IQ test found that she performed within the retarded range. A segregated class for children who were mentally retarded was recommended. Very upset, Maria's father referred her for an independent evaluation.

A home visit found that Maria's mother spoke only Italian. Her dad, an Italian American, spoke only Italian in the home until a year ago, when he realized that Maria needed to start learning English. One year of English was not enough, however, to allow Maria to perform well on the highly verbal intelligence test she had been given. In addition, Maria's mother—admitting that she was somewhat overprotective—explained that Maria had led a very sheltered existence. She had never used scissors or a knife, had never played unsupervised in a different room in the house, and never helped with simple cooking or other chores. Maria's mother was proud of her management of the household and boasted that Maria did not have to do anything for herself, even pick up toys. TV was not allowed in the home because of fears it would warp Maria's mind. Italian fairy tales were substituted for stories in English. As a result, Maria's understanding of American culture was limited, and she did not have the same fund of general information and experience as other children her age. On the adaptive behavior tests that measure a child's daily living skills, Maria naturally scored poorly. On a kindergarten readiness test her performance was no better. Maria could not identify Goldilocks, Little Red Riding Hood, and Ernie, popular American figures. She did, however, recognize more "advanced" characters to whom she had been introduced in her first few months of kindergarten such as George Washington and Abraham Lincoln.

It was obvious that the IQ test given to Maria had been linguistically and culturally inappropriate. It was suggested that Maria continue with kindergarten and also be allowed to watch some quality children's television programs (such as *Sesame Street*) at home to help her develop her language skills. Her parents were urged to read to her from English-language children's books and also to involve her in out-of-home activities such as trips to museums, children's plays, fairs, and the zoo to increase her exposure to American culture. Taking greater responsibility at home was discussed with her parents.

One year later, Maria's IQ test scores had increased, as had her adaptive behavior scores. However, Maria's English was still halting, even when playing with her friends. Maria could always comprehend teacher directions, but she had trouble segmenting words into their component sounds. Daily language therapy was instituted to try to remediate these weaknesses. Certainly, Maria's language and cultural background put her at a disadvantage in school—enough to nearly be identified as retarded. Maria's parents continue to do everything they can to help Maria succeed and, thanks largely to their love and encouragement, she is a happy, well-adjusted, charming little girl.

example, but has to do paper-pencil calculations on a group test, her poor score will not reflect her real math competencies. Because group tests don't allow for observing an individual's performance, they don't tell us about how a student tried to solve the problems. Individually administered tests, on the other hand, can inflate our estimates of a student's ability to perform in the classroom because these tests have an easier response format and they capitalize on the heightened attention and motivation of the one-to-one format.

Individual diagnostic achievement tests provide information about a student's strengths and weaknesses in reading, written language, and mathematics. However, the grade-equivalent scores they give are not very useful or accurate. All that a second-grade equivalent score tells us is that the child earned the same number of points as the average second grader who took the test. It doesn't tell us how an individual's performance across a range of items departs from what is typical. Therefore, just because a fifth grader, for example, tests as a third-grade equivalent reader, he or she may not be reading in all respects like a third grader.

*Standard scores and percentiles are better than grade-equivalent scores because they use a uniform metric to reflect the degree to which a student's performance departs from that of his or her peers.*

Another problem with grade-level scores is that minor successes or failures can create major fluctuations in grade-level estimates. It's possible, for instance, to score one or two grade levels higher or lower by getting just two or three more items right or wrong. These small differences are virtually meaningless, easily caused by high or low motivation or curriculum differences. Besides, as students get older, a spread of several grade levels is quite common among average students. Therefore, standard scores and percentiles are the measures of choice because they use a uniform metric to reflect the degree to which a student's performance departs from that of his or her peers.

*Scores on various achievement tests of the same skill can vary greatly because of different items, formats, and norms; therefore informal evaluation strategies should supplement formal testing.*

Assessors need to be sensitive to the fact that scores on various achievement tests of the same skill can vary greatly because of different items, formats, or norms. For example, one math test might require only computation, while another test requires understanding of geometric and measurement concepts, graphs, tables, budgeting, and time. One reading test requires oral reading; and another one, silent reading. One test assesses listening comprehension and reading rate; another test doesn't. One of these types of items or formats may be more difficult than another for particular students. Such variability among tests can greatly affect children's scores, the team's interpretations, and recommendations. Therefore, we must learn which tests score high or low at which ages and for which types of students. The test of choice is the one that best matches the student's curriculum, response style, and the specific questions being asked about the student's abilities.

Task analysis, trial teaching, assessing performance on classroom materials, and using books of varying interest and difficulty levels to assess reading skills are encouraged in order to gain the most valid information about a student's overall academic achievement. Informal writing samples, when analyzed for idea development, organization, coherence, language usage, and mechanics relative to classmates' performance, are extremely instructive because written language tests are particularly unsophisticated in helping with instructional recommendations in this area.

Finally, because the study and attending skill weaknesses of students with LD often contribute to their school failure, these learning styles also need to be a major focus of assessment. Informal assessment strategies, observational and interview data, and checklists such as those presented earlier in this chapter can provide very useful information in this regard.

## Intellectual Domain

It's important to remember that intelligence is not an immutable trait of the individual. It is a construct based on performance on a wide variety of tasks that predict school success. Intelligence tests are merely small samples of behavior, and scores do change with time. After the preschool years, IQ becomes more stable and a good predictor of success on schoolwork. As such, IQ tests are helpful in identifying learning disabilities when achievement falls below what would be expected. However, they measure only a portion of the variety of intelligent behavior needed in our complex world, and therefore tell us very little about a person's ability to form healthy relationships and find satisfying work—attributes that are critical to life adjustment.

*Intelligence is not an immutable trait of the individual. It is a construct based on performance on a wide variety of tasks that predict school success.*

The Wechsler Intelligence Scale for Children III is the most frequently used intelligence test. It measures skills in verbal comprehension, perceptual organization, attention, and processing speed with high reliability and validity. Various Wechsler Intelligence Scale profiles have been related to unique cognitive styles and processing patterns in students with reading and learning disabilities. Although these patterns do give hints of the strengths and weaknesses that have an effect on learning, they alone are not valid for diagnosing a specific type of learning disability or for generating remedial strategies. This is because students with LD who show similar Wechsler patterns can be very different in their academic strengths and weaknesses (they may have earned the same scores by approaching the tasks in very different ways), and those with different Wechsler patterns can be very similar in achievement (because the same school tasks can be learned in a variety of ways).

In fact, no one intelligence pattern on current tests has been identified as definitely unique to learning disabilities. For example, a significant 15-point standard score spread between verbal and performance (nonverbal) scales is something that one would expect to have an influence on achievement. Yet this spread is apparent in up to one-fourth of average achievers. Moreover, students with LD, who are uneven in their achievement, surprisingly show more even patterns between IQ subtests than do their nondisabled peers. The best use of IQ subtest profiles, therefore, is to generate hypotheses about the individual child's strengths that might be useful to teaching. These hypotheses then need to be explored further through trial teaching.

*No one intelligence pattern on current tests has been identified as unique to LD.*

Other popular measures of intelligence include the Stanford-Binet Fourth Edition and the Woodcock-Johnson III Tests of Cognitive Abilities. These sample more types of memory and information-processing abilities than do the Wechsler Scales.

As our concepts of intelligence broaden, new theories and tests are emerging. Sternberg, for example, is developing an IQ measure that taps more information-processing abilities, including our analytic reasoning, how automatic our learned skills are, and how well we apply what we know to everyday problems. Naglieri and Das have recently developed the Cognitive Assessment System, which shows promise in furthering our understanding of the information-processing patterns important to the achievement of children with different disabilities. The system assesses the cognitive processes of planning, attention, simultaneous (global) processing, and successive (sequential) processing and steers clear of items that could be directly influenced by school learning. Finally Gardner, concerned that American schools are wasting human potential with their nearly exclusive emphasis on linguistic and logical-mathematical intelligences urges educators to assess and program for the development of six additional types of intelligence: spatial (sculpting, surveying), musical (composing, singing), bodily-kinesthetic (athletics, arts and crafts, dancing), interpersonal (sensitivity to others), intrapersonal (awareness of one's own feelings), and natural (ability to discern patterns in nature). Although Gardner refers to these as discrete forms of intelligence, they actually are a set of competencies that depend on overlapping underlying abilities. Gardner suggests that we observe children's functioning in all these areas and encourage our schools to nurture this broader range of talents.

***When IQ tests are renormed, the student with LD is likely to earn a lower IQ than on prior testing because the new norm population is more knowledgable. This "Flynn Effect" must be accounted for in test interpretation.***

A final note of caution regarding IQ tests. These tests are renormed at periodic intervals, and with each new norm, the American population seems to get smarter. That is, it takes more raw score points to earn the same IQ score on the test (the same percentile standing) than it did using the old norms. This phenomenon has been called the "Flynn effect," after the professor who called attention to this upward creep. The upward creep in skills needed to earn IQ scores is caused by children bringing more sophisticated knowledge and problem-solving strategies to the test than in the past. This is related to a number of factors: exposure to a more complex society, more preschool programs, higher-quality educational opportunities since desegregation, better nutrition and prenatal care, reduction in family size among African American families (which increases the financial resources available per child), and an enormous increase in parental educational attainment, particularly among African Americans and Hispanics. The Flynn effect becomes problematical for a child like Melissa who is being retested for identification as learning disabled on the same IQ test, but using newer norms. If Melissa has been growing cognitively at a steady pace, instead of her IQ remaining the same as it was, it ends up 7 to 8 points lower than on the older test's norms. This difference is enough for a significant IQ-achievement discrepancy to disappear, and for identification as a student with LD and services to be withdrawn. Recognizing that the new norms are "stricter," psychologists need to consider adjusting the IQ scores of children like Melissa upward in recognition of the Flynn effect.

## Perceptual-Motor Domain

***Perceptual-motor measures are not valid for diagnosing a neurological impairment or for predicting school achievement, but they can guide remediation of handwriting and perceptually related academic weaknesses.***

Because motor problems are so common among the brain injured, fine-motor measures are often used to screen for students whose learning problems may have neurological roots. Although these measures aren't valid for diagnosing a neurological impairment or for predicting school achievement, they can be helpful in guiding remediation related to handwriting difficulties. They can also alert us to perceptual weaknesses that may be interfering with achievement, particularly in the early school years. These measures generally have inadequate norms, reliability, and validity.

## Medical-Developmental Domain

Evaluators need to determine whether medical, sensory, or health factors affect a child's learning problems. Medical records and medical-developmental history checklists completed by parents are helpful in this area of assessment, although some caution is wise because parental retrospective reports of events in a child's life sometimes have questionable accuracy. Also used within this domain are screening devices for visual or hearing impairments, physical and neurological problems, and attention-deficit hyperactivity disorder.

Neuropsychological assessment is helpful in clarifying the information-processing strength-weakness patterns of children with LD. These tests assess balance, coordination, and fine-motor dexterity as well as a broad range of intellectual, language, perceptual, problem-solving, and memory abilities. Often neuropsychological batteries make use of tests from other domains to compare left and right hemisphere integrity (linguistic and analytical-sequential processing vs. spatial and holistic processing) and front-back brain integrity (motor, sensory, and planning functions vs. visual-processing abilities). Although these procedures offer clues about the nature of the disorder underlying a learning disability, their validity for program planning is only now being researched.

***Neuropsychological assessment is helpful in clarifying children's information-processing strength-weakness patterns.***

Because of LD's genetic link, finding out about the learning histories of a student's relatives should not be overlooked. Interventions that succeeded for others may be worth attempting if the student's learning profile is similar.

***Because of LD's genetic link, the learning histories of a student's relatives should not be overlooked.***

## Adaptive Behavior Domain

*Adaptive behavior* is the degree to which a person meets the standards of personal independence and social responsibility expected of his or her age and cultural group in various settings, for example, self-help skills, independence, and responsibility. IDEA requires that assessment of adaptive behavior also address nonschool settings, and a special focus on this domain occurs during transition planning.

Adaptive behavior measures such as the Vineland Adaptive Behavior Scales are helpful in assessing nonschool role functioning. Peer sociometric scales that evaluate a child's popularity can also be used to see how a student adapts to a specific peer group (e.g., "Name three children with whom you would most/least like to do a project"). In addition, checklists can compare ratings from teachers, parents, the student, and sometimes peers. Because ratings are clearly influenced by the raters' attitudes, often ratings of the same student by different adults don't agree. This offers insights into those environments in which the adults' attitudes are likely to be most supportive of the student's emotional, social, and academic growth.

Adaptive behavior measures often are used when intelligence test estimates are questioned. When used in this way, evaluators need to be sensitive to factors that can underestimate adaptive skills, such as family overprotectiveness or not allowing children to handle currency or assume jobs around the house.

***Adaptive behavior measures often are used when IQ test scores are questioned.***

## Social-Emotional Domain

Personality assessment has undergone great change in the past two decades. The old assumption that problems exist solely within the individual has been challenged because different situations clearly have different influences on a person's personality. We know ourselves that we behave differently in different situations. We may be quite assertive with a grocery clerk and downright deferential with a police officer. Consequently, personality assessment now emphasizes assessment of people's interactions in different environments, rather than personality traits alone.

***Personality assessment emphasizes assessment of people's interactions in different settings, rather than personality traits alone.***

There are numerous behavior checklists that are helpful in examining social-emotional concerns. These can be completed by the student, parent, or teachers. Self-concept measures are also helpful in understanding how students feel about themselves in relation to home life, school, and peers, though students frequently inflate their self-evaluation—perhaps as a protective coping strategy.

Projective measures—which assume we will assign our feelings to essentially neutral stimuli like inkblots and drawings—have a long history of use but little or no reliability and validity. Behavior rating scales, checklists, and direct observation provide far more useful and verifiable information about how students feel about themselves, how they relate to others, and how they deal with stressful or unpleasant situations.

### Environmental Domain

*Because decisions about students with LD involve programming in multiple settings, we need to understand those settings and how their structure and climate can help or hinder students' development.*

Although it is obvious that environmental factors play a key role in learning, very few strategies have been developed to assess them. Nevertheless, because decisions about students who have learning disabilities involve consideration of programming in multiple settings, we need to thoroughly understand those settings and how their structure and social climate can help or hinder students' development.

Chapter 14 deals with the many school environment variables that need to be examined in comprehensive assessments, such as the openness of teachers to a student with learning problems, seating arrangements, how the curriculum is delivered, and classroom distractions. Chapter 13 addresses the important variables that need to be assessed in the student's most important setting, the home, in order to foster maximal academic and personal growth.

## Summary

The decisions that we make on behalf of students involve assessment, whether by means of informal consultation or by formal evaluation. The purpose for evaluation, whether screening, identification, instructional planning, or charting pupil progress, influences the kinds of assessment strategies chosen. Different models of assessment help evaluators focus on the student, the student's interactions with the curriculum, the student's interactions with various environments, or the student within broader sociocultural contexts. Each model tends to use a different set of assessment instruments, and is better suited to address a particular purpose for assessment. Evaluation with norm- and criterion-referenced measures, informal evaluation techniques, curriculum-based assessment strategies, or authentic assessment constitutes only a portion of the assessment process. Referral forms, records, interviews, consultation, and observation in natural or analogue settings also are important means of assisting decision making. Regardless of the method chosen to collect information, attention to issues of reliability, validity, relevance of content, and appropriateness of the comparison or norm group is important.

*A comprehensive evaluation analyzes the student's characteristics, the tasks the student is expected to accomplish, and the settings in which the student lives and learns to identify how the positive attributes of each can be capitalized on to foster the student's academic, personal, and social growth.*

Comprehensive assessment of students with LD is best implemented within a team approach that applies multiple perspectives to multiple assessment domains: primary language and sociocultural background, language skills, achievement, intelligence, perceptual-motor skills, medical-developmental history, adaptive behavior, social-emotional adjustment, and environments. With such a comprehensive analysis of the student's characteristics, the curriculum the student is expected to master, and the environments in which the student lives and learns, it is more likely that the positive attributes of each can be identified and capitalized on to promote the student's academic, personal, and social growth.

## Helpful Resources

### Assessment Purposes


Algozzine, B., & Ysseldyke, J. E. (1986). The future of the LD field: Screening and diagnosis. *Journal of Learning Disabilities, 19,* 394–398.

Fuchs, D., & Fuchs, L. S. (1986). Test procedure bias: A meta-analysis of examiner effects. *Review of Educational Research, 56,* 243–262.

Fugate, D. J., Clarizio, H. F., & Phillips, S. E. (1993). Referral-to-placement ratio: A finding in need of reassessment? *Journal of Learning Disabilities, 26,* 413–416.

Graden, J. L., Casey, A., & Bonstrom, O. (1985). Implementing a prereferral intervention system: Part II. The data. *Exceptional Children, 51* (6), 487–496.

Meltzer, L., & Reid, D. K. (1994). New directions in the assessment of students with special needs: The shift toward a constructivist perspective. *The Journal of Special Education, 28,* 338–355.

Salvia, J., & Ysseldyke, J. E. (2001). *Assessment* (8th ed.). Boston: Houghton Mifflin.

Shepard, L. A., & Smith, M. L. (1983). An evaluation of the identification of learning disabled students in Colorado. *Learning Disability Quarterly, 6,* 115–127.

Zigmond, N., & Miller, S. E. (1986). Assessment for instructional planning. *Exceptional Children, 52,* 501–509.


### Models of Assessment


Anastasi, A. (1982). *Psychological testing* (5th ed). New York: Macmillan.

Conoley, J. C. (1980). Organizational assessment. *School Psychology Review, 9,* 83–89.

Cronbach, L. J. (1975). Five decades of public controversy over mental testing. *American Psychologist, 30,* 1–14.

Eysenck, H. (1984). The effect of race on human abilities and mental test scores. In C. R. Reynolds & R. T. Brown (Eds.), *Perspectives on bias in mental testing.* New York: Plenum Press.

Frisby, C., & Braden, J. P. (1992). Feuerstein's dynamic assessment approach: A semantic, logical, and empirical critique. *The Journal of Special Education, 26,* 281–301.

Jensen, A. R. (1984). Test bias: Concepts and criticisms. In C. R. Reynolds & R. T. Brown (Eds.), *Perspectives on bias in mental testing.* New York: Plenum Press.

Keller, H. R. (1981). Behavioral consultation. In J. C. Conoley (Ed.), *Consultation in schools: Theory, research, technology.* New York: Academic Press.

Oakland, T., & Laosa, L. M. (1977). Professional, legislative, and judicial influences on psychoeducational assessment practices in schools. In T. Oakland (Ed.), *Psychological and educational assessment of minority children.* New York: Brunner/Mazel.

Walberg, H. J. (1977). Psychology of learning environments: Behavioral, structural, or perceptual? In L. S. Shulman (Ed.), *Review of research in education* (Vol. 4). Itasca, IL: F. E. Peacock.


### Assessment Methods


Archbald, D. A., & Newmann, F. M. (1988). *Beyond standardized testing: Assessing authentic academic achievement in the secondary school.* Reston, VA: National Association of Secondary School Principals.

Bell, P. F., Lentz, F. E., & Graden, J. L. (1992). Effects of curriculum-test overlap on standardized achievement test scores: Identifying systematic confounds in educational decision making. *School Psychology Review, 21,* 644–655.

Bigge, J. L., & Stump, C. S. (1999). *Curriculum, assessment, and instruction for students with disabilities.* NY: Wadsworth.

Bursuck, W. D., & Lessen, E. (1987). A classroom-based model for assessing students with learning disabilities. *Learning Disabilities Focus, 3,* 17–29.

Choate, J. S., Enright, B. E., Miller, L. J., Poteet, J. A., & Rakes, T. A. (1995). *Curriculum-based assessment and programming* (3rd ed.). Boston: Allyn & Bacon.

Deno, S. L. (1985). Curriculum-based measurement: The emerging alternative. *Exceptional Children, 52,* 219–232.

Elliott, S. N. (1991). Authentic assessment: An introduction to a neobehavioral approach to classroom assessment. *School Psychology Quarterly, 6,* 273–278.

Fuchs, L. S., Fuchs, D., & Stecker, P. M. (1989). Effects of curriculum-based measurement on teachers' instructional planning. *Journal of Learning Disabilities, 22,* 51–59.

Germann, G., & Tindal, G. (1985). An application of curriculum-based assessment: The use of direct and repeated measurement. *Exceptional Children, 52,* 244–265.

Good, R. H., III, & Salvia, J. (1988). Curriculum bias in published, norm-referenced reading tests: Demonstrable effects. *School Psychology Review, 17,* 51–60.

Gopaul-McNicol, S., & Armour-Thomas, E. (2002). *Assessment and culture: Psychological tests with minority populations.* New York: Academic Press.

Lidz, C. (1995). Dynamic assessment and the legacy of L. S. Vygotsky. *School Psychology International, 16,* 143–153.

Marston, D., Mirkin, P., & Deno, S. (1984). Curriculum-based measurement: An alternative to traditional screening, referral, and identification. *Journal of Special Education, 18,* 109–117.

*Mental Measurements Yearbook* series. Lincoln, NE: The Buros Institute of Mental Measurements. The University of Nebraska–Lincoln.

Popham, W. J. (1999). *Classroom assessment: What teachers need to know* (2nd ed.). Boston: Allyn & Bacon.

Reynolds, C. R., & Gutkin, T. B. (Eds.) (1999). Section 3: Psychological and educational assessment. *The handbook of school psychology* (3rd ed.) (pp. 291–595). New York: John Wiley & Sons.

Rueda, R., & Garcia, E. (1997). Do portfolios make a difference for diverse students? The influence of type of data on making instructional decisions. *Learning Disabilities Research & Practice, 12,* 114–122.

Shapiro, E. S., & Derr, T. F. (1987). An examination of overlap between reading curricula and standardized achievement tests. *Journal of Special Education, 21* (2), 59–67.

Shinn, M. R., Good, R. H., Knutson, N., Tilly, W. D., & Collins, V. L. (1992). Curriculum-based measurement of oral reading fluency: A confirmatory analysis of its relation to reading. *School Psychology Review, 21,* 459–479.

Shinn, M. R., Rodden-Nord, K., & Knutson, N. (1993). Using curriculum-based measurement to identify potential candidates for reintegration into general education. *The Journal of Special Education, 27,* 202–221.

Shinn, M. R., Tindal, G. A., & Spira, D. A. (1987). Special education referrals as an index of teacher tolerance: Are teachers imperfect tests? *Exceptional Children, 54,* 32–40.

Shinn, M. R., Tindal, G. A., & Stein, S. (1988). Curriculum-based measurement and the identification of mildly handicapped students: A research review. *Professional School Psychology, 3,* 69–85.

Shriner, J., & Salvia, J. (1988). Chronic noncorrespondence between elementary math curricula and arithmetic tests. *Exceptional Children, 55,* 240–248.

Smith, C. R. (1980). Assessment alternatives: Nonstandardized procedures. *School Psychology Review, 9,* 46–57.

Witt, J. C., Elliott, S. N., Kramer, J. J., & Gresham, F. M. (1994). *Assessment of children: Fundamental methods and practices.* Madison, WI: Brown & Benchmark.

## Multidimensional Assessment Approaches

Fuchs, D., Zern, D. S., & Fuchs, L. S. (1983). A microanalysis of participant behavior in familiar and unfamiliar test conditions. *Exceptional Children, 50,* 75–77.

Smith, C. R. (1999). Transdisciplinary training at Syracuse University's Psychoeducational Teaching Laboratory. In D. H. Evensen & P. B. Mosenthal (Eds.), *Advances in reading/language research: Reconsidering the role of the reading clinic in a new age of literacy* (pp. 149–173). Stamford, CT: JAI Press.

Taylor, L., Adelman, H. S., & Kaser-Boyd, N. (1985). Minors' attitudes and competence toward participation in psychoeducational decisions. *Professional Psychology: Research and Practice, 16,* 226–235.

## Assessment Domains

Alvarez, V., & Adelman, H. S. (1986). Overstatements of self-evaluations by students with psychoeducational problems. *Journal of Learning Disabilities, 19,* 567–571.

Coleman, M., & Harmer, W. R. (1982). A comparison of standardized tests and informal placement procedures. *Journal of Learning Disabilities, 15,* 396–398.

Collier, C., & Hoover, J. J. (1987). Sociocultural considerations when referring minority children for learning disabilities. *Learning Disabilities Focus, 3,* 39–45.

Daub, D., & Colarusso, R. P. (1996). The validity of the WJ-R, PIAT-R, and DAB-2 reading subtests with students with learning disabilities. *Learning Disabilities Research & Practice, 11,* 90–95.

Dennis, R. E., & Giangreco, M. F. (1996). Creating conversation: Reflections on cultural sensitivity in family interviewing. *Exceptional Children, 63,* 103–116.

Deyhle, D. (1987). Learning failure: Tests as gatekeepers and the culturally different child. In H. E. Trueba (Ed.), *Success or failure?* Rawley, MA: Heinle & Heinle.

Elliott, S. N., Busse, R. T., & Gresham, F. M. (1993). Behavior rating scales: Issues of use and development. *School Psychology Review, 22,* 313–321.

Flynn, J. R. (1987). Massive IQ gains in 14 nations: What IQ tests really measure. *Psychological Bulletin, 101*, 171–191.

Gardner, H. (1983). *Frames of mind: The theory of multiple intelligence.* New York: Basic Books.

Gottfredson, L. S. (1997). Mainstream science on intelligence: An editorial with 52 signatories, history, and bibliography. *Intelligence, 24*, 13–23.

Joschko, M., & Rourke, B. P. (1985). Neuropsychological subtypes of learning-disabled children who exhibit the ACID pattern on the WISC. In B. P. Rourke (Ed.), *Neuropsychology of learning disabilities.* New York: Guilford Press.

Kavale, K. A., & Forness, S. R. (1984). A meta-analysis of the validity of Wechsler Scale profiles and recategorizations: Patterns or parodies? *Learning Disability Quarterly, 7*, 136–156.

Kranzler, J. H. (1997). Educational policy issues related to the use and interpretation of intelligence tests in the schools. *School Psychology Review, 26*, 150–162.

Messick, S. (1995). Validity of psychological assessment: Validation of inferences from persons' responses and performances as scientific inquiry into score meaning. *American Psychologist, 50*, 741–749.

Mischel, W. (1979). On the interface of cognition and personality: Beyond the person-situation debate. *American Psychologist, 34*, 740–754.

Parmar, R. S., Frazita, R., & Cawley, J. F. (1996). Mathematics assessment for students with mild disabilities: An exploration of content validity. *Learning Disability Quarterly, 19*, 127–136.

Sattler, J. M. (2001). *Assessment of children: Cognitive applications* (4th ed). San Diego: Jerome M. Sattler, Publisher.

Sattler, J. M. (2001). *Assessment of children: Behavioral and clinical applications.* San Diego: Jerome M. Sattler, Publisher.

Slate, J. R. (1996). Interrelations of frequently administered achievement measures in the determination of specific learning disabilities. *Learning Disabilities Research & Practice, 11*, 86–89.

Sternberg, R. J. (1986). *Intelligence applied: Understanding and increasing your intellectual skills.* San Diego: Harcourt Brace Jovanovich.

Tombari, M. L., & Bergan, J. K. (1978). Consultant cues and teacher verbalizations, judgments, and expectancies concerning children's adjustment problems. *Journal of School Psychology, 16*, 212–219.

Wilen, D. K., & Sweeting, C. V. (1986). Assessment of limited English proficient Hispanic students. *School Psychology Review, 15*, 59–75.

CHAPTER TEN

# Planning Educational Interventions

*In regular education, the system tends to dictate the curriculum, but in special education the child dictates the curriculum. Because of the variation among children with LD in abilities and learning styles, no two children's problems will be exactly alike.*

**ARMED WITH INFORMATION** about learning disabilities in general and with the results of comprehensive assessments, the next task for those who teach and care for students with LD is to plan effective educational interventions. This is certainly not a simple process. It involves planning individualized instruction, adapting instruction to each student's learning ability and style, coordinating the roles of various professionals, and deciding how and where the instruction will be provided.

In regular education the system tends to dictate the curriculum, but in special education it is the child who dictates the curriculum. Because of the vast variation among children with LD, planning educational interventions that will match their abilities and learning styles is a highly individualized process, and each child's program will be different. Many of these students have severe skill or behavior deficits that make them especially difficult to teach. Others have milder weaknesses that respond rapidly to appropriately structured learning tasks and settings. As a consequence, teachers have to remain flexible, creative, and patient as they work with each unique pupil. Successes happen. But so do plateaus and backsliding. So teachers need to be ready to rethink and modify their programs as often as necessary, whatever it takes.

*Teachers must ask themselves questions like "How can I change* what *I am teaching and* how *I am teaching?" repeatedly throughout the school year.*

## Planning Individualized Instruction

Individualized instruction tailors an educational program to a student's specific needs. And once planned, programs aren't—or shouldn't be—static. Teachers must ask themselves questions like " How can I change *what* I am teaching and *how* I am teaching" not just once but repeatedly throughout the school year.

"The Animal School" story is an amusing and very revealing take on what happens when pupil and programs are mismatched. When students are forced to learn something they aren't ready to learn, or learn it in a way that is not natural for them, failure is predictable. If there are too many failures, too often, children learn to hate school and everything associated with learning. This in turn can deter achievement in academic, social, or extracurricular areas in which the child might have done well.

*When students are forced to learn something they aren't ready to learn, or learn it in a way that is not natural for them, failure is predictable.*

## The Individualized Education Program

The Individuals with Disabilities Education Act (IDEA) requires that each student who has been identified with LD receive an individualized education program (IEP). The specific program is set down in a written statement developed and reviewed annually by the student's parents or guardians, his or her special education teacher, regular classroom teacher, a professional who can interpret the instructional

*IDEA requires that each student identified with LD receive an individualized education program (IEP).*

### The Animal School

*A parable about the predictability of failure when students are forced to learn in a way that is not natural for them.*

Once upon a time, the animals decided they must do something heroic to meet the problems of "a new world." So they organized a school.

They adopted an activity curriculum consisting of running, climbing, swimming, and flying. To make it easier to administer the curriculum all the animals took all the subjects.

The duck was excellent in swimming, in fact better than his instructor; but he made only passing grades in flying and was very poor in running. Since he was slow in running, he had to stay after school and also drop swimming in order to practice running. This was kept up until his web feet were badly worn and he was only average in swimming. But average was acceptable in school so nobody worried about that except the duck.

The rabbit started at the top of the class in running, but had a nervous breakdown because of so much make-up work in swimming.

The squirrel was excellent in climbing until he developed frustration in the flying class where his teacher made him start from the ground up instead of from the tree top down. He also developed a "charlie horse" from over-exertion and then got C in climbing and D in running.

The eagle was a problem child and was disciplined severely. In the climbing class he beat all the others to the top of the tree, but insisted on using his own way to get there.

At year's end an abnormal eel that could swim exceedingly well, and also run, climb, and fly a little, had the highest average and was valedictorian.

The prairie dogs stayed out of school and fought the tax levy because the administration would not add digging and burrowing to the curriculum. They apprenticed their children to a badger and later joined the groundhogs and gophers to start a successful private school.

*Source:* Reavis, G. H. (1953). The animal school. *Educational Forum, 17* (2), p. 141. Reprinted by permission of Kappa Delta Pi Honor Society in Education.

implications of evaluation results, a school administrator such as the principal or pupil personnel director who is qualified to provide for special education programming and knowledgeable about the school's curriculum and resources, the student (when appropriate), and other related service personnel. The IEP should include:

1. The student's present level of educational performance and needs.
2. A statement of academic and behavioral goals for the year (e.g., complete the second-grade reading curriculum; attend to task for 20 minutes.)
3. A statement of short-term objectives (master the short vowel sounds; increase sight vocabulary from 50 to 100 words).
4. The specific education and related services to be provided, by whom, where, and how often (resource room for 1 hour a day; speech therapy for 45 minutes twice weekly).
5. Specification of materials and methods to be used and why.
6. Objective evaluation criteria and the timeline for determining whether instructional objectives are being met.
7. The projected date to begin services and how long they will be provided.
8. An explanation of how the student's disability affects his or her involvement and progress in the general curriculum, and the extent to which the student will be educated in a regular classroom or another least restrictive environment and participate in extracurricular activities.
9. Any modifications the student will need to participate in district or state-mandated regular assessments; if it is inappropriate for the student to participate in these assessments, a statement of why and what the alternative will be.
10. How the student's parents will be kept informed of progress and any proposed changes to the program.

Naturally the IEP is most effective when the planners can draw on the student's assessment findings to understand his or her abilities and learning styles, additional contributors to the learning problem, and the program characteristics that may best match the student's needs.

*By age 16, the IEP must put into place a comprehensive transition plan.*

By the time the student is 14 years old, the IEP must specify the anticipated academic or vocational course of study that the student will follow to prepare for life after high school. By age 16, and younger if necessary, the IEP must put into place a comprehensive transition plan. The responsibilities of various professionals and community agencies are laid out, and the student is invited to participate in the transition planning meetings. If students choose not to attend, school personnel must make sure their preferences and interests are considered.

*Class placement decisions during the IEP process consider the least restrictive settings in which the goals, materials, and methods specified in the IEP can best be implemented.*

Class placement decisions during the IEP process reflect the least restrictive settings in which the goals, materials, and methods specified in the IEP can best be implemented. Very important among these considerations are the degree of integration with nondisabled peers, and the training and personality of the teacher that will best serve the student. The inverted triangle in Figure 10.1 depicts the various class placement options for students with LD, from least to most segregated and specialized. Over 80 percent of students with LD are educated within the top four models in this figure. The more severe a student's learning disability, the more likely that the student will be placed in a setting that decreases the frequency of interaction with average achieving peers.

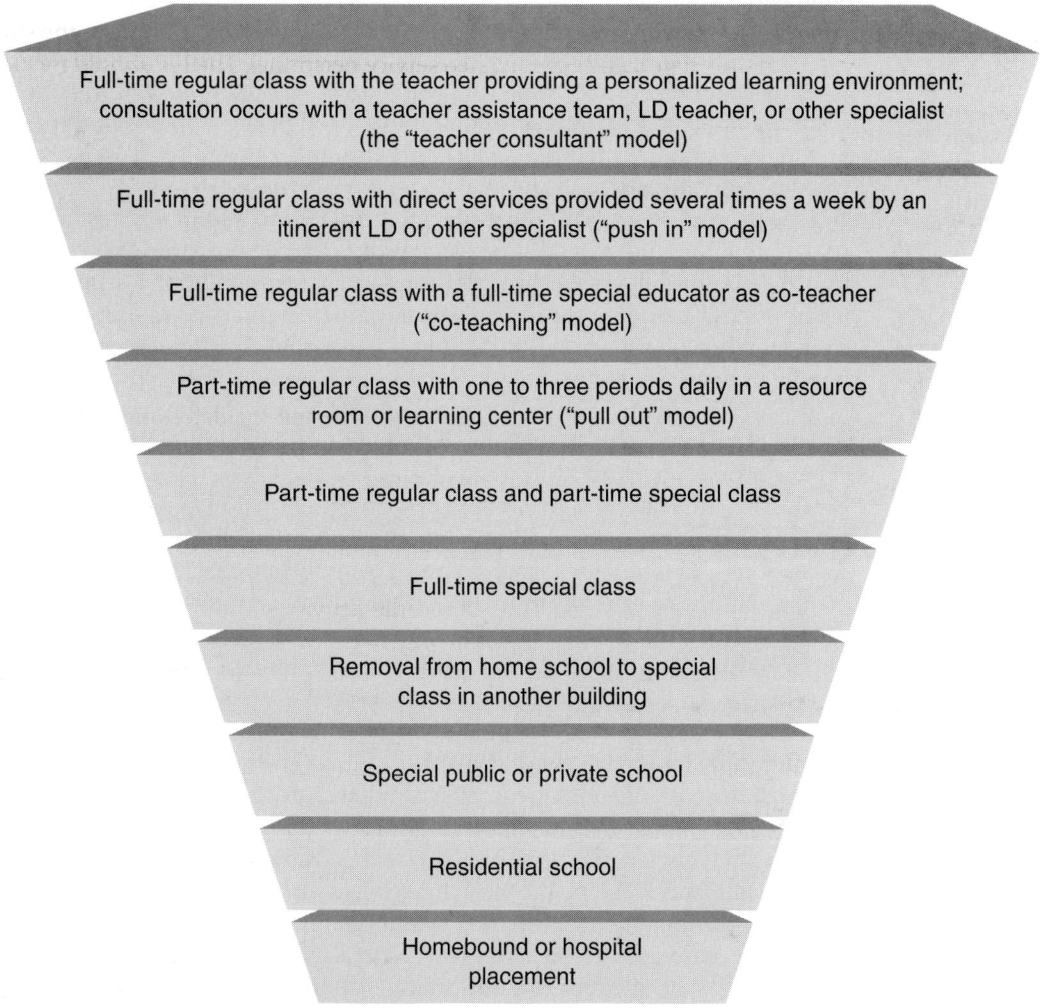

**Figure 10.1** Class placement options from least *(top)* to most *(bottom)* segregated and specialized.

The teacher is the most critical element in the class placement decision, far more important than any single method or material. When the teacher and student's styles conflict, even the most interesting and compelling material or peer group is unlikely to capture the student's attention, interest, and energy. An impulsive teacher, for example, might bombard some students with more information than they can handle. An overly detailed, reflective teacher is likely to bore the student who has attention weaknesses. A teacher who prefers teaching to the whole class will not benefit a child whose attention requires very precise direction within a

*The teacher is the most critical element in the placement decision, far more important than any single method or material.*

small group. A teacher who delegates teaching students with LD to an aide communicates his or her feelings to classmates, potentially deterring the academic and social opportunities of the learning disabled in that classroom.

*The classroom's peer group must be age appropriate and provide a positive academic and social model.*

The teacher-student relationship is fundamental to building the student's self-concept, interest in learning, and willingness to collaborate in the instructional planning process. It is equally important that the peer group be age-appropriate, provide a positive academic and social model, and be open to including students who learn in different ways.

*When the IEP calls for the student to be placed in a regular classroom, it's important that the student's skills be compatible with the instructional opportunities, given certain modifications and accommodations.*

When the IEP calls for the student to be placed in a regular classroom, it's important that the student's skills be compatible with the instructional opportunities in that setting. With certain modifications and accommodations, such as those in Figure 10.2, the student should be able to participate in class as fully as any other student. When it's time to study fractions, for example, the student with LD needs to be able to benefit from this instruction, but perhaps be allowed to use a calculator. Math word problems can be set up in numeral form for the child with reading deficits. A student who has trouble with written expression might take multiple-choice or oral American history tests instead of essay tests. Or a ninth grader with vocabulary and reading deficits could read an easier version of an earth science text, one that still makes it possible for him or her to participate knowledgeably in class discussions and laboratory experiments. It is important that modifications and accommodations be carefully thought out. Overuse of accommodations and modifications when they are unnecessary can deny the student important learning opportunities, hurt independence, and affect the student's motivation to take on challenges.

*Overuse of accommodations and modifications should be avoided so that learning opportunities, independence, and the motivation to take on challenges are not limited.*

The academic schedules of students with LD must be planned carefully so that they are included in those general education classes from which they can get the most benefit and enjoyment. Special education classes should be reserved for the times when inclusion in regular education is counterproductive.

As students get older, they become more sensitive to the stigma of leaving class for "pull out" special help. But "push in" services can be equally stigmatizing. Therefore, we are finding that co-teaching by a special educator in the regular classroom may be the option of choice. Better yet, a general education teacher who is also certified to teach special education can personalize the learning environment without calling special attention to the student with LD. When the co-teaching option is chosen, co-teachers should make sure to also teach high achievers in the classroom in order to avoid stigmatizing students with LD. Regardless of the system selected for ensuring special education help, the regular and special education teachers must regularly plan, coordinate, and evaluate a pupil's program so that teaching objectives, methods, and materials complement one another and facilitate the student's inclusion and progress in the regular curriculum.

All this said, in reality many professionals complain that the IEP is cumbersome and not worth the effort. They say that once written, the program is rarely consulted again until the next annual review. In addition, few teachers are well trained in translating assessment information into curriculum plans and writing instructional objectives. The truth is that the IEP can establish and monitor quantity and place of teaching but not quality. For example, it can mandate that Carlos must have untimed tests, but it can't ensure that Mr. Kram, the biology teacher, won't be so angered by what he sees as unfair practices that he grades Carlos lower

**Modifications and Accommodations for Students with LD**

Modifications and accommodations such as those listed below can be either formally specified on students' Individual Education Programs (IEPs) or worked out informally with teachers and school administrators. When they are specified on an IEP, all the child's teachers are legally required to comply with them. In most cases, accommodations and modifications specified on a high school IEP will continue to be honored by colleges and vocational programs. Students with documented disabilities are also allowed some accommodations on college entrance exams (SATs and ACTs) and state and national competency tests.

**In the Classroom**

- Allow preferred seating (near the teacher, close to the blackboard)
- Allow extra time to answer questions and to complete written work
- Provide copies of laboratory or lecture notes (notes can be provided by either the teacher or another student)
- Allow use of a tape recorder to record lectures
- Allow use of a calculator
- Provide access to a computer
- Allow alternative activities (e.g., ask student to prepare a video instead of writing a report)
- Highlight texts and worksheets to help student locate most important material
- Provide instructions both orally and in writing
- Provide more or fewer visual aids (depending on type of disability)
- Provide ready access to math tables, lists of formulas, maps, and so on (rather than requiring the student to memorize such material)
- Assign lab or study partners to help with particular tasks or subjects
- Preview written material (discuss contents of assigned texts in advance); pre-teach key vocabulary words
- Exempt student from selected requirements or activities (e.g., memorize periodic tables; oral math drills)

**Testing**

- Allow alternate settings (student may take tests in library, resource room, at home)
- Allow flexible scheduling (student may take tests after school, during study hall or resource period; test may be completed in two or more sessions)
- Extend or waive time limits
- Allow directions and test questions to be read to student
- Rephrase test questions in simpler language as necessary
- Allow student to answer questions orally instead of in writing
- Allow short-answer-only tests (true/false, multiple choice)
- Allow essay-only tests
- Allow use of calculator or math facts chart
- If student is unable to memorize, allow access to dates/facts/formulas on "cheat sheets"
- Allow tests to be taken on a computer (at school or at home)
- Allow student to circle answers in test booklet rather than use a computerized answer sheet

**Figure 10.2** Modifications are changes in course content, teaching strategies, testing, and student responses that fundamentally alter or lower expectations of the course, standard, or test. Accommodations are changes that do not fundamentally alter or lower the expectations of the course, standard, or test.

*Source:* Reprinted with the permission of The Free Press, a Division of Simon & Schuster Adult Publishing Group, from *Learning Disabilities A to Z: A Parent's Complete Guide to Learning Disabilities from Preschool to Adulthood* by Corinne R. Smith and Lisa W. Strick. Copyright © 1997 by Corrine R. Smith and Lisa W. Strick.

*(continued)*

- Reduce number of test questions or problems (student is tested on ten division problems or vocabulary words rather than twenty-five)

**Homework**
- Give students their homework assignments in writing on a daily or weekly basis (as opposed to giving assignments orally or expecting them to be copied from board)
- Arrange for textbooks on tape
- Allow all or part of assigned texts to be read to student
- Allow use of computers to scan and "read" written material
- Reduce total amount of material to be read (teacher highlights key passages, for example)
- Allow assigned texts to be rewritten in simpler language
- Allow text alternatives (permit student to watch movie version of Shakespeare's *Romeo and Juliet* instead of reading it)
- Allow students to record assignments on tape rather than writing
- Allow student to dictate reports to a "scribe" (often a parent) or give reports orally
- Reduce number of questions to be answered and/or length of written assignments (answer five comprehension questions instead of ten; write a three-page rather than a five-page report)
- Allow grading policy of no points off for spelling errors
- Allow assistance of proofreader to correct spelling/punctuation errors
- Allow use of computer with spell-checker
- Allow use of Cliff Notes or prepared outlines for previewing, organizing, and reviewing text material

**Figure 10.2** *Continued*

or treats him differently in class. Mrs. Small, a well-meaning resource teacher, may put into place the recommended phonological awareness strategies, but her lack of training only causes more confusion for the child as she jumps too quickly to higher-level tasks. Tamara may get her one hour of resource help and half-hour of speech and occupational therapy each day, but she may have to miss so much of the regular class that she can't keep up. The quality of instruction these children receive can only be guaranteed if teachers take the time to collaborate and engage in ongoing, diagnostic-prescriptive teaching.

## Diagnostic-Prescriptive Teaching

***Diagnostic-prescriptive teaching means trying out various instructional recommendations in a test-teach-test process.***

*Diagnostic-prescriptive teaching* means trying out various instructional recommendations according to a five-step process:

1. Observe and analyze the nature of the student's abilities and learning styles and how these relate to his or her performance on different academic tasks.
2. Scrutinize the nature of the curriculum and academic setting, and modifications that would better match what a student is ready to learn and his or her learning style.
3. Consult with the student whenever possible, present choices for curriculum and setting modifications, and decide together which ones to try.

4. Set short-term goals, make the modifications, and teach.
5. Evaluate progress after a reasonable time interval; if unsuccessful, go back to steps one to four.

Diagnostic-prescriptive teaching is essentially a test-teach-test process that is very important to instructional decision making. As Jake's story shows (page 358), when an intervention works one time we should not assume that it will always be necessary or that it will always work. The changing nature and complexities of the learning process are not easy to anticipate, and we should expect to return to the drawing board time and again. A case in point is evidence that elementary school students with LD find it helpful when we orally read math tests to them; yet this aural presentation tends to create confusion in the middle school years. Similarly, extra time may augment a child's performance, but sometimes it doesn't.

Diagnostic-prescriptive teaching involves a good deal of clinical intuition and guesswork, a skill that comes with training and many years of teaching experience. Curriculum-based measurement has been very helpful to this process because it offers teachers a systematic way to check whether their approaches are working. As teachers analyze their students' needs and match their curriculum and teaching approaches to these needs, their program design will follow a number of instructional models.

***Curriculum-based measurement is helpful to diagnostic teaching because teachers can systematically check whether their approaches are working.***

## Instructional Models

Several instructional models have come in and out of favor in the brief history of the learning disabilities field. The most prominent are the developmental, behavioral, information-processing, and cognitive psychology viewpoints, and more recently the constructivist school of thought. Each differs from the other on the question of what and how children should be taught.

The *developmentalists* believe that learning disabilities are mostly lags in the maturing process. They advocate teaching only those academic objectives that the student is absolutely ready to master. Mastering lower-level components of higher-level skills is thought to be essential because children will pass through the various learning stages in a set order and they need to build a solid foundation for higher-level learning. Learning from prior stages that becomes automatic will ready the child for the next stage. For example, learning to segment words into syllables, and syllables into phonemes, comes before learning to sound out and blend individual sounds into words. Learning the numbers 1 through 10 would come before learning 11 through 20. Though it is now popular to increase writing fluency by encouraging poor spellers to use "invented spellings," developmentalists would argue—and there is some evidence to support their concern—that this practice reinforces poor spelling habits that only have to be unlearned later on. Teaching the right material at the right time, not too much, too soon, too fast, is the developmentalist's mantra.

**Developmentalists** ***believe that learning disabilities are mostly lags in the maturing process. They advocate teaching only those academic objectives that the student is absolutely ready to master.***

Unlike the developmentalists, the *behaviorists* believe that a child can master even those skills that he or she is not prepared to understand, provided the academic tasks and environments are carefully designed with the right rewards and consequences. The focus is on direct instruction of key curriculum objectives. Thus Ruth could be taught to sound out words by imitating the teacher's model, even if she doesn't understand how and why all these sounds get strung together. The

**Behaviorists** ***believe that a child can master even those skills he or she is not prepared to understand, provided tasks and environments are carefully designed with the right rewards and consequences.***

## Jake

*The changing nature of this child's learning processes requires continual diagnostic-prescriptive teaching.*

Jake was delayed in language skills. At age 7, he could name only the letters that appeared in his name. His IEP listed learning letter names and sounds as one of its goals. When his teacher task-analyzed letter naming, she found that Jake did remember a great deal about letter names, but at a lower difficulty level from what she was requiring of him. When he was asked to point to letters as they were named, he was 100 percent accurate. He was also able to copy letters well. The problem came when he had to name letters or write them from memory.

The teacher experimented with methods that paired Jake's weaker naming skills with his stronger receptive language, visual discrimination, and copying abilities. She had him draw, trace, paste, construct, and copy letters as she named them and he repeated the letter names. He also used a computer program that named letters as he typed them. Because he was good at picking out the sounds of initial consonants in words, his teacher tried relating the letter form to a key word that began with the same letter and also had its shape. *Snake,* for example, begins with an ssss sound and an *s* looks like a snake. Similarly, *elephant* begins with a short *e* sound, and its trunk can be curled into an *e* shape. This method worked well. Jake was not introduced to phonetic reading until he became proficient at retrieving the individual letter sounds. Instead, he was encouraged to compensate for his disability by learning to recognize words by sight in pattern books where rhyming words were prevalent and the same sentence reappeared throughout the book.

All was well and good. But should Jake's teacher assume that he would be a poor namer on all tasks? Would these elaborate teaching modifications always be necessary? No. We can't generalize from one task to another unless we test our assumptions all over again. It turns out that Jake was excellent at naming numerals. Maybe numerals were more meaningful to him than letter names; after all, one apple is one real thing, whereas the letter *r* refers to nothing concrete. Maybe Jake found 9 numerals easier to master than all 26 letters. His teacher could test this hypothesis by reducing the number of letters she expected Jake to master at any one time. In diagnostic-prescriptive teaching, approaches that work in one set of circumstances are tried out on other teaching objectives as well.

Consider Jake four years later. He's a sixth grader who is reading at the third-grade level, progressing well in a series that teaches reading through word families (*sight, might; cable, table*). But math, always fun for him, has become troublesome. He can solve the multiplication problems the teacher drills on the board, but his homework papers are full of errors. A comparison of the two assignments shows that homework requires extensive reading of word problems. So Jake's parents began to read the problems and directions to him, and he once again excelled in math. Because of this, his teachers wondered whether they should limit or modify the reading in social studies and science. When they tested this idea, they found that social studies was indeed too difficult (he misread 4 out of every 10 words), but the science assignments, all group experiments, were a breeze for Jake. His classmates did the reading for him. When he took on independent science projects, Jake cleverly enlisted the help of the librarian to find books that were short and easier to read.

teacher's model attempts to make learning errorless, so Ruth won't learn from her mistakes (e.g., Ruth might repeat a word after she listens to the teacher read the word). Teacher planning and control is important in the behavioral approach, as when teachers set classroom rules and award points for compliance. Or when a remote-controlled device is placed on the desks of inattentive children so points can be credited for paying attention or deducted when children are off task. Often lessons in this model are highly scripted, with very precise explanations and examples and carefully structured demonstrations. Teachers reinforce appropriate answers, give corrective feedback, reteach when necessary, and help students apply the learned skills to new situations or problems.

The *information-processing* theorists stress that students can master higher-level skills best when their underlying information-processing deficits are remediated. They advocate capitalizing on the student's information-processing strengths for academic instruction, while devoting a good deal of time to shoring up their information-processing weaknesses. For example, for a student with a visual-processing deficit but language strengths, teachers emphasize a phonics approach to reading instruction and use books on tape to handle class texts; the words the child can sound out are then committed to sight recognition, which becomes the objective of remedial exercises. For this child's handwriting difficulties, language strengths could be used to dictate compositions, while handwriting remediation is approached by helping the child recall the images of letters and draw them accurately.

**Information-processing** ***theorists stress that students can master higher-level skills best when information-processing strengths are used for academic instruction and the information-processing weaknesses are remediated.***

The *cognitive psychology* focus is on improving the efficiency of students' learning strategies. Teachers teach specific strategies to help students activate their background knowledge, abilities, interests, and learning strategies so they will attend to, comprehend, store, and remember new material more effectively.

**Cognitive psychologists** ***focus on improving the efficiency of students' learning strategies.***

The *constructivist* perspective takes issue with the direct instruction approach, in which teachers dictate what is to be learned and how through rules, drill, and practice. Constructivists believe that children are active rather than passive "meaning makers" who learn more deeply and eagerly when encouraged to independently select, organize, connect, and make sense of information and ideas based on their prior knowledge and experiences. Children learn from their errors, and discovery approaches are encouraged. Instruction in the constructivist framework is best when it takes place in what Vygotsky described as the "zone of proximal development," just a bit beyond what the child already knows, that is, in the zone of their emerging abilities. This kind of active learning is "scaffolded" with teacher guidance and support, which is gradually withdrawn as the child's competence increases.

**Constructivists** ***believe that children learn more deeply and eagerly when they actively select and discover the meaning of information based on their prior knowledge and experiences.***

In actual classroom practice these different instructional models are combined to varying degrees. Easier skills are generally taught before more difficult ones (developmental model). New skills are usually approached through the student's stronger abilities and learning styles (information-processing and cognitive psychology models). Instruction frequently incorporates active, discovery learning (constructivist model) as well as learning strategy instruction (behavioral and cognitive psychology models) while important weaknesses are remediated (information-processing model).

***In actual classroom practice, the different instructional models are combined to varying degrees.***

Here's an example. We provide Jennifer, a student with language deficits, with texts that are written in easier language, but at the same time she is developing her vocabulary. Through peer reading and composing in cooperative learning groups, we expose Jennifer to literature related to a topic that's of high interest to her—dinosaurs, for instance; this helps to enrich her vocabulary skills. Lynn, who doesn't focus on details, may be allowed to study from the teacher's outline. But she also receives instruction on how to sort out the relevant information when taking notes. We could help Jonnie, who can't distinguish beginning, middle, and ending sounds in words, learn to read by emphasizing the visual features of words,

***Continuing to build the weaker areas while teaching through the strengths leads to more marked academic gains than when weaknesses are ignored.***

but at the same time we remediate his phonological awareness weaknesses. Encouraging Jonnie to use invented spellings in his writing helps him to discover some phonological principles. The practice of continuing to build the weaker areas while at the same time teaching through the strengths is supported by studies that show more marked gains when the weaker areas continue to be developed.

Ideally the skills taught, whether in stronger or weaker areas, should be those that students are ready and eager to succeed in and ones that will not present a tremendous struggle (developmental and constructivist models). The student practices at one level until he or she is proficient enough to move on to the next, more difficult level. This avoids the faulty learning and later need to unlearn error patterns that can happen when too much is presented before the child is ready to understand. For example, Nikko may find soft *a, e,* and *i* sounds confusing for a very long time because they were taught simultaneously. But if he is allowed to master one sound at a time, his rate of progress increases.

There will always be a small number of students with LD whose information-processing skills are so weak that they can't make much progress in the traditional developmental model. For them instruction must be forced in the same way teachers push students to take the next step in a skill hierarchy (behavioral model). Consider an adult who can't decode or calculate beyond the second-grade level. Despite this low reading ability, the adult must master survival reading and math skills in order to read road signs and bus directions, use the telephone directory, pass the written portion of the driver's exam, complete a job application, plan a budget, manage taxes, and count change. For this person, we must depart from the normal developmental goal of helping him understand math conceptually and how sounds get strung together to make words. Instead, we teach "survival" reading through repeated practice with sight words, and "survival" math by way of a calculator.

***Behavioral strategies are among the most consistently effective of all intervention approaches because they are so organized in presentation, and correct responses are rewarded immediately.***

No matter which of the instructional models are used, behavioral principles are evident in the way materials and methods are planned. Behavioral strategies are among the most consistently effective of all intervention approaches because they are so systematic and organized in presentation, and correct responses are rewarded immediately. These principles are summarized in Table 10.1.

Adelman's (1971) teaching model for students with LD incorporates the various instructional philosophies just described. Adelman describes three types of children:

Type I: No disorder, but learning is slow in a nonpersonalized instructional program.
Type II: Minor disorders can be compensated for in a personalized learning environment.
Type III: Severe ability and/or behavioral deficits require very intense and specialized intervention.

Because the difficulties of type I and II students can be helped by appropriately matching the learning environment to their needs, Adelman believes that these pupils' difficulties are due primarily to what we have described as curriculum or environmental causes. The source of their LD is seen as a deficiency in the learning environment that needs to be corrected. The type III student is the one whose learning disability is due to physiological and other contributors primarily within

**TABLE 10.1 Behavioral Principles That Guide Effective Instruction**

| *Principle* | *Example* |
|---|---|
| • Systematically reinforce (repeat, attend to, praise) appropriate responses and do not reinforce errors | • Praise "sitting in seat" behavior and ignore times out of the seat |
| • Pair neutral events with positive reinforcers so that the neutral behavior takes on positively reinforcing value | • Pair working hard with praise |
| • Highlight cues that differentiate stimuli and pair them with different responses | • The letter *b* points to the right, say "b"; and *d* points to the left, say "d"; make all *b*s red during instruction while *d*s remain black |
| • Model appropriate responses | • "Listen to how I would talk through this algebra problem aloud"; "watch how I organize my desk" |
| • Make positive outcomes contingent on the less valued behaviors, to encourage less valued behaviors | • Make free time contingent on one-half hour of library research |
| • Shape correct responses by means of successive approximations | • Ignore the fact that Juanita does not intersect the \| and o of the letter *b* until she can draw each individual element correctly; first teach Juanita to sit politely beside classmates in the lunchroom and then help her practice conversation entry skills |
| • Carefully control the rate of presentation of new materials | • Introduce only four new social studies concepts or spelling patterns daily |
| • Distribute practice over time rather than massing it | • Review class notes daily rather than cramming the night before the exam |
| • Preplan relearning and generalization of skills | • Periodically insert mastered material into classwork in order to review and encourage application of this information to new contexts |
| • Continually measure/evaluate interventions and outcomes | • Evaluate retention of spelling words when taught by different methods; evaluate time on task when different types of reinforcers are used |
| • Present information systematically so that easier subskills precede harder ones | • Teach subtraction before division |

the child. A student can be a type I, II, or III student in different subject areas, depending on the abilities and learning styles tapped by the curriculum, the match of the teacher, and the nature of the classroom.

For the type I child, a personalized learning environment in the regular classroom is sufficient to promote progress. A wide range of individual differences in development, motivation, and performance are accommodated in this setting, whether through active, discovery-oriented learning (constructivist model), or direct instruction methods (behaviorist and cognitive psychology models). This classroom environment becomes the prototype for prevention of LD because each child's strengths and desire to learn are fostered.

Type II youngsters may function well in this environment, but encounter occasional problems. At this point, the teacher must decide whether to delay some instruction (e.g., delay regrouping in addition problems) until the student becomes more ready to deal with it (developmental approach). When a decision is made not to delay the higher-level instruction, the student will require a different level of programming (behavioral approach).

First, the basic skills, content, and concepts of the school subject are retaught, such as number facts to 10. The reteaching process involves different explanations, techniques, and materials from those used previously (e.g., calculating with sticks instead of writing numerals). If reteaching is unsuccessful, the teacher reviews essential prerequisites needed for success, such as mastering comprehension of quantities to 5, and then 6 through 10. If this review is unsuccessful, the teacher remediates to any interfering behaviors or information-processing deficits. The teacher, for example, might assess the child's counting and one-to-one correspondence ability, comprehension of the concepts "more" and "less," and ability to copy numerals, and he or she works with the child on any identified problems.

The type III student has severe, pervasive learning difficulties that necessitate resolution of the interfering behaviors or information-processing deficits first (information-processing approach). For example, a student with severely delayed language development might be exposed to intensified language therapy instead of forcing reading instruction, because the child is unprepared to articulate or comprehend the language being read. Many type III children will still have some achievement areas that are developing normally or that require less intensive interventions.

Whereas the type I child may require the indirect services of a consultant in LD to the regular classroom teacher, the type II student usually requires some daily direct special education services. The type III child requires far more specialized and intensive special education services.

*To maximize motivation, students must understand how the program relates to their strengths, weaknesses, and interests, and how they are progressing.*

To maximize their motivation to put effort into achieving academically, students must understand how the program relates to their strengths, weaknesses, and interests, and how they are progressing. It is important that students be able to voice their preferences for various methods and materials in the planning process.

## Materials

*Teachers have to adapt materials before they teach students with LD because most materials are geared toward the learning pace and independence of the average student.*

Research on most special education programs is conducted catch as catch can, and many years after their publication. Although we know that most programs "teach," there are little data to substantiate any one program's approach as better than another's, or that one program works best for one or another type of student. Therefore, teachers tend to choose materials based on their experience with what worked in the past for students with similar learning challenges. In most cases, teachers have to adapt materials before they teach because most materials are geared toward the learning pace and independence of the average student. No one material is right for all the teachers' students, and no one program contains exactly the right material to meet all the needs of all students with LD. Therefore, teachers often mix parts of programs, modify them, and improvise as necessary.

*Programs prepared for the general education curriculum provide insufficient examples and tackle too many objectives rather than concentrating on essential information.*

Although programs prepared for the general education curriculum organize a complex set of skills and materials, they tend to be insufficient in many ways for students with LD. They provide too few examples and not enough background information. They tend not to deepen understanding by connecting new concepts to a variety of ideas and topics. They survey a field broadly by tackling too many objectives and information, rather than concentrating on mastery of essential skills. They do not help the teacher with detailed descriptions of teaching strategies, and they provide too little guided practice and active learning applications for the student with LD. Systematic reviews occur too infrequently. In short, many texts lack organization and coherence, leaving it to the students to fill in the gaps. This is something that students with LD, with their limited background knowledge and learning strategies, have a difficult time doing.

Because no published material is likely to be perfect, the experienced teacher devotes a good deal of time to scrounging, cutting, and pasting materials to meet the need for more in-depth explanations, practice, and review. Emmy's story (page 364) is a good illustration of how labor-intensive and exhausting that process can be if it is done well. The next academic year, Emmy's resource teacher had to transfer to a regular first-grade classroom to get a breather.

**Guidelines for Selecting Materials.** Students with LD make slow academic progress and therefore need to be taught the same objectives over and over again. Therefore, materials need to be innovative in how they present routine objectives yet expand a student's breadth of knowledge, curiosity, and thinking skills. The ideal curriculum integrates basic skills instruction with content-area instruction, in this way reinforcing student's abilities in math, reading, and writing. Teachers must look beyond attractive packaging to make sure that students have the readiness skills to benefit from the program, that the objectives are appropriate and the material of high interest, and that there is no bias toward a particular racial, ethnic, socioeconomic, gender, or disability group.

***Because students with LD need to be taught the same objectives over and over, materials must be innovative in presenting routine objectives yet expand a student's breadth of knowledge, curiosity, and thinking skills.***

The teacher must choose materials in which the content is conceptually challenging despite the student's weaknesses in taking in or communicating information. To maintain interest and success, subject matter, concepts, and language need to match the student's conceptual, vocabulary, and maturity levels. At the same time, the reading, spelling or composition requirements need to be geared toward the student's lower competencies in these areas. And, whenever possible, the material needs to be relevant, interesting, and entertaining—in short, no different qualitatively than the kind of materials their classmates use.

Here is an example of how reading material can be at a high content and abstraction level yet low reading level, and vice versa (Thypin, 1979):

| | Reading Level | Content Level |
|---|---|---|
| (1) The question is to be or not to be | First grade | High school |
| (2) Homo sapiens are omnivorous bipeds among the cohabiting stalagmites | High school | Fourth grade |

Just because a student can't read or write well does not mean he or she must be relegated to less intellectually stimulating content. Students with LD deserve to be just as knowledgeable as their peers, and our zeal to build their basic skills should not deny them this opportunity. After all, this knowledge is the necessary foundation for acquiring further knowledge and reasoning abilities and is a common ground for communication with classmates. This means that sometimes teachers need to find easier reading level texts, or even rewrite texts themselves, in order to present critical information. Figure 10.3 on page 365 presents additional criteria for good curriculum materials.

***Just because a student can't read or write well does not mean he or she must be relegated to less intellectually stimulating content.***

## Emmy

*The exhausting "rollercoaster" described by a teacher supporting this teenager in the general education classroom.*

I first met Emmy two years before I started working with her. She used to hang around outside my classroom door hoping to catch a glimpse of one of the boys that I worked with. She appeared to be a typical teenage girl. She was fashionably dressed, giggley, and persistent.

I came in contact with Emmy again during a summer meeting. She was to be one of my students come September. All I really knew about her was that she was coming from our self-contained classroom. I learned that she had been in a similar setting for all of her school career. Now she was a 13-year-old girl who read and wrote at a second grade level and whose math skills were at the fourth grade level. It was decided that it was time for an educational change. That September she was to be mainstreamed for English, science, and all of her specials. She would receive reading instruction and support for her courses in the resource room for three periods each day. She would receive individual math instruction by the math teacher.

My first reaction when I heard all this was no way. How could I meet all the needs of this child plus the needs of my other resource students? I was also very nervous about the situation because of all the attention her case was receiving. I thought for sure I would have six different people peering over my shoulder keeping an eye on my every move. Then I thought of Emmy. No one had ever given her the chance in a regular program. With modifications and the support of the people who were going to be working with her we might be able to help her be successful.

I met with all of Emmy's teachers the first week of school in order to ask for their input and review modifications. While all seemed more than willing to be flexible, I felt as if there was really no true understanding of Emmy's needs or what would be required of them in order for the program to work. We started out okay. Content area objectives were cut to the essential concepts and facts. I received notes ahead of time from the science teacher—once, and the books the English teacher would be using. I found out as weeks went by that her teachers were more than willing to allow modifications in her program, but no one was willing to do any of the modifying.

At first I thought I could do it all. As the year went on it became clear that one person could not be responsible for all of the changes. In science alone individual notecards had to be made for each chapter, vocabulary cards were made from class notes, separate readings from low level books had to be found, and tests had to be modified. In English short stories had to be taped, vocabulary units had to be retaught and modified along with all of the teacher's exams. Individual summaries were written for each chapter of the novels that were assigned and study guides were made to help prepare Emmy for the exams. Along with supplementing the content areas, I was also responsible for working on Emmy's reading and writing. If Emmy was one of five students, I know I could have done much more with her. But the truth was she was one of twenty-five.

At first the modifications helped Emmy be successful and feel good about herself. She worked hard and was into it. As the year went on, though, it became increasingly difficult to meet all of her needs by myself. Everyone was feeling overwhelmed, Emmy, myself, her teachers, and her mom. Every success was wonderful, but every disappointment was equally devastating and frustrating. Emmy was not always the easiest person to bring out of a bad or down mood. Many times she was unhappy with her grades, which was very frustrating for me. At times I could not blame her though; it had to be so frustrating. The most frustrating for me was the fact that the testing that I did at the end of the year showed little or no growth on the cognitive portion of the tests. I know that Emmy made a lot of gains that school

**Emmy** (Continued)

year, but the one thing everyone usually focuses on showed that she didn't.

I don't want people to think it was a terrible year, because it wasn't. It was exhausting and exhilarating all at the same time. A regular roller-coaster. The tests might not have shown any growth, but I knew better. I always look at my students as very unique individuals. They do not just grow as students, they grow as people. That's how I judge growth and success. Emmy, in my eyes, grew by leaps and bounds. When I see her once a week, now a freshman in high school, I am very proud of her. She helps me after school in my classroom. She has joined groups, works on committees, works with a tutor, and I think has come to realize that she's an okay person and can succeed at many things. I am very proud to have been a part of that.

*Source:* Reprinted by permission of Mary Ellen Koloski.

**Exemplary curriculum materials:**

1. Have a logical, hierarchical sequence of instructional objectives against which a student's current level of functioning can be compared
2. Incorporate styles of information presentation and reinforcement activities that are adaptable to different students' learning styles (projects, lectures, slides or transparencies, independent study modules, educational games, role-playing, workbooks, term papers, community service projects)
3. Rehearse the same objectives in multiple ways
4. Allow students to proceed at their own pace, backtracking over easier objectives when the student has difficulty learning the material, speeding up coverage of objectives that are mastered more easily, or skipping objectives already mastered
5. Present content and directions in a consistent and simple fashion
6. Offer teachers ideas for task analysis and individualization of teaching and reinforcement strategies
7. Pretest for where teaching should begin
8. Have built-in evaluation mechanisms for determining mastery of instructional objectives
9. Have built-in periodic rechecks on retention of previous learning, and provide opportunities for relearning in a novel format
10. Include several evaluation formats (projects; multiple-choice, essay, or open-book exams; oral reports; homework assignments; self-corrected assignments)
11. Include charts to facilitate student and teacher progress monitoring
12. Have components built-in that enhance student motivation
13. Be flexible so that different teaching methods may be used with the same materials
14. Be adaptable to individual, small-group, or large-group work
15. Help students transfer skills to related contexts and practice practical applications

**Figure 10.3** Selected criteria for exemplary curriculum materials.

Teachers can also make use of technology to help students with LD succeed. This includes talking calculators, a pocket speller or thesaurus, wireless transmitters and receivers to help the teacher's voice stand out from the classroom's background hum, and variable-speech-control tape recorders to slow down or speed up books on tape. Perhaps the most exciting development in recent years has been the growth of computer-assisted instructional tools for students with LD.

**Computer-Assisted Instruction.** A visit to Mr. Delman's resource room reveals an air of involvement and excitement. Mr. Delman is working with a group of 4 sixth graders, while 8 other students are engrossed at computer screens. At the first computer, 2 students take turns blowing up rockets by quickly typing answers to flashed multiplication facts. At the second terminal, a heavy game of "Rob the Boss's Office" requires students to compose sentences that direct the robber's actions. The computer recognizes most of their words and creates a matching graphic. Right now, however, the screen is flashing "Beg your pardon?" and the boys are busy searching for the correct spelling of a word in the dictionary. Michael and Alahandro have a spelling quiz tomorrow. At their terminal the spelling words they've entered flash one at a time; Michael and Alahandro have to type the word right after it has disappeared from the screen. At their computer, Alecia and Rupert are partners on a research project about quasars. They composed their paper on the word processor and are now making the changes suggested in an editing session with Mr. Delman. And finally, Laura just listened to the computer read a story and is now reading it aloud herself. When she doesn't know a word, she clicks on it and the computer highlights and reads each syllable aloud. The computer provides Mr. Delman with a list of words Laura had trouble reading, and Laura will be asked to incorporate these into an illustrated book that she will compose on the computer.

*Computer-assisted instruction is an effective aid to learning basic academic skills. Whether it is superior to traditional instruction depends on the study you read.*

As the cost of computers has come within reach of school district budgets, scenes such as this have become commonplace. There is no question that computer-assisted instruction is an effective aid to learning and practicing basic academic skills such as phonetic skills, word recognition, and elementary mathematics. But whether it is superior to traditional instruction depends on the study you read—sometimes yes and sometimes no.

*More learning occurs when computer-assisted instruction supplements rather than supplants classroom instruction, and when it is preceded by the teacher's explicit strategy instruction.*

There hasn't been sufficient research yet to determine exactly which skills are most benefited by computer-assisted instruction. There is some evidence that computer reading programs develop decoding and vocabulary skills better than comprehension skills. Children who are achieving well gain more from computer aided instruction than those with learning difficulties. We also know that more learning occurs when computer-assisted instruction supplements rather than supplants classroom instruction and when it is preceded by the teacher's explicit strategy instruction. For example, one study found that the quantity and quality of compositions improved faster when prewriting and editing conferences with the teacher were combined with work on the word processor, rather than using the word processor alone. The same is true for preteaching the necessary phonological skills before expecting children to learn to recognize sight words via computer presentation. Generalization of what has been learned also tends to be limited unless the teacher preplans for opportunities for students to apply and practice their new skills. And the more that computer programs mimic good teaching, as in providing a glossary, questions that link back to the answer in the text, highlighted main ideas, and explanations that summarize important ideas, the better these programs teach.

Computers with synthesized speech are enormously helpful to students with reading disabilities who can scan virtually any text into the computer, and the computer reads the text back to the student, highlighting each word as it reads. Students can highlight text on the computer and print the highlights to create notes. Speech recognition software also is a boon to students with writing difficulties because they can "talk" their stories into the computer. This technology is associated with gains in students' reading recognition, comprehension, reading rate, vocabulary, spelling, length and quality of compositions, and proofreading.

*Computers with synthesized speech are enormously helpful to students with reading disabilities. They scan text into the computer, which then highlights each word as it reads the text aloud.*

*Speech recognition software is a boon to students with writing difficulties because they can "talk" their stories into the computer.*

Computers have the advantage of systematically applying procedures known to enhance achievement: instruction and practice on carefully planned goals; individualized program development; assessing student responses and providing immediate feedback; mastery learning (practice continues until the skill is automatic); controlled rate/quantity/sequence of presentation; controlled response to answers; encouraging independent work; readjusting difficulty levels based on responses, and reviewing concepts in a format that simulates real-life decisions, thereby encouraging active learning and generalization.

One of the most important attributes of computerized instruction is the way it motivates students to persist. It's been demonstrated that, of the time allotted for instruction, children remain engaged on the computer from 80 to 90 percent of this time, compared to 15 to 50 percent of time on regular academic activities.

*One of the most important attributes of computerized instruction is the way it motivates students to persist: children remain engaged on the computer from 80 to 90 percent of the instructional time, versus 15 to 50 percent of the time on regular academic activities.*

Computer programs range from simple drill work, problem-solving practice, and word processing to complex database and design/drafting systems. Drill and practice programs reinforce rote material (such as math facts and spelling words) by requiring faster and faster response times, thereby helping students become more automatic in their retrieval and problem solving. And the more automatic these functions become, the more open and flexible a student will be in higher-order thinking. Put differently, as cognitive energy expended on basics such as spelling or decoding diminishes, more energy is freed for higher-level reasoning. These computer programs provide as much repetition as students require until they master the material, time that most teachers are unable to provide. The applications for the next generation of computer technology, virtual reality, are just now being explored.

*Drills.* Far from being dry and boring, drills on the computer can be in game formats complete with spectacular graphics, colors, moving objects, sounds, fast pace, and harder and harder challenges that keep the student involved. Touch-sensitive screens add to the excitement of these exercises.

*Problem-Solving Practice.* Problem-solving practice and exposure to new content also can occur in a gamelike format, with branching of material determined by the student's responses. Exciting simulations teach problem solving by pretending that the student is driving a car, conducting a science experiment, on a historical battlefield, or searching for hidden treasure while outsmarting an evil monster. Such simulations offer practice in basic skills such as reading instructions on the screen, composing grammatically correct and correctly spelled instructions for the computer to recognize, typing, calculating, and encouraging eye-hand coordination and rapid reaction time. More importantly, they offer wonderful problem-solving practice as the student evaluates risks (what is the risk of being captured if I enter the forbidden chamber?), plans ahead and organizes a strategy, draws maps, analyzes clues, interprets complex directions, takes notes to keep track of moves, uses logic, sustains attention, and so forth.

*Word Processing.* Word processing has made the difference between success and failure for many students with LD. Spell-checkers detect errors, and students are fairly good at choosing the correct suggested spelling of a word. Even homonyms pop up in color to warn the student to take another look. Revisions are easier on the computer because text can been added, deleted, moved, and simplified as necessary. A built-in thesaurus makes choosing new words simple, with the added benefit of growing the student's vocabulary. And proofreading programs suggest punctuation, capitalization, grammar, and style changes. Computers also help with slow typing by producing a word after its first letters are typed, or expanding phrases from their abbreviations. The computer offers choices for these words and phrases, and over time it learns the users' word preferences so they appear higher on the choice hierarchy.

***Many students with LD produce far more text on a computer than they would write by hand. But quantity doesn't always mean quality.***

Many students with LD produce far more text on a computer than they would write by hand. But quantity doesn't always mean quality. These students tend to limit revisions to mechanics and minor word changes unless teachers help them make the revisions that affect meaning, syntax, and organization and thus improve the finished product. Revision prompts provided by some software programs (e.g., "Does this paragraph make a clear point?") can be very helpful in this regard.

Computers lend themselves with ease to publishing student works and helping students learn to write for an audience. With monitors that are simultaneously visible to students and the teacher, they are also useful for collaborative writing projects in which students gather, organize, revise, write, and edit material for audiences such as the classroom or the school at large.

Of course, not all students with LD automatically take to the computer. Many need structured word-processing and keyboarding instruction to avoid frustration with confusing computer commands and slow typing. For many, keyboarding is even slower than their handwriting, which limits productivity and makes for more effort than it's worth.

*Database Management Systems.* Because database management systems are very common in business and daily life to track bank statements, sports scores, library holdings, organize lists, and so on, introducing them to students in a school setting can be helpful.

*Graphic Design.* The person who is interested in graphic or architectural design will be delighted with the time savings of computer-generated designs. Future landscapers, for example, can plot a garden and check on how the plants will "grow" over a virtual 10- or 15-year period.

*Authoring Systems.* Many students with LD are just as capable of creating their own computer programs as others, and the process of doing so reinforces many gains in academic, social, and self-confidence areas, including logical-analytical reasoning, task persistence, creativity, organization, cooperation, attention to detail, positive attitude toward learning, following directions, working independently, and asking for help. Not surprisingly, when students create their own quizzes they learn a great deal of content in the process.

*Concerns.* One of the problems with computer-assisted instruction is that it is all too easy for the busy teacher to occupy students with motivating programs and then offer little assistance. Magical as they are, computers are product oriented and can't substitute for the teacher's ability to observe the quality of a student's strategies. A computer never knows if a student gave the right answer, but for the wrong reason. Learning is meant to be an interactive process between the teacher and student, and teachers need to work with students at the computer reinforcing appropriate strategies and modifying those that don't work.

*Teachers need to work with students at the computer, reinforcing appropriate strategies and modifying those that don't work.*

Special educators are also concerned that computer software relies too much on drill and practice rather than more intellectually challenging material. Experts suggest that 10 to 15 minutes of drill is enough time for most students. Too much can be boring and reduce student enthusiasm for using the computer as a learning tool.

The success of any computer program depends on the teacher's ability to choose programs that address relevant curricular objectives with a presentation style and content appropriate to a student's background knowledge, interests, and needs. This includes making sure the graphics are not too confusing or overstimulating, the reading and comprehension requirements are appropriate to the student's instructional level, the memory demands are within a student's capabilities, that the presentation rate is suited to the student's information-processing speed, and that the typing process is not too cumbersome. As with any classroom instruction, this kind of instruction is most beneficial when teachers set performance criteria and chart student progress toward these goals.

Rather than using computers only to remedy deficits, educators also need to remember to use computers to enhance students' talents (e.g., musical composition, graphic design) and interest in topics about which they are passionate (by learning to conduct Internet searches, for example). If students concentrate only on their disabilities, their talents will remain underdeveloped and underappreciated.

*Computers should be used to enhance students' talents and interests, not just remedy deficits.*

## Adapting Instruction to the Student's Abilities and Learning Styles

*Matching goals, materials, and strategies to students' abilities and unique learning styles is more an art than a science.*

Translating assessment information into sound educational planning is easier said than done. Although matching goals, materials, and strategies to students' abilities and unique learning styles has been a goal since the beginning of the study of learning disabilities, it is still more an art than a science. Research Box 10.1 on page 370 explains why research on this matching process—officially called *aptitude by treatment interactions* (ATI)—is not easy to conduct.

*Individualization is important because only a few methods work with most children: teaching phonological awareness and phonics, teacher-directed instruction, heightening motivation, and developing learning strategies.*

We know there are a few methods that work with most children, such as teaching phonological awareness and phonics instruction, teacher-directed instruction, heightening motivation, and developing learning strategies. Beyond these, matching student and curriculum attributes is a highly individualized process: One method won't work for all children, the same method doesn't work

RESEARCH BOX 10.1

## Aptitude by Treatment Interaction Research

Aptitude by treatment interaction (ATI) research on how to match child and task characteristics is extremely difficult to conduct. To begin with, the tests used to categorize students as one or another type of learner often are not reliable or valid for the purpose. Besides, it is nearly impossible to categorize groups of children as similar learners for research purposes (e.g., auditory or visual, or simultaneous or successive learning preferences) because children can differ in so many ways that affect learning: for example, their motivation, their fund of information, and instructional background all will influence how they approach the research tasks. Therefore, the type of instruction being experimented with may have nearly as many effects on the children in a study as there are children. For these reasons, studies that make rather gross discriminations among children on the basis of a few test scores, and then compare the effects of different teaching methods, often show modest or no differences in outcomes between groups (Kavale & Forness, 1987; Larrivee, 1981). Most children will learn from the instruction given, and their preferred modalities and styles may direct learning, even when the teaching method is trying to involve their weaker modalities and styles (Tarver & Dawson, 1978). Although some children probably did benefit more from one type of instruction than they would have from another, because most studies don't give both types of instruction there is no way of

across the curriculum for any one child, and the same materials or methods may work for a while and then become ineffective.

The nature of classroom requirements plays an important role in augmenting or deterring student progress. For some children, a rigid curriculum may work. But as Liza's story on page 372 shows, inflexibility can lead to real or perceived failure. Liza's story also highlights the need for teachers to stay on top of curriculum content and method modifications in order to help their students stay on course and make steady progress.

## Matching Curriculum Content to Student Abilities

"Shana can't remember anything!" a parent may protest. But we know that's not really true. Shana may not remember all of the things we expect her to given her age and intelligence, but she certainly can learn more fundamental skills if we make sure they are easy enough for her. Matching content to what the student is absolutely ready to learn makes sense. The achievement of higher-level goals occurs more rapidly and completely when we build this background foundation first. As the developmentalists caution, teaching too much too soon may not only be overwhelming, it bypasses mastery of important basic skills and instills faulty habits that only need to be unlearned later on. Worse yet, the child who has put inordinate effort into learning but still fails may finally lose the motivation to try.

*Match content to what the student is ready to learn. Teaching too much, too soon may not only be overwhelming, it bypasses mastery of important basic skills and instills faulty habits.*

By comparing a student's skills with the scope and sequence charts in commercial curricula, teachers can locate the level of instruction that the student already has mastered, and the precise objectives the student has yet to learn. These charts, when

**RESEARCH BOX 10.1 (Continued)**

finding this out. The group data also mask the great gains of some children, with the less remarkable gains of others. To complicate the matter even further, most studies can't be compared because of differences in design and children studied. The majority of these studies have been conducted on a short-term basis in the laboratory. In most cases, researchers don't know whether this laboratory instruction will transfer to classroom skills and behaviors and how long its positive effects will persist.

A more recent and promising approach to ATI research is to administer extensive neuropsychological, information-processing, psychological, and educational batteries to students with LD and then apply statistical procedures to classify these children into subgroups. Such research has found, for example, that the more severe the language impairment, the less the benefit from phonics instruction, and that children with word-finding problems make more rapid reading gains from phonics, word pattern, and phonological awareness instruction than children with phonological awareness weaknesses (Lovett, Steinbach, & Frijters, 2000; Lyons, 1985).

More of this type of well-designed research is beginning to shed light on who will make the most gains with particular teaching techniques. Until ATI variables are better understood, trial teaching with continuous progress monitoring is the pragmatic way to make educational decisions. This involves teaching with one method and then switching methods, so that we discover what really works, and to what degree, for particular children.

used with task analysis, evaluation of past learning opportunities, and consultation with the student, help to determine the most logical goals for teaching.

*Scope and sequence charts, task analysis, evaluation of previous learning opportunities, and consultation with the student help us select the objectives that the student is most ready to learn.*

## Matching Curriculum Methods to Student Learning Styles

Besides modifying curriculum content, teachers must make sure that their methods fit students' learning styles. In the following pages, we explore how we modify instruction to match the most common learning styles among students with LD. In Chapters 7 and 8 we dealt with metacognitive weaknesses and low motivation, two other very common and important characteristics that require teachers to adjust how they go about teaching.

**Matching Tasks to Students' Attending Strategies.** As we have learned, students with LD tend to be so much more off task and distractible than their peers that they miss out on many learning opportunities. Compounding this fact is that, because their attention is so variable, they can be a whirling dervish for one period of time and then quiet and industrious at another. They will know something one day, but not the next. As a result, their performance and grades can fluctuate drastically, giving teachers the impression that if they've succeeded once, they can do it again if only they wanted to.

*Students with LD tend to be distractible and they miss out on many learning opportunities. Because their attention is so variable, they know something one day but not the next. Performance inconsistency is to be expected.*

But many children can't do it again even when they want to. Often their good days and bad days reflect the ups and downs of their attention. Performance inconsistency is to be expected. Students might stay engaged in a highly stimulating computer game for quite a long time, but not when tasks are harder, less interesting, and

## Liza

*A young woman whose weaknesses were perceived as disabilities due to inflexible curricula.*

Liza was born full term and healthy, although her mother was hospitalized with toxemia one week before delivery. At age 5, Liza was enrolled in a small private school because her listening and expressive language skills were weak. She had not uttered single words until age 2 and had not combined words until age 2½. When she entered speech therapy at age 3½, she could produce almost no consonant sounds. She referred to her sister Julie as "oo-ee," *bye-bye* was "i-i," and *bottle* was "o-u." She was able to say "ma-ma" and "da-ee."

Fearing that Liza might encounter academic difficulties, her parents thought that a private school's small-group setting would be to her benefit. By May of her kindergarten year, Liza's teacher's support of *any* verbalizations she made ended favorably. Liza had progressed from not even being brave enough to call out "Bingo" when she won a game at the beginning of the year, to constantly yelling "Hey Mrs. Thomas!" from anywhere in the room by the end of the year. All were delighted with this change.

But first grade required work and not talk. In early October the school's team told Liza's mother that she had an insolent, disobedient child who knew what to do but wouldn't do it and who destroyed the class with her disturbing chatter. Simply put, she was hyperactive and emotionally disturbed and was potentially excludable from school. The message was clear: the mother was to go home and have a talk with Liza. Liza should *pay attention* to the teacher, follow directions, and stop annoying others.

This type of behavior was a problem specific to the school. Although Liza chattered a lot at home, she was not a disturbance in that context. Her mother's message to the team was equally clear: "for my $9,800 a year it had better be your (teachers') attitudes and task modifications that alter my daughter's school behavior." Two hours later, the team and mother agreed on what types of modifications they would make to help Liza attend better and talk less: turn her desk to the wall with her back to the others, instruct her in small groups rather than all by herself so that she would have an opportunity to learn how to listen in a group, tell her the *rules* of when talking is allowed and not allowed, compliment her on good listening, get her attention before talking to her, and ask her to repeat directions. By the next conference the mother was amused to hear from the team, "I don't know what you did but Liza has been a changed child since the very day following our conference!"

Liza's idiosyncrasies followed her wherever she went. Her chatter and inattention were predictable. Her parents decided to explore second grade in their local public school. They found that although Liza had completed all her first grade work at the private school, most of her suburban peers in the public school had already completed second grade work. If enrolled with these children, Liza would be looked on as an underachiever among her peers. Liza's parents decided to enroll her in the public school's first grade instead. They reasoned that she had an August birthday and was somewhat immature anyhow. Liza became the brilliant class leader! She still talked a lot, didn't modulate her voice well, and couldn't judge when not to talk, but the teacher didn't notice in that large group. She still needed to hear directions twice, but the teacher repeated them automatically anyhow because of the noise in the classroom.

What is Liza?—emotionally disturbed, an underachiever relative to her peers and intelligence level (learning disabled), gifted? She is none of these; she is just a delightfully unique little girl who needed to find the right match between her strengths and weaknesses and school environment to facilitate her development.

The story doesn't end all that simply. Just as the resolved weaknesses of children with learning disabilities reappear periodically and interfere with

**Liza** (Continued)

progress, so Liza's uniqueness creates continual challenges. When in third grade, there was some concern that Liza was not being challenged enough in reading and math because she was being taught the curriculum of children one year younger. Her social maturity was excellent and in some ways distanced her from her peers. Yet she didn't seem to understand their joking. Her handwriting also did not progress, so she began seeing a resource teacher twice a week. Liza was not as adept at poetry, composition, and playing with words as her classmates. She also was too loud in the lunchroom.

Yet, even in third grade Liza's parents knew that she would be okay. Aware of her stumbling blocks, Liza nevertheless thought of herself as a lovable, beautiful, capable child. She tried very hard and seldom was defeated by disappointment. Liza's biggest trauma at the end of third grade was her strong desire to go to overnight camp at an age when most other children wouldn't consider it, but she didn't know whether camp was worth giving up thumbsucking or whether the energy of hiding the thumbsucking under her blankets for four weeks was worth it!

Liza is now 20 years old and a junior architecture student at an Ivy League college. Her language lags are evident even today in that her math SAT scores were 780, but the best she could do on the verbal SAT, even after $1,000 of tutoring, was 590. All SAT achievement tests were in the 600 to 700 range, but Spanish barely broke 450. Liza just finished a series of voice lessons with a radio/TV coach, because her sorority sisters commented once too often on how young her enunciation and voice quality sounded.

Liza's interest in architecture began in seventh grade when the math her friends were doing fascinated her. But the guidance counselor would not allow Liza into their honors class because of Liza's merely average academic record. Liza fought back tears with her counselor and, when in January a student moved away and left a vacant seat, the counselor gave in. Having missed half the content, and with private tutoring from the head of the high school math department, Liza mustered only an 80 average at the end of the year. Again her counselor wanted to drop her from the class, and again Liza protested. "I'd rather be the dumbest person in the honors class than the smartest person in the dumb class." It was in that next year that Liza became a 99th percentile math student eligible to try out for the Johns Hopkins Gifted and Talented Search.

Ninth grade brought with it 90s in all honors classes, although Spanish grades were in the 80s. Liza preplanned for Spanish vocabulary tests by systematically studying five flashcards per day. If she tried to cram the day before a test, it never worked. To improve her Spanish, she lived with a family in Spain that summer, and to improve her writing, the following summer she enrolled in a private school summer program. Well, her Spanish did not improve—the family had learned English at Liza's expense. But Liza's motivation to write and publish soared following the positive feedback she received in her writing program. By the time Liza applied to college, she had published 23 stories in national magazines and had won two national essay contests. How can that be, given her language lags? It seems that Liza's short sentences and simple vocabulary, coupled with her astute observations and quick wit, make for light, easy, enjoyable reading.

Liza panicked when she got to college because she was unaware that there was a two-year language requirement for graduation. She would not only have to pass four Spanish courses, and a written and oral exam, but she also would have to earn a 550 on the SAT Spanish achievement test. For the first time in her life she gave in and submitted her credentials regarding a language disability to the disability services office. In the meantime, Liza was required to enroll in the beginning Spanish class. So she enrolled in the third level class in an attempt to get through this requirement faster. The disability committee members said that they would not make a determination until the end of

*(continued)*

**Liza** (Continued)

the semester. Panicked throughout and motivated to move on, Liza studied hard, earned an A, and passed out of the language requirement at the end of the semester, the same day she received a letter from the disability office that waived her language requirement!

Liza's motivation pulls her through over and over again. She can't draw well, but practices and practices, and has improved to an A-level in her studio classes. She can't memorize art history facts well, so out come the flashcards again—this time ten per day. Having succeeded despite much frustration, Liza's attitude toward life is happy and optimistic. With effort she knows she can do anything. Her bubbly, cheery personality attracts many friends. She has suffered too much to speak ill of anyone—they know that—and they love the quirks that make her fun and unique.

more effortful such as seatwork or math drills. What they need are teachers who will make special efforts to modify settings, tasks, instructions, and explanations so that the class content engages their interest and participation more so than distracters.

Because these students' attention and activity levels vary greatly across settings, teachers need to observe children carefully in various settings and then develop the kind of environment in which each student shows the greatest tendency to focus and sustain attention. A hyperactive child, for example, isn't hyperactive all the time, or even most of the time. He or she might be much more active than peers during reading and math, but hardly distinguishable at lunch, recess, or gym class. In fact, it is quite common for a child's behavior to meet all the criteria for hyperactivity at school, but not at home. Therefore, taking time to learn about the environmental variables that are most likely to augment a child's attention is well worth the effort—situating the child in a classroom without big windows facing onto the busy playground or parking lot, for example, or with a teacher who likes to play background music. Among the environmental variables that can affect a child's attention in different classrooms are instructional methods such as individual versus cooperative work; peer characteristics such as helpfulness, boisterousness, or task orientation; visual distractions such as busy blackboards, a parachute draped from the ceiling; teacher attitude (positive and encouraging vs. negative); seating arrangements such as in rows versus clusters; and ambient noise, such as noisy talking or humming ultraviolet lights. Teachers need to observe children carefully in various settings and then develop the kind of environment in which the student will show the greatest tendency to focus and sustain attention. One mother's epiphany about learning the principles of managing her child with attention-deficit hyperactivity disorder (ADHD) at a Mexican restaurant (page 375) has much to teach us about environmental modifications that can augment the attention of children with weaknesses in this area.

***Implementing environmental modifications that are likely to augment a child's attention to task is well worth the effort.***

***Students with LD readily become engaged in free play and low-cognitive-demand tasks, but as tasks get harder and more effortful their time on task decreases.***

***Reducing Task Difficulty.*** Students with LD readily become as engaged in free play and low-cognitive-demand tasks such as drawing and painting as do their peers. But as tasks get harder and more effortful, their time on task decreases, such as when it's

## Wade

*(Almost) Everything His Mother Knows about Managing ADHD, She Learned at a Mexican Restaurant*

Who would have thought taking a dreaded trip to a restaurant would have uncovered so many ideas for managing ADHD (Attention-Deficit Hyperactivity Disorder)? When our son Wade was young, each visit to a restaurant became a nightmare for my husband David and me. Wade would fuss and fume, cry, scream, want to eat before the food came and not want to eat when the food finally was served. For several years, the only contact our family had with restaurants was in the drive-through lane. Finally, we received an invitation we could not decline to a Mexican restaurant.

We entered the restaurant early before many customers had arrived. We were led to a booth with wooden backs reaching all the way to the ceiling. Our son sat next to the wall. The waitress immediately served a generous basket of chips with salsa and our drinks. The lights were low. Lively Mexican songs played softly in the background. Colorful decorations hung from the walls and ceiling. After our dinner orders were taken, we munched on chips. Our food was delivered quickly. We ate in peace, with no outbursts from our son. We entered with apprehension; we exited in amazement.

What did we learn from this outing that we could apply at school or home?

1. ***Cut Out Distractions:*** We were tucked inside a booth with ceiling-high backs. Even though piñatas and a sombrero dangled from the ceiling, the decorations did not distract. Our son could not see them from the booth.

   By trial and error, we have found seating our ADHD son in the center of a restaurant full of diners will make his head spin around faster than Linda Blair's possessed head in *The Exorcist*. . . .
2. ***Low Lights:*** The Mexican restaurant used low lights and candles for a pleasant dining ambience. Harsh fluorescent lights can bother some ADHD students. By using softer lights at home, parents can create better homework environments.
3. ***Soft Music:*** This restaurant played lively music at low volume. I have often been asked by our son to turn down the volume on the car radio. He says it hurts his ears. Some ADHD students prefer to study to loud music, while others choose complete silence.
4. ***Instant Tasks:*** Our family was greeted immediately by the waitress with menus and chips. We did not have to wait a long time for something to eat. Giving an ADHD child a task to work on immediately when entering a classroom keeps him from seeking undesirable activities.
5. ***Work On One Task at a Time; Keep Hands Busy:*** We ate one course of food at a time: chips and salsa, tacos, and sopapillas and honey. We ate with our hands. At home or school, an ADHD child needs to concentrate on one lesson at a time. If he is trying to learn a new skill or master difficult material, using "manipulatives" can help.

   I once observed a special education teacher who covered all classroom shelves with soft-colored, solid (not printed) curtains. She only brought out materials for one lesson at a time. At the end of instruction, the students returned the games, charts, and flash cards to an assigned shelf and covered the shelf with its curtain. Then they proceeded to the next lesson. No posters or vivid bulletin boards covered the walls. No mobiles dangled from the ceiling. The classroom was a peaceful oasis for these ADHD and learning disabled students.
6. ***Be Friendly:*** At the Mexican restaurant, our family was welcomed with a friendly smile. Even our ADHD son was treated as a wanted guest. He responded appropriately, he behaved well. How well would ADHD students behave if they were handled as guests instead of hopeless troublemaker?

. . . we use the above practical tips every week.

*Source:* Morgan, B. W. (May, 2001). *Communiqué, 29*(7), p. 33.

time to copy letters from the board or join a reading group. This pattern has been attributed to these children's natural avoidance when task demands are too taxing. Some, unfortunately, also have learned to avoid tasks well within their capabilities because of their failure history. Therefore, sensitive adjustments of task difficulty by teachers can help students with LD maximize their attention. A general rule of thumb is that a student should be able to read 95 percent of words and respond correctly and with ease over 70 percent of the time in order to be motivated to stay on task on independent work; for teacher presentations, easily comprehending 70 to 85 percent of the information is sufficient to maintain attention yet challenge students with new learning.

*Sensitive adjustments of task difficulty by teachers can help students with LD maximize their attention.*

*Directed Instruction on How to Perform Tasks.* Teacher instructions must specifically direct the attention of students with LD to what is expected on required tasks. In one study, for example, telling a group of 11- to 13-year-olds with learning disabilities to read a story and "try to remember as much about the story as you can" resulted in better story comprehension than instructing students to read "as quickly and correctly as you can." Incorporating verbal labeling into tasks is also helpful, such as having students name and rehearse groups of states as the teacher points to them on the map.

*Teacher instructions must specifically direct the attention of students with LD to what is expected on tasks.*

Other ways to enhance focused attention and recall through teacher direction include helping students to apply the new ideas presented in the classroom to a practical problem; teaching mnemonic tricks, as in HOMES spells the first letters of the Great Lakes; memorizing information in categories rather than single items, for instance, a country's products categorized by occupation—transportation, mining, farming—versus a list of unrelated products; actively questioning the meaning of paragraphs as students read; silently repeating information students have seen or heard; recording the number of problems completed or minutes on task; reviewing small amounts of material at frequent intervals; and paying attention to the organization of information to discover main ideas (such as headings, topic and summary sentences).

*Activity-Based Instruction.* Students with LD respond well to active learning opportunities. Even when conducting whole class instruction, a teacher can have all children raise "response cards" (*yes, no, planet names, solid* or *liquid gas,* etc.) in response to questions so that everyone is actively involved, not just the one student who is called on by the teacher. We know that when a teacher demonstrates a task and then students imitate her behaviors, students learn and retain better than if only verbal instruction and worksheets are used. Building a ramp teaches algebraic principles better than working formulas. Football coaches certainly know that students learn by doing. So do art and music teachers. Learning by experience is equally important in the classroom in order to make the learning objectives more salient, meaningful, attention sustaining, and memorable.

*Students learn by doing. Active learning makes the objectives more salient, meaningful, attention sustaining, and memorable.*

*Avoiding Overloading.* Students with LD often get distracted by the perceptual characteristics of materials and then neglect to use their past knowledge to think through solutions. This is why they may say that ten pennies are more than a dime—because the pennies look like "more"—or why pictures in a book can cause distraction and reading errors. In addition, students with LD often become over-

*Students with LD often get distracted by the perceptual characteristics of materials and neglect to use their knowledge to think through solutions.*

loaded when they have to attend to more than 3 or 4 elements at a time—as in a 20-word spelling list, or learning the numbers 20 through 50 all at once. Because of all they must attend to while struggling to read, some children have no resources left to make meaning of what they've read; to work around this, they might tape their voices reading aloud, and then listen to the tape to get the meaning. The good student knows that a huge stack of index cards "works"—it simplifies what needs to be learned when you have to pay attention to only one item on a card. And research with the learning disabled has borne this out; give a child with LD a whole list and he or she can't memorize it—but give him or her each item on a different index card and learning is faster than the blink of an eye (well sort of). Children also learn better when they master one item at a time instead of running through the entire list repeatedly. Researchers believe that the list format creates internal distractions for students (prior items interfere with memorizing later items, and vice versa); this interference is eliminated when looking at and practicing only one item at a time. In a social studies study, South American countries were learned faster when information about each country was learned to mastery before moving on to another country; then information on all prior countries was reviewed before moving on to a new country. When these kinds of instructional modifications are made to reduce overloading, the learning of students with LD improves more than for average learners, which reflects their greater sensitivity to such task variables.

When a student is distracted or overloaded by the perceptual features of tasks or the sheer volume of what needs to be learned, teachers can easily divide the task into more manageable chunks. Reviewing only 4 math fact cards at a time, offering 2 versus 4 choices on a multiple-choice test, or cutting a calculation worksheet into fourths are easy solutions.

*Because overloading can happen when students must memorize or attend to too much at once, teachers need to break material into smaller segments to be learned at separate intervals. Young children's optimal unit size for new reading words may be 5 words at a time, but only 3 words for spelling.*

Because overloading can happen when students must engage in too much new learning or too many memory searches at once, teachers need to determine the optimum unit size for each pupil and limit material accordingly. Some research suggests that young children's optimal unit size for new reading words may be 5 words at a time, but only 3 for spelling. In one study, for example, two-thirds of children who were taught 3 different spelling words per day for three days learned all 9 words. However, when taught 4 words per day, only one-third learned the target 9 words. Five spelling words a day was disastrous, with fewer than 20 percent of the children demonstrating mastery of the target words. In a similar science study, students with LD remembered more about minerals—their name, color, use, etc.—if taught only 4 minerals at a time, rather than being overloaded with information on 8.

The benefit of reducing memory load comes up repeatedly in the literature on LD. For example, students learn more social studies content when teachers break lectures into natural segments and stop to ask students questions about each segment before moving on. Even computer-assisted vocabulary instruction is more effective in 10-word chunks rather than 25-word chunks.

The implication for the classroom is that in order to avoid overloading, students should not be given too much to look at, listen to, think about, or memorize at once. It is very important that information be broken into smaller segments to be learned at separate intervals—completely and deeply. Recent brain studies suggest that memory for the task actually consolidates and becomes stronger when practice is distributed at intervals.

*Teachers can assist their students by structuring tasks to draw attention to the curriculum's most critical features.*

*Drawing Attention to Distinctive Features.* Teachers can assist their students by structuring tasks in ways that draw attention to the curriculum's most critical features. For example, students' preferences for color, shape, or size (described in Chapter 7 as changing with age) can be used to facilitate attention. When teaching the numerals 1 and 2, the size of the numbers can be made different (smaller 1, larger 2), their shapes can vary (paste the 1 on a square, the 2 on a circle), or their colors can be distinctive (a red 1 and a yellow 2). Simply highlighting the last part of a text helps middle school children pay attention to and remember that information. Coloring certain letters in words, parts of letters, and signs in math problems improves children's spelling, letter formation, and math accuracy, respectively. Even high school students can be helped by writing the names of the leaders of democratic countries on circles and the names of dictators on squares, or writing foreign words with irregular conjugations on pink index cards and regular-conjunction words on white cards. Because vertical discriminations are easier than horizontals for young children, the teacher can help his or her students distinguish the difference between *b* and *d* by lining them up on top of one another:

b<br>d

(The up-down difference between *p* and *b* is more noticeable if the letters are placed next to one another.) Some research even suggests that giving children only one letter to consider at a time while scanning vertically facilitates early reading acquisition because interference from adjacent letters is eliminated. For example,

t<br>a<br>b<br>l<br>e

*Concrete objects make learning activities more compelling and meaningful.*

*Use of Concrete Objects.* It's well known that immature children respond much more readily to three-dimensional objects than to two-dimensional objects. A block with the number 3 painted on it is much more compelling than a paper with the number 3 printed on it. Because concrete references are so much more meaningful, children with LD find that counting on their fingers increases their accuracy, and all children improve their calculation accuracy when math problems are rewritten as stories. When they are confused about the operations to use in math word problems, giving children sticks or blocks to manipulate, or asking them to draw the problem, are most helpful. Even when students listen to stories, they remember much better if the teacher manipulates magnetic or flannel board figures that act out a story's events as the teacher reads aloud.

One experiment using computers found that children with LD couldn't anticipate in which direction to move an arrow to catch colored circles or squares as these moved across the screen. But when the circles and squares were transformed into bees or butterflies, and the arrow became a net, children could easily guide the net to where the bee or butterfly would fly. In fact, under these conditions these children did just as well as average students. Even teenagers are not beyond enjoying coins, buttons, poker chips, and beans to help them solve math problems, especially when part of a group problem-solving activity.

*Multimodal Learning.* Special educators have long held that teaching through several modalities at once helps draw attention to different elements of the task. Although helpful to most students, there are some students for whom this approach is overwhelming. They do much better when attention requirements are reduced to one stimulus in one modality at a time. For example, one study found that most secondary students with LD increased their comprehension to equal that of their nondisabled classmates when science and social studies material was highlighted word by word on a computer and read by a synthesized voice. However, some of the learning disabled did best by simply listening to the text, and others by only looking at the highlighted computer text. The nondisabled students learned no more from the multimodal presentation than they did from simply reading the material. Therefore, teachers need to be sensitive to which students will respond to a multimodal approach and which need more streamlined, unimodal instruction.

***Teaching through several modalities at once helps draw most students' attention to different elements of the task; some students, however, are overwhelmed by this approach.***

*Reducing Distracters.* Because of their distractibility, students with LD at times may learn just as much information as nondisabled students, but what they learn is incidental information—not the primary information that was intended. Their attention is drawn away to irrelevant aspects of tasks. Therefore, distracters must be minimized. For example, the pictures in a book distract many children with LD. They gather clues from the illustrations and then guess at the words rather than sounding them out. For them, books without pictures, dull though that may seem, may be the answer. For the same reason, researchers find that busy borders on math worksheets, while quite pretty, increase both learning disabled and nondisabled students' calculation errors. And the common practice of asking children to draw a picture about a topic before beginning to write can actually cut short the writing of many. There is some evidence that speeded presentations at times can increase the performance of children with ADHD, because this leaves less room for distraction. The direct instruction, focus, and energy involved in speeding a task along (such as the teacher quickly slapping flashcards onto the table and snatching up the next card) may help the child's attention be caught and recaught, crowding out distracters before they can get in the way. Clearly, attention on the teacher's part to reducing distracters can be most helpful to a student's learning.

***Reducing of distracters can be most helpful to a student's learning.***

*Increasing Task Organization.* One important way of reducing distractions is to organize information for students so that associations are built in that make the information more meaningful. Handouts that sort information into categories, for example, are very helpful, as is grouping together crops, religions, or rivers to be memorized. So is connecting a known vocabulary word with a new one—*fail/fallacy,* for example—or making a high-interest association of new with old information—for example, remembering the word *humiliated* with the sentence, "I feel *hum*iliated if people stare at me when I *hum* loudly while wearing my Walkman.")

Studies find that students with LD achieve more when the teacher organizes information so that key concepts are continually repeated, for example, state a concept, give an example, restate the concept, or when students understand the

*Organize information for students using associations, repetition, and elaboration to make the information more meaningful.*

order in which a lesson's concepts will be developed, as when given an outline sheet of headings. Memory for content increases when teachers organize and focus students by stopping during a story or lecture to tell students "Now you will hear the problem," and later "Now you will hear how to solve the problem." Adding elaborations to the text, or asking inference questions that force students to elaborate, augments their comprehension. The same lesson produces far more learning when the teacher explains the lesson's organization at the outset, announces transitions, points out how segments relate to one another, and reviews the organization at the end. The metacognitive strategies reviewed in Chapter 7 used organized study approaches to make information more meaningful and memorable.

***Reducing Similar Information.*** The presence of similar information can be far more distracting for the student with LD than for the nondisabled student. This is why a kindergarten teacher should avoid teaching *b* at the same time as *d*. One letter should be well learned before the other is introduced. The same is true for introducing 6 and 9, and sounding out short /e/ and /i/. Likewise, a junior high school teacher is better off teaching *longitude* first and the next week *latitude*, and *homogeneous* at a different time from *heterogeneous*. Teachers need to be especially attentive to separating in time the presentation of similar items that can confuse children's learning.

*Similar items that can confuse learning must be presented at separate times.*

**Matching Time Limits to Information-Processing Speed.** Professionals are becoming increasingly sensitive to the differences between students in the time they need to process information. Even when they read or write very accurately, students with LD often are not automatic at these tasks. They do so at a much slower pace than the average student. Simply turning a radio knob, moving a computer mouse, or putting books into the locker are slower for the learning disabled. And we already have noted that some students need phonemes to be sustained longer in order to "hear" them, or longer time to "register" visual material. Yet, when given extended time to show what they know, these students' performances can increase dramatically, often equaling that of their nondisabled peers. By comparison, more time benefits the average student only marginally.

*When given extended time, the performance of students with LD who process information slowly can increase dramatically, often equaling that of their nondisabled peers.*

Timed assignments and tests, then, tend to penalize students with LD. Therefore, we need to decide on time limits that will give each child a reasonable opportunity to show his or her knowledge. Lectures, for example, might require that the teacher speak more slowly and pause more often. This gives students time to repeat and organize what has been heard (e.g., a 10-minute lecture followed by 3-minute group work to discuss the main idea). Such pauses in lectures have been shown to help college students organize their notes and recall the information. Likewise, we need to wait longer after asking questions or making comments to give students time to comprehend what we've said and retrieve a response. In the typical classroom, teachers often wait less than one second for students to respond. For lower-achieving students, teachers wait even less time, as though they don't expect any response at all. But if we are just a bit more patient, we may be pleasantly surprised to learn that our students with LD know quite a bit more than we had anticipated.

**Matching Task Repetitions to Students' Practice Needs.** "Practice makes perfect" may not always work with the learning disabled. For instance, why can Josh easily read the word *friend* in the first paragraph but can't even guess at it two pages later? Why does the handwriting of students with LD deteriorate so rapidly in an essay? Why is it that Andrew's invented spellings and reversals get worse by the fifth line he writes (see Figure 10.4)? According to Andrew, his "brain went on pause." He's right. It appears that some students become overwhelmed and worn down with too much practice, to the point that they can no longer call to mind what they do know. Scanning our brains for verbal information (as in introducing ten friends to your mother—no doubt you will "block" on someone's name) seems more difficult than scanning for visual images.

*Some students become overwhelmed and worn down with too much practice, so they can no longer call to mind what they know. Repetitions need to be in small doses and at distributed intervals.*

Therefore, we must be careful that the number of repetitions of tasks won't overwhelm or exhaust students. Writing 20 spelling words ten times each, all in one sitting, may do more harm than good. Although students with LD do need far more repetitions than their peers for information to "stick," these need to be in small doses and at distributed intervals.

**Matching Tasks to Students' Stronger Information-Processing Modes.** The idea of matching task attributes to youngsters' stronger information-processing modes makes good sense, but only recently has research more consistently supported this practice (see Research Boxes 10.1 on page 370 and 11.1 on page 405). Phonics instruction works best for students with language strengths, for example. When written language is problematical, accepting oral recall of information in place of written renditions benefits that student. When auditory memory is a strength, listening to a taped version while following along in the text enhances the student's sight vocabulary, reading comprehension, and reading rate.

We also know that performance increases markedly when tasks are modified to work around students' weaker information-processing skills. For example, students

**Figure 10.4** Invented spellings, reversals, and handwriting get worse as writing continues. This exercise required Andrew, who is 9 years old, to compose sentences from a list of words containing *au*. Sadly his last sentence reads, "It will be my fault if I stay in 4th grade."

with LD commonly dictate longer and higher-quality essays compared to those they handwrite—and dictation is up to seven times faster!

However, we can't assume that such compensations will always produce better performance. In some cases, despite their reading difficulties these students understand more when they read than when they listen because of the heavy language and memory load required in listening. They also may do better at writing down answers than dictating them because writing allows more time for monitoring and revising one's language. Or when listening to tapes they might be able to focus best if they simultaneously highlight important text, take notes, or draw concept maps.

*Although most children benefit from learning new concepts through their information-processing strengths and working around weaker information-processing skills, it is important to strengthen the weaker skills as well.*

We are also reminded that even when instruction is proceeding well through the student's strengths, we can't ignore developing his or her weaknesses. A balanced focus is necessary. A child who is a good phonetic analyzer, for example, will continue to be a slow laborious reader unless he or she develops sight recognition skills. If the gap between these two skills isn't addressed, the gap between the child's processing strengths (phonetic analysis) and weaknesses (rapid visual recognition) will only widen, and reading will remain inefficient. Although we may introduce new concepts through the child's information processing strengths, it is important to strengthen the weaker of these skills as well.

*Teachers can help by altering their materials and methods to be more congruent with students' cognitive styles.*

*The teacher's model can be very influential in helping students to adopt more active, efficient, and effective learning styles.*

**Matching Tasks to Students' Cognitive Styles.** Many students have trouble breaking away from their preferred way of perceiving their environments, even when their problem-solving style is counterproductive to success on a task. Teachers can help by altering their materials and methods to be more congruent with their students' cognitive styles. For example, in one study students with LD who attributed success to their own efforts benefited more when allowed to self-correct papers and to study spelling words any way they wanted to. Students who attributed success to external factors, on the other hand, were helped when the teacher pointed out and corrected their errors and told them precisely how to study the spelling words ("Trace each word; write it three times"). The teacher's model is so powerful that teachers need to carefully examine their own styles and match these with appropriate goals for their students. There is evidence that students taught by reflective teachers will show greater increases in reflective style than those taught by impulsive teachers. And if inquiry is explicitly expected of students, they will become more independent in their learning than when conventional direct-instructional approaches are used. Therefore, as with information-processing strengths and weaknesses, a student's cognitive style preferences should be capitalized on to facilitate instruction, but the teacher's model can be very influential in helping students to adopt more active, efficient, and effective learning styles.

***Impulsive and Reflective Learners.*** Youngsters with impulsive cognitive styles don't stop to reflect about alternative answers. They quickly glance at words to read them, and care only about the gist of a story. They are done with tasks almost before they've begun. This tendency is due, in part, to their global rather than analytical approach to tasks.

Impulsive students usually don't double-check their work. They ignore details, write before thinking, leave off word endings, don't organize their compositions, copy sloppily from the board, and don't self-correct. But they are also adept at summarizing the main idea of a passage quickly, remembering general concepts, and providing an overview of situations with a great deal of insight. Unfortunately, our detail-oriented curricula don't favor the impulsive student, whose true capabilities remain untapped much of the time.

To modify tasks to suit this student's style, the teacher might adapt word attack instruction by modeling the whole word and then asking the student to describe why the word's phonemes combine to sound the way they do. Working from the parts (sounds) to the whole (word) would be difficult for the impulsive child. The teacher might approach the rules for regrouping in multiplication by pasting a number-fact chart and a list of calculation steps on the child's desk for use in organizing his or her problem-solving approach. To increase attention to story details, the child could skim a story's pictures and topic sentences, be encouraged to guess at the details, and finally read the story to see if he or she was right.

*Teaching impulsive students specific strategies for approaching school tasks, and why and when these are important, is very helpful in promoting success.*

Teaching impulsive students specific strategies for approaching school tasks, and why and when these are important, has been very helpful in promoting their success, for example outlining and note taking to increase attention to detail. We should not hesitate to give these students gentle but honest feedback when they are doing poorly, because they are naturally less attuned to their errors and need this feedback to increase both their effort and success.

The school's bias in favor of the reflective student doesn't mean that the reflective student always has an easy time of it. Main points are harder for this student to discover, and he or she becomes overwhelmed by trying to learn every detail in a textbook when only understanding of the major points is expected. These students get bogged down in a text's new terms when up to 80 percent of these are unimportant, appearing on only one page of the text. Reflectivity is also a clear disadvantage on timed tests when students ponder the ramifications of every possible choice on a multiple-choice test. Drills and games that call for rapid-fire responses are not their forté. For the reflective student, explicit directions about the concepts and vocabulary to study, group study sessions that help to highlight the most important information, lecture outlines that guide attention to relationships between themes and topics, instruction in note taking to organize details into broader categories, composition formats that emphasize main ideas, and extended time on tests can be helpful.

*Teachers need to adapt instruction for reflective students to help them grasp main ideas and themes.*

***Low and High Conceptual Learners.*** Many students with LD are *low conceptual learners*. That is, they prefer highly structured tasks and explicit teacher direction. They have trouble generating new ideas on their own or thinking of alternative solutions to problems. For them, directly teaching pertinent facts and key concepts, giving rules before instead of after examples, using lecture rather than discovery methods, instructing them to repeat facts or ideas in their own words, giving immediate feedback, teaching systematic ways to go about practicing, and simply giving them study guides (rather than expecting note taking) promote more learning. Instead of asking them "What do you think?" teachers need to expand these students' thinking by giving them more alternatives to ponder. In effect, we are increasing our students' conceptual flexibility by not leaving their learning to chance and by offering them specific ideas that will help them reason more intelligently.

All too often, teachers simply expect students to assimilate information and figure out how to go about learning on their own. Julian is a good example. He is a bright 12-year-old who attends private school with other bright youngsters. His reading, math, and comprehension skills are excellent. His spelling, however, is terrible. Julian's teachers referred him for evaluation for a learning disability. The evaluators used trial teaching approaches and discovered that Julian had no difficulty with learning to spell phonetic or nonphonetic words. He learned well with typical teaching methods and was even able to generalize spelling patterns from one word to new words, such as *commercial* to *superficial.* When these findings were shared with his teachers, they commented, "But we never teach spelling as a subject; these children just pick it up." That wasn't possible for Julian, however, who despite "soaking up" most information needed directed teaching of spelling all along.

Many studies have supported the effectiveness of teacher-directed instruction with well-sequenced, structured materials and high student involvement. This involves beginning a lesson with a statement of goals and a short review of relevant information from previous lessons, presenting material in short steps with practice after each step, giving clear and detailed instructions and explanations, asking questions to check for and deepen understanding, and guiding practice with explicit instruction. Teachers can help by guiding the student's attention to essential parts of the task, teaching appropriate strategies, allaying frustration, questioning to deepen comprehension, and modeling strategic processing such as shifting to a new approach when another hasn't worked. In the learning disabilities field, this is called teacher "scaffolding" to help students progress to the next higher level. As the student becomes more independent, the "scaffolding" is gradually pulled away.

Applying the careful sequencing and structure of direct instruction, teacher modeling, and "think alouds " to math problem solving has helped students with LD find the correct operations for solving word problems. Reading comprehension has improved when passages are organized deductively (main idea in the first sentence) rather than inductively (main idea stated at the end or implied). Critical reasoning training—for example, knowing that just because two things happened together doesn't mean that one caused the other, or that just because someone important said something, it's not necessarily true—has been found to transfer better to novel tasks when teachers specifically state the rules and follow these with examples than when they simply lead a discussion and rely on workbook exercises to help students discover the relationships.

Explicit direction from the teacher about the purpose for reading, which content to focus on, and how one will be tested are especially helpful for students with LD, as is activating their background knowledge about the topic prior to reading and highlighting associated events in their lives. When students have little background knowledge about the information they are reading, the text needs to be as explicit and coherent as possible and offer full explanations. Good learners, on the other hand, benefit when the text leaves out explanations and connecting inferences because they are forced to read more actively and elaborate in order to fill in the gaps.

***Direct instruction and teacher "scaffolding" are critical for the majority of students with LD. We can't expect these students to learn information incidentally or to generate their own strategies. The more explicit the teacher guidance, the more intelligently students will reason.***

Direct instruction is critical for the majority of students with learning disabilities. We can't expect students to learn information incidentally or to generate their own strategies unless they are quite ready to do so—or shown how. When Susie struggles to create a mnemonic for the 13 colonies, make one up for her. When Rufus can't get the point of a chemistry experiment, give him a list of what to expect will happen at every step and why. Instruction that gives these students direction on what to attend to and guides them in thinking about information will certainly give them more options with which to think more intelligently.

As students get older they will become able to operate at higher levels of conceptual complexity, reflectivity, and independence. Therefore, teachers need to be ready to reduce their support when appropriate—as in encouraging students to create their own mnemonics, study strategies, or memory tricks.

**Building Generalization into Tasks.** Students with LD have predictable problems automatically transferring knowledge, strategies, social skills, and behaviors to new situations. Clearly, any instruction is useful only if it can be applied when needed in new situations. Teachers must help make sure this happens.

We all use cues to generalize knowledge. Recall the last time you took a final exam in French, or any other subject, in a strange lecture hall. You may not have done as well as you expected because the room didn't have the right "French" cues. You couldn't scan the room trying to reconstruct the professor conjugating the verb *être* on the blackboard. With insufficient environmental cueing, you may not have been able to recover from memory what you knew you had put there. This is the same kind of frustration that students with LD experience. Therefore, teachers need to think of ways to help students generalize academic objectives, whether it involves transferring the use of headings learned in English class to biology assignments, or applying a math calculation at the grocery store.

Generalization is difficult for students with LD because it involves recognizing the sameness between a new situation and a familiar task in which a particular strategy, piece of information, or behavior had been useful. It also means reformulating these to fit the new situation. The more automatic that generalization becomes, the more capacity remains for higher-order analysis, planning, and monitoring of the work or situation at hand.

*Generalization is difficult for students with LD because it involves recognizing the sameness between a new situation and a familiar task in which a particular strategy, piece of information, or behavior had been useful, and reformulating these to fit the new situation.*

Figure 10.5 on page 386 presents several ways that generalization can be enhanced. Metacognitive strategies also can be effective because they help students learn how to learn on their own. When teachers give explicit metacognitive strategy instruction; explain when, where, and how to use these strategies; why each step is important; and how to modify strategies as needed, students are better able to generalize strategic approaches to new situations.

Checklists for students to monitor their own behavior can also be particularly helpful in facilitating transfer. They can ask themselves questions like "Did I volunteer to answer a question?", "Did I hand in my homework when it was due?", "Did I check for neatness and spelling errors?" Students record the use of a strategy and hand the checklist in with the assignment. The teacher's role is to remind the students to use the strategy, to identify contexts in which the strategy could be used, to determine the helpfulness of the strategy, and to point out cues that help trigger use of the strategy. Students brainstorm ways to adapt the strategies, and then report back on their success.

Deepening understanding of basic information and how it can be applied to new situations is especially important for students with LD. For many their difficulty generalizing information may be related to a lack of richness of meaning when information is being stored in the first place. Consider Alex, who met Dede at a school dance. If he had learned about her sports interests, her favorite music, her family, and her hardest school subjects, chances are he would remember her name when he runs into her in the hallway two weeks later. In other words, the more associations we can offer students to elaborate an idea or a piece of information, the

- Teachers should focus on conceptual models such as advance organizers that forecast what is to be learned and encourage students to meaningfully relate the forthcoming information to information that is already known.
- Teachers should teach fewer principles, but broadly develop these principles' general applications, rather than teaching more principles with fewer applications.
- Teachers should use many examples to deepen the potential application of the skills being learned. Examples should progress from easiest to most difficult.
- Problem-solving strategies should be taught and integrated within the regular curriculum. Teacher-guided exercises should help students reflect on why the strategies were helpful and where else they could be applied.
- Students should be taught to cue teachers when the students use appropriate task strategies, so that they can benefit from reinforcement.
- Teachers should use consistency and structure in initial teaching but then vary formats, procedures, and examples to promote generalization.
- The same information should be instructed by many people, in as many settings and conditions as possible.
- Teachers initially should use a consistent schedule to reinforce generalization but then change to delayed and intermittent reinforcement, so that the tendency to generalize independently is strengthened.
- Students should be taught to use verbal mediation to help them generalize.
- Students should be instructed to self-report generalization and to apply self-recording and self-reinforcement techniques.
- Information should be taught in connection with naturally occurring stimuli (peers, physical stimuli) and natural settings so that less generalization needs to occur. The teacher should build the connection between the standard curriculum and how this content is important to everyday life.

**Figure 10.5** Approaches that increase generalization of learning.

*Sources:* Adapted from Cronin, M. E. (1996). Life skills curricula for students with learning disabilities: A review of the literature. *Journal of Learning Disabilities, 29,* 53–68; Niedelman, M. (1991). Problem solving and transfer. *Journal of Learning Disabilities, 24,* 322–329; Stokes, T. F., and Baer, D. M. (1977). An implicit technology of generalization. *Journal of Applied Behavior Analysis, 10,* 349–367. Wong, B. Y. L. (1994). Instructional parameters promoting transfer of learning strategies in students with learning disabilities. *Learning Disabilities Quarterly, 17,* 110–120.

*The more associations that we offer students to elaborate an idea or a piece of information, and the more we help students think of ways to retrieve this information, the more accessible it will be to them in new situations.*

more likely that they will remember it in a new situation. Likewise, the more we help students think of ways to retrieve the information—visualize the setting where you learned it for example, focus on the first sound of the word, recall some associated information—the more accessible this information will be to them when needed in new situations.

## Defining and Coordinating Intervention Roles

With their variety of needs, students with LD require the expertise of many different kinds of professionals. Role definition is sometimes a problem when so many experts with overlapping talents and responsibilities converge. Nevertheless, most schools are able to effectively coordinate their services for the benefit of students. Professionals are encouraged to work as a team by loosening the boundaries between their fields of expertise and sharing responsibilities in a transdisciplinary fashion. Although the contributions of these committed men and women are essential and critical, we must never lose sight of the fact that the family is the primary monitor, advocate, teacher, and model for children. Parents know their child's needs best and over the longest period of time. They are the ones with the highest sense of urgency and commitment to keep all parties working together in their child's best interest.

*Role definition is sometimes a problem when so many experts with overlapping talents and responsibilities converge to serve the learning disabled.*

## School Personnel

The general education teacher, the learning disabilities specialist, reading and math specialist, speech-language pathologist, transition specialist, and school psychologist, among others, serve students with LD during the assessment, planning, and intervention processes. Team members need to be able to shift roles flexibly, depending on the students' needs and the specialists' area of expertise.

**The General Education Teacher.** Because nearly 85 percent of students with LD spend at least 40 percent of their time in the regular classroom, the general education teacher has responsibility for a good deal of their education. The general educator confers with teacher assistance teams, makes program modifications, and, if these are not successful, refers students for evaluation.

*Because more than 80 percent of students with LD spend more than 40 percent of their time in the regular classroom, the general education teacher has responsibility for a good deal of their education.*

Once a student is identified as learning disabled, the regular classroom teacher's responsibilities are detailed in the IEP. Unfortunately, more often than not general educators merely provide information on current student performance in the IEP process rather than becoming actively involved in instructional planning, despite the firsthand knowledge that comes from observing and teaching their students with LD for so many hours a week.

Although the classroom teachers bear considerable responsibility for students with LD, their day-to-day commitments rarely allow sufficient time for planning special programs. And, even if time were available, these teachers are often unprepared to meet the challenge.

To help them deal with a wider array of abilities and learning styles in their classrooms, university teacher-preparation programs are increasingly requiring special education and multicultural coursework. School districts in recent years have intensified in-service education to help teachers understand the unique needs of students with LD, how to adapt teaching methods and materials, and how to adapt programming to match the increasing cultural diversity in the classroom.

Nevertheless, general education teachers continue to feel they lack sufficient knowledge or skills to plan for and instruct the learning disabled. All too often they delegate instruction of children with LD to aides and volunteers who have less training than they do to teach this student population. They also rely heavily on the learning disabilities teacher instead of adapting instruction on their own.

*Despite coursework and in-service education, general education teachers feel they lack sufficient knowledge or skills to plan for and instruct the learning disabled.*

**The Learning Disabilities Specialist.** The specialist in LD is expected to be skilled in classroom observation, interviewing, assessment, specialized teaching, consulting with other professionals, and nurturing positive attitudes toward students with LD. The specialist in LD consults with the general education teacher and provides services to students with LD in the regular classroom or in a resource room for one or more periods each day. Approximately 14 percent of students with LD are taught by learning disabilities specialists.

*Approximately 14 percent of students with LD are taught primarily by learning disabilities specialists.*

Teachers of the learning disabled generally remediate basic academic weaknesses, teach learning strategies, and provide tutorial help in classroom subjects. The techniques these teachers use are intended to be special, not just a repetition of regular classroom instruction. After all, students have been identified as having LD because they require a quality and intensity of instruction different from that which benefits the average student. Unfortunately, too many learning disability teachers merely mimic what is being done in the general education class, rather than offering these students the quality and intensity of instruction they need.

*Special educators use techniques intended to be special, not just a repetition of regular classroom instruction.*

Specialists in LD also assess students and provide in-service training to school staff. Given the large numbers of youngsters with learning disabilities being educated in regular classes, the consultation role is of prime importance. Consultation does produce significant increases in student progress, but the need to help students pass minimum competency tests, the daily academic pressures, too few planning periods, and the reluctance of general educators to take responsibility for students with special needs make allocating time for consultation difficult.

*Teachers of the learning disabled often find themselves serving as tutors in regular class work rather than focusing on basic skill remediation.*

Teachers of the learning disabled often find themselves serving as tutors in regular class work because general educators are unable, unwilling, or don't have the time to accommodate the exceptional learner. Tutoring may well be needed, but other personnel, even peer tutors, could fill this role as well or better than the specialist in LD. For the most part teachers of the learning disabled are not experts in content-area subject matter, though some states now require such specialization or certification. The more they tutor, the less time that teachers of the learning disabled have to invest in remediating the weaknesses in math, reading, writing, and learning strategies that created the need for tutoring in the first place. Many teachers of the learning disabled try to do both by addressing the basic skills within the context of the classroom content. This is appropriate as long as the goal is clear: assisting basic academic skills more than teaching content. Gains in basic skills have more potential benefits than learning specific pieces of content.

Teachers of the learning disabled express frustration about the unrealistic expectations placed on them, inadequate support systems, inadequate accommodations for students with LD in the regular classroom, and insufficient time to consult effectively with teachers or instruct students intensively. They also worry that the more that they tutor, the more dependent students will become and the less initiative general education teachers will take to deal with individual differences in their classrooms.

Even though teachers of the learning disabled must address a broad spectrum of academic and social needs, state certification requires too little coursework in remedial reading, learning theory, curriculum development, speech-language development and disorders, math remediation, and consultation. Assessment training is also insufficient, resulting in learning disabilities teachers using technically inadequate instruments, not understanding the statistics necessary for test interpretation, and allowing tests rather than their clinical judgments to dictate their conclusions.

To address the need for more uniform training of teachers of the learning disabled, more uniform certification standards, criteria for employment, and standards for monitoring professional practices, the Council for Exceptional Children's Division for Learning Disabilities (DLD) published the DLD Competencies for Teachers of Students with Learning Disabilities.

**The Reading and Math Specialists.** In addition to remediating in their areas of expertise, these specialists also help organize and evaluate general education's reading and math programs. Because their remedial role overlaps that of the learning disabilities specialist, confusion sometimes results.

The specialist in LD has the advantage of IDEA requiring that students with learning disabilities receive services from a certified special education teacher. However, the learning disabilities specialist may have less expertise in math and reading than the specialists in these areas. Because the law doesn't require math and reading specialists to work with the learning disabled, these teachers often end up working with less severe underachievers who don't have disabilities. They are puzzled by a law that was designed to provide greater educational opportunities for students with LD but stipulates that these services be provided by special education teachers who may have less expertise in a specific area of remediation.

**The Speech-Language Pathologist.** The speech-language pathologist (sometimes called the communicative disorders specialist) is trained to evaluate and work with students who have articulation, voice, fluency (stuttering), and language development disorders. Because many students with LD have difficulties in these areas, the speech-language pathologist plays an important role. The speech-language pathologist also targets emerging literacy skills, such as comprehension and rhyming in young children, hoping that this will prevent learning difficulties in school.

There is some role confusion between the speech-language pathologist and the learning disabilities teacher because both engage in phonological awareness training to increase reading readiness, and comprehension exercises to increase listening and reading comprehension. In addition, because speech-language pathologists often handle caseloads of 50 to 90 pupils a week, language development instruction often falls to the less trained learning disabilities specialist who has a more reasonable caseload of 20 to 25 students.

***There is some role confusion between reading and math specialists, speech-language pathologists, and specialists in LD, with the latter often being less prepared to intervene in these specialized areas.***

**The School Psychologist.** The school psychologist traditionally provides assessment and counseling to students and consultation to the classroom teacher. IDEA states that the school psychologist must be involved in the multidisciplinary decision making that determines the presence of a handicapping condition, but he or she does not need to actually conduct the assessment for a learning disability. The school psychologist's knowledge of normal child development, handicapping conditions, and the attributes of the school environment that affect learning and behavior can be very helpful to the academic and social development of students with LD.

**The Vocational Educator.** For students with LD who choose not to pursue postsecondary education, high school vocational education offers invaluable opportunities to develop skills, explore careers, and learn how to get along on a job. Often employment prior to graduation is an excellent predictor of later vocational success. To be successful, vocational educators, who have little or no experience with students with LD, need to consult with special education teachers. Too often their classes focus on seatwork, large group instruction, lectures, textbooks, and workbooks, measures that have already failed with this student population.

In addition to vocational adjustment, students with LD need help with independent living, leisure time activities, and social adjustment. The IEP's transition plan is designed to assist in this process.

**Other Specialists.** School audiologists evaluate whether hearing or auditory processing problems are affecting students with LD and intervene accordingly. The occupational therapist, physical therapist, and adaptive physical education teacher can assist students with persistent coordination and self-help difficulties. Social workers address family issues that affect learning, and rehabilitation counselors can help students make the transition to work and independent living. School guidance counselors and administrators not only establish the organizational framework for service delivery but also provide important personal support to students and teachers.

## Medical Specialists

IDEA mandates that any medical factors relevant to a handicapping condition be explored and treated by appropriate medical personnel. These include the ophthalmologist and optometrist, who treat vision problems; the allergist, who can address physical conditions that distract from learning; the endocrinologist, who treats glandular disorders; the geneticist, who evaluates inherited learning patterns; the ear-nose-and-throat specialist, who treats hearing disorders; and others. The pediatrician and the neurologist are the most frequently consulted when learning disabilities are suspected.

**The Pediatrician.** One of the first professionals to see a child after birth, the pediatrician tracks children's development through adolescence. He or she deals with conditions that can affect learning such as vision and hearing disorders, malnutrition, and endocrine disorders. Parents naturally turn to their pediatrician for advice about their child's physical needs, academic and behavioral concerns, and advice on medication for attention deficits and hyperactivity. Pediatricians have a responsibility to report their findings to educators, to encourage parents to pursue assessment and special teaching programs, and to be knowledgeable about services in the community.

**The Neurologist.** Although not enough is known yet about brain-behavior relationships to have neurological assessment suggest more than the most general educational directions, neurologists can detect and treat ongoing neurological disease and seizure disorders, prescribe medication for attention deficits and hyperactivity, explore the family history of learning problems, and look for signs of brain injury or immature neurological development. The neurologist's job is complicated because the child's nervous system is still growing, and it is sometimes difficult to distinguish slow development from actual damage to the nervous system. In addition, neurological abnormalities are so common among average learners that it is difficult to know whether any abnormalities that may be found are related to the learning problems. Advances in techniques for studying brain structure, function, and neurochemistry forecast a more diagnostically and instructionally useful role for the neurologist in the future.

## The Family

Academic and social learning is a lifelong process that can be made easier or more difficult by family circumstances. The family system is the major source for positive interventions and influences on a child's life. That is why IDEA encourages parents to be involved in identification, placement, and programming decisions. It is also why the government funds special training for parents of children with LD.

As the ecological perspective on learning disabilities gains ground, more and more professionals see students' problems as part of a malfunctioning system rather than residing in the individual alone. Because the family network strongly shapes a child's attitudes and habits, resolving the child's problems is a family responsibility, not just the responsibility of the child and school. Chapter 13 is devoted to the critical role the family plays as model, advocate, and teacher in a student's life.

***The family system is the major source for positive interventions and influences on a child's life. Therefore, IDEA encourages parental involvement in identification, placement, and programming decisions. Systems changes often are necessary to promote the child's learning and development.***

## Summary

To develop appropriate individualized instructional programs for students, the assessment team's information is translated into an individualized education program (IEP). Through the planning process involved in writing the IEP, goals are set, evaluation criteria are established, and which types of services, by whom, and with how much participation in general education or another least restrictive environment are specified. A transition service component is designed for secondary students.

Daily lesson planning is the teacher's responsibility. This is not an easy task, especially considering that no one packaged program is likely to suit the uneven development of the student with LD. To determine precisely what and how to teach, teachers engage in ongoing, diagnostic-prescriptive teaching. They generally follow an eclectic instructional model that addresses both the student's weaker and stronger skill areas. Published materials must be creatively adapted to the unique needs of each student. In recent years, computer technology has added an exciting new dimension to teaching options.

Scope and sequence charts, task analysis, evaluation of previous learning opportunities, and consultation with the student help us select the objectives that the student is most ready and willing to learn. Factors such as the student's attention, information-processing speed, performance deterioration as practice continues, information-processing preferences, ability to generalize, and unique cognitive styles need to be considered when deciding how to approach instruction. The more we understand about the unique learning styles of students with LD, the better we can plan our teaching modifications.

The regular classroom teacher tends to spend more school hours with the student with learning disabilities than do other professionals. The learning disabilities teacher, reading and math specialists, speech pathologist, vocational educator, and school psychologist offer important assessment services, remedial and tutorial instruction, and teacher consultation. Medical personnel also play an important role in the service delivery network. Those with the greatest influence in shaping the course of a child's future, however, are the child's family members, from whom the child learns important attitudes and behaviors, and the willingness to persist when the going gets tough.

## Helpful Resources

### Planning Individualized Instruction

Cosden, M. A., Gerber, M. M., Semmel, D. S., Goldman, S. R., & Semmel, M. I. (1987). Microcomputer use within microeducational environments. *Exceptional Children, 53*, 399–409.

Elkind, J., Black, M. S., & Murray, C. (1996). Computer-based compensation of adult reading disabilities. *Annals of Dyslexia, 46*, 159–186.

Forness, S. R., Kavale, R. A., Blum, I. M., & Lloyd, J. W. (1997). Mega-analysis of meta-analysis: What works in special education and related services. *Teaching Exceptional Children, 29*, 4–9.

Hearne, J. D., Poplin, M. S., Schoneman, C., & O'Shaughnessy, E. (1988). Computer aptitude: An investigation of differences among junior high students with learning disabilities and their non-learning-disabled peers. *Journal of Learning Disabilities, 21*, 489–492.

Heward, W. L. (2003). Ten faulty notions about teaching and learning that hinder the effectiveness of special education. *The Journal of Special Education, 36*, 186–205.

Higgins, E. L., & Raskind, M. H. (1995). Compensatory effectiveness of speech recognition on the written composition performance of postsecondary students with learning disabilities. *Learning Disability Quarterly, 18*, 159–174.

Jones, K. M., Torgeson, J. K., & Sexton, M. A. (1987). Using computer guided practice to increase decoding fluency in learning disabled children: A study using the Hint and Hunt I program. *Journal of Learning Disabilities, 20*, 122–128.

Kintsch, W. (1994). Text comprehension, memory, and learning. *American Psychologist, 49*, 294–303.

Koscinski, S. T., & Gast, D. L. (1993). Computer-assisted instruction with constant time delay to teach multiplication facts to students with learning disabilities. *Learning Disabilities Research & Practice, 8*, 157–168.

Lieber, J., & Semmel, M. I. (1985). Effectiveness of computer application to instruction with mildly handicapped learners: A review. *Remedial and Special Education, 6*(5), 5–12.

MacArthur, C. A. (1988). The impact of computers on the writing process. *Exceptional Children, 54*, 536–542.

MacArthur, C. A., Graham, S., Haynes, J. B., & De La Paz, S. (1996). Spell checkers and students with learning disabilities: Performance comparisons and impact on spelling. *The Journal of Special Education, 30*, 35–57.

MacArthur, C. A., & Shneiderman, B. (1986). Learning disabled students' difficulties in learning to use a word processor: Implications for instruction and software evaluation. *Journal of Learning Disabilities, 19*, 248–253.

Macicini, P., Gagnon, J. C., & Hughes, C. A. (2002). Technology-based practices for secondary students with learning disabilities. *Learning Disability Quarterly, 25*, 247–261.

Malouf, D. B. (1987–88). The effect of instructional computer games on continuing student motivation. *Journal of Special Education, 21*(4), 27–38.

Raskind, M. H., & Higgins, E. L. (1998). Assistive technology for postsecondary students with learning disabilities: An overview. *Journal of Learning Disabilities, 31*, 27–40.

Simmons, D. C., Fuchs, D., & Fuchs, L. S. (1991). Instructional and curricular requisites of mainstreamed students with learning disabilities. *Journal of Learning Disabilities, 24*, 354–360, 353.

Smith, S. W. (1990). Individualized Education Programs (IEP's) in special education—From intent to acquiescence. *Exceptional Children, 57*, 6–14.

Swanson, H. L. (1999). Instructional components that predict treatment outcomes for students with learning disabilities: Support for a combined strategy and direct instruction model. *Learning Disabilities Research & Practice, 14*, 129–140.

Swanson, H. L., & Trahan, M. F. (1992). Learning disabled readers' comprehension of computer mediated text: The influence of working memory, metacognition and attribution. *Learning Disabilities Research & Practice, 7,* 74–86.

Taymans, J., & Malouf, D. (1984). A hard look at software in computer-assisted instruction in special education. *The Pointer, 28*(2), 12–15.

van Daal, V. H. P., & Van der Leij, A. (1992). Computer-based reading and spelling practice for children with learning disabilities. *Journal of Learning Disabilities, 25,* 186–195.

Vygotsky, L. S. (1962). *Thought and language.* Cambridge, MA: MIT Press.

Wise, B. W., Olson, R. K., Ring, J., & Johnson, M. (1998). Interactive computer support for improving phonological skills. In J. L. Metsala & L. C. Ehri (Eds.), *Word recognition in beginning literacy* (pp. 189–208). Mahwah, NJ: Lawrence Erlbaum.

Woodward, J. P., & Carnine, D. W. (1988). Antecedent knowledge and intelligent computer assisted instruction. *Journal of Learning Disabilities, 21,* 131–139.

Zigmond, N., & Miller, S. E. (1986). Assessment for instructional planning. *Exceptional Children, 52,* 501–509.

Instructional planning ideas: http://www.ldonline.com http://www.ideapractices.com

## Adapting Instruction to the Student's Abilities and Learning Style

Alster, E. H. (1997). The effects of extended time on algebra test scores for college students with and without learning disabilities. *Journal of Learning Disabilities, 30,* 222–227.

Anderson-Inman, L. (1986). Bridging the gap: Student-centered strategies for promoting the transfer of learning. *Exceptional Children, 52,* 562–572.

Bakker, D. J., & Vinke, J. (1985). Effects of hemisphere-specific stimulation on brain activity and reading in dyslexics. *Journal of Clinical and Experimental Neuropsychology, 7,* 505–525.

Belfiore, P. J., Grskovic, J. A., Murphy, A. M., & Zentall, S. S. (1996). The effects of antecedent color on reading for students with learning disabilities and co-occuring attention-deficit/hyperactivity disorder. *Journal of Learning Disabilities, 29,* 432–438.

Bendell, D., Tollefson, N., & Fine, M. (1980). Interaction of locus-of-control orientation and the performance of learning disabled adolescents. *Journal of Learning Disabilities, 13,* 83–86.

Brainerd, C. J., Kingma, J., & Howe, M. L. (1986). Long-term memory development and learning disability: Storage and retrieval loci of disabled/nondisabled differences. In S. J. Ceci (Ed.), *Handbook of cognitive, social, and neuropsychological aspects of learning disabilities* (Vol. 1). Hillsdale, NJ: Lawrence Erlbaum.

Bryant, N. D., Drabin, I. R., & Gettinger, M. (1981). Effects of varying unit size on spelling achievement in learning disabled children. *Journal of Learning Disabilities, 14,* 200–203.

Bryant, N. D., & Gettinger, M. (1981). Eliminating differences between learning disabled and non-disabled children on a paired-associate learning task. *Journal of Educational Research, 74,* 342–346.

Carnine, D. (1989). Designing practice activities. *Journal of Learning Disabilities, 22,* 603–607.

Case, L. P., Harris, K. R., & Graham, S. (1992). Improving the mathematical problem-solving skills of students with learning disabilities: Self-regulated strategy development. *The Journal of Special Education, 26,* 1–19.

Ceci, S. J., & Baker, J. G. (1989). On learning . . . more or less: A knowledge × process × context view of learning disabilities. *Journal of Learning Disabilities, 22,* 90–99.

Cermak, L. S., Goldberg-Warter, J., Deluca, D., Cermak, S., & Drake, C. (1981). The role of interference in the verbal retention ability of learning disabled children. *Journal of Learning Disabilities, 14,* 291–295.

Chan, L. K. S. (1991). Promoting strategy generalization through self-instructional training in students with reading disabilities. *Journal of Learning Disabilities, 24,* 427–433.

Coop, R. H., & Sigel, I. E. (1971). Cognitive style: Implications for learning and instruction. *Psychology in the Schools, 8,* 152–161.

Darch, C., & Kameenuî, E. J. (1987). Teaching LD students critical reading skills: A systematic replication. *Learning Disability Quarterly, 10,* 82–91.

Fuchs, L. S., & Maxwell, L. (1988). Interactive effects of reading mode, production format, and structural importance of text among LD pupils. *Learning Disability Quarterly, 11,* 97–105.

Gelzheiser, L. M., Shepherd, M. J., & Wozniak, R. H. (1986). The development of instruction to induce skill transfer. *Exceptional Children, 53,* 125–129.

Gheorghita, N. (1981). Vertical reading: A new method of therapy for reading disturbances in aphasics. *Journal of Clinical Neuropsychology, 3,* 161–164.

Gleason, M., Carnine, D., & Vala, N. (1991). Cumulative versus rapid introduction of new information. *Exceptional Children, 57,* 353–358.

Gold, J., & Fleisher, L. S. (1986). Comprehension breakdown with inductively organized text: Differences between average and disabled readers. *Remedial and Special Education, 7*(4), 26–32.

Graham, S. (1990). The role of production factors in learning disabled students' composition. *Journal of Educational Psychology, 82,* 781–791.

Hansen, J., & Pearson, P. D. (1983). An instructional study: Improving the inferential comprehension of good and poor fourth-grade readers. *Journal of Educational Psychology, 75,* 821–829.

Harber, J. R. (1983). The effects of illustrations on the reading performance of learning disabled and normal children. *Learning Disability Quarterly, 6,* 55–60.

Honea, J. M., Jr. (1982). Wait-time as an instructional variable: An influence on teacher and student. *Clearing House, 56,* 167–170.

Horton, S. V., Lovitt, T. C., & Christensen, C. C. (1991). Matching three classifications of secondary students to differential levels of study guides. *Journal of Learning Disabilities, 24,* 518–529.

Hudson, P. (1997). Using teacher-guided practice to help students with learning disabilities acquire and retain social studies content. *Learning Disability Quarterly, 20,* 23–32.

Hunt, D. E. (1974). Learning styles and teaching strategies. *High School Behavioral Science, 2,* 22–34.

Johnson, D. J. (1993). Relationships between oral and written language. *Social Psychology Review, 22,* 595–609.

Johnson, G., Gersten, R., & Carnine, D. (1987). Effects of instructional design variables on vocabulary acquisition of LD students: A study of computer-assisted instruction. *Journal of Learning Disabilities, 20,* 206–213.

Krupski, A. (1985). Variations in attention as a function of classroom task demands in learning handicapped and CA-matched nonhandicapped children. *Exceptional Children, 52,* 52–56.

Kurtz, B. E., & Borkowski, J. G. (1987). Development of strategic skills in impulsive and reflective children. A longitudinal study of metacognition. *Journal of Experimental Child Psychology, 43,* 129–148.

Lloyd, J. W., & Loper, A. B, (1986). Measurement and evaluation of task-related learning behaviors: Attention to task and metacognition. *School Psychology Review, 15,* 336–345.

Maier, A. S. (1980). The effect of focusing on the cognitive processes of learning disabled children. *Journal of Learning Disabilities, 13,* 143–147.

Marsh, L. G., & Cooke, N. L. (1996). The effects of using manipulatives in teaching math problem solving to students with learning disabilities. *Learning Disabilities Research & Practice, 11,* 58–65.

Mauer, D. M., & Kamhi, A. G. (1996). Factors that influence phoneme-grapheme correspondence learning. *Journal of Learning Disabilities, 29,* 259–270.

Montali, J., & Lewandowski, L. (1996). Bimodal reading: Benefits of a talking computer for average and less skilled readers. *Journal of Learning Disabilities, 29,* 271–279.

Porrino, L. J., Rapoport, J. L., Behar, D., Sceery, W., Ismond, D. R., & Bunney, W. E. (1983). A naturalistic assessment of the motor activity of hyperactive boys. I. Comparison with normal controls. *Archives of General Psychiatry, 40,* 681–687.

Radosh, A., & Gittleman, R. (1981). The effect of appealing distractors on the performance of hyperactive children. *Journal of Abnormal Child Psychology, 9,* 179–189.

Rose, T. L. (1986). Effects of illustrations on reading comprehension of learning disabled students. *Journal of Learning Disabilities, 19,* 542–544.

Rose, T. L., McEntire, E., & Dowdy, C. (1982). Effects of two error-correction procedures on oral reading. *Learning Disability Quarterly, 5,* 100–105.

Rose, T. L., & Sherry, L. (1984). Relative effects of two previewing procedures on LD adolescents' oral reading performance. *Learning Disability Quarterly, 7,* 39–44.

Rosenshine, B. V. (1986). Synthesis of research on explicit teaching. *Educational Leadership, 43* (7), 60–69.

Ruhl, K. L., & Suritsky, S. (1995). The pause procedures and/or an outline: Effect on immediate free recall and lecture notes taken by college students with learning disabilities. *Learning Disability Quarterly, 18,* 2–11.

Runyan, M. K. (1991). The effect of extra time on reading comprehension scores for university students with and without learning disabilities. *Journal of Learning Disabilities, 24,* 104–108.

Scruggs, T. E., & Mastropieri, M. A. (1993). Special education for the twenty-first century: Integrating learning strategies and thinking skills. *Journal of Learning Disabilities, 26,* 393–398.

Scruggs, T. E., Mastropieri, M. A., Bakken, J. P., & Brigham, F. J. (1993). Reading versus doing: The relative effects of textbook-based and inquiry-oriented approaches to science learning in special education classrooms. *The Journal of Special Education, 27,* 1–15.

Scruggs, T. E., Mastropieri, M. A., Levin, J. R., & Gaffney, J. S. (1985). Facilitating the acquisition of science facts in learning disabled students. *American Educational Research Journal, 22,* 575–586.

Suchman, R. G., & Trabasso, T. (1966). Color and form preference in young children. *Journal of Experimental Child Psychology, 3,* 177–187.

Szatmari, P., Offord, D. R., & Boyle, M. H. (1989). Ontario Child Health Study: Prevalence of attention deficit disorder with hyperactivity. *Journal of Child Psychology and Psychiatry, 30,* 219–230.

Torgesen, J. K. (1977). Memorization processes in reading-disabled children. *Journal of Educational Psychology, 69,* 571–578.

Torgesen, J. K., Dahlem, W. E., & Greenstein, J. (1987). Using verbatim text recordings to enhance reading comprehension in learning disabled adolescents. *Learning Disabilities Focus, 3*, 30–38.

White, W. A. T. (1988). A meta-analysis of effects of direct instruction in special education. *Education and Treatment of Children, 11*, 364–374.

Wilson, C. L., & Sindelar, P. T. (1991). Direct instruction in math word problems: Students with learning disabilities. *Exceptional Children, 57*, 512–519.

Wong, B. Y. L., Wong, R., & LeMare, L. (1982). The effects of knowledge of criterion task on comprehension and recall in normal achieving and learning disabled children. *Journal of Educational Research, 76*, 119–126.

Yando, R. M., & Kagan, J. (1968). The effect of teacher tempo on the child. *Child Development, 39*, 27–34.

Zentall, S. S. (1989). Attentional cuing in spelling tasks for hyperactive and comparison regular classroom children. *Journal of Special Education, 23*, 83–93.

Zentall, S. S., & Kruczek, T. (1988). The attraction of color for active attention-problem children. *Exceptional Children, 54*, 357–362.

Zigmond, N., Sansone, J., Miller, S. E., Donahoe, K. A., & Kohnke, R. (1986). Teaching learning disabled students at the secondary school level; What research says to teachers. *Learning Disabilities Focus, 1*, 108–115.

## Defining and Coordinating Intervention Roles

Carpenter, R. L. (1985). Mathematics instruction in resource rooms: Instruction time and teacher competence. *Learning Disability Quarterly, 8*, 95–100.

Haynes, M. C., & Jenkins, J. R. (1986). Reading instruction in special education resource rooms. *American Educational Research Journal, 23*, 161–190.

Houck, C. K., Geller, C. H., & Engelhard, J. (1988). Learning disabilities teachers' perceptions of the educational programs for adolescents with learning disabilities. *Journal of Learning Disabilities, 21*, 90–97.

Idol, L., & West, J. F. (1987). Consultation in special education (Part II): Training and practice. *Journal of Learning Disabilities, 20*, 474–494.

Idol-Maestas, L., & Ritter, S. (1985). A follow-up study of resource consulting teachers. *Teacher Education and Special Education, 8*(3), 121–131.

Knight, M. F., Meyers, H. W., Paolucci-Whitcomb, P., Hasazi, S. E., & Nevin, A. (1981). A four year evaluation of consulting teacher service. *Behavior Disorders, 6*, 92–100.

Mather, N., Bos, C., & Babur, N. (2001). Perceptions and knowledge of preservice and inservice teachers about early literacy instruction. *Journal of Learning Disabilities, 34*, 472–482.

McKenzie, R. G. (1991). Content area instruction delivered by secondary learning disabilities teachers: A national survey. *Learning Disability Quarterly, 14*, 115–122.

McKenzie, R. G., & Houk, C. S. (1986). Use of paraprofessionals in the resource room. *Exceptional Children, 53*, 41–45.

Nolen, P., McCutchen, D., & Berninger, V. (1990). Ensuring tomorrow's literacy: A shared responsibility. *Journal of Teacher Education, 41*, 63–72.

Pugach, M. (1987). The national education reports and special education: Implications for teacher preparation. *Exceptional Children, 53*, 308–314.

Vaughn, S., & Schumm, J. S. (1995). Responsible inclusion for students with learning disabilities. *Journal of Learning Disabilities, 28*, 264–270, 290.

Voltz, D. L., Elliott, R. N., & Cobb, H. B. (1994). Collaborating teacher roles: Special and general educators. *Journal of Learning Disabilities, 27*, 527–535.

Zigmond, N. (1990). Rethinking secondary school programs for students with learning disabilities. *Focus on Exceptional Children, 23*(1), 1–22.

Zigmond, N. (1996). Organization and management of general education classrooms. In Speece, D. L., & Keogh, B. (Eds.), *Research on classroom ecologies: Implication for inclusion of children with learning disabilities.* Mahwah, NJ: Lawrence Erlbaum.

CHAPTER ELEVEN

# Instructional Strategies: The Preschool and Elementary School Years

**THIS CHAPTER DISCUSSES** the general instructional approaches available to teachers of the learning disabled at the preschool and elementary levels. Because there are thousands of instructional strategies in use with more being created every year, we'll sample the most effective and widely used strategies.

The World According to Student Bloopers is a humorous look at the kinds of spelling, sequencing, and reasoning confusion that many students with LD experience. It's a reminder that, no matter how serious our efforts to assist these youngsters must be, a lighthearted approach helps maintain perspective with even the most challenging of students.

*We can't afford to wait and see whether preschoolers will outgrow developmental delays or cognitive style weaknesses—they may not.*

## Preschool Programming

We can't afford to wait and see whether preschoolers will outgrow developmental delays or cognitive style weaknesses; they may not. Intervention not only offers these children a head start in overcoming their weaknesses but also encourages growth in areas of strength that can help compensate for the weaknesses. We also

## The World According to Student Bloopers

*A humorous look at the spelling and reasoning confusion experienced by students with LD.*

One of the fringe benefits of being an English or history teacher is receiving the occasional jewel of a student blooper in an essay. I have pasted together the following "history" of the world from certifiably genuine student bloopers collected by teachers throughout the United States, from eighth grade through college level. Read carefully, and you will learn a lot.

The inhabitants of ancient Egypt were called mummies. They lived in the Sarah Dessert and traveled by Camelot. . . . The Egyptians built the Pyramids in the shape of a huge triangular cube. The Pramids are a range of mountains between France and Spain.

The Bible is full of interesting caricatures. In the first book of the Bible, Guinesses, Adam and Eve were created from an apple tree. . . . Jacob, son of Isaac, stole his brother's birth mark. . . . One of Jacob's sons, Joseph, gave refuse to the Israelites.

Pharaoh forced the Hebrew slaves to make bread without straw. Moses led them to the Red Sea, where they made unleavened bread, which is bread made without any ingredients. . . . David was a Hebrew king skilled at playing the liar. He fought with the Philatelists, a race of people who lived in Biblical times. Solomon, one of David's sons, had 500 wives and 500 porcupines.

Without the Greeks we wouldn't have history. The Greeks invented three kinds of columns—Corinthian, Doric, and Ironic. They also had myths. . . . One myth says that the mother of Achilles dipped him in the River Stynx until he became intollerable. Achilles appears in *The Iliad*, by Homer. Homer also wrote *The Oddity*, in which Penelope was the last hardship that Ulysses endured on his journey. Actually, Homer was not written by Homer but by another man of that name.

Socrates was a famous Greek teacher who went along giving people advice. They killed him. Socrates died from an overdose of wedlock.

In the Olympic Games, Greeks ran races, jumped, hurled the biscuits, and threw the java. . . . The government of Athens was democratic because people took the law into their own hands. . . .

Eventually, the Ramons conquered the Greeks. History calls people Romans because they never stayed in one place for very long. . . . Julius Caesar extinguished himself on the battlefields of Gaul. The Ides of March murdered him because they thought he was going to be made king. Nero was a cruel tyranny who would torture his poor subjects by playing the fiddle to them.

Then came the Middle Ages. King Alfred conquered the Dames, King Arthur lived in the Age of Shivery, King Harold mustarded his troops before the Battle of Hastings, Joan of Arc was cannonized by Bernard Shaw. . . . Finally, Magna Carta provided that no free man should be hanged twice for the same offense.

In midevil times most of the people were alliterate. The greatest writer of the time was Chaucer, who wrote many poems and verses and also wrote literature. . . .

The Renaissance was an age in which more individuals felt the value of their human being. Martin Luther was nailed to the church door at Wittenberg for selling papal indulgences. . . . It was an age of great inventions and discoveries. Gutenberg invented the Bible. Sir Walter Raleigh is a historical figure because he invented cigarettes. Another important invention was the circulation of blood. Sir Francis Drake circumcised the world with a 100-foot clipper.

The government of England was a limited mockery. . . . When Elizabeth exposed herself before her troops, they all shouted, "hurrah." Then her navy went out and defeated the Spanish Armadillo.

The greatest writer of the Renaissance was William Shakespeare. . . . He lived at Windsor with

*(continued)*

**The World According to . . .** (Continued)

his merry wives, writing tragedies, comedies, and errors. In one of Shakespear's famous plays, Hamlet rations out his situation by relieving himself in a long soliloquy. . . . Romeo and Juliet are an example of a heroic couplet. Writing at the same time as Shakespear was Miguel Cervantes. He wrote *Donkey Hote.* The next great author was John Milton. Milton wrote *Paradise Lost.* Then his wife died and he wrote *Paradise Regained.*

During the Renaissance America began. Christopher Columbus was a great navigator who discovered America while cursing about the Atlantic. His ships were called the Nina, the Pinta, and the Santa Fe. Later, the Pilgrims crossed the Ocean, and this was known as Pilgrims Progress. . . . Many of the Indian heroes were killed, along with their cabooses, which proved very fatal to them. The winter of 1620 was a hard one for the settlers. Many people died and many babies were born. Captain John Smith was responsible for all this.

One of the causes of the Revolutionary Wars was the English put tacks in their tea. . . . Finally, the colonists won the War and no longer had to pay for taxis.

Thomas Jefferson . . . and Benjamin Franklin were two singers of the Declaration of Independence. . . . Franklin died in 1790 and is still dead.

George Washington married Martha Curtis and in due time became the Father of Our Country. Then the Constitution of the United States was adopted to secure domestic hostility. . . .

Abraham Lincoln became America's greatest Precedent. . . . Abraham Lincoln wrote the Gettysburg Address while traveling from Washington to Gettysburg on the back of an envelope. He also freed the slaves . . . and the Fourteenth Amendment gave the ex-Negroes citizenship. But the Clue Clux Clan would torcher and lynch the ex-Negroes and other innocent victims. It claimed it represented law and odor. On the night of April 14, 1865, Lincoln went to the theater and got shot in his seat by one of the actors in a moving picture show. The believed assinator was John Wilkes Booth, a supposingly insane actor. This ruined Booth's career.

Meanwhile in Europe, . . .

Bach was the most famous composer in the world, and so was Handel. Handel was half German, half Italian, and half English. He was very large. . . . Beethoven wrote music even though he was deaf. He was so deaf he wrote loud music. . . .

France was in a very serious state. . . . During the Napoleonic Wars, the crowned heads of Europe were trembling in their shoes. Then the Spanish gorillas came down from the hills and nipped at Napolean's flanks. . . .

The sun never set on the British Empire. . . . Queen Victoria was the longest queen. She sat on a thorn for sixty-three years. Her death was the final event which ended her reign.

The nineteenth century was a time of many great inventions and thoughts. . . . Samuel Morse invented a code of telepathy. Louis Pasteur discovered a cure for rabbis. . . . Madman Curie discovered radium. . . .

The First World War, caused by the assignation of the Arch-Duck by a surf, ushered in a new error in the anals of human history.

*Source:* Lederer, R. (1987). *VERBATIM, The Language Quarterly.* Copyright 1987 by *VERBATIM®, The Language Quarterly.* Used by permission.

***We need to address social skills development at preschool ages, before negative behavior patterns become well-established and difficult to turn around.***

need to address social skills development at this early stage before negative behavior patterns become well-established and difficult to turn around. With appropriate programming the risk of a serious learning or behavior disorder may be reduced, so that the youngster has a greater chance of reaching his or her potential.

Preschool programming also needs to focus on the child's attending abilities, use of visual- and auditory-processing skills, and ability to communicate through language and motor skills. It's also a time to shape good learning strategies, motivation to learn, and positive attitudes toward one's self, peers, and authorities. For little children, all this learning takes place through play. Children develop at their own pace as we present them with learning opportunities they are ready to grasp. It's important to avoid rushing a preschooler into academic work. Expecting them to learn too much too soon may harm their overall development.

***It's important to avoid rushing a preschooler into academic work.***

Some preschoolers with delayed development can learn quite well when we personalize their learning environments by introducing objectives very systematically, and in ways that match their learning styles and developmental readiness to learn in different areas. For others, learning is harder. They need to be taught and retaught the very basic skills—the names of colors or shapes, for example, or classification skills—that will support higher academic knowledge.

Both types of children need directed instruction because they tend not to discover relationships for themselves or to generalize their knowledge to new situations. Richard, for example, may be able to count by rote to ten but not grasp how to count out four napkins for the snack table. Without very specific explanation and guidance, Richard is unlikely to discover this relationship for himself any time soon. These children also need very special encouragement and exciting activities to stay with a task because of their immature attention and information-processing skills.

Because preschoolers don't know how to go about trying to remember even when told to do so, teachers need to make the curriculum memorable through active, fun activities and by drawing children's attention to the most important elements of the task. Three-year-olds, for example, are drawn to colors more so than shapes, so the wise preschool teacher will teach the names of fruits by emphasizing the red of the apple or the green of the pear. At age 4, however, it is shape that captures attention, so that becomes the teaching focus (e.g., the shape distinctions among animals). Small children attend best when they can handle objects versus watching the teacher's demonstration, when objects are three-dimensional (alphabet blocks versus printed letters), and when relevant features are accentuated, (e.g., learning colors by hunting for animals hidden under colored "houses"—rather than simply naming color cards held up by the teacher.) Teaching sequences need to be kept short because of young children's short attention spans, but also because preschoolers recall best what comes last in a series and confuse what came earlier. So the numbers from 1 to 5 should be mastered first before tackling 1 to 10—or ABC before A through Z. When longer sequences are presented, the only way to overcome the interference of the later items with recall of earlier items is to verbally rehearse the earlier items, a strategy for which preschoolers are still too young.

***Because preschoolers don't know how to try to remember, teachers need to make the curriculum memorable through active, fun activities, keeping teaching sequences short, and by drawing children's attention to the most important elements of the task.***

Preschool is the ideal setting to build learning readiness through modeling adult and peer behavior, playing group games, playing with attention-getting materials, and taking part in teacher-directed lessons. Teachers need to set specific, individualized goals to help children acquire the needed skills, rather than letting development simply take its course. Early assessment and intensive remedial programming by specialists such as speech-language pathologists and occupational or physical therapists are very much in order for children with significant delays. Nonsensical approaches that have no direct relationship to preacademic goals, such as crawling, swinging on swings, eye movement exercises, trampolining, or memorizing strings of random words, should be avoided.

***Preschool teachers need to set specific, individualized goals to help children acquire needed skills, rather than letting development simply take its course.***

A child's preschool day is distributed among independent, teacher-child, small group, and large group developmentally appropriate activities. Group activities encourage such social behaviors as listening, sharing, taking turns, and attending through games, songs, circle time discussions, physical education, dancing, snack time, and listening to stories and tapes. Group time also is used to expand a child's preliteracy skills, breadth of knowledge, inquisitiveness, and problem-solving skills. Children might, for example, explore the principle of gravity by dropping objects of various sizes, or of temperature by making popsicles with fruit juice. They can listen to songs, poems, and stories containing rhymes ("We ride a bike with Ike," *Dr. Seuss* books), predictable patterns where the same sentence is repeated over and over again ("The sky is falling," "Are you sleeping, Brother John?"), alliteration ("Connie can catch cows," "We fiddle and fish with Farley Fox"), and sound sequences ("and the drum beat bumpety thumpety thump," "Old Macdonald had a farm—ee i ee i o"). Children enjoy it when the teacher pauses and they finish the rhymes, "read" the sentences, or reenact the story.

Individual class time is usually devoted to visual-motor activities such as clay work, coloring, cutting, and tracing; language activities such as labeling shapes, colors, and sizes, or categorizing and sequencing, or telling about events; and school readiness activities such as counting blocks, playing with "more" and "less," or matching alphabet letters. Frequently puppets named after letters and sporting the letter on their costume (*Mr. M*, for example) are used to relate prepared tales that reinforce letter-sound associations—for instance, "*Mr. M* likes to eat *m*arshmallows, *m*ilk, and *m*eat." Specific letters can be color-coded to draw attention and distinguish them from others (*b* from *d*, for example). Often teachers introduce letter-sound links by associating the letter with an object that is shaped like the letter and begins with that sound. The object and its shape help the child remember the letter's shape and sound, as in

and  (Isgur, 1975.) All of these activities enhance knowledge and readiness skills, and sharpen the child's information reception, expression, and thinking skills. Children also practice learning strategies such as self-instructing aloud and stopping, looking, and listening before responding.

Most activities have multiple purposes. Coloring, for example, is an eye-hand coordination activity, a language activity (naming colors), a visual-perceptual activity (noting the shades of colors), a following-directions activity, and a conceptual and planning activity (deciding whether to color objects as they appear in reality, and in what order to color).

***To engage preschoolers' attention and reinforce concepts in multiple ways, teachers frequently set themes to guide children's play.***

To engage children's attention and reinforce concepts in multiple ways, teachers frequently set themes to guide their students' play. Learning to label and sequence the animals in the Gingerbread Man story can come through the story itself, the Gingerbread Man song, a Gingerbread Man skit, baking gingerbread and animal cookies, and coloring or tracing gingerbread man and animal figures. If one activity doesn't capture a child's attention and interest, perhaps another one will.

When more than the usual preschool activities are needed, there are a number of packaged visual-motor and language development programs that can be adapted to preschoolers' learning needs and styles. In language development in particular, these structured, individualized programs have helped children make faster gains in their receptive, reasoning, and expressive language skills than through the language stimulation inherent in the preschool day. When teachers make a concerted effort to use extensive speech to mediate the child's preschool experience, this also leads to greater gains in language skills—especially when small group book reading is a priority. Simultaneous use of oral and sign languages has helped many children with severe language delays begin to see themselves as communicators. Average achievers also enjoy this addition to their communication repertoire.

*The earlier that individualized intervention begins, especially before age 3, and the longer it continues, the greater are the gains.*

The pioneers in the learning disabilities field—Frostig, Johnson, Myklebust, and Kephart, among others—suggested a wealth of ideas for encouraging language, visual-motor, and gross-motor development in children. Their teaching guides are outstanding even today, and they form the foundation for hundreds of preschool development books and programs.

*Children who attended preschool are less likely later on to be retained or assigned to special classes; they have higher achievement and motivation, greater homework completion and high school graduation rates, fewer early pregnancies and arrests, and they are more likely to go on to postsecondary education.*

The earlier that individualized intervention begins, especially before age 3, and the longer that it continues, the greater are the gains for the child. Research conducted in Head Start and other programs indicates that two years or more is better than one year of a preschool program, more hours per day and more days per year yield greater benefits, trained and quality teaching staff are more effective, low staff-to-child ratios are important to quality programming, and parent involvement is crucial to long-lasting success. Children who had the advantage of preschool are less likely to be retained or assigned to special classes once they begin formal schooling. Long-term follow-up studies show that these children demonstrate higher academic achievement and motivation; have greater homework completion and high school graduation rates; are more likely to go on to postsecondary education, are more competent in daily living skills; and have higher earnings and employment rates, lower welfare dependence, fewer encounters with the law, and fewer early pregnancies. When low socioeconomic status children attend intensive preschool programs, the positive effects on IQ (on average 9 points) and achievement have been evident even at 25 years of age.

*Preschool programs with highly structured goals, reinforcements, and teacher direction tend to benefit children more in intelligence, language, visual-perceptual skills, and school readiness than do more open, less academically structured programs. Programs that are less structured encourage responsibility for success, independence, and cooperativeness.*

Preschool programs with highly structured goals, reinforcements, and teacher direction tend to benefit children more in the important areas of intelligence, language, visual-perceptual skills, and school readiness than do more open, less academically structured programs. This is particularly true for children from low-income families. Several studies have found that lower-functioning preschoolers benefit most when teachers actively "mediate" their social and cognitive development by talking through, suggesting, and actively guiding children's awareness of memory strategies, making choices or comparisons, changing perspectives, planning ahead, using senses, identifying and understanding feelings, and the like. Higher-functioning children with developmental delays already engage in these types of reasoning and therefore benefit most from the direct instruction approach without the additional mediation. Programs that are less structured and more flexible, in contrast to the direct instruction approach, also encourage development of important personal attributes: responsibility for success, independence, and cooperativeness.

High-quality preschool programs result in readiness gains even if the quality of the home environment is not as nurturing as one would wish. Nevertheless, the

*A family-centered educational approach beginning before the child is 3 years of age has been found to be the most effective, especially when focussed on relationship building and satisfaction with the parenting role.*

family plays a critical role in the maintenance of gains made in preschool programs. Therefore, a family-centered, rather than a child-centered, approach beginning before the child is 3 years of age has been found to be the most effective. Family involvement that is focused on relationship building, rather than asking parents to become therapists or teachers, helps build parents' coping abilities and satisfaction with their parenting role, which in turn favorably affect their children's development and social competence. This kind of support is especially important given the circumstances faced by so many families today: unemployment, poverty, poor health care, drugs, violence in the home and street, to name just a few. When teachers work with both parents and children, their support strengthens the parent-child relationship and helps parents to become more competent and independent in their efforts to encourage their children's motivation and learning.

## Elementary School Programming

Elementary school students with LD have uneven achievement levels across academic areas because of the different information-processing skills, cognitive styles, and background experiences they bring to their studies. Therefore, teachers must to greater or lesser degrees adapt the curriculum to fit what the child already knows, what he or she needs to learn, what the child is ready to learn, and how he or she learns best. Most of the time they must mix and match from several programs to meet the child's precise needs.

Most schools adopt formal published reading, math, language arts, science, and social studies curricula. These contain scope and sequence charts of the objectives to be covered. The materials and strategies presented in this chapter help to individualize our approach to the teaching objectives in these programs. These intervention strategies generally use children's strengths to promote academic progress and work around the interference of information-processing weaknesses. Our strategies also aim at shoring up these weaknesses. The best way to discover what method will work best is to try them out one by one, chart progress, and evaluate the learning outcome after a trial period of a few weeks.

### Reading Decoding

*Both whole language and phonics approaches to reading should be used because each contributes something important to different stages of learning to read.*

Reading is a priority because it, more than any other skill, supports all other areas of academic progress. The whole-word, whole-language, and language experience approaches to reading instruction emphasize the meaning of the language being read. In contrast, phonics and linguistic approaches stress the ability to break the phonetic code. Most experts advocate using both approaches because fluent reading requires the skills promoted by each to work in unison: recognizing words at a glance; analyzing, sequencing, and retrieving sounds in words; and gaining meaning from the words that have been read. The two approaches each contribute something important to different stages of learning to read and thereby complement one another. If there is an overemphasis on one approach, this may result in the overuse of that strategy, which in turn can impede reading fluency.

The *whole-language approach,* with its focus on whole-word recognition and meaning, has enjoyed great popularity in recent years. This approach emphasizes exposure to real literature, which is meant to be savored and transformed by the reader, not read and memorized for tests. The whole-language movement has brought new life to many classrooms by immersing students in good literature and a language-rich environment, by emphasizing comprehension and daily writing, and by inspiring more creative learning activities. With these positives, however, has come intense debate about a one-sided emphasis on whole-language in beginning reading instruction. The whole-language assumption is that children learn phonetic rules naturally and without systematic instruction, by being immersed in a print-rich environment that invites guessing words from context and from one's own experiential and conceptual knowledge. Teachers may at times teach phonics, but not in a preplanned fashion—certainly not isolated word lists nor mundane vocabulary-controlled stories whose purpose is decoding instruction. Those of us old enough to remember still cringe at the memory of "see Spot run" and "jump Jip jump." In the whole-language approach, any phonics instruction is done in an authentic language context—for example, giving a phonetic spelling hint to aid in the writing process.

*Whole-language instruction immerses students in good literature and a language-rich environment by emphasizing comprehension and daily writing, and by inspiring creative learning activities. It is assumed that children will discover phonetic rules without systematic instruction.*

Most students do intuitively discover the relationship between the sounds of speech and the signs of print. They break the reading code regardless of the teaching method. This is especially true of children who enter school with good phonological awareness. Good readers use syntax and semantics (meaning-based) and graphophonic (code-based) cues to aid their word recognition and to gain meaning. Good readers have both avenues available to them when they fail to recognize a word.

But students with LD do not have this advantage. Without the backup skill of phonetic decoding when they don't recognize a word, most guess at words from context. Consequently, the whole purpose of reading—to gain meaning from printed words—suffers.

*Phonics* skills are critical to reading success. They are the key to unlocking new words. When children learn to read, they are faced with many different word types from which they infer many phonics rules on their own. Because students with LD often can't segment words into individual sounds or easily access the sounds even once they have been memorized, they are unlikely to intuit these phonetic skills without being systematically taught. Students who do not naturally crack the phonics code need systematic, explicit skill-by-skill phonics instruction to become proficient readers. This doesn't preclude a whole-language approach, as long as supplemental phonics instruction is offered and the literature that is read is appropriate to the student's language comprehension. Unfortunately for many children with reading delays, traditional basal readers that stress phonics and control the difficulty of the reading vocabulary do not also sufficiently control the order in which phonics is introduced—from easier to harder—and the frequency of practice so that mastery of one sound pattern is achieved before moving on to the next one. More specialized phonics instruction is necessary for the child with LD in order to master one phonics skill before becoming confused by another, and to practice the learned skills in stories with specially constructed vocabulary that follows these rules and is repetitive enough to build automaticity. Research Box 11.1 on page 405 further explores the importance of systematic phonics instruction for students with LD.

*Students who do not naturally crack the phonics code need systematic, explicit skill-by-skill phonics instruction to become proficient readers.*

For most children with learning disabilities, phonetic approaches that teach listening to, identifying, blending, and sequencing individual sounds in words

***Our alphabetical system is meant to help us figure out words that look very similar, as well as words we've never seen before.***

work better than methods that don't incorporate phonics instruction. Printed English is poorly suited to being accessed by the whole-word approach alone. It is confusing to learn the pronunciations for *hat/hit/hut, bat/bit/but, hit/hat* through this approach because these words all look so much alike. Phonics skills are essential to going beyond the visual shape of a word to its internal components. Our alphabetical system is meant to help us figure out words that look this similar, as well as words we've never seen before.

Research Box 11.1 explains that the optimal timing for the introduction of phonics instruction may depend on the student's specific strengths and weaknesses. If, for example, the child 's strengths are in language and auditory analysis, phonics instruction will likely lead to immediate success. At the same time, this student's weaker sight recognition skills would be remediated. If the student has weak phonological analysis, blending, or sound retrieval skills, then building a whole-word foundation first may be best, while at the same time sharpening the child's awareness of sounds in words and his or her ability to retrieve those sounds from memory. The danger with introducing a "look-say" habit, however, is that it may interfere with children applying their emerging phonics skills. Learning a great number of words by sight alone just won't work, and it can be quite confusing.

The same concerns that apply to the whole-language approach also apply to the *language experience approach,* in which the child dictates stories and personal experiences to the teacher, who writes them down verbatim. The teacher reads the resulting story aloud and then the child reads it, while the teacher draws attention to individual words. This approach motivates the child to read through activities such as illustrating, editing, and making permanent wall charts of his or her "writing." The language experience approach assumes that the more that the child dictates and reads the transcriptions, the more that he or she will absorb knowledge about how our alphabetical system works.

***Linquistic approaches, which cluster sounds into word families, are helpful to the child who has difficulty learning to analyze and sequence phonemes in words through phonics instruction.***

*Linguistic approaches,* which cluster sounds into word families (e.g., *pat, rat, cat*), are extremely helpful to the child who has difficulty learning to analyze and sequence the individual phonemes in words through typical phonics instruction. Word stems like *ick* are taught as sight words, and then individual sounds are added at the beginning of the stems—*p*ick, *k*ick, *s*ick. Students learn root words, and stems that are added at the beginning (*un, dis, re*) or end (*less, ful, ly*) of the root words. Words are presented in a definite sequence—regular spelling patterns first and then irregular patterns. Often the consonant and vowel that begin words are pronounced as a single unit (e.g., "*sa*"), and then the final letter is added (*g, t, p*). This method gets around the unnatural pronunciation when the first letter is sounded out in isolation before blending it with the stem (as in "*huh*" - *ike* for hike, or "*li*" - *ap* for lap). The confusion this can cause a child who already has difficulty analyzing and blending sounds in words is avoided because the isolated sound is added at the end, as in *hi* - "*k*" or *la* - "*p.*" In this approach the "at" family would be taught as "*pa - t,*" "*ra - t,*" "*ca - t,*" rather than "*p - at,*" "*r - at,*" and "*c - at.*" Linguistic approaches emphasize mastery of common *orthographic sequences* (common letter sequences in English), which in turn increases sight recognition. And once this system helps the child master the phonetic code, the child can focus on the real point of reading—understanding.

RESEARCH BOX 11.1

## Phonics and Whole-Language Approaches to Reading Instruction

Studies conducted in the classroom that examine the effectiveness of "code-emphasis" (phonological awareness and phonics) and whole-language (constructivist sight word) approaches to reading generally find that the code emphasis has an advantage, especially for children who are at risk for learning difficulties (Bateman, 1968; Bliesmer & Yarborough, 1965; Felton, 1993; Foorman, et al., 1998; Guyer & Sabatino, 1989; Juel & Minden-Cupp, 2000; O'Connor, Notari-Syverson, & Vadasy, 1998; Potts, 1968; Silberberg, Iversen, & Goins, 1973; Stahl & Miller, 1989). Developing the ability to break spoken words into syllables and syllables into their component sounds, blend these sounds together, and then link these phonological awareness skills with letter-sound correspondence is essential to reading achievement. Approaches that emphasize meaning (they expect children to intuit how to read words by simple exposure to whole words) rather than phonics have been found to be less successful than those that early on systematically teach decoding (Adams, 1990; Anderson et al., 1985; Chall, 1983; Finn, 1986; Juel & Minden-Cupp, 2000; O'Connor et al., 1998; Wise et al., 1998). Spelling also benefits more from an emphasis on how to break the reading code, whereas comprehension appears to develop equally well through either phonics or whole language methods (Adams, 1990).

Bateman's study was among the first in this line of research. It is of particular interest because it used several instructional approaches throughout first grade and analyzed the data separately for auditory and visual learners. Even the visual learners, who theoretically were mismatched with the phonics teaching technique, profited more in reading and spelling from a phonics approach than from a whole word approach. Even when phonics doesn't come easily to visual learners, it appears essential to reading progress and will benefit them in the long run.

Research concludes that, while helping children learn to read words automatically by sight is our goal in reading instruction, the method by which we get there is *not* a "sight" teaching approach. It is the learning of our alphabetic system—how sounds connect to letters and how sounds are sequenced in words—that, with practice, secures a "sight" word in memory. Reading efficiency, both sight word recognition and automatically connecting letters with their sounds and blending these together, is important because the more fluently one reads, the more effectively the text is comprehended (Shinn et al., 1992; Stanovich, 1982). When word identification is slow and cumbersome, comprehension suffers because cognitive resources need to be expended on decoding rather than on comprehension. Skilled readers automatically apply their visual recognition, orthographic awareness, familiarity with analogous letter patterns, and phonics skills to process nearly all the letters and words they see in a text. When these strategies fail, they can fall back on guessing strategies. But guessing is successful only about 25 to 30 percent of the time. Children have most success guessing words that don't affect meaning (for example, *to, the*), but are successful only 10 percent of the time guessing at words that carry meaning (such as *locomotive, wheat*). Therefore, guessing generally is not a very helpful strategy (in Ehri, 1998). Skilled readers seldom need to resort to guessing from context because word identification is so automatic (Vellutino, 1991).

*(continued)*

## RESEARCH BOX 11.1 (Continued)

There is abundant evidence of the positive effects on reading achievement when children are readied for phonics through phonological awareness instruction. The same results are found in studies conducted in a number of languages in different countries (Poskiparta, Niemi, & Vauras, 1999; Schneider et al., 1999). Phonological awareness facilitates the word recognition process, and is in turn itself facilitated by the improving word recognition (Torgesen, Wagner, & Rashotte, 1994). Facilitative effects on reading have been found even when teachers teach these skills for as little as two 15- to 20-minute sessions weekly. Teachers teach such basic skills as, from easiest to hardest, recognizing which word sounds longer (*spaghetti* or *train*—the "perceptual" confusion caused by the real lengths of these objects is purposeful here), segmenting sentences into words and words into syllables, rhyming, blending phonemes, syllable splitting, onset-rime (*b / ack*), segmenting phonemes within words, and substituting one phoneme for another within a word (Berninger, 1990; Bradley & Bryant, 1978, 1983; Castle, Riach, & Nicholson, 1994; Griffith & Olson, 1992; Hurford et al., 1994; Litcher & Roberge, 1979; Lundberg, Frost, & Petersen, 1988; O'Connor et al., 1998; Tornéus, 1984; Vandervelden & Siegel, 1997; Vellutino & Scanlon, 1987; Wallach & Wallach, 1979; Williams, 1984). These activities, especially when paired with the actual letters, lead to greater and more persistent reading gains than traditional letter-sound instruction and language activities (Ball & Blachman, 1991; Blachman, 1994; Bradley, 1988; Bradley & Bryant, 1985; Tangel & Blachman, 1995).

The segmenting, blending, and letter-sound correspondence tasks included in phonological awareness instruction appear to contribute most to children's reading gains (O'Connor, Jenkins, & Slocum, 1995). In spite of the generally facilitative effect of phonological awareness training, however, it is disappointing that most studies report that as many as 30 percent of their subjects are "treatment resisters." They do not benefit from this type of training and require far more intensive intervention (Fuchs et al., 2002; O'Shaughnessy & Swanson, 2000; Torgesen, 2000).

Younger and less skilled children progress much faster in reading when phonological awareness and phonics instruction shows them how to "crack the code" versus expecting them to discover these relationships from exposure to print and indirect teacher reinforcement of sound patterns in words (Blachman et al., 1999; Foorman et al., 1998; Hatcher, Hulme, & Ellis, 1994; Juel & Minden-Cupp, 2000; Torgesen et al., 1999). These skills are then applied to learning explicit strategies for attacking decodable and sight words (Fuchs et al., 2002; Hatcher et al., 1994; Juel & Minden-Cupp, 2000).

Juel and Minden-Cupp found that more skilled young readers made equal word recognition progress when exposed to either phonics skills or reading new words by analogy to known letter patterns (substituting stems—as in *f/b/r-ake and d/w/f-ish*), as long as they had been exposed to both approaches. However, less skilled students made only marginal progress if exposed to whole words, orthographic patterns, and rhyme patterns before they developed the phonics skills necessary to analyze these words. These children needed some initial letter sound analytical proficiency before they could benefit from attacking whole words by learning to detect known words and word parts within these words. The skills gained from direct phonics instruction facilitate reading of unknown phonetically regular words, while whole word decoding strategies enhance the reading of both regular and irregular words (Lovett et al., 1994).

## RESEARCH BOX 11.1 (Continued)

The 1980s and early 1990s "reading wars" between whole language and code-emphasis advocates have softened, with most experts now agreeing that incorporating phonological awareness and phonics instruction into print-rich learning environments speeds early reading progress, especially for the most at-risk students.

Code-oriented theorists now emphasize that reading instruction should balance systematic decoding instruction with a meaning emphasis approach, language enrichment, and extensive practice with text reading (Adams, 1990; Stahl, McKenna, & Pagnucco, 1994). Students benefit greatly from immersion in excellent literature that encourages vocabulary enrichment, reading for comprehension, use of context to monitor story lines and make predictions, and an understanding of how reading and writing are related (Chall, 1983; Hatcher et al., 1994; Mather, 1992; Pressley & Rankin, 1994; Spear-Swerling & Sternberg, 1994; Vellutino, 1991). Likewise, the best of today's whole language teachers infuse instruction in phonological awareness and phonics strategies directly into reading and writing activities in a deliberate, planned, intense, developmentally appropriate, and systematic manner (Dahl et al., 1999; Fitzgerald & Noblit, 2000).

Regardless of the method used to teach phonics skills, we should teach reading whenever possible in the context of good literature and enriching content, rather than using only controlled word lists. This not only makes sense in terms of fostering the child's linguistic development, but encouraging semantics and syntax development provides helpful cues to the poor reader when he or she can't recognize a word. This literature-based context for reading instruction also is important because too many poor readers have an impoverished understanding of what reading is all about. One researcher quotes a child who defined reading as "a piece of paper—on a piece of paper." Another child said that good readers were "fast and loud" (Palincsar & Klenk, 1992, p. 218). Teachers need to make sure that even the most severe learning disability doesn't stand in the way of the child being exposed to literacy experiences—even if aurally—that fulfill the purpose of reading: to gain meaning and knowledge.

***Teachers need to make sure that even the most severe learning disability doesn't stand in the way of children being exposed to literacy experiences—even if aurally—in order to gain meaning and knowledge.***

For many students, a wise match between their learning strengths and a reading program's approach will lead to reading progress. For those with severe deficits, however, dramatic modifications of the curriculum are necessary in the form of special reading strategies. Average ability young elementary school students require on average 35 presentations of a new word before they'll automatically recognize it. Students with LD require far more exposures for mastery, averaging anywhere from 40 to 70. Words are learned somewhat faster when they are concrete (for example *table,* vs. *about*), phonetically regular, and when presented in context versus isolation. What follows are descriptions of several special reading strategies available to educators.

***Young students with LD require far more exposures than average achievers to a reading word, from 40 to 70, before it is mastered.***

**Special Reading Strategies.** Written English is a tough code to crack. One letter, such as *a,* can have multiple sounds: the long *a* in b*a*ke; the short *a* in b*a*ck; an *e* sound as in langu*a*ge, *i* sound as in stom*a*ch, or *u* sound as in inf*a*my.

Several letters can be sounded as one letter (e.g., the *o* sound in alth*ough*). The same letter combinations can sound different depending on the word—b*ea*t, h*ea*lth. Half of all English words have silent letters, and only 50 percent follow phonetic rules. It's no wonder that many children with LD despair of ever learning to read well.

*Many of the specialized reading approaches follow multisensory formats.*

Many of the specialized reading approaches for children with LD follow multisensory formats similar to those advocated by the pioneers in the learning disabilities field. The premise is that when children actively involve all their senses in the learning process, they're more likely to pay attention to the important elements of the task. If one sense isn't grasping the task, perhaps the other will come to the rescue. These methods can be used to reinforce the objectives of the standard reading program, or replace it altogether. The choice of multisensory methods must be evaluated carefully in order to make sure that this isn't the kind of child who gets overloaded when bombarded by too much sensory involvement, to the point of literally tuning out.

***The Elkonin Method.*** Described most easily as the "say it and move it" method, this approach gives children chips, and a piece of paper with a picture at the top of the word (e.g., *jam, lamp*). On the bottom half is a rectangle divided into squares corresponding to the number of phonemes in the pictured word. Children are taught to say the pictured word slowly, pushing a chip into each square as each successive sound is articulated. Children begin by learning to use a chip to represent one phoneme ("*n*"), then two ("*an*"), and finally three phoneme combinations ("*man*") using a slow blending strategy. Eventually letters are substituted for the chips, and words can be built by substituting letters (e.g., "*sit*" becomes "*pit*," which then becomes "*pin*"). Because of children's slow information processing, sounds that can be sustained (e.g., *mmmm* and *ssss,*) are used before "stop" consonants that can't be sustained (such as *p* and *t*). The Elkonin method focuses on blending sounds because, without the ability to blend, knowledge of letter sounds is of no practical use in decoding a word. Children enjoy using a cookie tray with Scrabble tiles to create and modify words, or a pocket chart into which letter cards are placed. In time, picture cues, squares, and chips can be eliminated and replaced with simply saying the word slowly and then having the child write the sounds (letters) in the order he or she hears them. Many studies have shown this procedure to be more effective in increasing phonological awareness and generalizing the learned phonics skills to new words and spellings than more traditional instruction.

***The Fernald Approach.*** Grace Fernald developed the VAKT method (Visual-Auditory-Kinesthetic-Tactile) to teach reading through a multisensory approach that focuses on the whole word more than individual sounds. The child dictates a short story. The teacher then writes each word from the story that the child wants to learn on a strip of paper in large cursive writing. The child traces each word with his or her index and third fingers while slowly saying the word in syllables. The word to be traced can be made "bumpy" by placing the paper on top of a piece of window screen and using a grease pencil to write. The tracing continues until the child can write the word without the model. When all the words have been learned, the teacher types the story so the child can read it in print. Eventually the tracing is abandoned and the child learns words by looking at, saying, and copying them, and then writing them from memory without a model.

*The Gillingham-Stillman Method.* Based on Orton's pioneering work discussed in Chapter 1, this is an alphabetical system that stresses letters and their sounds. Spelling and writing are used to reinforce reading skills. It is a highly structured approach that requires the child to receive instruction five days a week for at least two years, working through a fixed sequence of phonetic rules.

Sounds are learned one at a time using auditory, visual, and kinesthetic stimuli and some tracing. The student learns all the possible pronunciations of a letter and then blends them into sound clusters and finally words. For example, the teacher will show the child the letter *a* on a flash card, and the student orally recites the different ways in which the *a* can be pronounced: *a* says /ă/ as in *sat*; *a* followed by a consonant and *e* says /ā/ as in *bake*, and so forth.

To aid word analysis, the teacher first reads aloud words that contain the phonemes the child has learned. The child points to these words as they are dictated by the teacher. Then the child reads the words. The teacher then creates reading passages using the phonics skills and words the student has mastered. Finally, the Simultaneous Oral Spelling process is introduced. The teacher says a word; the child repeats the word and then names the individual letters in the correct order. The child then writes the letters while naming them silently. Nonsense words (e.g., *tay*) are interspersed with real words in order to check on generalization of phonics rules. Research has found that this spelling approach is very effective for facilitating word recognition gains.

The Wilson Reading System is based on the Gillingham-Stillman model but incorporates more sentence reading, writing at the sentence level, reading of phonetically controlled passages, and listening comprehension. Lessons have a set order of component tasks, spending 2 to 5 minutes each on drilling sound cards, teaching/reviewing a reading concept, word cards, word list reading, sentence reading, spelling sound drill, teaching/reviewing a spelling concept, writing dictated words and sentences, followed by 10 to 15 minutes of controlled passage reading and 10 to 30 minutes for listening comprehension development.

*The Neurological Impress Method.* In this method, the teacher and the student read a passage aloud in unison while the child points to the words as they are read. The teacher sets a pace that matches the student's reading rate. At first the teacher's voice is faster and more dominant. As the child's confidence and sight recognition increase, the teacher's volume decreases and his or her pace lags behind the student's.

*Choral Reading.* Choral reading is modeled on the neurological impress method. Here several students read aloud as a group. A variation, having the student read along with a tape once each day, has been found to significantly improve the rate and accuracy of sight recognition, as well as independence in self-correction.

*Repeated Readings.* Improved reading performance occurs when the child rereads the same passage, sight word phrases, or letter-sound combinations. The child reads one-on-one with the teacher for about 15 minutes a day, and the teacher corrects the child's errors. If more than two errors are made per page, the child rereads the passage. Usually, three readings are sufficient to reach decoding proficiency, a good reading rate, and maximum comprehension. Children using this strategy generally are able to apply their newly developed word recognition skills to new passages that contain the same vocabulary.

***Previewing.*** Silent previewing of a reading selection has been shown to increase the number of words students subsequently read correctly in the passage. *Previewing by listening* is an even more effective strategy, with peers, aides, or tapes reading the passage to the child before the child attempts reading it alone. Previewing by listening, when followed by repeated readings, has proved to be an excellent strategy for improving reading rate. Children record their reading rate when they read a passage, and move on to a new passage after three successive improvements.

***Programs That Restrict the Memory Load.*** Several programs teach a prescribed sequence of phonics or linguistic skills while narrowing the memory load for students who can deal with only a limited amount of new information at a time. Programs like *Reading Mastery* (formerly *DISTAR*), *Corrective Reading,* and *Recipe for Reading* initially restrict the load to 9 to 11 sounds, with more sounds added as students master them. Reading gains in these tightly controlled programs are often well beyond that in a regular classroom phonics program.

***Patterned Books.*** Patterned books are made up of sentences and phrases that are repeated throughout. As the teacher reads these books aloud, students join in when they can predict what comes next. The child's aural memory for the sentences and phrases helps to develop word recognition skills.

***Reading Recovery.*** The Reading Recovery program slowly introduces the alphabet to beginning readers while they work one-on-one with the teacher for approximately 20 weeks. Hundreds of simple books, particularly patterned books, are read and reread; brief stories are written—cut up into single words—and reassembled; words are built with magnetic letters, and the teacher reinforces a variety of decoding strategies: sounding out and blending, using syntax cues, reading by analogy to known words and word parts, using picture and context cues. Reading Recovery books are not leveled according to decoding difficulty, but rather by text length, picture support, orthographic patterns, high-frequency words, text structure, and language complexity.

***Peabody Rebus Reading Program.*** When none of these systems has worked, and the child is not learning his or her letter sounds, teachers can turn to the Peabody Rebus Reading Program in which printed words are replaced with rebus symbols. For example, the word *bottlecap* may be represented by a  , *brain* by b-  , and *bread* by  . Gradually the symbols transition into sight words. For example, the rebus for the word *look,* which is eyeglasses, slowly begins to take the shape of the word *look.* Eventually the child can read over 100 printed words.

Today's teacher can also call on a number of reinforcement methods including the computer, tape recorder, educational games, filmstrips, books with accompanying tapes, and tachistoscopes that flash words at fixed rates. Educational TV is popularly used, as are teaching machines such as the Language Master, which plays back the child's recorded voice reading the printed word, as a card with that word on it is scanned by the machine. All of these, particularly talking computer programs, can add variety and excitement to the learning to read process. Research Box 11.2 reviews research on how we should go about responding to children's errors while they are reading aloud.

RESEARCH BOX 11.2

## Providing Feedback to Students on Their Reading Errors

What is the best way to respond when a child makes a decoding error? Pany and McCoy (1988) summarize the most common arguments against interrupting students to correct their oral reading errors: the child will rely increasingly on the teacher and diminish his or her self-monitoring during reading; correction draws the child's focus away from the real purpose of reading, which is gathering meaning; feedback is disruptive and impairs comprehension. Countering these arguments, however, Pany and McCoy found that third graders with LD who were corrected for every error decreased their oral reading errors, increased comprehension, and could recall the words 2 to 3 days later significantly better than students who received no feedback or were corrected only when their errors altered meaning (about half of all errors). Pany and McCoy's error correction procedure first cued the child to "try another way," then asked "What sounds does ______ make?"; if the child was still unsuccessful, the adult supplied the word. Rosy, McEntire, and Dowdy (1982) found that some students with LD profited best when, instead of having the chid sound out the word, the teacher simply supplied the correct word immediately after the reading error was made.

In the *constant time delay* technique, a reading word is presented to a student, and the teacher simultaneously reads the word aloud. On subsequent trials, the teacher waits a designated number of seconds (usually 3 to 5) for the student to read the word; if the student is unsuccessful, the teacher reads the word aloud. This nearly errorless method has resulted in more rapid learning of sight words; word definitions; math facts; spelling words; and science, social studies, and health facts than when teachers "prompt" students toward the correct response (Keel & Gast, 1992; Koscinski & Hoy, 1993; Mattingly & Bott, 1990; Wolery et al., 1991). Retention over time is good, and the material is generalized to other tasks and settings. When constant time delay procedures have been implemented within small elementary or high school groups, even the students who were not being "called on" learned a good deal through observation, provided that their attention was cued by writing the word or orally repeating the question while waiting for their peer's response.

Many of our special reading strategies are successful for the same reason as the technique of these researchers: They offer very precise feedback that immediately corrects errors and prevents a student from continuing to practice and learn his or her mistakes. Subsequent drills on these words help promote retention (Rosenberg, 1986).

## Written Language

*Language-rich programs in which reading and writing are used to reinforce one another find that the transfer of learning between the two is excellent, about 30 percent.*

Writing is often the biggest stumbling block for students with LD because writing involves applying the language processes needed for reading, spelling, listening, speaking, and thinking all at once. Language-rich programs in which reading and writing are used to reinforce one another find that the transfer of learning between the two is excellent, about 30 percent.

The whole-language approach offers an extremely rich environment for learning about writing. Good literature exposes students to ideas for writing and to superb models for the craft of writing, including how to organize the text, have it be coherent, and use the appropriate voice and style for a specific writing purpose.

*Good literature exposes students to superb ideas and models for the craft of writing, including how to organize the text, have it be coherent, and use the appropriate voice and style for a specific writing purpose.*

Vygotsky's theories of learning have had an important impact on the whole-language movement. Vygotsky viewed learning as a social event in which a teacher's modeling of strategies, through demonstration, discussion, and explanation, plays a critical role. The teacher's questioning and guidance provide the necessary "scaffolding" that supports the student progressing to the next higher level of development. Teachers and students discuss what they are learning and how they are going about learning, with the goal that these strategies will become the students' own in the teacher's absence.

In keeping with Vygotsky's thinking, *Literature Circles* are good ways to reinforce the reading-writing connection. Children choose a book from among those the teacher has recommended and form circles in which five or six students discuss the work. Through modeling and guided discussions, the teacher helps students relate the book to their own experiences, knowledge, other readings, and their own writing. Students might act out the story, rewrite it as a play, write a new ending, tell the story from another character's perspective, write a report on the setting of the story or one of its characters, or write a new story borrowing the same theme or characters. They may even choose to have their own writing be the subject of the literature circle. "Reader's" and "author's" chairs are popular ways for students to read to others in their group, especially their own works. The circle's discussion goes well beyond the literal meaning of the text and offers excellent opportunities for writing revisions based on peer feedback.

Literature circles can choose to read sets of texts on common themes (e.g., survival, women's roles); by certain authors; or organized around characters, cultures, or text structures (e.g., where one event causes a trickle-down effect). The Harry Potter phenomenon has inspired many such circles in schools across the country. Each student in the circle can read the same or a different text, or the teacher can read one book aloud while students read other members of the set independently. The teacher helps students make comparisons between texts and authors and relate this to their own writing.

*The best environment for developing writing skills is one that encourages students to use language for a variety of purposes and audiences through reading, writing, listening, and speaking.*

The best environment for developing writing skills is one that encourages students to use language for a variety of purposes and audiences through reading, writing, listening, and speaking. The scene described in Storytelling and Writing Time is an excellent example of this kind of environment. Such an integrated approach generates excitement, flexibility in materials and activities, an increase in students' recreational reading, encouragement to take risks by trying new readings and ways of writing, a focus on the child as a unique individual, an increase in

## Storytelling and Writing Time

*An example of a dynamic whole-language environment.*

One story the children worked with was entitled, "Franklin in the Dark" (Bourgeois & Clark, 1986). (Franklin is a turtle whose fear of dark places has led him to imagine that his own shell is inhabited by monsters, ghosts, and other unsavory characters.) Each child had been given a three-ring binder that served as a personal journal in which they would maintain their writings and revisions. As a prelistening activity, the children wrote journal entries about the things they were afraid of—or, in the case of 10-year-old boys who claimed to be fearless, about the fears of family members. After encouraging the children to share their journal entries (an opportunity for reading self-generated text), the teacher introduced the book. The children were asked to identify the genre, with supporting evidence, and to make predictions about the story. An illustration on the book cover, depicting a desolate turtle dragging his shell behind him, prompted the children to suggest that this would be a make-believe story.

After generating a series of predictions, the children listened as the teacher began to read . . . the children actively participated, spontaneously demonstrating their knowledge of story structure and their personal constructions of meaning: "Franklin is the name of the character." "His problem is he's afraid of the dark; that's my problem too!" "He oughta get hisself a night light." The student who made this suggestion later reminded everyone, with considerable pride, that he had predicted the author's solution.

As the teacher read the story, she called the children's attention to the story elements that they had been listening for in previous stories. She revisited their predictions, but she also called the children's attention to how Franklin might be feeling as he journeyed the world over, discovering that everyone he met had learned to deal with fear of some kind. "How would you feel if you were Franklin at this point?" "How," she asked, "does the author tell you that Franklin is surprised with what he is learning?" The teacher invited the children to join her in a second reading. The illustrations and predictable text supported the children in their choral reading.

Following the reading, the teacher introduced a writing activity by sharing her own fear of swimming, and by inviting the children to help her think of solutions to the problem. Then the children were asked to write a response to the story of Franklin in their journals. The response could be to write about solutions to the fear they had raised earlier, or to write a new story in which they were the character seeking help with a fear.

In a future session, the children shared their journal entries with their classmates. The writing process continued as, with the assistance of the teacher, the children edited their entries to substitute conventional spellings for inventions. Revisions were completed at this mechanical level over several months. . . . As we explored a variety of themes with the students, none seemed as appealing as those that dealt with people. Influenced by the topics the students chose to discuss and write about, we settled on themes related to friendship. This meant that we would explore friendship through both the writing and the reading that we did. Also, with this theme we chose to focus more systematically on planning, organizing, and revising one's writing. To facilitate this, the teachers began by composing a story with the children, first discussing some events they would possibly like to write about, then listing all the ideas they had for this story, and finally enlisting the children's help as they transformed the ideas into text. The children easily assumed ownership of the story, choosing ideas from their list and organizing these ideas into a story.

To foster a similar process of planning and organization among the students, we encouraged them to work in triads before they began their writing, to list—as the teacher had—ideas they would

*(continued)*

## Storytelling and Writing Time (Continued)

like to weave into their stories, and to help one another think of interesting ways to assemble those ideas. Following this pattern, with the teacher initially modeling, and the students planning collaboratively and then writing independently, the students were asked to select one from several writings that they would like to revise to make more interesting, exciting, or complete. The teacher once again used his writing and thought aloud, using a form of self-questioning, about how he might revise his writing. As the students began to get the gist of the teacher's activity, they added additional questions about the teacher's writing and suggested additional revisions.

To reinforce the concept of their classrooms as communities of inquiry, the students engaged in a variety of joint projects. For example, they assembled a class book entitled "Our School" for the purpose of informing new students about life at their school. They wrote a chapter about school rules, took photos of their favorite people and places in the school, planned and conducted interviews with significant people in the school, and wrote about those people and places. During a unit on whales, the students created a mural depicting the things they both wondered and learned about as they read and listened to information about whales from multiple sources, including books, newspapers, journals, videotapes, and tape recordings.

Throughout our instruction, we placed considerable emphasis on communicating to the children that they were capable of learning from print—even though they were not yet conventional readers—by listening to text, and studying the pictures from children's nature magazines, trade books, and newspaper articles.

*Source:* Palincsar, A. S., & Klenk, L. (1992). Fostering literacy learning in supportive contexts. *Journal of Learning Disabilities, 25,* 220–221. Copyright 1992 by PRO-ED, Inc. Reprinted by permission.

humor in the classroom, heightened interest in unsolicited writing and in reading one's own text, willingness to share one's knowledge, improvement in spelling and expression of thought in writing, and the fostering of pride in one's writing, even if it is less than perfect.

***In the whole-language approach, writing is viewed as a process of communication among a community of readers and writers.***

In the whole-language approach, writing is viewed as a process of communication among a community of readers and writers. Even before they can read or spell, children are encouraged to use *invented spellings* ("write it the way you hear it") to begin communicating through writing; in some studies encouragement of invented spellings in turn has speeded progress in phonetic decoding and spelling skills. Young children are amazed to find that what they wrote down is really "reading." Instruction continues on with well-defined writing objectives using very specific teacher-directed instruction.

Many children with LD don't plan their writing but rather simply write down whatever comes to mind. They seem to have a very limited view of writing. One researcher reports that a child described writing as, "good writers have strong muscles so that they can do cursive." Another said that the way to become a good writer is "to practice and hope and hold your pencil right." Still another defined writing as "copying the morning news " and "doing your five times each (spelling list)" (Palinscar & Klenk, 1992, p. 218). This lack of understanding contributes to depressed writing competence.

While a whole-language approach can build enthusiasm for writing, the majority of students with LD need very specialized additional instruction in written expression, spelling, and penmanship.

**Written Expression.** Written expression skills are not only necessary for compositions, poetry, short stories, and other kinds of expository writing, they contribute to good note taking, completing homework, essay exams, term papers, letter writing, and more. The knowledge of written story structure certainly enhances the student's ability to evaluate and appreciate literature, plays, movies, TV shows, and stories told by friends. Moreover, we've all experienced the therapeutic value of writing about plots, characters, thoughts, and feelings related to our personal experiences.

Besides the interference from reading disabilities, students' written expression difficulties can be due to language weaknesses, lack of experiences, or *production difficulties* with handwriting, punctuation, capitalization, and spelling. Since many instructional goals in written expression are similar to those for oral expression—vocabulary, logical organization of thoughts, inferential reasoning, syntax, synonyms, metaphors, idioms, etc.—if these are particularly poor, teachers need to seek the additional assistance of the speech-language specialist.

Students who have the experiences to write about but are reluctant to write them down may need help with idea and theme development, vocabulary, writing a logical and clear sequence of events, grammar, and the mechanics of writing (handwriting, punctuation, capitalization, and spelling). For students who lack motivating experiences to write about, the teacher can introduce exciting literature, enrichment experiences such as field trips, discussions, and movies, or encourage creative fantasies. Teachers can also encourage students to be creative about recounting everyday activities; provide magazines, newspapers, and other materials to stimulate ideas; and provide story enders (". . . and waved goodbye to their new friends." ". . . and no longer was afraid of the sea monster." ". . . and after the journey became a much wiser person."). Story enders tend to help students generate content leading toward a set goal or purpose more than do story starters.

***Story enders tend to help students generate content leading toward a set goal or purpose more than do story starters.***

Whichever approach the teacher chooses, it's best to avoid peppering student's writing with discouraging red marks. The feedback written on the student's work should reinforce what's good, and be followed up by constructive suggestions in one-to-one conferences. It's also good to focus on very specific writing goals in each assignment while overlooking others. When these goals are communicated to students before they write (e.g., concentrate on organization vs. mechanics), they're less overwhelmed by having to pay attention to all aspects of writing at once.

***The feedback written on the student's written work should reinforce what's good, and be followed by constructive suggestions in one-to-one conferences.***

Maintaining a writing notebook or personal journal is a popular way of encouraging written expression. Students enjoy writing down their experiences and their reactions to them. The teacher reads the notebook or journal every few weeks, adding occasional personal reflections but not corrections. Another way to promote writing is giving students ten minutes in class to write notes to each other, which are delivered immediately. Knowing that someone is going to read what you write is a strong motivator to sharpen one's skills. Using the World Wide Web to establish pen pals across the country, or in other countries, also is highly motivating. The message itself can be the focus of that day's written language instruction, before the child clicks "Send."

*Students with LD need clear strategy instruction to help them reflect on, plan, and improve the quality of their written work—on their own they tend to add elaborations on what was already said but generate few new ideas.*

Students with LD tend to cut their writing short, but they can be encouraged to persist with the simple suggestion to "write some more," which sometimes leads to higher-quality writing. They also need clear strategy instruction to help them reflect on, plan, and improve the quality of their work, because on their own they tend to add elaborations on what was already said but generate few new ideas. One example of such a strategy for persuasive essays is STOP:

> Suspend judgment to consider each side before taking a position,
> Take a side,
> Organize ideas,
> Plan more as you write.

Another is DARE:

> Develop your topic sentence,
> Add supporting ideas,
> Reject arguments for the other side,
> End with a conclusion.

Students whose dictated products are more sophisticated than the written versions can be encouraged to dictate into a tape recorder (which is later transcribed) or use a computer's voice recognition software. The teacher then uses this work for further development of specific written expression competencies.

A "shared writing" approach pairs the student and teacher in the writing process. The teacher writes the first sentence of a composition, the student the second, and so on. The teacher uses his or her sentences to model organization, thought development, punctuation, vocabulary, and spelling. A variation of this is the *dialogue journal,* which is a written conversation between the teacher and student over a period of time. The student usually initiates topics, and the teacher responds to the student's entry by adding ideas and questions. The teacher's entries help to expand on the areas in which the student demonstrates difficulty (e.g., in explaining the nature of a conflict). Again, corrections are suspended in favor of the teacher modeling good writing in the journal and maintaining the student's motivation.

One very helpful way to encourage written language development is by following the *writing process* model, especially when accompanied by direct instruction. Students write for at least 30 minutes a day on topics of their choice, focusing on the message, not the mechanics. Teachers set the right tone by writing at the same time as their students. A relaxed, informal atmosphere is set for the writing process. Students can work in small groups if they wish, read their works to each other, get feedback, and so forth. Their individual files contain works in progress, story ideas, lists of mastered goals and skills, etc.

*Writing conferences are essential to the success of the writing process.*

Writing conferences are essential to the success of the writing process. In conference, the student reads the piece to the teacher, describes difficulties, asks for input, and learns to self-evaluate. Teachers focus on a few well-chosen problem areas, reserving other problems for comment later on. The student takes the lead in suggesting which aspect of the piece he or she wants to work on together. Theme development always takes priority over mechanical errors. If the latter are focused on too soon, this can disrupt students' theme development and sentence flow in future writing. The teacher develops skill lessons for the classroom around the needs that become evident through these conferences.

*Mechanical errors, if focused on too soon, can disrupt students' theme development and sentence flow in writing.*

Experts describe five steps in the writing process: prewriting, composing, revising, editing, and publishing. *Prewriting* begins with topic selection. Many students struggle with this step because they believe they have nothing worth writing about. Teachers can help by having them list hobbies, activities they like, interesting things about themselves, their families and friends, and stories from their past. Students can share their lists with partners who can help them choose a topic as well as writing style: story, mystery, observation of a situation, description, and so on. Encouraging students to select their own topics communicates that not only are we confident in their choices but that they have something worthwhile to share. This is in stark contrast to the picture cues or story starters that typically are used in classrooms; these put the teacher, rather than the student, at the center of the writing task.

*The five steps in the* **writing process** *include prewriting, composing, revising, editing, and publishing.*

Also part of prewriting is the *brainstorming* phase in which students write down major ideas and put them in a logical sequence. Brainstorming might involve simply jotting down a title, notes on "where," "when," "who," "what happened," and an ending. Figure 11.1 on page 418 presents a tool to guide brainstorming that is very helpful to better-quality writing. Story grammar cue cards, shown in Figure 11.2 on page 419, have also helped students with LD produce higher-quality stories. Students check the appropriate story parts as they plan, and then again as they write.

*Story webs and story grammar cue cards have helped students with LD produce higher quality stories.*

*Composing* comes next. If teachers expose students to different literary genres and specifically instruct them to imitate an author's style, this can have a beneficial impact on their writing. It is helpful to read the resulting piece to others to elicit comments and questions that can stimulate revisions. *Revising* is the most difficult of all writing tasks. Many students are glad to get something, anything, on paper, let alone revise it. Too many are content to simply correct a few misspellings and pop in a comma or two. At this point, the student may have to go back to the prewriting phase to revisit ideas that need further elaboration or research. Again, comments from "peer editors" can be helpful. As students read their works to each other, they comment on what they liked best, ask questions, and give revision suggestions to increase clarity or detail. Revisions follow, but the focus of revisions is still on content, organization, and theme development, not mechanics.

In the *editing* phase, the student attends to spelling, capitalization, punctuation, and such language attributes as noun-verb agreement, synonyms, and complete sentences. Peer editors make this process more interesting.

*Publishing* is the last, very important step in the writing process because it recognizes a student's hard work by providing an audience for his or her thoughts. The piece is prepared with a cover and circulated in the classroom and beyond. Students have greater motivation to improve their composing and revising processes if they know that ultimately their work will be available to others.

The writing process just described takes a great deal of time and organization to set up. But once it is working, the payoff is evident. After a few years' experience with these steps, students wouldn't think of just sitting down and writing. They are willing and eager to put time into the preliminary phases and relaxed about the composing process, because they know what they want to say and in what order. They eagerly seek feedback from their peers, because of the mutual

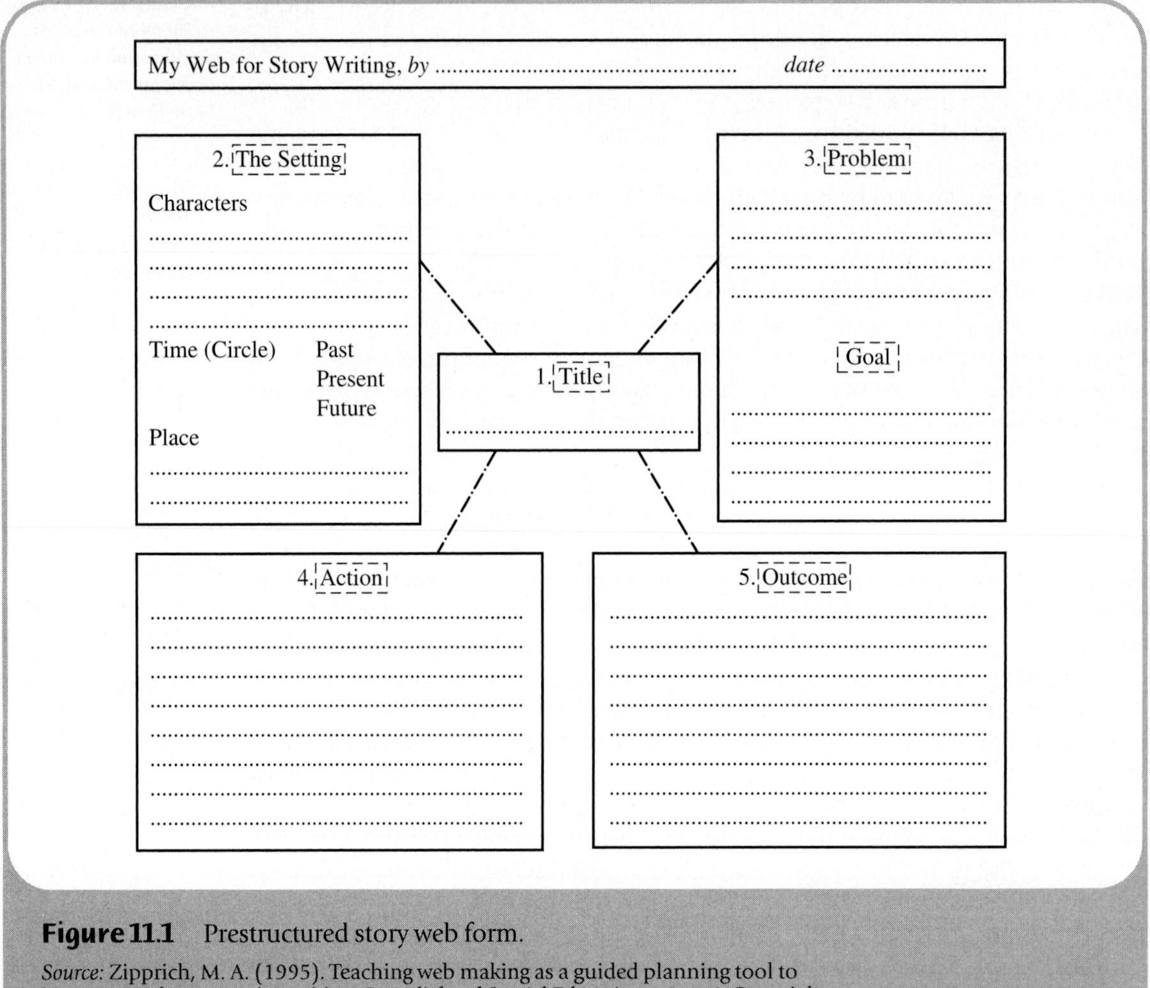


**Figure 11.1** Prestructured story web form.

*Source:* Zipprich, M. A. (1995). Teaching web making as a guided planning tool to improve student narrative writing. *Remedial and Special Education, 16,* p. 6. Copyright 1995 by PRO-ED, Inc. Reprinted by permission.

trust and respect built in the classroom. Best of all, they begin to see themselves as writers who have valuable thoughts to share, and control over how they communicate them.

***The majority of children with LD need very directed spelling instruction because they don't automatically discover spelling relationships through their reading, as average achievers do.***

**Spelling.** The majority of children with LD need very directed spelling instruction because they don't automatically discover spelling relationships through their reading, as average students do. Whereas elementary school students usually can spell 70 to 80 percent of words they can instantly read, the spelling accuracy of students with LD often is limited to 30 to 40 percent of the words they recognize by sight. The reasons are varied: trouble with recalling which letters go with which sounds, with discriminating the sequence of sounds in a word, with recalling standard orthographic patterns (letter pairs that follow one another in English), with visually recalling irregular spelling patterns (e.g., yacht, suede, pneumonia, and

| | Check as I plan | Check as I write |
|---|---|---|
| Characters | | |
| Setting | | |
| Problem | | |
| Plan | | |
| Ending | | |

**Figure 11.2** Story grammar cue card.

*Source:* Graves, A., & Montague, M. (1991). Using story grammar cueing to improve the writing of students with learning disabilities. *Learning Disabilities Research & Practice, 6,* p. 247. Reprinted by permission.

bouquet are words that must be memorized since they can't be sounded out), or with mastering spelling rules (as in "i before e except after c"). The specific reason for the spelling difficulties will dictate the instructional method chosen.

*Whereas elementary school students usually can spell 70 to 80 percent of words they can instantly read, the spelling accuracy of students with LD often is limited to 30 to 40 percent of the words they recognize by sight.*

*Spelling words to be learned are best selected from children's own essays, and best retained when integrated into the daily curriculum.*

Children learn to spell by first translating the sounds they hear in words to letters, and then by internalizing standard English orthography. They need to be able to read irregular words in order to spell them, because these can't be sounded out. Children improve faster in spelling when attention to orthography and other spelling supports are provided within the context of composition work. This is in lieu of practicing weekly spelling lists made up by the teacher. Spelling words to be learned are best selected from children's own essays, and best retained when integrated into the daily curriculum. Reviews can come in the form of computer games, filling in missing letters in words, and games like hangman, crossword puzzles, word searches, and word lotto. To strengthen retention of the word's image, children also enjoy imagining the word in black glossy letters on the chalkboard, the letters being pounded or illuminated letter-by-letter as on a theater marquis, and then writing it down. Children benefit from correcting their own spelling tests, having teacher guidance in comparing incorrectly with correctly spelled words, and using the dictionary to discover the right way to spell words they are unsure of.

What doesn't work is the old-fashioned "write each word ten times" method. It becomes a copying exercise rather than a chance to commit words to memory. Sara, for example, actually would copy the first letter of a word ten times, then the second letter, and so forth. Certainly, this accomplished nothing. One effective variation on this method is folding a sheet of paper accordion style into five columns. Sara copies the spelling word in the first column, then folds the paper and writes the word from memory in the second column, afterward checking for accuracy by referring to the first column again. Sara repeats this process until she can spell each word accurately three times.

Reading and language arts curricula usually include weekly spelling objectives that focus on word analysis, spelling rules and generalizations, syllabication

***It's important to limit spelling goals to only a few words, orthographic patterns, or phonics rules at a time to avoid overloading students.***

principles, and the six syllable types (consonant-vowel-consonant, vowel-consonant-e, etc.). These can be reinforced with special teaching strategies. For students who struggle with spelling, it's important to limit spelling goals to only a few words, orthographic patterns, or phonics rules at a time in order to avoid overloading students. Again, whenever possible, words should be drawn from the child's writing rather than standard word lists. Because children tend to reuse the same words again and again in their writing, these words have a greater likelihood of getting practiced and learned.

Research shows that as spelling and handwriting improve, so does writing quality. And as writing quality improves, so do spelling and handwriting. All three go hand in hand and, although composition is the most important of these skills to concentrate on, the others should not be ignored.

***The Elkonin Method.*** This "say it and move it" method of teaching phonemic awareness (see page 408) has proved very effective in enhancing spelling acquisition as well. Several studies have found marked improvement in both accurate spellings and invented spellings when using this method.

***The Fernald and Gillingham-Stillman Approaches.*** For students who have strong visual-processing skills, the Fernald approach (page 408), which emphasizes using all the senses through a whole word approach, might be appropriate. Students first trace the words they want to learn, and then write the word form memory. For students who are more adept at analyzing and sequencing the sounds in words, the Gillingham-Stillman approach, which uses oral and then written spelling, is more effective. The child listens to the word being pronounced very slowly, and then tells which letter sound is heard first, second, and so on. An oral misspelling might be written down so the student can read the misspelling and learn why it's incorrect. If the oral spelling is accurate, the letter order is reinforced by having the child find the letter card for the first letter, name the letter, and write it; this process is continued with subsequent letters. Techniques that simply have the child say the letters as they write the word a number of times have also boosted spelling acquisition.

***Linguistic Approach.*** This approach to spelling focuses on teaching word families (*bought, sought, thought; picture, torture, future*) and morphemes (such as common prefixes and suffixes added to words) in a set order. Teachers help children understand common spelling patterns by showing them that the parts of words that rhyme are spelled alike. This approach increases the child's ability to generalize word forms to others that follow the same orthographic patterns and rules (e.g., double the final consonant when adding *ing* if preceded by a short vowel.) The linguistic approach is helpful to teaching children to self-monitor their spellings, especially when combined with teaching of syntactic (*they're, their, there; it's, its*) and semantic (*new, knew; one, won*) spelling cues.

***Contingent Imitation Modeling.*** Teachers can improve children's spelling by pointing out and imitating misspellings, then writing the word correctly, and drawing a child's attention to the differences. In several studies this method significantly improved the spelling of children with LD.

*Other Methods.* The constant time delay strategy presented in Research Box 11.2, computer-assisted instruction, variations of a five-step procedure (say, write and say, check, trace and say, write and check), and naming letters while writing all benefit the spelling of students with LD. Writing, tracing, or keyboarding the words all appear to be equally effective. Wong's seven-step cognitive strategy is particularly interesting. The child asks (1) Do I know this word?; (2) How many syllables do I hear in this word? (3) I'll spell out the word; (4) Do I have the right number of syllables down?; (5) If yes, is there any part of the word for which I'm not sure of the spelling? (underline and try again); (6) Now, does it look right to me?; (7) When I finish spelling, I'll tell myself I'm a good worker. I've tried hard at spelling.

*Systematic approaches to writing, tracing, or keyboarding spelling words are equally effective.*

**Handwriting.** Word processing notwithstanding, students still need to be able to write by hand when they take notes, answer essay questions, and fill out job applications. For many students with LD, writing legibly and easily is a challenge.

Handwriting instruction focuses on holding and directing a writing utensil with appropriate grip, posture, and paper position as well as correctly, quickly, easily, and legibly forming manuscript (printing) and cursive writing. This includes attention to forming letters, spacing letters on the page, maintaining uniform size, crossing t's and x's, dotting i's, connecting lines within letters, closing looped letters, staying on a line, positioning the pencil (lightly between the thumb and adjacent two fingers) and paper (slanted 20 to 35 degrees to the left if right-handed, and the same angle to the right if left-handed), forearms on the table with elbows slightly extended, hips touching the back of the chair with feet on floor and torso slightly forward in a straight line. The diameter of the pencil doesn't seem to affect writing performance. Children should use the writing instrument most comfortable and motivating for them.

The instructional approach to handwriting varies depending on whether the child's weaknesses are due to poor revisualization of letter forms, motor incoordination, or spatial judgment. For example, when the difficulty is caused by a perceptual deficit, the student may need help recognizing and recalling the size, shape, and direction of letters. If the difficulty is due to poor attention and self-monitoring, simply asking students to "write as neatly as you can" increases handwriting quality, though speed suffers.

Workbook exercises typically have students copy a model or follow dotted lines. Frequently, this type of exercise is not enough to create fluent, legible handwriting for those with difficulties in this area. The teacher often needs to supplement these exercises with some of the following instructional steps, beginning with letter forms and progressing to short words and finally sentences:

I. Model the correct formation of one letter at a time, organized by type of stroke—circular, crossed lines, etc. Often *a, e, r,* and *t* are stressed because they account for nearly half of all malformed letters.

*a, e, r, and t account for nearly half of all malformed letters.*

II. Discuss the distinguishing features of letters—*h*'s and *m*'s look like hills, for example, while *u*'s and *w*'s look like valleys.

III. Highlight troublesome parts of letters in color and contrast these with other letters.

IV. The teacher models self-correction of his or her own errors, and helps students to recognize their own errors. Self-correction is reinforced.

V. Have children draw letters very large on a chalkboard or easel to let gravity aid in directing strokes; alternatively, use fingerpaints, draw in sand or shaving cream, trace bumpy letters written with grease pencil on paper that is laid on top of a mesh screen, and trace letters formed by glitter on glue. The letter name always should be said while tracing.

VI. Physically guide the child's hand or verbally prompt hand movements while the child says the letter's name and writes. Following dots, arrows, or associating the letter with a shape are very useful (as in b__d; the *b* represents the headboard of a bed, and the *d* the footboard).

VII. Show the child how to use self-talk to direct letter formation. Figure 11.3 shows the improvement in numeral formation and reversals when a child was taught to say "over and down" for 7s and "around and down" for 9s. The child found it easy to remember this verbal strategy, and the reversals seldom were seen again.

VIII. Have the child write a letter from memory several times after first copying it a few times (while saying the letter name).

IX. Have the child compare a letter with a model, describe areas for improvement, and praise correct features. Then do the same with letter combinations and words.

X. Once the child has achieved accuracy, increase fluency by periodically having the child chart the time it takes to copy a paragraph neatly.

The *trace and fade method* is another interesting modeling approach that has the advantage of gradually fading the visual prompt. The child traces a letter or word, then inserts a piece of tracing paper between the model and the first piece of tracing paper, and traces again. More and more tracing paper is inserted until the model's image fades away. At this point the child begins forming letters and words from memory. Successive layers of Scotch tape also can be used to fade a model as the child copies.

Teaching handwriting is an area in which the teacher can be especially creative by using stencils of letters, connecting dot-to-dot letters, completing incomplete letters, using acetate and markers for tracing, varying the color of paper for different letters, and using paper with different sized lines to help children stay within boundaries. In addition to sticks to trace letters in the dirt or sand, fingers for fingerpainting letters, paintbrushes for painting with water on the playground, dough to form letter cookies, pencil grips, and even Scotch tape to hold paper in the correct position, there are computer programs that let students draw letters on the screen and print out their own handwriting. Arrows help children practice strokes from up-to-down and left-to-right.

*If a child has struggled with manuscript, but mastered it, some experts recommend* **not** *switching to cursive; others advocate teaching cursive from the outset and avoiding manuscript.*

There is some controversy over whether children with handwriting weaknesses should be taught manuscript (printing) or cursive writing first. In third grade children typically transition to cursive from manuscript; manuscript has the advantage of more closely resembling text in books. If the child has struggled with manuscript, but finally mastered it, he or she might be encouraged to avoid yet another struggle by *not* switching to cursive—advocates of this position argue that one's signature is the only cursive writing that is essential in adult life. Others, however, advocate that the switch can be avoided by learning cursive writing from

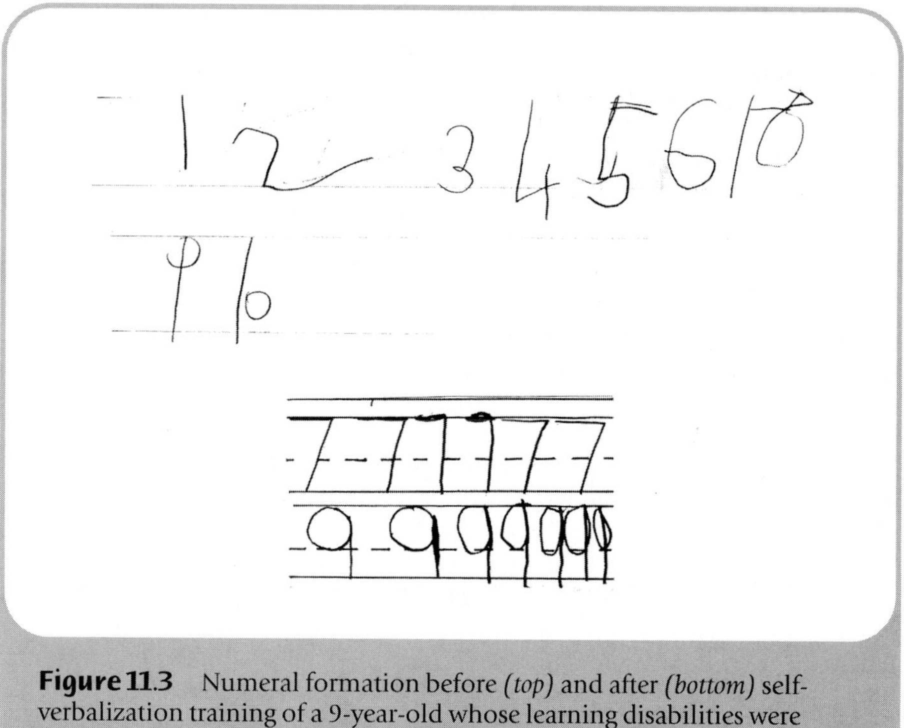

**Figure 11.3** Numeral formation before *(top)* and after *(bottom)* self-verbalization training of a 9-year-old whose learning disabilities were traceable to her mother's heavy drinking during pregnancy.

the very beginning, instead of manuscript. Cursive has the advantage of assisting with spacing and writing speed because letters are connected and writing starts and stops less often. Because all letters are formed form left to right in cursive, reversals also occur less often.

## Reading Comprehension and Content Area Instruction

By the fourth and fifth grades, students are introduced to more formal social studies and science instruction that come with textbooks and often assignments such as research projects and written reports. It is critical that the reading, written expression, and study skills weaknesses of the student with LD not be allowed to interfere with acquiring or demonstrating knowledge in these areas. If basic skills problems form a barrier to accessing the broader curriculum, students become less knowledgeable with time, less prepared to grasp the content of subsequent classes, and less able to interact with their peers on topics of mutual interest or concern.

*It is critical that reading, written expression, and study skills weaknesses of the student with LD not be allowed to interfere with acquiring or demonstrating knowledge in content areas.*

To evaluate a content area textbook for its appropriateness to the student with a learning disability, teachers need to check vocabulary, sentence complexity, extent of prior knowledge required, and readability level (readability formulas are described in Chapter 12.) Texts that teach well highlight important relationships, avoid overloading the student with less relevant concepts and details, give concrete examples of complex concepts, give practical applications of information, and provide visual aids, self-checks, and interesting content and style.

Too often students with LD are burdened with textbooks that are poorly organized, have an uninteresting writing style, and cover too many facts in too little conceptual depth. Moreover, the text publishers provide little information to the teacher on how to adapt lessons to include children with LD. The supplemental activities suggested are often inappropriate, impractical, and even dangerous (e.g., some science experiments).

*Texts are frequently too difficult for students with LD to read independently, necessitating taped texts, peer readers, outlines, or texts rewritten in easier language.*

Texts are also frequently too difficult for students with LD to read independently. In this case, it may be helpful for the teacher to read a section to the student before class, or help the student create an outline so that only key words need to be read. Peer readers and taped texts also can be used. If writing is a problem, the student could tape-record homework or test answers and have a parent or peer transcribe them. Because the transcription is in the student's natural language, it becomes ideal material for further instruction in reading, spelling, and written language.

Despite these accommodations, students may still have a difficult time understanding the text's material because the vocabulary and sentence structure are too difficult. One way to help is to adopt a "less is more" policy—that is, cover only essential points about essential topics and study them in greater depth, rather than overwhelming the child by trying to "cover the whole waterfront." This approach leaves students with some solid and useful higher-order concepts, rather than the few superficial and unconnected facts that "stick" almost by chance after bombardment by too much information. Teachers can rewrite texts, assignments, and tests in simpler vocabulary and sentences that the students can manage. The new material can be pasted over the original in the text so that the book appears to be the same as that used by the rest of the class.

*When learning content area material, "less is more." Cover only essential points about essential topics and study them in depth, rather than overwhelming the child.*

*Beyond poor reading, language, and information overload that impinge on comprehension, students with LD also have trouble identifying the main ideas, sequencing events, organizing ideas, drawing inferences, reaching conclusions, and applying information.*

Beyond poor reading, language, and information overload that impinge on comprehension, students with LD also have trouble identifying the main ideas, sequencing events, organizing ideas, drawing inferences, reaching conclusions, and applying information, especially when higher levels of problem solving and information evaluation are called for (as in comparison-contrast, cause-effect, if-then relationships, and dealing with idioms and metaphors). Students can benefit greatly from classroom discussions of readings and ideas that develop vocabulary, concepts, reasoning abilities, background to link with new ideas, and questions that stimulate a purpose for reading. Too often, though, comprehension development is relegated to worksheets and tests, leaving students with LD at a triple disadvantage—they have trouble with reading, writing, *and* comprehending.

Several approaches can aid comprehension. Most often, these methods apply schema theory to create a purpose for reading and a framework within which students can organize and interpret new information. They also teach self-questioning strategies and encourage the metacognitive goals and strategies described in Chapter 7.

**Schema Theory Approaches.** Schema theory states that, as the fund of relevant background information and awareness of text organization are heightened, comprehension will improve. Applying this theory has proved extremely helpful to students who find it difficult to locate, interpret, or remember important information and ideas in what they read.

Activating background knowledge is an important first step in increasing students' comprehension. The new information becomes more interesting, meaningful, and memorable because it is linked to information that is already familiar and understood. Activating background knowledge is particularly helpful in inferential comprehension because this kind of information is not literally stated in the text and the child's prior knowledge must help to infer what is meant. For example, a student might read, "Diane took a trip east. Although she had a phone within reach of her bed, she was upset to have to wait to call her mother about the exciting news." When asked why Diane had to delay calling, the student can respond only if he or she knows that "east" means that Diane is hours ahead of her mother, whose sleep she's reluctant to disturb.

***Activating background knowledge is an important first step in increasing students' comprehension. The new information becomes more interesting, meaningful, and memorable because it is linked to information that is already familiar and understood.***

There are several ways to help activate background knowledge before students read the text. In *brainstorming,* the teacher selects a word, phrase, picture, or excerpt from a reading passage and asks students to list as many words or phrases as they can associate with this stimulus. On the blackboard, the lists are compiled into categories, and the categories' underlying ideas are clarified. The *prereading plan* expands on brainstorming by asking students to reflect on what triggered their associations. Discussion generates further insights and associations. The *schema activation* strategy encourages students to discuss something they have done that is similar to the event they will read about, and to hypothesize about what will happen in the story. The teacher provides the main ideas before students read and leads them in thinking about what they might do, feel, or think in a similar circumstance.

Alerting students to the text's organizational structure can also increase comprehension. These strategies teach *story grammar,* the essential components of typical stories and how these usually are ordered. Students also can gain far more information when they simply ask themselves a series of questions that organizes the text as they read:

***Alerting students to the text's organizational structure can increase comprehension.***

1. *Who* is the story about?
2. *What* is he or she trying to do?
3. *What* happens when he or she tries to do it?
4. What happens *in the end*?

Another way to spur active involvement in the comprehension process is to teach children to diff1erentiate among answers that can be found easily in one place in the text, those that are hidden in the text, and those that require the reader to rely entirely on what he or she already knows. Comprehension is enhanced because children discover where to go for answers, including to their own minds.

The *RAP procedure,* described in Figure 11.4, has proved very effective in enhancing students' text comprehension. A variation of the RAP procedure has children paraphrase the main ideas and details of a paragraph into a tape recorder. In a similar process, students write a summary sentence after reading each paragraph. *Story retelling strategies,* or completing *story maps* such as the one shown in Figure 11.1 on page 418 help students track story components, for example, setting, problem, goals, sequence of events, reactions, and endings. All of these strategies markedly improve comprehension.

***The more we predict what is to come and question ourselves as we read, the more we comprehend.***

**Questioning Strategies.** The more we predict what is to come and question ourselves as we read, the more we'll comprehend. Because students with LD tend not

**Multipass: A Textbook Reading Strategy**

Survey the chapter using TISOPT

- T = Title read and paraphrased
- I = Introduction read verbatim and paraphrased
- S = Summary read verbatim and paraphrased
- O = Organization analyzed by reading headings
- P = Pictures examined
- T = Table of contents examined

Size up the information in the chapter using IQ-WHO

- I = Illustrations interpreted
- Q = Questions at the end of the chapter read and paraphrased
- W = Words in italics defined
- H = Headings: for each, do RASPN
  - R = Read a heading
  - A = Ask self a question based on heading topic
  - S = Scan for the answer
  - P = Put answer in own words
  - N = Note important information
- O = Other clues that textbook employs are identified and used

Sort out what has been learned from what needs to be learned using RAMS

- R = Read the question
- A = Answer the question if known
- M = Mark the question to indicate status
- S = SEARCH for the answer
  - S = Select a single heading
  - E = Examine the content carefully
  - A = Answer question if possible
  - R = Repeat under another heading if needed
  - C = Check with someone if still not found
  - H = Hassle questions clarified with teacher

**RAP: A Paraphrasing Strategy for Reading Comprehension**

- R = Read a paragraph
- A = Ask yourself what were the main idea and two details
- P = Put main idea and details in your own words

**Figure 11.4** Metacognitive strategies that enhance comprehension.

*Source:* Ellis, E. S., & Lenz, B. K. (1987). A component analysis of effective learning strategies for LD students. *Learning Disabilities Focus, 2,* 97–101.

to spontaneously monitor their comprehension as they read, teaching them questioning strategies makes sense. One such technique, Multipass, is described in Figure 11.4. *SQ3R* is another questioning strategy that teaches the child to *survey* the reading material first—chapter title, introductory statements, main headings, illustrations, summary, etc. Then the student reads the end-of-the-chapter *questions* to discover the purpose for reading, or creates some of his or her own questions (e.g., who, what, where, when, why, and how questions composed from the heading hints). The three *R*s follow: *read* the material to find the answers to the questions, *recite* the answers to the questions, and *review* the material for accuracy or to gain more information and ideas. In an adaptation of this method, *directed reading-thinking activities,* students begin by making predictions about what they will be reading and they generate questions. After children read the passage and answer their questions, the teacher follows up with questions requiring interpretation.

Also using questioning, teachers can assign short segments of passages to be read, which are followed by a *reciprocal questioning* technique between the teacher and pupil. The questions progress to higher levels as the child becomes ready to handle them, starting first with simple knowledge (facts, sequence, categories, methods), then comprehension (interpretation, inference), application, analysis (content, relationships, structure), synthesis (apply own ideas, generalize), and ultimately evaluation (analyze and make judgments about conclusions). In the *request* technique, the teacher and student each read a passage silently. First the child asks a question, giving the teacher an opportunity to model appropriate answers, including checking back in the text. Then it is the teacher's turn, and the child benefits from the modeling of appropriate questions. *Elaborative interrogation* involves the teacher leading students toward discovering why a fact is true through a series of questions, a technique that enhances comprehension more than simply providing the answers.

In a group questioning technique called *reciprocal teaching,* the teacher and students take turns leading class discussions on readings. Initially, the teacher models and labels different comprehension strategies to guide the leader's discussion: questioning, summarizing, clarifying, and predicting. The subsequent discussion focuses on the content of the text, inferences, disagreements in interpretation, arriving at a group summary of the gist of the piece, and predicting what will come next. The value of this strategy is that it sharpens the child's ability to engage in intentional learning from text, to use higher levels of discourse, and to monitor his or her own comprehension. Often several of these strategies are used in combination; all have greatly benefited the evaluation, recall, summarization, and application of the content material being read by students with LD.

## Mathematics

Many children with LD have difficulty understanding basic number concepts, time, measurement, money, fractions, and computational processes. Word problems pose an additional concern because they require reading and abstract reasoning in addition to computational skills.

In order to plan remedial instruction, teachers need to determine what is interfering with the child's mathematical progress, such as difficulty with size and spatial relationships, logical reasoning, writing numerals, reading, recalling number facts, attention to details, or poor past teaching. It's very helpful to listen to the child solve math problems out loud, to help identify the error in mathematical reasoning. Students' errors usually aren't random. They're trying to apply a rule that doesn't work in this specific context.

***Listen to the child solve math problems out loud, to help identify the error in mathematical reasoning. Students are usually trying to apply a rule that doesn't work in this specific context.***

Computations are only one part of a math curriculum. Students must learn how to apply this knowledge in everyday situations, estimate the reasonableness of their answers, read tables and graphs, reason about geometric principles, deal with time and measurement, and handle money. Therefore, it's important that math instruction for students with LD be put into a meaningful context to help these skills transfer to real-life problem solving.

*Math instruction should be put into a meaningful context to help these skills transfer to real-life problem solving.*

Like the reading curricula, the classroom math curriculum frequently doesn't meet the needs of students with LD. The reading vocabulary may be too difficult, too many concepts may be introduced at once, and there may be too few opportunities for practice. Typically, little practical application of these skills is built into the curriculum, and students may be unprepared for the concepts taught. Therefore, alternative approaches are necessary, and teachers need to practice ingenuity with students who demonstrate any number of problems that interfere with math success:

*Teacher adaptations of math curricula are necessitated by difficult reading vocabulary, too many concepts introduced at once, too few opportunities for practice, and little practical application.*

- Aligning calculations (teachers use graph paper, turn lined paper sideways).
- Remembering to calculate right to left (use graph paper for calculations and code each column a different color; green for the first column and red for the last cues the child to begin at green and stop at red).
- Remembering number facts (teachers use computer drills; paste a number line or fact sheet to the desk; teach how to count on from the highest number; teach rounding to the nearest 5 or 10 and then adding or subtracting from the answer the amount that was rounded; teach "count-bys" to calculate multiplication facts (counting by 2's, 3's, 4's, etc.); reduce the number of addition facts to be learned by teaching doubles for numbers one through nine (5 + 5), then double plus 1 (5 + 6 is calculated as 5 + 5 + 1), doubles plus 2 (5 + 7 is calculated as 5 + 5 + 2), add 1/subtract 1 before doubling [6 + 8 is calculated as (6 + 1) + (8 – 1) = 7 + 7], and going through 10 [9 + 5 is calculated as (10 + 5 = 15) – 1] (Pressley et al., 1990).
- Reading word problems (teachers transcribe the problems into numerals; teach cue words such as "altogether" and "left"; reduce sentence length and vocabulary complexity; eliminate extraneous information).
- Comprehending word problems (teachers paraphrase the problems; draw a diagram or picture of the problem; estimate an answer before calculating; personalize word problems to the child's interests and real-life surroundings).
- Attending to all elements of a problem (teachers set up lists of steps or self-checking devices).
- Becoming overloaded by too many problems on a page (teachers cut each worksheet into four segments).
- Understanding 10's and 1's places in borrowing (teachers enact the calculation using groups of 10 tongue depressors banded together and 1 or more single tongue depressor).
- Understanding what a numerical problem really means (teachers draw a picture of the problem, make up a story problem about it).
- Conceptualizing fractions (teachers demonstrate the fraction by sharing food or toys, using a measuring cup).

- Showing disinterest and lack of perceived relevance (teachers build math story problems into other subject matter lessons; read books in which the story lines are related to math concepts).
- Calculating, despite good conceptual and practical understanding of the problem (teachers encourage the use of calculators).

Although some educators still balk at the use of calculators in class, research consistently shows that in the early elementary years using these aids actually increases skill acquisition, attitudes toward math, and self-confidence. By using calculators to avoid being sidetracked by the arduous calculation process, children are freed to reason more intelligently about mathematical concepts. And it is mathematical reasoning, rather than calculation ability, that should be at the forefront of classroom math objectives. After all, even calculators are useless if a child can't reason about whether to add or subtract, or whether an answer seems in the right ballpark.

*Mathematical reasoning rather than calculation ability should be at the forefront of classroom math objectives.*

Traditional "drill and kill" math teaching, in which students memorize rules and do routine exercises, does little to prepare them for higher-order quantitative reasoning. It is not unusual, for example, for the young elementary school student to latch onto the numbers in a word problem and forego any reasoning about the mathematical relationships. One researcher found that 90 percent of second graders who scored above average on a standardized math test answered "36" when asked "There are 26 sheep and 10 goats on a ship. How old is the captain?" (Stipp, 1992). Our standard programs do nothing to help in this arena.

*Traditional "drill and kill" math teaching, in which students memorize rules and do routine exercises, does little to prepare them for higher-order quantitative reasoning.*

Better is the *constructivist model,* which encourages teachers to let students wrestle with personally engaging problems, thereby constructing their own knowledge and basic quantitative understandings. Students can also work as a group on interesting problems, working out solutions aloud, and trying different approaches. For example, students might build a scale model of a pencil from Gulliver's land of the giants, when given only the clue of the size of a paper clip. They might calculate in which year women swimmers' records will surpass men's, or when men's longevity will catch up to women's, given that the two are getting closer. Such active learning creates excitement and basic conceptual development. But it must be accompanied by teacher feedback and systematic calculation and application practice for students who don't discover relationships on their own. Besides such active learning, several special approaches using concrete materials and behavioral techniques have benefited students with LD.

*The constructivist approach to math instruction encourages students to wrestle with engaging math problems, thereby constructing their own quantitative understandings. This is accompanied by teacher feedback and systematic calculation and application practice for students who don't discover relationships on their own.*

**Concrete Materials.** Until children can understand that numerals on paper represent real things, paper-and-pencil addition of numerals is meaningless and confuses them further. Seeing and manipulating objects through play and structured practice builds the bridge between quantities and numerals, and later mathematical operations. Concrete materials help students reason about logical relationships represented by numerals: largest-smallest; first-last-next; more than–less than, and so forth. When impulsive students can touch objects as they count, they slow down and become more accurate.

Concrete objects should be used to teach all concepts, not just operations: clocks for telling time, calendars for blocks of time; real money; real tools to measure with. The more this practice can occur with real-life activities, as in running a class store or measuring fabric for a doll's blanket, the more likely that students will understand the usefulness of number concepts and apply them in practical circumstances. After introducing concepts with concrete manipulatives, the concept should be worked out with pictured objects and tallies, and finally numbers. *Cuisenaire rods* and *Stern's Structural Arithmetic* are commonly used concrete approaches that help children discover number facts and problem-solving approaches through active manipulation of concrete materials.

**Behavioral Techniques.** Behavioral methods systematically sequence the order of presentation of math skills and give students immediate feedback on accuracy. The *Sullivan Basal Math Program,* for example, is a series of programmed workbooks that teach basic math concepts. Students progress at their own rate, self-correcting along the way using answers provided in the workbook. When they finish a workbook, students take a teacher-administered test. The program doesn't require any reading, making it useful for the student with reading weaknesses. But it must be supplemented with instruction in the underlying concepts behind calculations.

In the *Distar Arithmetic Program I, II, III* the child is actively involved by responding orally and in writing to a rapid pace of problems presented in a set order by the teacher. The speed is attractive to some children with LD because it keeps them engaged. The program would not be appropriate for those who process information very slowly or have difficulty responding to aural directions. *Cawley's Project Math* teaches to mastery, reduces the level of reading demands, and ties ongoing assessment to a number of excellent instructional modifications.

*Constant time delay* is another effective technique. The teacher shows the child a math fact. If the child doesn't respond correctly in about three seconds, the teacher simply provides the answer. The child repeats the answer, and then the teacher moves on to the next math fact. Three to six facts are reviewed repeatedly in a session in a nearly errorless fashion. A variation of this strategy encourages the child to use his or her fingers, poker chips, or a number line as a backup when he or she can't provide the number fact within the allotted time.

Finally, cognitive behavior modification techniques work well with many children. After the teacher models a problem-solving procedure by talking it through aloud, the student and the teacher repeat the process together. Then the child self-instructs aloud while problem solving, and finally self-instruction becomes inaudible. For example, a child might be taught a structured five-step procedure that involves reading the problem, circling key words that hint at the operation to be used, drawing a picture of the problem, writing the equation, and finally solving it.

## Social-Emotional Adjustment

Oliver Wendell Holmes once attended a meeting in which he was the shortest man present. "Doctor Holmes," quipped a friend, "I should think you'd feel rather small among us big fellows." "I do," responded Holmes, "I feel like a dime among a lot of pennies" (Canfield & Wells, 1976, p. 55).

Perspective is everything. When teachers focus on the strengths of individuals with LD and on their many similarities to others, rather than on their differences (as did Holmes' friends), they can help counter many negative stereotypes. Because a student's feelings of self-worth and social skills play a significant role in present and future adjustment, teachers have an important responsibility to create programming that helps students face up to challenges and feel positively about themselves. There are a number of approaches.

***Because a student's feelings of self-worth and social skills affect present and future adjustment, teachers must help students face up to challenges and feel positively about themselves.***

**Multicultural Education.** All students must feel welcomed and valued in order to feel free to express their views, motivated, and able to learn. Yet too much of the current curriculum is neither culturally affirming nor culturally responsive. For the most part, our curriculum still is written from a white, middle-class perspective: white explorers, white generals, white inventors. Teachers need to balance this view to help students appreciate and take pride in the unique strengths and contributions of everyone's history and culture—including their own—and to send the message that all students have an important place in their classrooms. To appreciate and accommodate the similarities and differences among children with diverse cultural and linguistic backgrounds, teachers can do the following:

I. Incorporate ethnic information into topics, such as the roles of the culture, language, and national origin of African Americans and Native Americans in the Civil War.

II. Examine history and knowledge from different vantage points—the "discovery" of America from the Sioux perspective, for example.

III. Use teaching strategies that match children's different learning styles, such as cooperative learning.

IV. Help create school cultures that promote equity, such as rethinking instructional grouping practices or academic eligibility criteria for sports participation.

Multicultural education also recognizes the value of a child's native language. If speaking only English is required in Mr. Shulman's class, and Juan just arrived from Mexico, it won't be long before he feels that his language and culture are being denied, and that he is inferior. Incorporating Juan's language and culture into the classroom not only raises Juan's self-esteem and motivation, it also makes the classroom content more familiar, meaningful, and memorable to Juan, and enriches the experience for all students. Native American crafts can be part of art class; African drumming, the blues, and jazz in music class; traditional foods in health class; oral histories and folktales from grandparents in English class; and differences among peoples and cultures in social studies. All of these add color and dimension to learning for everyone. When it comes to exams, teachers must recognize that when children like Juan finally seem conversationally proficient in English, they still are unlikely to have mastered the test's vocabulary, so that allowing responses in both English and Spanish is in order.

Some teachers worry about opening the class to freewheeling discussions. They are concerned that one student's opinion may offend the class or that talking about differences will only make things worse. This doesn't happen as long as the teacher conveys that opinions matter to him or her, that there is no right or wrong opinion, that we don't need to agree on everything, that listening respectfully is essential, and that put-downs and preaching are not permitted. Open, honest conversations can be the beginning of greater understanding and promote the social integration and achievement of students from diverse cultural and linguistic groups.

*Teachers must be both culturally affirming and culturally responsive in their teaching.*

Teachers must be both culturally affirming and culturally responsive in their teaching. They need to recognize that different cultures value different behaviors in school from that which is the norm for white middle-income students. It is difficult to generalize about cultural beliefs because many subcultures exist within any one culture, and the variability within a culture often is equal to or greater than the variability between cultures. Nevertheless, some beliefs tend to be more prevalent in one or another culture, and teachers must be sensitive to when program modifications are necessary. For example, many Asian American children are socialized to solve problems privately within the family. Because seeking outside help for emotional concerns is shameful, a teacher prying by asking "what is wrong?" would be inappropriate. Many Asian Americans would have a problem with "assertiveness training," because their culture teaches them to avoid direct confrontation or arguments; instead they use a mediator to facilitate communication. Suppression of emotions is valued, and teachers need to "read between the lines" to recognize a problem. Advising the student to "let it all out—you'll feel better" will not go over well. Hugging too is not a prevalent greeting among Asian Americans, so an overly exuberant teacher may make the student uncomfortable. And teachers may be upset that some Asian parents don't attend their children's athletic events, but many Asian parents don't accept extracurricular activities or sports teams as part of the learning experience. Because these children live a bicultural lifestyle, we must be careful to help them feel that they can belong in and negotiate two cultures at once, comfortable both at school and at home.

"Multicultural Awareness" clubs in which students from different ethnic groups exchange ideas, share experiences, and learn from each other can provide an important support network that promotes socialization and self-esteem within the school environment. Also very affirming is to assign one day a year to each child to give the class a short talk about who they are, their talents, hobbies, interests—anything they wish. Children bring in artifacts from home to share, and their parents and relatives do the same. Classmates are fascinated by the new knowledge about their classmate, and relatives' stories about life journeys and beliefs—traditional dances, cooking, "how I became a doctor," "the life of an ironworker from 50 stories up," and more. A bulletin board is devoted to that child's story. Such activities help include the child in the classroom and also help the class develop a sense of community.

**Peer-Mediated Approaches.** Teachers can help students with LD be accepted and develop friendships by pairing them with average-achieving peers for instruction, seatwork, projects, and special privileges. The best pairings are those in which the children share some mutual interest, for example, baseball or a hobby, and in which the peer presents a positive role model, is willing to assist the student with LD, and is sensitive to the potential embarrassment of the student. *Peer tutoring* helps with building friendships, social skills, class work completion, and positive attitudes and interactions. This can often be a two-way process when the student with LD shares his or her strengths with the classmate or quizzes the partner on class work. Often the peer is coached by the teacher in how to praise appropriate effort (e.g., "you're really trying hard") and social behavior ("thank you for sharing"), or how to model a strategy ("watch how I do this"). Peer tutoring creates a situation of mutual give-and-take that goes a long way toward making youngsters

*Peer tutoring has academic benefits but also helps youngsters with learning disabilities feel worthwhile and that they have at least one friend to whom they are important.*

with LD feel worthwhile and that they have at least one friend to whom they are important. Students with LD can also become tutors for younger children.

*Classwide peer tutoring* is a variation in which the class is randomly divided into two or more teams that compete for points. At regular intervals during the week, tutor pairs within teams meet to ask one another questions from study guides, listen to each other read, dictate spelling words, and so on, for 20 or 30 minutes. Tutors award two points for correct answers on the first try and one point for the second attempt (after the tutor models the correct answer). Teachers circulate, awarding extra points for cooperation and appropriate behavior. In *peer-assisted literacy strategies* (PALS), a higher-achieving "coach" is paired with a lower-achieving "reader" for a variety of structured reading activities: the "reader" can give sounds to letters; segment words into phonemes; sound out words; read phrases; predict story outcomes from pictures; model the "coach's" reading of a story sentence by sentence, paragraph by paragraph; answer the coach's "wh" questions after reading for a few minutes, identify main ideas, "shrink" main ideas to ten words or less, summarize every half page; or retell stories. These systems have raised students' grades and self-concepts, increased time on task, decreased behavior problems, increased opportunities for academic feedback about correct responses and errors, and increased reading, spelling, and math accuracy. Like cooperative learning, which we will learn about in Chapter 14, classwide peer tutoring is a quite powerful intervention that benefits not only the child's academic achievement, but also his or her self-esteem.

**Social Skills Training Programs.** Social skills programs help children appreciate the worthiness of their own and others' ideas, feelings, and attributes. Through systematic teaching and discussion, children learn to define their personal and interpersonal problems, identify short- and long-range goals, generate alternative solutions to problems, choose the best option, take action, and evaluate the results. They also learn to cope with stressful situations, to be more sensitive to their own and others' feelings, to "read" environmental and interpersonal cues so they can pick the right response to a given situation, to resolve conflicts and negotiate with more effective and honest communication, to give positive feedback, to give and accept negative feedback, to initiate and maintain conversations, to resist peer pressure, and to maintain friendships.

An example of a technique that students are taught to avoid outbursts when they feel anxious, angry, or frustrated, and to behave in a way that helps them get what they need, is learning to identify the body reactions that reflect these feelings. When students identify that such a body reaction is occurring, they are taught to say three things:

(present) 1. *I feel* . . . (angry)
(past) 2. *because* . . . (Ronnie called me stupid)
(future) 3. *I want* . . . (him to stop)

Figure 8.6 on page 290 offers samples of additional objectives emphasized in social skills programs.

Many of these programs combine behavior modification and social-learning theory principles to achieve their goals. They reinforce appropriate behaviors and use contracts, modeling, role-playing, discussions, videotapes of students trying out the skill, self-evaluation, and self-management strategies. How long and how often a target behavior occurs is tallied, so progress can be observed. One technique, for example, is *script training,* in which teachers provide scripted roles for everyday situations: going to dinner, shopping, or waiting on a customer. The teacher models the behavior, is direct about what to do and say, and prompts children to stay in their roles and maintain communication as they act out the scene.

Another form of modeling is *self-modeling,* in which children are videotaped over time and all examples of negative behavior are edited out. Examples of compliant and nonaggressive behavior are then compiled, and the child views the tape(s). Shortly after beginning to view a series of tapes, undesirable behavior in the classroom diminishes because children begin to see themselves in a different light—and they model their more appropriate behavior!

*Developing Understanding of Self and Others* (DUSO) is a very different approach. It makes use of puppets, songs, and role-playing to help young elementary school age children discuss similarities and differences among children, helping, sharing, independence, decision making, feelings, and so forth. In the upper elementary grades, this program transitions to *Toward Affective Development,* which covers more sophisticated topics.

***Social skills training programs improve target skills during the training sessions, but are only moderately successful in generalizing the learned behaviors to everyday situations. The most successful programs also involve cognitive strategy training, tutoring, teacher consultation, and parent training.***

Research has shown that social skills training programs do improve target skills during the training sessions, but they are only moderately successful in generalizing the learned behaviors to everyday situations. This happens in part because the programs are short-lived and don't incorporate enough practice of very specific skills in real-life situations, and in part because students with LD may have the appropriate social repertoires but misjudge in which situations they should be applied. It has been suggested that these programs would be more successful if they emphasized how to apply the right skills in the right contexts and if they were taught in more natural relationship situations, for example, working with all members of a group in which the relationships have soured. The most successful programs are those that combine social skills training with cognitive strategies training, academic tutoring, teacher consultation, and parent training.

**Classroom Environment.** Of course, helping children appreciate themselves and others cannot be isolated to specific programs occurring in one time slot per day. Teachers must develop a civil and caring environment by modeling respect, trust, honesty, and communicating positive expectations throughout the day. They can do this by emphasizing what children do right and downplaying mistakes (e.g., marking correct items rather than errors on homework and tests, displaying progress charts), by encouraging participation in daily group problem solving, involving children in curriculum decisions, sharing children's individual successes with the group, role-playing, choosing a "student of the week," promoting a "social skill of the month" (such as listening without interrupting, or resisting peer pressure) or a "personality attribute of the month" (e.g., tolerance, humor, respect), writing something you value about the child next to you and the class guesses who that statement refers to, having students teach each other something they've learned outside of school, and so on. One of the best ways to promote positive self-esteem and social relationships is substituting cooperative for competitive learning systems, and by nurturing students' talents rather than focusing mostly on their weaknesses.

***One of the best ways to promote positive self-esteem and social relationships is to substitute cooperative for competitive learning systems, and to nurture students' talents rather than focusing mostly on their weaknesses.***

Helpfulness engenders gratitude, friendship, and good feelings about oneself. One interesting activity involves the teacher and children awarding one point at the end of the day to each classmate who has been helpful to them. The nature of the good deed is reported to the class, and the class can add an extra point if they deem the act especially noteworthy. When points accumulate, class auctions for trinkets are held, using the points as currency. Children go home happy, and ready to be helpful in school again the next day.

In the *Human Development Program* children sit in a "magic circle" and share their feelings and opinions with one another. The teacher acts as a facilitator to encourage participation and listening. Anyone can suggest topics for discussion, and no one is permitted to make value judgments about another's statements. Children can "pass" when it is their turn to contribute to the group. With such safety measures built in, most children eventually choose to participate.

With the help of such activities, children's self-confidence and trust in others is built, and they are more likely to try harder to succeed in all ways. Very important too in raising a child's motivation is the teacher giving the child direct feedback regarding the specific behaviors and efforts that led to success on a task. Finally, the guidance counselor's counseling, the custodian's friendship, the librar-

**Figure 11.5** Self-concept: An important goal of schooling.
*Source:* PEANUTS is reprinted by permission of United Feature Syndicate, Inc.

ian's guidance to books in which characters grapple with the same issues as these children, and the art, music, and physical educator's encouragement of talents all play critical roles in helping students to perceive themselves as worthy and likable. Figure 11.5 depicts the attitude with which we hope our students will leave school.

## Summary

Special interventions for students with LD begin when developmental delays are noticed in the preschool years and often continue into the secondary school years. The earlier that quality preschool intervention begins, the longer it continues, and the more involved the family is, the more that benefits persist—even into adulthood. When uneven developmental patterns continue into the elementary school years, the child is not prepared to benefit from the standard curriculum. Therefore, specialized materials and approaches need to be chosen on the basis of what these students already know, what they are prepared to learn, and how they learn best. All instructional materials and methods teach. But exactly which materials and approaches will teach which students best is the focus of much current research. Some students with LD require a personalized environment and moderate task modifications to be successful, whereas others require intense remedial efforts and altered curricula.

Phonological awareness and phonics instruction methods do much to help children with LD crack the reading code, and whole language methods help foster essential comprehension and written expression skills in a highly participatory and enthusiastic shared-learning environment. Content area texts often need to be revised for students with LD to be more consistent with the children's language levels and the number of new concepts and terms they can handle at one time. We have found that it is best to teach a few "big picture" ideas deeply, so they will be remembered and applied in new situations, than to overwhelm a child with hundreds of terms that are soon forgotten. Conceptual approaches to math instruction that use concrete materials and carefully sequenced learning objectives are far more helpful in the long run than traditional "drill and kill" calculation exercises.

All of the approaches to academic and social-emotional development reviewed in this chapter have been clinically validated as promoting student progress, but it is up to the teacher to determine which approach fits best in the classroom environment and which is most likely to match a particular child's learning abilities and styles. Such planning is challenging, especially as teachers try to juggle maintenance of the authentic, meaningful context for learning emphasized by constructivism with providing the level of direct, explicit instruction needed for students to gain important skills and strategies.

Although remediating basic reading, comprehension, math, and writing weaknesses in these formative years is critical, teachers also are urged to capitalize on students' strengths to nurture the talents, passions, general knowledge, and social skills that will help children feel that they belong and matter, that they are lovable and capable, and that their efforts are likely to be rewarded with success—no matter how hard the struggle.

## Helpful Resources

### Preschool Programming


Berk, L. E. (2002). *Child development* (6th ed). Boston: Allyn & Bacon.

Berrueta-Clement, J. R., Schweinhart, L. J., Barnett, W. S., Epstein, A. S., & Weikart, D. P. (1984). *Changed lives: The effects of the Perry preschool program on youths through age 19.* Ypsilanti, MI: High/Scope Press.

Bowman, B. T., Donovan, M. S., & Burns, M. S. (Eds.). (2001). *Eager to learn: Educating our preschoolers.* Washington, DC: National Academy Press.

Bronfenbrenner, U. (1975). *Is early intervention effective? Exceptional infant: Assessment and intervention* (Vol. 3). New York: Brunner/Mazel.

Bryant, D. M., Burchinal, M., Lau, L. B., & Sparling, J. J. (1994). Family and classroom correlates of Head Start children's developmental outcomes. *Early Childhood Research Quarterly, 9,* 89–309.

Campbell, F. A., & Ramey, C. T. (1994). Effects of early intervention on intellectual and academic achievement: A follow-up study of children from low-income families. *Child Development, 65,* 684–698.

Casto, G., & Mastropieri, M. A. (1986). The efficacy of early intervention programs: A meta-analysis. *Exceptional Children, 52,* 417–424.

Cole, K. N., Dale, P. S., Mills, P. E., & Jenkins, J. R. (1993). Interaction between early intervention curricula and student characteristics. *Exceptional Children, 60,* 17–28.

Frostig, M., & Maslow, P. (1973). *Learning problems in the classroom.* New York: Grune & Stratton.

Furth, H. G., & Wachs, H. (1974). *Thinking goes to school.* New York: Oxford University Press.

Gilliam, W. S., & Zigler, E. F. (2001). A critical meta-analysis of all evaluations of state-funded preschool from 1977 to 1998: Implications for policy, service delivery and program evaluation. *Early Childhood Research Quarterly, 15,* 441–473.

Gorey, K. M. (2001). Early childhood education: A meta-analytic affirmation of the short- and long-term benefits of educational opportunity. *School Psychology Quarterly, 16,* 9–30.

Guralnick, M. J. (1991). The next decade of research on the effectiveness of early intervention. *Exceptional Children, 58,* 174–183.

Johnson, D., & Myklebust, H. (1967). *Learning disabilities: Educational principles and practices.* New York: Grune & Stratton.

Kephart, N. C. (1960). *The slow learner in the classroom.* Columbus, OH: Charles E. Merrill.

Lazar, I., & Darlington, R. (1982). Lasting effects of early education: A report from the Consortium for Longitudinal Studies. *Monographs of the Society for Research in Child Development, 47* (Serial No. 195).

Neisser, U., Boodoo, G., Bouchard, T. J., Boykin, A. W., Brody, N., Ceci, S. J., Halpern, D. F., Loehlin, J. C., Perloff, R., Sternberg, R. J., & Urbina, S. (1996). Intelligence: Knowns and unknowns. *American Psychologist, 51,* 77–101.

Neuman, S. B., & Dickinson, D. K., (2001). *Handboook of early literacy research.* New York: The Guilford Press.

Newman, L. S. (1990). Intentional and unintentional memory in young children: Remembering vs. playing. *Journal of Experimental Child Psychology, 50,* 243–258.

Odom, S. L., McConnell, S. R., & McEvoy, M. A. (1992). *Social competence of young children with disabilities: Issues and strategies for intervention.* Baltimore: Paul H. Brookes.

Paris, S. G., & Lindauer, B. K. (1977). Constructive aspects of children's comprehension and memory. In R. V. Kail & J. W. Hagen (Eds.), *Perspectives on the development of memory and cognition.* Hillsdale, NJ: Lawrence Erlbaum.

Pick, A. D., Frankel, D. G., & Hess, V. L. (1975). Childrens' attention: The development of selectivity. *Review of Child Development Research, 5,* 325-383.

Stallings, J. (1974). *Follow through classroom observation evaluation, 1972–1973.* Menlo Park, CA: Stanford Research Institute.

Whitehurst, G. J., & Lonigan, C. J. (1998). Child development and emergent literacy. *Child Development, 69,* 848–872.

Winn, M. (1983). *Children without childhood.* New York: Pantheon Books.

Zigler, E. F. (1987). Formal schooling for four-year-olds? No. *American Psychologist, 42,* 254–260.

Zigler, E., & Styfco, S. J. (1994). Head Start: Criticisms in a constructive context. *American Psychologist, 49,* 127–132.

Zigler, E., Taussig, C., & Black, K. (1992). Early childhood intervention: A promising preventative for juvenile delinquency. *American Psychologist, 47,* 997–1006.

Early Childhood Research Institute on Culturally and Linguistically Appropriate Services. Materials and practices: htpp://www.clas.uiuc.edu


### Elementary School Programming


Adams, M. J. (1990). *Beginning to read: Thinking and learning about print.* Cambridge, MA: MIT Press.

Banks, J. A. (1993). Multicultural education: Characteristics and goals. In J. A. Banks & C. A. McGee Banks (Eds.), *Multicultural education: Issues and perspectives* (2nd ed.). Boston: Allyn & Bacon.

Beck, I. L., & Juel, C. (1995). The role of decoding in learning to read. *American Educator, 19*(2), 8, 21–25, 39–42.

Blachman, B. A. (1997). Early intervention and phonological awareness: A cautionary tale. In B. Blachman (Ed.), *Foundations of reading acquisition and dyslexia: Implications for early intervention* (pp. 409–430). Mahwah, NJ: Lawrence Erlbaum.

Blankenship, C. S. (1984). Curriculum and instruction: An examination of models in special and regular education. In J. F. Cawley (Ed.), *Developmental teaching of mathematics for the learning disabled.* Rockville, MD: Aspen.

Bos, C. S. (1991). Reading-writing connections: Using literature as a zone of proximal development for writing. *Learning Disabilities Research & Practice, 6,* 251–256.

Bos, C. S., & Vaughn, S. (2002). *Strategies for teaching students with learning and behavior problems* (5th ed.). Boston: Allyn & Bacon.

Carnine, D., & Kinder, D. (1985). Teaching low-performing students to apply generative and schema strategies to narrative and expository material. *Remedial and Special Education, 6*(1), 20–30.

Carnine, D., Miller, S., Bean, R., & Zigmond, N. (1994). Social studies: Educational tools for diverse learners. *School Psychology Review, 23,* 428–441.

Case, L. P., Harris, K. R., & Graham, S. (1992). Improving the mathematical problem-solving skills of students with learning disabilities: Self-regulated strategy development. *The Journal of Special Education, 26,* 1–19.

Cawley, J. F. (1984). An integrative approach to needs of learning disabled children: Expanded use of mathematics. In J. F. Cawley (Ed.), *Developmental teaching of mathematics for the learning disabled.* Rockville, MD: Aspen.

Ciborowski, J. (1995). Using textbooks with students who cannot read them. *Remedial and Special Education, 16,* 90–101.

Conduct Problems Prevention Research Group (2002). Using the Fast Track randomized prevention trial to test the early-starter model of the development of serious conduct problems. *Development and Psychopathology, 14,* 925–943.

Dimino, J. A., Taylor, R. M., & Gersten, R. M. (1995). Synthesis of the research on story grammar as a means to increase comprehension. *Reading & Writing Quarterly: Overcoming Learning Difficulties, 11,* 53–72.

Dohrn, E., & Bryan, T. (1994). Attribution instruction. *Teaching Exceptional Children, 26*(4), 61–63.

Durkin, D. (1984). Is there a match between what elementary teachers do and what basal reader manuals recommend? *The Reading Teacher, 37,* 734–744.

Ehri, L. C., & Wilce, L. S. (1987). Movement into reading: Is the first stage of printed word learning visual or phonetic? *Reading Research Quarterly, 20,* 163–179.

Elkonin, D. B. (1963). The psychology of mastering the elements of reading. In B. Simon & J. Simon (Eds.), *Educational psychology in the U.S.S.R.* London: Routledge & Kegan Paul.

Englert, C. S., Hiebert, E. H., & Stewart, S. R. (1985). Spelling unfamiliar words by an analogy strategy. *The Journal of Special Education, 19,* 291–306.

Englert, C. S., Tarrant, K. L., Mariage, T. V., & Oxer, T. (1994). Lesson talks as the work of reading groups: The effectiveness of two interventions. *Journal of Learning Disabilities, 27,* 165–185.

Fernald, G. M. (1943). *Remedial techniques in basic school subjects.* New York: McGraw-Hill.

Foorman, B. R., & Torgesen, J. (2001). Critical elements of classroom and small-group instruction promote reading success in all children. *Learning Disabilities Research & Practice, 16,* 203–212.

Forman, E. A. (1987). Peer relationships of learning disabled children: A contextualist perspective. *Learning Disabilities Research, 2,* 80–90.

Fox, C. L. (1989). Peer acceptance of learning disabled children in the regular classroom. *Exceptional Children, 56,* 50–59.

Frederickson, N., & Turner, J. (2003). Utilizing the classroom peer group to address children's social needs: An evaluation of the circle of friends intervention approach. *The Journal of Special Education, 36,* 234–245.

Fulk, B. M., & Stormont-Spurgin, M. (1995). Spelling interventions for students with disabilities: A review. *The Journal of Special Education, 28,* 488–513.

García, E. (1994). *Understanding and meeting the challenge of student cultural diversity.* Boston: Houghton Mifflin.

Gaskins, I. W. (1998). A beginning literacy program for at-risk and delayed readers. In J. L. Metsala & L. C. Ehri (Eds.), *Word recognition in beginning literacy* (pp. 209–232). Mahwah, NJ: Lawrence Erlbaum.

Gaustad, M. G., & Messenheimer-Young, T. (1991). Dialogue journals for students with learning disabilities. *Teaching Exceptional Children, 23,* 28-32.

Gerard, J. A., & Junkala, J. (1980). Task analysis, handwriting, and process based instruction. *Journal of Learning Disabilities, 13,* 49–58.

Gillingham, A., & Stillman, B. (1970). *Remedial training for children with specific disability in reading, spelling, and penmanship.* Cambridge, MA: Educator's Publishing Service.

Ginsburg-Block, M., & Fantuzzo, J. (1997). Reciprocal peer tutoring: An analysis of "teacher" and "student" interactions as a function of training and experience. *School Psychology Quarterly, 12,* 134–149.

Goldstein, H., & Gallagher, T. M. (1992). Strategies for promoting the social-communicative competence of young children with specific language impairment.

In S. L. Odom, S. R. McConnell, & M. A. McEvoy (Eds.), *Social competence of young children with disabilities: Issues and strategies for intervention.* Baltimore: Paul H. Brookes.

Goodman, K. S. (1986). *What's whole in whole language?* Portsmouth, NH: Heinemann.

Gopaul-McNicol, S-A., & Thomas-Presswood, T. (1998). *Working with linguistically and culturally different children: Innovative clinical and educational approaches.* Boston: Allyn & Bacon.

Goswami, U. (1989, March). *Orthographic units and transfer in reading.* San Francisco: American Educational Research Association.

Graham, L., & Wong, B. Y. L. (1993). Comparing two modes of teaching a question-answering strategy for enhancing comprehension: Didactic and self-instructional training. *Journal of Learning Disabilities, 26,* 270–279.

Graves, A., & Montague, M. (1991). Using story grammar cueing to improve the writing of students with learning disabilities. *Learning Disabilities Research & Practice, 6,* 246–250.

Griffey, Q. L., Zigmond, N., & Leinhardt, G. (1988). The effects of self-questioning and story structure training on the reading comprehension of poor readers. *Learning Disabilities Research, 4,* 45–51.

Griffith, P. L., & Olson, M. W. (1992). Phonemic awareness helps beginning readers break the code. *The Reading Teacher, 45,* 516–523.

Hargis, C. H., Terhaar-Yonkers, M., Williams, P. C., & Reed, M. T. (1988). Repetition requirements for word recognition. *Journal of Reading, 31,* 320–327.

Harniss, M. K., Hollenbeck, K. L., Crawford, D. B., & Carnine, D. (1994). Content organization and instructional design issues in the development of history texts. *Learning Disability Quarterly, 17,* 235–248.

Harris, K. R., & Graham, S. (1996). *Making the writing process work: Strategies for composition and self-regulation.* Cambridge, MA: Brookline Books.

Heckelman, R. C. (1969). A neurological impress method of remedial reading. *Academic Therapy, 4,* 277–282.

Hembree, R. (1986). Research gives calculators a green light. *Arithmetic Teacher, 34*(1), 18–21.

Hiebert, J., Carpenter, T. P., Fennema, E., Fuson, K. C., Wearne, D., Murray, H., Oliver, A., & Human, P. (1997). *Making sense: Teaching and learning mathematics with understanding.* Portsmouth, NH: Heinemann.

Jenkins, J. R., Heliotis, J., Haynes, M., & Beck, K. (1986). Does passive learning account for disabled readers' comprehension deficits in ordinary reading situations? *Learning Disability Quarterly, 9,* 69–76.

Juel, C., & Minden-Cupp, C. (2000). Learning to read words: Linguistic units and instructional strategies. *Reading Research Quarterly, 35,* 458–492.

Kilpatrick, W., Wolfe, G., & Wolfe, S. M. (1994). *Books that build character: A guide to teaching your child moral values through stories.* New York: Touchstone.

Koscinski, S. T., & Hoy, C. (1993). Teaching multiplication facts to students with learning disabilities: The promise of constant time delay procedures. *Learning Disabilities Research & Practice, 8,* 260–263.

Lederer, J. M. (2000). Reciprocal teaching of social studies in inclusive elementary classrooms. *Journal of Learning Disabilities, 33,* 91–106.

Lloyd, J. W., Forness, S. R., & Kavale, K. A. (1998). Some methods are more effective than others. *Intervention in School and Clinic, 33*(4), 195–200.

MacArthur, C. A., Schwartz, S. S., & Graham, S. (1991). Effects of a reciprocal peer revision strategy in special education classrooms. *Learning Disabilities Research & Practice, 6,* 201–210.

Marsh, L. G., & Cooke, N. L. (1996). The effects of using manipulatives in teaching math problem solving to students with learning disabilities. *Learning Disabilities Research & Practice, 11,* 58–65.

Manzo, A. V. (1969). The request procedure. *Journal of Reading, 13,* 123–126.

Mather, N., & Bos, C. S. (1994). Educational computing and multimedia. In C. S. Bos & S. Vaughn (Eds.), *Strategies for teaching students with learning and behavioral problems* (3rd ed.). Boston: Allyn & Bacon.

Mather, N., & Lachowicz, B. L. (1992). Shared writing: An instructional approach for reluctant writers. *Teaching Exceptional Children, 25,* 26–30.

Mathes, P. G., & Babyak, A. E. (2001). The effects of peer-assisted literacy strategies for first-grade readers with and without additional mini-skills lessons. *Learning Disabilities Research & Practice, 16,* 28–44.

McEvoy, M. A., Odom, S. L., & McConnell, S. R. (1992). Peer social competence intervention for young children with disabilities. In S. L. Odom, S. R. McConnell, & M. A. McEvoy (Eds.), *Social competence of young children with disabilities: Issues and strategies for intervention.* Baltimore: Paul H. Brookes.

Mercer, C. D., & Mercer, A. R. (2001). *Teaching students with learning problems* (6th ed.). Upper Saddle River, NJ: Merrill.

Miller, S. P., & Mercer, C. D. (1993). Using data to learn about concrete-semiconcrete-abstract instruction for students with math disabilities. *Learning Disabilities Research & Practice, 8,* 89–96.

Naglieri, J. A., & Gottling, S. H. (1997). Mathematics instruction and PASS cognitive processes: An intervention study. *Journal of Learning Disabilities, 30,* 513–520.

Newcomer, P. L., Barenbaum, E. M., & Nodine, B. F. (1988). Comparison of the story production of LD, normal-achieving, and low-achieving children under two modes of production. *Learning Disability Quarterly, 11*, 82–96.

O'Shea, L. J., Sindelar, P. T., & O'Shea, D. J. (1987). The effects of repeated readings and attentional cues on the reading fluency and comprehension of learning disabled readers. *Learning Disabilities Research, 2*, 103–109.

Palincsar, A. S., & Klenk, L. (1992). Fostering literacy learning in supportive contexts. *Journal of Learning Disabilities, 25*, 211–225, 229.

Parmar, R. S., & Cawley, J. F. (1993). Analysis of science textbook recommendations provided for students with disabilities. *Exceptional Children, 59*, 518–531.

Pressley, M., & colleagues. (1990). *Cognitive strategy instruction that really improves children's academic performance.* Cambridge, MA: Brookline Books.

*Report of the National Reading Panel: Teaching children to read.* (2000, December). NIH Pub. No. 00-4754. Washington, DC: US Dept. of Health & Human Services.

Rumelhart, D. E. (1980). Schemata: The building blocks of cognition. In R. J. Spiro, B. C. Bruce, & W. F. Brewer (Eds.), *Theoretical issues in reading comprehension.* Hillsdale, NJ: Lawrence Erlbaum.

Salend, S. J., & Nowak, M. R. (1988). Effects of peer-previewing on LD students' oral reading skills. *Learning Disability Quarterly, 11*, 47–53.

Schumm, J. S., Vaughn, S., Haager, D., & Klinger, J. K. (1994). Literacy instruction for mainstreamed students: What suggestions are provided in basal reading series? *Remedial and Special Education, 15*, 14–20.

Scruggs, T. E., Mastropieri, M. A., & Sullivan, G. S. (1994). Promoting relational thinking: Elaborative interrogation for students with mild disabilities. *Exceptional Children, 60*, 450–457.

Shanahan, T., & Tierney, R. J. (1990). Reading-writing connections: The relations among three perspectives. In J. Zutell & S. McCormick (Eds.), *Literacy theory and research: Analyses from multiple paradigms* (39th Yearbook). Chicago: National Reading Conference.

Shepard, T., & Adjogah, S. (1994). Science performance of students with learning disabilities on language-based measures. *Learning Disabilities Research & Practice, 9*, 219–225.

Slingerland, B. H. (1974). *A multi-sensory approach to language arts for specific language disability children.* Cambridge, MA: Educator's Publishing Service.

Smith, C. R. (1998). From gibberish to phonemic awareness: Effective decoding instruction. *Teaching Exceptional Children, 30*, 20–25.

Snow, C. E., Burns, M. S., & Griffin, P. (Eds.). (1998). *Preventing reading difficulties in young children.* Washington, DC: National Academy Press.

Spiegel, D. L. (1992). Blending whole language and systematic direct instruction. *The Reading Teacher, 46*, 38–44.

Stauffer, R. G. (1980). *The language experience approach to the teaching of reading* (2nd ed.). New York: Harper & Row.

Thorpe, H. W., & Borden, K. S. (1985). The effect of multisensory instruction upon the on-task behavior and word reading accuracy of learning disabled children. *Journal of Learning Disabilities, 18*, 279–286.

Treiman, R. (1998). Why spelling? The benefits of incorporating spelling into beginning reading instruction. In J. L. Metsala & L. C. Ehri (Eds.), *Word recognition in beginning literacy* (pp. 289–313). Mahwah, NJ: Lawrence Erlbaum.

Vygotsky, L. S. (1978). *Mind in society: The development of higher psychological processes.* Cambridge, MA: Harvard University Press.

Williams, D. M., & Collins, B. C. (1994). Teaching multiplication facts to students with learning disabilities: Teacher-selected versus student-selected material prompts within the delay procedure. *Journal of Learning Disabilities, 27*, 589–597.

Wong, B. Y. L. (1986). A cognitive approach to teaching spelling. *Exceptional Children, 53*, 169–173.

van Daal, V. H. P., & van der Leij, A. (1992). Computer-based reading and spelling practice for children with learning disabilities. *Journal of Learning Disabilities, 25*, 186–195.

Vaughn, S., McIntosh, R., & Spencer-Rowe, J. (1991). Peer rejection is a stubborn thing: Increasing peer acceptance of rejected students with learning disabilities. *Learning Disabilities Research & Practice, 6*, 83–88.

Character Education Partnership: http://www.character.org

United States Department of Education free publications: http://www.edpub.org

## Instructional Resources

http://www.teachingld.org

Ask Eric (Educational Resources Information Center): http://www.askeric.org

Mid-Continent Research on Education and Learning: http://www.mcrel.org

Council for Exceptional Children: http://www.col-ed.org/index.html

Eisenhower National Clearinghouse: http://www.enc.org/weblinks/lessonplans

The Library of Congress learning page: http://www.lcweb2.loc.gov

CHAPTER TWELVE

# Instructional Strategies: The Middle and Secondary School Years

**IF INDIVIDUALIZED INSTRUCTION** was difficult in elementary school, it is even more so in the middle and secondary school years. Gaps between a student's achievement and that of his or her peers often widen, and requirements are highly variable from one subject to another. Complicating matters is the fact that teenagers also are dealing with changes in their bodies, emotional needs, and social environments. Smooth passage through these years is not the norm. The school program must aim at developing strengths as well as compensations for continuing weaknesses, not merely "covering the curriculum." Provided the adolescent with LD is motivated to do so, remedial programming in reading, mathematics, written language, and survival skills can be quite successful, especially given the spurt in learning ability experienced by some teenagers. Academic tutoring is a must, as is transition planning and learning-strategy instruction. School personnel must also provide support in the important areas of speaking, thinking, and social skills development.

*The secondary school program must aim at developing strengths as well as compensations for continuing weaknesses. Provided the adolescent with LD is motivated to do so, remedial programming is important.*

## Reading

The tremendous pressure to "cover the curriculum" in middle and high school courses may result in teachers neglecting the basic reading instruction so necessary for students to function in life. At the secondary level, reading instruction is geared toward helping students cope with academic requirements, but it must also prepare them for everyday reading demands as adults, including postsecondary education. Students who are severely reading disabled still need to master basic decoding and comprehension strategies. Their struggle with decoding unfortunately diminishes the energy they can apply to understanding and remembering what's been read. But the situation is not hopeless at this age. Older students with severe reading disabilities can and do make gains when taught intensively, systematically, with a direct approach, "back to basics" objectives, and daily. Given their ongoing struggle, students with LD need special support in achieving positive attitudes toward reading, because the attitude with which they leave high school will tend to color their view of reading throughout their lives.

*Older students with severe reading disabilities can and do make reading gains when taught intensively, systematically, with a direct approach, "back to basics" objectives, and daily.*

As with anything, one of the best ways to become more proficient at reading is practice, practice, and more practice. This means engaging in independent reading—just for fun—something that students with LD rarely do. Students can learn to take more pleasure in reading, however, when taught to choose their reading materials wisely based on their comfort levels with several aspects of the text. Figure 12.1 presents a useful independent reading rubric for students to use after having read a page from the beginning of a book. If a suitable book cannot be found that is easy enough yet mature and interesting in content, *high interest-low reading level texts* have been developed to deal with this problem. These are content area books and classic works that look age-appropriate but have been rewritten at easier reading vocabulary levels and in simpler sentences, thereby providing students with materials which they can read that also convey sophisticated content. Even versions of popular magazines like *Time* and *Sports Illustrated* are available, abbreviated into short excerpts of news-breaking stories. Finally, parents need to be enlisted to encourage reading wherever and however possible in the course of negotiating the student's daily life: let the student help locate the car rental at the airport, the movies that are playing, the coupons for grocery items, upcoming rock concerts, department store sales, and so forth.

**High interest–low reading level** *texts are content area and classic works that are rewritten at easier reading vocabulary levels and convey sophisticated content.*

Besides continued direct and systematic reinforcement of decoding skills, reading instruction at the secondary level generally focuses on vocabulary, *fluency* (reading rate), and comprehension. These are taught in isolation, in the context of content area instruction, or both. Although some strategies developed for younger learners can be useful at the secondary level, most are too immature and require retailoring.

## Vocabulary

As we know, words guide our thinking, and the ability to name and verbally rehearse what we see and hear enhances our memory. If we can help students with LD build their vocabularies and the ability to translate new information into their own words, we strengthen their capacity to communicate orally, to read, to comprehend, to recall information, and to write meaningfully.

*Encouraging students to read whatever they want for a set period of time each day with no interruptions increases vocabulary, comprehension, and positive attitudes toward reading.*

A technique called *sustained silent reading* (SSR) stimulates vocabulary development by encouraging students to read whatever they want for a set period of time each day without interruptions. No tests or questions are permitted. This is reading for the pure pleasure of it. We've found that this simple measure can markedly increase vocabulary, comprehension, and positive attitudes toward reading.

**Independent Reading Rubric**

Book/Story/Chapter/Article Title: ______________________________

Author(s): ______________________________

| Readability Factors | Score 1 | Score 2 | Score 3 | Score 4 |
|---|---|---|---|---|
| Vocabulary<br>☐ Score | ☐ There are 10 or more words I do not know. | ☐ There are 7–9 words I do not know. | ☐ There are 4–6 words I do not know. | ☐ There are 3 or fewer words I do not know. |
| Sentences<br>☐ Score | ☐ Almost all of the sentences are long and complex. | ☐ A few sentences are easy but most are long and complex. | ☐ A few sentences are long and complex but most are easy. | ☐ Almost all of the sentences are short and easy. |
| Topics and Concepts<br>☐ Score | ☐ I am unfamiliar with the topic and most of the concepts are new to me. | ☐ I know a little about the topic and concepts. | ☐ I know much about the topic and concepts. | ☐ I am highly familiar with the topic and none of the concepts are new to me. |
| Clarity of Ideas<br>☐ Score | ☐ The ideas are presented unclearly and are difficult to understand. | ☐ A few of the ideas are presented clearly enough to understand without difficulty. | ☐ Most of the ideas are presented clearly enough to understand easily. | ☐ The ideas are presented very clearly and are easy to understand. |
| Level of Abstraction (including figurative language, metaphors, similes, slang, symbols, theories)<br>☐ Score | ☐ The author uses language and/or presents ideas that are highly abstract. | ☐ The author uses many abstract words and phrases and/or presents more than one abstract idea. | ☐ The author uses a few abstract words and phrases and/or presents an abstract idea. | ☐ The author uses language and/or presents ideas that are concrete. |
| Organization<br>☐ Score | ☐ I cannot figure out the organization. | ☐ It is difficult to follow the organization. | ☐ I can follow the organization but I have to concentrate. | ☐ I can follow the organization easily. |
| Design and Format (includes font, print size, paragraph length, use of columns, use of illustrations and other visuals, and other design issues.<br>☐ Score | ☐ The material is poorly designed and the format impedes reading. | ☐ The design and format create some problems for me. | ☐ The design and format create no serious problems for me. | ☐ The material is well designed and the format facilitates reading. |

**Figure 12.1** Independent reading rubric.

*Source:* Schirmer, B. R., & Lockman, A. S. (2001). How do I find a book to read? Middle and high school students use a rubric for self-selecting material for independent reading. *Exceptional Children, 34,* pp. 38–39. Copyright © 2001 by The Council for Exceptional Children. Reprinted with permission

*(continued)*

**Independent Reading Rubric (continued)**

| Readability Factors | Score 1 | 2 | 3 | 4 |
|---|---|---|---|---|
| Genre<br>☐ Score | ☐ I am not familiar with the writing form and style. | ☐ I have only read this kind of writing once or twice. | ☐ I have read this kind of writing a few times. | ☐ I am very familiar with the writing form and style. |
| Interest and Motivation<br>☐ Score | ☐ I am not interested in the topic and don't have any particular motivation or reason to read this material. | ☐ I am slightly interest-ed in the topic and would have difficulty explaining why I want to read this material. | ☐ I am somewhat interested in the topic and have a couple of ideas about why I want to read this material. | ☐ I am extremely interested in the topic, highly motivated, and have a definite reason to read this material. |
| Pacing and Fluency<br>☐ Score | ☐ If others watched and heard me read, they would describe me as tense and my reading was choppy. | ☐ If others watched and heard me read, they would describe me as uneasy and my reading as frequently hesitant. | ☐ If others watched and heard me read, they would describe me as comfortable but my reading as some-times unsure. | ☐ If others watched and heard me read, they would describe me as relaxed and my reading as fluent. |
| ☐ Total score | | | | |

*Directions:*
1. Read the first page of the book. If the first page is not a full page, read the next page also.
2. Check the box of the score most appropriate for each readability factor.
3. Write the score in the box under each readability factor.
4. Total the scores.
5. Determine if you can read the material independently.
   - If the total score is 30–40, the material can be read independently. If the score is 38–40, perhaps this material is too easy for you.
   - If the score is 20–29, the material is challenging. Decide which factors are most important to you. If you scored 3 or 4 on each of these factors, the material can be read independently. If you scored 1 or 2 on the most important factors, the material should be read only with assistance.
   - If the total score is < 20, the material is too difficult to read without assistance.

**Figure 12.1** *Continued*

In the *language experience approach,* the student discusses an event or idea that he or she would like to write about and then dictates the composition to the teacher. The teacher encourages the student to use new vocabulary and develops a classroom environment that supports experimentation with the new words and ideas. The student then transcribes the piece, which can be used for further instruction in comprehension, written organization, sentence structure, and so forth.

*Teachers must help students use new vocabulary in a variety of contexts to understand their connotations and extended meanings.*

Teachers need to plan for new vocabulary to be used in as rich a variety of meaningful contexts as possible in order to help the student understand the various connotations and extended meanings of words. Interactive techniques based on schema theory, like those in Figures 12.2, 12.3, and 12.4, are more helpful than

**Relationship Chart for the Chapter on Fossils**

| Key |
|---|
| + = positive relationship |
| − = negative relationship |
| 0 = no relationship |
| ? = uncertain |

| Important Words | Important Ideas: Type of life | | Location | | | Extinct? | |
|---|---|---|---|---|---|---|---|
| | *Plant* | *Animal* | *Sea* | *Land* | *Lakes* | *Extinct* | *Not extinct* |
| Trilobites | | | | | | | |
| Crinoids | | | | | | | |
| Giant cats | | | | | | | |
| Coral | | | | | | | |
| Bryozoans | | | | | | | |
| Guide fossils | | | | | | | |
| Dinosaurs | | | | | | | |
| Fresh water fish | | | | | | | |
| Brachiopods | | | | | | | |
| Small horses | | | | | | | |
| Ferns | | | | | | | |
| Enormous winged bugs | | | | | | | |
| Trees | | | | | | | |

**Figure 12.2** Semantic-feature analysis.

*Source:* Bos, C. S., & Anders, P. L. (1987). Semantic feature analysis: An interactive teaching strategy for facilitating learning from text. *Learning Disabilities Focus, 3,* p. 57. Reprinted by permission of the Division for Learning Disabilities.

typical definition instruction. These strategies are implemented as group or whole class activities. They are extremely powerful in activating background knowledge and deepening conceptual understanding about vocabulary words, thereby increasing students' comprehension.

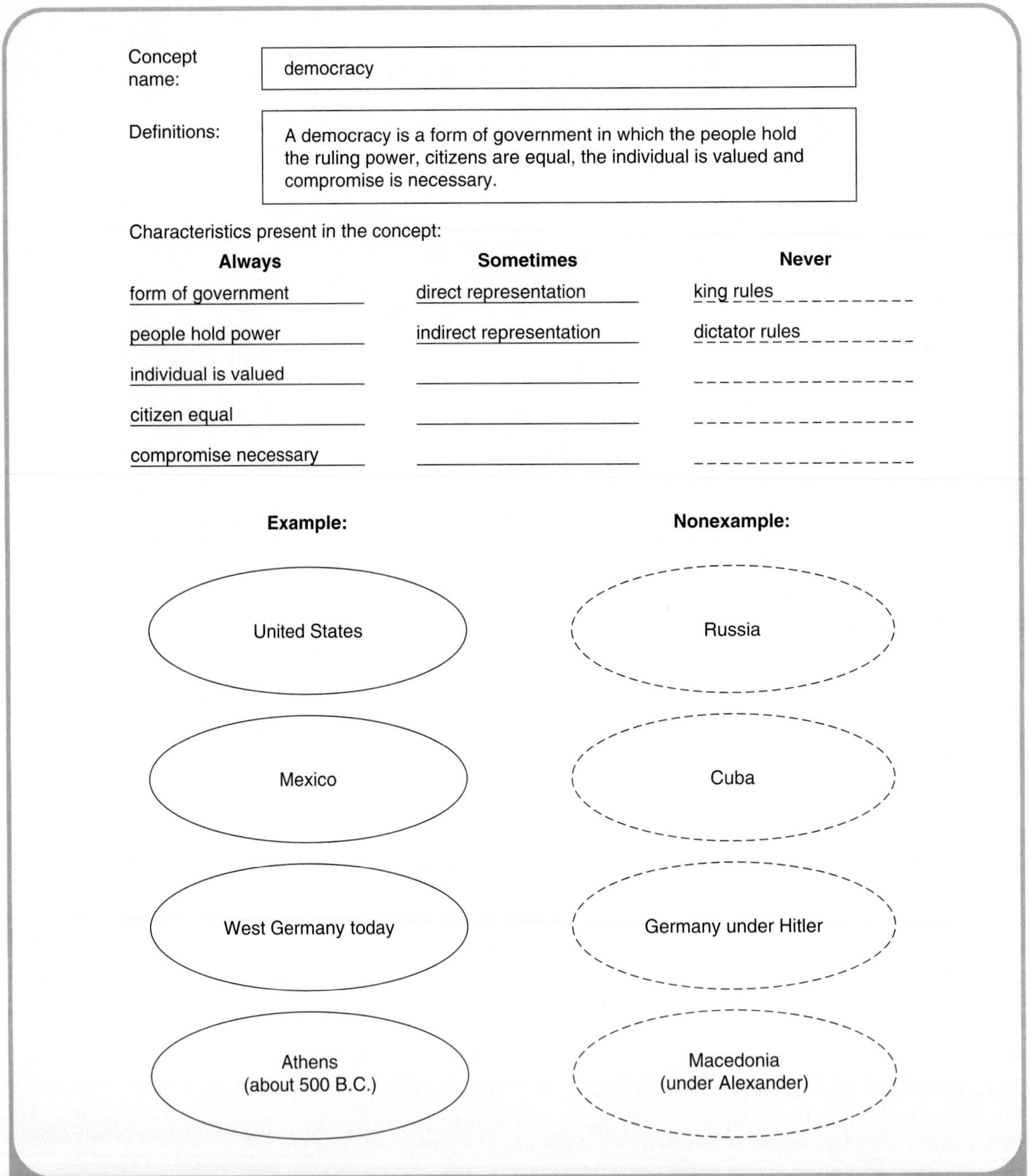

| Concept name: | democracy |
|---|---|
| Definitions: | A democracy is a form of government in which the people hold the ruling power, citizens are equal, the individual is valued and compromise is necessary. |

Characteristics present in the concept:

| Always | Sometimes | Never |
|---|---|---|
| form of government | direct representation | king rules |
| people hold power | indirect representation | dictator rules |
| individual is valued | | |
| citizen equal | | |
| compromise necessary | | |

| Example: | Nonexample: |
|---|---|
| United States | Russia |
| Mexico | Cuba |
| West Germany today | Germany under Hitler |
| Athens (about 500 B.C.) | Macedonia (under Alexander) |

**Figure 12.3** Concept diagram.

*Source:* Bulgren, J., Schumaker, J. B., & Deschler, D. D. (1988). Effectiveness of a concept teaching routine in enhancing the performance of LD students in secondary-level mainstream classes. *Learning Disability Quarterly, 11*, p. 6. Reprinted by permission.

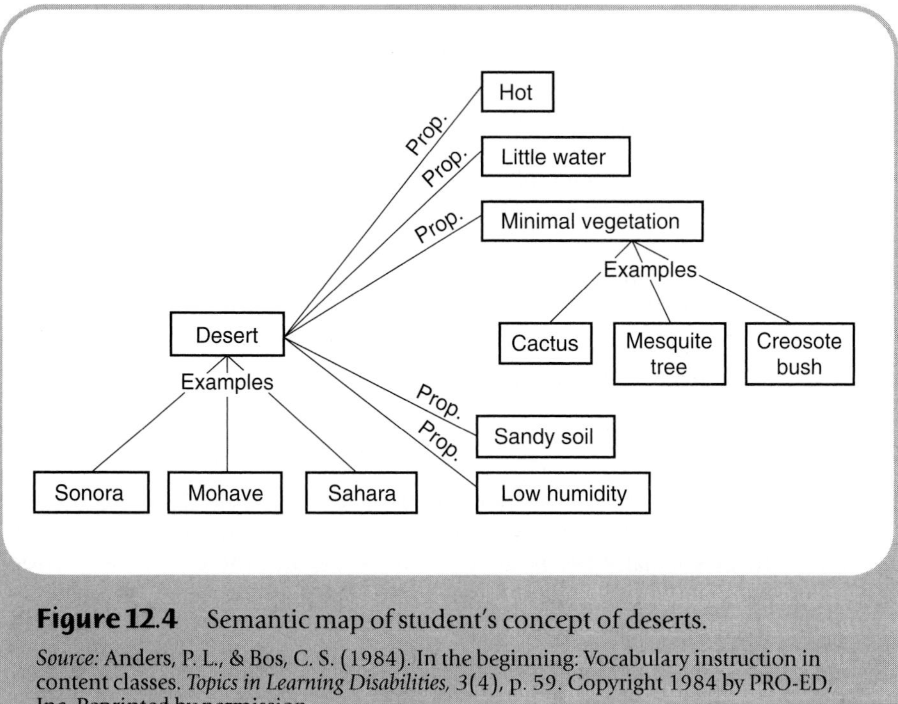


**Figure 12.4** Semantic map of student's concept of deserts.

*Source:* Anders, P. L., & Bos, C. S. (1984). In the beginning: Vocabulary instruction in content classes. *Topics in Learning Disabilities, 3*(4), p. 59. Copyright 1984 by PRO-ED, Inc. Reprinted by permission.

## Fluency

Secondary students with learning disabilities read far slower than the average teenager. In one study, teenagers with LD read about 30 to 150 words per minute compared to the approximately 90 to 190 words per minute of the average teenager. The faster you can read, the more attention can be freed for comprehension. Therefore, increasing their reading rate is an important goal for students with LD.

*Because the faster you can read, the more attention can be freed for comprehension, increasing reading rate is an important goal for students with LD.*

*Students with LD tend not to adjust their reading rates to the difficulty of the material or the purpose for reading.*

Students with LD tend not to adjust their reading rates to the difficulty of the material or the purpose for reading. Even simple assignments become major projects because students don't realize they can gain a great deal of information in a brief time from skimming. For the same reason, reading for pleasure is all too seldom attempted. There are three useful levels of skimming that should be taught to students with LD to encourage their engagement with reading materials:

**Level I** Scanning for points that are easy to find
**Level II** Scanning for an answer to a specific question
**Level III** Scanning for deeper information such as the main idea, the author's style, or reviewing class notes

You probably scanned at level I when you first opened this book by checking out the case studies, chapter titles, illustrations, and headings. You scanned at level

II if you wondered whether the text included information about adults with learning disabilities. It's at this level that students with LD start to have trouble. They often seem unaware of the usual organization of text material, and thus don't know where to look first. For this reason, they have trouble previewing end-of-chapter questions to gain a purpose for reading, and selecting the key words within questions so that paragraphs containing this information can be located. They need to be taught that chapter introductions and conclusions summarize content, as do each paragraph's topic or concluding sentences. Scanning at level III is the most difficult of all because it requires intensive reading and good comprehension. Students with LD need help judging which reading material requires their full attention and even rereading, and which can be scanned quickly, depending on the purpose for reading.

## Reading Comprehension

*Language weaknesses, inefficient learner strategies, and decoding struggles usually persist in some form beyond the elementary school years. All of these stand in the way of understanding what is read.*

*High school science and social studies texts often have incomprehensible lists of unnecessary details, or ramble from one topic to another. Anthologies can have a reading range of nine grade levels, and business and vocational texts are often written well above students' reading levels.*

Comprehension problems are the most frequent and debilitating reading difficulties at the secondary level. Language weaknesses, inefficient learner strategies, and decoding struggles usually persist in some form beyond the elementary school years. All of these stand in the way of understanding what is read.

Unfortunately, poorly written texts with widely varying readability levels tend to make the problem worse. Science and social studies texts often contain incomprehensible lists of unnecessary details, or ramble from one topic to another. Anthologies can have a reading range of nine grade levels, and business and vocational texts are often written well above students' reading levels. In addition, the texts' sentence patterns and vocabulary are not simply "talk written down"—they tend to differ considerably from students' customary language, and there are no social cues (such as a speaker's pauses, rate, emphasis) to help one understand.

Traditionally, the approach to reading comprehension has been "bottom up." That is, students read the words in the text, expecting to derive meaning from them. This works for the average student, but not for those with learning disabilities. Their language and reasoning weaknesses, combined with a slow reading rate, make this route to understanding difficult.

"Top down" approaches are much more effective. In these approaches, teachers help students use their prior knowledge and reasoning ability to guide the reading and comprehension process. For example, teachers can first help students learn to analyze a selection's conclusions in comparison with their own experiences, ideas, and feelings. Comprehension exercises are then geared toward a number of objectives, including the ability to

1. Deal with main ideas and details
2. Paraphrase information
3. Associate, generalize, and infer based on the information given
4. Make comparisons (e.g., relationships between elements, overall structure)
5. Interpret causal relations
6. Interpret figurative language (metaphors), ambiguous statements
7. Be sensitive to sequence (e.g., events, methods, processes)
8. Interpret anaphoras or pronominalization (a word or pronoun that substitutes for a preceding word or group of words; for example, "I did *it*")

9. Separate fact from fiction, reality from fantasy
10. Evaluate an author's bias and style
11. Be cognizant of the setting, theme, plot, character development, and resolution in stories

Applications of schema theory have proven that, if students discuss questions anticipating the text's content prior to reading, and their background associations are activated, they approach reading more ready to apply the comprehension skills listed above. Decoding too is less of an obstacle, as students are able to guess more accurately at the words because they already know the context.

*If students discuss questions anticipating the text's content prior to reading, and their background associations are activated, they approach reading more ready to comprehend.*

Students with learning disabilities generally have mastered story grammar by sixth grade. If they haven't internalized story structure as an aid to comprehension, however, using story grammar cue cards to guide reading continues to be helpful at the secondary level.

*Mutual questioning strategies* between teacher and student prior to reading can be helpful to the secondary student as well. In this approach, the teacher gradually increases the cognitive complexity of the questions and responses. In the *elaborative integration strategy,* the teacher asks questions and offers prompts that help students elaborate on information by relating it to their prior knowledge. For example, "Why would changes in climate have caused the dinosaur to become extinct? . . . (prompt) "Remember, we discussed that dinosaurs could have been cold-blooded." Such coaching is very effective in improving comprehension.

Students also benefit from learning to use self-questioning techniques. For example, they can ask themselves about the main idea; who, what, where, when, why, and how questions; and then read the passage, underline, and record answers.

Techniques that require generating main idea summary sentences are particularly helpful. Summarization techniques help students discriminate and organize information so that key points are condensed into units that are likely to be remembered. One method has students skim a passage, list the key points, combine related points into single statements, cross out less important points, number the points in logical order, and finally write these up in a cohesive paragraph.

Questioning and summarizing strategies aid comprehension by actively involving students in applying their reasoning skills to the reading material. As comprehension increases, so does memory for the material. The next section presents further examples of schema theory applications that can facilitate comprehension and memory of content area material.

*Questioning and summarizing strategies aid comprehension by actively involving students in applying their reasoning skills to reading material. As comprehension increases, so does memory for the material.*

**Reinforcing Reading and Comprehension through Content Area Instruction.** Several strategies are available for increasing reading and comprehension abilities while also enhancing content area learning. The content area teacher can easily incorporate these into his or her lesson plans.

***Reading Decoding.*** Just because a text is labeled for use at a certain grade level does not mean that it is written at a level appropriate for students in that grade. Studies have shown that first and second grade readers contain material that ranges from the 1.5 to 3.5 grade level in difficulty. Texts at the fourth and fifth grade levels can range in difficulty from the fourth to ninth grade levels, and high

*Just because a text is labeled for use at a certain grade level does not mean that it is written at a level appropriate for students in that grade.*

school texts can range into the college levels. Given this variability, the best way to ensure that the reading material is appropriate for a student is to apply a chart such as that shown in Figure 12.1, use a readability formula, conduct an informal reading inventory, or apply the Cloze procedure. The text's interest level and relevance to the student, as well as timeliness, are also important to consider. Controlling the interest and difficulty level of texts and assignments is critical so that students are appropriately challenged yet successful enough to remain task-oriented and motivated.

*Readability formulas* offer rough estimates of reading grade levels by considering such factors as average numbers of syllables or letters per word, sentence length, and the extent of unfamiliar vocabulary. Several such formulas exist. Each formula yields somewhat different grade-level estimates. Because readability formulas don't take the complexity of a passage's vocabulary, syntax, concepts, abstractness, clarity of presentation, design format, illustrations, literary style, cohesiveness, and organization into account, they should be used as only one piece of evidence in judging a text's appropriateness.

***If students comprehend over 90 percent of information after reading it silently, they are capable of independently comprehending the material. Roughly 75 to 90 percent comprehension represents an appropriate instructional level. Anything below 75 percent is far too difficult.***

***If the student orally reads less than about 93 to 95 percent of the words correctly, and understands even less, then the text is too difficult.***

The *Informal Reading Inventory* asks the student vocabulary, fact, sequence, and inference questions after he or she has read a passage silently. If over 90 percent of the responses are correct, the student is capable of independently comprehending the material. If roughly 75 to 90 percent of the responses are correct, the material is at an appropriate instructional level. Correct responses below 75 percent indicate reading material that is far too difficult and frustrating. When conducting an informal reading inventory, it also is appropriate to select a few passages for the student to read orally. If the student reads less than 93 to 95 percent of the words correctly, and understands an even lower percentage of the words, then the text is too difficult; the reading struggle is likely to deter comprehension even further, and perhaps even cause the student to give up. Students easily learn the "five finger test" to determine if a text or library book is too hard for them to handle. They read 100 words from a page in the middle of the book, and raise one finger for each word they can't read. If five fingers are up before the end of the page, the book is too difficult to read independently and enjoy. Finally, teachers need to check on whether the student can handle the text's table of contents, glossary, index, charts, and so forth independently.

***For homework, class assignments, and drill work, the student should be correct 70 to 85 percent of the time. This places the work somewhere between too easy and too difficult, enough to maintain attention.***

For homework, class assignments, and drill work such as spelling and sight word practice, the student's responses should be correct 70 to 85 percent of the time. This places the work somewhere between being too easy and too difficult. Either extreme usually means the student won't stay on task because he or she is either bored or frustrated.

In the *Cloze procedure,* every fifth word of a 250-word passage is blocked out. The student fills in the blanks orally or in writing. If the number of correct fill-ins approaches 50 percent, the student is anticipating enough of the text to make it appropriate for instructional purposes.

When the teacher concludes that the text is too difficult, an easier version can be assigned, such as *Hamlet* written in standard versus Elizabethan English. Although Libby may not be reading the same print as her classmates, this strategy nevertheless enables her to grasp the important themes and participate in class discussions. When no appropriate textbook is found, the teacher may need to rewrite the text, using shorter words and sentences, and less sophisticated vocabulary and sentence structure. Unnecessary detail should be eliminated. Once the content area reading material is established, it can be used to instruct basic reading, comprehension, vocabulary, spelling, and writing skills.

Tape-recorded texts are popular as a means of getting past decoding difficulties, but tapes alone are unlikely to solve the whole problem. Without adapting the text prior to taping, failure is still likely. This is because verbatim tapes do not help students with organizing or summarizing information, simplifying vocabulary and sentence structure, rereading, and so forth.

***Tape-recorded texts can help compensate for decoding difficulties, but often the text needs to be adapted prior to taping to be useful.***

When creating tapes, teachers may need to adapt the tape's content (reorganize it, present only the most important information, call attention to the most important information, use easier vocabulary and grammar), highlight the most important information in the text itself, develop accompanying study guides and worksheets focused on critical content, teach study skills (such as how to get an overview of chapters, take notes, self-test, rehearse important facts), and provide background knowledge and vocabulary. The following guidelines for recording tapes are important:

1. Do not record a chapter verbatim: read the key sections, but paraphrase those that are less important.
2. Provide a short advanced organizer on the tape (outline of what's to come).
3. Point out important points: "*The most important* cause of the war was . . . ").
4. Number the points that are being made (The political parties differ in four major ways: *1* . . . , *2* . . . , *3* . . . , *4* . . . ").
5. Insert questions or reminders that encourage the listener to stop and think.
6. Read at a comfortable rate and in a natural tone of voice.

Commercially available recorded books are useful when a student can benefit from listening to an original version of a novel or textbook, or simply as leisure time enjoyment. Most public libraries and bookstores carry an extensive collection of recorded books. Schools can register students with Recording for the Blind and Dyslexic (Princeton, NJ) to receive such texts free on tape. These also are available from the American Printing House for the Blind (Louisville, KY) and the Library of Congress (National Library Service for the Blind, Washington, DC). Even magazines and daily newspapers are available on tape. Use of such tapes should be encouraged, so that the poor reader can keep up to date with world events and access the rich history and culture explored in good literature. These organizations provide cassette players that play at half speed to accommodate the student who processes information slowly. Moreover, Recording for the Blind and Dyslexic's new "AudioPlusText" PC program displays text on a computer screen synchronized with narration, so that students can follow the words visually as they listen.

***Comprehension.*** Michael, a high school senior who sometimes struggled to comprehend lectures, was worried about the many lectures he'd encounter in college. Therefore, his high school resource teacher took him to a psychology lecture at a local university. After the lecture, she asked him several comprehension questions. He was 100 percent accurate, to her surprise, but she shouldn't have been. The lecture was on teenage sexuality! Not all lectures will be so captivating, of course, but

*Activating background knowledge, interest, and awareness of text organization can greatly enhance comprehension and memory of new material.*

Michael's story illustrates how by activating background knowledge and interest a teacher can greatly enhance comprehension and memory of new material. This is the objective behind schema theory approaches to comprehension.

A popular schema theory approach used in language arts classes is *literary discourse groups.* These are small groups in which students argue their interpretations of a text using evidence from the text and from their lived experience. The teacher sets a theme, such as "How far should you go to fit in?", and asks questions that lead students into literary discourses about characters' actions and motives, plot events, and so on. Each group builds a shared interpretation that is reported to the class, put into essay form, used in a debate, and more. The teacher incorporates the theme into further selections of books, plays, Internet research activities, and journal entries.

Another schema theory approach to comprehension is *semantic feature analysis.* The teacher gives each student a chart like the one shown in Figure 12.2 to list a text's main ideas and related vocabulary. The main ideas are introduced, and then students share their current knowledge about these concepts. The teacher then guides students in discovering the meaning of each vocabulary word or concept from their background knowledge or from looking in the text. The students predict whether each word might relate to the main idea by marking a +, –, 0 (no relationship), or ? in the appropriate grid. Finally, they read the text to test their predictions. Changes in the chart are made, and the reasons are discussed by the group. Students then fill in blanks in sentences using the chart as a reference (e.g., "Some extinct animals that lived in lakes are __________, __________, and __________"). Research has found semantic feature analysis to be more effective in building vocabulary and comprehension than teacher instruction of word meanings or looking words up in a dictionary and then writing sentences using the words.

The *concept diagram* is another useful comprehension strategy. The diagram shown in Figure 12.3 teaches the concept of democracy. Students define the concept and then list the attributes that always, sometimes, or never characterize it. Next students generate examples and nonexamples of the concept. They can also work up from the blanks in the examples, to the name of the concept, and finally its definition.

*Semantic mapping* is shown in Figure 12.4. Prior to reading, the teacher writes the key concept on the board and helps students generate ideas related to the main theme. "Tell me what you know about . . . " is an easy way to begin. After brainstorming, the students might consult the text's illustrations, headings, and bold print terms for additional clues. These are drawn branching from the key concept, and organized by category whenever possible. The map becomes an organizing guide for reading. After reading, the map is revised with greater detail.

When students have little background information to bring to a lesson, teachers can offer an *advance organizer,* which is an outline of the lesson's content. Students refer to the outline as the teacher relates the topic to previous lessons, forecasts the new information, clarifies the concepts to be learned, defines new terms, and builds interest and a purpose in reading. The advance organizer has been found to be very helpful to note taking, and the quantity and quality of learning improves.

*Structured overviews* are simple lists of lecture or text concepts written on the board to which students add related vocabulary words from their background knowledge. Along with technical information, the teacher lists the words and discusses the meaning of each. The vocabulary is then rearranged forming a map that links related ideas to each other. The map is revised while the class is reading the material, and then it serves as a blueprint for studying. These schema theory techniques work to improve comprehension, note taking, discussion of ideas and reactions, and test preparation for several reasons:

1. Familiarity with major ideas before reading helps students evaluate how each new sentence can be integrated with the text's overall theme and organization;
2. Readers don't have to identify the text's major ideas and organization, and therefore can pay more attention to monitoring their comprehension;
3. Readers who lack necessary background knowledge for comprehension are provided a schema to use as they read.

Charts, diagrams, and graphs, such as those in Figures 12.2, 12.3, and 12.4, can also help with comprehension. They help teachers be more systematic and thorough in presentations, compensate for disorganized texts, reduce the information to a manageable load, stimulate student interest, highlight important information, and provide a model for organizing notes. They aid memory because of the spatial arrangement. Such tools can be even more helpful when preparing for tests than study guides on which students answer a series of questions.

Presenting science and social studies passages using a computer with a digitized voice that reads the words aloud as they are highlighted (bimodal presentation) is another powerful strategy for increasing comprehension. There are other helpful strategies as well: filling in outlines provided by the teacher, underlining or using margin notes to highlight key points in the text, asking oneself "Who or what is the paragraph about . . . what happened?" after each paragraph, selecting or creating topic sentences that summarize a paragraph, contrasting key words while reading, differentiating important from unimportant details, orally summarizing a passage and thinking of two details to go with each main idea, recording answers to the "wh" questions as one reads, or simply rereading. Teachers also can create exercises in which students must detect a sentence in a paragraph that is irrelevant to the main idea, select which sentences could be added to the paragraph, and reorder sentences so that main ideas and subordinate information interrelate better. Finally, the thinking skills goals and metacognitive strategies described in Chapter 7 have been very helpful to the progress of teenagers with LD. When directly taught, students with LD can learn to reason logically, use analogies to prior knowledge to help them reason, and critically evaluate information based on the evidence at hand.

***When directly taught, students with LD can learn to reason logically, use analogies to prior knowledge to help them reason, and critically evaluate information based on the evidence at hand.***

In addition to comprehension exercises focused on reading, teachers need to use oral class time to increase understanding through listening exercises. Purposes for listening are set, the students listen, and then they respond to questions built on the 11 comprehension objectives listed earlier in this chapter. These exercises help with note taking as well, and can sharpen a youngster's ability to pick up information from the environment—an important asset in and out of school.

## Written Language

Written language remains one of the most unsuccessful areas for adolescents with learning disabilities. Spelling remediation and handwriting instruction need to continue when appropriate. Students also need to build compensations by learning to use the dictionary and the spell check on the computer, learning to check for homonyms and grammatical errors that their computers may not catch, and learning to proofread for spelling by scanning sentences backwards (try it; it works!). A misspeller's dictionary may be helpful (Figure 12.5) as may learning to type, provided typing doesn't present the same fine-motor difficulties as handwriting.

*The main priority in written language instruction for students with LD is to master conceptual writing.*

The main priority for students with LD is to master conceptual writing. Too often these students approach writing as though it were simply talk written down. They have a poor sense of the audience's perspective and therefore omit time, sequence, and organizational words that are meant to help the reader (such as "later," "first," "finally," "the reason . . . ," "the most important," "to summarize"). They need to learn to repeat words and synonyms for clarity when refer-

| *Incorrect* | *Correct* | *Incorrect* | *Correct* |
|---|---|---|---|
| kitastrofy | **catastrophe** | komfortable | **comfortable** |
| kitin | **kitten** | koming | **coming** |
| kleek | **clique** | kommunist | **communist** |
| klorine | **chlorine** | koris | **chorus** |
| knifes | **knives** | kraft | **craft** |
| knoted | **knotted** | kronic | **chronic** |
| knowlege | **knowledge** | kwik | **quick** |
| kolic | **colic** | kwire | **choir** |
| kolyumnist | **columnist** | | |

*Look-Alikes or Sound-Alikes*

**kernel** (seed) • **colonel** (officer)

**kill** (murder) • **kiln** (oven)

**knead** (to press) • **need** (must have)

**knew** (did know) • **gnu** (animal) • **new** (not old)

**knight** (feudal rank) • **night** (opposite of day)

**knot** (what you tie) • **not** (no)

**know** (to understand) • **no** (opposite of yes)

**Figure 12.5** Sample page from a misspeller's dictionary.

*Source:* Adapted from Krevisky, J., & Linfield, J. L. (1963). *The Bad Speller's Dictionary,* p. 81. New York: Random House. Copyright © 1963, 1967 by Innovation Press. Reprinted by permission of Random House, Inc.

ents such as *he, those, the same,* are unclear. Using transition words such as *therefore, however,* and *for example* to smooth the flow of their writing also is an important goal, as is using different sentence types (e.g., simple and complex, declarative and interrogative).

The most effective written language teaching activity for high school students is one that emphasizes the need to problem solve by gathering, analyzing, and reorganizing information. The traditional emphasis on handwriting, spelling, punctuation, and grammar does nothing to excite students about writing, nor does it stimulate them to develop conceptually or stylistically.

One useful technique for encouraging writing is *uninterrupted silent sustained writing.* Several times a week, for 5 or 10 minutes, students write about anything that comes to mind. They write quickly and without making corrections, and the product need not be shared with anyone. Keeping a personal journal also helps students get over the hurdle of even trying to write. *Interactive journal writing* is a variation in which the teacher and student converse in writing. Teachers avoid asking questions or evaluating the writing. The conversational give-and-take encourages students to use higher-level discourse in their writing and experiment with ideas.

Figure 12.6 on page 456 presents a more structured approach to writing in which the mechanics are disregarded until after the student works out ideas. This is a systematic technique that guides the student to express his or her own thoughts in a cohesive manner. Cue cards such as those in Figure 12.7 on page 457 also can be very helpful to paragraph development.

Writing instruction incorporating the steps of the writing process's prewriting, drafting, and revising stages, in combination with the word processor, can be particularly effective in improving writing quality, as can offering students story starters or story enders. The self-check statements in Figure 12.8 on page 458 also have helped students with LD with the difficult process of revising.

Story grammar cue cards such as the one shown in Figure 11.2 on page 419 can help students produce longer and higher-quality stories, especially when cues ask for more detail (e.g., "Tell the characters' thoughts, feelings, emotions, and reasons for doing what they do. Make sure they think and feel just as real people do"). Similarly, compare/contrast essays become clearer, more logical, and have more appropriate content when students follow a planning diagram that lists the topic, thesis, various compare/contrast ideas, and the conclusion. Also helpful are peer editing strategies that use interactive dialogues or respond to specific questions about each other's work, such as "Is there anything that is not clear?" "Where could more detail and information be added?" "Could you use a synonym?" "Did you use a million dollar word?" Research shows that gains from peer editor support are maintained even when the peer editor strategy is discontinued. Finally, simply listening to a taped version of one's writing can help students detect areas for revision, especially if the writing contains grammatical errors.

It is critical that teenagers with learning disabilities master basic writing skills. Ultimately, they will apply for jobs or go on to postsecondary education where the written product will play a large part in determining an individual's future options. Also, the better developed and organized that their writing becomes, the more that students become aware of the organization inherent in language. This, in turn, improves their memory for what they hear or read.

| Steps | Description |
|---|---|
| I | Write a short, simple, declarative sentence that makes one statement. This should be a sentence about an idea you have and not merely a description of how something looks or directions on how to make something. |
| II | Write three sentences about your subject in Step I that are clearly and directly about the entirety of that subject and not just some small aspect of it. A key to this step would be to think of the questions someone would typically ask about your subject.<br>A) ________<br>B) ________<br>C) ________ |
| III | Write four or five sentences about each of the three sentences in Step II.<br>A) ________<br>1) ________<br>2) ________<br>3) ________<br>4) ________<br>B) ________<br>1) ________<br>2) ________<br>3) ________<br>4) ________<br>C) ________<br>1) ________<br>2) ________<br>3) ________<br>4) ________ |
| IV | Make the material in the four or five sentences in Step III as concrete and specific as possible. Go into detail. Give examples. Don't ask, "What will I say next?" Say some more about what you have just said. Your goal is to say a lot about a little, not a little about a lot. Details are important. Avoid abstract terms. |
| V | In the first sentence of the second paragraph and every paragraph following, insert a clear reference to the idea in the preceding paragraph. In this step, relate each paragraph to the preceding paragraph and provide smooth transitions in the composition. |
| VI | Make sure every sentence in your theme is connected with, and makes clear reference to, the preceding sentence. |

**Figure 12.6** Method for teaching written composition skills.

*Source:* Adapted from Kerrigan, W. J., & Metcalf, A. A. (1987). *Writing to the point: Six basic steps* (4th ed.) New York: Harcourt Brace Jovanovich.

## Mathematics

In high school, mathematics becomes particularly difficult for even those students with learning disabilities who were able to manage math in elementary school. Al-

Introductory paragraph: Thesis statement first

- Answer the prompt in your first sentence.
- Write your first main idea in second sentence.
- Write your second main idea as the third sentence.
- Write your third main idea as the last sentence.

(1)

*Introductory paragraph: Thesis statement last*

- *Start with an "attention getter" and lead up to the thesis statement.*
- *Answer the prompt in your last sentence. Include your first, second, and third main ideas in a series.*

(2)

How to start with an "attention getter"

- *Use a series of questions.*
- *Use a series of statements.*
- *Use a brief or funny story.*
- *Use a mean or angry statement.*
- *Start with the opposite opinion from what you believe.*

(3)

First body paragraph: Use transition words to introduce ideas

- First (of all) . . .
- (The/My) first (reason/example) is . . .
- One (reason why/example is) . . .
- To begin with . . .
- In the first step . . .
- To explain . . .

(4)

Second and third body paragraphs: Use transition words to connect or add ideas, or give examples

- Second(ly) . . . Third . . .
- My second (reason/example) is . . .
- Furthermore . . .
- Another (reason) to support this is . . .
- What is more . . .
- The next step . . .

(5)

Concluding paragraph: Use transition words to summarize ideas

- In conclusion/To conclude . . .
- In summary/To sum up . . .
- As one can see . . ./As a result . . .
- In short/All in all . . .
- It follows that . . .
- For these reasons . . .

(6)

**Figure 12.7** Cue cards for paragraph development. These cards are followed to respond to a "prompt" given by the teacher, for example, "Where should the class go for a field trip and why?"

*Source:* De La Paz, S., Owen, B., Harris, K. R., & Graham, S. (2000). Riding Elvis's motorcycle: Using self-regulated strategy development to PLAN and WRITE for a state writing exam. *Learning Disabilities Research & Practice, 15,* p. 102.

gebra, geometry, and trigonometry demand a new vocabulary—*tangent* and *sine,* for example; new symbols ($\pi$ and $\sqrt{\ }$); more complex word problems; and sophisticated logical and perceptual reasoning. Mathematics remediation methods for this

**Evaluative Phrases**

A. Readers won't see why this is important.
B. People may not believe this.
C. People won't be very interested in this part.
D. People may not understand what I mean here.
E. This is good.
F. This could be said more clearly.
G. Even I am confused about what I am trying to say.
H. This doesn't sound quite right.
I. This sentence states the topic.
J. This sentence sums up what I have said.
K. This sentence doesn't follow a logical order.
L. This shows what I really think.
M. This does not sound like a conclusion.

**Directive Phrases**

1. I'd better leave this part out.
2. I'd better say more.
3. I'd better cross this sentence out and say it in a different way.
4. I'd better change the wording.
5. I think I'll leave it this way.
6. I'd better support what I'm saying with facts.
7. I'd better move this sentence.

**Figure 12.8** Evaluative and directive phrases to assist writing revisions (adapted from Bereiter & Scardamalia, 1982).

*Source:* Reynolds, C. J., Hill, D. S., Swassing, R. H., & Ward, M. E. (1988). The effects of revision strategy instruction on the writing performance of students with learning disabilities. *Journal of Learning Disabilities, 21*, p. 541. Copyright 1988 by PRO-ED, Inc. Reprinted by permission.

*Math remediation methods at the secondary level focus on making sense of the mathematical processes and developing problem-solving strategies.*

age group focus primarily on making sense of the mathematical processes, and developing problem-solving strategies, including self-checking techniques, listing problem-solving steps, enlisting the help of visual aids, and verbal self-instruction.

Word problems pose multiple challenges for students with learning disabilities. They must first read the problem. Then, because not all the information is usually given in the problem, they must apply some additional knowledge. They must also translate the math vocabulary imbedded in the problem into a numeric operation, then retranslate the problem's solution back into language. To complicate matters further, word problems usually include extraneous information that can sidetrack students.

Nevertheless, managing word problems is important because a good number of mathematical problems in real life are in word form, and they tend to be even more difficult because they are presented orally and solved mentally. For example, when the salesman tells you the cost of two items, you must mentally add the numbers and estimate whether you have enough money. The same is true for estimating whether you have enough time to make the train.

*Mastering functional math skills is critical for students with severe math reasoning weaknesses.*

For adolescents who continue to have great difficulty with very basic mathematical reasoning and computations, experts recommend focusing on the skills needed to function in adult life, such as those listed in Figure 12.9. It's particularly important to teach students to estimate answers before solving problems so they can evaluate the reasonableness of their answers. These "survival" skills are best practiced within real-life contexts. Science and social studies content also can be utilized to reinforce functional math skills, as in translating federal reserve rates

**Consumer Skills**
- Making change
- Determining cost of sale items utilizing percentages (e.g., "25% off")
- Determining tax amounts
- Doing cost comparisons
- Buying on "time"
- Balancing a checkbook
- Determining total cost of purchases

**Homemaking Skills**
- Measuring ingredients
- Budgeting for household expenses
- Calculating length of cooking and baking time when there are options (e.g., for a cake using two 9" round pans vs. two 8" round pans)
- Measuring material for clothing construction
- Doing cost comparisons

**Health Care**
- Weighing oneself and others
- Calculating caloric intake
- Determining when to take medication

**Auto Care**
- Calculating cost of auto parts
- Measuring spark plug gaps
- Determining if tire pressure is correct
- Figuring gas mileage

**Home Care**
- Determining amount of supplies (paint, rug shampoo) to buy
- Determining time needed to do projects
- Measuring rods and drapes
- Finding cost of supplies
- Finding cost of repairs

**Vocational Needs**
- Calculating payroll deductions
- Determining money owed
- Knowing when to be at work
- Doing actual math for various jobs

**Figure 12.9** Content for teaching functional math.

*Source:* Schwartz, S. E., & Budd, D. (1981). Mathematics for handicapped learners: A functional approach for adolescents. *Focus on Exceptional Children 13* (7), pp. 7–8. Reprinted by permission of Love Publishing, Denver, Colorado.

into practical implications for borrowing money, or the results of a drug study into the percentage of personal risk when taking a particular drug.

## Study and Test-Taking Skills

Students with learning disabilities, especially those with attention weaknesses, routinely forget to write down assignments, complete homework, or hand it in on time. They have great difficulty using their time wisely, breaking down long-term assignments into manageable pieces, developing reasonable timelines, and following through. Unless tasks are highly interesting or carry rewards or penalties, students have difficulty persisting or even getting started. If these students are to remember what they are taught and succeed, they need to develop good study skills such as note taking, outlining, library, and test-taking skills. The key word in each of these areas is *organization*.

A well-planned time schedule and a disciplined study approach are essential. Students can employ such organizational aids as 3 × 5 inch cards with reminders about what needs to be done today, in two weeks, or weeks from now. Post-it notes are also great for this purpose, provided they are placed judiciously where the student can see them. A well-organized notebook, complete with weekly and monthly calendars, is also essential. Consulting with parents and teachers on realistic daily and long-term goals is a must, as is rewarding oneself for meeting these goals (e.g., time to work out, go to a movie). Students with LD can also be assigned to observe their peers' study habits and adopt those they believe might work for them.

**Coaching** *is very effective in helping students with organization and study skills.*

*Coaching* is another approach that has proved very effective. Students who volunteer to meet with a "coach" determine long-term goals such as attending a moderately competitive college, making the soccer team, or getting a specific job. Then they meet with the coach for 10 to 15 minutes a day to monitor that day's progress and to plan exactly what to do tomorrow (Figures 12.10 and 12.11). The daily goals include not only task completion and good grades, but also behavioral commitments such as participating in class discussions. Barriers to reaching goals, such as skipping class or not doing homework, are discussed and worked on. Environmental supports, such as going to the library to study or asking mom to type a paper, also are decided on. The coach can be a caring teacher, an athletic coach, or teacher's aide—anyone with whom the student has a positive, trusting relationship. The students' self-evaluation and verbal commitment are keys to success, as is the coach's daily enthusiasm and encouragement. Hopefully, habits are modeled that will persist long after the coaching relationship has ended.

## Note Taking Skills

Most students find that underlining in the text is helpful to remembering key facts and important details. But students with language weaknesses may still need to go back and reread all the material before an exam in order to understand the context of the underlined phrases. Note taking can be an effective alternative strategy. It forces a student to paraphrase, organize, and elaborate on new information. It involves finding key concepts, separating the important from the less important, and summarizing pertinent information. Such active processing makes the information more meaningful and memorable. Students who take notes remember more than those who don't; the more information in the notes, the better is their test performance.

*Students who take notes remember more than those who don't.*

As in note taking from text, note taking during lectures frees the listener from trying to memorize what the speaker is saying. This is an important skill to develop because teacher lectures are the major source of information on which tests are based. Note taking during lectures, however, can be particularly problematical for students with LD. It requires attending, listening, comprehending, paraphrasing, identifying the most important information, and writing all at the same time. Students with LD tend to record less information, fewer units of information that the instructor had cued as important, use fewer abbreviated words, and write slower.

Although it is the student's responsibility to take notes, it is the teacher's responsibility to give lectures that are so well organized that relationships are clear

Long-Term Goals Planning Sheet

Student's Name: Leah Brody Date: November 18, 1997

What is your long-term goal?

Goal 1: Pass English in order to be eligible to try out for the volleyball team

What do you need to do to meet your goal?

1. take notes in class
2. write down all assignments
3. do homework
4. hand in homework
5. revew before tests

| Are there barriers you need to overcome in order to meet your goal? | How can you overcome these barriers? |
|---|---|
| 1. trouble taking notes and listening at the same time | ask the teacher for her notes. |
| 2. watching TV instead of doing homwork | watch TV only after finishing homework |
| 3. not studying for tests | study with a friend |

What environmental supports or modifications are necessary in order to help you meet these goals?

The teacher needs to share her notes
My parents need to drive me to my friend's home

What is your long-term goal?

Goal 2:

What do you need to do to meet your goal?

1.
2.
3.
4.
5.

| Are there barriers you need to overcome in order to meet your goal? | How can you overcome these barriers? |
|---|---|
| 1. | |
| 2. | |
| 3. | |

What environmental supports or modifications are necessary in order to help you meet these goals?

Do you think these are realistic goals?

✓ Yes

____ No—How can they be modified?

**Figure 12.10** Long-term goals planning sheet used in coaching.

*Source:* Adapted from Dawson, P., & Guare, R. (1997). Reproduced with permission of Multi-Health Systems, Inc. 908 Niagara Falls Blvd., North Tonawanda, NY 19120–2060. (800) 456-3003.

Coach Monitoring Sheet

Name: Leah Brody Date: November 28, 1997

THE BIG PICTURE:

| Upcoming tests/quizzes: | | Long-term assignments: | | Other responsibilities: | |
|---|---|---|---|---|---|
| Subject: | Date: | Assignment: | Date Due: | Task: | Date: |
| English | Dec. 1 | Shakespeare paper | Dec. 15 | Apply for x mas break job | Dec. 5 |
| Math | Dec. 3 | Science project | Dec. 17 | Invite friends to birthday party | Dec. 10 |
| Earth Science | Dec. 3 | | | | |

TODAY'S PLANS:

| What are you going to do? | When will you do it? | Did you do it? | How did you do?* |
|---|---|---|---|
| Academic Tasks: | | | |
| 1. English homework | 1. today 7:00 - 7:45 pm | (Yes) No | 1 2 3 (4) 5 |
| 2. Shakespeare note cards | 2. Saturday afternoon | Yes No | 1 2 3 4 5 |
| 3. go to library for science | 3. Thursday night | Yes No | 1 2 3 4 5 |
| 4. project | 4. | Yes No | 1 2 3 4 5 |
| 5. review for math quiz | 5. today 7:45 - 8:15 pm | (Yes) No | 1 2 (3) 4 5 |
| 6. | 6. | Yes No | 1 2 3 4 5 |
| Behavioral: | | | |
| 1. talk on phone only when | 1. every day | Yes (No) | (1) 2 3 4 5 |
| 2. homework is done | 2. | Yes No | 1 2 3 4 5 |

*Use this scale to evaluate: 1—Not well at all; 2—So-so; 3—Average; 4—Very well; 5—Excellent

GENERAL OBSERVATIONS REGARDING GOALS/PERFORMANCE:

I have trouble getting started with homework and then rush it so I can watch my favorite TV shows

**Figure 12.11** Coach monitoring sheet for daily tasks.

*Source:* Adapted from Dawson, P., & Guare, R. (1997). Reproduced with permission of Multi-Health Systems Inc., 908 Niagara Falls Blvd., North Tonawanda, NY 19120-2060. (800) 456-3003.

*It is the teacher's responsibility to give lectures that are so well organized that relationships are clear to students.*

to students. Teachers can incorporate several techniques that help students take notes: use advance organizers; link information from previous lectures to the current one; use words that cue an important concept—"in summary," "this is important to remember"; repeat key ideas and phrases and give students time to write them down; use voice quality to stress important ideas; number the points being made (*first, second*); use time cues (*next, finally*); write important ideas and technical terms on the board; ask questions periodically to see if students are understanding; ask questions to relate the new information to students' background knowledge; present examples and nonexamples of a concept; use pictures and diagrams to illustrate relationships among ideas; and allow time at the end of the lecture for students to review their notes and ask questions.

Beyond the teacher's organized lecture approach, structured lessons on note taking are important. Videotaped or audiotaped lessons are helpful because students can replay the tapes for different instructional purposes, for example, to listen for details or cue words that alert the listener to a major point. When practicing note taking from tapes, attention to detail and organization of the information can be taught by giving the student a form to complete that asks: What is today's topic? What do I already know about the topic? Record and number up to seven main points and list related details. List new terms. Summarize how the ideas relate to the topic.

Learning to recognize cues that signal important information in students' texts also is important: headings, bold print, italics, listed and numbered items, asterisks, and bullets. Some students prefer drawing "webs" or "maps" to the standard form of note taking, and the teacher can help them learn to organize information in this format.

When taking notes in the standard way, a two-column system is helpful. Students take notes in a broad right-hand column and use a narrower left-hand column to list key concepts that summarize the information in the right-hand column. When studying, the right-hand information is covered, and the left-hand column is used to ask oneself questions that trigger these details. In three-column systems, the far left column is used for recording related notes from the text, known information relevant to the topic, comments, questions for the teacher, future assignments, and so forth. Rereading notes immediately after taking them is important in order to fill in gaps and label key concepts. Reducing notes to the essential points, organizing the information, classifying ideas, reciting the material, and reviewing it are essential in order to have note taking benefit the student.

Students who take lecture notes learn more than students who don't, and they learn more from taking their own notes in their own words rather than using someone else's notes. Nevertheless, there are some students who benefit best from listening only. They tend to be those with poor short-term memory, low general ability, and little prior knowledge about the subject. For them, taking notes is an additional processing burden. Teachers can provide these students with copies of their lecture notes or permit students to use a copy of a peer's notes. Teacher-prepared guides on which the student merely fills in key words also can be helpful.

***Students learn more from taking their own notes in their own words rather than using someone else's notes. Nevertheless, for some students taking notes poses too much of an additional processing burden.***

## Outlining Skills

By design, outlines assist the adolescent in organizing ideas for writing, for taking notes on what's being read, and for note taking during lectures. Teachers can structure assignments into main ideas, subheadings, and details, so that outlining is simple and obvious, thereby giving students practice in using this helpful skill.

But many students find outlining, especially from a text, tedious. Sorting the material into superordinate categories may be difficult, or they may get bogged down in the mere mechanics of writing and spelling. An alternative is penciling notes in the margins. A method taught in a Brown University study skills course teaches that there are only seven types of questions the student is ever asked:

1. *Definition/identification:* explicit definition of ideas and the person/group who originated or supported the idea.
2. *Cause/effect.*
3. *Location/spatial relations:* geographical and nongeographical (e.g., molecular structure, location of cell types in the brain).
4. *Time/temporal relations:* specific dates or time periods and relationship (e.g., how the past influences the present).
5. *Method:* how something is accomplished or resolved (e.g., political policies that accomplish a goal).
6. *Type:* into which subtypes has the author subdivided the main idea?
7. *Motive.*

For about five minutes, the student prereads ten pages of topic sentences, introductions, summaries, and illustrations to forecast which of the above categories are most relevant to the content area. Next he or she reads the text, continually asking if the information is important enough to memorize for a test. If so, the student jots down the category in the margin and what it should trigger. For example, for Madame Curie, the student writes "ID (identification): discoverer of radium." For the date and cause of the Civil War, the student records "Time: Civil War" and "Cause: Civil War." As the student records these, he or she simultaneously verbalizes the answer. When the student reaches the bottom of the page, he or she reads all the notations to see if they trigger the answers. If not, the corresponding sentences are reread and a check placed next to the trigger to indicate a difficult item.

Students proceed like this for ten pages, and then review their recall of all the triggers. And then they take a well-deserved 15-minute break! Information that continues to be difficult to trigger is written in a notebook in sentence form.

This system is virtually foolproof in improving performance on exams if followed judiciously. This is because information is being organized into meaningful categories and rehearsed three times. Teenagers don't find it tedious because they are encouraged by how much they remember as they go along.

## Library Skills and Internet Searches

*Teachers must help students evaluate the validity of the information accessed in the library or over the Internet. Just because it's written down doesn't mean it's true.*

Libraries, with their computer catalogs, Dewey Decimal System, indexes, encyclopedias, dictionaries, almanacs, and so on, can be intimidating for anyone. Teachers can create activities to promote library use and help students understand what riches are contained inside those walls. Exploring libraries' multimedia materials may be a good way to stimulate student interest. For many students with LD, these materials and Internet searches, rather than reading, may become the primary tools for acquiring knowledge throughout life. When they don't become comfortable with a library during their school years, an important avenue for lifelong learning may be shut off. A key objective for the teacher is to help students evaluate the validity of the information they are accessing in the library or over the World Wide Web. Just because it's written down does not mean it's true.

### Test-Taking Skills

Most adolescents with learning disabilities need to be taught test-taking strategies to be able to, at the very least, accurately show what they do know. After learning these strategies their scores improve more than that of the nondisabled, because the average student already applies many of these approaches automatically. Figure 12.12 on page 466 illustrates two procedures that have helped students get ready for and take tests. Some experts have suggested that students star the 25 most important items in their notes and focus mostly on these. This makes the task more manageable by focusing on only essential details, allowing more time for repetition, and avoiding overloading. Mnemonic strategies are very useful as well, given that most teachers prepare exams that ask primarily for recall or recognition of facts. Students also can be permitted to bring one 8.5 × 11 inch "cheat sheet" to the test. By the time they've created this sheet, they've usually memorized the information anyway. And this method teaches students that understanding the main idea is more important than memorizing details, as long as you know where to go to find the specifics when you need them. Another alternative, though not as successful, is filling in blanks in diagrams while studying.

An important goal for teachers is to help students communicate what they know as competently as possible. Because of the learning disabled's poor performance on tests, many experts suggest that we substitute performance assessment whenever possible: demonstrations, projects, recitals, portfolios, and so forth. The variety of possible portfolio types and grading systems were explored in Chapter 8.

***Many experts suggest that we replace tests with performance assessment whenever possible: demonstrations, projects, recitals, portfolios.***

## Transition Planning

Planning ahead for postsecondary educational and career opportunities is an important part of the high school program. Teenagers also need to learn practical life skills for their entry into the adult world. Presumably this has been part of their schooling so far: reading—for menus, directions on prescriptions, credit card rules; comprehension—for figuring out the voting booth and whom to vote for; math—for budgeting, completing a tax return; written language—for completing job applications and writing a cover letter when returning a mail order item; and study skills—for the all-important driver's test. Yet many high school students with LD are weak in these basic skills or have trouble generalizing them from the classroom to real life. Compounded by social and emotional difficulties, the forecasts for life adjustment can be shaky. Therefore, transition planning is a necessity.

***Many students with LD have trouble generalizing learned skills from the classroom to real life.***

Career and vocational education and preparation for postsecondary schooling are priorities for transition planning. Students who have some vocational education or paid on-the-job experience tend to be more successful in the job market than those who don't. Vocational education programs can be helpful, but many of them are geared to less intelligent students or to delinquents. Thus many students who are learning disabled avoid them. Programs geared to the average student population, on the other hand, may be too academically oriented and geared toward higher-level occupations. Therefore, for students with LD a flexible class schedule that permits them to work a few hours a week may be the best answer. Participating in school-operated small businesses and job clubs also offers valuable opportunities to explore

***Students who have some vocational education or paid on-the-job experience tend to be more successful in the job market than those who don't.***

**Preparing for Tests**

1. The student should ask the teacher exactly what material will be on the test and what aspects of it will come from the notes, lectures, or textbooks. The student should also ask what the format of the test will be: true-false, essay, short answer, or multiple choice.
2. The student should obtain copies of previous exams (and their answer sheets) from other students who have taken the course or from teachers themselves. Students should be "test wise" and know what type of questions are usually on the exams and which topics are emphasized.
3. The student should be instructed in setting up and following a study schedule. This alleviates some of the necessity of cramming for tests, an ineffective method for all students—especially for students with LD who have reading problems. A brief review of the material following each class helps the student remember the content.
4. The student should understand testing terms such as *compare, contrast, illustrate, briefly describe, define,* and *elaborate.* The student should also note the relative point value the teacher places on different test items. This is an indication of how much information is needed to adequately answer the questions and how much time the student should spend answering it.
5. Students should be encouraged to approach the testing situation with a positive mental attitude. Discussing feelings ahead of time can be helpful and provides the teacher with an opportunity to reinforce the student's abilities and positive outlook toward the test.

**SCORER Technique**

S = *schedule* your time. How many questions are there, and how much time is there to complete the exam?

C = *cue* words. *All, never,* and *always* rarely indicate a true answer on a true-false test but *usually* or *sometimes* often do.

O = *omitting* or setting aside the difficult questions. Answer the easiest questions first and then go back.

R = *read* the directions and examples carefully.

E = *estimate* the approximate range of possible answers for a question; e.g., the area of a shoe box will be in square inches, so answers in square feet may be disregarded. You should also "guesstimate" the answer if credit is not taken off for doing so.

R = *review* your work. Make sure all questions are answered with the correct letter or number and be very cautious about changing answers without substantiation for the new choice.

**Figure 12.12** Procedure for preparing for tests and the SCORER technique.

*Sources:* Alley, G., & Deshler, D. (1979). *Teaching the LD adolescent: Strategies and methods.* Denver: Love Publishing Company; Carman, R. A., & Adams, W. R., Jr. (1972). *Study skills: A student's guide for survival.* New York: Wiley.

talents and careers, gain self-confidence, learn interviewing skills (timeliness, appearance, posture, politeness, conversational skills), resumé writing, and role-playing employment situations such as accepting a compliment, giving constructive criticism to a coworker, accepting instruction or criticism from a supervisor, and explaining a problem to a supervisor. All these skills can increase job retention.

Given that students with learning disabilities have so much to prepare for, teaching goals and materials must have very practical, everyday value. The more natural is the setting for learning adult survival skills, the better are the results for adolescents with LD. Money management, for instance, can be taught using an actual checking account or debit card. Reading, writing, and problem solving can be taught throughout the process of applying for, testing for, and earning a driver's license. And we can't forget about essential independent living skills such as cooking, cleaning, shopping, hobbies, leisure time interests, and "using" the community.

*Given that students with LD have so much to prepare for, teaching goals and materials must have very practical, everyday value, and be taught in as real life a setting as possible.*

Adult service organizations, postsecondary educational institutions, and potential employers need to be brought into the transition planning process as needed. Family involvement too is essential to the transition planning process, not only because students need and benefit from family support but also because many students with LD continue to live at home after graduation. The responsibility for continued guidance, then, falls primarily to the family.

*Transition planning includes the student, his or her family, adult service and educational organizations, and potential employers.*

## Social-Emotional Adjustment

Although we usually associate school with learning facts, it's also true that education is essentially a social process. It's the quality of human interactions, more than academic knowledge or even intelligence, that makes for a full and satisfying life. The more positive the student's social relationships and the higher his or her self-esteem, the more likely the student is to be successful in life. But positive social relationships and self-esteem don't come easily to many students with LD.

*It's the quality of human interactions, more than academic knowledge or even intelligence, that makes for a full and satisfying life. The more positive are students' social relationships and the higher their self-esteem, the more likely they are to be successful in life.*

The school's role in building social relationships, thinking skills, speaking skills, and self-esteem is vital to the social-emotional adjustment of the learning disabled. It is peers who choose to befriend students with LD or ignore them, thereby reducing their social learning opportunities. Therefore, interventions need to target both groups. Involving peers in social skills programming, or family members in counseling, and teachers in consultation is important when these individuals' behaviors and attitudes are affecting the self-esteem and social adjustment of students with LD.

### Social Relationship Programming

Many students with learning disabilities need directed practice with acceptable social behaviors. They do this best in environments that are conducive to sharing feelings and to learning about others' willingness to listen and help. Group discussions, for example, promote positive social-emotional growth and understanding among teenagers when they encourage students to engage in behavior that satisfies their personal needs without impinging on the needs of others. Classwide peer tutoring, described in Chapter 11, helps build social relationships while at the same time reducing failing quiz grades, tardiness, and truancy.

Good social skills involve so many reasoning skills with which the learning disabled may not be adept: thinking in a variety of ways about an issue, monitoring one's thoughts, evaluating choices and probable consequences, thinking positively (as in saying to oneself "I'm so *excited* about the job interview!" vs. "*nervous*"), recognizing similarities between old and new situations so proven strategies will be used, challenging assumptions so as to look at information in a new way and gain new insights, and being clear about personal values and connecting these to one's behavior choices. Promoting the thinking skills discussed in Chapter 7 is very helpful in developing these skills, especially when the lessons of formal thinking skills programs are connected with real-life situations to which these skills can immediately be applied. Goldstein's *Prepare Curriculum,* for example, uses modeling, role-playing, and videotaping to teach cooperation, interpersonal skills, anger control, stress management, moral reasoning, and empathy. Behaviors practiced in the group are assigned as homework to be tried out in real-life situations. Students report back at the next class. Brainstorming sessions also can help develop social reasoning skills when the following rules are followed:

1. Criticism is not allowed.
2. The wilder the idea is, the better, because freedom of expression stimulates more creative ideas.
3. Come up with as many ideas as possible, making sure that all are recorded on paper, videotape, or tape recorder.
4. Expand on each other's ideas and try combining and improving on other's suggestions.

Curricula that develop nonverbal skills for socially imperceptive students are also important. These students need to learn about body language cues, use of personal space, cosmetics, clothing, and sensitivity to vocal nuances.

***Due to short-lived programs or nonmeaningful goals, gains from formal social skills programs have been modest, and generalization to everyday circumstances limited. Skills taught must be personally meaningful, taught in as natural a setting as possible, and students must learn to recognize which social circumstances call for which behaviors.***

Unfortunately, gains from formal social skills training programs have been modest, for the most part, and generalization to everyday circumstances is limited. These programs tend to be too short-lived, poorly applied, and not targeted specifically enough to the needs of students to be able to turn around years of social skills deficits and missed social learning opportunities. Moreover, many students with LD have difficulty judging when a particular behavior that is already in their social repertoire, or that they just practiced "in group," is appropriate to use. Therefore, if we are going to teach these skills, it's important that the skills taught be socially meaningful to the student, taught in as natural a setting as possible, and that we help students analyze which social circumstances call for which behaviors. One way of doing this is by establishing networks of students without disabilities who provide social support during school activities to their learning disabled peers, with the goal of increasing their participation and acceptance. The nondisabled students must seriously commit to this activity, and meet weekly to problem solve and brainstorm strategies for mediating the social relationships of their classmates with learning disabilities.

## Speaking Skills Training

A wise man once said, "Never say anything that doesn't improve on silence." Unfortunately, students with LD often violate this adage. They may barge in on private conversations, talk nonstop, not listen, talk only about themselves, interrupt with irrelevant tangents, and more. Teaching the following strategies can help:

1. *Wait time.* Being sure to listen carefully and follow along with the thread of the conversation is important. Students need to organize their thoughts before they speak. Teachers can be helpful by reinforcing students when they respond appropriately and control irrelevant or inappropriate comments.
2. *Rehearsal.* Students rehearse what they want to say to a teacher, friend, potential employer, or in a speech and receive feedback from the class. Strategies for using "inner" language to rehearse in real-life situations are encouraged.
3. *Interpersonal sensitivity.* Teachers can help students learn how their speech affects listeners and then model what makes a person interesting to listen to—including maintaining good eye contact and showing genuine interest in what others have to say.
4. *Feedback.* Teachers provide accurate feedback to students by sharing what they have observed, which behaviors affected peers in particular ways, and how they personally reacted to the behaviors they saw.

## Building Self-Esteem

All of us have a general sense of self-worth, which is made up of very particular self-esteems: how we fare as students, athletes, singers, friends, artists, professionals, brothers, children, our physical attractiveness, and many more. When we intervene in school to raise a student's academic self-esteem, this may have some positive spillover on global self-esteem. However, increasing global self-esteem doesn't generalize in the opposite direction. In spite of the "don't worry, be happy" movement in recent years, people are smart enough to know that feeling good about oneself comes from having done well at some task, whether that's a hard-won B+ on a math quiz or a kind gesture toward someone in need.

***Everyone has a general sense of self-worth, which is made up of very particular self-esteems. When we intervene to raise a student's academic self-esteem, this may have some positive spillover on global self-esteem.***

Enhancing self-esteem among our students requires a targeted approach. Often students with LD are at a self-esteem disadvantage from the start. We are promoting *inclusive education*—including the disabled in general education environments and instruction—but research shows that when a student is in a scholastic environment in which the average student is academically superior, this results in lower academic self-concepts, lower grades, and lower educational and occupational aspirations. The activities suggested below can help to counteract this phenomenon, as can creating a cooperative rather than competitive class environment in which the emphasis is on mastery rather than grades, individuals' differences are valued, and social comparison is discouraged. Involving the whole class in a community service activity on a regular basis also can bolster social skills, self-esteem, confidence, and a sense of pride and belonging. And, of course, modifying and adapting the curriculum and assignments to ensure that a student can succeed is critical.

***Modifying and adapting the curriculum and assignments to ensure that a student can succeed is critical to his or her self-esteem.***

**Directed Writing Activity.** Teachers can encourage students to jot down their reactions to their daily lives in personal journals. Students are given time to write daily about their reactions to a positive and a negative event, and to focus on their own abilities and shortcomings. If the teacher reads the journals, issues raised can be followed up on through discussion with the student.

**Q-sort.** Students can sort descriptive adjectives into piles that represent their "existing" behavior and their "ideal" behavior. Students then select a behavior they wish to change and are reinforced for progress toward this goal.

**Bibliotherapy.** Often reading or listening to books in which the main character struggles with a dilemma in the student's own life serves as a superb counseling tool. The student learns how others have handled similar circumstances. An example of an excellent book that can help students feel that they're not all alone and strengthen their ability to cope is Sharon Flake's novel *Skin I'm In,* in which Maleeka, a teenager in an African American school struggles with ridicule for having darker skin and dressing in her individual style. *The Color Purple*'s theme is physical and sexual abuse; *Izzy, Willy, Nilly* deals with self-concept; *Julie of the Wolves* deals with resiliency; *The Solitary,* with self-determination; and so forth. Students dealing with similar challenges read a book revolving around that theme and discuss their feelings and ideas about the work with the help of a facilitator. The focus is on the characters and their dilemmas and coping strategies, rather than the student revealing his or her circumstances. This approach has assisted students in coping with stress, has helped build self-esteem and confidence, and improved student aspirations for the future.

**Self-Determination Training.** Many students with LD believe their lives are controlled by others and place the responsibility for their actions on someone else. "Peggy didn't sit with me at lunch because she's ashamed to be seen with me," a student might think. But a student who's been encouraged to accept more responsibility for his or her actions might say, "If I want to sit with Peggy at lunch, I'd better get there early enough so there's room for me at the table."

Role-playing and simulations can help students discover whether the locus of control is coming from outside or inside themselves. The value of internal control can be highlighted, and students can be supported as problems and action plans are identified. In one study, students learned to increase their math performance by using empowering statements: "I'm saying negative things that don't help. . . . I can stop and think more helpful thoughts." "Take it step by step." "I really did well in not letting this get the best of me." "Good for me! I did a good job!" (Kamann & Wong, 1993). Teachers can help a great deal when they give students opportunities for choice, model taking charge of one's destiny, help students attribute success to their own efforts, and positively reinforce motivation, self-esteem, and internal locus of control.

***Self-determination skills are essential to overcoming learned helplessness and to making important decisions about the future.***

Self-determination skills are essential to overcoming learned helplessness and to making important decisions about the future. Students who act according to their personal preferences and interests, make appropriate independent decisions about how to act in various situations (including safety and risk-taking), believe they can influence outcomes with their actions, set goals with appropriate plans to attain them, are good self-advocates, and who apply an accurate understanding of their strengths and limitations in making decisions are more likely to be employed one year out of high school, earn higher wages, have a bank account, and want to live independently. An important goal of schooling is to facilitate autonomy and the ability to govern one's life. You were introduced to Jeff and his frustrations in Chapter 8. Jeff's story continues on page 471. Jeff is the perfect example of how we

***An important goal of schooling is to facilitate autonomy and the ability to govern one's life.***

## Jeff

*A wonderful example of how we wish all students with LD would take charge of their lives.*

*Self-confidence (defined as belief in one's ability to influence events), persistence, and willingness to work hard are important contributors to success among young people with learning disabilities. Here, Jeff (a dyslexic adult whom you met in Chapter 8) describes how he went about getting into college:*

In my last couple years of high school, the whole idea of college seemed incredibly out of reach. Everybody sort of had the attitude that "Well, you're a bright guy, but, you know college is just not in the works for you." But that never sat right with me. Maybe it was because my father is Dean of a university, but I don't think that's the only reason. I just had ideas about what I wanted to do in life and they were going to require that somehow or other I get a handle on using my mind. But I had no study skills, and even after five years of high school I could not write. I had no clue as to where a period went or what commas were for. I had sort of got reading understood, but writing was overwhelming . . . So my senior year wound down and out of the blue I decided to call the new headmaster of a boarding school for students with learning disabilities where I had gone for seventh and eighth grade. I introduced myself and told him I had been a student at the school, and I didn't have a good plan for next year. And he said, "Well, come on down and we'll talk about it." So I hopped on a bus and spent the weekend at this school and we threw around some ideas. And the plan we came up with was that I would work at the school as a janitor, and they would give me a small salary plus room and board and tutoring from the faculty so I could take courses at the local community college.

In my first semester at the college I took two courses. It was an incredible experience, because I really started to feel that "Hey, I can do academic things." I never had that academic confidence in high school. I don't think my school had a very good idea of where they were going academically, let alone where they were going with someone who had disabilities. There was no plan, and when they saw I wasn't making progress they just let me do whatever I wanted. So high school was pretty much a lost situation. But my two years at the community college were great. They changed the way I perceived myself as a thinker. I took basic writing—like a pre-college writing course—and I really enjoyed it. We talked about structure—things like an introduction, and argument paragraphs and a conclusion. I found out once I had a *system* for writing I could do it. Another good thing I learned was to have someone proofread so I got credit for what I was saying and didn't get an inordinate number of points deducted for misspelling every other word (this was pre-computer for me, so I had to type everything out, which was a remarkably cumbersome process). I started getting A's and B+'s and learned that I could think, and that made me more confident. I liked working at the boarding school, too. The next year they gave me a position as a dorm master; I lived with thirty kids. They were all learning disabled one way or another and some had been so protected by their environments—well, they all had low self-esteem but some were completely incapable of handling basic tasks, like how to make a bed or get your shoes on the right feet or take a shower. So that was challenging, but I felt good because I could identify with these kids and the incredible satisfaction they got from learning to do things on their own. . . .

Then one of the teachers at the community college who had worked with me a lot suggested, "You know, you ought to apply to some four-year colleges." We wrote away and got some applications to some great schools. A lot of them seemed pretty overwhelming but I sent several in and went to one interview, which was actually very useful. I mean, a lot of students going through high school have everyone grooming them for college, but I

*(continued)*

**Jeff** (Continued)

had no clue. So this interviewer gave me a lot of tips about the application process, which was great. Still, I did not get into this very selective small college I wanted. When I got the rejection letter, I called the Dean of Admissions and I just said, "I'd like to drive there tomorrow and review my application with you." And to my total surprise he said, "Sure, what time will you be here?" So I met with him, and explained really simply that I had worked harder to have the opportunity to just sit down with him than any other student he would be accepting this year, and that no matter how carefully he screens all those applications somebody is going to drop out. So what did he have to lose? The worst thing that could happen was I would be one of those . . .

Anyway, halfway through the summer I got a letter from the college. And they accepted me.

*Source:* Interview by Jennifer Kagan.

*Source:* Reprinted with the permission of The Free Press, a Division of Simon & Schuster Adult Publishing Group, from *Learning Disabilities A to Z: A Parent's Complete Guide to Learning Disabilities from Preschool to Adulthood* by Corinne R. Smith and Lisa W. Strick. Copyright © 1997 by Corrine R. Smith and Lisa W. Strick.

wish all students with LD would take charge of their lives. Because of his belief in himself and his willingness to act on this belief, Jeff graduated from a highly competitive college and today is a successful computer programmer—and a wonderful advocate for his three little girls who are nonreaders.

## Assertiveness Training

***Assertive people are open, honest, direct, and spontaneous—but appropriate, positive, and respectful—in their communications with others. Nonassertive students often get hurt because they allow others to shape their goals.***

Assertive behavior is honest and straightforward expression to others and to ourselves about how we feel. Assertive people, students included, make their own decisions, and from this gain a great deal of self-satisfaction. They are open, honest, direct, and spontaneous—but appropriate, positive, and respectful—in their communications with others. With assertiveness training students learn to feel better about themselves and less anxious about sharing their feelings and ideas. By contrast, nonassertive students often get hurt because they allow others to shape their goals. The essential components of assertive behavior include

1. Good eye contact, appropriate body language, and a facial expression consistent with what's being said—for example, not smiling when you're really dissatisfied.
2. Spontaneous reactions to others' actions, but timing comments judiciously.
3. Honest communication about what one feels—"I am angry because you broke my watch" as opposed to "You are so clumsy!"
4. Matching the intensity of one's response to the situation—for example, not blowing up when someone bumps you in line.

When reinforced by the teacher, these skills can help markedly in boosting a student's self-esteem.

## Summary

Gaps between the basic achievement levels of students with learning disabilities and their peers generally widen at the middle and high school levels. Added to the tremendous pressure to "cover the curriculum" in these years, learning can be a frustrating and uphill battle for many students. If still motivated to continue remedial programming in reading, mathematics, and written language, these efforts can be quite successful, especially given the spurt in learning ability experienced by some teenagers. Basic skills also can be reinforced in the context of content area instruction. Curriculum adaptations and accommodations are critical in the secondary school years to help students with LD succeed in content area classes.

Teachers need to help students develop ways to compensate for their continuing weaknesses so as to minimize the interference with life success. Most importantly, strengths need to be developed, social skills and self-concept must be built, content needs to be made accessible to these students so their thinking and reasoning abilities are nurtured, and the student must be prepared for the transition to postsecondary schooling, employment, and independent living.

All this is not easy to plan and implement given the curriculum's demands and the great social and emotional changes experienced during the teenage years. Positive progress is most likely when teenagers understand their learning needs and become actively involved in their academic planning. Both the teacher and the family have the responsibility to attend as much to the teenager's affective and social development as to their academic development because success in life is linked far more to how we ultimately feel about ourselves than to our academic or intellectual levels.

## Helpful Resources

### Reading

Bergerud, D., Lovitt, T. C., & Horton, S. (1988). The effectiveness of textbook adaptations in life science for high school students with learning disabilities. *Journal of Learning Disabilities, 21*, 70–76.

Billingsley, B. S., & Wildman, T. M. (1988). The effects of prereading activities on the comprehension monitoring of learning disabled adolescents. *Learning Disabilities Research, 4*, 36–44.

Bos, C. S., & Anders, P. L. (1990). Effects of interactive vocabulary instruction on the vocabulary learning and reading comprehension of junior-high learning disabled students. *Learning Disability Quarterly, 13*, 31–42.

Bos, C. S., Anders, P. L., Filip, D., & Jaffe, L. E. (1989). The effects of an interactive instructional strategy for enhancing reading comprehension and content area learning for students with learning disabilities. *Journal of Learning Disabilities, 22*, 384–390.

Boyle, J. R. (1996). The effects of a cognitive mapping strategy on the literal and inferential comprehension of students with mild disabilities. *Learning Disability Quarterly, 19*, 86–98.

Bulgren, J., Schumaker, J. B., & Deshler, D. D. (1988). Effectiveness of a concept teaching routine in enhancing the performance of LD students in secondary-level mainstream classes. *Learning Disability Quarterly, 11*, 3–17.

Carr, S. C., & Thompson, B. (1996). The effects of prior knowledge and schema activation strategies on the inferential reading comprehension of children with and without learning disabilities. *Learning Disability Quarterly, 19*, 48–61.

Clark, F. L., Deshler, D. D., Schumaker, J. B., Alley, G. R., & Warner, M. M. (1984). Visual imagery and self-questioning: Strategies to improve comprehension of written material. *Journal of Learning Disabilities, 17*, 145–149.

Crank, J. N., & Bulgren, J. A. (1993). Visual depictions as information organizers for enhancing achievement of students with learning disabilities. *Learning Disabilities Research & Practice, 8*, 140–147.

Dale, E., & Chall, J. S. (1948, January 27). A formula for predicting readability. *Educational Research Bulletin*, pp. 11–20, 28, 37–54.

Flesch, R. (1951). *How to test readability.* New York: Harper & Row.

Fry, E. (1972). *Reading instruction for classroom and clinic.* New York: McGraw-Hill.

Gajria, M., & Salend, S. J. (1995). Homework practices of students with and without learning disabilities: A comparison. *Journal of Learning Disabilities, 28*, 291–296.

Gickling, E. E., & Thompson, V. P. (1985). A personal view of curriculum-based assessment. *Exceptional Children, 52*, 205–218.

Gurney, D., Gersten, R., Dimino, J., & Carnine, D. (1990). Story grammar. Effective literature instruction for high school students with learning disabilities. *Journal of Learning Disabilities, 23*, 335–342, 348.

Lenz, B. K., Alley, G. R., & Schumaker, J. B. (1987). Activating the inactive learner: Advance organizers in the secondary content classroom. *Learning Disability Quarterly, 10*, 53–67.

Leshowitz, B., Jenkens, K., Heaton, S., & Bough, T. L. (1993). Fostering critical thinking skills in students with learning disabilities: An instructional program. *Journal of Learning Disabilities, 26*, 483–490.

Malone, L. D., & Mastropieri, M. A. (1992). Reading comprehension instruction: Summarization and self-monitoring training for students with learning disabilities. *Exceptional Children, 58*, 270–279.

Manzo, A. V. (1975). Guided reading procedure. *Journal of Reading, 7*, 287–291.

Mastropieri, M. A., & Scruggs, T. E. (1997). Best practices in promoting reading comprehension in students with learning disabilities: 1976 to 1996. *Remedial and Special Education, 18*, 197–213.

McCormick, S., & Moe, A. J. (1982). The language of instructional materials: A source of reading problems. *Exceptional Children, 49*, 48–53.

McLaughlin, H. G. (1969). SMOG grading—A new readability formula. *Journal of Reading, 12*, 639–646.

Mercer, C. D., Campbell, K. U., Miller, M. D., Mercer, K. D., & Lane, H. B. (2000). Effects of a reading fluency intervention for middle schoolers with specific learning disabilities. *Learning Disabilities Research & Practice, 15*, 179–189.

Minton, M. J. (1980). The effect of sustained silent reading upon comprehension and attitudes among 9th graders. *Journal of Reading, 23*, 498–502.

Morocco, C. C., & Hindin, A. (2002). The role of conversation in a thematic understanding of literature. *Learning Disabilities Research & Practice, 17*, 144–159.

Rudman, M. K. (1995). *Children's literature: An issues approach* (3rd ed.). White Plains, NY: Longman.

Scanlon, D. J., Duran, G. Z., Reyes, E. I., & Gallego, M. A. (1992). Interactive semantic mapping: An interactive approach to enhancing LD students' content area comprehension. *Learning Disabilities Research & Practice, 7*, 142–146.

Schumaker, J. B., Deshler, D. D., & Denton, P. H. (1984). An integrated system for providing content to learning disabled adolescents using an audio-taped format. In W. M. Cruickshank & J. M. Kleibhan (Eds.), *Early adolescence to early adulthood.* Syracuse: Syracuse University Press.

Scruggs, T. E., & Mastropieri, M. A. (1993). Special education for the twenty-first century: Integrating learning strategies and thinking skills. *Journal of Learning Disabilities, 26*, 393–398.

Torgesen, J. K., Dahlem, W. E., & Greenstein, J. (1987). Using verbatim text recordings to enhance reading comprehension in learning disabled adolescents. *Learning Disabilities Focus, 3*, 30–38.

Vacca, R. T., & Vacca, J. L. (1999). *Content area reading: Literacy and learning across the curriculum* (6th ed.). NY: Longman.

Wong, B. Y. L., & Jones, W. (1982). Increasing metacomprehension in learning disabled and normally achieving students through self-questioning training. *Learning Disability Quarterly, 5*, 228–240.

Instructional resources: http://www.teachingld.org

## Written Language

Brown, A. S. (1988). Encountering misspellings and spelling performance: Why wrong isn't right. *Journal of Educational Psychology, 80*, 488–494.

Graves, A., Semmel, M., & Gerber, M. (1994). The effects of story prompts on the narrative production of students with and without learning disabilities. *Learning Disability Quarterly, 17*, 154–164.

Gregg, N. (1986). Cohesion: Inter and intra sentence errors. *Journal of Learning Disabilities, 19*, 338–341.

MacArthur, C. A., Graham, S., & Schwartz, S. (1991). Knowledge of revision and revising behavior among students with learning disabilities. *Learning Disabilities Quarterly, 14*, 61–73.

MacArthur, C. A., & Shneiderman, B. (1986). Learning disabled students' difficulties in learning to use a word processor: Implications for instruction and software evaluation. *Journal of Learning Disabilities, 19*, 248–253.

Montague, M., & Leavell, A. G. (1994). Improving the narrative writing of students with learning disabilities. *Remedial and Special Education, 15,* 21–33.

Reynolds, C. J., Hill, D. S., Swassing, R. H., & Ward, M. E. (1988). The effects of revision strategy instruction on the writing performance of students with learning disabilities. *Journal of Learning Disabilities, 21,* 540–545.

Rueda, R. S. (1992). Characteristics of teacher-student discourse in computer-based dialogue journals: A descriptive study. *Learning Disability Quarterly, 15,* 187–206.

Wong, B. Y. L., Butler, D. L., Ficzere, S. A., & Kuperis, S. (1997). Teaching adolescents with learning disabilities and low achievers to plan, write, and revise compare-and-contrast essays. *Learning Disabilities Research & Practice, 12,* 2–15.

## Mathematics

Bos, C. S., & Vaughn, S. (2002). *Strategies for teaching students with learning and behavior problems* (5th ed.). Boston: Allyn & Bacon.

Kameenuî, E. J., Carnine, D. W., Dixon, R. C., Simmons, D. C., & Coyne, M. D. (Eds.). (2002). *Effective teaching strategies that accommodate diverse learners.* (2nd ed.). Upper Saddle River, NJ: Merrill/Prentice Hall.

Mercer, C. D., & Mercer, A. R. (2001). *Teaching students with learning problems* (6th ed.). Upper Saddle River, NJ: Merrill/Prentice Hall.

Montague, M. (1997). Cognitive strategy instruction in mathematics for students with learning disabilities. *Journal of Learning Disabilities, 30,* 164–177.

## Study and Test-Taking Skills

Deshler, D., Ellis, E. S., & Lenz, B. K. (1996). *Teaching adolescents with learning disabilities: Strategies and methods.* (2nd ed.). Denver: London Publishing.

Hughes, C. A., & Suritsky, S. K. (1994). Note-taking skills of university students with and without learning disabilities. *Journal of Learning Disabilities, 27,* 20–24.

Mastropieri, M. A., Scruggs, T. E., Spencer, V., & Fontana, J. (2003). Promoting success in high school world history: Peer tutoring versus guided notes. *Learning Disabilities Research & Practice, 18,* 52–65.

Scruggs, T. E., & Mastropieri, M. A. (1988). Are learning disabled students "Test-Wise"?: A review of recent research. *Learning Disabilities Focus, 3,* 87–97.

Sheinker, J., & Sheinker, A. (1989). *Metacognitive approach to study strategies.* Gaithersburg, MD: Aspen Publishers.

Suritsky, S. K., & Hughes, C. A. (1991). Benefits of notetaking: Implications for secondary and postsecondary students with learning disabilities. *Learning Disability Quarterly, 14,* 7–18.

Woodward, J., & Noell, J. (1991). Science instruction at the secondary level: Implications for students with learning disabilities. *Journal of Learning Disabilities, 24,* 277–284.

How to Study: http://www.how-to-study.com

The Learning Toolbox: http://www.coe.jmu.edu/learning toolbox

Recording for the Blind and Dyslexic: http://www.rfbd.org

## Transition Planning

Cronin, M. E. (1996). Life skills curricula for students with learning disabilities: A review of the literature. *Journal of Learning Disabilities, 29,* 53–68.

Evers, R. B. (1996). The positive force of vocational education: Transition outcomes for youth with learning disabilities. *Journal of Learning Disabilities, 29,* 69–78.

Hammill, D. D., & Bartel, N. R. (Eds.) (1995). *Teaching students with learning and behavior problems: Managing mild-to-moderate difficulties in resource and inclusive settings* (6th ed.). Austin, TX: Pro Ed.

Lindstrom, L. E., Benz, M. R., & Johnson, M. D. (1996). Developing job clubs for students in transition. *Teaching Exceptional Children, 29*(2), 18–21.

Whang, P. L., Fawcett, S. B., & Mathews, R. M. (1984). Teaching job-related social skills to learning disabled adolescents. *Analysis and Intervention in Developmental Disabilities, 4,* 29–38.

National Center on Secondary Education and Transition: http://www.ncset.org

National Information Center for Children and Youth with Disabilites transition information: http://www.nichcy.org

National School-to-Work Learning Center: http://www.stw.ed.gov/wwwsites.htm

## Social-Emotional Adjustment

DuPaul, G. J., & Eckert, T. L. (1994). The effects of social skills curricula: Now you see them, now you don't. *School Psychology Quarterly, 9,* 113–132.

Elias, M. J., Zins, J. E., Weissberg, R. P., Frey, K. S., Greenberg, M. T., Haynes, N. M., Kessler, R., Schwab-Stone, M. E., & Shriver, T. P. (1997). *Promoting social and emotional learning: Guidleines for educators.* Alexandria, VA: Association for Supervision and Curriculum Development.

Fensterheim, H., & Baer, J. (1975). *Don't say yes when you want to say no.* New York: Dell.

Field, S. (1996). Self-determination instructional strategies for youth with learning disabilities. *Journal of Learning Disabilities, 29,* 40–52.

Forness, S. R., & Kavale, K. A. (1996). Treating social skill deficits in children with learning disabilities: A meta-analysis of the research. *Learning Disability Quarterly, 19,* 2–13.

Goldstein, A. P. (1999). *The prepare curriculum: Teaching prosocial competencies* (Rev. ed.). Champaign, IL: Research Press.

Goldstein, A. P., Glick, B., & Gibbs, J. C. (1998). *Aggression replacement training: A comprehensive intervention for aggressive youth* (Rev. ed.). Champaign, IL: Research Press.

Haring, T. G. (1992). The context of social competence: Relations, relationships, and generalization. In S. L. Odom, S. R. McConnell, & M. R. McEvoy (Eds.), *Social competence of young children with disabilities: Issues and strategies for interaction.* Baltimore: Paul H. Brookes.

Kamann, M. P., & Wong, B. Y. L. (1993). Inducing adaptive coping self-statements in children with learning disabilities through self-instruction training. *Journal of Learning Disabilities, 26,* 630–638.

Kilpatrick, W., Wolfe, G., & Wolfe, S. M. (1994). *Books that build character: A guide to teaching your child moral values through stories.* New York: Touchstone.

Kroth, R. (1973). The behavioral Q-sort as a diagnostic tool. *Academic Therapy, 8,* 317–330.

Minskoff, E. (1980). Teaching approach for developing nonverbal communication skills in students with social perception deficits. Part I: The basic approach and body language clues. *Journal of Learning Disabilities, 13,* 118–124.

Minskoff, E. (1980). Teaching approach for developing nonverbal communication skills in students with social perception deficits. Part II: Proxemic, vocalic, and artifactual cues. *Journal of Learning Disabilities, 13,* 203–208.

Niedelman, M. (1991). Problem solving and transfer. *Journal of Learning Disabilities, 24,* 322–329.

Perlmutter, B. F. (1986). Personality variables and peer relations of children and adolescents with learning disabilities. In S. J. Ceci (Ed.), *Handbook of cognitive, social, and neuropsychological aspects of learning disabilities* (Vol. 1). Hillsdale, NJ: Lawrence Erlbaum.

Shinn, M. R., Walker, H. M., & Stoner, G. (2002). *Interventions for academic and behavior problems II: Preventive and remedial approaches.* Bethesda, MD: National Association of School Psychologists.

Strein, W. (1993). Advances in research on academic self-concept: Implication for school psychology. *School Psychology Review, 22,* 273–284.

Wehmeyer, M., & Schwartz, M. (1997). Self-determination and positive adult outcomes: A follow-up study of youth with mental retardation or learning disabilities. *Exceptional Children, 63,* 245–255.

Yoder, D. I., Retish, E., & Wade, R. (1996). Service learning: Meeting student and community needs. *Teaching Exceptional Children, 28*(4), 14–18.

CHAPTER THIRTEEN

# The Family

**OF ALL THE SETTINGS** for children with learning disabilities, the family is by far the most important. Family members, especially the parents, nurture the student's learning abilities as well as social competencies, attitudes, and feelings of self-worth. Fostering intellectual competencies certainly is important, but so is supporting personal-social adjustment. No matter what children's abilities are, they will have a much easier time if they learn to trust others, listen and learn from others, and get along by telling the truth, following the rules, and being considerate, helpful, and altruistic. It is the family's example that teaches positive values, assertiveness, self-confidence, and the desire to achieve, all qualities that are important for school performance and life adjustment. Research finds that the child's satisfaction with family life is a far more important variable in the child's overall self-concept, motivation, achievement, and social extroversion than is the child's satisfaction with his or her friends or teachers.

*The family's example regarding values, self-confidence, and motivation, and the child's satisfaction with family life, are the most important influences on a child's school performance and life adjustment.*

Because the family's influence can help the child overcome learning disabilities and adjust socially or, unfortunately, exacerbate these problems, teachers need to get to know parents and encourage them to participate in the assessment, planning, and intervention process. Parents can be valuable resources to teachers; at the same time, parents need information and emotional support from teachers. Teachers must learn how to assess family systems and how to help parents with the often difficult and frustrating process of loving, caring for, teaching, and advocating for their child with learning disabilities.

# Families and Learning

*Although children enter this world with certain potentialities, it is how they learn in their "first school"—from their parents' modeling and encouragement—that will most affect their ultimate development.*

Parents are the child's first teachers and the home is the child's first school. Although children enter this world with certain potentialities, it is how they learn in their "first school"—from their parents' modeling and encouragement—that will most affect their ultimate cognitive development. The more teachers understand how the cognitive, academic, and social difficulties of the child with LD relate to the family environment, the more they can help plan effective family interventions aimed at increasing the child's learning and social opportunities.

## Cognitive and School Achievement

It is often during the preschool years that parents of a child with learning disabilities first note developmental delays in their child. They can do a great deal during this period to maximize opportunities for the child's cognitive and social-emotional growth. Many family factors play a role in this process:

- Parental value placed on achievement
- The quality of language modeled in the home
- Encouragement of independence and exploration beyond the home
- Intellectual interests and activities in the home
- Work habits modeled at home
- Involvement of both the mother and father
- Parental satisfaction with employment
- Quantity and quality of positive activities with adults
- Positive atmosphere in the home
- Avoidance of punishment
- Appropriate play materials
- Well-organized home (possessions, time management, etc.)
- Many books
- Behavior of siblings and secondary caregivers
- Traumatic events such as the death of a parent, divorce, birth of a sibling, moving

Also important are the parents' characteristics. Do they take initiative? Are they energetic? What are their teaching and learning styles? Do they stay with tasks until completed? How do they respond to their children emotionally and verbally? Do they have effective interpersonal skills? Are they involved with the school? The powerful influence of these and other factors in the family is evident in the intellectual, academic, and social-emotional declines observed in children who live with neglect, alcoholic or abusive parents, or divorce.

Perhaps the most telling data reflecting on the importance of the family come out of studies done with children raised in orphanages; these children were dramatically delayed in every area of development. But the home need not be as barren as an orphanage to produce children who fall behind. Parents who provide little auditory or kinesthetic stimulation to their infants; who are less responsive to their baby's cries for food or comfort; who don't talk to or spend time gazing at their babies often; who provide little variety in toys, social, and play activities; and who are not consistent in their responses can also produce children with significant delays. And these delays tend to persist through subsequent years.

*The home need not be as barren as an orphanage to produce children who fall behind.*

Fortunately, early intervention with children at high risk for school failure, through preschool programs such as Head Start and others, can produce gains in skills such as intellectual and perceptual-motor abilities, language, memory, and abstract reasoning. Lasting benefits frequently become apparent years later in higher school achievement, high school graduation rates, employment rates and earnings, and fewer retentions, special class placements, encounters with the law, and early pregnancies.

Home-based interventions also can be successful, even if begun as late as the sixth grade. The support, modeling, and information that parents receive from preschool educators' visits to their homes foster greater awareness of their child's abilities, commitment to becoming primary educators in their child's life, and confidence in their parenting skills. Mothers have increased their emotional and verbal responsiveness to their youngsters, use of appropriate play materials, and organization of the child's physical environment. Parents have been taught to enrich reading experiences by asking their child open-ended questions, expanding on the child's answers, suggesting alternative possibilities, and posing progressively more challenging questions. In one study, within one month of home-based intervention these parents' 2- and 3-year-olds had progressed 6 to 8 months more in verbal skills when compared to a control group. If parents continue to practice what they've learned, the children's gains continue.

*The support, modeling, and information parents receive from educators can foster greater awareness of their child's potential, commitment to becoming primary educators in their child's life, and confidence in their parenting skills.*

The earlier that either home-based or school-based intervention occur and the longer that they last, the greater are the benefits. Unfortunately, however, interventions don't happen often enough, especially for children from low-income families who are at high risk for developmental disabilities. While 56 percent of 3- to 5-year-olds currently attend preK programs, only 43 percent of low-income children participate compared to 73 percent of children from families with incomes over $50,000 per year.

*The earlier that either home- or school-based intervention occur and the longer that they last, the greater are the benefits.*

Clearly parents can be very successful change agents in their children's lives. That is why center-based preschool programs try to build a strong parent-involvement component, and why Public Law 99-457 provides for support services such as social skills training, parent consultation, and prevention activities with families of infants and preschoolers who show developmental delays. For school-aged children with identified disabilities, the Individuals with Disabilities Education Act (IDEA) of 1990 mandates involving parents in their children's program planning. Parents know their children best and, more than anyone else, have the sense of urgency and commitment to try to move mountains for their child.

In the following pages we explore the relationship of socioeconomic factors, parent-child interaction patterns, and physical surroundings to children's cognitive, academic, and social development. Socioeconomic factors forecast much more about the possibility of learning and adjustment problems than does a history of birth trauma. By far, though, the most powerful predictor is the nature of the parent-child relationship.

*Higher socioeconomic status homes can make up for poor schooling and the effects of birth trauma on school achievement, intelligence, and social skills.*

**Socioeconomic Status and Achievement.** Parents' socioeconomic status and educational levels are extremely predictive of children's developmental and academic outcomes, and even their educational and occupational success later in life. Just as the example in Research Box 13.1 illustrates how variables associated with higher socioeconomic status can make up for poor schooling, we have striking evidence that these factors can also overcome the impact of birth trauma on later school failure. One of the earliest of these studies followed every child born in 1955 on the island of Kauai, Hawaii. By 20 months of age, children who had experienced the most severe birth complications, but who grew up in upper-middle-income homes, nearly equaled the intelligence levels of children who did not experience birth trauma but were living in low-income homes. By age 10, the former children had achieved above average IQs. But the children from low-income homes who had experienced severe birth complications remained significantly delayed in intelligence, language, perceptual, reading, and social skills.

The Collaborative Perinatal Project, which followed about 50,000 children through age 8 whose mothers received prenatal care at 1 of 12 university medical centers, supports the Kauai findings. Again, learning disorders were more strongly related to socioeconomic status than to birth stress, and a greater proportion of children with LD came from lower-income families. Likewise, many studies show

RESEARCH BOX 13.1

## Home Teaching Helps Make Up for Poor Teaching

An interesting natural experiment regarding the value of encouraging whole word versus phonic approaches to reading occurred in Israel in the 1940s and 1950s (Feitelson, 1973). Because of the influence of a prominent educator, the whole-word, language experience approach was instituted in schools. Children were expected to infer the phonetic rules on their own. This method worked just fine for the largely middle-income European Jews living in Israel at the time. However, with mass immigration of lower-socioeconomic-status Jews from the Arab countries in the early 1950s, reading failure rates soared to 50 percent.

Investigation of the matter revealed that the whole-word method actually did not work well for most children. Children from European backgrounds nevertheless read well because their parents had taught them phonics at home. Because the families from Arab countries did not value education to the same extent and had lower parental educational levels, they did not supplement their children's schooling at home. Consequently, their children failed reading, and the failure of the whole-word teaching strategy finally became evident. The home press for education among the better-educated European Jews not only overcame their children's inadequate schooling but also masked the ineffectiveness of the teaching methods to which the children were being exposed.

that high-risk or malnourished adopted infants develop normally if they are raised in higher socioeconomic status families.

An unusual percentage of students with LD come from families in which educational stimulation is lacking and economic and family difficulties are pervasive. The 1999 National Household Education Survey found, for example, a significantly lower rate of literacy activities (reading, telling stories, arts and crafts) in the homes of preschoolers who lived in poverty, were ethnic minorities, whose mothers had no high school diploma or spoke a foreign language and limited English, and in which there was only one parent or no parents in the household. The national Early Childhood Longitudinal Study of the kindergarten class of 1998–99 found that children entered kindergarten with knowledge and skills that differed depending on their mother's educational levels. Gaps persisted or increased over the next two years, with children whose mothers had high school diplomas showing more rapid reading gains than children whose mothers had less education.

*An unusual percentage of students with LD come from families in which educational stimulation is lacking and economic and family difficulties are pervasive.*

Life can be harsh for the lower-income parent. Poorer nutrition, health care, overcrowded and ill-equipped homes, unsafe neighborhoods, stress, limited leisure activities, and emotional concerns such as low self-esteem take their toll. Many lower-income parents feel powerless on the job and unwittingly carry home the authoritarian model of their employers. They lack the higher education that would shift their focus to valuing the child's character development more than external behaviors such as obedience, neatness, and not interrupting. Studies find that lower-income parents tend to use authoritarian methods to enforce these external characteristics in their children. In contrast, higher-income parents tend to value internal characteristics such as curiosity, happiness, and self-control, which they encourage in their children through verbal praise, explanations, and mutual problem solving. These variations in child rearing certainly can set different educational paths.

*Life can be harsh for the lower-income parent. Even in the worst of conditions, however, there are families that produce resilient, eager, and thoughtful children.*

Some lower-income children must cope with far more than a lack of funds; they may live in urban "war zones" where fear for their safety, withdrawal, depression, and aggression sap motivation and concentration. But even in these conditions, there are families that rise to the occasion and produce resilient, eager, and thoughtful children. The more that a child's environment promotes intellectual stimulation, and feelings of personal value and control, the more likely that the child will be able to overcome the effects of a poor start in life.

*The more that a child's environment promotes intellectual stimulation, and feelings of personal value and control, the more likely that the child will be able to overcome the effects of a poor start in life.*

**Parent-Child Interaction and Achievement.** The attitudes and behavioral styles of many parents are very well suited to facilitating the development of their children with learning disabilities. However, there are certain parental interaction patterns that can greatly deter a child's intellectual, academic, and social-emotional development. Alcoholism, neglect and abuse, and parental absence for long periods of time are the most severe of these, but less obvious interaction difficulties can also have a negative effect.

The drawings in Figures 13.1 and 13.2 were created by two 8-year-olds, Eden and Rebecca. Both are of above average intelligence and come from middle-income homes. Every child in Eden's family has inherited a phonological processing disorder that leads to serious reading delays (Eden is Jeff's daughter, whom you met in Chapters 8 and 12). Eden's parents understand the nature of her disorder and are supportive and hopeful. Her family picture shows her father presenting

**Figure 13.1** Eden.

**Figure 13.2** Rebecca.

flowers to her pregnant mother, and a happy Eden playing ball with her sister. In her replies to incomplete sentence stems, Eden shows that she is satisfied with herself and her family and continues to maintain high academic and personal self-esteem: *Boys think I* am pretty; *My father never* shouts; *I know I can* read; *People are always* nice to me; *My family* is important to me; *At home* I like to play with my sisters; *Other children* play with me; *I wish I could stop* I don't know anything I wish I could stop.

Rebecca has the same kind and severity of learning disability as Eden, but her picture tells quite a different story. Rebecca's mother is a history professor, her father a physics professor, and her brother's academic career has been as stellar as might be expected in that family. Rebecca's parents cannot accept her differences. They are disappointed and angry, and they let her know it. Her pictures show it. While Eden's parents work cooperatively with the school to develop appropriate programming, Rebecca's parents demand this help. Their dissatisfaction with the school's slowness in responding to their requests has made Rebecca ambivalent about doing the work required by teachers whom her parents do not respect. In her drawing, the cats are more animated than the people. Although it is dinnertime, there is virtually no food on the table. Her parents and brother are together, but Rebecca is segregated, looking on from the doorway. She angrily scribbled over her self-portrait (which both girls drew on the upper left). In response to questions about her drawing, Rebecca stated: "I'm pretty stupid"; "I wish I could get out of the family"; "I'm sad because my mom and dad yell and scream"; "My brother's mean to me"; "I get spanked because I didn't change the cat's compost"; "My mom and dad wish for me to get away for real and in the picture"; "There's a blizzard outside but the sun's on the cat"; "My parents hate all of us."

***Parent-child interactions and stimulation in the home are far more powerful influences on child development than the effects of poverty or birth trauma.***

These two examples illustrate why parent-child interactions and stimulation in the home are far more powerful influences on child development than the effects of poverty or birth trauma. Compilation of data from many studies indicates that 60 percent of a child's achievement is related to family process variables and just 25 percent is predicted from health or socioeconomic status. Homes in which parents are rewarding and responsive, emphasize intellectual stimulation and emotional support, enjoy reading, talk a lot and use a varied vocabulary, have books, magazines, and learning supplies in the home, tell stories, are interested in the child's schooling and homework, discuss postsecondary educational plans, and use excursions (library, zoo) to augment their children's learning tend to produce children with the highest academic achievement and high school graduation rates, college attendance, success in independent living, and avoidance of drug use. Sadly, studies find that children not identified early on as at risk, but who show delays later on, often come from homes that provided less than optimal parent-child interactions and stimulation.

***School achievement and social adjustment are higher when children come from intimate and nurturing homes that instill a sense of competence, positive self-concept, stability, awareness, interest, and a mental set that values learning.***

School achievement and social adjustment are higher when children bring from home a sense of competence, positive self-concept, stability, awareness, interest, and a mental set that values learning. Southeast Asian "boat children" exemplify this point. Despite harrowing escapes from war-torn countries and relocation, their strong family support system, including the family's strong commitment to time spent on homework, has helped these children overcome nearly insurmountable odds and achieve well above their American-born peers. The positive effects of intimate, nurturing, and stimulating relationships between parents and their children are evident well into adolescence and beyond. Nick's story illustrates how important loving parents are in helping children get through the anger and frustration (and, in this case, misguided teaching) that often accompany a learning disability.

***Poor parent-child relationships affect all areas of a child's development.***

Poor parent-child relationships affect all areas of a child's development. Toddlers who grow up in noisy, confusing homes, for example, tend to develop more difficult temperaments—greater distractibility, mood shifts, withdrawal, intensity, activity level, and so forth. When a parent's style is to shift an engaged child's focus or to give many commands, requests, directions, and instructions, children have been slower to acquire vocabulary and other language skills. Parents who are constantly prohibiting with commands like "stop that!" or "don't . . . " rather than re-

## Nick

*This fifth grader expresses the importance of loving parents supporting him through the anger and frustration that accompanies his LD.*

*Nick's mother shares the following introduction to Nick's journal entry:*
Nick was in the fifth grade at the time of this journal entry, in complete despair over his inability to make any sense out of the class he was in. The teacher Nick had for the mainstreamed portion of his school day seemed certain she could handle Nick's slow work pace and misunderstanding of class assignments by making him sit on a bench during recesses. He didn't tell me about the benchings at first, apparently quite sad that the year was beginning so badly. That year remains in his memory as one of his worst, and he still shakes his head when he thinks of that teacher. Nick has shown us an incredible spirit in the face of many not so happy experiences and I tip my hat to him for his incredible determination.

*Nick's Journal Entry*
The hardest thing I ever had to do is get a good grade on my vocabulary test. Because I have a hard time remembering things. I study and study and I can't get it. I try hard but I need *more time.* My mom has been a big help. Now I have to do a poem. I can't do it see I told you now I have to sit on the bench. I wish I could slap myself and get rid of my learning problems, but Mrs. Saunders doesn't understand. My mom and my dad will talk to her and my dad has been a big help too. I've been on the bench for two weeks. This is getting me really mad. My friend understands why doesn't Mrs. Saunders understand. I hope I pass fifth grade. I'm really scared. Somebody help me. Alls Mrs. Saunders does is putting people on the bench. She yells at everybody. Now Matt is dead. I know Matt tried. He didn't mean to. I'm not having very much fun this year. I hate myself. Life isn't fair. I'm not happy. But when I'm around my dad he makes me feel really good. I love him very very much. He is the best dad in the world. I feel like I'm in jail and I will never get out. I want to tell her what I feel like but she will yell at me. I'm to get up my guts and tell her. I'm really sad with a capital S. I'm going to be dead again in about 3 seconds. I'm at the library now. Maybe I will talk to Mrs. Saunders.

Mom I hope you read this I love you mom and Dad. Now I'm going to study hall.

*Source:* Reprinted by permission of Rita and Nick Ter Sarkissoff.

sponding to the child's attempts at conversation or questions by repeating, paraphrasing, and expanding their child's statements, have children with lower IQs and language development. Likewise, parents who are less involved with their children; who communicate lower expectations; who neither monitor how constructively children spend their time nor set clear and consistent limits; and who are least accepting, nurturing, encouraging, involved with the school, and emotionally responsive to the child's needs have children with the most academic difficulties. An unusual percentage of children with LD come from homes that are unstable, controlling, negative, and that experience an unexpected number of tragedies such as job loss, serious illness, or death.

*An unusual percentage of children with LD come from homes that are unstable, controlling, and negative.*

In the Collaborative Perinatal Project, the 8-month-olds most likely to be identified as learning disabled or hyperactive seven years later had mothers who spoke harshly or negatively to their babies; made more critical comments about their babies; handled them in a remote, impersonal, rough, and clumsy manner; didn't help engage their babies' attention in the test materials; were slow to recognize and respond to their babies' needs for comfort, food, or a clean diaper; were indifferent to what or how their children were doing with the test materials; and neglected their children's physical needs (inadequately dressed, body odor, sores, rashes, didn't bring clean diapers).

On the other hand, there are parents at the other extreme. They are overly anxious and too involved with and understanding of their child's problems. The result ends up being the same. Their expectations aren't high enough, and they don't push their children to work to the best of their ability.

Given the strong relationship between language development and academic readiness, language modeling is a critical part of the parent-child relationship. This kind of modeling occurs when parents repeat a word the child has uttered—*ball*, for example—and expand it by saying "*Yes, that's a ball,*" or use it in a question, "*Did you find a ball?*" Conversations at home should be children's best source of linguistic and cognitive enrichment because the family's shared experiences and values can be explored in context and with a deeper personal meaning than interchanges with strange teachers who don't know the child's background experiences. Yet some mothers of language-impaired and hyperactive children may not be optimal language models because they tend to use lower-level language with their children—language that won't help their children's language development. One study found that professional mothers, regardless of ethnicity, spoke on average 2,100 words an hour to their 3-year-olds. In contrast, the child born to a lower-income parent heard 1,200 words an hour and mothers on welfare spoke 600 words an hour. Professional mothers used more different words, asked more questions, and repeated or expanded on the child's comments more often. Professional parents interacted with their children on average 42 minutes per hour, in contrast to the welfare family's 7 minutes per hour. The investigators in this study calculated the average number of words per year spoken to children in professional families to be 45 million. This contrasts with 26 million words in working class families and 3 million words in welfare families. Differences in the amount of parental interaction with their children add up quickly. The higher language and intellectual competencies of the children of professional mothers have to be related in part to this early language stimulation.

*Given the strong relationship between language development and academic readiness, language modeling is a critical part of the parent-child relationship.*

*Some mothers of language-impaired and hyperactive children tend to use lower-level language with their children —language that won't help their children's language development.*

Distinctive parent-child interaction patterns are already evident shortly after birth in the synchrony between the newborn's movements and the parents' reactions. The following example describes how the affective communications of mothers and their infants influence one another's emotional experiences and behavior:

> Imagine two infant-mother pairs playing the game peek-a-boo. In the first, the infant abruptly turns away from his mother as the game reaches its "peak" of intensity and begins to suck his thumb and stare into space with a dull facial expression. The mother stops playing and sits back watching her infant. After a few seconds the infant turns back to her with an interested and inviting expression. The mother moves closer, smiles, and says in a high-pitched, exaggerated voice, "Oh, now you're back!" He smiles in response and vocalizes. As they finish crowing together, the infant reinserts his thumb and looks away. The mother again waits. After a few seconds the infant turns back to her, and they greet each other with big smiles.
>
> Imagine a second similar situation except that after this infant turns away, she does not look back at her mother. The mother waits but then leans over into the infant's line of vision while clicking her tongue to attract her attention. The infant, however, ignores the mother and continues to look away. Undaunted, the mother persists and moves her head closer to the infant. The infant grimaces and fusses while she pushes at the mother's face. Within seconds she turns even further away from her mother and continues to suck on her thumb. (Tronick, 1989, p. 112)

Babies are clearly active, not passive, in signaling what they need from the environment. The first child' s mother, in tune with her infant's signals, provides a more positive, less stressful environment. The second mother disregards her baby's message—"Please stay away; I'm overaroused; I need time to quiet down and regulate my emotional state." Thus their interactions are likely to be more negative, with the baby disengaging herself from her mother.

Parents are responsible to turn babies' negative states into positive states and promote positive communication. Consider this example:

> The six-month-old infant stretches his hands out toward the object [which is just out of reach]. Because he cannot get hold of it, he becomes angry and distressed. He looks away for a moment and sucks on his thumb. Calmer, he looks back at the object and reaches for it once more. But this attempt fails too, and he gets angry again. The caretaker watches for a moment, then soothingly talks to him. The infant calms down and with a facial expression of interest gazes at the object and makes another attempt to reach for it. The caretaker brings the object just within the infant's reach. The infant successfully grasps the object, explores it, and smiles. . . . the caretaker is responsible for the reparation of the infant's failure into success and the simultaneous transformation of his negative emotion into a positive emotion. (Tronick, 1989, p. 113)

***Parents are guided by their baby's emotional state, and vice versa. When parents are depressed, intrusive, and don't turn infants' negative into positive moods, babies disengage, reduce interaction with objects and people, and compromise their cognitive development.***

Just as parents are guided by their baby's emotional state, infants use their parents' emotions to guide their own actions. It's not uncommon for babies to check out their parent's expression before exploring a new object or room—if the parent looks encouraging, the child goes ahead. If the parent looks fearful, the child doesn't venture forth. If the baby senses that the caretaker is continually depressed, intrusive, or has mistimed interactions, he or she is likely to reciprocate with negative moods. This infant gets little guidance on how to face stress and repair his or her negative states. The baby also doesn't learn to trust the parent's care taking, nor does he or she develop a sense of self as being effective, capable of positive interactions, and capable of turning negative into positive states. Instead, the infant regulates negative states by turning away, escaping, or "tuning out." The more comfortable that the baby finds disengagement, the more that it becomes a regular way of functioning. And as the baby reduces interactions with objects and people, his or her cognitive development can be compromised.

*The child learns from the caretaker a style of approach or withdrawal, and anticipation of pleasure or stress from new situations, which is likely to continue throughout childhood and into adulthood. The more securely attached the child is to the parent or caretaker, even if life is unstable, the better the outcome.*

The child learns from the caretaker a style of approach or withdrawal, and anticipation of pleasure or stress from new situations, which is likely to continue throughout childhood and even into adulthood. When parents are attentive, warm, stimulating, flexible, supportive, accepting, foster competence and self-esteem, have rules and structure in the home, engender trust, make opportunities available at major life transitions, and actively engage and support their children's problem solving, children have higher intellectual and academic competencies. These children feel safe exploring the wider world because they have their parents to count on as a stable emotional base. They become friendlier, more enthusiastic, and more attractive playmates. And later on they are likely to be responsible employees, have stable marriages, and be caring parents themselves. The more securely attached the child is to a parent or other caregiver, even if the child leads an unstable life, the more self-reliant, socially successful, academically competent, and confident the child is likely to grow up to be.

*Parent-child interaction is a two-way process. Characteristics of the child can hamper the relationship, too.*

It is important to remember that parent-child interaction is a two-way process. Characteristics of the child can hamper the relationship, too. If a child with a learning disability has a difficult or "slow to warm up" temperament, this makes the parent's responsibility more difficult. Central nervous system damage can disrupt the body movements that convey early nonverbal communication between children and their parents; this in turn can reduce parental responsiveness that stimulates cognitive and social development. Factors such as low birth weight, prematurity, serious neonatal illness and the resulting parent-infant separation, plus developmental delays and difficulty controlling behavior can predispose such a child to be the target of abuse or neglect in troubled families. In one study of infants who were born prematurely or were very ill at birth, their abnormal reactions to touch and other stimulation, coupled with their mothers' anxiety, shock, guilt, and powerlessness, led mothers to touch, smile at, look at, speak to, and hold their babies close less often than did parents of healthy newborns.

Because good parenting can do much to make up for a poor start in life or the realities of poverty, teachers must be sensitive to parents' circumstances, and, when appropriate, provide them with information on how to interact with their children more productively. That may be as simple as suggesting talking with their small children more, using different words, or taking turns in play. It might be recommended that parents regularly read and discuss stories with their children, or discuss future education plans with their teenagers, which is associated with lower dropout rates.

*If parents are not ready or able to provide the necessary supports, then children need other people in their lives who can provide nurturance and positive modeling.*

If parents are not ready or able to provide the necessary supports, then children need other people in their lives who can give positive attention—especially in times of crisis—provide nurturance, be positive role models, and establish close bonds. This could be a friend, relative, neighbor, or favorite teacher, or perhaps an acquaintance from church, the YMCA, 4-H, Big Brothers/Big Sisters, or other extracurricular activities. These supports help children in the most high-risk circumstances to be resilient enough to succeed academically and grow into fine young adults. The "Lifeguard" story illustrates how sometimes these supports come from the most unexpected sources.

## The "Lifeguard" Who Cared

*Emotional support for students with LD sometimes comes from the most unexpected sources.*

A child with a learning disability who also comes from a broken home, has attended three schools in his first four years of formal education, and somehow missed attending kindergarten may likely walk into his newest school with feelings of anger and lack of trust of both his fourth grade peers and school staff.

John is the student. In a small group setting, when he read orally, he would mimic the voice of a sassy 4-year old; when asked to complete a written task, his work was not legible; when contributing to an oral discussion, his answers were not appropriate. Finally, approximately six weeks after the school year began, John expressed his feelings of anger, sadness and fear through tears. The wall had finally been broken and there was a break through—a tiny twinkle at the end of the tunnel.

John described the playground rules as stupid, his peers as aggressive, and his new neighborhood without any friends. John said the classroom assignments were too difficult, and in general, life was rotten. When asked what he would like to do, he stated he wanted to build a go-cart assisted by the "lifeguard" who works in front of the school. The "lifeguard" happened to be the school crossing guard. Not only did he assist the students with pedestrian safety and serve as the "welcome wagon" to all entering the school, but Howard, the crossing guard, also displayed his handmade wooden toys on the school sidewalk.

Through several brief conversations and a letter to John's mother, arrangements were made for John to spend 30 to 45 minutes every Friday afternoon in the resource classroom with the school crossing guard, Howard. Howard was aware of John's needs and interests and gave John the opportunity to design something to be constructed out of wood. John chose a helicopter, drew a picture, and after the first session, Howard returned with the wooden pieces cut for a helicopter. The next five to six Fridays were spent sanding, hammering, and painting.

Of course, the final product, an army-green helicopter, went home with one happy boy. More importantly and throughout the weeks when John and Howard were a team, John's attitude changed in everything he did from reading to writing to oral responses to less aggression on the playground. The relationship John developed with Howard was not only a nurturing one for John, but served as a grandfather-grandson relationship for Howard. Their weekly session was not contingent upon anything, which eliminated any pressure for John, and also gave him a feeling of control. Howard was more than willing to give a little of his time each week and walked out of the resource room with a grin of satisfaction just as big as John's smile of success and security.

*Source:* Reprinted by permission of Ellen Peterson.

**Physical Surroundings and Achievement.** Jenkins and Bowen put forth a very simple but true formula for creating vocabulary- and book-rich environments for children: *lap method,* where "children sit in our laps and we talk and read and play games together" (1994, p. 37). Clearly books, magazines, learning supplies, community exposure (e.g., library, zoo, plays) and many more aspects of children's physical learning environments are related to school success. A survey of nearly 500 high school seniors with LD revealed that they had fewer and less adequate facilities for study and intellectual stimulation than their peers, and their parents were less interested in their schooling and personal lives.

Television is one part of a child's physical world that has received a great deal of attention, and with good reason. Estimates of children's average viewing time range from 11 to 28 hours a week. One nationwide study of fourth and eighth graders reported that over 40 percent watch 3 or more hours of television each day. That amounts to 6 solid days of waking hours per month, or 2 months per year. (At this rate, the child will have lost 10 years of waking hours to TV by the time he is 65!) Children spend more time watching television than any other activity except sleeping. Children from African American, less educated, or lower-income families rely most heavily on television for education, entertainment, aesthetics, and knowledge of the world. Yet commercial television offers only about 3 hours a week of educational programming geared toward children, as required by the Children's Television Act of 1997. This contrasts with public television's 27 hours a week of such programming. Cable television has added some fine children's programs, yet these often are financially inaccessible to low-income families. Experts judge that 75 percent of programming for preschoolers is of high quality in terms of learning and prosocial objectives, but only a quarter to a third of programming geared toward elementary children and teens are high in quality.

***Children spend more time watching TV (about 3 hours per day) than any other activity except sleeping.***

What is the effect of all this television viewing? Children do learn from high quality academically focused programming, and programming that promotes prosocial behaviors such as respect for others, friendliness, kindness, and sharing. But the lessons learned seem to be short-lived and not greatly generalized. The effects are greater when adults explicitly reteach and elaborate verbally on the content and behaviors modeled in the programs. Essentially, when parents use educational TV as a convenient baby-sitter, the children are unlikely to learn much at all. For educational programming to be effective, parents must watch with their children, discuss the TV content, and remind their children to apply these lessons in relevant situations.

***For educational TV to be effective, parents must watch with their children, discuss the content, and remind their children to apply these lessons in relevant situations.***

Most sobering is the large body of research finding that TV does a much better job of teaching violence than teaching academic or prosocial skills. There is a small but definite causal effect between television violence and children's aggressive behavior, acceptance of violence as a way to solve problems, reduced empathy with the suffering of others, reduced inclination to help victims of actual violence, and more fearfulness of the world. Children come to believe that the world is far more violent than is actually the case. Indeed, if the world were as violent as depicted on TV, many of us would hesitate to venture out our doors or to stroll on the streets.

***There is a small but definite causal effect between television violence and children's aggressive behavior, acceptance of violence as a way to solve problems, reduced empathy with the suffering of others, reduced inclination to help victims of actual violence, and more fearfulness of the world.***

About 60 percent of TV programs contain violence, and in about three-quarters of these there is no remorse, criticism, or punishment for the violence. On

TV, 55 percent of the victims show no pain or suffering, and another 36 percent experience unrealistically low levels of harm. Despite public outcries, TV programs continue to portray violence as "heroic"—40 percent of violent incidents are initiated by characters meant to be attractive role models for children. A case in point are cartoon "good-guys," who are often very violent, the violence is portrayed as justified, they show no remorse, and the victims suffer minimally if at all—a very poor message for children to be fed day in and out. Of violent scenes on TV, 40 percent are portrayed as humorous, antiviolence themes are rare, and only 15 percent of violent programs portray the long-term consequences of the violence to family, friends, and the community. Basically, children are taught that violence and killing are acceptable ways to vent frustration and anger and handle problems, that victims aren't harmed by these acts, that remorse is unnecessary, and that there may be no penalty for these actions.

***Children are taught by TV that violence and killing are acceptable ways to vent frustration and anger and handle problems, that victims aren't harmed by these acts, that remorse is unnecessary, and that there may be no penalty for these actions.***

The more true to life that children believe television aggression is, and the more that they identify with TV characters, the more they are likely to lower their inhibitions and give in to aggression. Young children accept much of what they see on TV as realistic, and do not distinguish fantasy from reality. Being too young to fully grasp the relationship between aggressive acts and the motives behind them, they may assume that a disobedient attitude and verbal or physical attacks are acceptable. In one study, the more violent were the TV programs watched at age 8, the more aggressive the youngsters were at age 19, the more serious the crimes for which they were convicted at age 30, and the more harshly they punished their own children.

By the time the average American child has graduated from elementary school, he has witnessed over 8,000 murders and over 100,000 other acts of violence on television, such as assault and rape. It is estimated that if a teenager watches just 9 hours of TV in a week, she'll be exposed to 27 sexual acts—1,400 per year. Not surprisingly, teenagers report that their greatest pressure to become sexually active comes from TV.

***Even one hour of TV a day can mean lower achievement and increased anxiety and depression.***

It is now apparent that even one hour of television a day can mean lower academic achievement. As viewing time increases, verbal fluency, reading fluency, and imaginativeness decrease; there is an increase in anxiety, depression, sleep disturbances, fear, and ethnic- and sex-stereotyped attitudes.

Despite efforts to more accurately represent diverse family types and roles, such as single-parent families and women and minorities in professional positions, many television programs continue to imply that one must be male, white, young, or beautiful to be acceptable. The predominant theme remains one of men seeing women as sexual objects, and women not setting limits on male advances. Often sexual harassment is portrayed as humorous, with little harm done. Research shows that TV stereotypes contribute to prejudice regarding the social contributions of ethnic minorities, females, and members of low socioeconomic groups. This prevents these groups from seeing new role possibilities for themselves, and society from accepting these as goals. Moreover, classic animated movies that children are encouraged to watch as part of American folklore present archaic views of gender roles, with heavy doses of fair maidens waiting for handsome princes to rescue them—but only if they are beautiful *(Snow White, Cinderella)*; powerful women being wicked (the queen in *Snow White*, Ursula in *The Little Mermaid)*; men needing women to tame them *(Lady and the Tramp)*; and women's independence requiring paternal approval (*The Little Mermaid*). Parents need to mediate children's watching of these classics by pointing out that these movies were made a long time ago, when men's and women's roles were much different than they are today. Parental mediation also helps moderate the moral judgments teenagers learn from exposure to TV violence and the greater frequency of premarital than marital sex scenes on TV.

***Parents need to mediate their children's TV watching in order to turn around the role definitions, stereotypes, and poor moral judgments they are learning.***

Although the research on children and the media has not focused specifically on the learning disabled, the results are troubling and suggest that the choices of these children in particular must be monitored carefully. Children with LD have a hard enough time already, without risking picking up additional attitude and behavior problems. Parents need to be encouraged to limit the number of hours their children watch TV, ban some programs, discuss violent and stereotypical episodes, and encourage shows that teach valuable lessons depicting cooperative and nonstereotypical behavior—children should model these attitudes and behavior. Shows that are proven to teach language, pre-reading, and math skills (such as *Sesame Street*) or prosocial reasoning such as helping, cooperation, obeying rules, task persistence, and delaying gratification (e.g., *Barney and Friends, Blue's Clues, Mister Rogers's Neighborhood*) are to be encouraged. Parents also need to be aware that rapid-fire presentation formats enhance a child's arousal and attention, but if the information load is too high then the child's attention capacities become overburdened. It seems that the frequent attention shifts in high paced programs can reduce the processing of content when this material is too much or too hard for the child to automatically comprehend.

To mitigate the negative effects of TV viewing, school curricula have been developed to demystify what students are seeing. They describe how shows are produced (the ship sinking in the storm is actually a toy boat in a washtub), distinguish between fantasy and reality (if a car were dropped on a "live" cartoon character, the character would die, not "bounce back"), examine special effects to show, for example, that violence isn't really happening, and they explore the consequences of TV behavior if it were real (jail, death penalty). These curricula also help children understand the real motives behind television advertising. Any parent will testify to the "I want" family discord stemming from children viewing more than 40,000 TV ads per year, in addition to product promotions embedded in program content. Children don't recognize the persuasive intent of TV advertising until about 8 years old, and even then don't absorb the "disclaimer language" such as "assembly required," "doll not included." Given their maturational lags, it is likely to take children with LD even longer to become savvy consumers of commercial advertising.

***To mitigate the negative effects of TV viewing, school curricula have been developed to demystify what students are seeing.***

Finally, we can't forget about the myriad other ways in which the media bombard children and teach lessons we don't want them to learn. Cigarette and alcohol advertising, for example, is a significant factor in adolescents' use of these substances. One half of ads are sexually suggestive. Video and computer games involve the child actively in violent simulations. Today's music and music videos increasingly communicate themes that are sexually explicit, violent, racist, and glorifying of drugs and alcohol. By fifth and sixth grade, listening to popular music begins to surpass TV as the most important of media to children. Research shows that the 3 to 4 hours of daily exposure to today's popular music increases children's acceptance of violence and defiant behavior, sex stereotypes, and anti-establishment attitudes.

***Exposure to today's popular music increases children's acceptance of violence and defiant behavior, sex stereotypes, and anti-establishment attitudes.***

Moreover, the Internet has over 1,400 racist, anti-Semitic, and other hate sites, in addition to websites specializing in police photos and morgue shots. About 25 percent of American teenagers have visited websites promoting information by hate groups. Nearly half have visited sites that are X-rated or include sexual content. Some 15 percent of teens have seen websites that teach how to build bombs or buy a gun. While only 13 percent of teens put a great deal of trust in information received from the Internet, this is less likely to be the case for those with LD. Given the myriad "lessons" coming at today's children daily, the parental role as primary teacher, model, monitor, discussant, and encourager of appropriate media choices is more important than ever.

## Social Development

*Although not every student with LD has social problems, they nevertheless are more prevalent among this group. Intervention involves attending to the environmental as well as student aspects of the problem because social difficulties never exist in a vacuum.*

Although not every student with a learning disability has problems with parents, teachers, or peers, social problems nevertheless are more prevalent among this group than among students having no academic difficulties. Intervention requires attending to the environmental as well as student aspects of the problem because social difficulties never exist in a vacuum.

**Normal Patterns of Prosocial Development.** In order for children to behave in a socially acceptable manner, they must be able to judge what is right and wrong. As with other areas of development, moral judgments change with age.

Piaget noted that children less than age 7 or 8 often don't understand why something is right or wrong; rather, they accept an external source such as a parent or older child as an authority. Thus they tend to be very rigid about interpreting rules. If David takes April's toy, he is wrong because adults say so. The fact that he's taking the toy out of retaliation for April's taking his toy isn't considered. Likewise, a lie is a lie, whether or not it was told in an attempt to spare someone's feelings. Children at this age are concrete in judging the magnitude of a misdeed. If you accidentally drop a tray of six glasses and they break, this is deserving of a more severe punishment than if you dropped and broke just one glass. And children base their judgments of a lie on how far it departs from the truth. It's worse to say you saw a cow in the street when it really was a dog, than pretending to have better grades than you do in school.

*Children less than age 7 or 8 often don't understand why something is right or wrong; rather, they accept an external source such as a parent or older child as an authority.*

In children over age 8, Piaget noted a gradual shift toward conforming to the behavioral rules of the group and greater self-reliance on following these rules. The parent is no longer considered the final authority. Motives are sometimes considered, and sometimes not.

By age 11 or 12, the child begins to understand that rules come from mutual consent and that rules make life easier for people. Lying begins to be regarded as wrong because if everyone told lies there could be little trust—how could families, classrooms, and the world operate if people couldn't be believed? The 12-year-old connects the magnitude of punishments to the perpetrator's motives and justification. In late adolescence, young people begin to fully understand that rules preserve society and that we are obliged to follow them for that reason. From Kohlberg's research with adults, we have learned that a small percentage eventually come to recognize that not all laws are just, and will act to change these laws to better society.

*The 12-year-old understands the importance of social rules and connects the magnitude of punishments to the perpetrator's motives and justification.*

This developmental progression in moral reasoning is extremely important for teachers and parents to understand. An understanding of a child's level of moral reasoning helps us deal with behavioral infractions "at their level" and encourages growth in their social maturity.

*An understanding of a child's level of moral reasoning helps us deal with behavioral infractions "at their level" and encourages growth in their social maturity.*

**Prosocial Development and the Student with Learning Disabilities.** Just as students with LD are academically delayed, their ability to make social judgments also may be like that of younger children. A 9-year-old, for example, may still rely heavily on authority figures for cues about how to act. This makes it almost impossible to function in school where numerous situations arise that demand immediate decisions and actions, on many of which the child's parents or teachers have never made a ruling.

Consider the dilemma of Oliver, a 10-year-old impulsive child who must decide whether telling a lie to avoid hurting someone is more correct than telling the truth. He has trouble focusing on several aspects of the problem at once and delaying a response until alternatives and consequences have been considered. Among other things, Oliver must look at the situation from another's perspective, evaluate verbal and nonverbal cues, and choose which words to use, all skills with which students who are learning disabled have trouble. That Oliver might make the wrong decision and get negative feedback is understandable.

Teachers need to understand the students' stage of moral reasoning and help them progress to higher moral reasoning levels. Their responses to misbehavior must fit the children's moral reasoning levels, as in simply "stating the rule" to Eron who is too aggressive in his bear hugs, or to Shira who overstays her welcome with friends because of her excessive teasing and roughhousing. Both children are old enough to know better, but reasoning with them about the other children's perspective would not have worked. For young children, behavior modification techniques and simply stating what is right and wrong work well. These children choose their behaviors based on adults' rules and stated consequences. Older elementary school children, very aware of social obligations to their groups, benefit from explicit reminders about these expectations and from instruction to model their peers' behavior. Older youngsters, who recognize the benefits of society's laws, may respond to negotiated agreements, such as not talking out in class, or setting goals for grades and contracting for positive consequences (e.g., more free time) if they live up to their end of the agreement.

*For young children, behavior modification techniques and simply stating what is right and wrong work well.*

Parents are powerful influences on their children's moral reasoning and social development. Research has found that those children who are more competent socially with their peers are the ones who experience more attachment and emotional security in their homes, and less family dysfunction. Children learn from their parents through identification (wanting to be like them), modeling (imitating them), and direct training through parental teaching and discipline.

*Older elementary school children, very aware of social obligations to their groups, benefit from explicit reminders about these expectations and from instruction to model their peers' behavior. Adolescents begin to understand that rules preserve society, and therefore respond to negotiation and contracting.*

***Identification and Modeling.*** Parents are high-status people in their children's lives, and children learn by simply observing what their parents do. If a father is always willing to lend a helping hand in the neighborhood, his son sees this model and, wanting to be like dad, is helpful to younger children. A daughter may be tempted to lie, but resists because she knows her parents would be disappointed in her if she did so. These processes of identification and modeling are fostered by parents' warmth and support, which in turn encourage prosocial traits in their children such as kindness, honesty, generosity, obedience to the rules, resistance to cheating and lying, and consideration of the rights and welfare of others.

*Parents must draw their children's attention to modeled behavior, help them rehearse and apply the behavior, and give incentives for adopting the behavior.*

Bandura's classic modeling studies showed that parents need to do more than model good behaviors. They must first of all begin with positive attitudes toward their children, and then draw the children's attention to the modeled behavior, help them remember through rehearsal, encourage them to practice the behavior, and give incentives for adopting the behavior. Most parents do this unconsciously and inconspicuously. But many children with LD don't pick up on these messages. Therefore, parents have to be far more intentional about these teachings. To complicate matters, their children often don't understand the emotions the model is expressing and have difficulty attending to, interpreting, and retaining the modeled behavior and verbal explanations. Consequently, parents may need to explain more, highlight important aspects, help the child verbally rehearse and role-play, and provide support when information-processing or motivational problems present obstacles.

*Many children with LD come from homes where warm and supportive modeling of prosocial behaviors and positive expectations are in short supply.*

Unfortunately, many children with LD come from homes where warm and supportive modeling of prosocial behaviors is in short supply. Their family systems can be more chaotic, disturbed, less structured, less emotionally stable, less cohesive, more rigid, and more disengaged than other families. Parents often react more negatively to their children with learning disabilities, are more harsh and remote, communicate lower expectations, and provide less affection and care giving. More affection is shown to the sibling who has higher verbal ability, perseveres in school tasks, and is less worrisome. Parents may view the successes of the child with LD less positively (caused by luck rather than ability) and the failures more negatively (caused by inability rather than bad luck) than do parents of nondisabled children. Parents frequently expect less of their children with LD than the children expect of themselves.

An additional difficulty for children with LD is that some parents may themselves be poor models. Many evaluate their own social skills as poorly as they do their children's. Because learning disorders often show a hereditary pattern, children and parents can share similar cognitive problems and inappropriate behavioral styles. Therefore, parents may need to evaluate and modify their own behavior before being able to be of maximum help to their children.

*Direct Training.* Direct training, through teaching and discipline, is another way in which parents can influence their children's attitudes and behaviors. Clear expectations offer a consistent family structure that has a stabilizing influence on children's development. Threats of punishment or power plays are less effective than explanations about why certain behaviors are better than others, and positively reinforcing these behaviors.

Baumrind's classic research on child-rearing practices among middle-income parents identified three general patterns: authoritative, authoritarian, and permissive. *Authoritative parents* were controlling and demanding. They had high demands for obedience, academic achievement, and sharing household tasks. At the same time, they were warm, open to discussion and negotiation with their children about why they didn't want to comply, and responded positively to their children's independent behavior. *Authoritarian parents* were more punitive and rejecting. They, too, had high standards for behavior, but these were absolute. Power, unaccompanied by reasoning and communication, was used to compel compliance. They valued obedience for its own sake and there was little give-and-take with their children. By contrast, *permissive parents* were very accepting of all their children's impulses and didn't enforce rules or standards for behavior and achievement.

*Authoritative parents tend to produce children who are socially responsible, independent, friendly to peers, cooperative, achievement oriented, dominant, and purposeful.*

Authoritative parents tended to produce children who were socially responsible, independent, friendly to peers, cooperative, achievement-oriented, dominant, and purposeful. In contrast, children of authoritarian parents tended to be discontent, withdrawn, and distrustful. Permissive parents raised children who were the least self-reliant, self-controlled, and explorative.

*Children of authoritarian parents tend to be discontent, withdrawn, and distrustful. Permissive parents raise children who are the least self-reliant, self-controlled, and explorative.*

Baumrind identified several parent practices and attitudes that help develop children whose behavior is socially responsible, assertive, cooperative, purposeful, confident, altruistic, creative, cognitively challenging, and independent:

1. Modeling socially responsible and self-assertive behavior.
2. Firmly enforcing policies that reward socially responsible behavior and punish deviant behavior, and that are accompanied by explanations consistent with the parents' principles.
3. Accepting, but not overprotective or passive, parental attitudes; approval is contingent on the child's behavior.
4. High demands for achievement and conformity with parental policies, accompanied by openness to the child's rationale and encouragement of independent judgment.
5. Provision of a complex, stimulating environment that offers challenge and excitement as well as security.

Many of Baumrind's authoritative parents' behaviors correlated with greater autonomy in their youngsters: parents being accepting, empathic, supportive, self-aware, curious, appreciative of individual's differences yet building connectedness within the family, and using family discussions to solve problems. Parents who tell children *why,* not just *what,* to do help give children a rationale for the future when they face not only a similar situation but also new problems.

*Authoritative parents, who tell children* why, *not just* what, *help moderate peer influence and give children a rationale for decision making when faced with new problems.*

Authoritative parenting helps to moderate peer influence in that these children are more strongly influenced by high-achieving friends and less influenced by drug-using friends. These parents directly influence their adolescents' friendships through such means as giving advice on which teenagers to steer clear of, inviting over prosocial friends, and encouraging activities that draw socially appropriate peers. The authoritative parent knows to "pick the battles" carefully, overlooking harping on the child's sloppy dress habits, for example, in favor of promoting the value of studying. These teenagers have lower drug use than do teenagers whose parents use lower levels or too controlling levels of management.

Research shows that overprotective parents tend to delay their children's development. Mothers in the Collaborative Perinatal Project who were overdemonstrative to their 8-month-old infants—frequently fondling and caressing them, using terms of endearment, talking only about their child's good qualities while glossing over or explaining away less desirable behaviors—seven years later more often had children who had learning difficulties or were hyperactive.

Keeping a balanced view is important in order to know when to step in and help a child, and when to encourage independence from the sidelines. In Robynn's story, Robynn's mother describes how her daughter let her know that she had to begin letting go.

A great deal of the child's ability to identify, model, and learn from his or her parents depends on the interaction of the child's unique temperament with that of family members. Unfortunately, at times the disorganization of children with LD and their families becomes a vicious cycle; the child's behavior causes disruption in the family, which in turn is increasingly unable to provide the structure, model, and discipline the child needs.

***A good fit between parent and child can go a long way toward modifying a child's hard-to-live-with temperament; a poor fit can make a difficult situation much worse, or create a difficult situation when the child's temperament is just fine.***

***Parent-Child Temperament Match.*** Although many children are born with difficult temperaments, a good fit between parent and child can go a long way toward modifying a child's hard-to-live-with temperament. Conversely, a poor fit can make a difficult situation much worse, or create a difficult situation when the child's temperament is just fine. For example, when parents expect concentration for long periods of time, they put undue stress on a distractible child. When parents of a highly active child insist that he or she sit still all through dinner, rather than being permitted to help serve and clear the table, they make life harder for everyone. When parents abruptly interrupt a goal-directed, persistent child in the midst of a project to engage in a family activity, that child will be in no mood to be cooperative or pleasant. When parents don't value the hard work of a very capable child, they diminish

## Robynn

*A teenager tells her mother that it's time to let go.*

Although students with learning disabilities don't always say or do things the way others do, they certainly get their points across.

My teenage daughter was diagnosed as learning disabled when she was three years old. Our suspicions were first aroused by her lack of verbal expression. Of course, this turned out to be just a symptom of a far greater problem.

Verbal aptitude has always eluded Robynn. She speaks slowly and often the right words just don't come. But when she wants to get a point across, she figures out which words to put together.

Being an overprotective mother, I have always monitored Robynn's comings and goings. In trying to protect her from the world, I have often hovered too long over her.

One day she had had enough. She wanted to tell me that she wanted some more independence, that I was smothering her with my protective arms. For lack of those words, she said, "You make me feel like I'm still inside of you." I understood exactly what she was feeling. She couldn't have said it better.

*Source:* Reprinted by permission of Irene Hershkowitz.

his or her incentive to achieve. And when parents expect unreasonable academic achievement of a child with LD, they make a tough situation even worse.

One expert has likened a child's temperament to the fault lines that can lead to earthquakes. Environmental events, particularly parenting styles, are the strain. And just as earthquakes result from the match between faults and strains, so behavior difficulties can arise from a mismatch between certain child temperaments and certain styles of parenting. Norman's story is a good illustration of such a mismatch. His temperament and life experiences are like those frequently associated with children with learning disabilities. When these children grow up in homes that are hostile or critical, and parental expectations are be-

## Norman

*This 17-year-old's impatient and hypercritical father created a self-fulfilling prophecy.*

Norman was seen at age 17 by one of us (S. C.), who had followed him since age 4½ because of persistent behavior disturbance. At age 17 he had already dropped out of two colleges in one year, and was planning to go abroad for a work-study program. He was in good contact but dejected and depressed. He was extraordinarily self-derogatory, said he could not finish anything he started, was lazy, and didn't know what he wanted to do. "My father doesn't respect me, and let's face it, why should he." He talked of "hoping to find myself" in a vague, unplanned way.

Norman had always been a highly distractible child with a short attention span. Intelligent and pleasant, the youngest in his class throughout his school years due to a birth date, he started his academic career with good mastery. However, at home his parents were impatient and critical of him even in his preschool years because of his quick shifts of attention, dawdling at bedtime, and apparent "forgetfulness." By his fifth year he showed various reactive symptoms such as sleeping difficulties, nocturnal enuresis, poor eating habits, and nail tearing. Year by year his academic standing slipped. His father, a hard-driving, very persistent professional man, became increasingly hypercritical and derogatory of Norman. The father equated the boy's short attention span and distractibility with irresponsibility and lack of character and willpower. He used these terms openly to the boy and stated that he "disliked" his son. The mother grew to understand the issue, but no discussion with the father as to the normalcy of his son's temperament and the impossibility of the boy's living up to his standards of concentrated hard work succeeded in altering the father's attitude. He remained convinced that Norman had an irresponsible character and was headed for future failure—indeed a self-fulfilling prophecy. There were several times when the boy tried to comply with his father's standards and made himself sit still with his homework for long periods of time. This only resulted in generalized tension and multiple tics and Norman could not sustain this effort so dissonant with his temperament—another proof to himself and his father of his failure. Direct psychotherapy was arranged in early adolescence, but Norman entered this with a passive, defeated attitude and the effort was unsuccessful. His subsequent development was all too predictable.

*Source:* Thomas A., & Chess, J. (1977). *Temperament and development,* pp. 167–169. New York: Brunner/Mazel. Reprinted by permission.

yond the children's capabilities, then the outcome can be bleak. But if the children have warm, supportive homes where the environment is arranged to help them rather than imposing unreasonable pressures and standards, they have a better chance of avoiding such secondary problems as poor self-image and depression.

*The same home environment affects different children in different ways.*

It is also true that the same home environment affects different children in different ways. A number of factors make the home environment unique for each child: differences in parental behavior and affection toward different children, the child's perception of differences in treatment, birth order and gender differences, experiences outside the family, peer interactions, and so forth. It may happen that a parent-child match was perfect for all the other siblings in terms of shaping their personalities and facilitating cognitive gains but, because of the challenges posed by a child with a learning disability, the match needs to be reworked for this child.

## Family Assessment

One of the most difficult tasks for a teacher is to assess family factors that may exacerbate a student's difficulties. But these assessments are important because the family plays such a key role in fostering the intellectual stimulation and social skills needed in and out of school. Recognizing this, in 1986 Public Law 99-457 amended the Education for All Handicapped Children Act to mandate assessment of family strengths and needs as they relate to the development of the preschool child. The law required that an individualized family service plan address any identified issues.

*An ecological approach to family assessment is important because the student's behavior is affected by family members, relatives, friends, and neighbors.*

An ecological approach to family assessment is important because the student's behavior is affected not only by individual family members but also by relatives, friends, and neighbors. For example, 6-year-old Becky was nearly always fearful and withdrew from academic and social participation in school. A visit by her teacher to her home revealed that an exconvict had moved his trailer next door to the family's property. The man, who had been jailed for child molestation, frequently paraded nude outside, built bonfires on his property, and peered into neighbors' windows. Becky became so fearful that she would enter only those portions of her mobile home that faced away from the man's trailer. Knowing this helped her teacher decide to relax academic pressures and create opportunities for Becky to draw and talk about her fears. The teacher also helped the family obtain representation through legal aid services.

*Family assessment centers on the family's emotional atmosphere, methods of discipline, prosocial modeling, attitudes toward learning, and the student's broader social context.*

Ideally, family assessment centers on the family's emotional atmosphere, methods of discipline, prosocial modeling and attitudes toward learning, as well as the student's broader social context. Emotional factors include the warmth and affection between family members; stressors such as finances, illness, divorce, or job dissatisfaction; the support and encouragement given to children; the fostering of independence; hostility between individuals; and attitudes toward the student's disability. Methods of discipline include factors such as how rules are established and maintained, negotiation, coercion, compliance, and the use of corporal punishment. Prosocial modeling involves behaviors and attitudes that the child may imitate or be reinforced for on the part of parents, siblings, babysitters, relatives, and others. Attitudes toward learning include feelings about different school subjects, teachers, the school administration, and whether academic achievement is valued.

The assessment process also needs to identify the support systems available to help families cope during difficult times. Coping with the stress of a child with LD is often more difficult for lower-income families and single-parent households. Sixteen percent of children in the United States now live in poverty; this figure rises to 43 percent for African American children. Over half of children born in the last decade have spent at least part of their childhood in a single-parent family. The great majority—more than 85 percent—of single-parent families are headed by mothers, about one-third of whom have not completed high school, 50 percent are unemployed, and over 60 percent have incomes below $10,000. For all these reasons and more, these mothers are at greater risk than married mothers for anxiety, depression, and health problems that can affect their relations with their children.

***Assessment needs to identify the support systems available to help families cope during difficult times; coping with the stress of a child with a disability is often more difficult for lower-income families and single-parent households.***

The subject of mothers working outside the home has received a great deal of attention, given that 75 percent of mothers of school-age children now work outside the home, as do over one-half of mothers of infants under 12 months of age. About one-third of children less than age 5 are cared for by child-care centers, 20 percent by relatives, 15 percent in homes with other children, and the rest by babysitters in their own homes. Seriously disadvantaged and at risk children garner very positive benefits from child-care programs. Aside from some short-term social benefits, the social competence and academic achievement of children from more advantaged families, however, is predicted directly from their family background—the child-care program has no long-term effect one way or the other for these children. Provided mothers are sensitive and responsive to their infants, child care does not impair the mother-infant bond regardless of the number of hours spent per week with a hired caregiver or the number of times new care arrangements are necessary.

In addition to child-care programs at the least *not* causing harm and at best accelerating child development, benefits accrue to children when their mothers are more satisfied with their lives because of employment. Studies find that working outside the home is beneficial to most women's self-esteem and sense of satisfaction, provided they wish to be employed, are satisfied with their jobs, and have stable child-care arrangements. If the father shares child-care responsibilities, this further relieves the strain and enhances the mother's mental health. Psychosomatic symptoms, depression, and stress are lower among employed mothers. Employment offers them an important buffer during times of stress, and when their infants have difficult temperaments. Working mothers' greater overall satisfaction spills over to perceiving their children more positively, engaging their children with a higher level of interaction and verbal stimulation, adopting warm but authoritative parenting styles, and emphasizing independence. These positive interactions are reflected in children's higher achievement, adjustment, and even accomplishments as adults. Children of working mothers are more independent and have fewer stereotypical views on sex roles. Several studies have found that maternal employment is especially beneficial to daughters, perhaps because it reinforces the concept of women being as competent as men.

***Working outside the home can increase women's self-esteem and sense of satisfaction, which can spill over into more positive mother–child interactions, and higher student achievement, better adjustment, and independence.***

Research has shown, however, that a mother's employment can be detrimental to the child's emotional or academic adjustment under the following circumstances: the mother works more than 40 hours a week, child-care arrangements are inadequate, there is no father or other adult support, the father resents the child-care responsibilities, the child is disabled or chronically ill, the mother wishes she didn't have to work, her work hours are inflexible, the father worries that his career will suffer or he interprets his wife's employment as failure in his breadwinner role. These situations create stress and dissatisfaction, and in turn affect the children.

*Mothers who are full-time homemakers, but who would rather work, experience greater stress and depression, are less responsive toward their infants, and encourage dependency.*

Studies find that mothers who are full-time homemakers, but who would rather work, experience greater stress and depression, are less responsive toward their infants, and encourage dependency. Part-time maternal employment seems to mediate the stress of full-time homemaking or work.

*The greater is the father's involvement in child care, the higher is the child's intelligence, academic achievement, and social maturity.*

In both single- and dual-wage families, the greater is the father's involvement in child care, the higher is the child's intelligence, academic achievement, and social maturity. This has been related to the positive effects of the father's gain in self-esteem from the parenting role.

Family variables are so critical in a child's life that family assessment should not be neglected. It can be done not only by the teacher but also by the school social worker or psychologist using such tools as home observation, interviews, and questionnaires completed by parents and significant others in the child's life. Variations among different respondents' answers shed light on the interaction patterns, attitudes, and messages that may be promoting or deterring a youngster's academic and social-emotional adjustment.

As parents get to know and trust the teacher through informal contacts, they may become more willing to share their family experiences and more open to ideas on how to be better models, teachers, and advocates for their children. With the benefit of the parents' information, teachers also can try to provide for the intellectual stimulation and emotional support that may be lacking in the home.

## Family Adjustment to a Learning Disability

Families can have any number of reactions to having a child with LD, some of which may contribute to poor family relationships and create barriers to the child's achievement. Other reactions may interfere with the evaluation and delivery of services to the student. Teacher sensitivity to these reactions is important in order to offer the family the support needed to help the child progress.

*Many parents are superb observers of their child's behavior. Even before the evaluation results are in, they can pinpoint their child's problems and areas of strength. Confirmation of their suspicions comes as a relief.*

### Parental Adjustment

Many parents are superb observers of their child's behavior. Even before the evaluation results are in, they can pinpoint their child's problems and areas of strength. They are thankful that there is finally an explanation for their child's struggle in school, and confirmation of their suspicions comes as a relief. One mother describes her relief at finding out that she's not to blame for her son's hyperactivity:

> For seven years it seemed like everybody was looking to me to control this kid. My husband, my mom, my friends all seemed to think I should be able to manage him, because I was the mother. People made "helpful" suggestions hinting at where they thought I was going wrong: "Do you feed him a lot of processed food? Does he get enough sleep? Maybe if you weren't working and could spend more time with him." I felt like wearing a sign: "I'm a good mother! I breast-fed him! I read to him every day!" But the bottom line was I did feel responsible. Scott was repeating first grade when we learned he had ADHD. The first thing I thought when they told me was, "Thank God! It's not all my fault!" ADHD isn't the easiest thing to live with, but I find I can deal with it a lot more effectively since I've educated myself about it and let myself off the hook. (Smith & Strick, 1997, p. 40)

*Some parents may be shocked, angry, sad, feel guilty, or be in denial on first learning about their child's learning disability.*

Other parents, however, may be shocked, angry, sad, feel guilty, or be in denial on first learning about their child's learning disability. These reactions have been likened by some experts to the cycle of emotions experienced when a loved one suddenly dies. Some parents may react by being angry with the school personnel as the bearers of bad tidings, or they may turn the anger inward by blaming themselves or each other—"if I had only done _________ differently" is a frequent lament. If they deny that the problem exists at all, they may well seek another opinion. In a field that has so many unanswered questions, a second opinion may make sense, but this "shopping" becomes problematic when it interferes with making definitive intervention plans and accepting the child no matter what his or her abilities.

*"Shopping" for second opinions becomes problematic when it interferes with making definitive intervention plans and accepting the child no matter what his or her abilities.*

As they come to grips with the reality of a learning disability, some parents need to "mourn" the loss of the ideal concept they had envisioned for their child. And some parents react to their anger and disappointment by becoming overprotective or overinvolved, which deprives their child of important learning experiences. Their parents' controlling and hovering attitudes make the children feel fragile, weak, and incapable. The parents' interference creates a situation in which the child is withdrawn from having to learn to solve his or her own problems and deal with conflict; and important opportunities for learning are lost (e.g., when parents don't let siblings settle their own arguments). The parent who reacts with overindulgence, on the other hand, doesn't provide the guidance and limits all children need.

*Some parents react to their anger and disappointment by becoming overprotective or overinvolved, which deprives their child of important learning experiences. Others push the child until he or she rebels; other parents blame the school.*

Some parents react to the diagnosis of a learning disability by "blaming" the child, comparing the child to a higher-achieving older or younger sibling ("why can't you be like Andrea?"), and withdrawing themselves. Others push the child until he or she rebels. Some, who perhaps had bad experiences at school themselves, communicate a hostile attitude toward teachers and other authorities to the child, who in turn resists teacher efforts to help because "the school is to blame for my problems." Other parents deny the gravity of the problem and don't hold the child responsible for learning in an active and motivated way. Still other families may actually work to preserve the child's learning disability in order to deflect attention from other family problems or to have a mission that makes them feel needed. It is easy to see how these parental attitudes can complicate a child's learning and attitudinal problems.

It is to be expected that having a child with a learning disability will stress a family system in some way. When teachers are alert and sensitive to parental feelings, are patient with the family's emotional crisis, and remain available for support, they can become invaluable resources.

## Sibling Adjustment

*When parents are honest in their explanations to children about the strengths and weaknesses of a sibling with LD, they can dispel potential guilt, fright, or confusion.*

*Siblings of children with LD do experience greater stress, but they also can show psychological benefits.*

Siblings are affected by their learning-disabled brothers or sisters, and they in turn influence the behavior of the affected child. If they are given no information, they may come up with such far-fetched ideas as they caused the problem or that LD is catching like an infectious disease, or even fatal. When parents are honest in their explanations about the strengths and weaknesses of a sibling with a learning disability, they can dispel much of the guilt, fright, or confusion.

Common sibling reactions include anger, resentment of the extra parental attention and time required by the child who is learning disabled, feelings of unfairness over different rules and expectations, diminished self-concept because the sibling does not feel "special," reducing one's own expectations because of identification with the disabled sibling, and embarrassment over their brother or sister's behavior. In Eli's story, he describes his own mixed feelings toward his brother.

Teachers and parents need to understand that siblings of students with LD typically experience greater stress than if their sibling were not disabled. They often are asked to assume some responsibility for their sibling with LD, while at the same time facing decreased parental support for themselves. And it is disconcerting that the needs of the child with LD can dictate family life, whether it be daily schedules, vacation decisions, or monetary allocations. Parents can put undue pressure on the nondisabled siblings to achieve academically, athletically, or socially, as if to compensate for the child with LD. Studies have shown that up to 25 percent of siblings of children with a wide variety of LD have experienced increased anxiety, depression, aggression, poor peer relations, and reduced academic and cognitive efficiency. On the other hand, siblings can show psychological benefits such as greater tolerance and understanding of differences, greater patience and compassion, dedication to altruistic goals, and even enhanced self-concepts because of their feelings of normalcy and competence in comparison with their siblings.

Parents need to be alert to their nondisabled children's potential adjustment problems, accept their negative feelings, and take time to listen to and respond to their needs. Including them as appropriate in discussions and planning makes them feel less neglected and invites their help in promoting their sibling's development. In doing so, however, parents need to carefully guard against the child assuming a mediator role between the parents and his or her disabled sibling.

*Special care must be taken so that every child in the family gets all the nurturing that he or she needs. Fairness doesn't mean that everyone gets the same thing.*

*The sibling relationship needs to be nurtured. Siblings' love and acceptance can make the home a happy and safe haven, one where the child with LD feels important.*

Special care must be taken so that every child in the family gets all the nurturing that he or she needs. Lavoie (1998) points out that fairness doesn't mean that everyone gets the same thing. If dad is sick and mom serves him chicken soup in bed, that doesn't mean that the whole family hops into their beds and expects the same privilege. Jonathan, who has a learning disability, may have mom's help with homework for an hour each night. Stacey, his sibling, has the whole family cheering for her volleyball games each Wednesday evening. Mom and dad are being "fair" to both children because, by treating them differently, both are getting what they need.

The sibling relationship also needs to be nurtured by parents. The child who is learning disabled has much to gain from modeling his or her brothers and sisters as they study and relate to peers and adults. Their love and acceptance can do much to make the home a happy and safe haven, one where the child with LD feels important.

## Eli

*A college student expresses his mixed feelings growing up with a brother with LD.*

Being the younger child is not easy—especially in a family of two boys. My memories are filled with competition and jealousy. In some ways, my older brother's learning disability made our relationship even more complicated and difficult.

I admit, when I was first told my brother had a learning disability I was thrilled. He's two years older than I am and had been ahead of me in almost everything. Now *I* was going to be better at a few things! When I was angry with my brother (which was pretty often), I sometimes felt like taunting him with his handicap: "I'm smarter than you are in school! You have brain damage and I don't!" I never said it; I knew it would be a low blow. I thought it, though, and I think he knew I did.

But at times I had trouble believing in this disability. I couldn't see anything in my brother that was "different." At my elementary school there were a lot of students with disabilities, and he didn't look or act like any of them. He didn't have distorted features or make odd noises or need a wheelchair or walk with a tilt. He looked about as normal as a big brother can get.

I watched for signs of his handicap. It was taking him a long time to learn his times tables, but I knew lots of kids who were bad at math. Nobody was making excuses for them! I began to wonder if having a learning disability wasn't more of an advantage than a disadvantage. My brother got to use a calculator for math tests (blatant cheating, it seemed to me) and was given extra time for some assignments and exams. He didn't even have to take a language in high school. Hey, I had some trouble with social studies and Spanish, but nobody was giving me any breaks! At one point in high school, my brother and I landed in the same math class (I was a year ahead in math, and he was a year behind). I worked hard and got 90s while he got 70s. My parents seemed equally pleased with those grades (because the learning disability made math especially hard for him, they were happy my brother had passed). They expected each of us to do our best and maybe that was the fairest way to look at it, but it sure didn't feel right to me at the time.

When my brother got extra time to take his college SATs, I thought, "These learning disabilities sure are handy!" It seemed like I was going to have to do twice the work to get into college that he did. One day when I was swamped with homework, I remember telling my mom I wished I had a learning disability so I could get all kinds of help and forgiveness if I screwed up. (Nobody was happy with *me* when I brought home a C on a test!) She told me to be grateful that I could succeed in every class if I worked hard—small comfort to a kid who thought he had too much to do.

Today I can think of my brother's learning disability with a little more compassion. It couldn't have been easy for him, sharing a class with a cocky younger brother. Looking back, he handled that situation with an amazing amount of dignity. I understand also that I do have more options than he does. When I look at my college catalogue, for example, my choices are unlimited, and there are no roadblocks between me and my choice of a career. My brother has a lot of talents, so I know he will succeed, but I wonder if he'll have to explain learning disabilities to his employers. That's going to be a lot harder than explaining to teachers at school. I know from experience how difficult it is to make people believe in something they can't see. No matter how much my mother told me about learning disabilities, the extra help and attention my brother got always seemed unfair. I was never 100 percent sure he wasn't just fooling everybody and coasting.

*Source:* Reprinted with the permission of The Free Press, a Division of Simon & Schuster Adult Publishing Group, from *Learning Disabilities A to Z: A Parent's Complete Guide to Learning Disabilities from Preschool to Adulthood* by Corinne R. Smith and Lisa W. Strick. Copyright © 1997 by Corrine R. Smith and Lisa W. Strick.

## Family Intervention

The more involved parents become with their children's education, the better their children do in school, the more appropriately they behave, and the more positive their attitudes toward learning. Three approaches have worked to increase parent involvement: a focus on improving the parent-child relationship in the context of the family; a focus on integrating parents into the school program, and a focus on building a strong relationship between the school, family, and the larger community.

*Because different cultures interpret LD in different ways, we need to be sensitive to parents' belief systems.*

One of the best ways to involve parents and help them to become more able models, teachers, and advocates is by listening to their perspectives and then offering feedback and information. Because different cultures, and subcultures within cultures, interpret LD in different ways, we need to be sensitive to parents' belief systems. For example, many Hispanic parents may not see their children as having LD because their children's command of English may already exceed their own, and their definitions of "normalcy" may be much wider than those used by our educational system. In fact, the very term LD can stigmatize the whole family because of their strongly enmeshed family identity. So we must value these different perspectives even as we also help parents to understand the school's responsibility toward children with LD.

*Parents need clear language and concrete definitions at the IEP meeting; the student's strengths must be the first thing mentioned, rather than focusing just on weaknesses.*

Even if parents understand what we mean by "learning disabilities," many have never heard terms like phonics, receptive language, and simultaneous learning style. They need clear language and concrete definitions at the evaluation conferences. At the IEP meeting, the student's strengths should be the first thing mentioned, instead of focusing just on his or her weaknesses. Too often, school personnel start off on the wrong foot by focusing on what children can't do, rather than valuing what they can do—and building from there. At the IEP meeting recommendations must be offered and, most important, the meeting must elicit information and participation from the parents and whenever possible, the student. These are times to start building a relationship of trust and understanding between home and school; one of the best ways to do this is to encourage parents to talk about their dreams for their child—and then plan together to get there.

*It is most important for parents to be heard, considered, and valued for the unique information and perspectives they bring to the problem-solving process.*

It is most important for parents to be heard, considered, and valued for the unique information and perspectives they bring to the problem-solving process. Their insight on their children's learning styles, likes, and dislikes can be invaluable in helping to shape a teacher's intervention plans. And if teacher and parents are "on the same page," parents can do much to reinforce at home the school's goals for a child (e.g., awarding privileges at home when the eighth grader brings home ten points earned for speaking courteously to the teacher, or handing in homework). Mary Sheedy Kurcinka, an educator and parent of a boy "who could scream for forty-five minutes because his toast has been cut in triangles when he expected rectangles" notes that parents can do much to turn around the negative vocabulary used at planning meetings and elsewhere, which results in biases and colors teacher perceptions of their children: they might purposely use the adjective "enthusiastic" rather than describing the child as "loud," for example, or "tenacious" rather than "stubborn," "cautious" rather than "anxious," and "spirited" rather than "difficult."

Based on their experiences when they were first told about their child's learning disability, parents have recommended the following: the fewer are the school personnel at the meetings, the less intimidated that parents feel; professionals should avoid anger or defensiveness and spouting of regulations that imply parents must do as they say; professionals should use less jargon and make bilingual translators available if necessary; both parents should be included at the meetings and transportation provided if needed; relevant reading material should be available; parents should receive written evaluation reports; parents should be invited to present their own report on their child's progress and needs; advice on home management should be offered; and information about the child's social progress should also be covered. At Syracuse University's Psychoeducational Teaching Laboratory, parental partnership in the recommendation process begins by visiting the family in their home prior to the assessment, encouraging parents to observe and comment on the assessment through a one-way mirror, and inviting them to edit a "draft" report that they read prior to the conference.

At parent-school meetings, professionals should be ready to discuss the possible reasons for the child's learning difficulty. Samples of the child's work should be available to illustrate areas of concern. Parents are very familiar with the schoolwork their children bring home and find it much easier to deal with these examples than with obtuse standardized scores. Parents also want to know what services are available in the school and the community. They are eager for long-range forecasts for their child's school, work, and life adjustment. Although this is always difficult to do given the many factors that can influence learning progress, parents should be told about research results in a way that is hopeful and instructive about what they can do to help. Educators also need to warn parents about quack "cures" and quick fixes that not only won't help their child but may also cause further harm. Parents need to be encouraged to actively intervene, yet at the same time have patience because there are no quick solutions.

***Parents should be told about research results in a way that is hopeful and instructive about what they can do to help, and warned about quack "cures" and quick fixes that won't help or may cause further harm.***

Teachers need to be especially sensitive to parents who are reluctant to come to meetings or engage actively in brainstorming solutions. Remember that much of learning disabilities is hereditary. Many parents bear deep-seated scars from their own school days. They recall poor grades and social rejection or isolation. The only time their parents were contacted by the school was when they were in trouble. They anticipate hearing that now they're the ones who are doing a poor job of parenting, and they are afraid their child will be labeled "dumb"—as they were. They feel ill-equipped to help with homework and have little confidence in their ability to talk with "educated" people.

***Teachers need to be especially sensitive to parents who are reluctant to come to meetings or engage actively in brainstorming solutions—many parents bear deep-seated scars from their own school days.***

Many Hispanic and Asian parents, on the other hand, have such deep respect for teachers and the authority of the school that they don't see any relevance to their presence at school meetings. Schools impart knowledge. Families socialize children. It would be rude to intrude in school affairs, just as it would be rude for school personnel to intrude in the family's private matters.

Teachers may need to go to unusual lengths to gain parents' trust, alleviate fears, and open doors. They can hold meetings after work hours at night (and provide babysitting), visit parents at home or in the workplace, and meet on neutral ground that is less intimidating, such as a coffee shop. Complimenting parents on some of their children's behaviors helps, as does sending home frequent "happy grams" praising their child's accomplishments. Opening the school's computer lab at night so students can teach their parents computer skills; scheduling a parent month in which parents spend a half day with their child at school and eat lunch with them; and inviting parents to chaperone a field trip, make costumes or sets for plays, or come in to share with the class how the family came to the United States or interesting things about their job can help a great deal.

*Teachers and parents need feedback from one another about how things are going.*

Once lines of communication are opened and a course of action decided on, teachers and parents need feedback from one another about how things are going. Besides formal conferences, periodic phone calls and notes back and forth are to be encouraged—a message notebook can be useful. Informal exchanges while the parent drops his or her child off or chaperones a class outing are most helpful. Open houses that accommodate the parent's work schedule, family nights that include dinner and babysitting, and parent bulletin boards all encourage parent-teacher information sharing. A homework hotline phone number, assignment notebook, and a letter sent periodically from the teacher informing parents of class expectations and upcoming events are important communication vehicles. Parent "tip" sheets also are helpful, such as tips on helping with homework or reading aloud with their child.

Many parents ask for help with increasing their child's academic motivation, providing structure for a child with an attention deficit, organizing their child's approach to homework, and improving methods of discipline. The teacher can help parents model academic interest by suggesting that the parents read more in front of their child, talk favorably about academic achievement, show an interest in their child's schoolwork by reviewing school papers, praise academic effort and independence, establish a set homework time and area, provide learning games and activities at home, and talk aloud about different ways to approach solving a problem. For the inattentive hyperactive child, for example, the teacher could recommend a more structured and consistent daily routine. Because anxiety can increase impulsivity, parents can work to eliminate stressors in the home. Parents can also learn to match their behaviors with their child's abilities. For a child who has difficulty with auditory processing or organization, for example, the parent can speak slower, use shorter sentences, and repeat often. For the teenager who is perpetually forgetting things, the parents can suggest memory strategies. If Robert insists that listening to "his" music helps him with his homework, his parents can suggest a test period to see whether this is actually true, rather than nixing the idea automatically. Teachers can encourage parents to adopt the role of coach, thereby helping their children to work more systematically and independently. Stepping back and letting go may be the most difficult task of all.

*Teachers can encourage parents to adopt the role of coach, thereby helping their children to work more independently.*

Most important, the teacher must stress how important parents are in promoting their child's self-worth. By providing a warm and supportive home, they help their child feel loved and wanted, rather than a disappointment to them because of academic failure. Ben's story illustrates what a lifesaver it can be to a child's self-concept when parents go out of their way to encourage the development of talents in their children, thus shifting the focus from weaknesses to competencies.

## Ben

*Joining the track team increased his confidence, base of friends, and openness to try new things.*

*Ben is an anthropology major and an officer of the photography and outing clubs at Bates College. His hobbies include fly fishing, drawing, ballroom dancing, mountain biking, and guitar (an instrument he says helps him make friends wherever he goes).*

When I started high school, my father insisted that I go out for a team sport. It was part of his scheme to get me involved in my new school. I remember feeling very disgruntled about being forced to occupy my time according to my father's plans. I was tall, gangly, not in terribly good shape, and certainly not interested in organized physical activity. I saw myself being hit by balls, crushed by 300-pound freaks with no necks, and being told to grin and bear it when I was in pain. My interests strayed more toward the arts spectrum, where my coordination could be put to use in a manner that did not involve damaging my limbs. But for me it was a sport I must choose, or risk the wrath of my father standing tall and dark above me.

I consulted my gym teacher. She introduced me to her nephew Joe, a senior who had run on the cross-country team since middle school. Joe introduced me to his coach, who told me to show up for practice the next day with shorts and running shoes. Thus my career as a runner began.

When I showed up for practice, the coach sent me out on a 5-mile run. I woke up the next morning hardly able to walk. When I hobbled into school, the muscles in my legs felt like they were being flayed by red hot pokers. Other members of the team noticed and sympathized with my condition. Older team members encouraged me to keep running and told me it would get better.

As I continued to attend practices, I discovered that I was not so different from these other runners. Yes, there were some stereotypical "jocks" on the team, but there were also artists, drama enthusiasts, and mathematicians participating for various reasons. Some of us ran for fun, some ran for fitness, and some ran for scholarships. We all hurt at the top of the hill, and when the race was done.

Often experienced members of the team would help new members. They offered encouragement when exhaustion set in and passed on bits of advice about warming up, reducing fatigue, getting rid of cramps. I liked the fact that even if you weren't a "star," you were accepted and respected as a member of the team. I remember one runner who was obese. Every year he ran to lose weight. He wasn't any good—in fact, he usually came in last—but he always finished. And every time he crossed the finish line, his teammates would clap and cheer.

As I began to get in shape, my times started coming down. I became more interested in how I was running; I enjoyed setting personal records and breaking them. I wasn't running because my father said I had to any more—I was running because I liked it. I developed a friendly rivalry with another freshman as we competed for the same spot on the team roster. I found myself wanting to win. I made sure I got plenty of sleep before race day and ate spaghetti for dinner so I would have plenty of energy.

At the end of my first semester, I made varsity. My mother had promised me that if I earned a varsity letter, she would get me a jacket like some of the older members of the team wore. We went to the mall, picked out the jacket, and had it monogrammed. At home, Mom sewed on the bright orange letter. The next day I felt great wearing that jacket to school, like I'd made the big league! Looking back, I guess I must have looked pretty funny, a skinny freshman "art geek" in a size-too-big varsity jacket. But I felt proud of

*(continued)*

**Ben** (Continued)

earning it, and that jacket still keeps me warm on autumn days.

I know now my father was right to have me go out for a team. In addition to becoming a source of confidence and personal pride . . . I also learned to be more open-minded about trying new things. . . . I went on to become involved in many other school activities. I joined the ski club. I helped build sets for the drama club and eventually worked up the courage to audition for parts in the school plays. I became a photographer—and ultimately photo editor—for the yearbook. Each of these activities involved a different kind of teamwork, and each gave me opportunities to make new friends. These experiences added so much to my enjoyment and growth in my high school years that I really hate to think of what they would have been like for me if my father had not insisted that I become a member of a team.

*Source:* Reprinted with the permission of The Free Press, a Division of Simon & Schuster Adult Publishing Group, from *Learning Disabilities A to Z: A Parent's Complete Guide to Learning Disabilities from Preschool to Adulthood* by Corinne R. Smith and Lisa W. Strick. Copyright © 1997 by Corrine R. Smith and Lisa W. Strick.

School personnel can provide workshops and newsletters on LD, recommend books that are written in understandable language, and provide background information on learning disabilities, home and school management ideas, and the various types of professionals who can be of help. Long-term, more comprehensive approaches to home-school collaboration are even more successful, such as the parent becoming a paid classroom aide, visiting the classroom weekly, or volunteering as class "mother." These arrangements need to be initiated soon after a child enters school, because parent participation tends to decline when children get older. Research shows that active parent involvement with the school facilitates student achievement, attendance, homework completion, and positive attitudes toward learning.

***Active parent involvement with the school facilitates student achievement, attendance, homework completion, and positive attitudes toward learning.***

Parents themselves have organized informational meetings to support one another and to advocate for quality services for their children. These groups are invaluable in providing a forum for parents to share their feelings, information about strategies and behavior management techniques they have tried, and the names of agencies and professionals that can be helpful. When teachers join these groups, they can be excellent resources in helping parents become more effective teachers and advocates for their children.

## Parents as Teachers

***Some parents just naturally take on the role of teacher and provider of services.***

Some parents just naturally take on the role of teacher and provider of services. Considering the gap between the numbers of children needing learning disabilities services and the limited time available to professionals, parents can be important additional resources if they get appropriate training. Very successful structured programs exist, for example, to teach parents how to attend to their children's positive behaviors, ignore their negative behaviors, use time-out procedures, manage their child's behavior in public, and so forth.

Preschool programs that incorporate a home-based parent-training component promote long-lasting gains because parents have become better teachers and reinforcers of appropriate behavior. Parents trained as tutors have improved their children's reading rate, comprehension, and visual-motor performance. And parent involvement in academic activities, especially homework completion, can noticeably affect achievement.

Nevertheless, there are some good reasons why some parents should not serve as their children's teachers. Some parents are so focused on academic success that they make teaching sessions torture for both parent and child, getting more upset with every error the child makes. Often such parents actually diminish their child's effort and willingness to tackle challenges, and increase dependency by communicating low expectations, being negative and highly directive, and not encouraging higher-level thinking. Other parents may share the same learning disability as their child, making the tutoring role impractical. Some parents may feel ill-equipped to help with homework, preferring instead to help their children acquire practical life skills. And still other parents may be too overwhelmed with trying to keep a roof overhead and food on the table to have energy for the teaching role.

*Some parents may share the same learning disability as their child, making the tutoring role impractical. Others' interactions are too negative to make tutoring productive or are overwhelmed with more basic priorities.*

Even if they don't directly help their child with homework, parents can establish a routine time and place for homework, gather the necessary materials to assist with homework, monitor distractions (e.g., shutting off the TV and keeping noise down), provide snacks, help the child organize which assignments to tackle first, and praise homework completion.

Teachers must be careful not to undermine parents' important nurturing role by advocating tutoring, for which some parents may have little inclination and few skills. The home should be the primary source of love and support for each child, not a place where they fail once again on their schoolwork. A youngster needs time to refuel and, depending on the individual situation, this may be a more appropriate function for the family.

## Parents as Advocates

Committed to the child from birth to maturity, parents are the most important advocates a child will ever have. The parent advocate role begins when a problem is recognized, which leads to an evaluation and then a search for services. IDEA's mandate for parental involvement throughout the assessment and planning process supports this role. Research teaches that when parents are involved in their children's schooling, grades, attendance, achievement, behavior, self-esteem, attitude toward schoolwork, homework completion, and class participation all improve.

*Committed to the child from birth to maturity, parents are the most important advocates a child will ever have.*

Unfortunately, school participation levels of parents whose children have learning disabilities have tended to be low. Many believe they have little to contribute. This is particularly true of parents from minority backgrounds and lower-income and lower educational levels, who tend to have an incomplete understanding of educational issues and due process rights. Even when they do participate, these parents tend to be too passive during the conferences, asking too few questions and contributing little.

*Unfortunately, school participation levels of parents whose children have LD have tended to be low; many believe they have little to contribute.*

Parental advocacy involves far more than the annual IEP meeting. Parents need to watch over evaluations to ensure that they are done adequately by competent

*There is a powerful spillover into academic and social arenas when a child's talents are supported.*

*Parents can be especially helpful with advocating for the creation of services where none existed before.*

personnel, that subsequent instructional programming is appropriate, that progress is evident, and that school personnel are planning for the future. They also need to push for compensations so that their children keep up with learning content, despite their reading and writing lags. And areas of strength need to be developed to the fullest extent possible. Sarah's story speaks to the powerful spillover into academic and social arenas when a child's talents are supported.

Parents can be especially helpful with advocating for the creation of services where none existed before. It was out of frustration over lack of services and the strains of daily life with children diagnosed as having LD or ADHD that parents

## Sarah

*Music taught her self-discipline and rewarded her with friends and teachers who supported her.*

*Sarah is a 21-year-old college senior who has an auditory processing disability. She began studying the flute in fourth grade.*

It's funny: I have a very hard time remembering things people say to me, but remembering music is no problem. I've always loved it. Some years music was the only thing that kept me going to school. For example, when I was in middle school I did very poorly academically. I don't mean in just math or English; I was doing horribly in *everything.* I was unhappy and unmotivated—except in band and chorus. I made an effort for my music teachers, and they gave me a lot of encouragement. When I was in eighth grade, the high school band director came and auditioned all the kids who wanted to play in the band the next year. It seemed like besides me, there were about a hundred other kids who wanted to play the flute, and we all had to play solos. The director chose me for the second seat in the high school band! That success lifted my self-esteem tremendously. I was a lot less afraid of high school, knowing I had such a good place in band waiting for me . . .

In high school, music turned my life completely around. I eventually became involved in the Pep Band, the Marching Band, and the Concert Orchestra; I participated in three different choral groups and sang and acted in musical theater performances. I won awards for musical achievement—when our concert band was invited to play at the Epcot Center at Disney World, I even got to play the featured solo. The amazing thing, though, was the way success in music carried over to my other studies. At some point it clicked that I was successful in music *because I worked at it*—and that working hard could make a difference in my other classes. I started to apply myself, and my grades went up. When I graduated, my first-choice college awarded me an academic scholarship.

Music did wonderful things for me socially also. I would guess that 85 percent of the people I feel close to and keep in touch with today are friends I met through musical theater or band. Looking back, it's easy to see that without music my high school career would have been nothing. Music gave me friends and teachers who supported and believed in me. It taught me the value of effort and self-discipline and gave me self-confidence. I think I would be a very different person now if my family and my school hadn't supported my love of music the way they did.

*Source:* Reprinted with the permission of The Free Press, a Division of Simon & Schuster Adult Publishing Group, from *Learning Disabilities A to Z: A Parent's Complete Guide to Learning Disabilities from Preschool to Adulthood* by Corinne R. Smith and Lisa W. Strick. Copyright © 1997 by Corrine R. Smith and Lisa W. Strick.

formed the parent-professional organizations that continue to be major sources of information today. The most prominent among these are the *Learning Disabilities Association of America* (LDA) and CHADD (*Children and Adults with Attention Deficit Disorders*). Local affiliates of these and other groups provide support for parents and have been powerful advocates for legislation of services to the learning disabled, including vocational training and transitional living services.

No one can put in as many hours, be as committed to a child with a learning disability or be as potent an influence as a parent. Professionals must do all they can to encourage parents to become and remain involved and to enhance their advocacy and intervention efforts.

***No one can put in as many hours, be as committed to a child, or be as potent an influence as a parent. Professionals must encourage parents to become involved and to enhance their advocacy and intervention efforts.***

## Summary

In this chapter we explored the most important influence on the development and competence of individuals with LD—their family. Learning disabilities can be made worse, helped, or perhaps even prevented by the family. The impact of the family, especially the parents, on a youngster's intellectual, academic, and social development is great. Parents have the responsibility to stimulate and oversee the development of their offspring with kindness, respect, and warmth. Parents influence their children's attitudes, work habits, values, and learning through their own attitudes toward learning, through the intellectual stimulation provided in the home, through the modeling they provide, and through their warmth, acceptance, and support. Higher-socioeconomic-status homes are more successful when it comes to producing academically achieving children, even when these children had experienced severe trauma at birth. Far more powerful than the influence of socioeconomic status, however, is the nature of the parent-child relationship. The probability for overcoming the risk factors posed by biological and socioeconomic conditions is excellent in homes that offer high-quality family environments.

Teachers have a responsibility to support parents through emotional crises and help parents work through their feelings about having a child with LD. Teachers also can provide information about learning disabilities and methods for modeling, discipline, and making the home more conducive to learning. Parents as both advocates and teachers are a natural answer to the shortage of services and personnel to teach students with LD. But the teacher role does not suit every parent, so professionals need to be careful not to place added burdens on already burdened parents unsuited to this role.

## Helpful Resources

### Families and Learning

Amerikaner, M. J., & Omizo, M. M. (1984). Family interaction and learning disabilities. *Journal of Learning Disabilities, 7*, 540–543.

Austin, A. M. B., & Peery, J. C. (1983). Analysis of adult-neonate synchrony during speech and nonspeech. *Perceptual and Motor Skills, 57*, 455–459.

Bandura, A. (1969). *Principles of behavior modification.* New York: Holt, Rinehart and Winston.

Barkley, R. A., Cunningham, C. E., & Karlsson, J. (1983). The speech of hyperactive children and their mothers: Comparison with normal children and stimulant drug effects. *Journal of Learning Disabilities, 16,* 105–110.

Bayley, N., & Schaeffer, E. S. (1964). Correlations of maternal and child behaviors with the development of mental abilities. *Monographs of the Society for Research in Child Development, 29*(6).

Bee, H. L., Barnard, K. E., Eyres, S. J., Gray, C. A., Hammond, M. A., Spietz, A. L., Snyder, C., & Clark, B. (1982). Prediction of IQ and language skill from perinatal status, child performance, family characteristics, and mother-infant interaction. *Child Development, 53,* 1134–1156.

Berk, L. E. (2002). *Child development* (6th ed). Boston: Allyn & Bacon.

Blair, C., & Scott, K. G. (2002). Proportion of LD placements associated with low socioeconomic status: Evidence of a gradient? *Journal of Special Education, 36,* 14–22.

Borkowski, J. G., Ramey, S. L., & Bristol-Power, M. (Eds.). (2002). *Parenting and the child's world: Influences on academic, intellectual, and socio-emotional development.* Mahwah, NJ: Lawrence Erlbaum.

Bradley, R. H., & Caldwell, B. M. (1978). Screening the environment. *American Journal of Orthopsychiatry, 48,* 114–130.

Bushman, B. J., & Anderson, C. A. (2001). Media violence and the American public: Scientific facts versus media misinformation. *American Psychologist, 56,* 477–489.

Calvert, S. L., Jordan, A. B., & Cocking, R. R. (Eds.). (2002). *Children in the digital ages: Influences of electronic media on development.* Westport, CT: Praeger.

Cameron, J. R. (1977). Parental treatment, children's temperament, and the risk of childhood behavioral problems: 1. Relationships between parental characteristics and changes in children's temperament over time. *American Journal of Orthopsychiatry, 47,* 568–576.

Cameron, J. R. (1978). Parental treatment, children's temperament, and the risk of childhood behavioral problems: 2. Initial temperament, parental attitudes, and the incidence and form of behavioral problems. *American Journal of Orthopsychiatry, 48,* 140–147.

Campbell, F. A., & Ramey, C. T. (1994). Effects of early intervention on intellectual and academic achievement: A follow-up study of children from low-income families. *Child Development, 65,* 684–698.

Caplan, N., Choy, M. H., & Whitmore, J. K. (1992). Indochinese refugee families and academic achievement. *Scientific American, 266*(2), 36–42.

Chapman, J. W., & Boersma, F. J. (1979). Learning disabilities, locus of control, and mother attitudes. *Journal of Educational Psychology, 71,* 250–258.

Collins, W. A., Macoby, E. E., Steinberg, L., Hetherington, E. M., & Bornstein, M. H. (2000). Contemporary research on parenting: The case for nature and nurture. *American Psychologist, 55,* 218–232.

Eron, L. D., & Huesmann, L. R. (1987). Television as a source of maltreatment of children. *School Psychology Review, 16,* 195–202.

Estrada, P., Arsenio, W. F., Hess, R. D., & Holloway, S. D. (1987). Affective quality of the mother-child relationship: Longitudinal consequences for children's school-relevant cognitive functioning. *Developmental Psychology, 23,* 210–215.

Garber, H. L. (1987). *The Milwaukee Project: Preventing mental retardation in children at risk.* Washington, DC: American Association on Mental Deficiency.

Gelardo, M. S., & Sanford, E. E. (1987). Child abuse and neglect: A review of the literature. *School Psychology Review, 16,* 137–155.

Hart, B., & Risley, T. R. (1992). American parenting of language-learning children: Persisting differences in family-child interactions observed in natural home environments. *Developmental Psychology, 28,* 1096–1105.

Hart, B., & Risley, T. R. (1995). *Meaningful differences in the everyday experience of young American children.* Baltimore, MD: Paul H. Brookes.

Haskins, R. (1989). Beyond metaphor: The efficacy of early childhood education. *American Psychologist, 44,* 274–282.

Haywood, H. C., & Switzky, H. N. (1986). The malleability of intelligence: Cognitive processes as a function of polygenic-experiential interaction. *School Psychology Review, 15,* 245–255.

Huston, A. C., Watkins, B. A., & Kunkel, D. (1989). Public policy and children's television. *American Psychologist, 44,* 424–433.

Kato, T., Takahaski, E., Sawada, K., Kobayashi, N., Watanabe, T., & Ishi, T. (1983). A computer analysis of infant movements synchronized with adult speech. *Pediatric Research, 17,* 625–628.

Kohlberg, L. (1984). *The psychology of moral development: The nature and validity of moral stages.* San Francisco: Harper & Row.

Lazar, I., & Darlington, R. (1982). Lasting effects of early education: A report from the Consortium for Longitudinal Studies. *Monographs of the Society for Research in Child Development, 47* (Serial No. 195).

Lorsbach, T. C., & Frymier, J. (1992). A comparison of learning disabled and nondisabled students on five at-risk factors. *Learning Disabilities Research & Practice, 7,* 137–141.

Matheny, A. P., Jr., Wilson, R. S., & Thoben, A. S. (1987). Home and mother: Relations with infant temperament. *Developmental Psychology, 23,* 323–331.

McLoughlin, J. A., Clark, F. L., Mauck, A. R., & Petrosko, J. (1987). A comparison of parent-child perceptions of student learning disabilities. *Journal of Learning Disabilities, 20,* 357–360.

National Television Violence Study (Vol. 2). (1998). Thousand Oaks, CA: Sage.

Nichols, P., & Chen, T. (1981). *Minimal brain dysfunction: A prospective study.* Hillsdale, NJ: Lawrence Erlbaum.

O'Connor, S. C., & Spreen, O. (1988). The relationship between parents' socioeconomic status and education level, and adult occupational and educational achievement of children with learning disabilities. *Journal of Learning Disabilities, 21,* 148–153.

Odom, S. L., McConnell, S. R., & McEvoy, M. A. (1992). *Social competence of young children with disabilities: Issues and strategies for intervention.* Baltimore: Paul H. Brookes.

Osofsky, J. D. (1995). The effects of exposure to violence on young children. *American Psychologist, 50,* 782–788.

Park, J., Turnbull, A. P., & Turnbull, H. (2002). Impacts of poverty on quality of life in families of children with disabilities. *Exceptional Children, 68,* 151–170.

Pearl, R., & Bryan, T. (1982). Mothers' attributions for their learning disabled child's successes and failures. *Learning Disability Quarterly, 5*(1), 53–57.

Piaget, J. (1948). *The moral judgment of the child.* Glencoe, IL: Free Press.

Powers, S. I., Hauser, S. T., & Kilner, L. A. (1989). Adolescent mental health. *American Psychologist, 44,* 200–208.

Provence, S., & Lipton, R. C. (1962). *Infants in institutions.* New York: International Universities Press.

Singer, D. G., & Singer, J. L. (Eds.). (2001). *Handbook of children and the media.* Thousand Oaks, CA: Sage.

Sprafkin, J., Gadow, K. D., & Kant, G. (1987–1988). Teaching emotionally disturbed children to discriminate reality from fantasy on television. *Journal of Special Education, 21*(4), 99–107.

Svanum, S., Bringle, R. G., & McLaughlin, J. E. (1982). Father absence and cognitive performance in a large sample of six- to eleven-year-old children. *Child Development, 53,* 136–143.

Taverne, A., & Sheridan, S. M. (1995). Parent training in interactive book reading: An investigation of its effects with families at risk. *School Psychology Quarterly, 10,* 41–64.

Tharinger, D. J., & Koranek, M. E. (1988). Children of alcoholics—At risk and unserved: A review of research and service roles for school psychologists. *School Psychology Review, 17,* 166–191.

Thomas, A., & Chess, S. (1984). Genesis and evolution of behavioral disorders: From infancy to early adult life. *American Journal of Psychiatry, 141,* 1–9.

Tollison, P., Palmer, D. J., & Stowe, M. L. (1987). Mothers' expectations, interactions, and achievement attributions for their learning disabled or normally achieving sons. *Journal of Special Education, 21,* 83–93.

Toro, P. A., Weissberg, R. P., Guare, J., & Liebenstein, N. L. (1990). A comparison of children with and without learning disabilities on social problem-solving skill, school behavior, and family background. *Journal of Learning Disabilities, 23,* 115–120.

Walberg, H. J., & Marjoribanks, K. (1976). Family environment and cognitive development: Twelve analytic models. *Review of Educational Research, 46,* 527–551.

Werner, E. E. (1989, April). Children of the Garden Island. *Scientific American, 260,* 106–111.

Werner, E. E., & Smith, R. (1977). *Kauai's children come of age.* Honolulu: University of Hawaii Press.

Williams, T. M. (1986). *The impact of television: A natural experiment in three communities.* Orlando, FL: Academic Press.

Winick, M., Meyer, K. K., & Harris, R. C. (1975). Malnutrition and environmental enrichment by early adoption. *Science, 190,* 1173–1175.

Yarrow, L. J., Rubenstein, J. L., & Pederson, F. A. (1975). *Infant and environment: Early cognitive and motivational development.* Washington, DC: Hemisphere Publishing.

Children's Defense Fund poverty figures: http://www.childrensdefense.org

## Family Adjustment

Atkins, S. P. (1991). Siblings of learning disabled children: Are they special, too? *Child and Adolescent Social Work, 8,* 525–533.

Dyson, L. L. (1996). The experiences of families of children with learning disabilities: Parental stress, family functioning, and sibling self-concept. *Journal of Learning Disabilities, 29,* 280–286.

Faerstein, L. M. (1986). Coping and defense mechanisms of mothers of learning disabled children. *Journal of Learning Disabilities, 9,* 8–11.

Falik, L. H. (1995). Family patterns of reaction to a child with a learning disability: A mediational perspective. *Journal of Learning Disabilities, 28,* 335–341.

Ferguson, P. M. (2002). A place in the family: An historical interpretation of research on parental reactions to having a child with a disability. *The Journal of Special Education, 36,* 124–130, 147.

Hannah, M. E., & Midlarsky, E. (1985). Siblings of the handicapped: A literature review for school psychologists. *School Psychology Review, 14,* 510–520.

Lavoie, R. D. (1986). Toward developing a philosophy of education: A re-examination of competition, fairness and the work ethic. *Journal of Learning Disabilities, 19,* 62–63.

Michaels, C. R., & Lewandowski, L. J. (1990). Psychological adjustment and family functioning of boys with learning disabilities. *Journal of Learning Disabilities, 23,* 446–450.

Owen, F. W., Adams, P. A., Forrest, T., Stolz, L. M., & Fisher, S. (1971). Learning disorders in children: Sibling studies. *Monographs of the Society for Research in Child Development, 36* (4, Serial No. 144).

## Family Assessment

Barrett, B. V., & Depinet, R. I. (1991). A reconsideration of testing for competence rather than for intelligence. *American Psychologist, 46,* 1012–1024.

Guidubaldi, J., Perry, J. D., Cleminshaw, H. K., & McLoughlin, C. S. (1983). The impact of parental divorce on children: Report of the nationwide NASP study. *School Psychology Review, 12,* 300–323.

Harry, B. (2002). Trends and issues in serving culturally diverse families of children with disabilities. *The Journal of Special Education, 36,* 131–138, 147.

Hoffman, L. W. (1989). Effects of maternal employment in the two-parent family. *American Psychologist, 44,* 283–292.

Huebner, E. S. (1991). Correlates of life satisfaction in children. *School Psychology Quarterly, 6,* 103–111.

McLoyd, V. C. (1989). Socialization and development in a changing economy: The effects of paternal job and income loss on children. *American Psychologist, 44,* 293–302.

Scarr, S. (1998). American child care today. *American Psychologist, 53,* 95–108.

Translation of English vocabulary for use with bilingual families: http://www.world.altavista.com

## Family Intervention

Barkley, R. A. (1987). *Defiant children: A clinician's manual for parent training.* New York: Guilford Press.

Christenson, S. L., Hurley, C. M., Sheridan, S. M., & Fenstermacher, K. (1997). Parents' and school psychologists' perspectives on parent involvement activities. *School Psychology Review, 26,* 111–130.

Dembrinski, R., & Mauser, A. (1977). What parents of the learning disabled really want from professionals. *Journal of Learning Disabilities, 10,* 578–584.

Gopaul-McNicol, S.-A. (1997). *A multicultural/multimodal/multisystems approach to working with culturally different families.* Westport, CT: Praeger.

Hanson, M. J., & Carta, J. J. (1995). Addressing the challenges of families with multiple risks. *Exceptional Children, 62,* 201–212.

Harry, B. (1992). Making sense of disability: Low-income, Puerto Rican parents' theories of the problem. *Exceptional Children, 59,* 27–40.

Harry, B. (1992). Restructuring the participation of African-American parents in special education. *Exceptional Children, 59,* 123–131.

Henderson, A. T. (Ed.) (1987). *The evidence continues to grow: Parent involvement improves student achievement.* Columbia, MD: National Committee for Citizens in Education.

Kay, P. J., Fitzgerald, M., Paradee, C., & Mellencamp, A. (1994). Making homework at home: The parent's perspective. *Journal of Learning Disabilities, 27,* 550–561.

Keith, T. Z., Keith, P. B., Troutman, G. C., Bickley, P. G., Trivette, P. S., & Singh, K. (1993). Does parental involvement affect eighth-grade student achievement? Structural analysis of national data. *School Psychology Review, 22,* 474–496.

Lynch, E. W., & Stein, R. C. (1987). Parent participation by ethnicity: A comparison of Hispanic, Black, and Anglo families. *Exceptional Children, 54,* 105–111.

Lyytinen, P., Rasku-Puttonen, H., Poikkeus, A. M., Laskso, M. L., & Ahonen, T. (1994). Mother-child teaching strategies and learning disabilities. *Journal of Learning Disabilities, 27,* 186–192.

Marcon, R. A. (1999). Positive relationships between parent school involvement and public school inner-city preschoolers' development and academic performance. *School Psychology Review, 28,* 395–412.

Maryam, M., & White, K. R. (1988). Parent tutoring as a supplement to compensatory education for first-grade children. *Remedial and Special Education, 9*(3), 35–41.

Rockowitz, R. J., & Davidson, P. W. (1979). Discussing diagnostic findings with parents. *Journal of Learning Disabilities, 12,* 11–16.

Smith, C., & Strick, L. (1997). *Learning disabilities A to Z: A parent's complete guide to learning disabilities from preschool to adulthood.* New York: The Free Press.

Thurston, L. P., & Dasta, K. (1990). An analysis of in-home parent tutoring procedures: Effects on children's academic behavior at home and in school and on parents' tutoring behaviors. *Remedial and Special Education, 11*(4), 41–52.

Annenberg Public Policy Center: http://www.appcpenn.org

Children and Adults with Attention Deficit Disorder: http://www.chadd.org

Learning Disabilities Association of America: http://www.ldamerica.org

National Information Center for Children and Youth with Disabilities: http://www.nichcy.org

No Child Left Behind Parent Guide: http://www.nclb.gov/parents

Parent advice: http://www.schwablearning.org

U.S. Education Department Helping Your Child series: http://www.ed.gov/pubs/parents

CHAPTER FOURTEEN

# The School

**THE SCHOOL EXERTS** a powerful influence on the academic achievement and social-emotional adjustment of all students. It is, after all, the place where the average youngster spends some 14,000 hours in the classroom from kindergarten through twelfth grade. And it is the school's academic expectations that cause children with LD to be singled out from their peers.

From a social systems perspective, students with learning disabilities are victims of the demands society places on its citizens to achieve academically, a demand that is evident in compulsory education laws and minimum competency standards for graduation. When children can't acquire these skills, they're viewed as failures. Unfortunately, the school setting emphasizes academic skills while valuing less other skills that may be strengths for children with LD, such as street smarts, musical or artistic talent, and mechanical abilities.

*The school setting emphasizes academic skills while valuing less other skills that may be strengths for children with LD, such as street smarts, musical or artistic talent, and mechanical abilities.*

As Chapter 13 illustrated, environment matters a great deal, and a person's behavior is strongly influenced by the context or setting. Frustration that could lead a child to a temper tantrum at home, for example, might not in school, where the opinion of peers can be harsher than that of loving parents.

*The learning and behavior of students with LD are influenced by hundreds of variables operating in a classroom at any given time.*

The learning and behavior of students with LD are influenced by hundreds of variables operating in a classroom at any given time. Consider Paul and Dale, for example. They are of similar ages and family backgrounds. And they share the label of learning disabled because of their short attention span and the academic difficulties that it has caused. Paul attends a private school for children with LD. His classroom is very traditional with seats placed in neat rows where most of the work must be done. Dale, on the other hand, is assigned to an open classroom in her public school that believes strongly in including students with LD full time in general education classes.

Paul's school setting has helped him focus attention and make academic progress. Significant course modifications and accommodations have fostered success in advanced content area classes. However, Paul has not learned the social skills of his age peers, and even strangers notice how immature he acts. At family reunions Paul hangs out with the little kids. Dale, on the other hand, seems to be slipping further and further behind academically. She is continually distracted and has trouble problem solving and learning on her own. She has been tracked into lower-level courses where she struggles to get by. She expects learning to be a challenge and is not afraid to try because her efforts do in the end lead to passing grades. Dale is a very popular girl with above average numbers of social contacts with different children each day. Her classmates enjoy her company and she has learned to dress and act just as they do. She's interested in the same celebrities and TV shows they're interested in. Hours each night are spent on the phone doing homework together with her friends—she's cleverly figured out which friend to call for which subject.

Over the years, the differences between their two schools influence Paul and Dale's similarities to fade. By the time they are ready to apply to college, Dale chooses to "go for it" and applies to four-year noncompetitive schools at some distance from home. Paul is more wary of making it in the "regular" world and chooses to live at home and attend a community college that has an excellent record for transferring students to highly competitive colleges. Clearly, Paul and Dale's school environments have made a real difference in their lives. This chapter explores how the effects of the school's physical, organizational, teacher, and peer characteristics can foster or constrain the academic success and social-emotional adjustment of students like Paul and Dale.

## Physical Characteristics

Educators once assumed that if the minimum standards for class size, acoustics, lighting, and heating were fulfilled, the classroom would be ready for learning. But we know now that it matters psychologically, instructionally, and socially where a child sits, what shape the classroom is, whether there is noise in the background, and more. An even more paramount concern is safety, especially since only 30 to 35 percent of parents feel that their children are very safe when in school or walking to school.

*Only 30 to 35 percent of parents feel that their children are very safe when in school or walking to school.*

### The Ambient Classroom Environment

Studies find that visual and noise distractions, especially intense or meaningful noise, are disruptive to students' performance. Generally, the level of disruption tends to be similar for children with and without LD.

*Visual and noise distractions, especially intense or meaningful noise, are disruptive to students' performance.*

**Background Noise.** Quieter classroom environments benefit most students, whether learning disabled or not. Research has found that background noise, especially meaningful background noise such as public address announcements or the soundtrack of a movie being played in the classroom next door, lowers performance for most children, especially when working on difficult tasks. Reasons given for the depressed performance include the following:

1. The noise interferes with communication in the classroom so that children can't attend to or hear the teacher. They miss out on important instruction.
2. Less communication is possible in noisy than in quiet environments, as illustrated by urban classrooms near elevated trains that require instruction to stop every few minutes as the train passes.
3. Children in perpetually noisy environments learn to screen out both irrelevant and relevant sounds.
4. Very noisy environments affect a child's emotional state negatively because this stress is beyond the child's control, annoying, distressing, and perhaps even seen as threatening. Distractibility and less persistence result. At Syracuse University's Psychoeducational Teaching Laboratory, one child asked each time a plane passed overhead whether it was going to drop a bomb. It was not difficult to understand why, with these concerns, he had difficulty attending to academic tasks.

***Surprisingly, listening to one's favorite rock music may improve performance for children with ADHD; it has no effect, positive or negative, for nondisabled children.***

Parents frequently call to their children to "turn down that music" when studying. Contrary to what our intuition might lead us to believe, listening to one's favorite rock music may actually improve performance for some children with attention-deficit hyperactivity disorder (ADHD); it has no effect, positive or negative, for nondisabled children. Music may have this positive effect for children with ADHD because it adds stimulation for children whose central nervous systems are underaroused. It could also be that stimuli they experience as pleasant help keep these children focused on the task at hand.

**Visual Distractions.** As with noise, both students with LD and average achievers tend to be hampered on educational tasks by excessive visual distractions. Experimenters have tested this point by using visual distractions such as reading the word "blue" printed in green ink, or asking children to copy figures on a background of wavy lines or to trace geometric forms obscured within a background of lines and shading. Although experts have long advocated the use of three-sided study carrels to minimize visual distractions in the classroom, research suggests that whether this leads to better performance is an idiosyncratic matter that must be assessed for each child.

***Whether study carrels will lead to better performance is an idiosyncratic matter.***

Besides visual distractions such as busy bulletin boards, clutter, and eye-catching jewelry on the teacher, classroom lighting deserves attention because it may not always be optimal for learning. For example, the light on either side of a room with a standard ceiling fixture is often 50 percent of that at the center of the room, and fluorescent lighting is only one-tenth as bright as being in the shade on a sunny day. Early speculation about the relationship between fluorescent lighting and hyperactivity, however, has proven untrue. Color is another aspect of the visual environment, but it has received little research attention. Although some people claim that pink helps calm aggressive behavior and that light green relaxes muscles, these claims have yet to be verified.

## The Designed Environment

We have learned that students with LD benefit from designed aspects of the environment such as smaller schools and class sizes, open-space designs, small-group seating arrangements, pleasant surroundings, and sitting front and center.

**School and Class Size.** Larger school size is associated with decreased attendance, lower grade point average and achievement test scores, higher dropout rates, and higher crime rates than smaller schools. The effect of larger school size is worse for schools serving lower-income students. Overcrowded schools also have a negative effect on achievement.

Small schools appear to give students a better chance to participate in many aspects of school life, thereby fostering a spirit of challenge, action, close cooperation with peers, and high self-esteem. They also enable the teacher to use more of the effective teaching strategies discussed later in this chapter and to develop more powerful, intense interactions with their students. When large schools develop a "house" model or a "school-within-a-school," this does seem to help socially and affectively, but achievement gains remain only moderate.

*Small schools give students a better chance to participate in many aspects of school life, thereby fostering a spirit of challenge, action, close cooperation with peers, and high self-esteem. Interactions with teachers are more powerful.*

Students in classrooms of 15 to 20 or fewer pupils have been shown to have significantly higher academic achievement than students in classes of 25 children or more. These students also have higher graduation rates. It seems that in smaller classes, teachers are more likely to individualize instruction and to have higher morale and more favorable attitudes toward students, which in turn relate to higher student self-concept, interest, and participation. Even if children experience smaller class size only in elementary school, the positive effects on their achievement tend to persist at least into the middle school years.

*In smaller classes, teachers are more likely to individualize instruction and to have higher morale and more favorable attitudes toward students, which relate to higher student self-concept, interest, and participation.*

**School and Classroom Design.** Classroom designs convey messages to children about who they are supposed to be, and how they are expected to learn. The rectangular classroom design of the turn of the century reflected the then-current notion of the child as an "empty" learner who must sit still and be "fed" information that others deem important. These early classrooms featured long rows of chairs and desks bolted to the floor with a raised platform in the front of the room for the teacher. By the 1930s these had given way to square classrooms with movable seats and the teacher's desk at the side of the room, reflecting the progressive education movement's view of the child as an active learner. The open-plan classroom of the 1960s reflected yet another concept of the child as perpetually in motion, the motion being important to learning. Studies of school and classroom design variables show that these do indeed influence students' attitudes, behaviors, and achievement.

*Open-Space Schools.* More than half the schools built in the late 1970s were open in design, and many still exist. Open-space schools are characterized by a lack of interior walls and by instructional areas ranging in size from 2 ordinary classrooms to over 30. There is an important distinction between *open space* and *open education.* The former is an architectural variable, whereas the latter is an instructional variable in which students self-pace and self-initiate educational activities while the teacher facilitates their learning.

In open-space schools, studies show that students use more classroom areas, particularly library areas, and spend less time at their desks. They interact with peers more often, but at some expense to individual contact with the teacher. Less time is spent reading and writing than in traditional classrooms, though no consistent differences have been found in academic achievement or student creativity between the two designs.

*Both teachers' and students' attitudes toward school appear to be favorably influenced by open-space schools.*

Both teachers' and students' attitudes toward school appear to be favorably influenced by open-space schools, particularly feelings of enthusiasm, satisfaction, ambition, autonomy, willingness to take risks, and cooperation and caring among teachers and students. Some of these benefits, however, may be due to teacher self-selection, rather than the open plan itself, in that teachers with these positive feelings may gravitate to open-space schools in the first place and their attitudes influence their selection to teach in these settings.

*Students with LD who are hyperactive or distractible are not necessarily at a disadvantage with the increased freedom of the open-space classroom.*

Contrary to popular wisdom, students with LD who are hyperactive or distractible are not necessarily at a disadvantage with the increased freedom of the open-space classroom. Nevertheless, teachers need to be sensitive to students who need greater structure and teacher direction through modifications of the open-space format.

*Seating students at tables or in rows is associated with reduced task focus and more student interruption.*

*Furniture Arrangement.* The arrangement and use of space in classrooms also affect student behavior. Seating students at tables, for example, has been associated with reduced task focus and more student interruption of one another. One study found that in a third-grade classroom in which as many as 12 student desks were clustered together and there were no clear boundaries or barriers for specific classroom activities, students had shorter attention spans, louder conversations, and more inappropriate movement around the classroom. In this classroom, the teacher's desk was in the center of the room, enabling her to manage most activities without getting up, thus decreasing her individual contact with students.

In another third-grade classroom, where there were fewer behavior problems, desks were in less accessible areas of the room, providing students with a degree of privacy. Desks were arranged so that only two or three children could work together. The teacher's desk was in a corner, necessitating her moving around the classroom to direct activities. Bookcases served as barriers limiting movement and activity. In another study, students seated in clusters or circles of desks showed significantly more on-task behavior and less disruptiveness or withdrawal than when desks were arranged in rows. Arranging the furniture so as to leave clear paths that don't intrude on working spaces reduces interruption of work and encourages student entry into some classroom areas but not others. Findings like these have clear implications for the learning disabled, who need facilitative seating arrangements and personal contact with the teacher to stay on task.

*Students who sit in the front-center portion of the classroom seem to place a significantly higher value on learning, are more attentive, stay on task longer, have more positive attitudes toward learning, learn more, and interact more with the teacher.*

*Seating Location.* There is something known as the "front and center phenomenon." That is, students who sit in the front-center portion of the classroom seem to place a significantly higher value on learning, are more attentive, stay on task longer, have more positive attitudes toward learning, learn more, and interact more with the teacher. If students' seating has an important effect on their classroom experience, teachers need to reexamine the common practice of isolating children with LD at the outer reaches of the classroom because of their distractibility. Because the teacher spends most class time in the front of the room, a front-and-center placement may result in more teacher supervision and encouragement, despite this being a busier place to sit.

*Pleasantness of Surroundings.* Achievement suffers in school buildings with substandard structural and cosmetic conditions. This is related in part to fewer teaching resources, and in part to the negative effect of these conditions on teacher and student morale. Studies in the 1950s found a relationship between ugly environments and fatigue, discontent, and a desire to escape. A number of subsequent studies have shown that children tend to persist longer at educational tasks in pleasant surroundings. One study in fact found that first and second graders worked longer at a motor task when the schoolroom was decorated with "happy" pictures than they did in rooms with pictures of neutral or sad scenes. When teachers simply induce positive moods by asking students to close their eyes and picture something that makes them happy, accuracy, rate of learning, and retention improve.

***Children tend to persist longer at educational tasks in pleasant surroundings.***

## Organizational Characteristics

Organizational aspects of school settings include the procedures for allocating resources, developing curriculum, identifying students in need of special services, assigning pupils and teachers to classrooms, and setting rules. The assumption that it is good to identify students as having LD and provide special education services for these students outside the regular classroom must be weighed against the stigma and isolation that these practices sometimes create. Because of these concerns and the negative effect of "tracking," the model of co-teaching by general and special educators has been promoted of late so that the student can be educated entirely with his or her peers in the regular classroom. In the "push-in" model, special education teachers come to the classroom to provide services; in the consultation model, special educators consult with the regular classroom teacher on how to meet student needs. These approaches meet the needs of many students with LD and comply with the Individuals with Disabilities Education Act (IDEA) of 1990's mandate that students with disabilities be educated in the "least restrictive environment." Of course, the mainstream environment may not be the least restrictive for every student with a learning disability. Therefore, each pupil's needs must be assessed carefully before deciding which setting will help the student spend the most time on the most appropriate tasks, feel good about himself or herself, and reach the highest possible levels of academic, social, and prevocational adjustment. In this section we explore the impact of identification, placement, and various instructional organization decisions on the academic and social-emotional growth of students with LD.

***The mainstream environment may not be the least restrictive for every student with LD. Each pupil's needs must dictate which setting will help the student spend the most time on the most appropriate tasks, feel good about himself or herself, and reach the highest possible levels of academic, social, and prevocational adjustment.***

### Identification

Identification of students as having LD qualifies the students for special education services, and it also qualifies the school systems for funds distributed by federal and state education agencies, though these funds cover only a fraction of the real cost of educating these students (which is usually double that of educating the average student). Identification also helps schools project the personnel needed, and the number of students needing special assistance, and it serves as a rallying point for advocacy to increase research, funding, and services.

However, identification of a student as learning disabled has a number of potential disadvantages. Parents and educators may reduce their expectations of identified children and fail to challenge them, and peers may harbor negative biases. After identification as having LD, research has found that some mothers reduce their assessment of their child's well-being when compared with mothers' judgments of equally low-achieving children who are not identified as having LD. In one study when children were told that a classmate had ADHD, they tended to be less friendly in their interactions with that child—talking less, disengaging from a mutual task, and making the child with ADHD work harder. In turn, the children with ADHD saw themselves as less capable and the other children as "mean." The label "LD" itself can negatively bias the attitudes of teachers and affect their interactions with the identified student.

*The label "LD" can reduce parent and teacher expectations, negatively bias the attitudes of teachers and peers, and affect their interactions with the student.*

The negative judgment resulting from learning disability identification is troubling because a sizable and controversial body of research has found that in some, though not all, cases a teacher's expectations about a student's ability can influence the teacher's behavior toward that student, the student's classroom behavior, and the student's ultimate academic performance. This "self-fulfilling prophecy" happens when the teacher knows the child is learning disabled but does not yet know the child well. Once teachers have had a chance to work with the child, they often revise their expectations based on their observations and experience. Teacher perceptions of student capabilities and students' own self-perceptions move closer to one another's as the academic year progresses. Nevertheless, this shift in expectations can take time. Think about the last time you heard a nasty rumor about an acquaintance. Even after you've learned that the story is untrue, you may doubt that person for some time to come. Although the effect of the "self-fulfilling prophecy" is smaller than originally thought, the achievement of low achievers is more susceptible to teacher expectancies, whether positive or negative, than is the achievement of high achievers.

*Teachers' self-fulfilling prophecies about students with LD are revised once they have had a chance to work with the child, but in the interim student achievement can be affected.*

Another disadvantage of classification as LD is that the identification often leads to "tracking," that is, homogeneous instructional grouping for all classes according to ability. When "tracked," students frequently miss out on much of the standard school curriculum. Often schools make the mistake of assuming that *ability grouping*—grouping low-achieving children together for all academic instruction—results in more homogeneity and therefore easier planning and instruction for the teacher. In fact, when students, whether learning disabled or not, are grouped for instruction on the basis of one criterion (e.g., reading level), this doesn't make them any more alike on any other characteristic, such as math achievement. Thus, the teacher needs to plan and teach at multiple levels anyhow. Even in the area thought to be homogeneous (such as reading), the teacher instructing a "homogeneous" group of low achievers often needs to plan a different lesson for each child, because each child has unique learning needs. The result is far more preparation than if a teacher plans one lesson for the child with LD included in a regular education class and a handful of lessons for the rest of the class. Teaching a different lesson to each child in an ability-grouped class cuts short the

*When students, whether LD or not, are grouped for instruction on the basis of one criterion (e.g., reading level), this doesn't make them any more alike on any other characteristic, such as math achievement. The teacher needs to plan multiple lessons at multiple levels.*

individual time a teacher can devote to each child. The day is spent getting through 12 individual reading lessons, 12 individual math lessons, and so on. Because the general education teacher is used to planning for a wide range of student variability in the classroom (in the typical second-grade classroom children range from the mid-first to seventh-grade reading levels; children in sixth grade range from third- to twelfth-grade reading levels), the teacher should be able to address the needs of children with LD in this context. A final argument against ability grouping is that this complicates classroom management because the behavior problems have been aggregated into the one setting.

Often the teachers of lower-tracked classes are not trained special educators. Isolated basic skills become the focus of teaching rather than a curriculum rich in literature and content. The pace of instruction can be as much as 13 times slower for lower ability groups than for higher ones. Therefore students in higher tracks are exposed to much more of the curriculum, and lower-track students fall farther and farther behind. Ability-grouped students become less knowledgeable over time about science, social studies, and current issues of concern such as drugs, pollution, women's issues, politics, and terrorism. Their sparse background knowledge reduces their ability to integrate a wide array of information, and they become less able to communicate with peers because they have less in common. In addition to the reduced richness of content, course selection in lower tracks is limited and instruction in lower ability groups often includes more teacher interruptions, more teacher time managing the class, less clarity of directions, lower teacher enthusiasm and task orientation, and poorer student attention to task, confidence, work habits, and independence. All of this fosters an inferior quality of education.

***The instructional pace can be as much as 13 times slower for lower ability groups than for higher ones. Therefore, students in higher tracks are exposed to much more of the curriculum, and lower-track students fall further and further behind.***

Not surprisingly, self-esteem and motivation of tracked students suffer as a result of reduced expectations. Tracking also restricts friendship choices and contact with a wide range of peers, and it results in a social caste system with an overrepresentation of minorities. Research shows that ability grouping results in lower achievement and higher dropout rates than had these children been educated with their nontracked peers and received a few minutes of extra help each day.

***Tracking results in lower achievement and higher dropout rates than had these children been educated with their nontracked peers and received a few minutes of extra help each day.***

Besides the evidence just reviewed, tracking makes no sense conceptually in that, despite their label, pupils with LD remain just as diverse in learning styles, behavior, and instructional needs as many of their nondisabled peers. In a number of studies as many as 1 in 4 of these children in fact score above average in some skill areas. And their achievement test scores are often indistinguishable from those of low achievers who are neither identified as disabled nor tracked—and who progress faster in more heterogeneous groupings.

The justification for labeling is to afford special teaching for the child with LD. Yet in actual practice special teaching objectives, methods, and materials simply don't happen. Grouping for instruction that separates pupils from the mainstream can make sense only if there is something very compelling about the education offered.

***Grouping for instruction that segregates pupils from the mainstream can make sense only if there is something very compelling about the education offered.***

A final disadvantage of identification as LD is that it implies that inborn characteristics are sufficient to explain why these students have so much difficulty learning. In some instances, the real reasons for the student's lack of success can be found in the instructional strategies and human interactions in the pupil's classroom, more so than the learning disability.

*LD classifications by themselves tell us nothing about how to intervene. Therefore, class placement must be based on instructional needs rather than disability classifications or reading levels.*

Clearly, learning disability classifications by themselves do not describe the student, and they tell us nothing about how to intervene. That is why assigning pupils to programs according to their instructional needs, rather than their learning disability classifications or reading levels, has gained greater acceptance in recent years. A "one-size-fits-all" approach is inappropriate.

## Placement

An important aspect of the organizational environment concerns how schools arrange classroom placements for students with special learning needs. These placements can range from a regular classroom with no support services to special residential schools for students with LD. The place of instruction is less important than what goes on in these placements, and the skills and attitudes of the teacher. There are many reports of positive academic, social, and self-esteem outcomes in every placement choice, from special class to full inclusion in the general education class. Research to date suggests that students with LD tend to benefit more academically, socially, and emotionally the more special education they receive. This often means pulling the student out of the mainstream for some portion of the day for specialized instruction, in addition to the instruction and special support received in the general education setting. General education teachers appear more satisfied with this "pull-out" arrangement than with providing all instruction within the general education class. IDEA's mandate to educate children in the least restrictive environment has spurred increased collaboration between special and general educators in recent years in order to provide children with LD the benefit of specialized instruction while also maximizing access to the general education curriculum and integration with nondisabled peers.

*Students with LD benefit more academically, socially, and emotionally the more special education they receive. This can mean pulling the student out of the mainstream for some specialized instruction, or receiving special support in the general education setting.*

**The Least Restrictive Environment.** IDEA mandates that students with LD be educated in the most normal setting possible. Its "least restrictive environment" provision states that:

> to the maximum extent appropriate, children with disabilities . . . [be] educated with children who are not disabled, and [that] . . . removal. . . . from the regular educational environment [occur] only when the nature or severity of the disability of a child is such that education in regular classes with the use of supplementary aids and services cannot be achieved satisfactorily. (PL 105-17; IDEA reauthorization of 1997)

The law states that "where a child with disabilities is so disruptive in a regular classroom that the education of other students is significantly impaired, the needs of the child with disabilities cannot be met in that environment" (34 C.F.R. ss 33.552, comments). The courts have ruled that if schools must move students to more restrictive settings, they must justify those placements with concrete data. If gaps in the continuum of services exist, and the appropriate placement for a particular child isn't available in the district, the school must make other arrangements such as paying for private school or contracting with another school district.

*IDEA supports the view that, although most students with special needs can be educated in the regular classroom, some have needs best met in some form of alternative setting.*

IDEA supports the view that, although most students with special needs can be educated in the regular classroom, some have needs best met in some form of alternative setting. It is important to remember that full-time "inclusion" in the general education classroom and "least restrictive" are not synonymous. Any setting, including the general education classroom, that prevents a child from receiving an appropriate education is not the "least restrictive environment" for that child. Sometimes education in the mainstream can be restrictive, such as when a teacher is poorly prepared to deal with the student's needs, when the teacher is unwilling to individualize instruction, the class structure or curriculum are inappropriate, or when the class composition itself would provide poor modeling for a student with LD. Sometimes education in special classes is restrictive when teachers don't challenge students and when behavior management issues disrupt instruction and modeling of appropriate social skills. Therefore, placement decisions must be based on student needs, student preferences, and the quality of the actual resources available.

*"Inclusion" and "least restrictive" are not synonymous. Any setting, including the general education classroom, that prevents a child from receiving an appropriate education is not the "least restrictive environment" for that child.*

**Special Class Placement for Students with LD.** A backlash against special classes began when research showed that children of below average intelligence developed no better socially, and often worse academically, when taught in special classes than in regular classes. And many studies have found that students with LD who are educated in special classes have lower self-concepts than those attending general education classes. The explanation is that these students feel demeaned intellectually, segregated from their peers, and less challenged by the curriculum.

Nevertheless, an equal number of studies report that academic and social gains in fact can be quite favorable in special education settings for children with LD. These gains seem to be related to these students having the cognitive potential to make rapid academic progress when exposed to more intense, individualized instruction. In special classes for the learning disabled, the teacher-pupil ratios are 2 to 3 times lower than in regular classes. And a trained special educator is doing the teaching. When compared with the general education classroom, studies have shown greater on-task behavior in special classes, less time waiting for the teacher to get organized, more direct instruction, more comfortable pacing, more breaking of lessons into smaller units, more strategy instruction, more positive reinforcement from the teacher, more completed interactions (student spoke–teacher responded), fewer instructions geared to the whole group, more individual and small group instruction, more adult initiations to which children responded, and more frequent and longer interactions with the teacher.

Students with learning disabilities also have been shown to benefit socially and emotionally from special classes. In some research students in special classes maintained as good a self-concept as average achievers in general education classes, despite significantly lower reading achievement, which usually correlates with lower self-concept. In contrast, students with LD who remained in the regular classroom and received daily tutoring tended to have significantly lower self-concept scores, even when their reading achievement scores or IQs were higher than those of students in the special classes. The reason for this disparity may be that students compare themselves unfavorably with higher-functioning classmates, and in the general education class the learning disabled often are ignored or rejected. The competitive climate of many general education classrooms, in which students with LD fear critical evaluation by their academically superior peers, doesn't help matters. All students are sensitive to peer evaluation. In one study, for example, students with LD made significantly more oral reading errors when reading in a group of more skilled peers than in a group of peers similar in ability. It is in the intermediate grades that exposure to more competent peers is most likely to begin to undermine a child's perception of competence, because the ability to make social comparisons against group norms develops around age 10. In line with this reasoning, several studies suggest that the more hours the child is away from the general education classroom receiving special education services, the higher is his or her self-concept. No matter how well a youngster is doing academically or socially in the general education classroom, there's always another student with better math scores or more birthday party invitations. It's easy to see why, for some children, being grouped in special classes with children who also experience learning difficulties increases the possibility for positive judgments of self-worth.

***Several studies suggest that, due to more favorable social comparisons, the more hours the child is away from the general education classroom receiving special education, the higher is his or her self-concept.***

Why different placement models are effective in different ways for different children is something that future research needs to sort out. Currently, approximately 14 percent of students with LD are educated for most (over 60 percent) of the school day in special class settings.

**Inclusive Service Models.** Studies showing poor gains made by mildly retarded students placed in special education classes, coupled with civil rights activism in decades past, led to the embrace of *mainstreaming* as an educational concept. It was argued that it is simply ethically wrong to segregate children with LD from the regular classroom content and from a broad range of peer models. Mainstreaming meant at least part-time placement of students with LD in regular classrooms, as defined by PL 94-142, now IDEA. Many advocates of mainstreaming have become strong proponents of *inclusion,* or including students with LD full-time in regular classrooms with appropriate special education supports provided in that setting.

Although the long-term effects of part-time mainstreaming or full-time inclusion have not been fully evaluated, this is what we know so far:

***Regular classroom teachers are positive about the concept of inclusion but are hesitant about providing for the needs of special students in their classrooms.***

1. Regular classroom teachers are positive about the concept of inclusion but tend to be hesitant about providing for the needs of special students in their classrooms. This is especially true for secondary level teachers. Despite positive attitudes about including these students, in reality teachers make few instructional adaptations (such as special grading systems, modifying a test's reading level), resist making adaptations (in part because it calls attention to the student with LD and nondisabled students perceive it as unfair), give little individual attention or feedback, feel inadequately prepared, fear lawsuits, complain about workload and added paperwork, are not enthusiastic about team teaching, "move on" in the curriculum before the student is ready, feel that the necessary adaptations aren't feasible in the regular classroom, and often feel that the regular class is inappropriate for students with learning disabilities.
2. Regular classroom teachers rely on whole class instruction and differentiate instruction only minimally for students of different ability levels. A "one sizes fits all" approach does not provide the intensity of explicit instruction required by children with LD.
3. Regular classroom teachers are willing to make adaptations for students with LD that benefit the whole class (such as using study guides or typed tests),

but they are reluctant to provide modifications geared toward individual students' needs. They argue that adapting instruction to a wide range of differences is unrealistic given the pressure to have students meet minimum competency standards.

*Regular classroom teachers are willing to make adaptations for students with LD that benefit the whole class, but are reluctant to provide more individualized modifications.*

4. Academic gains in the general education classroom appear to be greater when both the regular and special education teacher take responsibility for teaching, and when students receive additional pull-out individualized instruction.
5. Students with LD tend to be less popular in regular classrooms and they are more frequently rejected.

*Students with LD tend to be less popular in regular classrooms and they are more frequently rejected.*

6. General education placement may or may not result in greater social interaction with nondisabled students, or modeling of these classmates' behavior. For students with LD to benefit from inclusion, the classroom organization must be planned for social interaction and modeling to occur by using cooperative learning principles, for example, peer tutoring, or assigning modeling roles to nondisabled students.
7. General education teacher perceptions of students with LD tend to be lower than special educators' perceptions in more segregated environments. And students are sensitive to these perceptions. Even when mainstreamed students' physical ability, appearance, and friendship self-concepts equal those of their classmates, their academic, intellectual, and social self-concepts tend to be low.
8. Some experts wonder whether the primary goal of exposure to the regular curriculum is far too narrow for students with LD given their weak social skills and cognitive strategies, and less than satisfactory postschool employment and adjustment histories. Especially at the secondary level, intensified vocational preparation and transition services may benefit some students more, raising again the issue of separate programs and segregation.
9. Sharing their child's stigma, parents may feel less respected or accepted by other parents. In addition, because their interests and concerns are different from those of nondisabled students' parents, their isolation may grow over time. Bulletin board displays of student work and open-house curriculum presentations are painful reminders to parents of the discrepancy between their child with LD and his or her classmates.
10. Some parents and teachers have expressed concerns—unjustified as it turns out—that the average children's achievement may suffer if students with LD are included in the regular classroom.

*Class placements should be determined by what is right for each individual given his or her age, desires, needed curriculum modifications, social skills, numbers of pupils in the class, role models in different settings, the attitudes and competencies of the teachers, and the family support system.*

The bottom line is that class placements should be determined by what is right for each individual child given his or her age, desires, needed curriculum modifications, social skills, numbers of pupils in the class, role models in different settings, the attitudes and competencies of the general education and special education teachers, and the family support system. All national learning disabilities and special education organizations have issued statements emphasizing that indiscriminate placement of all students with LD in regular education is inappropriate because some students need to learn different content in different ways; and these specialized services and techniques are simply not available in regular class settings. Even if they spend the bulk of their day in special education classes, it is argued that students still can be mainstreamed with same age peers for art, physical education, music, library, field trips, and homeroom. When they are ready to be included in academic subject area classes, they are mainstreamed for these as well.

***If inclusion is to work for students with LD, special education intervention or general educator training to help plan teaching modifications is necessary.***

In general, research suggests that if inclusion is to work for students with LD, special education intervention or general educator training to help plan teaching modifications is necessary. General education teachers cannot merely add the child with LD into the existing program. They must be willing to forego the rigid lock-step system dictated by each grade's curriculum and be flexible about what students will be taught, how they will learn, the rate at which they will learn, and grading. The system must be ready to make adjustments to accommodate the individual with special needs.

Extensive in-service training is essential to modify general education teachers' attitudes, build a repertoire of accommodations that require little teacher preparation time, and teach useful interventions that can be implemented for the class as a whole. For example, students with LD do better when regular educators teach the whole class memory strategies, note taking, organization, time management, and how to read in content areas. Success in general education placements can be maximized if teachers and students jointly set instructional goals, measure progress toward these goals, and meet weekly to discuss progress and revise plans.

Inclusive service models also are more likely to succeed if nondisabled students are prepared to serve as friends, role models, peer tutors, and teammates on projects. Disability simulations, discussions, films, and books can help foster positive attitudes toward the learning disabled among classmates. But the student with LD also needs to be specifically prepared for the regular class by teaching him or her social skills, such as interacting positively with others, obeying class rules, and maintaining appropriate work habits. Encouragement of talents, athletic abilities, game playing, and conversational skill also is important, as classmates' perceptions of competence in these areas facilitate the child's social integration and popularity.

The most common method for providing special education services to mainstreamed students with LD has been through the "pull-out" model, which provides services in a resource room. Alternative models in which the special educator co-teaches with the general educator, "pushes" into the class to deliver services, or consults on program modifications have recently become popular.

***Pull-Out Model.*** Currently, nearly 85 percent of students with LD are educated in mainstream classes for 40 percent or more of the school day. Just over half are "pulled out" for special instruction in a resource room for 20 percent of the school day or less. The other half receives resource room instruction for up to 60 percent of the school day.

The *resource room* has emerged as an alternative to the segregated special classroom. It is a *pull-out* service that allows the student to leave the regular classroom for one or more periods a day for individual and small group instruction from a special education teacher. Often children with different types of disabilities but similar instructional needs are grouped together for resource room instruction.

Research supports the effectiveness of resource room services as a means of increasing students' on-task behavior and rate of achievement, as well as teacher and student perceptions of progress and personal-social adjustment. Because of the generalization difficulties of children with LD, however, gains in the resource setting don't always transfer to the regular classroom. Pull-out services do not appear to be detrimental to the peer acceptance or the overall self-concept of mainstreamed students with LD.

*Resource room services are associated with increases in students' on-task behavior and rate of achievement, as well as teacher and student perceptions of progress and personal-social adjustment.*

Despite the success of resource programs, pulling students out of their regular classes can have disadvantages. When this happens, students may feel disconnected and confused by the disruptions and may miss out on important class assignments, thereby getting a watered-down curriculum. Extra time must be spent playing catch-up. They may also miss out on enjoyable subjects like art and physical education, in which success could provide just the motivation needed to persist with more difficult academic challenges. Time is wasted moving from class to class. In addition, some children are sensitive to the stigma of leaving class and may fabricate reasons for their absences to save face with their peers. One researcher reports that Kim, for example, told her friends that she had to leave for piano lessons. She kept up the story for more than two years, all the while hoping that no one would ask her to play! Finally, the pull-out model makes it difficult for special and general educators to coordinate instruction, and may absolve regular classroom teachers of the need to take their responsibilities toward low-achieving students seriously.

When assigning students to resource programs, school personnel must remember that there should be something very special, intense, individualized, and qualitatively different about the pull-out program to justify uprooting students from their regular classes. Although many resource programs fit this description to a T, others do not. Many times the same materials and practices that didn't work in the regular classroom are continued in the resource room. In addition, instead of remediation or study skills training, resource teachers all too often find themselves tutoring students to help them pass quizzes and state competency tests. Students may pass, but they haven't picked up the skills they need to function more independently in the regular classroom.

*There should be something very special, intense, individualized, and qualitatively different about the pull-out program to justify uprooting students from their regular classes; many times the same materials and practices that didn't work in the regular classroom are continued in the resource room, and tutoring predominates over remediation or study skills training.*

***Push-In Models.*** To counter criticism of the pull-out model, *push-in models* have been developed to try to provide high-quality, individualized educational experiences for children right in their general education classrooms. Special education teachers may come into the regular class to instruct one or more children, or they may teach their own regular class, or team teach in an integrated general education class, of which one-third may be children with LD. Children benefit academically, socially, behaviorally, and in self-esteem from these arrangements. The few controlled studies done on push-in models indicate that academic gains generally are equivalent to those in the resource room model. When push-in services are combined with pull-out services, however, academic gains are even greater. Current push-in models are meeting with more success at the elementary and middle school grades than at the high school level.

*Academic gains in push-in models are equivalent to those in the resource room model.*

Several models can be followed when co-teaching in a general education classroom. One teacher can teach while the other assists individual students, and the teachers may or may not take turns as lead teachers. In another model, the general educator teaches the majority of students while the special educator teaches a smaller group that needs reteaching of concepts and previewing of lessons to come. The teachers also can split the class into two heterogeneous groups and teach the same content in parallel; all children benefit from the smaller instructional groups. Or the teachers can each instruct one-third of the children, while the remaining students do seatwork; groups rotate to the different teachers for different subject area instruction. The most commonly used model is the first, in which the special educator supports students while the general educator instructs. The special educator is in a helper role: explaining requirements, keeping students on task, interpreting the text, reteaching main ideas, and supervising group assignments. In this subordinate position, it's unfortunate that special educators seldom take responsibility for active teaching of whole classes or even small groups, given their unique expertise for delivering specialized instruction. It takes an especially compatible pair of teachers in terms of teaching philosophy and personality to create a truly shared teaching experience.

When special educators choose the model of coming into the general education classroom to teach specific children, they must take great care to avoid embarrassing their students by being stigmatized as the teacher of "dummies." To counter this possibility, the special education teacher often works with a group of high-achieving students daily, coaches an athletic team, advises the yearbook staff, or some other valued activity. One organizational framework that has been reported to improve achievement and avoid stigma is the nongraded, multiage class, in which students are grouped in each subject according to skill level. Another alternative is to assign every student in the school, disabled or not, to one period a day devoted to special education and enrichment activities.

In the *teacher consultant model,* the stigma for the student is reduced because the special educator doesn't serve students directly. Rather, the consultant works to improve the general education teacher's skills, who in turn directly teaches the students with LD. Several studies have found that these students make equivalent gains in academic performance under the teacher consultant and resource room models.

Perhaps because of the embarrassment, elementary school students tend to prefer their classroom teachers for special help rather than specialists, which highlights an additional value of the co-teaching model. And while students of all ages like their general education teachers to make instructional accommodations for them, they are more sensitive about adaptations in tests, textbooks, and homework assignments that make them look different. When homework assignments differ, this takes away an important catalyst for children to interact after school hours—this socialization is very important for students with LD.

The pull-out, push in, co-teaching, and teacher consultant models are organizational characteristics of the school that can benefit students with LD when done right: instructional accommodations make it possible for the student to participate meaningfully with the curriculum, the environment is conducive to social inclusion, and special education services help build basic skills and learning strategies. The strength of these models lies in the fact that students can receive support from special educators yet maximize the time they spend with their nondisabled peers.

***Including students in the placement decision and hearing out their concerns is important.***

When there's a choice of service models, it makes sense to consult the student to see what he or she would prefer. Several recent interview studies report that some students with LD prefer resource to regular classes, and others prefer the opposite. Those who prefer the pull-out arrangement talk about work that is easier and more fun, the quieter setting, their greater sense of accomplishment, and not being embarrassed; in the inclusion class they were picked on, called names, pushed around, and teachers didn't "look out for them." They also found the inclusion class too hard, and complained about confusion caused by all the noise and activity. Those who prefer the inclusion setting talk about their boredom covering the same material year in and year out in the resource room—they feel they learn more in the regular class. They also like being treated as "normal" and not reminded of their learning disability. Children sometimes express preference for the friendships in the regular class, and sometimes for those in the resource room.

On page 532, Emmy describes the hard work and pleasure that accompanied her transition from special class to regular class—her "baptismal day." In Chapter 10, Emmy's resource teacher told of the grueling effort it took to serve Emmy in regular classes. But it was worth it. Emmy had been placed in a special class in first grade because she could not read. Her self-confidence diminished year by year, in part because of a teacher who overprotected rather than challenged students. Because her basic skills had not progressed, Emmy's parents argued that for sixth grade she should be included in a regular class. For the remainder of her schooling Emmy received significant resource room support and spent three hours a day on homework. Very different from her elementary school years, Emmy joined after-school activities, walked with more of a bounce, smiled, spoke spontaneously to others rather than staring at her feet when spoken to, had a date for the senior prom, and in twelfth grade celebrated another "baptismal day"—her election to the National Honor Society. An email from Emmy just three weeks ago informed me that she would be graduating from a state university this spring, and is pursuing the goal of a social work masters degree! Emmy's parents and evaluation team were wise to include Emmy in the placement decision from the start, and listen carefully to her aspirations and concerns. As for all students with LD, Emmy's "buy in" was critical to her motivation to do her best in the selected educational settings.

## Organization of Instruction

Teachers differ from one another in the way they use class time, pace instruction, structure and deliver the curriculum, help students progress through the curriculum, and group students for instruction. The decisions that teachers make in each of these areas influence their effectiveness in promoting student learning. The system and instructional factors that have been found most effective in maximizing student learning in the classroom are listed in Figure 14.1 on page 533.

*In most classrooms there is too little time spent in direct instruction, too little time on task, too little active student responding, too little teacher feedback to students, and too little teacher attention or praise contingent on appropriate student behaviors.*

Much of the research on what makes schools effective has been done with only a few references to students with special education needs. The limited information we do have, however, suggests disappointing implementation of effective teaching strategies by both regular and special educators. There is too little time spent in direct instruction, too little time on task, too little active student responding, too little teacher feedback to students, and too little teacher attention or praise contingent on appropriate student behaviors.

## Emmy

*Transitioning from the special to regular class was hard work, but well worth it—a "baptismal day"*

A baptismal battle for me was when I got out of being in one class all day. Now I am in regular classes this year. Last year I had no homework, and this year I have alot. Last year if I did not want to do something I did not have to do it. If I do not do something this year I lose grades and only get half credit. I like this year alot better But it is a lot harder for me. I did not think I would ever get out of being in the same room all day. my grades have been very good. I have been really happy with them.

Now all I have to do is get my Reading and my other skills up there, and I will feel better about myself and school. maybe it will help me do better. I guess I have come a long way so far. I wish I could come even farther. I wish I was smart.

*Source:* Reprinted by permission of "Emmy."

**Educational Leadership and Support**

- Principal and teachers believe that academic achievement is possible for all pupils, and they create a school climate conducive to learning
- Principal demonstrates commitment to goals and flexibility in pursuing them
- A sense of shared values and culture is developed among students and staff
- Clear, reasonable, orderly, safe, disciplined, and consistent school policies and rules are enforced
- The staff is committed to emphasizing basic skills, evaluation of pupil progress, and program adaptations as necessary
- Support for small class size
- Staff development through in-service programs that address skills, techniques, attitudes, and behavior
- Principal protects the school day for teaching, minimizing teachers' administrative chores and classroom interruptions
- Principal makes sure teachers have necessary materials and assistance
- Principal builds morale of teachers and encourages a high level of professional collegiality
- Encouragement of teacher involvement in formulating school teaching policies and selecting textbooks
- Schoolwide recognition of academic success through symbols, ceremonies, and official recognition of accomplishments
- Encouragement of parental involvement and support
- Encouragement of a strong sense of student identification and affiliation with the school

**Orderly and Positive School Climate**

- "Withitness": teachers are aware of and responsive to what is going on in their classrooms at all times. Their awareness is communicated to students, and problems are anticipated and managed before they escalate
- High levels of informal student interaction with desirable activities
- School policies emphasize shared responsibility for the overall school climate
- Students perceive the school's expectations for academic success
- Positive, enthusiastic, pleasant, friendly, safe, and orderly classroom environment
- Teacher conveys enthusiasm, "hams" it up, uses humor and vocal expressiveness
- Rewards are content related rather than global praise ("That's right, a triangle has three sides" vs. "you're the best"); activity reinforcers are used (free time, time with athletic coach), exchangeable reinforcers (points, holes punched in a ticket), tangible reinforcers (pencils, magazines); when possible choices of reinforcers are offered; effort is reinforced
- Teacher is sparing rather than effusive in use of praise; praising easy responses is potentially embarrassing to the student, intrusive, and distracting

*(continued)*

**Figure 14.1** Characteristics of effective schools, classrooms, and instruction.

*Sources:* Berliner (1984); Bickel & Bickel (1986); Brigham, Scruggs, & Mastropieri (1992); Brophy (1982); Brophy & Good (1986); Carnine (1994); Dawson (1987); Englert (1984); Elbaum et al. (2000a, 2000b); Fisher, Berliner, Filby, Marliave, Cahan, & Dishaw (1980); Gersten, Woodward, & Darch (1986); Gickling & Thompson (1985); Glass, Cahan, Smith, and Filby (1982); Good (1983); Good & Brophy (1986); Gottlieb (1984); Hudson (1996); Lipham (1981); Lloyd & Loper (1986); Lou et al. (1996); Purkey & Smith (1983); Rademacher, Schumaker, & Deshler (1996); Samuels & Miller (1985); Shapiro (1992); Shavelson (1983); Sikorski, Niemiec, & Walberg (1996); Simmerman & Swanson (2001); Stevens & Rosenshine (1981); White (1986); Wilson & Wesson (1986).

- Avoid overcriticizing, especially via sarcasm or personal attacks
- Reward group task completion at times instead of each individual; encourage self-praise
- Correct papers marking accurate answers rather than errors; errors are then corrected by students to yield perfect papers
- Small-group and individualized instruction establishes closer teacher-student social ties and involvement than recitations, which place the teacher at the center of control
- Incorporate students' ideas into lessons as a way of letting them know their ideas are interesting and respected
- Encourage creative experiences, variety, and challenge
- Encourage student roles, such as homework monitor and team captain, to foster responsibility and involvement in management of students' school lives

**High Achievement Expectations**

- Set high but attainable goals; assign appropriate and frequent homework
- The staff is serious, businesslike, and purposeful about the task of teaching
- The staff expects students to learn, holds them accountable for learning, and rewards it
- High expectations are communicated by seating lower-ability students close to the teacher
- Call on low-ability as much as high-ability students and give them equal quality of feedback
- Wait up to 5 seconds for low-ability students to respond to questions; sustain the interaction by rephrasing the question, providing clues, follow-up questions, and explanations when students have difficulty answering questions
- Provide feedback to parents about the quality of student work

**Systematic Monitoring of Student Performance**

- Performance is monitored through classroom questions, homework, frequent essays, and quizzes
- Continual monitoring of individual and class progress; rapid feedback on homework
- Weekly and monthly reviews of student progress
- Graph student progress
- Monitor independent work to increase time that student is engaged (move about to check accuracy, ask questions, give feedback)
- Grading motivates students if tied to objective performance and used judiciously

**Emphasis on Basic Skills**

- Increase silent reading time, which increases vocabulary and reading fluency (elementary school students average only 7 to 8 minutes a day of silent reading); increase time spent on writing more than one sentence in length
- Teach basic and lower-level skills to mastery to build a foundation for higher-level objectives

**Organization of Instruction**

- Establish, communicate, and teach reasonable and workable class rules for conduct, procedures, and routines; clearly communicate consequences for infractions
- Adopt a systematic, preplanned structure to the learning process and time management
- Pace as briskly as possible with clear activity demands that sustain student momentum
- Allocate time for instruction in proportion to the priority of the subject area
- Increase time allocated to instruction (teachers deliver instruction about 80 percent of the time they allocate; large variability exists across teachers)
- Increase time that student is engaged during time allocated for instruction

**Figure 14.1** *Continued*

- Transitions and time spent getting organized should be brief and orderly (e.g., reinforce students for getting materials quickly, rearrange seating to make access to materials easier)
- Shorten recess or free time
- Streamline organizational activities (e.g., passing out papers; correcting papers) by increasing student self-management (e.g., correcting own spelling papers, charting own progress)
- Increase practice related to materials on which evaluation will occur
- Maintain 90 to 100 percent success on independent activities before moving on
- Make assignments neither too easy nor too hard or on-task behavior will decrease
- The more content covered, the more is learned; as much as 80 percent of reading achievement can be related to pacing, with higher-ability groups being paced up to 15 times faster than lower-ability groups
- Pace instruction briskly, in small steps, and with moderate to high rates of success; slow the pace as necessary to allow students time to absorb the material
- Use both whole class and small group instruction
- Determine number and size of instructional groups based on student skill and characteristics
- Use different groupings for different subjects, and based on frequent reassessment
- Teaching in smaller groups maintains attention better than large groups of 10 or more
- Achievement in small groups of 3 to 4 members is greater than in groups of 5 to 7 members
- Small group instruction has an advantage over one-to-one instruction because of increased peer interaction, more teacher time available for instruction per pupil, and more opportunities for skill generalization
- Low-ability students benefit the most from small group instruction
- Small group instruction enhances general self-concept
- One-to-one instruction is equally effective when skilled instructors are teaching, or well-supervised volunteers and paraprofessionals
- Classes should be heterogeneous with one-third or less being low-ability students
- Large or small heterogeneous groups are well suited to teaching material requiring little prior knowledge, such as social studies or science
- Small heterogeneous learning groups are effective for low-ability students because they benefit from peer explanations and guidance. Average learners progress faster in homogeneous small groups because they participate at higher rates in giving and receiving explanations than in heterogeneous groups. High-ability students fare well in either group.
- Homogeneous grouping for reading instruction augments achievement. Related heterogeneous activities further enhances achievement. Grouping also may be done by interest in different topics
- Avoid extreme heterogeneity in classes (e.g., ten grade levels)
- Limit ability grouping to only a few groups, to allow adequate direct instruction time and preparation of differentiated lesson plans
- Experiential learning can augment achievement to the same extent as small group instruction
- Decrease the use of worksheets to 50 percent (these often constitute 70 percent of daily reading time yet contribute little to yearly reading gains)
- Teach important subjects in both the morning and the afternoon

*(continued)*

**Figure 14.1** *Continued*

- Hold two reading sessions a day for low-ability groups rather than one long session
- Develop cooperative learning environments, peer tutoring

**Teacher Strategies**

- Take an active, teacher-directed role in instruction, including extended time blocks to develop concepts and actively elicit student responses
- There should be greater teacher-directed and supervised instruction than independent work or peer tutoring
- Carry the content to the student instead of relying on materials to do so (as in independent learning modules or workbooks); brief presentations are the method of choice, followed by recitation and application opportunities
- Check for understanding of new content and assignments by reviewing the previous day's lessons through questioning and quizzes; redundancy reinforces new learning
- Give oral or written frequent, detailed, and meaningful feedback, correction, and reteaching
- Correct student errors immediately; keep corrections to 30 seconds or less to avoid the rest of the class becoming off task
- Use spread-out, periodic, varied, and cumulative review of lessons
- Explicitly teach strategies and scaffold instruction
- Provide guided practice and drill; use a variety of activities and learning strategies
- Clarify criteria for quality work and how the work will be judged
- Provide choices so students have options for how to complete assignments; solicit student suggestions
- Begin work on assignments in class so assistance can be provided
- Use many detailed and redundant explanations when introducing a new concept, especially concrete and everyday examples and nonexamples
- Relate new academic content to a student's own life and previous learning
- Circulate among students as they do independent work, check student work, and give frequent, brief contacts to on-task students
- Provide daily opportunities to read easy material (96 percent accuracy level or higher)
- Keep learning at close to 80 percent accuracy (more frequent errors are expected when introducing new skills and content, but this quickly transitions to minimal errors); homework and seatwork should require effort and thought yet result in over 90 percent accuracy
- Unknown material should range from 15 to 30 percent of the total material presented
- Fifty or more repetitions, spread over several teaching sessions, may be necessary
- Give clear instructions and demonstrate often; signal transition between key ideas
- Actively elicit student responses in small group discussion (avoid passive listening)
- Use games and exercises that have a high response format rather than activities that require students to wait for a turn and listen to others
- Use a variety of learning modalities
- Use frequent comprehension checks, at least one question every two minutes; call on a student after rather than before the question has been asked in order to maintain class attention and give students time to think; call on both nonvolunteers and volunteers
- Increase opportunities to participate by calling on students in a predetermined order; calling on students randomly usually results in higher-achieving and assertive students being called on, and those who most need practice and feedback have fewer opportunities

**Figure 14.1** *Continued*

- When students are reticent to respond to questions, encourage "call-outs"
- Waiting three or more seconds after asking a question leads to more appropriate and higher-level responses, greater variety of responses, and more confidence in responding
- Seventy-five percent of questions should elicit correct answers; even if incorrect (as will happen on generalization, application, and evaluation questions), responses should be substantive
- Use more lower-order questions (knowledge, comprehension)—these will stimulate higher-level comprehension (application, analysis, synthesis, evaluation); follow with higher-level questions
- Teacher "talk" should involve more questions and feedback than lecturing
- Encourage students to paraphrase and summarize
- Follow a structured teaching sequence: begin instruction with overviews and outlines, advance organizers, and review of objectives; outline the content, main ideas, summarize completed parts of the lesson; signal transitions, provide relationship to prior learning through analogies and organization of concepts; model problem-solving processes that involve judgment and decision making; review main ideas; ask key questions; demonstrate; use concrete and meaningful examples, guided practice and progress monitoring, test, review, feedback, reteaching
- Attention and success are increased by spending time discussing the goals of a lesson, how they fit with the scheme of things, and what to focus on for success

**Figure 14.1** *Continued*

Research on effective schools refutes the notion that schools are relatively powerless in the face of other variables that affect achievement, such as a youngster's dysfunctional family situation. Schools can do much to enhance student achievement when they promote appropriate changes in the system itself, the organization of instruction, and teaching strategies. Two of the effective school variables most highly related to academic outcome are the amount of teacher structure provided through direct instruction and the amount of student engaged time spent productively on task.

**Direct Instruction.** We have emphasized throughout this book that students with LD generally need very structured, carefully sequenced instruction that concentrates on a few major criteria in depth (so this knowledge will be applied beyond the classroom), rather than teaching many concepts superficially. Depending on their goals, teaching styles, and the students' needs, teachers may organize instruction into teacher-directed group or individual activities, free-play situations in which students can choose from all available activities, or free-choice situations in which students are free to choose from among the activities their teacher has prepared.

***Students with LD generally need very structured instruction and teaching that concentrates on a few big ideas in depth. When teachers teach for exposure rather than depth, little of the information is remembered.***

The *open-education* instructional system popularized in the 1960s and 1970s contrasted with teacher-directed approaches by taking a self-paced, self-initiated approach to student learning. It was expected to foster more creativity

*The expected psychological gains from open-education classes were not realized, and academic achievement in reading, math, and other subjects was inferior to the traditional classroom.*

and psychological well-being, and yet be as effective as the traditional approach in promoting academic achievement. Hyperactive and distractible children were expected to be less disruptive and thrive in an environment in which they were free to move and set their own learning pace. However, study after study has shown that the expected psychological gains were not realized and that academic achievement in reading, math, and other subjects was inferior to the traditional classroom.

*Time spent on task in class and outside of the classroom is one of the most powerful predictors of achievement.*

Students seem to fare better in traditional classrooms because they spend more time working directly on academic tasks instead of wondering what their goal should be, waiting for teacher direction, or socializing with peers. It is time spent on task in class and outside the classroom that is one of the most powerful predictors of achievement in all areas. Therefore, more traditional organization of instruction, or more teacher guidance in classrooms with constructivist philosophies, may benefit students with LD who generally require consistent teacher direction to focus their attention appropriately, to remain on task, and to comprehend and remember what they are taught.

Given the huge amount of material covered in textbooks—on average 300 science words per text in sixth grade and 3,000 new terms and symbols in tenth grade—teachers are advised to select among topics, simplify the material, and teach a few "big" ideas well rather than cover many topics poorly. It's been found that because texts "mention" so much, teachers can devote less than 30 minutes in instructional time per year to 70 percent of the topics covered. When teachers teach for exposure rather than depth, little of the information is remembered and applied in practical situations.

*When greater amounts of time are allocated to instruction, when students spend more of this time engaged on task, and when more of the engaged time results in successful learning experiences, the greater are the academic gains.*

**Engaged Time on Tasks.** We know that when greater amounts of time are allocated to instruction, when students spend more of this time engaged on task, and when more of the engaged time results in successful learning experiences, the greater are the academic gains. Yet students spend far too little time each day devoted to academic learning. Studies show that only 50 to 60 percent of the school day at best is allocated to instruction, students are taught for only 40 percent of the day, and they are attending to task for only about one-quarter of the day—that's 1½ hours out of a 6-hour school day! Almost 3 hours each day are devoted to activities such as procedural matters (distributing worksheets, collecting materials, managing behavior, announcements, clarifying rules); waiting for instruction or one's turn; transitions from one subject or room to the next; free time; interruptions by the teacher, students, or the public address system; and eating or snack time. In a study that observed regular classes for 6 months, one-third of the allocated instructional time was spent waiting for teacher directions, getting and putting away materials, and lining up and moving to new activities. Observational studies in classrooms find that children spend on average 6 to 10 minutes per day reading silently and 3 to 13 minutes reading orally. Very little instruction is devoted to reading comprehension. Over half of the time allotted to reading instruction is typically spent in seatwork and worksheet completion. Even in a 30-minute reading group, one study found that students got only 12 to 88 seconds each to read aloud. In another study, time spent writing was found to be equally dismal, with only 3 percent of class time being spent in writing activities of a paragraph or more in length; short sentences were the norm for answering questions. One study found that only 20 minutes of a school day on average was spent writing; 60 percent of this time was spent filling out worksheets, practicing handwriting, and completing spelling activities. The amount of time spent on task in the resource room or special class often is reported to be similarly bleak; too many opportunities for learning are wasted.

***The amount of time spent on task in the classroom is bleak; too many opportunities for learning are wasted.***

If students could spend only a few of the wasted minutes in additional reading each day, their reading achievement would very likely improve considerably. Simple mathematics dramatizes this point. Beginning with the assumption that the student with LD may lose 15 minutes of learning time each day when transferring from the regular class to resource room, one expert figured that:

> Fifteen minutes a day is not much time but it translates into forty-five hours a year—a full two weeks of instructional days. Over a K–12 school experience, a total of 130 days are lost at 15 minutes a day—more than two-thirds of a school year! Nearly a year of instruction lost just in the time it takes to leave the regular education class, walk to the resource room, be greeted and have the day's instructional activity commence, and then to return to the regular classroom and begin to work there. (Allington, 1984, p. 95)

Time spent on homework is another avenue for increasing time on task, opportunities to learn, and academic achievement. A series of national surveys of over a third of a million seniors in more than 1,000 high schools finds that grades and achievement test scores increase as the number of homework hours increase. These studies found that homework was able to compensate partially for low ability, in that the average low-ability student who completed 3 to 5 hours of homework a week achieved higher grades than the average-ability student who did no homework. Yet over half the seniors reported doing less than 3 hours of homework a week. Almost 20 percent studied less than 1 hour per week. Only about one-third of students spent 6 or more hours a week studying or doing homework. In other surveys of fourth, eighth, and twelfth graders, only one-third to one-half devoted as much as 1 hour or more to homework each evening, yet 40 to 50 percent watched television 3 to 5 hours per day. Survey results from nearly 500 seniors with LD are equally discouraging. These students did significantly less homework than their peers (1 to 3 hours per week), yet devoted 2 to 3 hours daily to "the tube," and another 2 to 3 hours a day to extracurricular activities. When asked, most students perceive extracurricular activities and being with friends as more important than doing homework.

***Grades and achievement test scores increase as the number of homework hours increase.***

Several issues related to homework are common among students with LD: reluctance to do homework as evidenced by complaining, avoiding getting started, and taking too long to complete it; distractibility caused by daydreaming, being drawn off task by noises, or studying only if someone else is in the room or working with them; poor study skills; forgetting to bring home assignments and materials; poor planning for the time needed to complete homework; not checking to see whether all the homework is done; not handing in homework; frustration with task difficulty and quitting; failing to break projects and reports into manageable pieces and working on these a little at a time; getting less help and encouragement from parents, but more criticism. Several recommendations can help these students with homework completion: have teachers and parents sign a "homework notebook" of assignments daily; focus assignments on practice and maintenance activities rather than new learning, so that the student is sure to be successful on at least 80 percent of the items; assign meaningful tasks; help parents set schedules and contingencies that encourage homework completion; have students graph homework completion; and teach students independent study skills. If practice and maintenance homework continues to be trying for students and parents, the teacher can shift to "preparation" homework, in which parents preview with their children material that will be covered at school, thereby priming them for success and participation in the classroom. Homework also can be in the form of applying classroom concepts in "real life" and encouraging creativity: making a collage or poster of good nutrition, taping interviews for a family history story to be written in school, clipping coupons and calculating the savings after grocery shopping.

Assigning more homework does positively affect the achievement of students with LD. So does making a concerted effort to decrease classroom time spent on class management, waiting, making transitions, and so on. Aides, foster grandparents, and student teachers can help increase the time students actively spend engaged in instructional programs. And after-school homework support programs have been very successful in improving reading and math performance.

***Decreasing classroom time spent on class management, waiting, and making transitions increases achievement.***

Another promising approach is daily *classwide peer tutoring,* in which student pairs take turns listening to one another read and asking questions. Not only do the number of minutes devoted to reading aloud and silently increase about tenfold, but so does reading, spelling, math, and comprehension accuracy. In one method, the stronger reader reads for five minutes, after which the weaker reader reads the same text. Tutors point out reading errors, and encourage tutees to figure out the word and reread the sentence before giving them the word. The lower achiever retells what had been read, and after every paragraph summarizes the main idea in ten words or less. This student then predicts what will be read in the next paragraph, and the process begins anew. Studies find that peer tutoring is effective for increasing the academic skills of both tutors and tutees; students with LD benefit from the tutoring role and many do it quite well with appropriate training and supervision. Training is important, however, because often the stronger student will dominate, cut short explanations, and convey faulty logic that could hamper the learning process.

***Peer tutoring is effective for increasing the academic skills of both tutors and tutees.***

Some have argued for a longer school day and year as a way to address the issue of time on task. Extended-year programs (210 school days vs. 180 for example) do effect academic gains. Most experts believe, however, that there is plenty of opportunity to make much better use of the allotted time during the current school day by decreasing busywork, waiting, and disruptions, increasing the amount of direct instruction, and increasing the rigor of homework assignments that lead to academic achievement for all students.

## Human Characteristics

The character of the school environment, which reflects the attitudes and behaviors of classroom teachers and peers, can affect the academic and social success of students. Because students with LD have a harder time making friends and may have more negative interactions with teachers and peers, we need to find ways to help them be more valued, accepted, and befriended. If we do, their rising self-esteem will help them persist with their studies and make better life adjustments. Carol Blatt's story—The Force IN Me—is a wonderful example of how personal strength, and one special teacher at the right time, can help a student with a severe learning disability find satisfaction.

## Teacher Characteristics

There is no question that a teacher's personality, style, and attitudes can strongly influence daily life in a classroom. Springtime often finds parents and students

### The Force IN Me That Said—You Are a Fighter and Survivor So Don't Give Up Regardless How Difficult Success Is

*Personal strength and one special teacher helped this individual persevere and succeed.*

My name is Carol. I was born on March 27, 1955. I could not complete anything that I had to write down in elementary school and I was a very slow writer and reader however as the school system I was in was concerned I did not exist. When I entered the Sixth Grade and mathematically I had the skills of a sixth grader but I could not write anything down on paper and yet I had no trouble verbalizing what should have been written down on paper. My family was told by a school system who had not woken up until I had completed the sixth grade for the first time that they sensed that a problem existed and I could not enter Junior High School. My mother said you have just woken up now and told us that there is problem well you will not hold her over and she will go onto Junior High School. In Junior High School Grade Seven I was placed in a class whereby all that the other children did not want to learn. After be exposed to one more year of the School systems inability to educate me my parents placed me in a private school.

Now to chapter two of my life—Grade Eight and the initial installment of you are a fighter, you will never give up and you will succeed regardless how difficult success is for you I walked into my Eighth Grade Homeroom and gradually came to know someone one who was also my Eighth Grade English teacher who continually instilled in me that you can learn regardless how difficult the work gets, you can be taught anything regardless how difficult and that even if it takes you twice as long or even three times as long you will succeed. She became the person who helped me with anything in Grades 8 to 12 that was difficult and frustrating for me to achieve and throughout all this and what she wrote in my school year book in Grade 12—DESPITE HOW DIFFICULT THE TASK, YOU ARE A FIGHTER AND YOU WILL NOT JUST SURVIVE BUT SUCCEED.

Now onto part three my parents had no expectations of my becoming anything but I told my sister that I wanted to go onto college and she told my parents that I had to be given that chance. . . . With the voice within in me that comes through everytime I come upon an obstacles that says you will succeed and don't give up. I have continued to make many strives until today. . . . I am today a teaching for 15 years with a Master's Degree, 4 City Education Licenses, Permanent State Certification . . . The End.

*Source:* Reprinted by permission of Carol Blatt.

jockeying to get into (or out of) a particular teacher's class for the next school year based on their perceptions that "her classes are always happy and high achieving" or that "he is too mean and plays favorites" or that "she is too lazy to challenge students."

*Teachers set the tone—positive or negative—in the classroom.*

Teachers set the tone—positive or negative—in the classroom. One study, for example, found that teachers whose styles were predominantly positive spent about 10 percent of their time dealing with behavior problems, whereas those whose styles were predominantly negative spent about 42 percent of their time managing students' inappropriate behavior. We next explore a number of variables that influence teacher attitudes and behavior toward students with LD, all of which contribute to the classroom climate experienced by the student.

**Attitudes Toward Special Students.** Much of the success of inclusion efforts hinges on the attitudes of general education teachers toward youngsters with LD. The more special education courses or workshops in which a teacher has participated, the more co-teaching with special educators, and the greater the confidence

## Dear Regular Education Teacher

*A mother appeals to her son's teacher to put aside her biases and help him to flourish in class.*

My son will be in your class next year. He has just finished a wonderful year in the Resource Room, and with the Regular Education Initiative at the doorstep of our school, he will be mainstreamed into your class. You will be the one who touches his life most in school, even though the special education teacher will be there to help you.

My son is a fine boy. You will like him. He wants to do well but he does not read well. His language skills are also quite low. He doesn't spell well and he doesn't know all his math facts yet. He sometimes has a hard time understanding when instructions are given too fast and too many are given at once. He may get mixed up at times, but he always tries hard. He won't cause any trouble. Please don't let him give up; the special education teacher is still there to help him. He won't often ask for your help. He'll be quiet.

For his sake, please don't accept sloppy work. His markovers and misaligned work are part of his learning disability but he can copy the work. Maintain high standards for him. Give pencil grades and expect him to improve. Use the improved grade as the permanent grade. He can do well if we set high standards for him.

It might be a helpful realization for you, as a regular education teacher, to consider the area of fairness. When a special education student is only required to do ten questions or half the homework, the other students often resent this. The realization that this may be the fair way must come from the heart of the teacher and be explained to the class from the beginning. Fairness is not having everything the same for every student, fairness is providing what each student needs to be successful. All students need to know that this is the standard.

Another idea which may be helpful is to talk to all students about individual strengths and weaknesses. Some strengths are very visible, like academics and sports. Some strengths are less obvious, like kindness and the desire to work hard.

Learning disabilities are handicaps that others may not be able to see but are very real. These in his or her teaching ability, the more willing the teacher is to include students with LD and to adapt instruction.

*Special education teachers tend to have a more favorable attitude than general education teachers toward the intelligence, task orientation, and motivation of students with LD and are more convinced that they can succeed in the regular classroom.*

General education teachers tend to accept students with milder disabilities more easily, especially when those students fit nicely into established instructional groupings. Special education teachers, however, tend to have a more favorable attitude than general education teachers toward the intelligence, task orientation, and motivation of students with LD and are more convinced that they can succeed in the regular classroom.

General education teachers prefer students with LD who are approachable, persistent, and adaptable. They would prefer to transfer out of their classes children with more active and distractible temperaments. If students with LD sense the teacher's ambivalence, negativism, or lack of understanding and support, their performance can be affected.

Building sensitivity among the school staff toward students with learning disabilities is very important. One study found that students with LD who

### Dear Regular Education Teacher (Continued)

hidden handicaps are affecting every part of my son's life. No student wants to fail and failing is what he and others like him have done. They need to achieve success at their own level and to be able to be proud of their effort. Praise the effort!

School is often a tough time for these kids and it is important that some part of each school day is enjoyable, or at least that students like my son understand the reason they are there: to teach them how to learn, to teach them the job skills they will need, to teach them how to get along with others, and to teach them how to follow instructions. Often these students will not learn or retain the information offered in the regular education classroom as readily as other students. They need to know there are reasons to keep trying. Always praise their efforts!

My last suggestion for you comes from the heart of a mother. I am working very hard to give you a whole human being. He is sensitive, loving, hard working, and desires very much to please you, his teacher. He'll try hard for you. Please help me give this child a sense of self-worth, of value to his life. He has faith in his family to love and support him and faith in his school to teach him the best way they can. He will learn at his own rate and in time he will get there. Please don't be frustrated or discouraged. He feels that enough for both of you. Try as hard as you can to help me build that self-esteem he so desperately needs to survive. Offer information; you may find a spark of interest there. Try to share your love of learning with him, and if you find that spark, encourage him to branch out even if his specific interest does not fit into the curriculum.

Next to his parents, I believe you, his teacher, have the hardest job. Thank you for helping me to shape a positive, productive, whole person through your understanding, love, and encouragement.

Thank you for being willing to listen to the mother who is sharing her son with you this school year, so we can be prepared and confident through the sometimes tough but successful days together.

*Source:* Eddinger, B. A. (1990, July/August), *LDA Newsbriefs*, p. 15. Reprinted with permission of *LDA Newsbriefs*.

acknowledged their academic problems, yet saw their teacher's feedback and grading as positive, rated themselves as just as smart and good at schoolwork as their non-disabled classmates. In another study, a teacher's positive, accepting attitude helped her students with LD be as well liked by peers as others in the classroom; nearly everyone had a mutual friend. Barbara Eddinger's poignant letter to her son's teacher, on page 542, is an especially moving appeal to set aside typical biases, and give her son a chance to grow and develop in that teacher's classroom.

*Generally, teacher-student interactions are more numerous, more positive, and of higher quality with special education teachers.*

**Teacher-Student Interaction.** Although children with learning disabilities are not purposely singled out or made to feel different in the regular classroom, generally teacher-student interactions are more numerous, more positive, and of higher quality with special education teachers. These students tend to have a lower rate of interaction with general education teachers in part because they ask for less assistance and answer fewer questions, and in part because teachers tend not to check as much on these students' learning. When more frequent interactions do occur, they are often criticisms, corrections, or warnings elicited by student behaviors such as distractibility and low frustration tolerance. In one study, a hyperactive child's presence in the classroom was associated with increased disruptiveness in classmates and negative feedback from the teacher toward both the hyperactive child and the class as whole.

*General education teachers tend to offer little praise for their students with LD, have lower expectations, give less extended feedback, and ask them fewer academic questions.*

Many studies find that general education teachers offer little praise for their students with learning disabilities, have lower expectations, give less extended feedback (e.g., shorter explanations, fewer cues, fewer repetitions of questions), and ask them fewer academic questions. Some teachers appear to avoid such interactions in whole class situations because they think that slower students take longer to arrive at answers or bore their classmates, in either case increasing the risk of class disruption.

Many studies have found that regular class teachers tend not to individualize instruction for students with learning disabilities or to systematically monitor their learning, even though they know this is a good thing to do and have been taught how to do so. When they do make adaptations, these tend not to be "special"; instead, teachers simply extend timelines to reach certain objectives, delete an objective, lower goals, or move the child out of the regular class for instruction. A recent national survey found that 66 percent of general education teachers think it is unfair to adapt tests for the learning disabled alone.

*Students with LD benefit from cooperative learning systems, though direct instruction and peer tutoring have more powerful effects.*

Because teaching to the whole group is the norm, teachers are more apt to adopt practices that improve instruction for all learners, rather than implement a plan that meets the needs of only the student with LD. They seem to be quite willing, for example, to implement the cooperative learning strategies described in Research Box 14.1. The average student responds to cooperative learning strategies with higher achievement and more positive social interactions than in traditional competitive learning systems. Students with LD also can learn from cooperative learning systems, though direct teacher instruction and peer tutoring have more powerful effects on their achievement. Their achievement increases when cooperative learning is designed to include individual accountability and group rewards. Cooperative learning is an attractive alternative to the competitive learning environment and can positively affect the behavior and social acceptance of a student with LD.

RESEARCH BOX 14.1

## Cooperative Learning Techniques

In cooperative learning every member of a group participates in academic activities that can be successfully completed only through interdependent and cooperative behavior. Students must master material initially presented by the teacher, and ensure that others in their group do so as well. Cooperative learning strategies have been very successful in promoting social interaction, while avoiding the competitive atmosphere of the typical classroom. When compared with traditional competitive and individual learning structures, positive effects from the cooperative reward structure have been apparent on student achievement, creative writing, ethnic relations, mutual concern, social and academic self-esteem, internal locus of control, behavior, friendships, time on task, perspective taking, and cooperativeness. Studies also report that cooperative learning facilitates critical thinking and higher-level reasoning, generation of new ideas and solutions to problems, transfer of what is learned in one situation to another, positive attitudes toward the subject matter and the instructional experience, greater motivation to pursue learning about the subject, and positive attitudes toward the teacher (Johnson & Johnson, 1994; Margolis & Freund, 1991; Slavin, 1995, 1996; Stevens & Slavin, 1991).

The positive effects of cooperative learning have been attributed to motivational increases resulting from the group reward; students modeling the higher-level problem solving of more capable peers; increased social cohesion; giving explanations; peer discussions and feedback; elaboration and summarizing of material; peer editing; students learning to care and feel responsible for one another's achievement; and following of teacher-directed strategies for learning. High, average, and low achievers and students of all ages and different ethnicities tend to benefit equally from cooperative learning strategies when compared with traditional competitive or individualistic learning approaches.

Cooperative learning techniques can differ in subject matter, the way in which students help one another, the way in which groups interact, whether students or teachers choose the groups, whether grades or rewards are based on individual or group performance, and the amount of environmental modification or teacher preparation required. It is common for students to be graded individually; however, group scores are computed to determine which team has excelled. Individual grades may be assigned on the basis of test performance, accuracy of homework, individual effort, individual contribution to the group, individual improvement, or cooperativeness in the group. Group goals and rewards have been shown to enhance achievement outcomes, but only if team scores are based on the individual learning contributions of *all* group members; if the performance of each individual isn't counted in some way, there is little incentive for group members to explain concepts to one another, help one another out, and encourage teammates to put forth maximum effort—a handful of group members may end up doing all the work.

When individual scores are used to compute the group's score, it is wise to compare each student's performance against that of a student of equal ability in each of the other groups (e.g., the top scorer in each team on the previous quiz, the second best scorers, and so forth). The highest scorer is assigned the maximum number of points, for example, 10; the second highest scorer is scored 1 or 2 points lower; and so on. In this way each student, whether of high or low ability, is equally valued within the group because he or she has the opportunity to contribute the same number of points to the group's

*(continued)*

## RESEARCH BOX 14.1 (Continued)

overall performance as anyone else. Because the group outcome depends on every individual's success, group members are motivated to encourage and help one another to excel (e.g., explain information in a way that makes more sense than the teacher's explanations, quiz one another, demonstrate how to go about researching a topic). A modification of this approach is to assign students to heterogeneous groups to coach one another for a test. When the test is taken, "improvement points" are awarded to each student based on comparison with past test grades. The improvement points are then tallied for each group. Because the student with LD has a good chance of contributing more improvement points to group scores than do consistently excellent students, teammates are motivated to help the student prepare.

Groups of four students have been found to be optimum, composed of one high achiever, two average achievers, and one low achiever. When first instituting cooperative learning, pairs and threesomes are recommended in order to help students manage the interpersonal dimensions of small group work. Groups should not grow to more than six members, in order to promote every one's engagement and active participation. A group may remain together for one class period, 4 to 6 weeks, or even a whole marking period. Team cohesion and interdependence is encouraged by having students take on roles such as "recorder," "observer," "researcher," or "summarizer." The social skills necessary for successful collaboration must be taught, such as clearly communicating ideas and feelings, listening skills, sharing of materials, supportiveness, refraining from interruption, how to disagree agreeably, responding to others' suggestions, how to reach consensus, abiding by time limits, generating strategies, asking for ideas or help, expanding on someone else's ideas, and managing controversy.

Because students with LD often are not active participants in these groups, and at times are ignored or rebuffed, they need to be coached on ideas to contribute to the group and on how to ask their peers for help or feedback ("How am I doing?"). New concepts need to be reinforced, and the teacher must help them rehearse their reports to the class. In turn, the nondisabled need to learn how to offer constructive criticism in a way that won't make the learning disabled feel anxious or embarrassed. The nondisabled also need reassurance that their grades will not be negatively affected by such inclusion. This can be accomplished by keeping the requirements for the student with LD reasonable, offering bonus points to groups that include members with disabilities, and training students in peer-tutoring strategies (Johnson & Johnson, 1986). Bohlmeyer and Burke (1987) and Slavin (1995) offer comprehensive reviews of cooperative learning techniques. We explore several of these below.

### Jigsaw

In Jigsaw, students are assigned heterogeneously (gender, race, ability levels) to groups of 3 to 6 students to teach each other some classroom content. Each person in the group is given a specific set of information to teach the others. In a social studies unit, for example, one student may be assigned social customs, another the nation's agriculture, another religious beliefs, and so forth. A biography might be divided into the person's youth, family, schooling, accomplishments, and so on. Students responsible for the same lessons across different groups get together to clarify their understanding of the materials and discuss how to make their teaching most interesting. Then they return to their groups to teach their sections. Finally, all students are quizzed on the entire content. Team scores may or may not be used. A variation of this technique is for all students

RESEARCH BOX 14.1 (Continued)

to study all the content, but individuals are responsible for focusing on different aspects on the test.

**Group Investigation and Co-op Co-op**

In Group Investigation, the class is assigned a general area of study and groups actively decide what they will study and how. In Co-op Co-op each group is responsible for researching a specific topic; students can choose the group that most interests them, although the teacher does encourage heterogeneity of ability, gender, and ethnicity within groups. The teacher sets up learning stations in order to facilitate the students' research activities. Group members can divide the work among themselves, each carrying out a different piece of the investigation. Once each group has gathered sufficient information, the group plans a report and presents it to the class. The class members are responsible for learning the materials presented by all groups.

**Student Teams-Achievement Divisions and Teams-Games-Tournament**

In Student Team Learning, group members are responsible for teaching one another the content, and the groups compete for mastery via academic quizzes or games. If the groups are heterogeneously formed, the average quiz grade or "improvement points" of team members can be the basis for group points. At other times students of equal ability engage in an academic tournament. The score each student earns is added to an overall team score. The winning team is recognized in some fashion, such as an announcement in the school newspaper. Grades, however, are based on students' individual quiz performance.

**Circles of Learning**

As in Student Teams, group members teach one another from a packet of information provided to each group. Group members sit in a circle facing each other and are responsible for sharing materials and helping one another. Although individual tests are administered, group rewards also can be earned. For example, bonus points can be awarded to each member of a group if all members reach a certain criterion. Classwide cooperation can be encouraged by giving the entire class a reward if each group reaches a set criterion.

**Small Group Mathematics**

Here the teacher decides on homogeneous or heterogeneous groupings and assigns students to groups after students submit names indicating whom they would and would not prefer to work with. Groups are composed of four members who work as a group to solve each math problem. Students are encouraged to share leadership, build on others' ideas, and confirm that everyone understands the problem's solution before moving on.

**Team-Assisted Individualization (Team-Accelerated Instruction)**

Also designed for mathematics instruction, Team-Assisted Individualization teams consist of 4 or 5 heterogeneously placed students. Students within teams are divided into dyads or triads. Students work their own problems. Then their partners check their accuracy. When students have questions, they consult their team members first. If still unclear, they consult the teacher. The program is individually paced so that when they feel they are ready, students take the test that matches their instructional objectives. At the end of each week, team scores are compiled based on the average number of units covered by each team's members. The team reaching the criterion established by the teacher wins some form of recognition (e.g., a certificate).

The willingness of a teacher to implement special strategies makes a big difference to a child with LD in that classroom, as will the teacher's sensitivity to his or her reactions to students based on their gender, attractiveness, social class, and achievement level.

*Teacher Nonverbal Behavior.* Teachers communicate positive and negative judgments to children through their facial expressions, body movements, and posture. These in turn affect students' self-esteem, how well they like their teachers, and their judgments of teacher performance. Testimony to the power of teachers' nonverbal behaviors is one study's finding that direct and frequent teacher eye contact alone improved student attention and participation, increased the amount of information retained, and boosted students' self-esteem.

***The lower social status or students with LD in their general education classrooms is highly correlated with teacher attitudes toward these children.***

There is evidence that the lower social status of students with LD in their classrooms is highly correlated with teacher attitudes toward these children. Teachers ignore these students' verbal initiations more often than the initiations of good learners. They more often avoid eye contact, frown, and provide less physical contact and encouragement. These nonverbal "judgments" are not lost on nondisabled classmates, who frequently adjust their attitudes about the social desirability of the learning disabled accordingly. This in turn affects how students with LD feel about themselves.

***Children who give teachers more positive nonverbal communication are often more liked by teachers and judged to be brighter.***

Communication is a two-way process. Children who give teachers more positive nonverbal communication are often more liked by teachers and judged to be brighter. Unfortunately, many students with LD don't pick up and practice these positive nonverbal behaviors as well as their peers, and they may suffer as a result.

*Gender Differences.* In both elementary and secondary schools, boys are disciplined more often than girls, and they receive more teacher criticism. Surprisingly, they also receive more teacher praise. Teachers are more likely to use harsh or angry tones with boys than girls for the same misbehavior, and to grade boys lower than their achievement warrants. More boys are referred to special education.

***Boys' more active behavior attracts more attention and criticism from the teacher.***

Some experts maintain that it is the disruptive behavior of boys that brings them more negative feedback, not an overt gender bias on the part of teachers. Boys who behave like boys—rowdy, loud, and impulsive—stand out more and therefore attract more attention from the teacher, whether positive or negative. Regardless of the reason, sex is likely to play a role in teachers' interactions with students who are learning disabled, the majority of whom are boys.

The gender of the teacher is also an important factor. It has been found that female teachers are far more likely to refer children displaying high levels of problem behaviors for alternative education services. These were more likely to be males, given their higher activity levels.

*Attractiveness.* Students whose appearance is odd or unattractive are more likely to receive poor grades, to be involved in negative interactions with the teacher, to elicit lower teacher expectations, and to be referred to special education. Some children with LD fall into this category because their social imperceptiveness leads them to be unkempt, or because their cognitive disabilities are accompanied by subtle physical differences. Unfortunately, the physical appearance of students with LD also appears to be an important influence on social status among their peers.

***The physical appearance of students with LD appears to be an important influence on social status among their peers.***

***Social Class, Race, and Cultural Differences.*** Several studies have found that teachers hold more negative attitudes toward and have lower expectations of African American, Hispanic, and lower-income students. All other factors being equal, these students are referred for special education services at higher than expected rates. Teachers seem to give more praise, rewards, approval, support, and nonverbal reinforcement to middle-income children; they more often neglect, punish, and misunderstand lower-socioeconomic-status and African American children, especially boys. In one study, experienced white teachers listening to taped responses to school questions assigned significantly higher grades to white boys than to African American boys even though the boys gave identical answers. Another study found that teachers' attitudes toward Hispanic third and fourth graders became less favorable as these children's accents thickened. This held true, though to a lesser extent, even for Hispanic teachers. Studies find that teachers more often isolate Hispanic and African American students, communicate lower expectations, avoid interaction and eye contact, leave them out of class activities, call on and praise them less often, don't help them to develop their ideas as fully, respond less positively to their comments, and ask them fewer questions.

***Teachers hold more negative attitudes toward and have lower expectations of African American, Hispanic, and lower-income students. All other factors being equal, these students are referred for special education services at higher than expected rates.***

This type of bias against children from lower-socioeconomic-status and racial or culturally different backgrounds is particularly relevant to learning disabilities because the characteristics associated with learning disabilities are prevalent among students in these groups. Children from these groups are disproportionately represented in the LD population.

Teachers need to learn to honor and value the contribution that students from diverse backgrounds bring to class and find ways for these students to feel comfortable sharing their rich heritages. Multiculturalism built into the curriculum, and respect for differences among those in the classroom, foster personal self-worth and academic motivation for those in the minority. We can encourage students to use their native language among themselves at school. Signs in both English and other languages can be posted and books in these languages made available. We can recruit tutors and guest speakers who share similar backgrounds, hold international food fests, study the history of various countries, and so forth. As teachers begin to appreciate the origins of children's individual styles, they will be less quick to wrongly judge students as indifferent, insolent, or arrogant (e.g., when they look away from the teacher and don't respond); teachers understand that these children are responding differently than we would expect because of their cultural upbringing.

***Teachers need to honor and value the contribution that students from diverse backgrounds bring to class, and modify programs to fit these students' learning and behavior preferences.***

It helps a great deal when teachers modify their programs to fit the learning and behavioral preferences of students from culturally and linguistically diverse backgrounds. This includes learning which cultures tend to respect competitiveness and which cooperation, which cultures operate "by the clock" and which have an expanded sense of time (this can affect time limits on tests, for example), which cultures value remaining passive much of the time and which must talk and be on the move nearly constantly, which prefer to stand close and touch and which value personal space, which cultures believe that eye contact is a measure of respect and which find it offensive, and so on. In a Chicago school, achievement motivation and the number of students continuing their educations after graduation increased when peer tutoring and mentoring was designed to build on the "brotherhood" and "sisterhood" that united these African American students. In a Hawaiian school, student pride and participation increased when teachers adopted these students' mothers' expectations: that children will organize among themselves to get a job done, without supervision and with minimal verbal direction. As teachers accommodate their classes to draw children's home and school lives closer together, thereby affirming their culture, they must also be cautious not to assume that all children of one race or ethnic background share the same cultural teachings and values. There is great heterogeneity within each culture; each child must be approached as an individual within a belief system that may be uniquely his or her own.

***Teachers must be cautious not to assume that all children of one race or ethnic background share the same cultural teachings and values. There is great heterogeneity within each culture.***

When classrooms become responsive to the unique and culturally bound skills and behaviors students bring with them, students are more likely to perceive the schooling experience as relevant and meaningful. Feeling less alienated, more respected, and not pressured to reject their culture in favor of the attitudes of the dominant culture, these students can devote more positive energy toward managing the social and academic challenges of the school.

*Achievement Differences.* Most research suggests that teacher behavior toward high- and low-achieving students differs more in quality than quantity of interaction. Higher-achieving students are more active participants in class and receive more positive teacher contact and feedback. Teachers smile, nod, maintain eye contact, call on, and lean forward toward the student more often when they are told that he or she is a high achiever versus a low achiever.

***Higher-achieving students are more active participants in class and receive more positive teacher contact and feedback.***

Teachers tend to pay less attention to lower-achieving students, to seat them farther away, to require less work and effort, to wait less time for them to answer questions, to interrupt them more frequently, to not provide cues or follow-up questions when the student is uncertain, to criticize incorrect answers more often and praise correct answers less, and to provide them with less lengthy, accurate, and detailed feedback. Naturally, because students with LD tend to fall into the low-achieving category, they are more likely to trigger such teacher biases. General education teachers are less likely to find teaching these students a joy, and more likely to wish they could be removed from the class, even if the teachers have formal training and experience in including children with special needs. These children often are quite aware of the lower expectations conveyed by their teachers' behaviors.

## Peer Characteristics

***Students with LD do form friendships with students like themselves, but have a harder time relating with their nondisabled peers.***

Peer relationships are pivotal human aspects of the classroom setting. We know that students with learning disabilities do form friendship clusters with students like themselves. However, they have a harder time with relationships with nondisabled peers. They are less interactive in the classroom and therefore less "known" to their peers, have fewer friends, draw fewer positive responses from peers, and are more often rejected than their nondisabled classmates. Sometimes children with LD are aware of their lower social status, and sometimes not.

You have only to observe the high social status held by cheerleaders, basketball players, and student government officers to know that popularity is often related to academic and athletic ability. In these respects, students with learning disabilities are disadvantaged right from the start. Low achievement, physical incoordination, reluctance to try out for sports, and school "no pass—no play" policies limit their social status. Further, some students with LD have problems that make social communication difficult, such as comprehension and oral language problems, social imperceptiveness, learned helplessness, immaturity, and impulsiveness. And we know from research that the more unusual a child is relative to the peer group, the more likely that he or she will be rejected.

*The more unusual a child is relative to the peer group, the more likely that he or she will be rejected.*

Rejection of students with LD may also be a function of the learning disabilities identification process. When classmates know that these students have been labeled by the school as academically less adequate than others, they may be less friendly and welcoming to students with learning difficulties.

It may be tempting to give in to the law of the playground in these matters, but exciting possibilities for modifying peer attitudes toward classmates with special needs are provided through *cooperative learning,* in which each individual contributes to the group activity to ensure success. Cooperative learning strategies counter the tendency to ignore or reject students with LD by helping them to be viewed by their classmates either neutrally or as worthwhile, competent people. Teacher ratings of student self-concept and behavior also improve when these strategies are used. Cooperative learning strategies have increased the nondisabled students' openness to sitting by and playing, talking, or working with students with LD. And the learning disabled student in turn seems to exhibit more positive social behaviors such as listening, questioning, and working with his or her peers.

*Cooperative learning strategies have increased the nondisabled students' openness to sitting by and playing, talking, or working with students with LD, who in turn learn more positive social behaviors.*

Peer tutoring has also been successful in enhancing social acceptance and interaction among nondisabled and disabled students, particularly when specific social interaction directives are given to the tutor pairs such as "Talk with your friend," "Stay with your friend," or "Play with your friend." Teachers can help friendships along by pairing children for activities, designing activities that invite interaction among classmates, placing certain students' desks next to each other, allowing quiet talk in the classroom, not scheduling academic remediation during times of high peer interaction (e.g., during a science experiment), not carrying out punishments during recess or play time, and by encouraging students to "first ask three others your questions, and then ask me." These types of strategies help children be better "known" to their classmates—and the more that students with LD are known, the more they tend to be liked.

*Peer tutoring has been successful in enhancing social acceptance and interaction among nondisabled and disabled students.*

Because "likes attract" when it comes to friendship groups, and even preschoolers choose nondisabled or more mature children as play partners, teachers need to make very concerted efforts to help students with LD become befriended by their peers. The affective education strategies described in Chapters 11 and 12 can do much to facilitate these children's social integration.

## Summary

The culture of the school, its organizational and interaction patterns, plays a significant role in students' academic and social adjustment. It is in this context that students are identified as learning disabled; schools can and do make a difference.

The physical and organizational environments of school settings can affect students either positively or negatively. Although background noise and visual distractions tend to diminish performance of all pupils equally, students with LD are the ones who can least afford any more lost opportunities for learning. Small schools seem to promote greater participation and feelings of responsibility among students, and small classes promote higher achievement. Open-space schools provide opportunities to develop students' self-direction in learning, but their decreased structure and consistency may be just the opposite of what some students with LD require. Studies in classroom design and seating arrangement show that students seated near the front and center of the room interact more with the teacher, and seating in small clusters best facilitates achievement. In addition, teacher-directed instructional approaches benefit students with LD more than do free-choice instructional approaches.

Students with LD generally benefit academically and socially from separate instruction by special educators. Concerns with segregation, however, together with poor outcomes in tracked classrooms, have resulted in inclusion of students with LD in regular classes whenever possible, with the necessary support services. Inclusion enables these students to benefit from interaction with their nondisabled peers and to more fully access the regular curriculum.

Human attributes of the school setting include the attitudes and behaviors of teachers and peers. General education teachers and classmates often do not view students with learning disabilities in a particularly positive manner. Curricula that are sensitive to the various cultural backgrounds in the classroom, cooperative learning strategies, and peer tutoring have been helpful in enhancing the acceptance and social integration of students with LD.

The climate of the school setting is an important factor in "making it or breaking it" for students with learning disabilities. Attention to the physical, organizational, and human attributes of school settings is important to provide more academically and socially productive environments for these students.

## Helpful Resources

### Physical Characteristics

Abikoff, H., Courtney, M. E., Szeibal, P. J., & Koplewicz, H. S. (1996). The effects of auditory stimulation on the arithmetic performance of children with ADHD and nondisabled children. *Journal of Learning Disabilities, 29*, 238–246.

Barker, R. G., & Gump, P. (1964). *Big school, small school.* Stanford, CA: Stanford University Press.

Beeken, D., & Janzen, H. L. (1978). Behavioral mapping of student activity in open-area and traditional schools. *American Educational Research Journal, 15*, 507–517.

Bronzaft, A. L., & McCarthy, D. P. (1975). The effect of elevated train noise on reading ability. *Environment and Behavior, 7*, 517–527.

Bryan, T., Mathur, S., & Sullivan, K. (1996). The impact of positive mood on learning. *Learning Disability Quarterly, 19*, 153–162.

Carter, J. L., & Diaz, A. (1971). Effects of visual and auditory background on reading test performance. *Exceptional Children, 38*, 43–50.

Cherry, R. S., & Kruger, B. (1983). Selective auditory attention abilities of learning disabled and normal achieving children. *Journal of Learning Disabilities, 16*, 202–205.

Flynn, N. M., & Rapoport, J. L. (1976). Hyperactivity in open and traditional classroom environments. *Journal of Special Education, 10*, 285–290.

George, P. S. (1975). *Ten years of open space schools: A review of the research.* Gainesville, FL: Florida Educational Research and Development Council, University of Florida.

Getzels, J. W. (1974). Images of the classroom and visions of the learner. *School Review, 82*, 527–540.

Glass, G. V., Cahan, L. S., Smith, M. L., & Filby, N. N. (1982). *School class size: Research and policy.* Beverly Hills, CA: Sage.

Hygge, S. (1993). A comparison between the impact of noise from aircraft, road traffic and trains on long-term recall and recognition of a text in children aged 12–14 years. In H. Ising & B. Krupp (Eds.), *Larm und Krankheit: Noise and disease.* Stuttgart, Germany: Gustav Fischer Verlag.

Mintz, N. L. (1956). Effects of esthetic surroundings: II. Prolonged and repeated experience in a "beautiful" and "ugly" room. *Journal of Psychology, 41,* 459–466.

O'Leary, K. D., Rosenbaum, A., & Hughes, P. C. (1978). Fluorescent lighting: A purported source of hyperactive behavior. *Journal of Abnormal Child Psychology, 6,* 285–289.

Rosenfield, P., Lambert, N. M., & Black, A. (1985). Desk arrangement effects on pupil classroom behavior. *Journal of Educational Psychology, 77,* 101–108.

Somervill, J. W., Warnberg, L., & Bost, D. E. (1973). Effects of cubicles vs. increased stimulation of task performance by 1st-grade males perceived as distractible and nondistractible. *Journal of Special Education, 7,* 169–185.

Staples, S. L. (1996). Human response to environmental noise: Psychological research and public policy. *American Psychologist, 51,* 143–150.

Trickett, E. J. (1978). Toward a social ecological conception of adolescent socialization: Normative data on contrasting types of public school classrooms. *Child Development, 49,* 408–414.

Weinstein, C. S. (1979). The physical environment of the school: A review of the research. *Review of Educational Research, 49,* 577–610.

Zentall, S. S., & Zentall, T. R. (1976). Activity and task performance of hyperactive children as a function of environmental stimulation. *Journal of Consulting and Clinical Psychology, 44,* 693–697.

Zifferblatt, S. M. (1972). Architecture and human behavior: Toward increased understanding of a functional relationship. *Educational Technology, 12,* 54–57.

National Center for Education Statistics alternative schools and programs: http://www.nces.ed.gov

## Organizational Characteristics

Affleck, J. Q., Madge, S., Adams, A., & Lowenbraun, S. (1988). Integrated classroom versus resource model: Academic viability and effectiveness. *Exceptional Children, 54,* 339–348.

Algozzine, B., Morsink, C., & Algozzine, K. M. (1988). What's happening in self-contained special education classrooms? *Exceptional Children, 55,* 259–265.

Baker, J. A., Derrer, R. D., Davis, S. M., Dinklage-Travis, H. E., Linder, D. S., & Nicholson, M. D. (2001). The flip side of the coin: Understanding the school's contribution to dropout and completion. *School Psychology Quarterly, 16,* 406–426.

Bell, A. E., Sipursky, M. A., & Switzer, F. (1976). Informal or open-area education in relation to achievement and personality. *British Journal of Educational Psychology, 46,* 235–243.

Bender, W. N., Vail, C. O, & Scott, K. (1995). Teachers' attitudes toward increased mainstreaming: Implementing effective instruction for students with learning disabilities. *Journal of Learning Disabilities, 28,* 87–94, 120.

Boudah, D. J., Schumacker, J. B., & Deshler, D. D. (1997). Collaborative instruction: Is it an effective option for inclusion in secondary classrooms? *Learning Disability Quarterly, 20,* 293–316.

Brophy, J. E. (1983). Research on self-fulfilling prophecy and teacher expectations. *Journal of Educational Psychology, 75,* 631–661.

Bryan, T., & Sullivan-Burstein, K. (1997). Homework how-to's. *Teaching Exceptional Children, 29,* 32–37.

Butler, R., & Marinov-Glassman, D. (1994). The effects of educational placement and grade level on the self-perceptions of low achievers and students with learning disabilities. *Journal of Learning Disabilities, 27,* 325–334.

Carlberg, C., & Kavale, K. (1980). The efficacy of special versus regular class placement for exceptional children: A meta-analysis. *Journal of Special Education, 14,* 295–309.

Chandler, T. A. (1966). The fallacy of homogeneity. *Journal of School Psychology, 5,* 64–67.

Clark, M. D. (1997). Teacher response to learning disability: A test of attributional principles. *Journal of Learning Disabilities, 30,* 69–79.

Coleman, J. M. (1983). Handicapped labels and instructional segregation: Influences on children's self-concepts versus the perceptions of others. *Learning Disability Quarterly, 6,* 3–11.

Dusek, J. B. (1975). Do teachers bias children's learning? *Review of Educational Research, 45,* 661–684.

Elbaum, B. (2002). The self-concept of students with learning disabilities: A meta-analysis of comparisons across different placements. *Learning Disabilities Research & Practice, 17,* 216–226.

Epstein, M. H., Polloway, E. A., Foley, R. M., & Patton, J. R. (1993). Homework: A comparison of teachers' and parents' perceptions of the problems experienced by students identified as having behavioral disorders, learning disabilities, or no disabilities. *Remedial and Special Education, 14,* 40–50.

Fuchs, D., Fuchs, L. S., & Burish, P. (2000). Peer-assisted learning strategies: An evidence-based practice to promote reading achievement. *Learning Disabilities Research & Practice, 15,* 85–91.

Gajria, M., & Salend, S. J. (1995). Homework practices of students with and without learning disabilities: A comparison. *Journal of Learning Disabilities, 28,* 291–296.

Gajria, M., Salend, S. J., & Hemrick, M. A. (1994). Teacher acceptability of testing modifications for mainstreamed students. *Learning Disabilities Research & Practice, 9,* 236–243.

Gettinger, M. (1988). Methods of proactive classroom management. *School Psychology Review, 17,* 227–242.

Greenwood, C. R., Terry, B., Utley, C. A., Montagna, D., & Walker, D. (1993). Achievement, placement, and services: Middle school benefits of classwide peer tutoring used at the elementary school. *School Psychology Review, 22,* 497–516.

Guralnick, M. J., & Groom, J. M. (1988). Peer interactions in mainstreamed and specialized classrooms: A comparative analysis. *Exceptional Children, 54,* 415–425.

Gutierrez, R., & Slavin, R. E. (1992). Achievement effects of the non-graded elementary school: A best evidence synthesis. *Review of Educational Research, 62,* 333–376.

Haynes, M. C., & Jenkins, J. R. (1986). Reading instruction in special education resource rooms. *American Educational Research Journal, 23,* 161–190.

Howard, K. A., & Tryon, G. S. (2002). Depressive symptoms in and type of classroom placement for adolescents with LD. *Journal of Learning Disabilities, 35,* 185–190.

Jenkins, J. R. & Heinen, A. (1989). Students' preferences for service delivery: Pull-out, in-class, or integrated models. *Exceptional Children, 55,* 516–523.

Jenkins, J. R., Jewell, M., Leicester, N., O'Connor, R. E., Jenkins, L. M., & Troutner, N. M. (1994). Accommodations for individual differences without classroom ability groups: An experiment in school restructuring. *Exceptional Children, 60,* 344–358.

Keith, T. Z., & Page, E. B. (1985). Homework works at school: National evidence for policy changes. *School Psychology Review, 14,* 351–359.

King-Sears, M. E. (1997). Best academic practices for inclusive classrooms. *Focus on Exceptional Children, 29*(7), 1–22.

Kistner, J., Haskett, M., White, K., & Robbins, F. (1987). Perceived competence and self-worth of LD and normally achieving students. *Learning Disability Quarterly, 10,* 37–44.

Klingner, J. K., Vaughn, S., Hughes, M. T., Schumm, J., & Elbaum, B. (1998). Outcomes for students with and without learning disabilities in inclusive classrooms. *Learning Disabilities Research & Practice, 13,* 153–161.

Lee, V. E., & Bryk, A. S. (1988). Curriculum tracking as mediating the social distribution of high school. *Sociology of Education, 62,* 78–94.

Madon, S., Jussim, L., & Eccles, J. (1997). In search of the powerful self-fulfilling prophecy. *Journal of Personality and Social Psychology, 72,* 791–809.

Madon, S., Smith, A., Jussim, L., Russell, D. W., Eccles, J., Palumbo, P., & Walkiewicz, M. (2001). Am I as you see me or do you see me as I am? Self-fulfilling prophecies and self-verification. *Personality and Social Psychology Bulletin, 27,* 1214–1224.

Manset, G., & Semmel, M. I. (1997). Are inclusive programs for students with mild disabilities effective? A comparative review of model programs. *The Journal of Special Education, 31,* 155–180.

Marston, D. (1996). A comparison of inclusion only, pull-out only, and combined-service models for students with mild disabilities. *The Journal of Special Education, 30,* 121–132.

Mathes, P. G., & Fuchs, L. S. (1994). The efficacy of peer tutoring in reading for students with mild disabilities: A best-evidence synthesis. *School Psychology Review, 23,* 59–80.

McKee, W. T., & Witt, J. C. (1990). Effective teaching: A review of instructional and environmental variables. In T. B. Gutkin & C. R. Reynolds (Eds.), *The handbook of school psychology* (2nd ed.) (pp. 821–846). New York: Wiley.

Milich, R., McAninch, C. B., & Harris, M. J. (1992). Effects of stigmatizing information on children's peer relations: Believing is seeing. *School Psychology Review, 21,* 400–409.

Minke, K. M., Bear, G. G., Deemer, S. A., & Griffin, S. M. (1996). Teachers' experiences with inclusive classrooms: Implications for special education reform. *The Journal of Special Education, 30,* 152–186.

Morrison, G. M. (1985). Differences in teacher perceptions and student self-perceptions for learning disabled and nonhandicapped learners in regular and special education settings. *Learning Disabilities Research, 1,* 32–41.

Radencich, M. C., & McKay, L. J. (Eds.) (1995). *Flexible grouping for literacy in the elementary grades.* Needham Heights, MA: Allyn & Bacon.

Raudenbush, S. W. (1984). Magnitude of teacher expectancy effects on pupil IQ as a function of the credibility of expectancy induction: A synthesis of findings from 18 experiments. *Journal of Educational Psychology, 76,* 85–97.

Rich, H. L., & Ross, S. M. (1989). Students' time on learning tasks in special education. *Exceptional Children, 55,* 508–515.

Rosenberg, M. S. (1989). The effects of daily homework assignments on the acquisition of basic skills by students with learning disabilities. *Journal of Learning Disabilities, 22,* 314–323.

Rosenshine, B. V. (1980). How time is spent in elementary classrooms. In C. Denham & A. Lieberman (Eds.), *Time to learn.* Washington, DC: National Institute of Education.

Rosenthal, R., & Jacobson, L. (1968). *Pygmalion in the classroom: Teacher expectations and pupils' intelligence development.* New York: Holt, Rinehart & Winston.

Schumm, J. S., Moody, S. W., & Vaughn, S. (2000). Grouping for reading instruction: Does one size fit all? *Journal of Learning Disabilities, 33,* 477–488.

Sizer, T. R. (1996). *Horace's hope: What works for the American high school.* Boston: Houghton Mifflin.

Slavin, R. E. (1987). Ability grouping and student achievement in elementary schools: A best evidence synthesis. *Review of Educational Research, 57,* 293–336.

Thurlow, M. L., Ysseldyke, J. E., Graden, J. L., & Algozzine, B. (1983). What's "special" about the special education resource room for learning disabled students? *Learning Disability Quarterly, 6,* 283–288.

Vaughn, S., Elbaum, B. E., & Schumm, J. S. (1996). The effects of inclusion on the social functioning of students with learning disabilities. *Journal of Learning Disabilities, 29,* 598–608.

Vaughn, S., & Klinger, J. K. (1998). Students' perceptions of inclusion and resource room settings. *The Journal of Special Education, 32,* 79–88.

Vaughn, S., Levy, S., Coleman, M., & Bos, C. S. (2002). Reading instruction for students with LD and EBD: A synthesis of observation studies. *Journal of Special Education, 36,* 2–13.

Vaughn, S., & Schumm, J. S., Jallad, B., Slusher, J., & Saumell, L. (1996). Teachers' views of inclusion. *Learning Disabilities Research & Practice, 11,* 96–106.

Vaughn, S., & Schumm, J. S., & Kouzekanani, K. (1993). What do students with learning disabilities think when their general education teachers make adaptations? *Journal of Learning Disabilities, 26,* 545–555.

Walther-Thomas, C. S. (1997). Co-teaching experiences. The benefits and problems that teachers and principals report over time. *Journal of Learning Disabilities, 30,* 395–407.

Wright, R. J. (1975). The affective and cognitive consequences of an open-education elementary school. *American Educational Research Journal, 12,* 449–465.

Yell, M. L. (1994). Least restrictive environment, inclusion, and students with disabilities: A legal analysis. *The Journal of Special Education, 28,* 389–404.

Zigmond, N. (1990). Rethinking secondary school programs for students with learning disabilities. *Focus on Exceptional Children, 23*(1), 1–22.

Zigmond, N., Jenkins, J., Fuchs, L. S., Deno, S., Fuchs, D., Baker, J. N., Jenkins, L., & Couthino, M. (1995). Special education in restructured schools: Findings from three multi-year studies. *Phi Delta Kappan, 76,* 531–540.

Zigmond, N., Sansone, J., Miller, S. E., Donahoe, K. A., & Kohnke, R. (1986). Teaching learning disabled students at the secondary school level: What research says to teachers. *Learning Disabilities Focus, 12,* 108–115.

## Human Characteristics

Alves, A. J., & Gottlieb, J. (1986). Teacher interactions with mainstreamed handicapped students and their nonhandicapped peers. *Learning Disability Quarterly, 9,* 77–83.

Bear, G. G., & Minke, K. M. (1996). Positive bias in maintenance of self-worth among children with LD. *Learning Disability Quarterly, 19,* 23–32.

Brophy, J., & Good T. (1974). *Teacher-student relationships.* New York: Holt, Rinehart, & Winston.

Bruininks, V. L. (1978). Actual and perceived peer status of learning disabled students in mainstream programs. *Journal of Special Education, 12,* 51–58.

Chaikin, A. L., Gillen, B., Derlega, V. S., Heinen, J. R. K., & Wilson, M. (1978). Students' reactions to teachers' physical attractiveness and non-verbal behavior: Two exploratory studies. *Psychology in the Schools, 15,* 588–595.

Conderman, G. (1995). Social-status of sixth- and seventh-grade students with learning disabilities. *Learning Disability Quarterly, 18,* 13–24.

Cook, B. G., Tankersley, M., Cook, L., & Landrum, T. J. (2000). Teachers' attitudes toward their included students with disabilities. *Exceptional Children, 67,* 115–135.

Cook, L., & Friend, M. (1996). Co-teaching: Guidelines for creating effective practices. In E. L. Meyen, G. A. Vergason, & R. J. Whelan (Eds.), *Strategies for teaching exceptional children in inclusive settings* (pp. 155–182). Denver: Love Publications.

Crowl, T. K., & MacGinitie, W. H. (1974). The influence of students' speech characteristics on teachers' evaluation of oral answers. *Journal of Educational Psychology, 66,* 304–308.

Doll, B. (1996). Children without friends: Implications for practice and policy. *School Psychology Review, 25,* 165–183.

Farmer, T. W., & Farmer, E. M. Z. (1996). Social relationships of students with exceptionalities in mainstream classrooms: Social networks and homophily. *Exceptional Children, 62,* 431–450.

Fuchs, L. S., Fuchs, D., Hamlett, C. L., Phillips, N. B., & Karns, K. (1995). General educators' specialized adaption for students with learning disabilities. *Exceptional Children, 61,* 440–459.

Garrett, M. K., & Crump, W. D. (1980). Peer acceptance, teacher preference, and self-appraisal of social status among learning disabled students. *Learning Disability Quarterly, 3*(3), 42–48.

Good, T., & Brophy, J. (1978). *Looking in classrooms.* New York: Harper & Row.

Good, T. L. (1981), Teacher expectations and student perceptions: A decade of research. *Educational Leadership, 38,* 415–422.

Gottlieb, B. W. (1984). Effects of relative competence on learning disabled children's oral reading performance. *Learning Disability Quarterly, 7,* 108–112.

Jayanthi, M., Epstein, M. H., Polloway, E. A., & Bursuck, W. D. (1996). A national survey of general education teachers' perceptions of testing adaptations. *The Journal of Special Education, 30,* 99–115.

Jordan, C., Tharp, R. G., & Baird-Vogt, L. (1992). "Just open the door": Cultural compatibility and classroom rapport. In M. Saravia-Shore & S. F. Arvizu (Eds.), *Cross-cultural literacy: Ethnographies of communication in multiethnic classrooms.* New York: Garland.

LaGreca, A. M., & Stone, W. L. (1990). LD status and achievement: Confounding variables in the study of children's social status, self-esteem, and behavioral functioning. *Journal of Learning Disabilities, 23,* 483–490.

Lyon, S. (1977). Teacher nonverbal behavior related to perceived pupil social-personal attributes. *Journal of Learning Disabilities, 10,* 173–177.

Mastropieri, M. A., & Scruggs, T. E. (2001). Promoting inclusion in secondary classrooms. *Learning Disability Quarterly, 24,* 265–274.

McIntosh, R., Vaughn, S., Schumm, J. S., Haager, D., & Lee, O. (1993). Observations of students with learning disabilities in general education classrooms. *Exceptional Children, 60,* 249–261.

McIntyre, L. L. (1988). Teacher gender: A predictor of special education referral? *Journal of Learning Disabilities, 21,* 382–383.

McMaster, K. N., & Fuchs, D. (2002). Effects of cooperative learning on the academic achievement of students with learning disabilities: An update of Tateyama-Sniezek's review. *Learning Disabilities Research & Practice, 17,* 107–117.

Mitchell, V. (1992). African-American students in exemplary urban high schools: The interaction of school practices and student actions. In M. Saravia-Shore & S. F. Arvizu (Eds.), *Cross-cultural literacy: Ethnographies of communication in multiethnic classrooms.* New York: Garland.

Montague, M., & Rinaldi, C. (2001). Classroom dynamics and children at risk: A followup. *Learning Disability Quarterly, 24,* 75–83.

Parker, I., Gottlieb, B. W., Davis, S., & Kunzweiller, C. (1989). Teacher behavior toward low achievers, average achievers, and mainstreamed minority group learning disabled students. *Learning Disabilities Research, 4,* 101–106.

Perlmutter, B. F., Crocker, J., Cordray, D., & Garstecki, D. (1983). Sociometric status and related personality characteristics of mainstreamed learning disabled adolescents. *Learning Disability Quarterly, 6,* 20–30.

Pullis, M. (1985). LD students' temperament characteristics and their impact on decisions by resource and mainstream teachers. *Learning Disability Quarterly, 8,* 109–122.

Richey, H. W., & Richey, M. N. (1978). Nonverbal behavior in the classroom. *Psychology in the Schools, 15,* 571–576.

Rist, R. C. (1970). Student social class and teacher expectations: The self-fulfilling prophecy in ghetto education. *Harvard Educational Review, 40,* 411–451.

Rodden-Nord, K., Shinn, M. R., & Good, R. H., III. (1992). Effects of classroom performance data on general education teachers' attitudes toward reintegrating students with learning disabilities. *School Psychology Review, 21,* 138–154.

Ross, M. B., & Salvia, J. (1975). Attractiveness as a biasing factor in teacher judgments. *American Journal of Mental Deficiency, 80,* 96–98.

Sale, P., & Carey, D. M. (1995). The sociometric status of students with disabilities in a full-inclusion school. *Exceptional Children, 62,* 6–19.

Shinn, M. R., Tindal, G. A., & Spira, D. A. (1987). Special education referrals as an index of teacher tolerance: Are teachers imperfect tests? *Exceptional Children, 54,* 32–40.

Siperstein, G. N., & Goding, M. J. (1985). Teachers' behavior toward LD and non-LD children: A strategy for change. *Journal of Learning Disabilities, 18,* 139–144.

Vaughn, S., & Schumm, J. S. (1996). Classroom interactions and implications for inclusion of students with learning disabilities. In Speece, D. L., & Keogh, B. (Eds.), *Research on classroom ecologies: Implications for inclusion of children with learning disabilities.* Mahwah, NJ: Lawrence Erlbaum.

Weiss, M. P., & Lloyd, J. W. (2002). Congruence between roles and actions of secondary special educators in co-taught and special education settings. *Journal of Special Education, 36,* 58–68.

Wiener, J. (1987). Peer status of learning disabled children and adolescents: A review of the literature. *Learning Disabilities Research, 2,* 62–79.

Woolfolk, A. E., & Brooks, D. M. (1985). The influence of teachers' nonverbal behaviors on students' perceptions and performance. *The Elementary School Journal, 85,* 513–528.

# REFERENCES


Ackerman, P. T., & Dykman, R. A. (1993). Phonologic processes, confrontational naming, and immediate memory in dyslexia. *Journal of Learning Disabilities, 26,* 597–609.

Ackerman, P. T., Dykman, R. A., & Gardner, M. Y. (1990). Counting rate, naming rate, phonological sensitivity, and memory span: Major factors in dyslexia. *Journal of Learning Disabilities, 23,* 325–327, 319.

Adams, M. J. (1990). *Beginning to read: Thinking and learning about print.* Cambridge, MA: MIT Press.

Adelman, H. S. (1971). The not so specific learning disability population. *Exceptional Children 37,* 528–533.

Adelman, H. S., & Taylor, L. (1986). Moving the LD field ahead: New paths, new paradigms. *Journal of Learning Disabilities, 19,* 602–608.

Adelman, H. S., & Taylor, L. (1990). Intrinsic motivation and school misbehavior: Some intervention implications. *Journal of Learning Disabilities, 23,* 541–550.

Alajouanine, T., & Lhermitte, F. (1965). Acquired aphasia in children. *Brain, 88,* 653–662.

Allington, R. L. (1984). So what is the problem? Whose problem is it? *Topics in Learning & Learning Disabilities,* 3(4), 91–99.

American Psychiatric Association. (1994). *Diagnostic and statistical manual of mental disorders* (4th ed.). Washington, DC: American Psychiatric Association.

Amunts, K., Schlaug, G., Jäncke, L., Steinmetz, H., Schleicher, A., Dabringhaus, A., & Zilles, K. (1997). Motor cortex and hand motor skills: Structural compliance in the human brain. *Human Brain Mapping, 5,* 206–215.

Anderson, R. C., Hiebert, E. H., Scott, J. A., & Wilkinson, I. A. G. (1985). *Becoming a nation of readers: The report of the Commission on reading.* Pittsburgh, PA: National Academy of Education.

Argulewicz, E. N. (1983). Effects of ethnic membership, socioeconomic status, and home language on LD, EMR, and EH placements. *Learning Disability Quarterly, 6,* 195–200.

Artiles, A. J., & Trent, S. C. (1994). Overrepresentation of minority students in special education: A continuing debate. *The Journal of Special Education, 27,* 410–437.

Baddeley, A. D. (1986). *Working memory.* London: Oxford University Press.

Bakker, D. J. (1970). Temporal order perception and reading retardation. In D. J. Bakker & P. Satz (Eds.), *Specific reading disability: Advances in theory and method.* Rotterdam: Rotterdam University Press.

Bakker, D. J. (1972). *Temporal order in disturbed reading: Developmental and neuropsychological aspects in normal and reading retarded children.* Rotterdam: Rotterdam University Press.

Bakker, D. J. (1984). The brain as dependent variable. *Journal of Clinical Neuropsychology, 6,* 1–16.

Bakker, D. J., Bouma, A., & Gardien, C. J. (1990). Hemisphere-specific treatment of dyslexia subtypes. A field experiment. *Journal of Learning Disabilities, 23,* 433–438.

Bakker, D. J., Moerland, R., & Goekoop-Hoefkens, M. (1981). Effects of hemisphere-specific stimulation on the reading performance of dyslexic boys: A pilot study. *Journal of Clinical Neuropsychology, 3,* 155–159.

Bakker, D. J., & Vinke, J. (1985). Effects of hemisphere-specific stimulation on brain activity and reading in dyslexics. *Journal of Clinical and Experimental Neuropsychology, 7,* 505–525.

Ball, E. W., & Blachman, B. A. (1991). Does phoneme awareness training in kindergarten make a difference in early word recognition and developmental spelling? *Reading Research Quarterly, 26,* 49–66.

Barkley, R. A. (1977). A review of stimulant drug research with hyperkinetic children. *Journal of Child Psychology and Psychiatry, 18,* 137–165.

Barrett, G. V., & Depinet, R. L. (1991). A reconsideration of testing for competence rather than for intelligence. *American Psychologist, 46,* 1012–1024.

Bateman, B. (1968). The efficacy of an auditory and a visual method of first grade reading instruction with auditory and visual learners. In H. Smith (Ed.), *Perception and reading.* Newark, DE: International Reading Association.

Bayley, N. (1943). Size and body build of adolescents in relation to rate of skeletal maturing. *Child Development,* 14, 47–89.

Bayley, N., & Jones, M. C. (1955). Physical maturing among boys as related to behavior. In W. E. Martin & C. B. Stendler (Eds.), *Reading in child development.* New York: Harcourt, Brace & Co.

Begley, S. (October 11, 2002). Survival of the busiest. *The Wall Street Journal,* B1 & B4.

Bentzen, F. (1963). Sex ratios in learning and behavior disorders. *American Journal of Orthopsychiatry, 33,* 92–98.

Bereiter, C., & Scardamalia, M. (1982). From conversation to composition: The role of instruction in a developmental process: In R. Glaser (Ed.), *Advances in instructional psychology: Vol. 2* (pp. 1–64). Hillsdale, NJ: Lawrence Erlbaum.

Berk, L. E. (1997). *Child development* (4th ed). Boston: Allyn & Bacon.

Berliner, D. C. (1984). The half-full glass: A review of research on teaching. In P. L. Hosford (Ed.), *Using what we know about teaching.* Alexandria, VA: Association for Supervision and Curriculum Development.

Berninger, V. W. (1990). Multiple orthographic codes: Key to alternative instructional methodologies for developing the orthographic-phonological connections underlying word identification. *School Psychology Review, 19,* 518–533.

Bickel, W. E., & Bickel, D. D. (1986). Effective schools, classrooms, and instruction: Implications for special education. *Exceptional Children, 52,* 489–500.

Bigler, E. D. (1992). The neurobiology and neuropsychology of adult learning disorders. *Journal of Learning Disabilities, 25,* 488–506.

Blachman, B. A. (1994). What we have learned from longitudinal studies of phonological processing and reading, and some unanswered questions: A response to Torgesen, Wagner, and Rashotte. *Journal of Learning Disabilities, 27,* 287–291.

Blachman, B. A., Tangel, D. M., Ball, E. W., Black, R. S., & McGraw, C. K. (1999). Developing phonological awareness and word recognition skills: A two-year intervention with low-income, inner-city children. *Reading and Writing: An Interdisciplinary Journal, 11,* 239–273.

Bliesmer, E. P., & Yarborough, B. H. (1965). A comparison of ten different beginning reading programs in first grade. *Phi Delta Kappan, 46,* 500–504.

Bohlmeyer, E. M., & Burke, J. P. (1987). Selecting cooperative learning techniques: A consultative strategy guide. *School Psychology Review, 16,* 36–49.

Bos, C. S., & Fletcher, T. V. (1997). Sociocultural considerations in learning disabilities inclusion research: Knowledge gaps and future directions. *Learning Disabilities Research & Practice, 12,* 92–99.

Bourgeois, P., & Clark, B. (1986). *Franklin in the dark.* New York: Scholastic.

Bradley, L. (1988). Making connections in learning to read and spell. *Applied Cognitive Psychology, 2,* 3–18.

Bradley, L., & Bryant, P. E. (1978). Difficulties in auditory organization as a possible cause of reading backwardness. *Nature, 271,* 746–747.

Bradley, L., & Bryant, P. E. (1983). Categorizing sounds and learning to read—A causal connection. *Nature, 301,* 419–421.

Bradley, L., & Bryant, P. (1985). *Rhyme and reason in reading and spelling.* Ann Arbor, MI: University of Michigan Press.

Brigham, F. R., Scruggs, T. E., & Mastropieri, M. A. (1992). Teacher enthusiasm in learning disabilities classrooms: Effects on learning and behavior. *Learning Disabilities Research & Practice, 7,* 68–73.

Brophy, J. (1982). Successful teaching strategies for the inner-city child. *Phi Delta Kappan, 63,* 527–530.

Brophy, J., & Good, T. L. (1986). Teacher behavior and student achievement. In M. C. Wittrock (Ed.), *Handbook of research on teaching* (3rd ed.) (pp. 328–375). New York: Macmillan.

Brosnan, F. L. (1983). Overrepresentation of low-socioeconomic minority students in special education programs in California. *Learning Disability Quarterly, 6,* 517–525.

Brown, R. T., Reynolds, C. R., & Whitaker, J. S. (1999). Bias in mental testing since *Bias in Mental Testing. School Psychology Quarterly, 14,* 208–238.

Bruno, R. M., Johnson, J. M., & Simon, J. (1987). Perception of humor by regular class students and students with learning disabilities or mild mental retardation. *Journal of Learning Disabilities, 20,* 568–570.

Bruno, R. M., Johnson, J. M., & Simon, J. (1988). Perception of humor by learning disabled, mildly retarded, and nondisabled students. *Learning Disability Focus, 3,* 114–123.

Bryan, T. (1986). Personality and situational factors in learning disabilities. In G. Th. Pavlidis & D. F. Fisher (Eds.), *Dyslexia: Its neurology and treatment.* New York: John Wiley.

Cain, L., Melcher, J., Johns, B., Ashmore, J., Callahan, C., Draper, I., Beveridge, P., & Weintraub, T. (1984). Reply to "A Nation at Risk." *Exceptional Children, 50,* 484–494.

Canfield, J., & Wells, H. C. (1976). *100 ways to enhance self-concept in the classroom: A handbook for teachers and parents.* Englewood Cliffs, NJ: Prentice-Hall.

Caplan, P. J. (1977). Sex, age, behavior, and school subjects as determinants of report of learning problems. *Journal of Learning Disabilities, 10,* 314–316.

Caplan, P. J., & Kinsbourne, M. (1974). Sex differences in response to school failure. *Journal of Learning Disabilities, 7,* 232–235.

Carlberg, C., & Kavale, K. (1980). The efficacy of special versus regular class placement for exceptional children: A meta-analysis. *Journal of Special Education, 14,* 295–309.

Carnine, D. (1994). Introduction to the mini-series: Diverse learners and prevailing, emerging, and research-based educational approaches and their tools. *School Psychology Review, 23,* 341–350.

Castle, J. M., Riach, J., & Nicholson, T. (1994). Getting off to a better start in reading and spelling: The effects of phonemic awareness instruction within a whole language program. *Journal of Educational Psychology, 86,* 350–359.

Ceci, S. J., & Williams, W. M. (1997). Schooling, intelligence, and income. *American Psychologist, 52,* 1051–1058.

Chall, J. (1983). *Stages of reading development.* New York: McGraw-Hill.

Chase, C. (1996). A visual deficit model of development dyslexia. In C. Chase, G. Rosen, & G. Sherman

(Eds.), *Developmental dyslexia: Neural, cognitive, and genetic mechanisms.* Baltimore: York Press.

Chinn, P. C., & Hughes, S. (1987). Representation of minority students in special education classes. *Remedial and Special Education, 8,* 41–46.

Coleman, J. C., & Sandhu, M. (1967). A descriptive relational study of 364 children referred to a university clinic for learning disorders. *Psychological Reports, 20,* 1091–1105.

Collier, C., & Hoover, J. J. (1987). Sociocultural considerations when referring minority children for learning disabilities. *Learning Disabilities Focus,* 3, 39–45.

Conners, C. K. (1975). Controlled trial of methylphenidate in preschool children with minimal brain dysfunction. *International Journal of Mental Health,* 4, 61–74.

Corina, D. P., Richards, T. L., Serafini, S., Richards, A. L., Steury, K., Abbott, R., Echelard, D. R., Maravilla, K. R., & Berninger, V. W. (2001). fMRI auditory language differences between dyslexic and able reading children. *Neuroreports, 12,* 1195–1201.

Coulter, W. A., Morrow, H. W., & Tucker, J. A. (1978). *What you always wanted to know about adaptive behavior but were too hostile and angry to ask.* Paper presented at the meeting of the National Association of School Psychologists, New York, NY.

Critchley, M. (1970). *The dyslexic child.* Springfield, IL: Charles C. Thomas.

Cunningham, J. W., Cunningham, P. M., & Arthur, S. V. (1981). *Middle and secondary school reading.* New York: Longman.

Dahl, K. L., Scharer, P. L., Lawson, L. L., & Grogan, P. R. (1999). Phonics instruction and student achievement in whole language first-grade classrooms. *Reading Research Quarterly, 34,* 312–341.

Davidoff, J. B., Cone, B. P., & Scully, J. P. (1978). Developmental changes in hemispheric processing for cognitive skills and the relationship to reading ability. In A. M. Lesgold, J. W. Pellegrino, S. Fokkema, & R. Glaser (Eds.), *Cognitive psychology and instruction.* New York: Plenum.

Dawson, M. M. (1987). Beyond ability grouping: A review of the effectiveness of ability grouping and its alternatives. *School Psychology Review, 16,* 348–369.

Denckla, M. B. (1979). Childhood learning disabilities. In K. M. Heilman & E. Valenstein (Eds.), *Clinical neuropsychology.* New York: Oxford University Press.

Denckla, M. B., & Cutting, L. E. (1999). History and significance of rapid automatized naming. *Annals of Dyslexia, 49,* 29–42.

Denckla, M. B., & Heilman, K. M. (1979). The syndrome of hyperactivity. In K. M. Heilman & E. Valenstein (Eds.), *Clinical neuropsychology.* Oxford: Oxford University Press.

Denckla, M. B., LeMay, M., & Chapman, C. A. (1985). Few CT scan abnormalities found even in neurologically impaired learning disabled children. *Journal of Learning Disabilities, 18,* 132–135.

Dennis, M. & Whitaker, H. A. (1976). Language acquisition following hemidecortication: Linguistic superiority of the left over the right hemisphere. *Brain and Language, 3,* 404–433.

Devine, R., & Rose, D. (1981). *To learn to learn, or to learn to read.* Proposal to produce a one-hour, broadcast-quality videotape on dyslexia. Rochester, New York.

Duffy, F. H., & McAnulty, G. B. (1985). Brain electrical activity mapping (BEAM): The search for a physiological signature of dyslexia. In F. H. Duffy & N. Geschwind (Eds.), *Dyslexia: A neuroscientific approach to clinical evaluation.* Boston: Little, Brown.

Dunn, L. M. (1968). Special education for the mildly retarded—Is much of it justifiable? *Exceptional Children, 35,* 5–22.

Education for all Handicapped Children Act. (1975). PL 94-142. *Federal Register,* Dec. 29, 1977.

Ehri, L. C. (1998). Grapheme-phoneme knowledge is essential for learning to read words in English. In J. L. Metsala & L. C. Ehri. (Eds.), *Word recognition in beginning literacy* (pp. 3–40). Mahwah, NJ: Lawrence Erlbaum.

Eisenberger, R., & Cameron, J. (1996). Detrimental effects of reward: Reality or myth? *American Psychologist, 51,* 1153–1166.

Elbaum, B., Vaughn, S., Hughes, M. T., & Moody, S. W. (2000a). How effective are one-to-one tutoring programs in reading for elementary students at risk for reading failure? A meta-analysis of the intervention research. *Journal of Education Psychology, 92,* 605–619.

Elbaum, B., Vaughn, S., Hughes, M. T., Moody, S. W., & Schumm, J. S. (2000b). How reading outcomes of students with disabilities are related to instructional grouping formats: In R. Gersten, E. Schiller, & S. Vaughn (Eds.), *Contemporary special education research: Syntheses of the knowledge base on critical instructional issues* (pp. 105–135). Mahwah, NJ: Erlbaum.

Elbert, T., Pantev, C., Wienbruch, C., Rockstroh, B., & Taub, E. (1995). Increased cortical representation of the fingers of the left hand in string players. *Science, 270,* 305–307.

Ellis, E. S., & Lenz, B. K. (1987). A component analysis of effective learning strategies for LD students. *Learning Disabilities Focus, 2,* 94–107.

Englert, C. S. (1984). Effective direct instruction practices in special education settings. *Remedial and Special Education, 5*(2), 38–47.

Epstein, H. T. (1980). Some biological bases of cognitive development. *Bulletin of the Orton Society, 30,* 46–62.

Erikkson, P. S., Perfilieva, E., Bjork-Erikkson, T., Alborn, A. M., Nordborg, C., Peterson, D. A., & Gage, F. H.

(1998). Neurogenesis in the adult human hippocampus. *Nature Medicine, 4,* 1313–1317.

Eysenck, H. (1984). The effect of race on human abilities and mental test scores. In C. R. Reynolds & R. T. Brown (Eds.), *Perspectives on bias in mental testing.* New York: Plenum Press.

Farmer, M. E., & Klein, R. M. (1995). The evidence for a temporal processing deficit linked to dyslexia: A review. *Psychonomic Bulletin & Review, 2,* 460–493.

Farnham-Diggory, S. (1978). *Learning disabilities: A psychological perspective.* Cambridge: Harvard University Press.

Feitelson, D. (1973). Israel. In J. Downing (Ed.), *Comparative reading: Cross-national studies of behavior and processes in reading and writing.* New York: Macmillan.

Felton, R. H. (1993). Effects of instruction on the decoding skills of children with phonological-processing problems. *Journal of Learning Disabilities, 26,* 583–589.

Finger, S., & Almli, C. R. (1984). *Early brain damage: Vol. 2. Neurobiology and behavior.* New York: Academic Press.

Finn, C. E. (1986). *What works: Research about teaching and learning.* Washington, DC: U.S. Department of Education.

Fisher, C. W., Berliner, D. C., Filby, N. N., Marliave, R., Cahan, L. S., & Dishaw, M. M. (1980). Teacher behaviors, academic learning time, and student achievement: An overview. In C. Denham & A. Lieberman (Eds.), *Time to learn.* Washington, DC: National Institute of Education.

Fisher, D. F., & Athey, I. (1986). Methodological issues in research with the learning disabled: Establishing true controls. In G. T. Pavlidis & D. F. Fisher (Eds.), *Dyslexia: Its neuropsychology and treatment.* New York: John Wiley.

Fitzgerald, J., & Noblit, G. (2000). Balance in the making: Learning to read in an ethnically diverse first-grade classroom. *Journal of Educational Psychology, 92,* 3–22.

Flavell, J. H., & Wellman, H. (1977). Metamemory. In R. V. Kail & J. W. Hagen (Eds.), *Perspectives on the development of memory and cognition.* Hillsdale, NJ: Lawrence Erlbaum.

Fletcher, J. M., Levin, H. S., & Landry, S. H. (1984). Behavioral consequences of cerebral insult in infancy. In C. R. Almli & S. Finger (Eds.), *Early brain damage; Vol. 1. Research orientations and clinical observations.* New York: Academic Press.

Flynn, J. M., & Rahbar, M. H. (1994). Prevalence of reading failure in boys compared with girls. *Psychology in the Schools, 31,* 66–71.

Flynn, T. M. (1984). IQ tests and placement. *Integrated Education, 21,* 124–126.

Foorman, B. R., Fletcher, J. M., Francis, D. J., Schatschneider, C., & Mehta, P. (1998). The role of instruction in learning to read: Preventing reading failure in at-risk children. *Journal of Educational Psychology, 90,* 37–55.

Forness, S. R. (1985). Effects of public policy at the state level; California's impact on MR, LD, and ED categories. *Remedial and Special Education, 60*(3), 36–43.

Frame, R. E., Clarizio, H. F., & Porter, A. (1984). Diagnostic and prescriptive bias in school psychologists' reports of a learning disabled child. *Journal of Learning Disabilities, 17,* 12–15.

French, J. N., & Rhoder, C. (1992). *Teaching thinking skills: Theory and practice.* New York: Garland.

Frumkin, R. M. (1997). Significant neglected sociocultural and physical factors affecting intelligence. *American Psychologist, 52,* 76–77.

Fuchs, D., Fuchs, L. S., Thompson, A., Al Otaiba, S., Yen, L., Yang, N. J., Braun, M., & O'Connor, R. E. (2002). Exploring the importance of reading programs for kindergarteners with disabilities in mainstream classrooms. *Exceptional Children, 68,* 295–311.

Galaburda, A. M. (1986). Animal studies and the neurology of developmental dyslexia. In G. Th. Pavlidis & D. F. Fisher (Eds.), *Dyslexia: Its neuropsychology and treatment.* New York: John Wiley & Sons.

Garner, R., & Alexander, P. A. (1989). Metacognition: Answered and unanswered questions. *Educational Psychologist, 24,* 143–158.

Gersten, R., & Woodward, J. (1994). The language-minority student and special education: Issues, trends, and paradoxes. *Exceptional Children, 60,* 310–322.

Gersten, R., Woodward, J., & Darch, C. (1986). Direct instruction: A research-based approach to curriculum design and teaching. *Exceptional Children, 53,* 17–31.

Geschwind, N., & Behan, P. (1982). Left-handedness: Association with immune disease, migraine, and developmental learning disorder. *Proceedings of the National Academy of Sciences USA, 79,* 5097–5100.

Gickling, E. E., & Thompson, V. P. (1985). A personal view of curriculum-based assessment. *Exceptional Children, 52,* 205–218.

Glass, G. V., Cahan, L. S., Smith, M. L., & Filby, N. N. (1982). *School class size: Research and policy.* Beverly Hills, CA: Sage.

Goethe, K. E., & Levin, H. S. (1984). Behavioral manifestations during the early and long-term stages of recovery after closed head injury. *Psychiatric Annals, 14,* 540–546.

Goldman, P. S., Crawford, H. T., Stokes, L. P., Galkin, T. W., & Rosvold, H. E. (1974). Sex-dependent behavioral effects of cerebral cortical lesions in the developing rhesus monkey. *Science, 186,* 540–542.

Good, T. L. (1983). Classroom research: A decade of progress. *Educational Psychologist, 18,* 127–144.

Good, T. L., & Brophy, J. E. (1986). School effects. In M. C. Wittrock (Ed.), *Handbook of research on teaching* (3rd ed.) (pp. 570–602). New York: Macmillan.

Gopnik, A., Choi, S., & Baumberger, T. (1996). Cross-linguistic differences in early semantic and cognitive development. *Cognitive Development, 11*, 197–225.

Gottfredson, L. S. (1997). Mainstream science on intelligence: An editorial with 52 signatories, history, and bibliography. *Intelligence, 24*, 13–23.

Gottlieb, B. W. (1984). Effects of relative competence on learning disabled children's oral reading performance. *Learning Disability Quarterly, 7*, 108–112.

Gottlieb, J., Alter, M., Gottlieb, B. W., & Wishner, J. (1994). Special education in urban America: It's not justifiable for many. *The Journal of Special Education, 27*, 453–465.

Gottlieb, J., Rose, T. L., & Lessen, E. (1983). Mainstreaming. In K. T. Kernan, M. J. Begab, & R. B. Edgerton (Eds.), *Environments and behavior: The adaptation of mentally retarded persons.* Baltimore: University Park Press.

Gould, E., Reeves, A. J., Graziano, M. S. A., & Gross, C. G. (1999). Neurogenesis in the neocortex of adult primates. *Science, 286*, 548–552.

Graham, S., Schwartz, S. S., & MacArthur, C. A. (1993). Knowledge of writing and the composing process, attitude toward writing, and self-efficacy for students with and without learning disabilities. *Journal of Learning Disabilities, 26*, 237–249.

Greenough, W. T. (1976). Enduring brain effects of differential experience and training. In M. R. Rosenzweig & E. L. Bennett (Eds.), *Neural mechanisms of learning and memory.* Cambridge, MA: MIT Press.

Gregory, J. F., Shanahan, T., & Walberg, H. (1986). A profile of learning disabled twelfth-graders in regular classes. *Learning Disability Quarterly, 9*, 33–42.

Gresham, F. M., MacMillan, D. L., Beebe-Frankenberger, M. E., & Bocian, K. M. (2000). Treatment integrity in learning disabilities intervention research: Do we really know how treatments are implemented? *Learning Disabilities Research & Practice, 15*, 198–205.

Griffith, P. L., & Olson, M. W. (1992). Phonemic awareness helps beginning readers break the code. *The Reading Teacher, 45*, 516–523.

Guyer, B. P., & Sabatino, D. (1989). The effectiveness of a multisensory alphabetic phonetic approach with college students who are learning disabled. *Journal of Learning Disabilities, 22*, 430–434.

Harris, A. J. (1962). *Effective teaching of reading.* New York: David McKay.

Harry, B., & Anderson, M. G. (1994). The disproportionate placement of African American males in special education programs: A critique of the process. *Journal of Negro Education, 63*, 602–619.

Hartlage, L. C., & Telzrow, C. F. (1986). *Neuropsychological assessment and intervention with children and adolescents.* Sarasota, FL: Professional Resource Exchange.

Hatcher, P. J., Hulme, C., & Ellis, A. W. (1994). Ameliorating early reading failure by integrating the teaching of reading and phonological skills: The phonological linkage hypothesis. *Child Development, 65*, 41–57.

Hécean, H., & Albert, M. L. (1978). *Human neuropsychology.* New York: Wiley.

Heilman, K. M., & Valenstein, E. (1979). *Clinical neuropsychology.* Oxford: Oxford University Press.

Herrnstein, R. J., & Murray, C. (1994). *The bell curve: Intelligence and class structure in American life.* New York: Free Press.

Hier, D. B. (1979). Sex differences in hemisphere specialization: Hypothesis for the excess of dyslexia in boys. *Bulletin of the Orton Society, 29*, 74–83.

Hier, D. B., LeMay, M., Rosenberger, P. B., & Perlo, V. P. (1978). Developmental dyslexia: Evidence for a subgroup with a reversal of cerebral asymmetry. *Archives of Neurology, 35*, 90–92.

Hines, M. (1990). Gonadal hormones and human cognitive development. In J. Balthazart (Ed.), *Hormones, brains, and behaviors in vertebrates: 1. Sexual differentiation, neuroanatomical aspects, neurotransmitters, and neuropeptides.* Basel, Switzerland: Karger.

Hinshelwood, J. (1898). A case of "word" without "letter" blindness. *Lancet, 1*, 422–425.

Hinshelwood, J. (1899). "Letter" without "word" blindness. *Lancet, 1*, 83–86.

Hudson, P. (1996). Using a learning set to increase the test performance of students with learning disabilities in social studies class. *Learning Disabilities Research & Practice, 11*, 78–85.

Hurford, D. P., Johnston, M., Nepote, P., Hampton, S., Moore, S., Neal, J., Mueller, A., McGeorge, K., Huff, L., Awad, A., Tatro, C., Juliano, C., & Huffman, D. (1994). Early identification and remediation of phonological-processing deficits in first-grade children at risk for reading disabilities. *Journal of Learning Disabilities, 10*, 647–659.

Huttenlocher, P. R. (1979). Synaptic density in human frontal cortex: Developmental changes and effects of aging. *Brain Research, 163*, 195–205.

Hynd, G. W., & Willis, W. G. (1988). *Pediatric neuropsychology.* New York: Grune & Stratton.

Individuals with Disabilities Education Act. (IDEA). (1997). PL 105-17, amendment to IDEA 1990, PL 101-476. *Federal Register,* March 12, 1999.

Isaacson, R. L., & Spear, L. P. (1984). A new perspective for the interpretation of early brain damage. In S. Finger & C. R. Almli (Eds.), *Early brain damage: Vol 2. Neurobiology and behavior.* New York: Academic Press.

Isgur, J. (1975). Establishing letter-sound associations by an Object-Imaging-Projection method. *Journal of Learning Disabilities, 8*, 351.

Jacklin, C. N., & Maccoby, E. M. (1982). Length of labor and sex of offspring. *Journal of Pediatric Psychology, 7*, 355–360.

Jenkins, R., & Bowen, L. (1994). Facilitating development of preliterate children's phonological abilities. *Topics in Language Disorders, 15*, 26–39.

Jensen, A. R. (1984). Test bias: Concepts and criticisms. In C. R. Reynolds & R. T. Brown (Eds.), *Perspectives on bias in mental testing.* New York: Plenum Press.

John, E. R., Karmel, B. Z., Corning, W. C., Easton, P., Brown, D., Ahn, H., John, M., Harmony, T., Prichep, L., Toro, A., Gerson, I., Bartlett, F., Thatcher, R., Kaye, H., Valdes, P., & Schwartz, E. (1977). Neurometrics. *Science, 196,* 1393–1410.

Johnson, D. W., & Johnson, R. T. (1986). Mainstreaming and cooperative learning strategies. *Exceptional Children, 52,* 553–561.

Johnson, D. W., & Johnson, R. T. (1994). *Learning together and alone: Cooperative, competitive, and individualistic learning* (4th ed.). Boston: Allyn & Bacon.

Juel, C., & Minden-Cupp, C. (2000). Learning to read words: Linguistic units and instructional strategies. *Reading Research Quarterly, 35,* 458–492.

Kail, R., Hall, L. K., & Caskey, B. J. (1999). Processing speed, exposure to print, and naming speed. *Applied Psycholinguistics, 20,* 303–314.

Kail, R., & Leonard, L. B. (1986). Sources of word-finding problems in language-impaired children. In S. J. Ceci (Ed.), *Handbook of cognitive, social, and neuropsychological aspects of learning disabilities* (Vol. 1). Hillsdale, NJ: Lawrence Erlbaum.

Kamann, M. P., & Wong, B. Y. L. (1993). Inducing adaptive coping self-statements in children with learning disabilities through self-instruction training. *Journal of Learning Disabilities, 26,* 630–638.

Karni, A., Meyer, G., Jezzard, P., Adams, M. M., Turner, R., & Ungerleider, L. G. (1995). Functional MRI evidence for adult motor cortex plasticity during motor skill learning. *Nature, 377,* 155–158.

Kaufman, A. S., & Kaufman, N. L. (1983). *Kaufman Assessment Battery for Children.* Circle Pines, MN: American Guidance Service.

Kavale, K. A., & Forness, S. R. (1987). Substance over style: Assessing the efficacy of modality testing and teaching. *Exceptional Children, 54,* 228–239.

Keel, M. C., & Gast, D. L. (1992). Small-group instruction for students with learning disabilities: Observational and incidental learning. *Exceptional Children, 58,* 357–368.

Keogh, B. K. (1987). Response [to Senf]. In S. Vaughn & C. S. Bos (Eds.), *Research in learning disabilities: Issues and future directions.* Boston: College-Hill.

Keogh, B. K., & Babbitt, B. C. (1986). Sampling issues in learning disabilities research: Markers for the study of problems in mathematics. In G. Th. Pavlidis & D. F. Fisher (Eds.), *Dyslexia: Its neuropsychology and treatment.* New York: John Wiley.

Keogh, B. K., Major-Kingsley, S., Omori-Gordon, H., & Reid, H. P. (1982). *A system of marker variables for the field of learning disabilities.* New York: Syracuse University Press.

Ketchum, E. G. (1967). Neurological and/or emotional factors in reading disabilities. In J. Figural (Ed.), *Vistas in reading.* Newark, DE: International Reading Association.

Kinsbourne, M., & Caplan, P. (1979). *Children's learning and attention problems.* Boston, MA: Little, Brown.

Kinsbourne, M., & Warrington, E. K. (1963). Developmental factor in reading and writing backwardness. *British Journal of Psychology, 54,* 145–156.

Klingberg, T., Hedehus, M., Temple, E., Salz, T., Gabrieli, J. D., Moseley, M. E., & Poldrack, R. A. (2000). Microstructure of temporo-parietal white matter as a basis for reading ability: Evidence from diffusion tensor magnetic resonance imaging. *Neuron, 25,* 493–500.

Koh, T., Abbatiello, A., & McLoughlin, C. S. (1984). Cultural bias in WISC subtest items: A response to Judge Grady's suggestion in relation to the PASE case. *School Psychology Review, 13,* 89–94.

Kolb, B. (1989). Brain development, plasticity and behavior. *American Psychologist, 44,* 1203–1212.

Koscinski, S. T., & Hoy, C. (1993). Teaching multiplication facts to students with learning disabilities: The promise of constant time delay procedures. *Learning Disabilities Research & Practice, 8,* 260–263.

Lambert, N. M., & Sandoval, J. (1980). The prevalence of learning disabilities in a sample of children considered hyperactive. *Journal of Abnormal Child Psychology, 8,* 33–50.

Larrivee, B. (1981). Modality preference as a model for differentiating beginning reading instruction: A review of the issues, *Learning Disability Quarterly, 4,* 180–188.

Lavoie, R. D. (1986). Toward developing a philosophy of education: A re-examination of competition, fairness and the work ethic. *Journal of Learning Disabilities, 19,* 62–63.

Lavoie, R. D. (1998). That's life in the jungle. Presentation at the International Meetings of the Learning Disabilities Association of America. Washington, DC.

Lehrer, G. M. (1974). Measurement of minimal brain dysfunction. In C. Xintras, B. L, Johnson, & I. de Groot (Eds.), *Behavioral toxicology.* Washington, DC: U.S. Department of Health, Education, and Welfare.

Lenneberg, E. H. (1967). *Biological foundations of language.* New York: John Wiley & Sons.

Levin, H. S., Handel, S. F., Goldman, A. M., Eisenberg, H. M., & Guinto, F. C., Jr. (1985). Magnetic resonance imaging after "diffuse" nonmissile head injury: A neurobehavioral study. *Archives of Neurology, 42,* 963–968.

Liberman, I. Y. (1985). Should so-called modality preferences determine the nature of instruction for children with reading disabilities? In F. H. Duffy & N.

Geschwind (Eds.), *Dyslexia: A neuroscientific approach to clinical evaluation.* Boston: Little, Brown.

Lieberman, L. M. (1986). Profiles: An interview with Laurence M. Lieberman. *Academic Therapy, 21,* 421–425.

Liepert, J., Bauder, H., Wolfgang, H. R., Miltner, W. H., Taub, E., & Weiller, C. (2000). Treatment-induced cortical reorganization after stroke in humans. *Stroke, 31,* 1210–1216.

Lipham, J. M. (1981). *Effective principal, effective school.* Reston, VA: National Association of Secondary School Principals.

Litcher, J. H., & Roberge, L. P. (1979). First grade intervention for reading achievement of high-risk children. *Bulletin of the Orton Society, 29,* 238–244.

Lloyd, J. W., & Loper, A. B. (1986). Measurement and evaluation of task-related learning behaviors: Attention to task and metacognition. *School Psychology Review, 15,* 336–345.

Lord-Maes, J., & Obrzut, J. E. (1996). Neuropsychological consequences of traumatic brain injury in children and adults. *Journal of Learning Disabilities, 29,* 609–617.

Lou, Y., Abrami, P. C., Spence, J. C., Poulsen, C., Chambers, B., & d'Appollonia, S. (1996). Within-class grouping: A meta-analysis. *Review of Educational Research, 66,* 423–458.

Lovett, M., Stainbach, K. A., & Frijters, J. C. (2000). Remediating the core deficits of developmental reading disability: A double-deficit perspective. *Journal of Learning Disabilities, 33,* 334–358.

Lovett, M. W., Borden, S. L., DeLuca, T., Lacerenza, L., Benson, N. J., & Brackstone, D. (1994). Treating the core deficits of developmental dyslexia: Evidence of transfer of learning after phonologically and strategy-based reading training program. *Developmental Psychology, 30,* 805–822.

Lundberg, I., Frost, J., & Petersen, O. (1988). Effects of an extensive program for stimulating phonological awareness in preschool children. *Reading Research Quarterly, 23,* 263–284.

Luria, A. R. (1976). *The neuropsychology of memory.* New York: John Wiley & Sons.

Luria, A. R. (1977). Cerebral organization of conscious acts; A frontal lobe function. In L. Tarnapol & M. Tarnopol (Eds.), *Brain function and reading disabilities.* Baltimore: University Park Press.

Luria, A. R. (1980). *Higher cortical functions in man.* New York: Basic Books.

Lynn, R. (1997). Direct evidence for a genetic basis for black-white differences in IQ. *American Psychologist, 52,* 73.

Lyon, G. R. (1985). Educational validation studies of learning disability subtypes. In B. P. Rourke (Ed.), *Neuropsychology of learning disabilities.* New York: Guilford Press.

MacMillan, D. L., Gresham, F. M., & Bocian, K. M. (1998). Discrepancy between definitions of learning disabilities and school practices: An empirical investigation. *Journal of Learning Disabilities, 31,* 314–326.

MacMillan, D. L., Hendrick, I. G., & Watkins, A. V. (1988). Impact of Diana, Larry P., and P. L. 94–142 on minority students. *Exceptional Children, 54,* 426–432.

Malouf, D. (1983). Do rewards reduce student motivation? *School Psychology Review, 12,* 1–11.

Margolis, H., & Freund, L. A. (1991). Implementing cooperative learning with mildly handicapped students in regular classrooms. *International Journal of Disability, 38,* 117–133.

Mather, N. (1992). Whole language reading instruction for students with learning disabilities. Caught in the cross fire. *Learning Disabilities Research & Practice, 7,* 87–95.

Mathinos, D. A. (1988). Communicative competence of children with learning disabilities. *Journal of Learning Disabilities, 21,* 437–443.

Mattingly, J. C., & Bott, D. A. (1990). Teaching multiplication facts to students with learning problems. *Exceptional Children, 56,* 438–449.

McIntyre, L. L. (1988). Teacher gender: A predictor of special education referral? *Journal of Learning Disabilities, 21,* 382–383.

McMillen, M. M. (1979). Differential mortality by sex in fetal and neonatal deaths. *Science, 204,* 89–91.

Meiners, M. L., & Dabbs, J. M., Jr. (1977). Ear temperature and brain blood flow: Laterality effects. *Bulletin of the Psychonomic Society,* 10, 194–196.

Mercer, J. R. (1970). The ecology of mental retardation. In *The proceedings of the first annual spring conference of the Institute for the Study of Mental Retardation* (pp. 55–74). Ann Arbor, MI.

Mercer, J. R. (1973). *Labeling the mentally retarded: Clinical and social system perspectives on mental retardation.* Berkeley: University of California Press.

Mercer, J. R. (1979). *Technical manual: System of multicultural pluralistic assessment.* New York: Psychological Corp.

Mercer, J. R., & Lewis, J. F. (1978). *The system of multicultural pluralistic assessment.* New York: Psychological Corp.

Morris, R., Lyon, G. R., Alexander, D., Gray, D. B., Kavanagh, J., Rourke, B. P., & Swanson, H. L. (1994). Editorial: Proposed guidelines and criteria for describing samples of persons with learning disabilities. *Learning Disability Quarterly, 17,* 106–109.

*A Nation at risk: The imperative for educational reform. A report to the Nation and the Secretary of Education.* (1983). Washington, DC: U.S. Department of Education, The National Commission on Excellence in Education.

National Center for Educational Statistics. (1992). *NELS: 88: A profile of parents of eighth graders.* Washington, DC: U.S. Government Printing Office.

National Joint Committee on Learning Disabilities. (1997). Operationalizing the NJCLD definition of learning disabilities for ongoing assessment in schools. *Perspectives: The International Dyslexia Association, 23*(4), 29–33.

Natriello, G., Pallas, A. M., & McDill, E. L. (1990). *Schooling disadvantaged children: Racing against catastrophe.* New York: Teachers College Press.

Neisser, U., Boodoo, G., Bouchard, T. J., Boykin, A. W., Brody, N., Ceci, S. J., Halpern, D. F., Loehlin, J. C., Perloff, R., Sternberg, R. J., & Urbina, S. (1996). Intelligence: Knowns and unknowns. *American Psychologist, 51,* 77–101.

Novitski, E. (1977). *Human genetics.* New York: Macmillan.

O'Connor, R. E., Jenkins, J. R., & Slocum, T. A. (1995). Transfer among phonological tasks in kindergarten: Essential instructional content. *Journal of Educational Psychology, 87,* 202–217.

O'Connor, R. E., Notari-Syverson, A., & Vadasy, P. (1998). First-grade effects of teacher-led phonological activities in kindergarten for children with mild disabilities: A follow-up study. *Learning Disabilities Research & Practice, 13,* 43–52.

Office of Civil Rights. (1992). *1992 Office of Civil Rights elementary and secondary school survey.* Washington, DC: U.S. Office of Education.

O'Leary, D. S., & Boll, T. J. (1984). Neuropsychological correlates of early generalized brain dysfunction in children. In C. R. Almli & S. Finger (Eds.), *Early brain damage: Vol. 1. Research orientations and clinical observations.* New York: Academic Press.

Osgood, C. E., & Miron, M. S. (1963). *Approaches to the study of aphasia.* Urbana, IL: University of Illinois Press.

Oswald, D. P., Coutinho, M. J., Best, A. M., Singh, N. N. (1999). Ethnic representation in special education: The influence of school-related economic and demograhic variables. *The Journal of Special Education, 32,* 194–206.

Palincsar, A. S., & Klenk, L. (1992). Fostering literacy learning in supportive contexts. *Journal of Learning Disabilities, 25,* 211–225, 229.

Pany, D., & McCoy, K. M. (1988). Effects of corrective feedback on word accuracy and reading comprehension of readers with learning disabilities. *Journal of Learning Disabilities, 21,* 546–550.

Paris, S. G., & Lindauer, B. K. (1977). Constructive aspects of children's comprehension and memory. In R. V. Kail & J. W. Hagen (Eds.), *Perspectives on the development of memory and cognition.* Hillsdale, NJ: Lawrence Erlbaum.

Pascual-Leone, A., Dang, N., Cohen, L. G., Brasil-Neto, J. P., Cammarota, A., & Hallett, M. (1995). Modulation of muscle responses evoked by transcranial magnetic stimulation during the acquisition of new fine motor skills. *Journal of Neurophysiology, 74,* 1037–1945.

Pascual-Leone, A., Tarazona, F., Keenan, J., Tormos, J. M., Hamilton, R., & Catala, M. D. (1999). Transcranial magnetic stimulation and neuroplasticity. *Neuropsychologia, 37,* 207–217.

Pascual-Leone, A., & Torres, F. (1993). Plasticity of the sensorimotor cortex representation of the reading finger in Braille readers. *Brain, 116,* 39–52.

Patrick, J. L., & Reschly, D. J. (1982). Relationship of state educational criteria and demographic variables to school system prevalence of mental retardation. *American Journal of Mental Deficiency, 86,* 351–360.

Penfield, W., & Roberts, L. (1959). *Speech and brain mechanisms.* Princeton: Princeton University Press.

Pennington, B. F. (1995). Genetics of learning disabilities. *Journal of Child Neurology, 10,* Supplement #1, s69–s77.

Poskiparta, E., Niemi, P., & Vauras, M. (1999). Who benefits from training in linguistic awareness in the first grade, and what components show training effects? *Journal of Learning Disabilities, 32,* 437–446, 456.

Potts, M. (1968). The relative achievement of first graders under three different reading programs. *The Journal of Educational Research, 61,* 447–450.

Pressley, M., & associates. (1990). *Cognitive strategy instruction that really improves children's academic performance.* Cambridge, MA: Brookline Books.

Pressley, M., & Rankin, J. (1994). More about whole language methods of reading instruction for students at risk for early reading failure. *Learning Disabilities Research & Practice, 9,* 157–168.

Purkey, S. C., & Smith, M. S. (1983). Effective schools: A review. *The Elementary School Journal, 83,* 427–452.

Rademacher, J. A., Schumaker, J. B., & Deshler, D. D. (1996). Development and validation of a classroom assignment routine for inclusive settings. *Learning Disability Quarterly, 19,* 163–177.

Reitan, R. M. (1974). Methodological problems in clinical neuropsychology. In R. M. Reitan & L. A. Davison (Eds.), *Clinical neuropsychology: Current status and applications.* Washington, DC: Winston.

Reschly, D. J., Kicklighter, R., & McKee, P. (1988). Recent placement litigation. Part II: Minority EMR overrepresentation: Comparison of Larry P. (1979, 1984, 1986) with Marshall (1984, 1985) and S-1 (1986). *School Psychology Review, 17,* 22–38.

Resnick, L. B. (1989). Developing mathematical knowledge. *American Psychologist, 44,* 162–169.

Reynolds, C. R., & Brown, R. T. (Eds.). (1984). *Perspectives on bias in mental testing.* New York: Plenum.

Richards, T. L. (2001). Functional magnetic resonance imaging and spectroscopic imaging of the brain: Application of fMRI and fMRS to reading disabilities and education. *Learning Disability Quarterly, 24,* 189–203.

Richards, T. L., Berninger, V. W., Aylward, E. H., Richards, A. L., Thomson, J. B., Nagy, W. E., Carlisle, J. F., Dager, S. R., & Abbott, R. D. (2002). Reproducibility of Proton MR Spectroscopic Imaging (PEPSI): Comparison of dyslexic and normal-reading children and effects of treatment on brain lactate levels during language tasks. *American Journal of Neuroradiology, 23*, 1678–1685.

Rodier, P. M. (1984). Exogenous sources of malformations in development: CNS malformations and developmental repair processes. In E. S. Gollin (Ed.), *Malformations of development.* New York: Academic Press.

Rose, T. L., McEntire, E., & Dowdy, C. (1982). Effects of two error-correction procedures on oral reading. *Learning Disability Quarterly, 5*, 100–105.

Rosenberg, M. S. (1986). Error-correction during oral reading: A comparison of three techniques. *Learning Disability Quarterly, 9*, 182–192.

Rosenberg, M. S., Bott, D., Majsterek, D., Chiang, B., Gartland, D., Wesson, C., Graham, S., Smith-Myles, B., Miller, M., Swanson, H. L., Bender, W., Rivera, D., & Wilson, R. (1993). Minimum standards for the description of participants in learning disabilities research. *Journal of Learning Disabilities, 26*, 210–213.

Rourke, B. P., Bakker, D. J., Fisk, J. L., & Strang, J. D. (1983). *Child neuropsychology: An introduction to theory, research, and clinical practice.* New York: Guilford Press.

Rumsey, J. M. (1996). Neuroimaging in developmental dyslexia. In G. R. Lyon & J. M. Rumsey (Eds.), *Neuroimaging: A window to the neurological foundations of learning and behavior in children* (pp. 57–77). Baltimore: Paul H. Brookes.

Rushton, J. P. (1997). Race, IQ, and the APA report on *The Bell Curve. American Psychologist, 52*, 69–71.

Ryan, R. M., & Deci, E. L. (2000). Self-determination theory and the facilitation of intrinsic motivation, social development, and well-being. *American Psychologist, 55*, 68–78.

Salvia, J., & Ysseldyke, J. E. (2001). *Assessment* (8th ed.). Boston: Houghton Mifflin.

Samuels, S. J., & Miller, N. L. (1985). Failure to find attention differences between learning disabled and normal children on classroom and laboratory tasks. *Exceptional Children, 51*, 358–375.

Sattler, J. M. (2001). *Assessment of children: Cognitive applications* (4th ed.). San Diego: Jerome M. Sattler, Pub.

Schneider, W., Ennemoser, M., Roth, E., Küspert, P. (1999). Kindergarten prevention of dyslexia: Does training in phonological awareness work for everybody? *Journal of Learning Disabilities, 32*, 429–436.

Schneider, W., & Pressley, M. (1997). *Memory development between two and twenty* (2nd ed.). Mahwah, NJ: Erlbaum.

Schumaker, J. B. (1992). Social performance of individuals with learning disabilities. Through the looking glass of KU-IRLD research. *School Psychology Review, 21*, 389.

Searleman, A. (1977). A review of right hemisphere linguistic capabilities. *Psychological Bulletin, 84*, 503–528.

Segalowitz, S. J., & Bryden, M. P. (1983). Individual differences in hemispheric representation of language. In S. J. Segalowitz (Ed.), *Language functions and brain organization.* New York: Academic Press.

Segalowitz, S. J., & Lawson, S. (1995). Subtle symptoms associated with self-reported mild head injury. *Journal of Learning Disabilities, 28*, 309–319.

Senf, G. M. (1987). Learning disabilities as sociologic sponge: Wiping up life's spills. In S. Vaughn & C. S. Bos (Eds.), *Research in learning disabilities: Issues and future directions.* Boston: College-Hill.

Shapiro, E. S. (1992). Use of Gickling's model of curriculum-based assessment to improve reading in elementary age students. *School Psychology Review, 21*, 168–176.

Shavelson, R. J. (1983). Review of research on teachers' pedagogical judgments, plans, and decisions. *Elementary School Journal, 83*, 392–413.

Shaywitz, S. E., & Shaw, R. (1988). The admissions process: An approach to selecting learning disabled students at the most selective colleges. *Learning Disabilities Focus, 3*, 81–86.

Shaywitz, S. E., Shaywitz, B. A., Fletcher, J. M., & Escobar, M. D. (1990). Prevalence of reading disability in boys and girls: Results of the Connecticut Longitudinal Study. *Journal of the American Medical Association, 264*, 998–1002.

Shaywitz, S. E., Shaywitz, B. A., Pugh, K. R., Fulbright, R. K., Constable, R. T., Mencl, W. E., Shankweiler, D. P., Liberman, A. M., Skudlarski, P., Fletcher, J. M., Katz, L., Marchione, K. E., Lacadie, C., Gatenby, C., & Gore, J. C. (1998). Functional disruption in the organization of the brain for reading in dyslexia. *Proceedings of the National Academy of Sciences USA, 95*, 2636–2641.

Shinn, M. R., Good, R. H., Knutson, N., Tilly, W. D., & Collins, V. L. (1992). Curriculum-based measurement of oral reading fluency: A confirmatory analysis of its relation to reading. *School Psychology Review, 21*, 459–479.

Siegler, R. S. (1989). Mechanisms of cognitive development. *Annual Review of Psychology, 40*, 353–379.

Siegler, R. S. (2000). The rebirth of children's learning. *Child Development, 71*, 26–35.

Sikorski, M. F., Niemiec, R. P., & Walberg, H. J. (1996). A classroom checkup: Best teaching practices in special education. *Teaching Exceptional Children, 29*(1), 27–29.

Silberberg, N. E., Iversen, I. A., & Goins, J. T. (1973). Which remedial reading method works best? *Journal of Learning Disabilities, 6*, 547–556.

Silver, L. B. (1971). Familial patterns in children with neurologically-based learning disabilities. *Journal of Learning Disabilities, 4,* 349–358.

Simmerman, S., & Swanson, H. L. (2001). Treatment outcomes for students with learning disabilities: How important are internal and external validity? *Journal of Learning Disabilities, 34,* 221–236.

Simos, P. G., Breier, J. I., Fletcher, J. M., Bergman, E., & Papanicolaou, A. C. (2000). Cerebral mechanisms involved in word reading in dyslexic children: A magnetic source imaging approach. *Cerebral Cortex, 10*(8), 809–816.

Simos, P. G., Fletcher, J. M., Bergman, E., Breier, J. I., Foorman, B. R., Castillo, E. M., Davis, R. N., Fitzgerald, M., & Papanicolaou, A. C. (2002). Dyslexia-specific brain activation profile becomes normal following successful remedial training. *Neurology, 58,* 1203–1213.

Slavin, R. E. (1995). *Cooperative learning: Theory, research, and practice* (2nd ed.). Boston: Allyn & Bacon.

Slavin, R. E. (1996). Research on cooperative learning and achievement: What we know, what we need to know. *Contemporary Educational Psychology, 21,* 43–69.

Smith, C. R. (1980). Assessment alternatives: Non-standardized procedures. *School Psychology Review, 9,* 46–57.

Smith, C. R. (1994). *Learning disabilities: The interaction of learner, task, and setting* (3rd ed). Boston: Allyn & Bacon.

Smith, C. R. (1999). Transdisciplinary training at Syracuse University's Psychoeducational Teaching Laboratory. In D. H. Evensen & P. B. Mosenthal (Eds.), *Advances in reading/language research, Vol. 6: Reconsidering the role of the reading clinic in a new age of literacy* (pp. 149–173). Stamford, CT: JAI Press.

Smith, C., & Strick, L. (1997). *Learning disabilities A to Z: A parent's complete guide to learning disabilities from preschool to adulthood.* New York: The Free Press.

Snyder, L. S., & Downey, D. M. (1995). Serial rapid naming skills in children with reading disabilities. *Annals of Dyslexia, 45,* 31–49.

Spear-Swerling, L., & Sternberg, R. J. (1994). The road not taken: An integrative theoretical model of reading disability. *Journal of Learning Disabilities, 27,* 91–103, 122.

Sperry, R. W. (1968). Hemisphere deconnection and unity in conscious awareness. *American Psychologist, 23,* 723–733.

Spiker, C. C., & Cantor, J. H. (1983). Component in the hypothesis testing strategies of young children. In T. J. Tighe & B. E. Shepp (Eds.), *Perception, cognition, and development: Interactional analyses.* Hillsdale, NJ: Lawrence Erlbaum.

Sporns, O. (1994). Selectionist and instructionist ideas in neuroscience. In O. Sporns & G. Tononi (Eds.), *Selectionism and the brain.* New York: Academic Press.

Sprague, R. L., & Sleator, E. K. (1973). Effects of psychopharmacologic agents on learning disorders. *Pediatric Clinics of North America, 20,* 719–735.

Springer, S. P., & Deutch, G. (1997). *Left brain, right brain: Perspectives from cognitive neuroscience* (5th ed.). San Francisco: Freeman.

Stahl, S. A., McKenna, M. C., & Pagnucco, J. R. (1994). The effects of whole-language instruction: An update and a reappraisal. *Educational Psychologist, 29,* 175–185.

Stahl, S. A., & Miller, P. D. (1989). Whole language and language experience approaches for beginning reading: A quantitative research synthesis. *Review of Educational Research, 59,* 87–116.

Stanovich, K. E. (1982). Individual differences in the cognitive processes of reading: I. Word decoding. *Journal of Learning Disabilities, 15,* 485–493.

Stanovich, K. E. (1988). Explaining the differences between the dyslexic and the garden-variety poor reader: The phonological-core variable-difference model. *Journal of Learning Disabilities, 21,* 590–604.

Stevens, R., & Rosenshine, B. (1981). Advances in research on teaching. *Exceptional Education Quarterly, 2*(1), 1–9.

Stevens, R. J., & Slavin, R. E. (1991). When cooperative learning improves the achievement of students with mild disabilities: A response to Tateyama-Sniezek. *Exceptional Children, 57,* 276–280.

Stipp, D. (1992, September 11). Reinventing math. *The Wall Street Journal,* p. B4.

Strauss, A. A., & Kephart, N. C. (1955). *Psychopathology and education of the brain-injured child: Vol. 2. Progress in theory and clinic.* New York: Grune & Stratton.

Strauss, A. A., & Lehtinen, L. E. (1947). *Psychopathology and education of the brain-injured child.* New York: Grune & Stratton.

Swanson, H. L. (1983). Relations among metamemory, rehearsal activity and word recall of learning disabled and non-disabled readers. *British Journal of Educational Psychology, 53,* 186–194.

Tangel, D. M., & Blachman, B. A. (1992). Effect of phoneme awareness instruction on kindergarten children's invented spelling. *Journal of Reading Behavior, 24,* 233–261.

Tangel, D. M., & Blachman, B. A. (1995). Effect of phoneme awareness instruction on the invented spelling of first-grade children: A one-year follow-up. *Journal of Reading Behavior, 27,* 153–185.

Tarnopol, L., & Tarnopol, M. (1977). Introduction to neuropsychology. In L. Tarnopol & M. Tarnopol (Eds.), *Brain function and reading disabilities.* Baltimore: University Park Press.

Tarver, S. G., & Dawson, M. M. (1978). Modality preference and the teaching of reading: A review. *Journal of Learning Disabilities, 11,* 5–17.

Taylor, H. G. (1984). Early and long-term recovery from brain damage in children and adults: Evolution of concepts of localization, plasticity, and recovery. In C. R. Almli & S. Finger (Eds.), *Early brain damage: Vol. 1. Research orientations and clinical observations.* New York: Academic Press.

Thompson, R. A., & Nelson, C. A. (2001). Developmental science and the media. *American Psychologist, 56,* 5–15.

Thypin, M. (1979). Selection of books of high interest and low reading level. *Journal of Learning Disabilities, 12,* 428–430.

Tomlinson, J. R., Acker, A., Canter, A., & Lindborg, S. (1977). Minority status, sex, and school psychological services. *Psychology in the Schools, 14,* 456–460.

Torgesen, J. K. (1987). Thinking about the future by distinguishing between issues that have resolutions and those that do not. In S. Vaughn & C. S. Bos (Eds.), *Research in learning disabilities: Issues and future directions.* Boston: College-Hill.

Torgesen, J. K. (2000). Individual difference in response to early interventions in reading: The lingering problem of treatment resistance. *Learning Disabilities Research & Practice, 15,* 55–64.

Torgesen, J. K., & Houck, D. G. (1980). Processing deficiencies of learning disabled children who perform poorly on the digit span test. *Journal of Educational Psychology, 72,* 141–160.

Torgesen, J. K., Wagner, R. K., & Rashotte, C. A. (1994). Longitudinal studies of phonological processing and reading. *Journal of Learning Disabilities, 27,* 276–286.

Torgesen, J. K., Wagner, R. K., Rashotte, C. A., Rose, E., Lindamood, P., Conway, T., & Garvan, C. (1999). Preventing reading failure in young children with phonological processing disabilities: Group and individual responses to instruction. *Journal of Educational Psychology, 91,* 579–593.

Tornéus, M. (1984). Phonological awareness and reading: A chicken and egg problem? *Journal of Educational Psychology, 76,* 1346–1358.

Townes, B. D., Trupin, E. W., Martin, D. C., & Goldstein, D. (1980). Neuropsychological correlates of academic success among elementary school children. *Journal of Consulting and Clinical Psychology, 48,* 675–684.

Tronick, E. Z. (1989). Emotions and emotional communication in infants. *American Psychologist, 44,* 112–119.

Tucker, J. A. (1980). Ethnic proportions in classes for the learning disabled: Issues in nonbiased assessment. *Journal of Special Education, 14,* 93–105.

*Twenty-third Annual Report to Congress on the Implementation of the Individuals with Disabilities Education Act.* (2001). Washington, D.C.: U.S. Department of Education.

Tzavaras, A., Kaprinis, G., & Gatzoyas, A. (1981). Literacy and hemispheric specialization for language: Digit dichotic listening in illiterates. *Neuropsychologia, 19,* 565–570.

Vandervelden, M. C., & Siegel, L. S. (1997). Teaching phonological processing skills in early literacy: A developmental approach. *Learning Disability Quarterly, 20,* 63–81.

Vellutino, F. R. (1991). Introduction to three studies on reading acquisition: Convergent findings on theoretical foundations of code-oriented versus whole-language approaches to reading instruction. *Journal of Educational Psychology, 83,* 437–443.

Vellutino, F. R., & Scanlon, D. M. (1987). Phonological coding, phonological awareness, and reading ability: Evidence from a longitudinal and experimental study. *Merrill-Palmer Quarterly, 33,* 321–363.

Wallach, M. A., & Wallach, L. (1979). *Teaching all children to read.* Chicago: University of Chicago Press.

Walsh, K. W. (1978). *Neuropsychology: A clinical approach.* Edinburgh: Churchill-Livingstone.

Welch, M. (1992). The PLEASE strategy: A metacognitive learning strategy for improving the paragraph writing of students with mild learning disabilities. *Learning Disability Quarterly, 15,* 119–128.

Welton, D. A. (1990). Language as a mirror of culture. *Houghton Mifflin/Educators' Forum,* p. 7.

Werner, H., & Bowers, M. (1941). Auditory-motor organization in two clinical types of mentally deficient children. *Journal of Genetic Psychology, 59,* 85–99.

Werner, H., & Strauss, A. A, (1941). Pathology of figure-background relation in the child. *Journal of Abnormal and Social Psychology, 36,* 236–248.

White, O. R. (1986). Precision teaching-precision learning. *Exceptional Children, 52,* 522–534.

Whorf, B. L. (1956). *Language, thought, and reality.* New York: John Wiley & Sons.

Wiig, E. H., & Semel, E. M. (1980). *Language assessment and intervention for the learning disabled.* Columbus, OH: Charles E. Merrill.

Willcutt, E. G., & Pennington, B. F. (2000). Comorbidity of reading disability and attention-deficit/hyperactivity disorder: Differences by gender and subtype. *Journal of Learning Disabilities, 33,* 179–191.

Williams, J. P. (1984). Phonemic analysis and how it relates to reading. *Journal of Learning Disabilities, 17,* 240–245.

Williams, W. M., & Ceci, S. J. (1997). Are Americans becoming more or less alike? Trends in race, class, and ability differences in intelligence. *American Psychologist, 52,* 1226–1235.

Wilson, H. R. (1988). Development of spatiotemporal mechanisms in infant vision. *Vision Research, 28,* 611–628.

Wilson, R., & Wesson, C. (1986). Making every minute count: Academic learning time in LD classrooms. *Learning Disabilities Focus, 2,* 13–19.

Wise, B. W., Olson, R. K., Ring, J., & Johnson, M. (1998). Interactive computer support for improving phonological skills. In J. L. Metsala & L. C. Ehri (Eds.), *Word recognition in beginning literacy* (pp. 189–208). Mahwah, NJ: Lawrence Erlbaum.

Witelson, S. (1977). Developmental dyslexia: Two right hemispheres and none left. *Science, 195,* 309–311.

Witelson, S. F. (1976). Sex and the single hemisphere: Specialization of the right hemisphere for spatial processing. *Science, 193,* 425–427.

Wolery, M., Cybriwsky, C. A., Gast, D. L., & Boyle-Bast, K. (1991). Use of constant time delay and attentional responses with adolescents. *Exceptional Children, 57,* 462–474.

Wolf, M., Bowers, P. G., & Biddle, K. (2000). Naming-speed processes, timing, and reading: A conceptual review. *Journal of Learning Disabilities, 33,* 387–407.

Wolff, P. H., & Melngailis, I. (1996). Reversing letters and reading transformed text in dyslexia: A reassessment. *Reading and Writing: An Interdisciplinary Journal, 8,* 341–355.

Wright, P., & Santa Cruz, R. (1983). Ethnic composition of special education programs in California. *Learning Disability Quarterly, 6,* 387–394.

Yakovlev, P. I., & Lecours, A-R. (1967). The myelogenetic cycles of regional maturation of the brain. In A. Minkowski (Ed.), *Regional development of the brain in early life* (pp. 3–70). Oxford, England: Blackwell.

Zelniker, T., & Jeffrey, W. E. (1976). Reflective and impulsive children: Strategies of information processing underlying differences in problem solving. *Monographs of the Society for Research in Child Development, 41* (5, Serial No. 168).

Zihl, J. (1981). Recovery of visual functions in patients with cerebral blindness: Effect of specific practice with saccadic localization. *Experimental Brain Research, 44,* 159–169.

# NAME INDEX

# SUBJECT INDEX